Randi W.

P9-DUF-547

Readings in
CHRISTIAN
HUMANISM

Readings in
CHRISTIAN
HUMANISM

Edited by Joseph M. Shaw, R.W. Franklin,
Harris Kaasa and Charles W. Buzicky

Foreword by Martin E. Marty

AUGSBURG Publishing House • Minneapolis

Contents

Acknowledgments

We wish to thank the following publishers for permission to quote from these copyrighted sources:

AMBROSE. "Aeterne rerum conditor," in *Hymns of Breviary Missal*, © 1948 Glencoe Publishing Co.

ANONYMOUS. "Creator alme siderum" and "Te lucis ante terminum" in *Hymns of Breviary Missal* © 1948 Glencoe Publishing Co.

ARISTOTLE. From *The Philosophy of Aristotle*, tr. by Werdman and Creed, © 1963 New American Library.

AQUINAS, THOMAS. From *On the Truth of the Catholic Faith, Summa Contra Gentiles*, tr. by Anton C. Pegis © 1955 by Notre Dame Press. "Lauda, Sion, Salvatorem," in *Hymns of Breviary Missal*, © 1948 Glencoe Publishing Co.

AUGUSTINE. From *City of God* in *Fathers of the Church*, Vols. 14 and 24, © Catholic University of America Press. From "The Way of Life of the Catholic Church" in *Fathers of the Church*, Vol. 56, © Catholic University of America Press.

BENEDICT. From *The Rule of Benedict*, Copyright © 1981 by The Order of St. Benedict, Inc., Collegeville, Minnesota, used with the permission of The Liturgical Press.

BERNARD OF CLAIRVAUX. "Jesu, dulcis memoria," in *Hymns of Breviary Missal*, © 1948 Glencoe Publishing Co.

BONHOEFFER, DIETRICH. From *Letters and Papers from Prison*, rev., enlarged ed. Copyright © 1953, 1967, 1971 by SCM Press, Ltd. Reprinted with permission of Macmillan Publishing Co., Inc.

BRUNNER, EMIL. From *Christianity and Civilization*, Vol. I. Used by permission of Charles Scribner's Sons. Copyright 1948 Charles Scribner's Sons.

CALVIN, JOHN. From *Institutes of the Christian Religion*, ed. by John T. McNeill, tr. by Ford Lewis Battles. Copyright © MCMLX W. L. Jenkins. Reprinted by permission of The Westminster Press.

THE CREEDS. From International Consultation on English Texts.

DANTE ALIGHIERI. From *Monarchy*, tr. by Donald Nicholl, © 1954 Hyperion Press, 1954. From *Divine Comedy*, tr. by Dorothy L. Sayers, © 1962. Reprinted by permission of David Higham Associates, Ltd.

DOCUMENTS OF THE SECOND VATICAN COUNCIL. From *Vatican Council II: The Conciliar & Post Conciliar Documents*, ed. by Austin Flannery, © 1975 Costello Publishing Co.

Foreword

I am, as always, eager to speak out on the subjects of humanism and the humanities. But I yield the floor first to someone who rather typically poses the problem that lies behind this book and the whole project of "Christian Humanism." Philosopher Frederick A. Olafson, near the end of an elaborate defense of the humanities, faces up to the problems of humanism and religion. His words will help illumine everything that follows:

> The relationship between humanism and religious belief is one that has given difficulties for centuries and has caused a good deal of personal anguish to those humanists like St. Jerome and Petrarch who have aspired to be sincere Christians. There have been forms of religious belief that are radically incompatible with humanism because they proclaim the nothingness of man and transfer to their gods every possible form of agency or achievement with which man might otherwise be tempted to credit himself. Then, too, there are forms of religious belief in which natural forces have not yet reached the degree of personification that would permit human beings to understand themselves as persons through their relationship to their superhuman counterparts. But there are also religions that teach that there is something, however limited, that human beings as individuals and as societies can do and that thus concede a measure of significance and value to the achievements of human culture and even allow a modicum of human pride, as well as of shame, stemming from the contemplation of what has been done. (*The Dialectic of Action: A Philosophical Interpretation of History and the Humanities.* Chicago: University of Chicago Press, 1979, pp. 155-56.)

The relationship between Christianity and humanism still gives difficulty and "a good deal of personal anguish." When I as a humanist pursue my goals, I am doing what I as a politician, a business person, a professional must always be doing. I must know that there is some tension between that vocation, which I live under God, and the pull of specific saving activity. Humanism, like politics, does not save souls or make sad hearts glad or bring in the kingdom of God. Yet the humanities—philosophy, literature, the study of religion, history, and the like—have their lure and are part of God's creation. The Christian humanist says, "I must know that whatever I touch on the pages of human production is tainted by the fact that it will turn to dust. It belongs to an order of existence that is not only God's creation, but is also tinged with the power of the demonic." Yes, there is anguish.

Olafson moves on to a second point, however, one that can help remove false anguish today. Despite some conflict, it would be a mistake, he says, to write off all humanism as "atheistic or even antireligious." Today such writing off has been going on. Some well-intentioned, but frustrated and shortsighted persons have been used by less than well-intentioned exploiters of frustration. Together they have formed a kind of political crusade against all humanisms as being secular, atheistic or at least antireligious. This is short-sighted because it yields some of God's ground to the enemy, and unfair because it groups together people who do not belong in the same camp. I might add that it is even theologically unsound, because God can work also in the secular sphere, through people who do not know him.

This book is part of an effort to reclaim space and a voice for Christian humanism. The cause is not helped by people who dismiss all humanisms as secular and then turn that into a code word for atheistic or antireligious. This book does not gripe about secular humanism; it does something about it.

Olafson is correct, further, when he says that there *are* belief systems that are radically incompatible with humanism. They misread, in the Christian case, the need to see human life as creaturely, with the need to see it as always and only corrupt and irredeemable, as if God has lost power to work through the creature. In our time much Christian antihumanism comes from forms of "Second Coming" theology, millennialisms that urge the worthlessness of the world because it will end. They give up on the world before God does, and act as if Jesus did not mean it when he sent people forth into that world. Whoever reads the chapters anthologized here will find that for many centuries Christian humanists, fully aware of the evil potential of fallen humanity, make clear that they are members of the race that God chose to visit, the human race, hence humanism.

Humanism is rooted in the humanities, and humanists speak for a culture rooted in literacy, based in traces and texts. One of the theological traditions that produced this volume stems from a rereading of the Bible by Martin Luther. Luther knew what Olafson called the "anguish" of Christian humanism, as he worked with the benefits of classic literature in order to use what he learned for translating and understanding the Bible. He knew the limits of the human venture. But he came out as a Christian humanist:

> I am persuaded that without knowledge of literature pure theology cannot at all endure, just as heretofore, when letters have declined and lain prostrate, theology, too, has wretchedly fallen and lain prostrate; nay, I see that there has never been a great revelation of the Word of God unless he has first prepared the way by the rise and prosperity of languages and letters, as though they were John the Baptists. . . . Certainly it is my desire that there shall be as many poets and rhetoricians as possible, because I see that by these studies, as by no other means, people are wonderfully fitted for the grasping of sacred truth and for handling it skillfully and happily. . . . Therefore I beg of you that at my request (if that has any weight) you will urge your young people to be diligent in the study of poetry and rhetoric. (Preserved Smith and Charles M. Jacobs, eds. *Luther's Correspondence.* Philadelphia: United Lutheran Publication House, 1918. Vol. 2, pp. 176-77.)

I would call that a rather emphatic charter for Christian humanism. In many respects, the riches in the present collection are to show how literature is a "John the Baptist" that prepares and points the way for Christ. They do not make the move of explicit witness, and are not written to convert people to Jesus. They are not proselytizing documents. I make that point because it is necessary to remind the pluralist culture that this Christian voice has a full claim, *as humanism,* to be heard in public classrooms. Christian humanism is not a churchly affair, but a cultural one.

To try to understand Western civilization while screening out the greatest, oldest, wisest, most convincing voices (alongside those of the Greco-Roman world, which have a privileged place) is an educational folly, a pedagogical scandal. Yet the attempt has often gone on, thanks to Christian abdication, thoughtlessness, organized obtuseness, and ganging up by humanists-in-general.

But whenever one sets out to make a case for Christian humanism in the public forum or the classroom, there is always a challenge from a culture that lives off texts: show us the texts! At that point one mumbles a bit about Petrarch and Erasmus and John Henry Newman, and the curriculum committee moves on. It has not time to go rummaging through libraries. There must be convenient materials. From now on there is little room for shuffling off, because materials are now at hand.

This anthology boldly sets claims to the ground Christian humanism once so willingly and forthrightly claimed. It brings together some highlights from the almost unlimited gallery of Christian humanist thinkers. They are stimulants to our own not yet exhausted imaginations. It could be that Christians in the humanistic culture and humanists who do not call themselves by the name of Christ alike will profit from the stimulus of people who enjoy being part of the race that God honored by choosing to dwell in it.

MARTIN E. MARTY
University of Chicago

Preface

This book presents a selection of writings on humanism from the perspective of Christian faith. Beginning with Plato, Aristotle, and the Old Testament, as forerunners of the Christian tradition of humanism, the readings range from early Christianity to modern times. Included are such important thinkers as Augustine, Francis of Assisi, Petrarch, Erasmus, Galileo, Reinhold Niebuhr, Dorothy Sayers, and Martin Luther King, Jr. Excerpts from the works of such influential persons show how Christians in different historical periods have addressed themselves to significant human problems.

The purpose of the book is to bring into plain view the enduring strength and amplitude of the humanism found in historic Christianity. The selections are not intended to trace the development of Christian doctrine, nor to review the history of the church, but rather to unfold before the reader the main elements in the tradition of Christian humanism. Of each contribution the reader is invited to ask, "What does this writer say about the meaning of being human?" A related question is, "How does the writer's Christian faith affect the understanding of humanism?"

As used in this book, the term "Christian humanism" refers to a long-standing feature, especially of Western civilization, in which Christian insight and practice have yielded certain basic understandings about human nature, its powers, limits, purpose, and destiny. Christian humanism has been a fluid rather than a fixed element in Western culture. It embraces disagreements among Christians regarding various human actions and aspirations. Sometimes it must take issue with other types of humanism, but at other times it may join non-Christians in supporting goals for the protection and enhancement of human life. In its fundamental attitudes, Christian humanism is moved by a profound appreciation of the distinctiveness of human existence and a desire to enable all human persons to attain their fulfillment, as individuals and in community with others.

Christian humanism bases its regard for human beings on the central affirmations of the Christian faith. Persons owe their existence and true nature to the action of a Creator God. History reveals a universal and persistent tendency on the part of humankind to rebel against the Creator, with disastrous consequences for human society and the world. But God in his love for his creatures has acted to restore human beings and their environment. The coming of Jesus Christ into the world, so Christians believe, is not only God's move to rescue humans from their fallenness, but is the ultimate affirmation of the human race and the personal pledge of its fulfillment.

This particular way of looking at human existence is not merely a page from a Christian catechism; it is the source of much of the substance and energy of the Western humanistic tradition. Christian humanism is as much a part of the cultural background of every person touched by Western culture as are, for example, the development of modern science and the ideal of democracy, both of which were nourished on Christian soil.

In past generations, educated people, whether committed Christians or not, usually had a general familiarity with the tradition of Christian humanism. In recent times, however, knowledge of Christian humanism has grown faint, in the institutions of higher learning and even in the churches. The conviction guiding the preparation of this book is that younger and older adults are entitled to know about this profound and fascinating humanism, an outgrowth of historic religion and a vital part of their intellectual and moral heritage.

The present volume has grown out of a joint academic program partially supported by the National Endowment for the Humanities. Four colleges of the Upper Midwest, two Roman Catholic and two Lutheran, have collaborated in introducing students and the wider public to the heritage of Christian humanism. The four colleges—the College of St. Catherine in St. Paul, Minnesota; Luther College in Decorah, Iowa; St. John's University in Collegeville, Minnesota; and St. Olaf College in Northfield, Minnesota—are all liberal-arts institutions devoted to the study of the humanities and consciously related to the Christian community. The grants from the National Endowment for the Humanities have enabled these colleges to introduce new courses on Christian humanism on the respective campuses, to present a series of public festivals and seminars, and to make study materials on Christian humanism available to other colleges, universities, and adult discussion groups through publication.

The editors wish to acknowledge their great debts to colleagues and students at the four colleges without whose help the Christian Humanism Project never could have been launched nor this book assembled:

At the College of St. Catherine: Presidents—Sr. Alberta Huber c.s.j. and Sr. Catherine McNamee c.s.j.; Academic Deans—Sr. Karen Kennelly, c.s.j. and Sr. Anita Pampusch, c.s.j.; Professors—Sr. Eileen Gavin, c.s.j., Rev. John Ginsterblum, s.j., Alan Graebner, George Rochefort, and Ms. Jane Lamm Carroll.

At Luther College: President E. D. Farwell, Dean Glenn Nelson, Associate Dean Jane Borelli, Professors Bruce Wrightsman and Leigh Jordahl, and Ms. Jane Kemp.

At St. John's University: Abbot Jerome Theisen, o.s.b., President Michael Blecker, o.s.b., Vice-President Gunther Rolfson, o.s.b., Dean Robert Spaeth, Bro. Alcuin Francis, o.s.b., Mr. Peter Gathje, Ms. Maxine Richmond, Mr. Patrick Murphy, Ms. Ann Coughlin, Ms. Mary Flood, Ms. Mary Fox O'Boyle, Mr. Michael O'Keefe.

At St. Olaf College: President Harlan F. Foss, former President Sidney A. Rand, Vice-President David E. Johnson, Dean Keith O. Anderson, former Dean William C. Nelson, Professors Harold H. Ditmanson and William H. K. Narum, Ms. Sharon Bishop.

And the two evaluators of the Christian Humanism Project: Dean H. J. Hanham of M.I.T. and former President Edward A. Lindell of Gustavus Adolphus College.

Introduction

The Tradition of Christian Humanism

Christian humanism is the interest in human persons and the positive affirmation of human life and culture which stems from the Christian faith. It shares with other humanistic philosophies the motive of discovering and supporting whatever enhances human existence, but is distinctive in finding the source and goal of human powers in God, the Creator, Redeemer, and Spirit. Where secular forms of humanism focus on "merely" human interests, deliberately excluding transcendent factors from consideration, Christian humanism seeks an understanding of the whole range of human experience in the light of God's revelation to humanity in the person and work of Jesus Christ.

Christian Humanism and Its Sources

One does not find numerous references to Christian humanism in textbooks. It is not as readily identified as a cultural influence as, for example, Platonism, Stoicism, Thomism, rationalism, or existentialism. It is more of a pervasive and creative presence in history especially in the development of Western civilization, though one of its most important sources, the Bible, is not strictly a Western document. For many, Christian humanism has an unfamiliar ring because when the word "humanism" first entered the English language it was understood in certain circles as the designation of an unorthodox theological view in which the doctrine of the divinity of Christ was denied.[1] Furthermore, "humanism" is associated historically with the period of the Renaissance which is popularly understood as having taken up the study of human beings as rational creatures set free from all theological determinations.[2]

Actually, Christian humanism emerged with Christianity itself. As soon as Christian people reflected on the new criteria for determining the meaning of their lives, the criteria given through faith in Christ, Christian humanism made its appearance. If humanism is an attitude centering on human interests or values, then the first Christians were indeed humanists in their own way. It is a modern misunderstanding that regards ultimate loyalty to God as irreconcilable with a lively concern for human interests and values. As the Danish churchman N. F. S. Grundtvig wrote, "We are human beings first, and only then Christians." Or, in the words of John Locke, "God, when he makes the prophet, does not unmake the man." [3]

One of the major purposes of the present volume is to show that faith in God, far from reducing the sense of how noble and important human beings are, issues in a larger, richer humanism than nontheistic perspectives are able to offer. Discussions of human nature and potential have been impoverished needlessly in modern times by ignorance of what a long line of Christian thinkers and writers have contributed to the understanding of what Reinhold Niebuhr called, in the title of his greatest work, "the nature and destiny of man."

Christian humanism has continued through the centuries, not as a separate, structured, historical movement, but as a leaven or influence making its mark whenever Christianity confronted the cultural situation around it, directing the light of Christ on the question of what it means to be human. The influence has not always been steady and consistent; Christianity experiences its own internal changes in clarifying its faith and applying it to the human scene. Sometimes Christians and churches become aligned with antihumanistic forces, and therefore need to be reformed. Reform and renewal are made possible by the fact that Christianity is defined by a self-critical, renewing power at its heart, namely, the good news about Jesus the Christ.

The good news, or gospel of Christ, is the primary source of Christian humanism, not Christianity as an historical religion nor the church as a hierarchical, authoritarian institution. Stated in brief form, the gospel is the good news that the living God, the ruler of the universe, is favorably disposed toward humankind, and that in his love for his human creation he has sent Jesus Christ into the world to restore and fulfill all that belongs to human existence.

Through careful study of New Testament texts modern biblical authorities—superseding older views that equated the Christian message with platitudes about Jesus, love, and brotherhood—have shown in some detail what the early Christians announced to the world when they proclaimed the "gospel." They declared that (1) the new age of God's rule had arrived; (2) the main sign of its arrival was the appearance of Jesus of Nazareth, who declared that God's rule was at hand, healed the sick and possessed, taught in parables, called disciples, clashed with religious leaders, was arrested, and put to death on a cross; (3) on the third day God raised him from the dead, thereby certifying that Jesus was Lord and Christ; (4) all people, Jews and Gentiles, were summoned to put their trust in this Jesus as the Savior sent from God for the liberation and restoration of the entire human race; (5) trusting in Jesus meant to turn from sin, join the community of Christ by receiving baptism, receive the forgiveness of sins, and experience the revitalizing power of the Holy Spirit; (6) this Jesus, the Risen One, Lord of all and head of his body, the church, will come again as God's emissary to bring history to its conclusion, judge the nations, and make the ultimate sovereignty of God known to every part of creation.

This summary of early Christian preaching starts with the deeds of God as of first importance. "Grace," God's overture to humanity in Christ, creates a new relationship which, viewed from the human side is "faith" or "trust." Thus Christian humanism takes its starting point, not within the human situation as such, but within the fact of divine activity extended toward the human race in Jesus. The next implication for Christian humanism is that God has committed himself to the good of humankind in the most complete and radical way imaginable: he has come to the human family in the person of his own Son, Jesus of Nazareth, an authentic human person. The theological term for this revolutionary fact is *incarnation*. A further important implication is that Jesus, by accepting lowliness, sufferings, and death, made the new life he offered open to all persons, not just to some who have special qualifications. In his public ministry Jesus himself preached good news to the poor, proclaimed release to prisoners, and gave recovery of sight to the blind. The impetus toward humanism, then, is traced to the relationship of faith, the human response to the loving actions of Jesus Christ.

In addition to the gospel as the primary source of Christian humanism one moves naturally to the creeds developed by the church, especially the Apostles' and Nicene Creeds. They resemble the summary of early Christian preaching, especially in their concentration on the figure of Jesus Christ. The humanistic aspect of Christian faith is strikingly expressed when the Nicene Creed says of Christ: "For us and for our salvation he came down from heaven: by the power of the Holy Spirit he became incarnate from the Virgin Mary, and was made man. For our sake he was crucified under Pontius Pilate."

The summary of the gospel and the reference to the creeds might suggest that Christian humanism is identical with theology; rather, theology may be counted as another source of Christian humanism.

Theology defines the content of the church's faith; it places in systematic order the doctrines of the church. St. Augustine, St. Thomas
Aquinas, John Calvin, and H. Richard Niebuhr are good examples of
theologians who can be regarded as Christian humanists as well.
When theologians take up the doctrine of creation, for example, Christian humanism is attentive to what this doctrine, reinterpreted for
each generation, implies for the nature, possibilities, and responsibilities of the human creatures. Christian humanism does not attempt to
formulate doctrinal statements for the church. To take another example, it does not offer a particular interpretation of the person of Christ,
but it takes a keen interest in how certain Christological developments
affect the determination of various human concerns.

So it is with such theological disciplines as church history and ethics. Issues of humanism are numerous in the history of the church, to
be sure, but they also appear in interesting byways outside the usual
orbit of church history. Christian ethics inquires, in Paul Lehmann's
words, into "what God is doing in the world to make and to keep human life human." [4] The affinity with humanism is obvious. On the other
hand, Christian humanism does not set for itself the considerable program of producing solutions to ethical problems. It is often in the
neighborhood of ethics, but it remains free to travel along other roads
as well.

One other source of Christian humanism is suggested in a phrase
from a prayer of the church in which the worshippers give thanks for
"the lives of all faithful and godly people." Besides drawing upon the
central message of Christianity, the gospel, the great creeds of Christendom, and the theological fields, Christian humanism draws suste-
nance from a huge but often unknown company of people, past and
present, who have talked, sung, written, and preached about human
life imbued with divine reality. The names of many are known:
Saints Benedict and Francis, Dante Alighieri, Marsilio Ficino, Johann
Sebastian Bach, John Henry Newman, Dorothy Sayers, and others.
Among the unknown are writers of letters, composers of hymns, obscure
poets, preachers, and professors who spoke or wrote a timely word
that helped someone move a step closer to true humanness.

The sources of Christian humanism suggested above do not exhaust
the possibilities; in every generation men, women, and children will
discover new regions of experience from which further contributions
to humanism will be drawn. The reflections of thoughtful persons
weighing the needs and opportunities of their age will always be an
important resource for all who examine the human story from the
perspective of Christian faith.

Features of Christian Humanism

In the discussion of any world view, definitions serve only a limited purpose. They indicate partially what the conversation is about; they provide some preliminary pointers. In time, however, definitions must give way to descriptions. The following paragraphs describe some of the features of Christian humanism.

1. Human nature under God. From the book of Genesis, to St. Augustine, to the Renaissance scholar Pico della Mirandola, and to the twentieth century theologian Emil Brunner, the topic of human nature remains fresh and salient. Created in the image of God, human beings are perceived by the Christian humanist as closely related to God, dependent upon him, part of a "good" created order, but distinct from all other creatures in nature, abilities, freedom, vocation, and destiny. Emil Brunner maintains that the biblical notion of *imago Dei* (image of God) is not the same as the Greek idea of man's participation in the divine *nous* or *logos* which dwells in his reason. He writes, "Christian humanism . . . as distinguished from the Greek, is of such a kind that the humane character of existence is not automatically a possession of man, but is dependent on his relation to God, and remains a matter of decision." [5]

2. Human sinfulness. Non-Christians are often repelled by the biblical doctrine of original sin, and Christians vary widely in how they treat the idea. Tertullian, an early Christian teacher, acknowledges the corrupt origin of the soul but adds, "Still there is a portion of good in the soul, of that original, divine, and genuine good, which is its proper nature." [6] Augustine took a more drastic view of the disobedience of the first two humans: "The sin which they committed was so great that it impaired all human nature—in this sense, that the nature has been transmitted to posterity with a propensity to sin and a necessity to die." [7] For the modern mind, the universality of sin is the issue, not so much the origin or the mode of transmission of this "propensity." For Christian humanism, not only is it part of realism to acknowledge human sin, but it is part of faith and freedom to know the power of forgiveness in personal existence before God and among human persons.

3. An orderly universe. Marred as it is by sin, the world was created good, and the Creator's work of creating and governing continues. The Genesis creation stories show the human figures as responsible stewards of the created order, not plunderers. In recent times an ancient idea has reappeared: that humans are expected to live in harmony with nature; the order or disorder of the world owes a great deal to human decisions. In that connection, humanism does not con-

fine itself narrowly to the human sphere alone. It is essential to humanism that the relationship between humans and their world not be
allowed to deteriorate into indifference or exploitation.

In the Christian view, the basic order of the universe reflects the
providence of a God who cares for his creatures, placing them in a
world which they inhabit as their home. In keeping the world safe for
human habitation, humans are asked to take up their delegated role
as co-workers with God in the continuing process of creation. Dorothy
Sayers remarks that in the human soul's desire for creativeness lies its
"substantial likeness to the Divine Christ who in this world suffers and
creates continually." [8] Sayers also underscores the church's insistence
"that the whole material universe is an expression and incarnation of
the creative energy of God." [9]

4. *Human responsibility.* Christian humanism rejects on biblical
grounds the passivity which withdraws us from the historical struggle
to await the final intervention of God. It upholds responsibility, for
the neighbor and for the world, as a noble sign of humanity. In the
ancient world Christians had to assert themselves against a deaden-
ing sense of fate; in the contemporary world the voices of Christian
humanism are raised against other determinisms which regard humans
as controlled by hereditary or environmental factors. There is also need
to affirm responsibility in the face of advertising, political propaganda,
and other mass influences which threaten to deprive persons of their
right to exercise independent judgment in important decisions.

5. *The human will and its freedom.* Against determinism and behaviorism, Christian humanism seeks freedom for all persons, but not
under the illusion that human freedom is absolute. Human life is always set within limits, though humanists generally react strongly
against determinism. For the Christian humanist, the question of
human will and freedom begins with the sovereign freedom of God
and human freedom as a gift.

A famous historical dispute on free will took place between Erasmus
and Luther. Luther granted the exercise of free will in all matters
"below" humankind, the ordinary decisions of daily life. But "those
things pertaining to eternal salvation" were a different matter. Erasmus
claimed that persons had some freedom of will to turn to or away from
that which leads to salvation. Luther replied, "With regard to God, and
in all things pertaining to salvation or damnation, man has no free will,
but is a captive, servant and bond-slave, either to the will of God, or to
the will of Satan." [10]

It is an ancient question, occupying the minds of Augustine and Paul
long before the Luther–Erasmus debate, but the nature and extent of
the will's freedom continues to challenge thoughtful people. For Chris-

tians a paradox exists: the more fully one surrenders the will to God, the more freedom one may experience. According to St. Paul, those who are called to freedom are asked to be servants, through love, of one another (Gal. 5:13).

6. *Community.* Non-Christian humanisms tend to revel in individualism, but uninformed Christians are also attracted by the image of the solitary, autonomous hero. Renaissance humanism is frequently praised for its individualistic spirit. But Christian humanism, rooted in the Old Testament and carried forward by the apostolic church, pictures the individual, the person, as part of a community. "Man cannot become truly human except by entering into community," writes Emil Brunner.[11] Romano Guardini anticipated much later Christian thought about community when in 1922 he wrote: "There are human beings like myself. Each one is akin to me, but each one is also a separate world of his own, of unique value. And from this realisation springs the passionate conviction that we all belong one to another; are all brothers. It is now taken as self-evident that the individual is a member of the community. . . . the task of building up the community is just as primary and fundamental as that of perfecting personality." [12]

7. *Human gifts and talents.* All humanistic philosophies stand for the fostering of each person's unique endowments, whether strength, intelligence, or talents. In a competitive society, however, these individual endowments too often are perceived as setting individuals against one another. Popular culture consciously urges persons and groups to covet what is regarded as the highest distinction, to rise to pre-eminence over all the others. The irony of this drive to excel is that those who succeed in achieving the desired superiority are those who most fully reflect the commonly held values. Theirs is the triumph of conformity, though hailed ritualistically as uniqueness.

In the tradition of Christian humanism, human talents are appreciated as gifts to be shared in the community for the benefit of others. Differences in abilities need not be viewed in a competitive way, but welcomed for the diversity they lend to the community's life. Such was the case, for instance, in the Benedictine monastic communities. The abbot, out of responsibility for the good of the flock, was charged to treat the brothers "according to each one's character and understanding," and in the daily life of the monastery the brothers were encouraged to apply their talents to work that would be useful for the community.[13] But even more important in the Benedictine way of life was humility, the injunction to consider oneself lower and of less account than anyone else.[14]

8. *History and human destiny.* Christian humanism seeks to understand human experience within a context of history because Christian-

ity understands itself as arising from God's redeeming actions in history. Seeing all of world history under the guidance of God, the author of the book of Revelation, and St. Augustine, whose *City of God* was influenced by this apocalypse, and Christians of all centuries have lived in confidence that God will bring history to its intended culmination. Christian humanism shares the conviction that history has a purpose for which Christ is the key, but it does not share the views of those who use the Bible to issue detailed predictions about the future course of history. It is enough to know that the future is in God's hands.

Earlier in this century, Reinhold Niebuhr rejected liberalism's optimism about human history and its belief in the law of progress. He wrote, "History points to a goal beyond itself, and not merely to an eternity which negates history. . . . God transcends history and yet makes himself known in history." [15] Christian hope in its fullness gives the individual confidence in a new existence with Christ after death, but the individual believer's hope is also related to belief in the redemption of both creation and history, signaled by the resurrection of Christ from the dead. Moreover, the Christian already experiences in this life the powers and qualities of "the age to come." Therefore life in this world is not simply the marking of time until the end comes; it is rather a time for vigorous, creative activity energized by the present power of the Holy Spirit.

Some of the features of Christian humanism have been indicated in the preceding pages, but others could be named. Once the basic perspective is established that the central factor for Christian humanism is the incarnation of divine power through Christ in the textures of this world, it will be seen that the spheres of experience feeling the impact of Christ are virtually without limit. In summarizing the important features of Christian humanism, one observes that certain basic themes are present in the form of dialectical pairs of ideas. From ancient to modern times, Christian humanism is always concerned with the relationship of the individual to the community; it expresses in a variety of ways the unique Christian insight that both matter and spirit are in the service of human purposes; it acknowledges that faith implies both freedom and authority; finally, Christian humanism holds that the incarnation of Christ gives significance to both time and eternity.

Other Types of Humanism

Since the purpose of this volume is to provide readings and commentary to show the meaning of Christian humanism, it will be useful by way of comparison to mention some other humanistic viewpoints. One need not assume that other humanisms are sharply at odds with

Christian humanism at every point, but it is essential to recognize certain differences.

For well over a thousand years, the Western world was familiar with a humanism combining Christian and biblical elements with the idealism of the classical world. With the Renaissance and Reformation, the humanistic stream began to separate, the Renaissance pursuing the classical view of humanity which gloried in human freedom and potential, the Reformation emphasizing divine grace and human dependence upon God. Rudolf Bultmann, a prominent New Testament scholar of this century, has characterized the difference between classical humanism of the Greco-Roman tradition and Christian faith. The former, he writes, "expresses the conviction that man by virtue of his spirit is able to shape his life in freedom and to subject to himself the world in which he has to live his life." By contrast, "the Christian faith expresses the conviction that man is not his own master, that this world is an alien country to him, and that he can gain his freedom from the world only with the help of divine grace, which is freely given to the world from the beyond." [16]

The context of Bultmann's comments indicates that he sees Western culture in need of both types of humanism to make a stand against the nihilism and totalitarianism of the twentieth century. Historically, the two major humanisms drew further apart from one another in the time of the Enlightenment. Scientific discoveries and a new philosophical interest in human nature created an increased confidence in human powers. When the empirical method was combined with philosophical anthropocentrism, the door was opened for secular humanisms to make their appearance.

Secularization did not happen overnight, but from the eighteenth to the twentieth century the gap gradually widened between Christian and secularist viewpoints about human existence, partly because of the developments in science, but more through the association of science with a naturalistic philosophy. In addition, the new demands of nationalism and industrialization gave a different focus to human energies. The social as well as the natural sciences contributed to secularization in the nineteenth and twentieth centuries. Auguste Comte, the father of sociology, propounded a philosophy of positivism which was of enormous influence in laying the groundwork for modern secularism. According to Comte's Law of the Three Stages, human society outlives the theological and metaphysical stages and moves inevitably toward the final positive–scientific stage in which a new "religion of humanity," a religion without God, is created.

Accompanied by powerful social and political movements, the ideas of scientists and other thinkers seemed to bend the Western world inexorably toward a firmly secularist view of life. By the middle of the nineteenth century religion seemed superfluous to many. Some voices even declared, "God is dead!" and life on earth continued much as it had before. That human beings could handle their affairs without reference to God and the church seemed self-evident, so various secular humanisms appeared on the scene.

From a historical perspective the rise of secular humanisms does not appear as striking as the survival of any kind of humanism through the shattering destruction and brutalities of the twentieth century. Two major wars followed by decades of further assaults on every human sensibility might well have spelled the end of every humanistic dream. But human beings are resilient and capable of astonishing tenacity. In the contemporary world one can identify at least four types of humanism devoted to preserving humanity from destruction and to unfolding more humane patterns of existence. They overlap one another somewhat, making the attempt to find suitable names for them an exercise in approximation. The four to be described here may be called *academic, scientific, secular,* and *religious–ethical* humanism.

Academic humanism pays homage to the Greeks and the Renaissance as its key historical predecessors. Usually found in the humanities divisions of colleges and universities, it moves with cosmopolitan interest among a wide range of sources for the study of mankind, tapping the riches of prose, poetry, philosophy, and the arts. Academic humanism needs no persuading to include such Christian luminaries as Erasmus, Milton, and T. S. Eliot in its search for significant aspects of human understanding. In an age heavily dominated by the scientific point of view, academic humanism strives to prevent the aesthetic, imaginative powers of the personality from being stifled by narrow, pragmatic approaches to truth.

Scientific humanism is both old and new. Enlightenment thinkers adopted science as an effective tool to be applied by reason to the solving of human problems. What is new in recent times is a scientific naturalism which proclaims itself capable of explaining the human mind, human qualities, and religious faith itself, entirely by means of physical laws. The discipline of sociobiology aims at producing a mythology which will replace the role now played by traditional religion.[17] Some critics say that scientific humanism does not really stand in the humanistic tradition because it does not believe in a human nature possessing intrinsic and inalienable qualities.[18]

Secular humanism is a broad term applicable, at times, to scientific humanism, and inclusive of such variations as naturalistic, Marxist–socialist, rationalist, and behaviorist humanism. The adjective "secularistic" could be used to apply to humanisms which are militantly atheistic. In general, secular humanism refers to those interpretations that seek the full meaning of human existence within the boundaries of this age and this world. What humans are and ought to be can be determined without reference to any powers or gods outside the pale of verifiable human knowledge. Naturalistic humanism seeks the welfare of all persons with reference to such strictly natural forces as heredity, environment, and physical needs. It rejects both religious supernaturalism and metaphysical idealism. Problems can be solved through reason, science, and the principles of democracy.

Marxist or socialist humanism also renounces dependence upon powers outside the empirical, known processes of life. Marx regarded religion as antihumanistic. For him the central human problem was alienation, from the self, from the work process, and from other persons. In his view capitalism dehumanized people, and religion gave its assent to oppressive forces instead of opposing them. Humans are to transform the world, to free humankind from all forms of enslavement and alienation, especially the economic exploitation based on class antagonisms.

Rationalist humanism obviously follows the Greek idealistic view that reason is the definitive feature of human existence. No higher authority exists. It can be assumed that human beings are capable of those decisions and actions which reason stipulates. Behaviorist humanism finds the clue to human action, not in reason and self-awareness, but in the social environment. B. F. Skinner, a leading behaviorist, writes: "I would define a Humanist as one of those who, because of the environment to which he has been exposed, is concerned for the future of mankind." [19] Skinner's writings stress the control of human behavior based on a scientific study of the environment.

Religious–ethical humanism is not to be confused with Christian humanism, despite the words with which its proponents have chosen to describe it. According to this style of humanism, religion may have value in inspiring people to ethical responsibility, and ethics has value as long as it arises from human need and is guided by human experience. But religion is rejected if it expresses belief in transcendent power, traditional dogmas, creeds, or specific theological views on divine revelation. The *Humanist Manifestos* issued in 1933 and 1973 set forth the character of this nontheistic humanism which "begins with humans not God, nature not deity." [20]

The religion and ethics of which this viewpoint speaks are subservient to human experience and judgment. Traditional religions are faulted for failing to foster independence and courage, and even for being antihumanistic. "Humanism cannot in any fair sense of the word apply to one who still believes in God as the source and creator of the universe," writes one of its spokesmen.[21] Religious–ethical humanism is another version of secular humanism since it is very explicit in ruling out theism and in limiting human meaning to earthly, historical existence. "Humans are responsible for what we are or will become. No deity will save us; we must save ourselves." [22]

As stated, there is considerable overlapping among the above types of humanisms. Closer examination of their tenets would reveal a common respect for human reason, a call to responsibility, a typical admiration of science and its role in the humanizing process, a fundamental desire to secure human happiness, and skepticism—if not outright hostility—toward traditional religion, from which, ironically, they derive their notions of the sacredness of human personality. Among the values and goals of these differing humanisms are ideas which a Christian humanist might well endorse, but some with which he or she would have to disagree. By that same token, the humanisms described above would not necessarily reject all features of Christian humanism, though it is clear that for the most part they deny any human relationship to transcendent powers.

Humanism on Trial

The purpose of this volume is to present the tradition of Christian humanism as a significant resource available to thoughtful men and women as they seek to understand their humanness and to serve more effectively the needs of humanity. But there are other humanisms in the field. A more extended examination of differences would reveal, among other things, that Christian humanism offers a framework for affirming the uniqueness of human nature, whereas most secular humanisms, approaching the human phenomenon empirically, are at a loss to explain why human beings are different from other creatures.

The point to be taken up now is the current threat to all humanism. In view of the dangerous, dehumanizing forces at work in the world today, the question, What is humanism? is far from being an academic one, as the following statement by Floyd Matson indicates:

> Not only Humanism and humaneness, but humanity itself, is in clear and present danger of extinction—on one side from the technology of violence, which has given us an irresistible armory of doomsday machines and collective self-destructive devices; on the other side from the technology of industry, which has given us (as an accidental by-product of its enterprise) a chemical fallout which promises the slow death of the environ-

ment. Indeed, the physical threat to life and existence appears to many so compelling as to override all concerns and considerations other than that of survival itself.[23]

But even if humanity survives, saving itself by computer programming, systems analysis, and biological engineering, contends Matson, the survival of humanism would not thereby be assured, for underlying industrial, technological society with its mechanical picture of the world is a conception of human nature which is fundamentally antihumanistic. Matson calls it the image of *mass man*, "of man as the passive creature of ulterior forces working through and upon him, either from without (stimulus-response psychologies) or from within (instinct and drive psychologies)."[24] This image of mass man has become so deeply ingrained and so fully harmonized with the dictates of the industrial state "that it has remained largely an unchallenged and inarticulate assumption both in the public mind and in the behavioral sciences."[25]

Humanism is on trial in the present era, in events which threaten humanity itself, in the ideas which often provide the rationale for antihuman actions, and in certain religious circles which have made humanism the object of a determined attack. Looking back on the history of the twentieth century, one sees the plain and brutal record of actual destruction of human beings through major wars, genocides, totalitarian oppression, growing poverty, disastrous famine, and the spread of violence. If one thinks of humanism quite simply and noncontroversially as respect for human life and well-being, one can only conclude that it has been under severe attack throughout most of the course of this century. There are always calamities over which human beings have little or no control, but the events mentioned above are those involving conscious human decisions.

Humanism is also under attack in the world of ideas. Those who perpetuate cruelty and oppression against human beings operate from their own perverted kind of "humanism." Tyrants like Hitler claim the right to determine who is human and who is not, and to liquidate the latter. The so-called super powers amass their arsenals of indescribable destructive power with the justification that they are only seeking to preserve a form of human existence superior to that of the enemy. Business interests which spend more on advertising than is spent by the whole nation on education are promoting a pallid sort of "humanism": human beings as consumers.

Humanism also suffers from the current confusion about the meaning of humanism; the term is adopted by ideologies which have little in common with the tradition of humaneness once universally recognized by every sensitive person. Debate over the meaning of humanism is to be encouraged, but always in the hope that the dialog will expose the difference between authentic humanisms which embody a respect for the human person and those would-be humanisms which ultimately stifle the human spirit.

It is evident that the topic of humanism needs to receive a thorough airing when one observes, for example, that one writer insists that scientific humanism *is* humanism, rejecting religious humanism as a contradiction in terms. In another case, one person declares that Marxism is humanism, while a colleague questions whether the term properly can be used by orthodox Marxist–Leninists. The same commentator decides to exclude Pope Paul VI from the humanist circle because the Holy Father's faith and piety seemed to take precedence over reason and reliance on human powers.[26]

Further indications of the erosion of the values of humanism are found in the public marketplace of ongoing events and ideas where "unchallenged and inarticulate assumptions" about human nature are often as strong and influential as consciously held opinions. For example, the issue of abortion is vigorously debated, with persons of conscience to be found on both sides of the question. But in the meantime, one and one-half million abortions are being performed each year in the United States. As the practice increases, the haunting question is how a society can avoid becoming calloused regarding human life.

A similar concern must be voiced about increasing private and public violence. There are a few modest gains for humanism when such acts as rape and the battering of women and children, once concealed from view, are being brought to the attention of appropriate public authorities, and the help of counselors and therapists is made available to the victims. Nevertheless, what alarms the humanist is the growing attitude of acceptance shown by the public toward acts of violence. As so often happens, the dangerous dimensions of increasing crime are minimized by journalists and politicians who invoke the comforting, chauvinistic myth that the people of the United States are "basically good." This societal self-deception is supported by powerful commercial interests with their active lobbyists who contrive to undercut any humane measures of reform, whether it is a case of beating down sensible restrictions on the use of firearms or producing statistics designed to "prove" that crime and violence on television have no detrimental effects on human conduct.

The status of humanism in the colleges and universities is an ambiguous one. Within the humanities divisions of the institutions the good fight for the humanist cause continues to be waged, but even there the fullness of the humanistic tradition gives way at times to narrow specialization. The field of philosophy, which traditionally interpreted humanity with reference to metaphysical and ethical considerations, tends now, from the influence of logical positivism and the philosophy of Wittgenstein, to concentrate on questions of linguistic analysis. The social sciences using empirical methods have amassed new data about human behavior and its causes, but such studies tend to regard human beings as organisms subject to conditioning by their environment. The more "humanistic" social scientists point out that their colleagues have adopted the mechanistic models of a physics which is now outmoded.

The public schools in general are weak in offering students an acquaintance with the humanistic heritage. Functional illiteracy affects millions of young adults. Language study has fallen off drastically. The great literary works which their parents grew up on are no longer read by high-school students. History has become "social studies" in many places. The important question of what it means to be human is not approached through an exposure to the works of great humanists of the past and present, but through filmstrips and movies dealing with "lifestyles," drug abuse, sex education, and the like. Since teachers are constrained from making moral judgments, all points of view are given equal standing in theory. In practice, students are left in confusion, receiving little or no help in formulating their ideas about human values.

According to theologian Emil Brunner, all true humanism is doomed when cut off from its metaphysical base. He argues that the humanism of the Renaissance and early Enlightenment was still in touch with the metaphysical substance of the Christian tradition until the movement of positivism replaced metaphysics with naturalism. The way was thus cleared for philosophies which regarded humans, not as unique personal beings, but as "nothing but" highly differentiated animals.[27] This reductionistic understanding of humankind produces such slogans as "Man is nothing but a high-brain-capacity, low-instinct organism"; "Human behavior is nothing but a physiological stimulus-response pattern"; or "Human values are nothing but products of society."[28]

A measure of the deterioration of humanism in the twentieth century is what has happened to the category of "the human," which traditionally was distinguished both from the divine and from the bestial. As the great humanistic systems have been attacked by naturalistic positivism, materialism, behaviorism, and other nonmetaphysical ideologies, the uniqueness of human beings has been placed in jeopardy. Early in the century, liberal optimism tried to elevate humans virtually to divine status; later in the century came the opposite threat, treating

persons as subhuman, subjecting them to totalitarian control, environmental conditioning, psychological manipulation, and biological determinism.

In the first case, the problem of evil and the fact of limits are ignored.
In the other instance, "being human" is equated with weakness. Persons
are thus absolved of responsibility, their aggressiveness excused, their
animalistic behavior rationalized, and their freedoms curtailed "for
their own good." In both cases, the wonder and complexity of human
personality are not fully honored.

In recent times humanism has been placed on trial both by the shattering events of a turbulent world and by some of the changing ideas
of what it means to be human. What individuals and societies think
about the meaning of humanity is directly related to the private and
public events that affect human beings. Humanism, therefore, is not an
isolated intellectual topic of interest only to scholars and students. It
is a subject worthy of broad public attention, especially when there no
longer seems to be a consensus that humans are unique, free, and
responsible beings whose lives and dignity should be protected at
all costs.

Humanism is also under attack from still another quarter. The source
of this challenge is a constellation of "conservative" religious forces
which has defined humanism simply as secular humanism. These forces
have singled out humanism as the enemy of such cherished institutions
as the home, the public school, and the nation itself. At an earlier stage
in history these religious groups fastened upon communism as the chief
threat to the United States, but more recently they have traced the
moral and political ills of American society to humanism.

This movement differs from predecessors in that it actively seeks
political power and specific legislation to remove from public life certain practices which it labels as immoral: homosexuality, abortion, sex
education in the public schools, and what is perceived as a general
moral laxity in the entire culture. Representatives of this religious
moralism attack secular humanism by appealing to the reputed Christian character of the United States and to certain moral teachings of
the Bible, which is held to be inerrant and interpreted literalistically.
The religious right, usually called the Christian Right because it lays
claim to the Christian tradition, aims to support and elect political
candidates who agree with its conception of what is moral; it has had
striking success in this endeavor.

There could be significant gains for society if the leaders of the religious right were to analyze the weaknesses of secular humanism and
instruct their followers in the meaning of Christian humanism, but that
is not the case. Ironically, proponents of this particular viewpoint un-

derstand the concept of humanism as defined by secular humanists—or, more accurately, by those relatively few secular humanists who add atheism to their belief that human life is determined solely by the known phenomena of this world. The religious right is not interested in distinguishing between varying kinds of humanism; in its thinking, the very concept of humanism is unacceptable because humanism by definition and necessarily must be atheistic as well as secular.

An attack on secular humanism is in order in view of its exclusive claim to represent the humanistic tradition. The problem, however, is that in its anxiety about atheistic humanism the religious right fails to recognize that there are other humanisms which are not necessarily atheistic, including what was referred to earlier as academic humanism, and even certain forms of secular humanism which do not find it necessary to deny religion. Society can benefit from such humanisms as well as from Christian humanism. There is a danger that the religious right, in aiming its weapons at secular humanism, may also wound endeavors which it might embrace in the common struggle for the life, dignity, and freedom of all human persons.

Christian Humanism for a New Day

In spite of the fact that humanism is on trial, there are signs in the late twentieth century that the tradition of Christian humanism may have a better opportunity to make an impact on culture than was the case earlier. But in noting such signs, one must take special care to avoid triumphalism and not to predict the cultural ascendancy of Christian humanism. The latter has its source in the gospel of a humiliated, crucified Christ and thus its power, like that of the gospel, is hidden; its support of humanity must be commensurate with the principle of grace whereby "power is made perfect in weakness." Christian humanism takes its place in the world as a witness to the truth, not as an ideological system designed to vanquish all rivals and establish its dominance over culture.

Christian insights regarding human beings have been available for centuries, to be sure, but in the present stage of human history there are indications of a new readiness to let Christian humanism make its case. Christian humanism offers to all persons a way of understanding and appropriating a fully human life based on the good news of God's love embodied in Jesus Christ. Such words may have a conventional ring, but the possibility at hand is that the form of Christianity's mission to the future may be one, not of conversion in the usual sense, but of presenting to the world a fresh articulation of humanism.

Humanism has been on trial and under attack, as noted above, yet the disasters of recent times have not smothered the yearnings for peace and justice. On the contrary, men and women of all nations recognize the futility of relying on military power to resolve differences among peoples, with the experience of the United States in Vietnam as a telling case in point. The image of beating swords into plowshares is more compelling than it has ever been.

The painful economic disorders in the world are giving new weight to the need for cooperative planning among the nations, taking the concept of a worldwide family of brothers and sisters out of the sphere of utopian dreaming into that of finding concrete measures to relieve human need. Some still pin their hopes on the old economy of greed and expansion, but wiser heads understand the unyielding facts of limitations, which can only mean that human beings throughout the globe must learn to share resources in order that all may live.

Recent ecological discussions have placed in focus the interesting and valuable insight that a sound humanism does not simply concentrate on humans as such, but is vitally concerned about the total environment in which human fulfillment is pursued. In one of his books René Dubos nominated St. Benedict as patron saint of ecology. He writes, "Benedict of Nursia, who was certainly as good a Christian as Francis of Assisi, can be regarded as a patron saint of those who believe that true conservation means not only protecting nature against human misbehavior but also developing human activities which favor a creative, harmonious relationship between man and nature." [29]

A humanistic care for the treasures of nature has its corollary in the stewardship of personal wealth. Christian humanism shares the longstanding wisdom that fullness of life does not depend upon the abundance of one's possessions. At the same time, a clear mandate summons believers to regard the poor and the deprived as those among whom the living Christ will be found. Many churches in the affluent countries have been slow in acting on the fundamental biblical commands to feed the hungry and clothe the naked. Nevertheless, the Christian community, inspired by such significant symbolic gestures as the visits of Pope John XXIII and his successors to prisoners in Rome, is being led to recognize as never before that its calling in a world of poverty and injustice is to be a fellowship of service in the midst of suffering humanity.

One of the significant gains for humanism in the church during this century has been the ecumenical movement, the recognition that the church is a family of persons from many nations, diverse backgrounds, and all races. The drive toward Christian unity among Roman Catholics, Orthodox, and Protestants has underscored the humanistic insight that God's creative and redemptive work in the world is intended to bring the children of God together in one community of faith. Since the vision of the unity of all humanity is a prominent feature of the Hebrew Bible that the first Christians adopted, it follows that the people of God is a community in which the Jews are the older brothers and sisters. How to understand this wider unity of God's family is one of the church's immediate tasks.

In pursuing its mission, the church has learned a great deal about its responsibility toward the whole of humanity. The documents of the Second Vatican Council are replete with such expressions as "the supremely human character of the mission of the Church." "Nothing genuinely human fails to raise an echo" in the hearts of the followers of Christ. Warning against "a humanism which is merely earth-bound," the fathers of the Council said, "Christians cannot yearn for anything more ardently than to serve the men of the modern world ever more generously and effectively." They affirmed the quest for "a world more genuinely human." [30]

In helping to build a more fully human world, churches of diverse backgrounds have rejected the false choice between a mission confined to proclaiming the gospel and one directed toward the furtherance of social justice. It must be both. Preaching and nurture cannot be carried out with integrity if the poor, the sick, and the prisoners are neglected. In short, a new concern for basic human well-being increasingly has characterized the life and mission of many churches in the closing decades of the century.

Theological developments have assisted the church in recovering the human character of its mission. To put the matter briefly, theological thought has come to grips with the humanity of Christ, the humanity of the Bible, and the humanity of the world. The humanity of Christ is appreciated anew, not simply as part of an ancient theological formula, but as an integral feature of the total significance of Christ. As God's servant, he identified himself completely with humanity. The incarnation of the Word of God is the definitive sign of God's unconditional, loving concern for humankind.

The humanity of Christ is the key to a fresh appreciation of the human context and history of Holy Scripture; the divine message is presented in human form. Thus biblical criticism can trace the various human factors—personal, social, and historical—which have influenced the form and content of the Bible, not for the purpose of denying the Bible's credibility as the Word of God, but of more fully understanding its message. Because of a remarkable era of productive biblical scholarship and the dissemination of its results to the general public, deep and detailed knowledge of the Bible is at hand for all who choose to make use of it.

The humanity of the Bible permits its message to be seen for what it is, the story of the actions of a loving God to reconcile the whole human family and to redeem the world. Christ is not only the key to human redemption but the central clue, precisely in his death and resurrection, to the ultimate liberation of the entire created order. According to the New Testament letter to the Colossians it is God's intention through Christ "to reconcile to himself all things, whether on earth or in heaven, making peace by the blood of his cross" (Col. 1:20). A similar thought is expressed by St. Paul in his letter to the Romans: the creation "will be set free from its bondage to decay and obtain the glorious liberty of the children of God" (Rom. 8:21). These statements imply that the process of humanization centered in Jesus Christ, the standard of what it is to be human, anticipates the fulfillment of God's purpose for the entire universe.

Modern theologies are manifesting a fresh interest in the possible relationships between the human and the cosmic. No one can predict where such ideas will lead, challenging as they are to the faith and imagination, but it may be noted that these notions have ancient roots, in the Bible, in Greek philosophy, and in early Christian thought. In ways not as yet clear to modern persons, the history and destiny of humanity is related to the history of nature.

In the meantime and on a more popular level, one finds further encouragement for humanism in the fact that there is public discussion of the values by which people live. A penetrating social criticism is offered by such writers as Christopher Lasch in *The Culture of Narcissism* and Robert Sennett in *The Fall of Public Man* who point up the dangers inherent in popular philosophies of individualism and self-indulgence. Through television programs, movies, and many voluntary agencies the public is being educated concerning famine, poverty, mental illness, chemical dependency, unemployment, the plight of migrants, the condition of refugees, and many other social problems which cry out for compassion and responsible action.

Here and there it is apparent that previously unquestioned assumptions about what makes for the good life are at least challenged if not rejected. There is less unqualified praise of scientific technology as humankind's benefactor; in solving some problems it has created new ones. Thoughtful people see the difference between authentic civil liberty within a social framework and unrestricted personal freedoms which impose on others. While it seems tragically slow in coming, a new sobriety about violence is emerging as Americans face the fact that since 1963 more people, some 400,000, have been killed by fellow Americans wielding guns than were killed in World War II.[31]

Considering that by the middle of this century 50 million people had been killed in wars in Europe alone, it does not seem amiss to suggest that a more realistic view of human nature, which includes its darker side, is in order. It was a Jew, Rabbi Richard Rubenstein, who reminded his largely Christian audience at a university convocation some years ago of "the old Augustinian-Calvinist notion of original sin" when other speakers had been waxing enthusiastic over American messianism and the coming of the new age.[32]

The university world seems more open to serious dialog about profound human questions than was once the case. In 1925 a significant trend began when the University of Iowa established a school of religion. By 1960 over 90 percent of the nation's public-supported colleges and universities were offering courses in religion. Once citadels of secularism, these institutions discovered, belatedly, that in their zeal to exclude "sectarian" viewpoints they had deprived students of a great body of human experience and learning. As Harold Schilling wrote, "Clearly, an institution of higher learning that is without specialists who are conducting research and giving instruction in religion can not be regarded as a real university any more than if it had no productive physicists or philosophers." [33]

For some time, whether through formal courses in religion or through other forums, the colleges and universities have felt the impact of biblical scholarship, the history of religions, and the work of such great theological minds as Karl Barth, Martin Buber, Abraham Heschel, H. Richard and Reinhold Niebuhr, and Paul Tillich. The walls of positivism and scientific humanism are beginning to erode. Some philosophers now argue that metaphysics cannot be removed from philosophical thought. Humanists are challenging the elevation of science to a philosophy, "scientism." Some social scientists are recoiling from a behavioralism which reduces human beings to responding organisms. These few indicators hardly presage the "victory" of Christian humanism, but they suggest an openness to those great and permanent issues —the nature of God, of human personality, and of the universe—which have always been the concern of Christian humanism, itself one of the original architects of the university in the Western world.

The paragraphs above have pointed to a number of signs that Christain humanism may have a fresh opportunity to present its understanding of the human story to receptive minds. Without exaggerating the prospects, one detects a new readiness to consider a Christian interpretation of human life and destiny in the world at large, in the church, and in the academic community. In whatever way one chooses to document the case, the world of the 1980s and 1990s is a different world from that of the opening of this century. In the words of Ernest Becker, the new scientific Faustian man has failed, first in eliminating economic inequality, second in trying to triumph over nature. "Once he had eclipsed the sacred dimension, he had only the earth left to testify to the value of his life." [34]

The tradition of Christian humanism is not a set of answers to specific political, economic, and moral problems of the day, but it holds before the world a perspective on God, the universe, history, and the human spirit which can guide people in their search for the meaning of human existence. At the heart of Christian humanism is the conviction, supported by centuries of experience in the lives of men and women of all cultures and races, that the fullest realization of what it means to be human can be known through personal communion with Jesus Christ, the Word of God who entered the arena of human life to bring wholeness and freedom to every human being.

Notes

1. Geddes MacGregor, *The Hemlock and the Cross: Humanism, Socrates and Christ* (Philadelphia and New York: J. B. Lippincott Company, 1963), p. 15.

2. John A. Symonds, *Renaissance in Italy: The Revival of Learning* (New York: Charles Scribner's Sons, 1915), p. 52.

3. Grundtvig lived from 1783 to 1872. The Locke statement is from *An Essay Concerning Human Understanding,* "Of Enthusiasm," p. 14.

4. Paul L. Lehmann, *Ethics in a Christian Context* (New York and Evanston: Harper & Row, Publishers, 1963), p. 14.

5. [Heinrich] Emil Brunner, *Christianity and Civilisation* (London: Nisbet & Co., Ltd., 1948-49), I, 79. (See Reading.)

6. Tertullian, "On Prescription Against Heretics," *The Ante-Nicene Fathers,* Vol. III, Chapter XLI. (New York: Scribner's, 1903) (See Reading.)

7. Augustine, *City of God,* Book Fourteen, Chapter 1. (See Reading.)

8. Dorothy L. Sayers, "Creed or Chaos?" in *Christian Letters to a Post-Christian World,* edited by Roderick Jellema (Grand Rapids, Michigan: Wm. B. Eerdmans Publishing Co., 1969), pp. 40-41. (See Reading.)

9. *Ibid.,* p. 42.

10. Martin Luther, *The Bondage of the Will,* 638, cited in *Erasmus-Luther: Discourse on Free Will,* translated and edited by Ernst F. Winter (New York: Frederick Ungar Publishing Co., Inc., 1961, 1978), p. 113.

11. Emil Brunner, p. 95. (See Reading.)

12. Romano Guardini, "The Awakening of the Church in the Soul," *The Church and the Catholic and the Liturgy,* tr. Ada Lane (New York: Sheed and Ward [now Andrews and McMeel] 1953) (See Reading.)

13. *The Rule of St. Benedict* (Collegeville: The Liturgical Press, 1948), Chapter 2. (See Reading.)

14. *Ibid.,* Chapter 7. (See Reading.)

15. Reinhold Niebuhr, "Ten Years That Shook My World," *The Christian Century,* April 26, 1939, p. 544. (See Reading.)

16. Rudolf Bultmann, "Humanism and Christianity," *The Journal of Religion*, XXXII:77 (1952), cited by Roger L. Shinn in *Man: The New Humanism*, Volume 6 of *New Directions in Theology Today* (Philadelphia: The Westminster Press, 1968, 1974), p. 174.

17. Edward O. Wilson, *On Human Nature* (Cambridge, Massachusetts: Harvard University Press, 1978), pp. 192, 209.

18. MacGregor, p. 53.

19. B. F. Skinner, "Humanism and Behaviourism," in *The Humanist Alternative: Some Definitions of Humanism*, edited by Paul Kurtz (Buffalo, N.Y.: Prometheus Books, 1973), p. 103.

20. *Humanist Manifestos I and II* (Buffalo, N.Y.: Prometheus Books, 1973, 1977), p. 16.

21. Paul Kurtz, "Is Everyone a Humanist?" in *The Humanist Alternative*, p. 177.

22. *Humanist Manifestos I and II,* p. 16.

23. Floyd Matson, "Toward a New Humanism," in *The Humanist Alternative*, p. 94.

24. *Ibid.*, p. 95.

25. *Ibid.*

26. Kurtz, "Is Everyone a Humanist?" p. 184. Cf. also *The Humanist Alternative*, pp. 82, 151.

27. Emil Brunner, p. 85. (See Reading.)

28. James Woelfel, "Two Types of Humanism," *The Christian Century*, March 1, 1972, p. 251.

29. René Dubos, "Franciscan Conservation versus Benedictine Stewardship," in *Ecology and Religion in History*, edited by David and Eileen Spring (New York: Harper & Row, Publishers, 1974), pp. 130-131.

30. Citations from Vatican II documents in Shinn, *Man: The New Humanism*, p. 48.

31. *Time*, April 13, 1981, p. 51.

32. Shinn, *Man: The New Humanism*, p. 157.

33. Harold K. Schilling, "The University and the Church," lecture delivered at University of Chicago to "The Fellowship of Campus Ministry" of Congregational Christian Churches and Evangelical and Reformed Church, 1955.

34. Ernest Becker, *Escape from Evil* (New York: The Free Press, 1975), p. 72.

Part One

Foundations of Christian Humanism:

Jerusalem and Athens

Introduction

A significant facet of the culture of the 1970s was a fascination with a phenomenon known as "roots." The fascination continues and shows few signs of abating. Though some facets of its present manifestation may be different from what occurred in the past, the phenomenon itself is not new. What is being experienced is a form of historical consciousness. It is always appropriate and worthwhile to investigate the circumstances, or roots, from which any great idea or movement has sprung. This is certainly the case with Christian humanism, whose religious origins are rooted in Old Testament religion and whose sociopolitical context is to be found in the Roman Empire. In their respective ways these two elements provided a kind of heredity and environment crucial for the growth of Christian humanism.

In its own inimitable manner Christianity absorbed and synthesized two remarkable earlier humanistic traditions: the religious outlook of the Hebrew people recorded in what Christians came to refer to in their own Bible as the Old Testament and the philosophical outlook of classical antiquity, which set a high value on human reason.

Christian humanism, which addresses the question, "Viewed from a Christian perspective, what does it mean to be human?", has its origin in the first book of the Old Testament, where its essential features are delineated. In Genesis there is an unmistakable sense of the dignity of human nature: human nature is said to have been created in the image of God. Moreover, human beings have a special relationship to the rest of creation, as well as to their creator, and with that special relationship, special responsibilities. This relationship is described in the story of Adam and Eve, who disobeyed their creator and thus deserved expulsion from their earthly paradise; despite their disobedience God continued to manifest his love and concern for them. This act of human rebellion against the will of the creator is frequently referred to as the "fall" and has been perceived to have significant implications for human nature. Many Christian writers have undertaken to explore what the fall meant for human nature and the human condition; for some of them—Augustine, Luther, and Calvin—this exploration had consequences of utmost importance for the freedom of the human will.

49

Even in the fallen state, however, human beings remained the noblest of God's creatures, and that nobility seemed capable of being developed. Human nature possessed a dignity sufficient to warrant redemption. The creator's covenant with his people, a mark of his esteem for them, carried with it the promise of redemption by a messiah whom he would send. Despite a persistent and seemingly ineradicable tendency to rebel against their creator, God's people continued to hope and long for their redeemer, while questioning in the words of Psalm 8, "What is man that thou art mindful of him?" and answering, "Yet thou hast made him little less than God, and dost crown him with glory and honor." This explicit recognition of the dignity and potential of human nature is frequently encountered in the Old Testament where it is present like a musical *leitmotiv*.

Another essential element of Christian humanism found in the Old Testament, again in Genesis, is the dignity of nature itself. In recounting the story of creation, the author of Genesis calls attention to God's satisfaction with what he has created; the words, "And God saw that it was good," run like a refrain through the description of the process of creation. The sense of dignity of nature is again revealed in Psalm 8 where the author says, "When I look at the heavens, the work of thy fingers, the moon and the stars which thou hast established. . . ." It is clear from the Old Testament that the human being has a unique place in creation and a special responsibility toward the rest of creation; the creator has provided the rest of creation for human use and has conferred upon the human being stewardship over what has been created. The function of the Old Testament prophets was to remind Israel of its responsibility toward the covenant with the creator. The dignity of nature is an important Christian humanist theme and is indissolubly linked to the dignity of the human being. As Richard Southern aptly observes, ". . . the power to recognize the grandeur and splendour of the universe is itself one of the greatest expressions of the grandeur and splendour of man." (*Medieval Humanism and Other Studies*, Oxford: Blackwell, 1970, p. 31.)

For Christians the hope and anticipation of their redemption was fulfilled in the first century A.D. in the Roman Empire, a state virtually surrounding the Mediterranean Sea. Often referred to simply as "Rome," the Empire was a political federation of peoples of diverse backgrounds and customs. Indeed, one of the distinguishing characteristics of the Roman Empire was its diversity; the genius of the Roman imperial system lay in being able to take advantage of the numerous opportunities afforded by this diverse cultural heritage while at the same time maintaining a sense of unity and loyalty under Rome. The first two centuries of the Christian era from 27 B.C. to A.D. 180 became known as the period of the *Pax Romana*—the Roman Peace—because the Roman government was perceived as providing security and stability. At any rate during, perhaps because of, the *Pax Romana*, the Roman Empire was as successful as it was ever to be.

In the context of the Roman Empire, the Jewish people and religion were only one of numerous national and religious groups that had come under the political tutelage of Rome. At times the Jews did clash with the Roman political authorities, but on the whole the Romans remained remarkably tolerant of Jewish ideas and customs. Among the various cultural influences in the Roman Empire, the Jewish influence was far less important than the 300 years of Greek influence. Ever since the time of Alexander the Great (d.323 B.C.) and the establishment of his empire, Greek culture had been paramount in the eastern Mediterranean area. Greek was the language of philosophy, literature, and commerce, and consequently that of the New Testament. Greek philosophy with its emphasis on reason, with its search for explanations, with its insistence that the questions "how" and "why" be asked, had a profound impact on Roman life and thought. The Greek element in Roman culture was so significant that it has been argued that it should be referred to as Greco-Roman culture, to give appropriate status and recognition to its Greek source. While hailing reason as the distinguishing characteristic of the human being, Greek philosophy could make use of reason in ways as different as those of Plato and Aristotle, each of whom gave a particular bent to philosophizing. The Greek emphasis on reason was destined to pose great problems for Christianity; it presented a great dilemma: should this emphasis be accepted or rejected? How far and in what ways was reason consonant with the Christian faith?

The Greeks also had a profound impact on thinking about the *cosmos.* Ancient Greek thought indeed had several different, even widely divergent, views of the universe. Ultimately it was Aristotle's integrated picture of the structure of the universe that won Christian favor during the Middle Ages. Rival cosmologies from antiquity were either unknown to or refuted by Christian thinkers interested in matters cosmological. Though there were some noteworthy exceptions on specific points, the cosmology of Aristotle proved capable of being successfully harmonized with Christian thought. Efforts to accomplish this were especially prominent in the thirteenth century. The Aristotelian notion of a spherical earth at the geometric center of a vast, spherical universe was popularized in the second century A.D. by Ptolemy, who wrote the greatest treatise on astronomy before Copernicus. Many aspects of this Aristotelian–Ptolemaic cosmology proved intellectually challenging as well as satisfying to Christian thinkers for well over a millenium.

PLATO

Plato (428-347 B.C.) was one of the greatest and most influential thinkers of all time. He represents what was noblest and best in ancient classical

Greek civilization. Perhaps the most outstanding pupil of Socrates (469-399 B.C.), Plato was able to build upon the philosophical foundation laid by his beloved master and inspired teacher. Indeed, the works of Plato are some of the most important sources for evaluating the achievement of Socrates. Though a native of Athens, Plato traveled extensively throughout the eastern Mediterranean region, including visits to Egypt, Italy, and Sicily. Plato's legacy to posterity included the great school he founded at Athens, known as the Academy, and a magnificent group of writings which constitute one of the glories of ancient Greek thought.

As a teacher Socrates had called attention to himself by his persistent questions and questioning. To question everything was the essence of Socrates' methodology. For the Greeks in general and especially for Socrates, the feature which distinguished the human from the rest of creation was reason. By his constant questioning Socrates simply meant to put reason to the test. But in 399 B.C. after a disastrous war which Athens lost, those in power in Athens felt threatened by a philosopher who asked questions about the true nature of virtue, morality, patriotism, and wisdom. Socrates was brought to trial on a charge that he had corrupted the youth of Athens. He was found guilty and died by his own hand. The trial and death of Socrates are detailed in two moving works by Plato, the *Apology* and the *Phaedo*. Like most of Plato's works, these are in the form of dialogs. Frequently in Plato's dialogs, Socrates is made to play the part of an interrogator.

In the *Republic* Plato sets forth what he has to say on the ideal form of government. Not only does he show himself to be a stimulating philosopher, but he also displays a fine literary style. In Plato's view, good government is achieved only when leadership rests with persons of knowledge and wisdom. Wisdom is to know that reality consists in the ordering principles of the world, namely, *ideas*. These *ideas* are not at all the same as subjective opinions, but are the permanent structures of existence. Physical objects come and go; the senses provide only a partial grasp of the constantly changing scene. Reason, or mind or intelligence, however, is akin to the permanent realities.

From Plato, **Republic**

BOOK VI

"Now, then, understand," I said, "that by the other part of things thought I mean what the arguing process itself grasps by power of dialectic, treating assumptions not as beginnings, but as literally hypothesis, that is to say steps and springboards for assault, from which it may push its way up to the region free of assumptions and reach the beginning of all, and grasp it, clinging again and again to whatever clings to this; and so may come down to a conclusion without using the help of anything at all that belongs to the senses, but only ideals themselves, and, passing through ideals, it may end in ideals."

"I understand," said he, "though not sufficiently, for you seem to me to describe a heavy task; but I see that you wish to lay down that a clearer perception of real being and the world of mind is given by knowledge of dialectic, than by the so-called 'arts' which start from pure assumptions. It is true that those who view them through these are compelled to view them with the understanding and not the senses, but because they do not go back to the beginning in their study, but start from assumptions, they do not seem to you to apply a reasoning mind about these matters, although with a first principle added they belong to the world of mind. The mental state of geometricians and suchlike you seem to call understanding, not reason, taking understanding as something between opinion and reason."

"You have taken my meaning quite sufficiently," I said. "Now then, accept these four affections of the soul for my four divisions of the line: Exercise of Reason for the highest, Understanding for the second; but Belief for the third and Conjecture for the last. Then arrange the divisions in proportion, believing they partake of clearness just as the affections which they represent partake of truth."

"I understand," said he, "and I agree, and I arrange them as you tell me."

BOOK VII

"Next, then," I said, "take the following parable of education and ignorance as a picture of the condition of our nature. Imagine mankind as a dwelling in an underground cave with a long entrance open to the light across the whole width of the cave; in this they have been from childhood, with necks and legs fettered, so they have to stay where they are. They cannot move their heads round because of the fetters, and they can look forward, but light comes to them from fire burning behind them higher up at a distance. Between the fire and the prisoners is a road above their level, and along it imagine a low wall has been built, as puppet showmen have screens in front of their people over which they work their puppets."

"I see," he said.

"See, then, bearers carrying along this wall all sorts of articles which they hold projecting above the wall, statues of men and other living things, made of stone or wood and all kinds of stuff, some of the bearers speaking and some silent, as you might expect."

"What a remarkable image," he said, "and what remarkable prisoners!"

"Just like ourselves," I said. "For, first of all, tell me this: What do you think such people would have seen of themselves and each other except their shadows, which the fire cast on the opposite wall of the cave?"

"I don't see how they could see anything else," said he, "if they were compelled to keep their heads unmoving all their lives!"

"Very well, what of the things being carried along? Would not this be the same?"

"Of course it would."

"Suppose the prisoners were able to talk together, don't you think that when they named the shadows which they saw passing they would believe they were naming things?"

"Necessarily."

"Then if their prison had an echo from the opposite wall, whenever one of the passing bearers uttered a sound, would they not suppose that the passing shadow must be making the sound? Don't you think so?"

"Indeed I do," he said.

"If so," said I, "such persons would certainly believe that there were no realities except those shadows of handmade things."

"So it must be," said he.

"Now consider," said I, "what their releases would be like, and their cure from these fetters and their folly; let us imagine whether it might naturally be something like this. One might be released, and compelled suddenly to stand up and turn his neck round, and to walk and look towards the firelight, all this would hurt him, and he would be too much dazzled to see distinctly those things whose shadows he had seen before. What do you think he would say, if someone told him that what he saw before was foolery, but now he saw more rightly, being a bit nearer reality and turned towards what was a little more real? What if he were shown each of the passing things, and compelled by questions to answer what each one was? Don't you think he would be puzzled, and believe what he saw before was more true than what was shown to him now?"

"Far more," he said.

"Then suppose he were compelled to look towards the real light, it would hurt his eyes, and he would escape by turning them away to the things which he was able to look at, and these he would believe to be clearer than what was being shown to him."

"Just so," said he.

"Suppose, now," said I, "that someone should drag him thence by force, up the rough ascent, the steep way up, and never stop until he could drag him out into the light of the sun, would he not be distressed and furious at being dragged; and when he came into the light, the brilliance would fill his eyes and he would not be able to see even one of the things now called real?"

"That he would not," said he, "all of a sudden."

"He would have to get used to it, surely, I think, if he is to see the things above. First he would most easily look at shadows, after that images of mankind and the rest in water, lastly the things themselves. After this he would find it easier to survey by night the heavens themselves and all that is in them, gazing at the light of the stars and moon, rather than by day the sun and the sun's light."

"Of course."

"Last of all, I suppose, the sun; he could look on the sun itself by itself in its own place, and see what it is like, not reflections of it in water or as it appears in some alien setting."

"Necessarily," said he.

"And only after all this he might reason about it, how this is he who provides seasons and years, and is set over all there is in the visible region, and he is in a manner the cause of all things which they saw."

"Yes, it is clear," said he, "that after all that, he would come to this last."

"Very good. Let him be reminded of his first habitation, and what was wisdom in that place, and of his fellow-prisoners there; don't you think he would bless himself for the change, and pity them?"

"Yes, indeed."

"And if there were honours and praises among them and prizes for the one who saw the passing things most sharply and remembered best which of them used to come before and which after and which together, and from these was best able to prophesy accordingly what was going to come—do you believe he would set his desire on that, and envy those who were honoured men or potentates among them? Would he not feel as Homer says, and heartily desire rather to be serf of some landless man on earth and to endure anything in the world, rather than to opine as they did and to live in that way?"

"Yes, indeed," said he, "he would rather accept anything than live like that."

"Then again," I said, "just consider; if such a one should go down again and sit on his old seat, would he not get his eyes full of darkness coming in suddenly out of the sun?"

"Very much so," said he.

"And if he should have to compete with those who had been always prisoners, by laying down the law about those shadows while he was blinking before his eyes were settled down—and it would take a good long time to get used to things—wouldn't they all laugh at him and say he had spoiled his eyesight by going up there, and it was not worthwhile so much as to try to go up? And would they not kill anyone who tried to release them and take them up, if they could somehow lay hands on him and kill him?"

"That they would!" said he.

"Then we must apply this image, my dear Glaucon," said I, "to all we have been saying. The world of our sight is like the habitation in prison, the firelight there to the sunlight here, the ascent and the view of the upper world is the rising of the soul into the world of mind; put it so and you will not be far from my own surmise, since that is what you want to hear; but God knows if it is really true. At least, what appears to me is, that in the world of the known, last of all, is the idea of the good, and with what toil to be seen! And seen, this must be inferred to be the cause of all right and beautiful things for all, which gives birth to light and the king of light in the world of sight, and, in the world of mind, herself the queen produces truth and reason; and she must be seen by one who is to act with reason publicly or privately."

"I believe as you do," he said, "in so far as I am able."

"Then believe also, as I do," said I, "and do not be surprised, that those who come thither are not willing to have part in the affairs of men, but their souls ever strive to remain above; for that surely may be expected if our parable fits the case."

"Quite so," he said.

"Well then," said I, "do you think it surprising if one leaving divine contemplations and passing to the evils of men is awkward and appears to be a great fool, while he is still blinking—not yet accustomed to the darkness around him, but compelled to struggle in law courts or elsewhere about shadows of justice, or the images which make the shadows, and to quarrel about notions of justice in those who have never seen justice itself?"

"Not surprising at all," said he.

"But any man of sense," I said, "would remember that the eyes are doubly confused from two different causes, both in passing from light to darkness and from darkness to light; and believing that the same things happen with regard to the soul also, whenever he sees a soul confused and unable to discern anything he would not just laugh carelessly; he would examine whether it had come out of a more brilliant life, and if it were darkened by the strangeness; or whether it had come out of greater ignorance into a more brilliant light, and if it were dazzled with the brighter illumination. Then only would he congratulate the one soul upon its happy experience and way of life and pity the other; but if he must laugh, his laugh would be a less downright laugh than his laughter at the soul which came out of the light above."

"That is fairly put," said he.

"Then if this is true," I said, "our belief about these matters must be this, that the nature of education is not really such as some of its professors say it is; as you know, they say that there is not understanding in the soul, but they put it in, as if they were putting sight into blind eyes."

"They do say so," said he.

"But our reasoning indicates," I said, "that this power is already in the soul of each, and is the instrument by which each learns; thus if the eye could not see without being turned with the whole body from the dark towards the light, so this instrument must be turned round with the whole soul away from the world of becoming until it is able to endure the sight of being and the most brilliant light of being: and this we say is the good, don't we?"

"Yes."

"Then this instrument," said I, "must have its own art, for the circumturning or conversion, to show how the turn can be most easily and successfully made; not an art of putting sight into an eye, which we say has it already, but since the instrument has not been turned aright and does not look where it ought to look—that's what must be managed."

"So it seems," he said.

"Now most of the virtues which are said to belong to the soul are really something near to those of the body; for in fact they are not already there, but they are put later into it by habits and practices; but the virtue of understanding everything really belongs to something certainly more divine, as it seems, for it never loses its power, but becomes useful and helpful or, again, useless and harmful, by the direction in which it is turned. Have you not noticed men who are called worthless but clever, and how keen and sharp is the sight of their petty soul, and how it sees through the things towards which it is turned? Its sight is clear enough, but it is compelled to be the servant of vice, so that the clearer it sees the more evil it does."

"Certainly," said he.

"Yet if this part of such a nature," said I, "had been hammered at from childhood, and all those leaden weights of the world of becoming knocked off—the weights, I mean, which grow into the soul from gorging and gluttony and such pleasures, and twist the soul's eye downwards—if, I say, it had shaken these off and been turned round towards what is real and true, that same instrument of those same men would have seen those higher things most clearly, just as now it sees those towards which it is turned."

"Quite likely," said he.

"Very well," said I, "isn't it equally likely, indeed, necessary, after what has been said, that men uneducated and without experience of truth could never properly supervise a city, nor can those who are allowed to spend all their lives in education right to the end? The first have no single object in life, which they must always aim at in doing everything they do, public or private; the second will never do anything if they can help it, believing they have already found mansions abroad in the Islands of the Blest."

"True," said he.

"Then it is the task of us founders," I said, "to compel the best natures to attain that learning which we said was the greatest, both to see the good, and to ascend that ascent; and when they have ascended and properly seen, we must never allow them what is allowed now."

"What is that, pray?" he asked.

"To stay there," I said, "and not be willing to descend again to those prisoners, and to share their troubles and their honors, whether they are worth having or not."

"What!" said he, "are we to wrong them and make them live badly, when they might live better?"

"You have forgotten again, my friend," said I, "that the law is not concerned how any one class in a city is to prosper above the rest; it tries to contrive prosperity in the city as a whole, fitting the citizens into a pattern by persuasion and compulsion, making them give of their help to one another wherever each class is able to help the community. The law itself creates men like this in the city, not in order to allow each one to turn by any way he likes, but in order to use them itself to the full for binding the city together."

ARISTOTLE

Aristotle (384-322 B.C.) spent twenty years in the Academy and was Plato's outstanding student. He lived at a time when Greek civilization was in transition from its Hellenic phase to its Hellenistic phase. This was when Macedon was coming into its own in leading the Greek states. Aristotle's lifetime witnessed the spectacular leadership of Philip of Macedon and the still more brilliant exploits of his son, Alexander the Great. When Aristotle was in his forties, he was called to the Macedonian capital by King Philip to serve as a tutor to Alexander, who came to hold him in high regard. Several years after the death of Philip, when Alexander was king of Macedon and beginning his career of military conquest, Aristotle returned to Athens, where he founded his own school, the Lyceum. Though popular as a teacher, he was not well liked by many Athenians who resented his friendship with Alexander.

Aristotle always claimed to respect Plato highly, although in large part he emancipated himself from his master just as Plato had freed himself from Socrates. His life's work was studying and organizing in logical form all the knowledge then available. No mere encyclopedist or compiler of information, he was able by a process of careful observation to add much to the body of knowledge available for study. Aristotle's writings are witness to the wide range of his interests, the depth of his knowledge, and his intellectual power. Considered the inventor of formal logic, Aristotle also contributed to the fields of ethics, politics, aesthetics, rhetoric, natural history, and metaphysics.

When examining the appropriate political environment for human existence, Aristotle, like Plato, focuses on what was most familiar to him, the city-state. Where Plato in the *Republic* tended to be idealistic, Aristotle in his *Politics* had a more realistic outlook. Plato had neither denied nor ignored the existence of the material world. On the contrary, it bothered him. Yet he was committed to a propostion which he considered irrefutable. If the non-material world of *ideas* was real, then the material world of the senses could not be real. In Plato's mind this statement was logical. On the other hand, Aristotle's experience as an apprentice to his father, a physician, had convinced him of the value of what could be learned through observation and even through trial and error, and thus predisposed him toward a compromise with the world of the senses. His eventual conclusion that reality consisted of both the *idea* and its material expression meant that there was truth in nature after all.

From Aristotle, **Politics**

BOOK I

1. We see that every state is a sort of partnership, and that every partnership is formed in order to attain some good. After all, it is universally true that people do act with a view to obtaining what they think good for them. Clearly, then, all partnerships have some good as their objective; and the highest, most authentic of all partnerships, the one that includes all others. This is the state: political partnership.

Some thinkers, however, suppose that statesman, king, estate manager, and master of a family have a common character. This is a mistake; they think that the distinction between them is not a difference in kind, but a simple, numerical difference. For example, if a man rules over a few, they call him a master; if more, a manager; and so on with the statesman and king—as though there were no difference between a large estate and a small estate. As for the terms statesman and king, they use the latter when a person holds power on his own; and they use statesman when a person follows the principles of the science of statesmanship and takes his turn with others in governing and being governed. However, these views are not true.

Our meaning will become clearer if we follow our usual method. In other cases, too, one must analyze a complex whole into its elements; similarly, if we look at the constituent parts of the state, we shall be clearer about the differences between the different functions mentioned above, and we shall see whether it is possible to arrive at a precise distinction, as in a science.

2. The best way of studying the matter, as in other cases, will be to see how things develop right from the start. First of all, there has to be an association of those persons who cannot exist apart from each other, namely, male and female, in order to reproduce. This is not a matter of choice, but, as with other animals and with plants, it is part of nature to desire to leave something like oneself behind.

There must also be an association between that which naturally rules and that which is ruled, with a view to security. That which is able to plan and to take forethought is by nature ruler and master, whereas that which is able to supply physical labor is by nature ruled, a slave to the above. This is why master and slave have a common interest.

Female and slave are marked off from each other by nature. Nature does not operate like the smiths who made the Delphic knife a multi-purpose tool. There is nothing niggardly about her: she assigns a single function to a single thing. An instrument is at the peak of perfection when it serves a single end, not a number of ends. But among barbarians, female and slave occupy the same position. The reason is that a natural ruler is not to be found among barbarians. Association there is a partnership between slaves, female and male. All the more reason, then, for the poet to say: "It is right for Greeks to rule over barbarians," since barbarian and slave are by nature identical.

The first product of these two partnerships is the household. Hesiod was right when he wrote, "First a house and a wife and an ox to plow"; the point being that for poor people an ox is equivalent to a slave. The partnership established by nature for satisfying all daily needs is the household. The members are humorously called "mess-mates" by Charondas, and "trough-fellows" by Epimenides the Cretan.

The first partnership that is (a) the product of several households and (b) not meant just for satisfying daily needs is a village. By nature, the village seems to be par excellence a development of a household: its members are called "fellow-sucklings," "one's children and one's children's children." This is why, to start with, states were run by kings; and it is the reason why "tribes" (as opposed to states) are still ruled by kings. They arose from social forms that were themselves monarchic. Every household has a "king," the eldest member; so too, therefore, does its offshoot or development, because the members are related. This is the point made by Homer about the Cyclopes: "each of them rules over his wives and children." They all live apart from one another; and indeed, in antiquity, this scattered living was prevalent. Besides, everybody says that the gods too are ruled by a king, because some people are still so ruled and others were once; and human beings imagine the gods to live like human beings, just as they imagine the gods to be like men in appearance.

A partnership of several villages is a state; and with that the process is complete. It is a partnership that has already reached the high point of self-sufficiency; it originated so that people could live, but its *raison d'etre* now is that people can live the good life. All states therefore are natural, since the very first partnerships are natural. The state is their end, or the goal they aim at, and nature means end; we use the expression "the nature of a thing" with regard to what it is like when its development is complete, as with "man," "horse," and "house."

Also, the end of an activity, the reason why it is done, is the highest good; and self-sufficiency is the objective of the state and is the highest good.

Clearly, then, the state is natural, and man is by nature an animal designed for living in states. The person who by nature, not accident, does not belong to a state is either an inferior creature or better than a mere human being. He is like the man criticized by Homer: "without a clan, without law, and without a home." Such a person has also a passion for war; he is on his own, like an isolated piece in a game.

It is now clear why the term "animal designed for living in states" applies to man more than to bees or to any other animal living in herds. Nature, we are always saying, does nothing without a purpose. Now, man is the only animal with the power of speech. The mere voicing of sounds is an indication of pleasure and pain, which is why it is found among animals other than man; the point being that their nature has reached the point where they perceive what is pleasant or painful and can indicate this to one another. But speech is for pointing out what is useful or hurtful; it points out also what is just or unjust. This is peculiar to man, as compared with the other animals—the fact that he is the only animal to have a sense of good and evil, just and unjust, and so on. It is a common partnership in such ideas that brings about a household, and eventually a state.

The state is, clearly, by nature prior to the household or to the individual human being; for the whole must be prior to the part. If the whole body is destroyed, there will not be, for example, a foot or a hand, except in the ambiguous sense in which one speaks of the hand of a statue as "the stone hand": if that hand is destroyed, it will still be stone. But things are characterized by their function and capacity: when they no longer have their particular character, they cannot be described unequivocally as the same thing. Clearly, then, the state is a natural thing, prior to the individual: an individual is not self-sufficient when separated; and, therefore, the relation between him and the whole (the state) will be that of part to whole. The man who is unable to join in partnerships or does not need to because he is himself sufficient is not part of a state; he is either a beast or a god.

There is therefore a natural and universal impulse toward such partnerships. The man who first formed one was responsible for great benefactions. Man, when he is at the goal of his development, is the best of all animals; but he is the worst of all when he is detached from customs and justice. Injustice, given weapons, is the most oppressive thing there is; and man is given weapons at birth, which are meant to serve prudence and goodness but can easily be turned to the opposite ends. Man without goodness is the most wicked and savage of animals, the most subject to lust and gluttony. Justice, however, is part of the state, since it settles what is just; and political partnership is regulated by legal justice.

From Aristotle, **Ethics**

BOOK I

7. Let us return to the good we are looking for and ask what it is. It appears to vary according to the activity or craft: it is different in medicine from what it is in generalship, and so with the rest. Then, what is meant by "the good" in each and every art? It is that toward which all other activities are means. In medicine, this is health; it is victory in generalship, a house in architecture, and so on. In every activity and choice of action, it is the end: everything else that people do, they do because that is their object. If there is an ultimate end in all matters of action, that will be the good in matters of action; or if there is more than one, then the sum of these. By a different approach, then, the argument has reached the same result. But we must try to be still clearer about this.

There seem to be a number of ends. Some of these we choose on behalf of yet another end—like wealth, flutes, and instruments in general. Not all ends, therefore, are ultimate ends, whereas the supreme good is something final. So if there is one thing that is alone ultimate, this is what we are looking for; and if there are more than one, it will be the most complete or final among these. That which is sought for its own sake is more complete than that which is sought as a means to something else. That which is never sought as a means to something else is more complete than things sought both on their own account and on account of the former. By absolutely final, we mean that which is sought for its own sake, and never as a means to something else. Happiness seems to be something of that sort. We always pursue that for its intrinsic value, never as a means; whereas we pursue honor, pleasure, wisdom and all the virtues, both for their own sakes (we would want them even if they led to nothing further) and for the sake of happiness, since we think we shall attain happiness by means of them. But no one wants happiness as a means to these other things, or indeed as a means to anything else at all.

The same conclusion is reached from the notion of the self-sufficient. The final good is thought to be something self-sufficient. The term "self-sufficient" does not refer to an individual living a hermit's life; it embraces parents, children, wife, friends, and citizens, since man is naturally a social animal. But there should be a limit to these; if we extend the term to ancestors, descendants, and friends of friends, there will be an infinite series. However, we must look into that at another time. We regard as self-sufficient that which, just by itself, makes life worth choosing, and lacking in nothing. We think that happiness has that character. Also, we think it the object of choice *par excellence,* even when other things are not taken into account. For when other goods are reckoned in, happiness *and* the least of them is superior to happiness by itself. The extra makes an increment of good, and the greater good is always preferable to the lesser. Happiness, therefore, seems to be something final and self-sufficient, the ultimate object of matters of action.

It may be that in calling happiness the highest good, we are only stating a platitude. It needs to be defined more clearly still. We might achieve this by ascertaining the specific function of man. In the case of flute players, sculptors, and all craftsmen—indeed, of all who have some function and activity—"good" and "excellent" reside in their function. Now, the same will be true of man, if he has a function peculiar to himself. Do builders and cobblers have functions and activities, but man not, being by nature idle? Or, just as the eye, hand, foot, and every part of the body has a function, similarly, is one to attribute a function to man over and above these? In that case, what will it be? Living is something shared by man even with plants, whereas we are after something specific. Therefore, we must rule out nutritive living, life as growth. Next comes perception; but this too is shared—in this case by horses, cows, and all animals. We are left with a life concerned with action, belonging to the rational part of man. This has two parts: that which obeys reason, and that which has reason and thinks. This kind of life, concerned with action, is itself twofold; and we must take the part that is actually operative, as this is the more correct sense.

The function of man is activity of soul in accordance with reason, or at least not without reason. Now, we say that function is generically the same when we speak of an individual and of an individual good at his job, as in the case of a lyre player and a good lyre player. This is generally true in all cases. Function comes first, and superiority in excellence is superadded. As an example, playing the lyre is the function of the lyre player, playing it well belongs to the good lyre player. If this is so, the good for man proves to be activity of soul in conformity with excellence; and if there is more than one excellence, it will be the best and most complete of these. Also, it requires a complete lifetime: one swallow does not make a spring, nor does a single fine day; similarly, one day or a short time does not make a man blessed or happy.

This is our outline of the good. I say outline advisedly, since perhaps we should make a sketch first and put in the details later. Anyone can then develop the outline and fill in what is appropriate to it; time itself seems to be a discoverer and a good workmate. This is how progress has been made in the arts and crafts, since anyone can fill in what is missing. We should also recall our earlier remarks, and not look for the same degree of accuracy in everything, but only according to the subject matter and as far as is appropriate to the inquiry. Both builders and geometricians look into the right angle, but in different ways: the former does so, so far as it is useful for the job in hand; but the latter studies what it is, or what kind of thing, as he studies truth. We must behave in the same way in other things too, so that side issues do not overshadow the main ones.

Not even the cause should always be precisely accounted for. In some cases, it is enough if we show clearly that something is so, as with principles. That something is so is itself a starting point and principle. Some principles are gathered by induction, some by perception, some by a sort of habituation, and so on. We should inquire into each in the way natural to it, and be serious about distinguishing them rightly, since they have a great bearing on what follows. The principle or beginning is thought to be more than half of the whole, and to provide solutions to many of our questions.

8. We should examine happiness not only on the basis of the conclusion and the parts of the definition but also by what is said about it. All the available facts are in harmony with the truth; whereas, when something is false, the discord between it and the facts is soon apparent.

Goods are divided into three groups. Some are called external, others goods of the soul, and others goods of the body. Goods of the soul are the ones we call goods proper, and we take it that acts and activities of the soul are of the soul. So, according to this view, which is of some antiquity and meets with agreement among philosophers, we are right to define happiness as we do.

It is correct, too, that certain acts and activities are asserted to be the end. In that way they belong to goods of the soul, not to external goods.

The view about the good life and "successful living" of the happy man agrees with our definition. For we have really spoken of a sort of good life and "successful living."

It seems as though everything that people look for in connection with happiness resides in our definition. Some think it to be excellence or virtue; others wisdom; others special skill; whereas still others think it all these, or some of these together with pleasure, or at least not without pleasure. Others incorporate external goods as well. Some of these views are held by numerous venerable authorities, others by a few distinguished men. It is likely that neither group will be totally wrong, but rather that they will get some part of most of it right. Our definition agrees with those who call it virtue or a virtue; for activity in conformity with virtue shows that virtue is present.

There is probably a big difference between treating the supreme good as possession and as use, between the state and the activity. It is possible for the state to be there but achieve nothing, as when one is asleep or inactive for some other reason. But this is not possible for the activity of good: it will necessarily act, and act well. At the Olympic Games, it is not the handsomest and strongest who are crowned, but actual competitors, some of whom are the winners. Similarly, it is those who act rightly who get the rewards and the good things in life.

THE BIBLE

The central message of the Bible is that the God of heaven and earth is at work in this world to liberate humanity from everything that harms human life and ultimately to bring to fulfillment all the powers and joys that he intends for human beings as his children. The Bible tells us, writes Karl Barth, how God has sought and found the way to us.

The Genesis creation stories show how God honors the human creation with dignity, creative power, and responsibility. Despite human rebellion, God continues to provide for human welfare. Servitude in Egypt is met by God's work of deliverance followed by the gift of a covenant enabling his ancient people to live in loyalty to him and with justice in the community.

The Hebrew psalmists praise God for the goodness of creation and the wonder of being human.

None of this is difficult to detect in the biblical records, but many Bible readers have been taught to look only for signs of the divine and the miraculous in Scripture, the human elements being regarded either as incidental features or as occasions for moralizing. But the genius of the Bible is the claim that God expresses his loving purpose for humanity in and through human persons and circumstances. The Bible is utterly realistic about human sinfulness and at the same time totally confident concerning the power of God's forgiving and healing love.

The Sermon on the Mount shares that astonishing spectrum of cleareyed realism and steady hope. Jesus' healings and exorcisms declare that faith in God can overcome the deadliest foes; his deeds make visible what he teaches in the parables concerning the kingship or rule of God. The message is that divine power is at work recreating this flawed world. But the mode of divine power is that of suffering love, which means that Jesus seals his message of the rule of God by going obediently to the cross.

The New Testament writers employ a variety of words and images to state their conviction that Jesus of Nazareth is the one appointed by God to be the central figure in the redemption of the human race. He is the Messiah, the Anointed One. He is the *Logos*, the Word of God coming into the human family in the flesh. He is the one who comes to serve, not to be served. And he is preeminently the Risen One: the resurrection of Jesus from the dead is God's signal that the new age has begun. The benefits of this new age— life, wholeness, freedom, and peace—can be realized now, on this earth, through the working of God's Holy Spirit in the lives of all who believe this good news.

A profoundly "humanistic" claim issued by St. Paul is that in this new age of Christ every person can be made right, justified, given a sense of worth—not by the old age's formula of competitive struggle, but by faith, that is, by personal attachment to Christ, the unique Son of God and the definitive human being. To believe in Christ is thus to receive the meaning of one's humanity from "the man of God's own choosing." To believe in Christ is to be incorporated into the community of faith, the body of Christ, the fellowship of the Spirit, where the more excellent way of love finds concrete expression.

The student of humanism will notice that at the very end of the Bible, the seer's vision of the holy city, the new Jerusalem, is not of something in a remote heaven, but rather of a city "coming down out of heaven from God." Likewise, the voice heard by the seer declares that God himself comes to be with mankind. "He will dwell with them, and they shall be his people." From Genesis to Revelation, the Bible is consistently attentive, not simply to God, but to God in relation to humanity.

Selected Readings

Genesis, chapters 1—3. The creation stories and the fall
Exodus 13:1—15:21; 19:1-6; 20:1-20. Deliverance from Egypt; covenant; decalog
Psalm 8. A psalm extolling creation and man's place in it
Psalm 32. A psalm of praise to the Creator
Matthew, chapters 5—7. The Sermon on the Mount
Matthew, chapter 9. Examples of Jesus' healings
Matthew, chapter 13. Jesus teaches in parables
Matthew, chapters 24 and 25. Examples of Jesus' eschatological teachings
Mark 8:27—9:8. The confession of Jesus' Messiahship; discipleship
Mark 14:1—16:8. Jesus' final days, arrest, trial, death, resurrection
Luke, chapter 2. The Christmas story
Luke, chapter 15. Three stories on the lost and found
Luke, chapter 24. Jesus' resurrection appearances and ascension
John 1:1-18. Prolog to Gospel of John; the Logos (Word)
Romans, chapters 1—3. Mankind's accountability and God's righteousness
Romans, chapter 8. Life in the Spirit; creation to be set free
1 Corinthians, chapter 12. The community in the Spirit, the Body of Christ
1 Corinthians, chapter 13. The more excellent way of love
1 Corinthians 15:1-11. Paul's understanding of the gospel
Galatians 2:11-21. Justification is by faith in Christ
Galatians, chapter 5. The freedom of the Christian
Colossians, chapter 3. The new life in Christ
Revelation 21:1—22:5. Vision of the holy city, the new Jerusalem

Part Two

The Emergence of Christian Humanism

Introduction

The tradition of Christian humanism assigns a unique position to the person and mission of Christ. Jesus Christ—to Christians the promised Redeemer of the Old Testament—was born in the Jewish state, a subject territory of the Roman Empire, when that empire was near the height of its power and influence. The founder of the empire and one of its greatest rulers, Augustus (27 B.C.–A.D. 14), was guiding the destiny of Rome. While he lived, Christ meant little or nothing to the Romans. Jesus came from Galilee in the north and made his way to Jerusalem to begin his public life when he was about 30. He gathered around him a small group of followers, the apostles, most of whom had formerly been fishermen. Jesus went about the countryside preaching and teaching, and what he had to say appealed to many of the Jews of his time who were disaffected by various conditions of Roman rule. Some have found what Jesus had to say radical or revolutionary, and in some senses that may have been so. But there was also a deep vein of common sense and moving compassion to be found in the utterances of this bewildering Nazarene.

Rather than emphasizing social revolution or national aspirations, Jesus announced that the kingdom, the rule of God, was breaking in upon the human order. This message was startling good news of both cosmic and personal import. God was exerting his kingly power in the world so that human beings could know love, goodness, joy, and peace in their present experience. Love divine gave power to love the neighbor. Jesus also declared that God in his own time would bring world history to a climax. The appropriate human responses to the gracious pressure of the present and coming kingdom were repentance and faith; no other qualifications were needed. The greatest in the kingdom were the poor, the humble in spirit, and the children. It was a simple message, but nonetheless powerful.

What Jesus had to say not only disturbed some of the Roman authorities when they became aware of his preaching, but also some of the leaders of the Jewish people who distrusted his intentions, felt threatened by his influence, and feared Roman retaliation for what he had said or might do. Lest things get out of hand and Jesus become too difficult to deal with, it was expedient to get him out of the way. Thus he was arrested, tried by the Jews, and executed by the Romans. As his passion and death are recounted in the Gospel narratives, there is an emotional crescendo as these events are related. To add to the ignominy of his crucifixion, Christ was deserted by all except a single follower and his mother.

Then after three days it was reported that Jesus had risen from the dead. He was seen by some of his followers, who recognized him when he broke bread with them, a ritual he had commended to them at the Last Supper on the night before he died. Forty days after his resurrection Christ again took leave of his followers, but not before promising them that he would send the Holy Spirit, who would remain with them forever.

Slowly the news about Jesus and what he had said and done spread in the Jewish communities scattered throughout the Roman Empire. Important as Christ's preaching to the Jews had been, the greatest impact of Christianity was in its universal appeal.

For Christian humanism the person of Christ is crucial. The New Testament asserted the uniqueness of Jesus of Nazareth as the climactic revelation of God. The basic New Testament idea of human dignity is that God himself saw fit to be born in this world as a human being. The writer of the Fourth Gospel ascribed to Christ (the Logos) identity with the one God of the Old Testament and with this God's creative action (John 1:1-3). What Christ said and did is recorded in the Gospels, and among these there are some interesting differences in emphasis and outlook, especially between Matthew, Mark, and Luke on the one hand, and John, on the other.

It is readily evident that Christ could serve as a model in many ways. He has elements in his teaching very close to orthodox Judaism: a strict and uncompromising monotheism and great respect for the Scriptures. However, the Jewish groups of Christ's time tended to be quite exclusive, but Christ enjoined his followers to go forth and teach all nations. This emphasis was to result in Christian universality. While it is possible to stress the connections Christianity has with Judaism, there are also elements of morality in Jesus' teachings that have an affinity with contemporary teachings of the Stoics. The more one examines the New Testament, the more one learns its contents are not easily harmonized, though its main message is clear. This was a lesson learned by the early Christians.

An important question for early Christians involved how they should react to the Roman state and to the Greco-Roman culture in which they found themselves. Christ said, "Render to Caesar, the things that are Caesar's, and to God, the things that are God's" (Mark 12:17), and this is echoed in Paul's Letter to the Romans (13:1) where he enjoins obedience to legitimately constituted political authority. On the other hand the book of Revelation suggests a different pattern that involves utter rejection of this world in the firm expectation of the imminent replacement of the present world order with a new one. Following the counsels of the New Testament, the Christian could legitimately undertake two rather different courses of action.

Paul of Tarsus has been recognized as the earliest of the great Christian missionaries as well as the first Christian theologian. At first a persecutor of Christians, then an illustrious convert to Christianity, and finally an indefatigable missionary and inspiration throughout the Roman world, Paul exerted tremendous influence on the early Christian church. In his letters addressed to various Christian communities throughout the Roman world, Paul explores and reflects on God's relationship to human beings.

This process of intellectualizing Christianity has sometimes been called the "Hellenization of Christianity." What was begun by Paul in the first century A.D. continued for centuries, reaching a climax in the third and fourth centuries in the so-called patristic age.

The work of Paul left an indelible mark on the early Christian church and furnished it with an enduring legacy: an emphasis on intellectual truth as well as on ethical concerns. Paul broadened the humanistic concerns of the early Christians by elaborating what Christ meant in and for the lives of his followers. Christ, the firstborn of creation, has inaugurated a new age. The possibilities of a more fully human life through Jesus Christ, indeed a new life in Christ, are set out by this dynamic missionary who claimed from his own personal experience, "By the grace of God I am what I am" (1 Cor. 15:10). It was Paul who enunciated the idea that Christ, the new dispensation, fulfilled the old law; he also preached that it was through faith that the human being is justified; he taught that Jesus was the divine son of God through whose sufferings human beings were saved; and finally he elaborated the idea that all Christians are one with Christ in a mystical body.

During the first three centuries of the Christian era the relationship between Christianity and the Roman Empire was an uneasy one. On the whole, Roman imperial policy was tolerant of the Christians and their ways; it was customary for the Romans to be tolerant in matters of religion. Departures from this customarily tolerant attitude toward the Christians might occur under individual Roman emperors who were hostile to Christianity, for example, under Nero (A.D. 54-68), Domitian (A.D. 81-96), and Diocletian (A.D. 284-305), or in circumstances where Christian practices were perceived as disloyalty to the Roman state, for example, the refusal of Christians to worship the emperor. Though the early Christians would have been reluctant to admit that such was the case, Roman persecutions of the Christians were generally sporadic, local, and brief, and probably did more good than harm for Christianity. As Tertullian, an implacable foe of Rome, wrote, "The blood of the martyrs is the seed of the church."

Tertullian's stand was simply another chapter in the prolonged struggle of Christian writers over the question of the proper relationship between the Christian religion and its cultural context. This patristic writer in his famous query, "What has Athens to do with Jerusalem?" expressed his hostility to pagan learning. Somewhat conditioned by the persecutions raging around him, Tertullian feared that Christianity would be corrupted by the contact with Greco-Roman culture, but more to the point, he believed that since the Christians had Christ, classical culture was unnecessary.

Somewhat earlier than Tertullian, another Christian writer, Justin Martyr, had adopted a different tack in dealing with Roman thought and ways. He sought to persuade the Roman emperor not to persecute Christians, and he did so on the basis of one of the values the Roman cultural establishment held dear—reason. A learned man trained in Greek thought, Justin skillfully set forth his case that the emperor ought not kill Christians based on the rational arguments so dear to philosophers. Since he is known as Justin *Martyr*, it is evident that his arguments were not sufficiently persuasive. Nevertheless, Justin's legacy from the Greeks, the insistence that reason was a distinguishing characteristic of being human, was to remain in the mainstream of Christian humanism. In considering Tertullian and Justin it is worthwhile to note that early Christian thought as a whole was characterized by considerable diversity of opinion on many matters.

The fortunes of Christianity changed rather suddenly in the early fourth century. Violent persecution of the Christians, which had been particularly intense around A.D. 300 abruptly ceased, and in 313 the Roman emperor Constantine promulgated an edict of toleration which changed the legal status of Christianity in the Roman Empire. Before the end of the century, in 380, another emperor, Theodosius, established Christianity as the official religion of the empire. Clearly the tables were turned. The process whereby Christianity accommodated itself to its cultural context continued, as it had been doing for centuries, but now Christianity was in a position to shape society to itself.

The change in the status of Christianity had profound implications for Christian humanism. While persecutions raged or were possible and Christianity faced exterior threats, internal divisions or dissensions were kept to a minimum. With the exterior threats removed in the fourth century, differences within the Christian community came to the fore. The Christian church had to define precisely what it believed in and stood for. Issues crucial to the development of Christian humanism were raised, discussed, disputed in church councils and by eminent patristic writers: What is Christian morality? What are the sacraments? Are human beings saved by their own efforts or solely by the action of God?

Significant as the above issues were, they pale in comparison with the most significant of all the controversies: those involving Christ himself. How was Christ related to the Father? Was Christ truly God? Was he truly man?

Ecumenical councils formulated orthodox teaching in these matters. The most famous formulations were those related to the nature of Christ and the Trinity, namely the Apostles' Creed and the Nicene Creed. These controversies over doctrinal matters called for scholarship of a high order and did much to bring reason into the service of revelation. On the other hand, Christian theology was fixed in the language and thought forms of Greek philosophy. Out of extensive theological discussion there eventually emerged two separate and distinct scholarly traditions, one in Latin and one in Greek. The Latin tradition, which flowered in the West, emphasized practical theological questions and administrative centralization under the Roman bishop. The Greek tradition, which flourished in the East, placed an emphasis on theological speculation and considerable local autonomy in matters of church jurisdiction.

Christian study of the human being and human relationships with the divine led to a high value being placed on education. There was new interest in and need for Christian scholarship, and its pursuit became a distinguished calling. This is evident in the careers of two of the greatest Latin writers of the patristic age, Jerome (340-420) and Augustine (354-430); both men discussed the issue of the relationship between Christianity and classical culture. Their involvement with this question is significant because it came about at just the time when classical culture seemed destined for extinction as the political power of the Roman Empire headed toward collapse in the western half of the empire. Both Jerome and Augustine had deep, personal experiences in the process often referred to as the "fall of Rome."

Jerome is a good example of a scholar, sincerely converted to Christian values, who continued to experience the pull of his scholarly calling and yet perceived the possibility of a conflict with his Christian values. Jerome had the best secular education available in the fourth century, was known as a lover of Cicero and Vergil, and was widely considered a splendid teacher of the pagan authors. Then came a renunciation of the classics—his famous dream in Epistle 22 gives some valuable clues to his state of mind—and his espousal of asceticism. But try as he might, and sometimes he did not try, Jerome could not give up his training in the pagan classics. He drove himself as biblical commentator, translator, and theological controversialist, almost overwhelming himself with work, yet his letters throughout his life abound with quotations from pagan authors. Even in his biblical commentaries he cites Horace, Plautus, and Vergil. His literary style clearly betrays his knowledge and love of the classics.

Jerome's outstanding literary and linguistic talents were ultimately employed on the supreme achievement of his career, the Latin translation of Scripture known as the Vulgate Bible, which was to stand for over a thousand years as the standard text of the sacred book of Christian revelation. Even under the spell of the pagan classics and faithful to the ancient insis-

tence on reason as characteristically human, Jerome concluded that to interpret the Bible rightly one must have had an education similar to the one he
himself had received. Jerome, like Benedict and later Erasmus, rightly perceived that the proper foundation for the Christian life was to be found in
the Bible, and to lay that foundation it was necessary to have as accurate
and intelligible a text as possible. As with Erasmus over a millenium later,
Christian humanism received an invaluable boost from an increased interest
in and attention to biblical studies.

Augustine of Hippo (354-430) is one of the giants in the history of Western civilization. In Christian thought only Jesus and Paul are figures of
comparable eminence. Augustine's lifetime embraces the period of the twi-
light of Roman civilization in the West and the beginning of the Middle
Ages. In some senses he may be regarded as a transitional figure, but his
life and work defy most efforts to put them in neat categories. In Augustine's writings there are some important clues to suggest his key role in the
transition from the Greco-Roman culture of the ancient world to a new
Christian orientation during the Middle Ages (c.400–c.1300).

Like his somewhat older contemporary, Jerome, Augustine was fortunate
to have a splendid secular education, though, unlike Jerome, he never mastered the writing of Greek. For years Augustine taught rhetoric and acquired
something close to reverence for Cicero, whom he was able to admire for the
rest of his life. The shift in his values is clearly perceptible in his work. His
estimate of the purpose of pagan learning comes through in *De Ordine*, a
treatise he wrote early in his career: "All those liberal arts are learned
partly for the conduct of life, partly for the understanding and contemplation of the universe." Years later when he wrote *De Doctrina Christiana*,
he referred specifically to the *De Ordine* and said that he regretted "the
emphasis that I laid on the liberal arts of which many saints are greatly
ignorant, whilst some who are familiar with them are not saints." He goes
on to suggest that all the disciplines of pagan antiquity should be closely
studied by Christians, but for the purpose of interpreting the Bible. Indeed,
Augustine's learning made popular his method of interpreting the Bible as
having meaning on four distinct levels: 1) the historical, 2) the etiological,
3) the analogical, 4) the allegorical.

In many significant ways Augustine is a key figure in the history of Christianity. He has important links with the early Christian church; he was a
model and guide for later pilgrims and reformers like Anselm, Petrarch,
Luther, Calvin, and Pascal. Like Paul he underwent a conversion to Christianity and became one of the most tireless workers on its behalf. Like Justin
Martyr he tried and was disappointed by one philosophy after another,
though his study of Plato left its mark on his Christian writings. Ultimately
a conversion experience brought him to Christianity, the result perhaps of
the earlier prompting of Christians like his mother, Monica, and the great

preacher Ambrose. Augustine's spiritual autobiography, *Confessions,* is a deeply moving document and displays well the emotional side of his nature. There were few issues of importance to the Christian world on which Augustine did not express himself, and therefore it is difficult to sum up the wide range of his interests and influence. For more than a thousand years after his death, Augustine was a veritable mine of ideas to pursue and undoubtedly the dominant figure in the development of Christian thought.

It is quite clear that the letters of Paul provided the point of departure for many of Augustine's most provocative discussions. He elaborated and developed such matters in Paul as the nature of God, the nature of the world, and the relationship between God and the human being. Thus Augustine's work is of special importance to any study of Christian humanism. From Neoplatonism he took the notion of the universe organized as a great chain of being, with God, perfect being, at the top; angels, pure spirits, and the highest created beings, next below God; then human beings, the most spiritual of material creatures, who possess self-knowledge, understanding of good and evil, and have an immortal soul. Below human beings are animals ordered according to their intelligence; vegetables are below animals, and inanimate objects are below vegetables. The derivation of this system from the thought of Plato is obvious; it was widely used and admired throughout the Middle Ages.

Augustine also explored other topics of central concern to the Christian humanist: sin and grace, the fall, original sin, evil, predestination, and free will. In dealing with nature and the material world Augustine draws upon the tradition of classical humanism. In agreement with Plato, he believed that the material world was less real than the world of ideas, but not that it was evil. After all, a good God had created the material world; therefore it must be good. In accepting the goodness of the material world Augustine helped to create a climate favorable to the scientific study of the material world and saved Christianity from a completely otherworldly outlook.

Likewise Augustine performed a valuable service for historical thought. He did not accept the ancient classical notion of cycles of time, but instead chose to elaborate the biblical view that time was a gift of God and had meaning. This so-called linear view of time marked another significant break with the classical past. This view gives meaning to historical events because they now take on a sense of movement and direction. Augustine's view of time makes possible a sense of historical development and emphasizes a process of change. An important consequence of this linear view of time is that it makes possible the notion of human progress, an idea which came of age in the era of Enlightenment.

Like the civilization itself, the ideas of Augustine were in a state of flux. His most famous, perhaps greatest, work, *City of God,* was the product of a lifetime of experience in which Christian faith had become the dominant influence. Against the background of the decay of the classical world and its values, he held out the hope that Christianity offered something better and more enduring. Augustine was the most influential thinker in the West; his attitudes toward learning and life molded educational values for the next six centuries.

JUSTIN MARTYR

Justin, known as the martyr, was born early in the second century and met a martyr's death in A.D. 163. Little is known of his life except what can be gleaned from his writings. He was born in Palestine of pagan parents and was educated in turn in contemporary pagan philosophies: first that of the Stoics, then that of the Peripatetics, and finally that of the Pythagoreans. Each of the philosophies left him unconvinced and dissatisfied; he claimed that none of them provided him with the truth. The quest for truth led him to Christianity, which he embraced with enthusiasm and heroic courage. He traveled about the Roman Empire as a teacher of Christianity and came to Rome during the reign of the emperor Antoninus Pius (A.D. 138-161). Justin lectured on the Christian faith while at Rome and founded a school there. During the reign of Marcus Aurelius (A.D. 161-180), he was brought to trial, an account of which fortunately has survived, found guilty, and martyred along with a group of companions in A.D. 163.

The writings of Justin Martyr have a special place in early Christian literature. They are classified with the writings of the apologists who worked on the frontier of the church and the world and sought to defend the Christian faith from misrepresentation and attack. The apologists also sought to commend Christianity to the interested inquirer and to demonstrate the falsity of polytheism. Most of the surviving apologies are in the form of legal documents petitioning the Roman authorities to investigate what Christianity was really about. The apologists took pains to challenge current calumnies and were particularly eager to answer the charge that the Christian church endangered the Roman state. They insisted that the Christian faith was a force for the maintenance and welfare of the world.

Evidently Justin was a rather prolific writer, although only three of his works have survived. There are two *Apologies* against the pagans (Romans) and a *Dialogue with the Jew Trypho*, the oldest Christian apology against the Jews. These works are written in Greek and lack literary grace or style. They possess, however, compelling power. Justin suggests that the Roman authorities err under Roman law when punishment is imposed although a defendant is not actually convicted of a crime. The first section of the *First Apology* demonstrates the folly of the official Roman attitude toward the

Christians. The second section provides a justification of the Christian religion and gives a detailed description of the church's doctrine and worship.

From Justin Martyr, **First Apology**

1. To the Emperor Titus Aelius Adrianus Antoninus Pius Augustus Caesar, and to his son Verissimus the philosopher, and to Lucius the philosopher, the natural son of Caesar, but the adopted of Pius, the lover of learning; and to the sacred senate, and to all the people of Rome, in the behalf of men of all ranks and nations unjustly loaded with public odium and oppression, I, Justin, the son of Priscus, and grandson of Bacchius, Natives of Flavia Neapolis of Palestine, Syria, I, who am one of this suffering multitude, humbly offer this Apology.

2. It is the voice of reason, and ever attended to by men truly pious and worthy the name of philosopher, that truth alone is the thing to be had in the highest honour, and to hold the first place in our affections, and the ancients to be followed not one step further than they are followers of truth. The same right reason dictates also that we are not only to strike in with any sect of men, unjust either in practice or principle, but, moreover, that a lover of the truth must by all means, and before life itself, and in defiance of all the menaces of death, choose to square his words and actions by the rules of justice whatever it cost him. And whereas you wear the glorious titles of pious and philosophers, and guardians of justice and lovers of learning, though these, I say, are the darling characters you affect to be distinguished by everywhere, yet whether you make them good or no shall be seen by the following discourse; for we come not here with a design to flatter or ingratiate by the power of fine words, but we come in plain terms to demand judgment according to the strictest and exactest rules of justice, that neither prejudice nor the vanity of getting into the good graces of superstitious men, nor blind passion, or a scandalous report which has so long prepossessed you, might any longer prevail with you to pass sentence against yourselves by condemning the innocent; for it is a maxim among us Christians that we cannot possibly suffer any real hurt, if we cannot be convicted of doing any real evil: "You may kill indeed, but you cannot hurt us."

6. And thus far we frankly confess the charge, that with respect to the gods in worship among you we are atheists; but far otherwise in respect of the most true God, the Father of righteousness, purity, and every virtue, a God infinitely removed from the least mixture or spot of evil: Him and His only-begotten Son (Who has instructed us in what I just now mentioned concerning these evil spirits, and likewise acquainted us with another host of good and godlike ministering spirits), both

these, I say, together with the Spirit Who spake by the prophets, we worship and adore, and our way of worshipping is in spirit and truth; and as we have been taught, so are we ready to communicate the same freely to every one that is willing to learn.

7. But perhaps it will be objected that some Christians have been taken up and convicted as evil-doers. Well, I might grant the objection and more; not only that some, but many, and at many times, have been thus duly convicted upon a fair trial; but then I must tell you again that you condemned not the persons aforesaid as criminals, but as Christians. Moreover, we confess that as all the sects in general among the Greeks went under the common name of philosopher, though extremely different in opinions, so truly among the barbarians the professors of this new wisdom, whether in reality or appearance only, go all by the same title, and are denominated Christians; wherefore we pray that all those who are indicted by the name of Christian may be examined as to their actions, and that every person may suffer as an evil-doer, and not as a Christian; and if he be found not guilty, that he may be discharged as a Christian who has done nothing worthy of punishment. And as to our false accusers, far be it from us to desire you to punish—their own painful wickedness, and utter ignorance of all that is good and amiable, is punishment in abundance.

8. I could wish you would take this also into consideration, that what we say is really for your own good; for it is in our power at any time to escape your torments, by denying the faith when you question us about it. But we scorn to purchase life at the expense of a lie; for our souls are winged with a desire of a life of eternal duration and purity, of an immediate conversation with God the Father and Maker of all things; we are in haste to be confessing and finishing our faith, being fully persuaded that we shall arrive at this beatific state if we approve ourselves to God by our works, and express our passion by our obedience for that divine life which is never interrupted by any clashing evil. But to lay before you, in short, what we expect, and what we have learned from Christ, and what we teach the world, take it as follows: Plato and we are both alike agreed as to a future judgment, but differ about the judges—Rhadamanthus and Minos are his judges, Christ ours. And moreover we say that the souls of the wicked, being reunited to the same bodies, shall be consigned over to eternal torments, and not, as Plato will have it, to the period of a thouasnd years only. But if you will affirm this to be incredible or impossible, there is no help but you must fall from error to error, till the day of judgment convinces you we are in the right.

9. But we cannot vouchsafe to worship with numerous victims, and garlands of flowers, the work of men's hands,—what you must help

into the temple, and being so placed think fit to dub them gods; for we know them to be senseless, inanimate idols, and in nothing resembling the form of God (for we cannot conceive God to be anywise like what is drawn to represent and honour Him by), but in imitation only of those evil spirits who have imposed upon the world under such titles and apparitions. But what need I mention to such knowing persons as you are how the artists manage the subject-matter of their gods, how they hack and hew it, and cast it and hammer it, and not seldom form vessels of dishonour; by changing their figure only, and giving them another turn by the help of art, out comes a worshipful set of things you call gods. This we look upon not only as the highest flight of human folly, but as the most injurious affront to the true God, Who is a God of glory and form ineffable, thus to transfer His incommunicable Name upon such corruptible and helpless things as wood and stone. Besides, the artificers of what you worship are the lewdest of men, and, not to mention particulars, practised in all sorts of wickedness, as you your-selves are very sensible of; men who debauch the girls while they are helping them to make your gods. Oh! stupidity of men as thunder-struck! that ever you should let such beasts have a hand in making your gods, and put them and the temples which hold them under the protection of such villains, never reflecting what an execrable crime it is, either to think or say, that men have the care and keeping of the gods!

10. And while we look upon God as the Giver of all good things, we can never think He stands in need of the material and gross obla-tions of men; but we are taught, and most firmly believe and know, that they only are the acceptable worshippers of God who form their minds by the mind eternal, and express it in temperance, justice, hu-manity, and such other virtues as are the essential excellence of the Divine Nature, or the more proper inmost perfections of Him Who is a God unnameable; and this Almighty Being, so good in Himself, made all things in the beginning for the good of man out of a chaos of rude ill-favoured matter; and they who walk according to His will, and demonstrate their worthiness by their works, we are sure will be ad-mitted into the Divine presence, there to reign with Him, where cor-ruption and suffering never come. For as He created us at first, when we were not, so by the same power will He restore us to begin again, and crown with the immortal enjoyment of Himself such as have made it their choice to please their Maker; for though we had no choice in our creation, yet in our regeneration we have; for God persuades only, and draws us gently in our regeneration, by co-operating freely with those rational powers He has bestowed upon us. And we are verily of opinion that it would be for the interest of all men living not only to

tolerate the learning of the Christian faith, but to give it all the public encouragement possible; for that inward conscientious discharge of our several duties, which human laws can never reach, the wisdom which is from above would bring about effectually, were it not for those false and atheistical accusations which are sowed about the world by diabolical spirits, who take advantage to strike in with that original sin and proneness to all evil that reigns in our nature, and which is sure to enter into confederacy with them; but of all their accusations we are entirely innocent.

11. But upon the first word you hear of our expectations of a kingdom, you rashly conclude it must needs to be a kingdom upon earth, notwithstanding all we can say that it is one in Heaven, and though you have such an experimental proof to the contrary from our professing ourselves Christians upon examination, when we know death to be the certain consequence of such a profession. But were our thoughts fixed upon a kingdom of this world, we would surely deny our religion for the safety of our lives, and have recourse to all the methods of concealment to secure us in a whole skin against that good day we expect. But since our hopes do not fasten upon things present, the preservation of our lives is the least of our concern, because we know our murderers can cut us short but a few days; for all must die.

16. In the first place, then, it is certain we cannot justly be branded for atheists, we who worship the Creator of the universe, not with blood, libations, and incense (which we are sufficiently taught He stands in no need of); but we exalt Him to the best of our power with the rational service of prayers and praises, in all the oblations we make unto Him; believing this to be the only honour worthy of Him; not to consume the creatures which He has given us for our use, and the comfort of those that want, in the fire by sacrifice, but to approve ourselves thankful to Him, and to express this gratitude in the rational pomp of the most solemn hymns at the altar in acknowledgment of our creation, preservation, and all the blessings of variety in things and seasons; and also for the hopes of a resurrection to a life incorruptible, which we are sure to have for asking, provided we ask in faith. Who that knows anything of us will not confess this to be our way of worshipping? And who can stigmatize such worshippers for atheists? The Master Who instructed us in this kind of worship, and Who was born for this very purpose, and crucified under Pontius Pilate, procurator of Judea, in the reign of Tiberius Caesar, is Jesus Christ, Whom we know to be the Son of the true God, and therefore hold Him the second in order, and the Prophetic Spirit the third; and that we have good reason for worshipping in this subordination, I shall show hereafter. For here they look upon it as downright madness to assign to a crucified man the

next place to the immutable, eternal God, Parent of all things, being entirely in the dark as to the mystery of this order; and therefore I advise you to give diligent attention while I expound it to you.

17. But first I am to caution you against those spirits, which I have already accused for practising upon you, that they do not delude and pervert you from reading and understanding what I am now proposing to your consideration; for to hold you in slavery and bondage is the prize they contend for, and sometimes by visions in sleep, sometimes by magical imposture they make sure of all such as are little concerned about their salvation. I could wish you would follow our example, who by the persuasions of the Logos have revolted from these spiritual wickednesses, and come over to the obedience of the only begotten God, through His Son Jesus Christ. We, who heretofore gave ourselves a loose to women, now strictly contain within the bounds of chastity; we, who devoted ourselves to magic arts, now consecrate ourselves entirely to the good unbegotten God; we, who loved nothing like our possessions, now produce all we have in common, and spread our whole stock before our indigent brethren; we, who were pointed with mutual hatred and destruction, and would not so much as warm ourselves at the same fire with those of a different tribe upon the account of different institutions now since the coming of Christ cohabit and diet together, and pray for our enemies; and all our returns for evil are but the gentlest persuasives to convert those who unjustly hate us, that by living up to the same virtuous precepts of Christ they might be filled with the same comfortable hopes of obtaining the like happiness with ourselves, from that God Who is the Lord of all things.

30. As to the Son of God called Jesus, should we allow Him to be nothing more than man, yet the title of the Son of God is very justifiable upon the account of His wisdom; for is not God styled by your own writers, Father of Gods and Men? But now if we say that the Logos of God is properly the begotten of God, by a generation quite different from that of men, as I have already mentioned, yet even this I say is no more than what you might very well tolerate, considering you have your Mercury in worship under the title of the Word and Messenger of God. As to the objection of our Jesus being crucified, I say that suffering was common to all the fore-mentioned sons of Jove, but only they suffered another kind of death; so that Christ does not seem at all inferior to them upon the score of the difference of His suffering, but much superior even in this very respect of His passion, as I shall prove in the following discourse, or rather indeed have proved already; for the excellence of every one is to be judged of by the nature and end of his actions. As to His being born of a Virgin, you have your Perseus to balance that; as to His curing the lame and the paralytic, and such

as were cripples from their birth, this is little more than what you say of your Aesculapius.

31. But in order to make it more plain that whatever we have declared from Christ and His preceding prophets is true and older than any of your writers, and that we desire to be believed, not because we deliver many the same things with them, but because we deliver the truth, and nothing but the truth, and that Jesus alone is properly the Son of God, as being the Logos, and First-begotten, and Power of God, and by His counsel was made man, and taught these doctrines for the conversion and restoration of mankind, before Whose coming in our flesh these same evil spirits, by their instruments, the poets, dressed up fables to represent these things as already past and over, on purpose to defeat the good designs of His coming; just such another pack of scandalous wicked lies they have at present invented to render Christians odious, for which they cannot produce one witness, nor anything like proof, as I shall presently make appear.

36. But we who are truly Christians are so far from maintaining any unjust or ungodly opinions, that exposing of infants, which is so much in practice among you, we teach to be a very wicked practice; first, because we see that such children, both girls and boys, are generally all trained up for the service of lust; for as the ancients bred up these foundlings to feed cows, or goats, or sheep, or grass-horses, so now-a-days such boys are brought up only to be abused against nature; and accordingly you have a herd of these women and effeminate men, standing prostitute for sale in every nation; and you traffic with such kind of cattle, and take toll and custom for their wickedness, when all such monstrous practices ought to be quite and clean rooted out of the world. And besides, whoever has to do with such wicked creatures, not only defiles himself with a mixture repugnant to all the laws of religion and temperance, but it is a great chance that the sinner does not pollute himself with some of his own children or nearest relations. Some there are who prostitute their own wives and children, and others are cut publicly for pathic obscenity, and their instruments made a sacrifice to the mother of the gods. And of all the established deities among you, a painted serpent is the greatest symbol and mystery. And such actions as you commit in the face of the sun, and are creditable vices among you, as if you had not one spark of divine light left, those you charge upon us; though this charge will do no harm to us, who are entire strangers to such sins, but to the doers of them only, and to such as falsely lay them to the charge of Christians. But the ringleader and prince of evil spirits is by us called the serpent, and Satan, and false accuser, as you may easily find from our Scriptures, who together with all his host of angels, and men like himself, shall be thrust into

fire, there to be tormented, world without end, as our Christ has foretold; and the reason why God has not done this already is out of mercy
to such of mankind as He foresees will repent and be saved; some of
which are now in being, and others as yet unborn. And from the beginning He made mankind intelligent and free creatures, fit for the
choice and practice of truth and goodness, so that every sinner should
be without excuse before God; for we are endued with reason, and
formed for contemplation. If any one, therefore, shall disbelieve the
providence of God, or shall deny His existence, notwithstanding the
evidence of His world, or assert Him to be a Being delighted with
wickedness, or as unactive as a stone, and that vice and virtue are
nothing in themselves, and depend only upon the opinions of men; this,
I say, is a consummate piece of impiety and injustice. And another
reason against exposing infants is, that we are afraid they should perish
for want of being taken up, and so bring us under the guilt of murder.

44. That the prophets were inspired by nothing but the Divine Wisdom of Logos, Who would forsee things at such a distance, is what I
believe you yourselves will grant me; but where this Logos was to be
born, hear what Micah, another prophet, says, and thus it stands: "And
thou, Bethlehem, in the land of Judah, art not the least among the
princes of Judah; for out of thee shall come a Governor That shall
rule My people Israel." Now this Bethlehem, where Christ Jesus was
born, is a certain village in Judaea, about thirty-five furlongs from
Jerusalem, as you may see in the censual tables of Cyrenius, the first
Prefect of Judaea; and how Christ after He was born lived in obscurity, and how this obscurity of life was foretold likewise, we have
our prophets to show, for thus they speak; —————.

46. We have been taught that Christ is the first-begotten of God,
and . . . He is the Reason of which every race of man partakes. Those
who lived in accordance with Reason are Christians . . . such as . . .
Socrates, Heraclitus and . . . Abraham . . . those who lived without
Reason were ungracious and enemies to Christ. . . . But those who
lived by Reason, and those who so live now are Christians. . . .

56. Moreover, the Holy prophetic Spirit has instructed us in the doctrine of free-will by Moses, who introduces God, speaking to the new-
made man in this manner: "Behold good and evil is before you; choose
the good." And again, by another prophet, Isaiah, He speaks to the
same effect in the person of God, the Father and Lord of the universe:
"Wash ye, make you clean, put away the evil of your doings, learn to
do well, judge the fatherless, and plead for the widow. Come now,
and let us reason together, saith the Lord: Though your sins be as
scarlet, they shall be as white as snow; though they be red like crim-
son, they shall be as wool. If ye be willing and obedient, ye shall eat

the good of the land: But if ye refuse and rebel, the sword shall feed upon you; for the mouth of the Lord hath spoken it" (Isa. i. 16-20). And whereas it is said that the "sword shall feed upon you," and not that the disobedient shall be cut off by swords, I must tell you, by the by, that the "sword of God" is fire, which shall prey upon those who have made wickedness their choice, and therefore He says, "The sword shall feed upon you; the mouth of the Lord hath spoken it." Whereas had He spoken of a common sword which cuts off, and despatches in a moment, He would not have used the word "feeding upon," which intimates a gradual destruction.

57. When Plato therefore said "that the blame lies at his door who wills the sin, but God wills no evil," he borrowed the saying from Moses; for Moses is older than any of your Greek writers; and as to all their notions about the immortality of the soul, and punishments after death, and their divine theories, and such-like doctrines, the philosophers and poets plainly took their hints from the prophets, which they consulted and built upon, and by this means the seeds of truth seem to be scattered about the world; but it is evident they understood them not as they should do, from the manifold contradictions amongst them.

58. By maintaining, therefore, that future events have been foretold by the prophets, we do not maintain that the things foretold came to pass by any necessity, but from that divine prescience which foresees all the actions of men, without necessitating them to act. And since a just retribution of rewards and punishments is a current opinion in the world, God has been pleased to second this motion by the prophetic Spirit, the more to awaken mankind and to print a future judgment perpetually upon their minds, and withal to show that His providence is concerned about us, and observes all our actions.

66. Since therefore we thus demonstrably prove that the things now come to pass were proclaimed by the prophets long before the events, how can we withhold from believing that the prophecies as yet unfulfilled will as verily be accomplished in their season as those we now see verified with our own eyes? For as these were once foretold and disbelieved, and yet came to pass, so the remainder will be brought to as certain an issue, in spite of ignorance and infidelity; for the very same prophets have foretold a twofold Advent of Christ, one wherein He was to come in the guise of an inglorious suffering mortal, and this is over; the other, wherein He shall come in His own form, encircled with celestial glory, and His host of angels, when He shall raise from the dead all the men that ever had a being, and shall invest the righteous with bodies incorruptible, and make the ungodly, together with these wicked spirits, feel His vengeance in fire everlasting.

68. I have a great many other prophecies in store, but I forbear, concluding what has been produced to be enough in reason for the conviction of such as have ears that will admit them to a fair hearing, and understandings prepared for truth. I can hardly persuade myself that you can take us for such romancers as those who dress up stories about the factitious progeny of Jove, mighty talkers, but able to prove nothing. For what motive could ever possibly have persuaded us to believe a crucified man to be the First-begotten of the Unbegotten God, and that He should come to be the judge of all the world, had we not met with those prophetic testimonies of Him proclaimed so long before His incarnation? Were we not eye-witnesses to the fulfilling of them? Did we not see the desolation of Judaea, and men out of all nations proselyted to the faith by His apostles, and renouncing the ancient errors they were brought up in? Did we not find the prophecies made good in ourselves, and see Christians in greater number and in greater sincerity from among the Gentiles than from the Jews and Samaritans? For all sorts of people are by the prophetic Spirit styled Gentiles; but the Jews and Samaritans stand distinguished by the name of the house of Israel and Jacob.

70. So many, therefore, and such mighty proofs as your own eyes are witnesses to cannot fail, methinks, of generating a firm and rational faith in the minds of those who are lovers of truth, and not carried away with opiniatrety and passion; but the instructors of your youth, who read them lectures out of the fables of the poets, never let them into the ground of these fictions. And that they are the work of devilcraft only, the better to delude mankind and hold them in darkness, I shall now prove. For these devilish spirits no sooner understood by the prophets that Christ was to come, and the ungodly to be punished with fire, but they trumped up that crew of Jove's sons abovesaid, imagining by this forgery to debauch the world into an opinion, that these prophecies concerning Christ were just such another pack of lies as the fables of the poets; and these stories they divulged among the Greeks and all the Gentiles, when they learned from the prophets that these were the people that should mostly come over to the Christian faith; but not diving far enough into the sense of the prophets, they attempted to copy after them, and, like men in the dark, blundered in their imitation, as I shall now show you.

90. And so far as these things shall appear agreeable to truth and reason, so far we desire you would respect them accordingly, but if they seem trifling, despise them as trifles; however, do not proceed against the professors of them, who are people of the most inoffensive lives, as severely as against your professed enemies; for, tell you I

must, that if you persist in this course of iniquity, you shall not escape
the vengeance of God in the other world.

TERTULLIAN

Tertullian (*c.* 160-230) is in many ways an ambiguous and elusive character. When he was born and when he died are not known with any degree
of precision. He seems to have burst into prominence amid the controversy
he loved so well and then faded out of sight. His activity as a writer seems
to be confined to the quarter-century from 195-220. Tertullian was associated
with the flourishing church in north Africa and is often considered to have
been its first real star. His birthplace seems to have been Carthage, and off
and on he was associated with that city. On the authority of Jerome it is
suggested that he was a presbyter. He himself reveals the fact that he had
been a pagan and was converted to Christianity; he may have been a jurist,
and if so, he attained some eminence in that field as witness the citations in
Justinian's *Corpus Juris Civilis.* What he did as presbyter remains shadowy,
and most of what is known about him and his work emerges through his
writings, of which a number of important products remain.

Tertullian has been called the creator of ecclesiastical Latin, and many,
indeed most, commentators agree that this is an accurate assessment. His
Latin is fluent and stylish; he seems to have had to create religious terminology in Latin because little or none had existed before. What he created
became the foundation for continued discussion in Latin and came to be
regarded as the proper theological vocabulary of the West. Tertullian's sentences are short and crisp and clearly influenced by the knowledge of good
Latin style. The passion of his rhetoric is something that clearly distinguishes
Tertullian. He loved to attack an opponent and then proceed to demolish
him. His opponents were always wholly in the wrong; there seems to have
been no room for compromise in his temperament. Tertullian believed himself to have been morally reborn through Christianity. Thus he defended his
faith with all the passion he could muster. He hated the persecutors of Christianity violently; he seems always to have sought moral rigor. Frequently he
attacks the moral laxness of his opponents. Any form of Christianity that
seemed to be an ally of philosophy was Tertullian's enemy. Tertullian did
not hide his feelings or prejudices; they are everywhere in his work!

From Tertullian, **On Prescription Against Heretics**
CHAPTER III
The Soul's Origin Defined Out of the Simple Words of Scripture
Would to God that no "heresies had been ever necessary, in order

that they which are approved may be made manifest!" We should then never be required to try our strength in contests about the soul with philosophers, those patriarchs of heretics, as they may be fairly called. The apostle, so far back as his own time, foresaw, indeed, that philosophy would do violent injury to the truth. This admonition *about false philosophy* he was induced to offer after he had been at Athens, had become acquainted with that *loquacious* city, and had there had a taste of its huckstering wiseacres and talkers. In like manner is the treatment of the soul according to the sophistical doctrines of men which "mix their wine with water." Some of them deny the immortality of the soul; others affirm that it is immortal, and something more. Some raise disputes about its substance; others about its form; others, again, respecting each of its several faculties. One school of philosophers derives its state from various sources, while another ascribes its departure to different destinations. *The various schools reflect the character of their masters,* according as they have received their impressions from the dignity of Plato, or the vigour of Zeno, or the equanimity of Aristotle, or the stupidity of Epicurus, or the sadness of Heraclitus, or the madness of Empedocles. The fault, I suppose, of the divine doctrine lies in its springing from Judaea rather than from Greece. Christ made a mistake, too, in sending forth fishermen to preach, rather than the sophist. Whatever noxious vapours, accordingly, exhaled from philosophy, obscure the clear and wholesome atmosphere of truth, it will be for Christians to clear away, both by shattering to pieces the arguments which are drawn from the principles of things—I mean those of the philosophers—and by opposing to them the maxims of heavenly wisdom—that is, such as are revealed by the Lord; in order that both the pitfalls wherewith philosophy captivates the heathen may be removed, and the means employed by heresy to shake the faith of Christians may be repressed. We have already decided one point in our controversy with Hermogenes, as we said at the beginning of this treatise, when we claimed the soul to be formed by the breathing of God, and not out of matter. We relied even there on the clear direction of the inspired statement which informs us how that "the Lord God breathed on man's face the breath of life, so that man became a living soul"—by that inspiration of God, of course. On this point, therefore, nothing further need be investigated or advanced by us. It has its own treatise, and its own heretic. I shall regard it as my introduction to the other branches of the subject.

CHAPTER IV

In Opposition to Plato, the Soul Was Created and Originated at Birth

After settling the origin of the soul, its condition or state comes up next. For when we acknowledge that the soul originates in the breath of God, it follows that we attribute a beginning to it. This Plato, indeed, refuses to assign to it, for he will have the soul to be unborn and unmade. We, however, from the very fact of its having had a beginning, as well as from the nature thereof, teach that it had both birth and creation. And when we ascribe both birth and creation to it, we have made no mistake: for being *born,* indeed, is one thing, and being made is another,—the former being the term which is best suited to living beings. When distinctions, however, have places and times of their own, they occasionally possess also reciprocity of application among themselves. Thus, the being made admits of being taken in the sense of being brought forth; inasmuch as everything which receives *being* or *existence,* in any way whatever, is in fact generated. For the maker may really be called the parent of the thing that is made: in this sense Plato also uses the phraseology. So far, therefore, as concerns our belief in the souls being made or born, the opinion of the philosopher is overthrown by the authority of prophecy even.

CHAPTER V

Probable View of the Stoics, that the Soul Has a Corporeal Nature

Suppose one summons a Fubulus to his assistance, and a Critolaus, and a Zenocrates, and on this occasion Plato's friend Aristotle. They may very possibly hold themselves ready for stripping the soul of its corporeity, unless they happen to see other philosophers opposed to them in their purpose—and this, too, in greater numbers—asserting for the soul a corporeal nature. Now I am not referring merely to those who mould the soul out of manifest bodily substances, as Hipparchus and Heraclitus [do] out of fire; as Hippon and Thales [do] out of water; as Empedocles and Critias [do] out of blood; as Epicurus [does] out of atoms, since even atoms by their coherence form corporeal masses; as Critolaus and his Peripatetics [do] out of certain indescribable *quintessence,* if that may be called a body which rather includes and embraces bodily substances;—but I call on the Stoics also to help me, who, while declaring almost in our own terms that the soul is a spiritual essence (inasmuch as breath and spirit are in their nature very near akin to each other), will yet have no difficulty in persuading (us) that the soul is a corporeal substance. Indeed, Zeno, defining the soul to be a spirit generated with [the body], constructs his argument in this way: That substance which by its departure causes the living being to die is a corporeal one. Now it is by the departure of the spirit, which is generated with [the body], that the living being dies; therefore the spirit which is generated with [the body] is a corporeal substance. But this spirit which is generated with [the body] is the soul: it follows, then, that the soul is a corporeal substance. Cleanthes, too, will have it that family likeness passes from parents to their children not merely in bodily features, but in characteristics of the soul, as if it were out of a mirror of a [a man's] manners, and faculties, and affections, that bodily likeness and unlikeness are caught and reflected by the soul also. It is therefore as being corporeal that it is susceptible of likeness and unlikeness. Again, there is nothing in common between things corporeal and things incorporeal as to their susceptibility. But the soul certainly sympathizes with the body, and shares in its pain, whenever it is injured by bruises, and wounds, and sores: the body, too, suffers with the soul, and is united with it (whenever it is afflicted with anxiety, distress, or love) in the loss of vigour which its companion sustains, whose shame and fear it testifies by its own blushes and paleness. The soul, therefore, is [proved to be] corporeal from this inter-communion of susceptibility. Chrysippus also joins hands in fellowship with Cleanthes, when he lays it down that it is not at all possible for things which are endued with body to be separated from things which have not body; because they have no such relation as mutual contact or coherence. Accordingly Lucretius says:

"Tangere enim et tangi nisi corpus nulla potest res."
"For nothing but body is capable of touching or of
being touched."

(Such severance, however, is quite natural between the soul and the body); for when the body is deserted by the soul, it is overcome by death. The soul, therefore, is endued with a body; for if it were not corporeal, it could not desert the body.

CHAPTER VII

Pagan Philosophy the Parent of Heresies. The Connection Between Deflections from Christian Faith and the Old Systems of Pagan Philosophy

These are "the doctrines" of men and "of demons" produced for itching ears of the spirit of this world's wisdom: this the Lord called "foolishness," and "chose the foolish things of the world" to confound even philosophy itself. For [philosophy] it is which is the material of the world's wisdom, the rash interpreter of the nature and the dispensation of God. Indeed heresies are themselves instigated by philosophy. From this source come the Aeons, and I know not what infinite forms, and the trinity of man in the system of Valentinus, who was of Plato's school. From the same source came Marcion's better god, with all his tranquillity; he came of the Stoics. Then, again, the opinion that the soul dies is held by the Epicureans; while the denial of the restoration of the body is taken from the aggregate school of all the philosophers; also, when matter is made equal to God, then you have the teaching of Zeno; and when any doctrine is alleged touching a god of fire, then Heraclitus comes in. The same subject-matter is discussed over and over again by the heretics and the philosophers; the same arguments are involved. Whence comes evil? Why is it permitted? What is the origin of man? and in what way does he come? Besides the question which Valentinus has very lately proposed—Whence comes God? Which he settles with the answer: From *enthymesis* and *ectroma*. Unhappy Aristotle! who invented for these men dialectics, the art of building up and pulling down; an art so evasive in its propositions, so farfetched in its conjectures, so harsh in its arguments, so productive of contentions—embarrassing even to itself, retracting everything, and really treating of nothing! Whence spring those "fables and endless genealogies," and "unprofitable questions," and "words which spread like a cancer?" From all these, when the apostle would restrain us, he expressly names *philosophy* as that which he would have us be on our guard against. Writing to the Colossians, he says, "See that no one beguile you through philosophy and vain deceit, after the tradition of men, and contrary to the wisdom of the Holy Ghost." He had been at Athens, and had in his interview [with its philosophers] become acquainted with that human wisdom which pretends to know the truth, whilst it only corrupts it, and is itself divided into its own manifold heresies, by the variety of its mutually repugnant sects. What indeed has Athens to do with Jerusalem? What concord is there between the Academy and the Church? What between heretics and Christians? Our instruction comes from "the porch of Solomon," who had himself taught that "the Lord should be sought in simplicity of heart." Away with all attempts to produce a mottled Christianity of Stoic, Platonic, and dialectic composition! We want no curious disputation after possessing Christ Jesus, no inquisition after enjoying the gospel! With our faith, we desire no further belief. For this is our palmary faith, that there is nothing which we ought to believe besides.

CHAPTER XXII

Recapitulation. Definition of the Soul

Hermogenes has already heard from us what are the other natural faculties of the soul, as well as their vindication and proof; whence it may be seen that the soul is rather the offspring of God than of matter. The names of these faculties shall here be simply repeated, that they may not seem to be forgotten and passed out of sight. We have assigned, then, to the soul both that freedom of the will which we just now mentioned, and its dominion over the works of nature, and its occasional gift of divination, independently of that endowment of prophecy which accrues to it expressly from the grace of God. We shall therefore now quit this subject of the soul's disposition, in order to set out fully in order its various qualities. The soul, then, we define to be sprung from the breath of God, immortal, possessing in its own nature, developing its power in various ways, free in its determinations, subject to the changes of accident, in its faculties mutable, rational, supreme, endued out of one [archetypal soul]. It remains for us now to consider how it is developed out of this one original source; in other words, whence, and when, and how it is produced.

CHAPTER XL

The Body of Man Only Ancillary to the Soul in the Commission of Evil

Every soul, then, by reason of its birth, has its nature in Adam until it is born again in Christ; moreover, it is unclean all the while that it remains without this regeneration; and because unclean, it is actively sinful, and suffuses even the flesh (by reason of their conjunction) with its own shame. Now although the flesh is sinful, and we are forbidden to walk in accordance with it, and its works are condemned as lusting against the spirit, and men on its account are censured as carnal, yet the flesh has not such ignominy on its own account. For it is not of itself that it thinks anything or feels anything for the purpose of advising or commanding sin. How should it, indeed? It is only a ministering thing, and its ministration is not like that of a servant or familiar friend—animated and human beings; but rather that of a vessel, or something of that kind: it is body, not soul. Now a cup may minister to a thirsty man; and yet, if the thirsty man will not apply the cup to his mouth, the cup will yield no ministering service. Therefore the *differentia,* or distinguishing property, of man by no means lies in his earthy element; nor is the flesh of the human person, as being some faculty of his soul, and a personal quality; but it is a thing of quite a different substance and different condition, although annexed to the soul as a chattel or as an instrument for the offices of life. Accordingly the flesh is blamed in the Scriptures, because nothing is done by the soul without the flesh in operations of concupiscence, appetite, drunkenness, cruelty, idolatry, and other works of the flesh,—operations, I mean, which are not confined to sensations, but result in effects. The emotions of sin, indeed, when not resulting in effects, are usually imputed to the soul: "Whosoever looketh on a woman to lust after, hath already in his heart committed adultery with her." But what has the flesh alone, without the soul, ever done in operations of virtue, righteousness, endurance, or chastity? What absurdity, however, it is to attribute sin and crime to that substance to which you do not assign any good actions or character of its own! Now the party which aids in the commission of a crime is brought to trial, only in such a way that the principal offender who actually committed the crime may bear the weight of the penalty, although the abettor too does not escape indictment. Greater is the odium which falls on the principal, when his officials are punished through his fault. He is beaten with more stripes who instigates and orders the crime, whilst at the same time he who obeys such an evil command is not acquitted.

CHAPTER XLI

Notwithstanding the Depravity of Man's Soul by Original Sin, There Is Yet Left a Basis Whereon Divine Grace Can Work for Its Recovery by Spiritual Regeneration.

There is, then, besides the evil which supervenes on the soul from the intervention of the evil spirit, an antecedent, and in a certain sense natural, evil which arises from its corrupt origin. For, as we have said before, the corruption of our nature is another nature having a god and father of its own, namely the author of [that] corruption. Still there is a portion of good in the soul, of that original, divine, and genuine good, which is its proper nature. For that which is derived from God is rather obscured than extinguished. It can be obscured, indeed, because it is not God; extinguished, however, it cannot be, because it comes from God. As therefore light, when intercepted by an opaque body, still remains, although it is not apparent, by reason of the interposition of so dense a body; so likewise the good in the soul, being weighed down by the evil, is, owing to the obscuring character thereof, either not seen at all, its light being wholly hidden, or else only a stray beam is there visible where it struggles through by an accidental outlet. Thus some men are very bad, and some very good; but yet the souls of all form but one genus: even in the worst there is something good, and in the best there is something bad. For God alone is without sin; and the only man without sin is Christ, since Christ is also God. Thus the divinity of the soul bursts forth in prophetic forecasts in consequence of its primeval good; and being conscious of its origin, it bears testimony to God (its author) in exclamations such as: *Good God! God knows! Good-bye!* Just as no soul is without sin, so neither is any soul without seeds of good.

Therefore, when the soul embraces the faith, being renewed in its second birth by water and the power from above, then the veil of its former corruption being taken away, it beholds the light in all its brightness. It is also taken up (in its second birth) by the Holy Spirit, just as in its first birth it is embraced by the unholy spirit. The flesh follows the soul now wedded to the Spirit, as a part of the bridal portion—no longer the servant of the soul, but of the Spirit. O happy marriage, if in it there is committed no violation of the nuptial vow.

From Tertullian, **Against Praxeas**

CHAPTER IV

God's Honour in the Incarnation of His Son Vindicated, Marcion's Disparagement of Human Flesh Inconsistent as Well as Impious. Christ Has Cleansed the Flesh. The Foolishness of God Is Most Wise.

Since, therefore, you do not reject the assumption of a body as impossible or as hazardous to the character of God, it remains for you to repudiate and censure it as unworthy of Him. Come now, beginning from the nativity itself, declaim against the uncleanness of the generative elements within the womb, the filthy concretion of fluid and blood, of the growth of the flesh for nine months long out of that very mire. Describe the womb as it enlarges from day to day,—heavy, troublesome, restless even in sleep, changeful in its feelings of dislike and desire. Inveigh now likewise against the shame itself of a woman in travail, which, however, ought rather to be honoured in consideration of that peril, or to be held sacred in respect of [the mystery of] nature. Of course you are horrified also at the infant, which is shed into life with the embarrassments which accompany it from the womb; you likewise, of course, loathe it even after it is washed, when it is dressed out in its swaddling-clothes, graced with repeated anointing, smiled on with nurse's fawns. This reverend course of nature, you, O Marcion, [are pleased to] spit upon; and yet, in what way were you born? You detest a human being at his birth; then after what fashion do you love anybody? Yourself, of course, you had no love of, when you departed

from the Church and the faith of Christ. But never mind, if you are
not on good terms with yourself or even if you were born in a way
different from other people. Christ, at any rate, has loved even that
man who was condensed in his mother's womb amidst all its unclean-
nesses, even that man who was brought into life out of the said womb,
even that man who was nursed amidst the nurse's simpers. For his sake
He came down [from heaven], for his sake He preached, for his sake
"He humbled Himself even unto death—the death of the cross." He
loved, of course, the being whom He redeemed at so great a cost. If
Christ is the Creator's *Son*, it was with justice that He loved His own
[creature]; if He comes from another god, His love was excessive,
since He redeemed a being who belonged to another. Well, then,
loving man He loved his nativity also, and his flesh as well. Nothing
can be loved apart from that through which whatever exists has its
existence. Either take away nativity, and then show us *your* man; or
else withdraw the flesh, and then present to our view the being whom
God has redeemed—since it is these very conditions which constitute
the man whom God has redeemed. And are *you* for turning these conditions into occasions of blushing to the very creature whom He has
redeemed, [censuring them], too, as unworthy of Him who certainly
would not have redeemed them had He not loved them? Our birth He
reforms from death by a second birth from heaven; our flesh He restores from every harassing malady; when leprous, He cleanses it of
the stain; when blind, He rekindles its light; when palsied, He renews
its strength; when possessed with devils, He exorcises it; when dead,
He reanimates it,—then shall *we* blush to own it? If, to be sure, He
had chosen to be born of a mere animal, and were to preach the kingdom of heaven invested with the body of a beast either wild or tame,
your censure (I imagine) would have instantly met Him with this
demurrer: "This is disgraceful for God, and this is unworthy of the
Son of God, and simply foolish." For no other reason than because
one thus judges. It *is* of course, foolish, if we are to judge God by
our own conceptions. But, Marcion, consider well this Scripture, if
indeed you have not erased it: "God hath chosen the foolish things
of the world, to confound the wise." Now what are those foolish
things? Are they the conversion of men to the worship of the true
God, the rejection of error, the whole training in righteousness, chastity, mercy, patience, and innocence? These things certainly are not
"foolish." Inquire again, then, of what things he spoke, and when you
imagine that you have discovered what they are will you find anything to be so "foolish" as believing in a God that has been born, and
that of a virgin, and of a fleshly nature too, who wallowed in all the
before-mentioned humiliations of nature? But some one may say,

"These are not the foolish things; they must be other things which God has chosen to confound the wisdom of the world." And yet, according to the world's wisdom, it is more easy to believe that Jupiter became a bull or a swan, if we listen to Marcion, than that Christ really became a man.

CHAPTER V

Christ Truly Lived and Died in Human Flesh. Incidents of His Human Life on Earth, and Refutation of Marcion's Docetic Parody of the Same.

There are, to be sure, other things also quite as foolish [as the birth of Christ], which have reference to the humiliations and sufferings of God. Or else, let them call a crucified God "wisdom." But Marcion will apply the knife to this *doctrine* also, and even with greater reason. For which is more unworthy of God, which is more likely to raise a blush of shame that *God* should be born, or that He should die? that He should bear the flesh, or the cross? be circumcised, or be crucified? be cradled, or be coffined? be laid in a manger, or in a tomb? *Talk of "wisdom!"* You will show more of *that* if you refuse to believe this also. But, after all, you will not be "wise" unless you become a "fool" to the world, by believing "the foolish things of God." Have you, then, cut away all sufferings from Christ, on the ground that, as a mere phantom, He was incapable of experiencing them? We have said above that He might possibly have undergone the unreal mockeries of an imaginary birth and infancy. But answer me at once, you that murder truth: Was not God really crucified? And, having been really crucified, did He not really die? And, having indeed really died, did He not really rise again? Falsely did Paul "determine to know nothing amongst us but Jesus and Him crucified." Falsely has he impressed upon us that He was buried; falsely inculcated that He rose again. False, therefore, is our faith also. And all that we hope for from Christ will be a phantom. O thou most infamous of men, who acquitest of all guilt the murderers of God! For nothing did Christ suffer from them, if He really suffered nothing at all. Spare the whole world's one only hope, thou who are destroying the indispensable dishonour of our faith. Whatsoever is unworthy of God, is of gain to me. I am safe, if I am not ashamed of my Lord. "Whosoever," says He, "shall be ashamed of me, of him will I also be ashamed." Other matters for shame find I none which can prove me to be shameless in good sense, and foolish in a happy one, by my own contempt of shame. The Son of God was crucified; I am not ashamed because men must needs be ashamed *of it*. And the Son of God died; it is by all means to be believed, because it is absurd.

And He was buried, and rose again; the fact is certain, because it is impossible. But how will all this be true in Him, if He was not Himself true—if He really had not in Himself that which might be crucified, might die, might be buried, and might rise again? *I mean* this flesh suffused with blood, built up with bones, interwoven with nerves, entwined with veins, *a flesh* which knew how to be born, and how to die, human without doubt, as born of a human being. It will therefore be mortal in Christ, because Christ is man and the Son of man. Else why is Christ man and the Son of man, if he has nothing of man, and nothing from man? Unless it be either that man is anything else than flesh, or man's flesh comes from any other source than man, or Mary is anything else than a human being, or Marcion's man is *as* Marcion's god. Otherwise Christ could not be described as being man without flesh, nor the Son of man without any human parent; just as He is not God without the Spirit of God, nor the Son of God without having God for His father. Thus the nature of the two substances displayed Him as man and God—in one respect born, in the other unborn, in one respect fleshly, in the other spiritual; in one sense weak, in the other exceeding strong; in one sense dying, in the other living. This property of the two states—the divine and the human—is distinctly asserted with equal truth of both natures alike, with the same belief both in respect of the spirit and of the flesh. The powers of the Spirit, proved Him to be God, His sufferings attested the flesh of man. If His powers were not without the Spirit in like manner, were not His sufferings without the flesh. If His flesh with its sufferings was fictitious, for the same reason was the Spirit false with all its powers. Wherefore halve Christ with a lie? He was wholly the truth. Believe me, He chose rather to be born, than in any part to pretend—and that indeed to His own detriment—that He was bearing about a flesh hardened without bones, solid without muscles, bloody without blood, clothed without the tunic *of skin,* hungry without appetite, eating without teeth, speaking without a tongue, so that His word was a phantom to the ears through an imaginary voice. A phantom, too, it was of course after the resurrection, when, showing His hands and His feet for the disciple to examine, He said, "Behold and see that it is I myself, for a spirit hath not flesh and bones, as ye see me have"; without doubt, hands, and feet, and bones are not what a spirit possesses, but only the flesh. How do you interpret this statement, Marcion, you who tell us that Jesus comes only from the most excellent God, who is both simple and good? See how He *rather* cheats, and deceives, and juggles the eyes of all, and the senses of all, as well as their access to and contact with Him! You ought rather to have brought Christ down, not from heaven, but from some troop of mountebanks, not as God besides man, but simply as a man, a magician; not as the High Priest of our salvation, but as the conjurer in a show; not as the raiser of the dead, but as the misleader of the living,—except that, if He were a magician, He must have had a nativity!

THE CREEDS

Creeds such as the Apostles' Creed and the Nicene Creed can be described as terse summaries of the essentials of Christian belief. It is known that such summaries of belief existed in New Testament times. It is also most likely that there was no fixed wording for such summaries until the middle of the second century. Early references to what may be described as creeds emphasize an oral tradition known as the "rule of faith." The earliest use of creeds by Christians is recorded in connection with baptism, where they served as interrogatory statements of faith. What began as interrogatory statements about the faith eventually became declaratory statements used to instruct those preparing for baptism. From the surviving evidence it does not seem that the creeds originated as a defense of the faith, though they did indeed come to serve that purpose. From early Christian times to the present these creeds have served as statements of what it is essential that a Christian must believe. For many Christians the recital of the creed has become part of the Eucharistic liturgy.

The Apostles' Creed is so-called because Rufinus, in the early fifth century, recorded the tradition that the twelve apostles around the time of Pentecost composed a uniform statement of belief which all would teach as they went about their missionary work. A later account of the composition of the Apostles' Creed embroidered on the account furnished by Rufinus by adding the point that each apostle contributed one of the twelve clauses. This account of the composition of the Apostles' Creed and the formula that had been preserved were not questioned until the fifteenth century when doubts were raised at the church council held at Ferrara-Florence in 1438-39. Soon after the Council it was demonstrated that the wording of the Apostles' Creed could not have been apostolic in origin. It was agreed, however, that the Apostles' Creed did represent the teaching of the apostles. In the form in which it has survived to the present day, the wording of the Apostles' Creed is no older than the eighth century.

The Nicene Creed came into being as part of an effort to combat heresy in the early Christian church. In the fourth century the Arian heresy, involving the relationship of the Father and the Son in the Trinity, threatened to split the church irreparably. Consequently the Roman emperor Constantine, in an effort to pacify the warring factions, called the first Ecumenical Council at Nicea in 325. The council promulgated a creed meant to exclude Arianism, although the formula arrived at, the insertion of the key word *homoousios* did not settle the controversy. It was only after the Arians were subdued that a universally acceptable formula was set forth. This formula, or statement of the creed, is referred to as the Nicene Creed and was approved and issued by the second Ecumenical Council at Constantinople in 381.

Apostles' Creed

I believe in God the Father Almighty, creator of heaven and earth.
I believe in Jesus Christ, his only Son, our Lord. He was conceived by
the power of the Holy Spirit, and born of the virgin Mary. He
suffered under Pontius Pilate, was crucified, died, and was buried.
He descended into hell. On the third day he rose again.
He ascended into heaven, and is seated at the right hand of the
Father. He will come again to judge the living and the dead.
I believe in the Holy Spirit, the holy catholic Church, the communion
of saints, the forgiveness of sins, the resurrection of the body, and
the life everlasting. Amen.

Nicene Creed

We believe in one God,
the Father, the Almighty,
maker of heaven and earth,
of all that is, seen and unseen.
We believe in one Lord, Jesus Christ,
the only Son of God,
eternally begotten of the Father,
God from God, Light from Light,
true God from true God,
begotten, not made,
of one Being with the Father.
Through him all things were made.
For us and for our salvation
he came down from heaven;
by the power of the Holy Spirit
he became incarnate from the Virgin Mary, and was made man.
For our sake he was crucified under Pontius Pilate;
he suffered death and was buried.
On the third day he rose again
in accordance with the Scriptures;
he ascended into heaven
and is seated at the right hand of the Father.
He will come again in glory to judge the living and the dead,
and his kingdom will have no end.

We believe in the Holy Spirit, the Lord, the giver of life,
   who proceeds from the Father and the Son
   With the Father and the Son he is worshiped and glorified.
He has spoken through the prophets.
We believe in one holy catholic and apostolic Church.
We acknowledge one Baptism for the forgiveness of sins.
We look for the resurrection of the dead,
   and the life of the world to come. Amen.

JEROME

Jerome (*c.* 340-420) was a great scholar of the patristic age. He was born in Dalmatia to Christian parents of considerable means. Educated at Rome under the famous grammarian Donatus, Jerome took time to enjoy some of the pleasures for which the Roman capital had become notorious. However, he also displayed considerable interest in the early Christian heroes, whose resting places he visited in the Roman catacombs. Gradually he developed a liking for theology and studied at Trier, where a fine theological school was to be found. During the 370s he traveled rather extensively in the eastern Mediterranean area and became acquainted with such centers of Greek culture as Antioch, Alexandria, and Constantinople. In 382 he went to Rome at the request of Pope Damasus and also, at his request, agreed to prepare a Latin text of the Scriptures. This task was to occupy him intermittently for the rest of his life. After 386 Jerome settled in Palestine and made his home at Bethlehem, where he gathered around him a community of monks and became a model of the ascetic life. In his old age Jerome had to cope with ill health, failing eyesight, and privation. He died in 420.

Jerome left an enormous literary legacy. Writing seems to have been his favorite activity. Among his most significant literary efforts are his letters, biblical commentaries, homilies, monastic rules, and his Latin translation of the Scriptures, the Vulgate Bible. Perhaps the letters reveal him best; they are witty, sarcastic, fiery, and stylish. This great scholar prided himself on his fine Latin style and constantly strove to refine it. Jerome was at his best when engaging in controversy, especially of a theological nature, which he did at the slightest provocation. From the writings of Jerome we can see that he was steeped in classical culture and loved it. His efforts to renounce or eschew his Roman heritage were unsuccessful. The Vulgate Bible was truly a labor of love. Working from the oldest Greek, Hebrew, and Chaldaic manuscripts he could locate, Jerome prepared a Latin translation of the Bible that was clear, straightforward, and popular. Indeed, by its excellence, the Vulgate Bible rendered other Latin translations of the Bible obsolete.

Jerome was among the first to acquaint the West with the monastic life. His life focused on two goals: his scholarship and the practice of asceticism. He was especially irritated by the laxity and worldliness of the clergy and denounced them in matchless terms. He saw the practice of asceticism as a useful corrective for the deficiencies of ecclesiastics. He made his point so strongly, however, that he was several times forced to flee the wrath of an enraged clergy. For Jerome it was often best to be alone.

From Jerome, **Letter XXII**

Many years ago for the sake of the kingdom of heaven, I cut myself off from home, parents, sister, relations, and, what was harder, from the dainty food to which I had been used. But even when I was on my way to Jerusalem to fight the good fight there, I could not bring myself to forego the library which with great care and labour I had got together at Rome. And so, miserable man that I was, I would fast, only to read Cicero afterwards. I would spend many nights in vigil, I would shed bitter tears called from my inmost heart by the remembrance of my past sins; and then I would take up Plautus again. Whenever I returned to my right senses and began to read the prophets, their language seemed harsh and barbarous. With my blind eyes I could not see the light: but I attributed the fault not to my eyes but to the sun. While the old serpent was thus mocking me, about the middle of Lent a fever attacked my weakened body and spread through my inmost veins. It may sound incredible, but the ravages it wrought on my unhappy frame were so persistent that at last my bones scarcely held together.

Meantime preparations were made for my funeral: my whole body grew gradually cold, and life's vital warmth only lingered faintly in my poor throbbing breast. Suddenly I was caught up in the spirit and dragged before the Judge's judgment seat: and here the light was so dazzling, and the brightness shining from those who stood around so radiant, that I flung myself upon the ground and did not dare to look up. I was asked to state my condition and replied that I was a Christian. But He who presided said: 'Thou liest; thou art a Ciceronian, not a Christian. "For where thy treasure is there will thy heart be also." ' Straightway I became dumb, and amid the strokes of the whip—for He had ordered me to be scourged—I was even more bitterly tortured by the fire of conscience, considering with myself the verse: 'In the grave who shall give thee thanks?' Yet for all that I began to cry out and to bewail myself, saying: 'Have mercy upon me, O Lord, have mercy upon me': and even amid the noise of the lash my voice made itself heard. At last the bystanders fell at the knees of Him who presided, and prayed Him to pardon my youth and give me opportunity to repent of my error, on the understanding that the extreme of torture should be inflicted on me if ever I read again the works of Gentile authors. In the stress of that dread hour I should have been willing to make even larger promises, and taking oath I called upon His name: 'O Lord, if ever again I possess worldly books or read them, I have denied thee.'

After swearing this oath I was dismissed, and returned to the upper world. There to the surprise of all I opened my eyes again, and they were so drenched with tears, that my distress convinced even the incredulous. That this experience was no sleep nor idle dream, such as often mocks us, I call to witness the judgment seat before which I fell and the terrible verdict which I feared. May it never be my lot again to come before such a court as that! I profess that my shoulders were black and blue, and that I felt the bruises long after I awoke from my sleep. And I acknowledge that henceforth I read the books of God with a greater zeal than I had ever given before to the books of men.

AUGUSTINE

Augustine of Hippo (354-430), so-called because of his long service as its bishop, is undoubtedly the greatest of the fathers of the Western church. Perhaps no one after St. Paul has exerted anything approaching his influence on the evolution of Christian thought. He was born in North Africa to a Christian mother, Monica, who hoped and prayed that someday he might become a Christian. Her hopes and prayers were fulfilled when, after much experimentation with various modes of life and thought, he ventured to hear the preaching of Ambrose and later experienced conversion to Christianity. The story of his conversion is told in a most moving manner in his spiritual autobiography, the *Confessions*. He was ordained a priest and then became bishop of Hippo, where he served until his death in 430. His activities as bishop show him to have been a sensitive and completely dedicated pastor to his flock, yet somehow he found time to write a whole library of books, some of which are among the "great books" of all time.

Augustine's greatest work, the *City of God*, was begun shortly after the sack of Rome in 410 by the Goths in order to acquit the Christians of the charge that Christianity had brought about the fall of Rome. Augustine claimed that Rome had fallen because of her vices and that, great as she was, Rome was, after all, only a material city. What really mattered was the City of God. What God intended was that the world should serve as a proving ground where men should have the opportunity to prove their fitness to become permanent residents of this eternal city. In the *City of God*, and in other writings, Augustine works out the essential role of the church in the salvation of souls. He stresses the compelling importance of God's grace in the salvation of the soul. Augustine's insistence upon the indispensable nature of God's grace has led scholars to stress his belief in predestination; Luther and Calvin were to pay much heed to Augustine's thought on this matter. Augustine was a prolific writer, and his advice was continually being sought and given in letters and handbooks. Of the latter the *Enchiridion*, the oldest theological textbook for laymen, is one of the most celebrated. Augustine's *De Doctrina Christiana* is a handbook for preachers and is meant to be a guide for instructing Christians in the Bible.

From Augustine, **The Way of Life of the Catholic Church**
CHAPTER 3

(4) Let us inquire, then, how according to reason man ought to live. Certainly, we all wish to live happily. There is no human being who would not assent to this statement almost before it is uttered. However, in my opinion, neither he who lacks what he loves can be called happy, whatever it be, nor he who has what he loves if it be harmful, nor he who does not love what he has although it be the best. For he who desires what he cannot obtain is tormented, and he who has attained what he should not have desired is deceived, while he who does not desire what he should seek to attain is diseased. To souls such as these, there remains nothing but misery, and since misery and happiness are not accustomed to dwell in the same man simultaneously, none of these men can be happy.

As I see it, however, a fourth alternative remains in which the happy life may be found—when that which is best for man is both loved and possessed. For what else is meant by enjoyment but the possession of what one loves? But no one is happy who does not enjoy what is supremely good for man, and whoever does enjoy it is not unhappy. We must possess our supreme good, therefore, if we intend to live happily.

(5) It follows that we must seek to discover what is man's supreme good, and it cannot, of course, be anything inferior to man himself; for whoever strives after something inferior to himself becomes himself inferior. But all men are obliged to seek what is best. Therefore, man's supreme good is not inferior to man.

Will it then perhaps be something similar to man himself? It might well be so, provided there is nothing superior to man that he can enjoy. If, however, we find something that is both more perfect than man and which can be attained by the one loving it, who would doubt that he should, in order to be happy, strive to possess this thing, which is more

excellent than he himself who seeks it? For if happiness is the possession of a good than which there is no greater, and this is what we call
the supreme good, how can a person be said to be happy who has not
yet attained his supreme good? Or how can it be called the supreme
good if there is something better that he can attain? Such being the
case, it follows that one cannot lose it against his will, for no one can
be confident of a good he knows can be snatched from him even though
he wishes to keep and cherish it. And if he lacks this confidence in the
good which he enjoys, how can he, in such fear of loss, be happy?

CHAPTER 4

(6) Let us, then, attempt to discover what is better than man. And
this will be very difficult unless we first discuss what man himself is.
But I do not think I should be expected to give a definition of man here.
Rather, it seems to me that since nearly everyone agrees (or at least,
and it is sufficient, those with whom I am now dealing agree) that we
are composed of body and soul, what should be determined at this
point is what man himself is. Of the two which I have mentioned, is
he body alone or soul alone? For although they are two things, soul
and body, and neither could be called man were the other not present
(for the body would not be man if there were no soul, nor would the
soul be man were there no body animated by it), it might happen,
nevertheless, that one of these would be looked upon and be spoken
of as man.

What do we call man, then? Is he soul and body like a centaur or
two horses harnessed together? Or shall we call him the body alone
in the service of a governing soul, as is the case when we give the name
lamp, not to the vessel and flame together, but to the vessel alone on
account of the flame within it? Or shall we say that man is nothing
but the soul, inasmuch as it rules the body, just as we say that the
horseman is not the horse and man together, but the man alone from
the fact that he guides the horse? This is a difficult problem to solve,
or, at any rate, even if its solution were simple, it would require a
lengthy explanation involving an expense of time and labor which
would not profit us here. For whether it be both body and soul or soul
alone that goes by the name of man, that is not the supreme good of
man which constitutes the supreme good of the body. But whatever is
the highest good either of body and soul together or of the soul alone,
that is the supreme good of man.

CHAPTER 5

(7) If we ask what is the supreme good of the body, reason compels us to admit it is whatever causes the body to be at its best. But of

all things that give vigor to the body, none is better nor more important than the soul. Hence, the supreme good of the body is not sensual pleasure, nor absence of pain, nor strength, nor beauty, nor swiftness, nor whatever else is ordinarily numbered among the goods of the body, but the soul alone. For by its very presence, the soul provides the body with all the things we have enumerated and with that which excels them all besides, namely, life. Therefore, it does not seem to me that the soul is the supreme good of man, whether we call man soul and body together, or soul alone. For, as reason declares, the greatest good of the body is that which is better than the body and by which the body is given life and vigor, so, too, whether the body and soul together be man or the soul alone, we must still find out whether there is anything beyond the soul itself which, when sought after, makes the soul more perfect in its own order. If we can discover some such thing, all of our doubts will be removed, for it will unquestionably merit the name of the supreme good of man.

(8) If the body be man, it cannot be denied that the supreme good of man is the soul. But, surely, when it is a question of morals—when we ask what kind of life we must lead in order to attain happiness—the commandments are not for the body, and we are not concerned with bodily discipline. In a word, good morals pertain to that part of us which inquires and learns, and these are acts of the soul. Therefore, when we are dealing with the attainment of virtue, the question is not one which concerns the body. But if it follows, as it does, that the body when ruled by a virtuous soul is ruled both better and more worthily and is at its best because of the perfection of the soul ruling it rightly, then that which perfects the soul will be man's supreme good even though we call the body man. For if at my command the charioteer feeds and properly manages the horses in his care, and enjoys my generosity in proportion as he is obedient to me, who can deny that not only the charioteer but the horses, too, owe their well-being to me? And so, whether body alone, or soul alone, or both together be man, the important thing, it seems to me, is to discover what makes the soul perfect, for when this is attained, a man cannot but be perfect, or at least much better than if it were lacking to him.

CHAPTER 11

(18) To strive after God, then, is to desire happiness; to reach God is happiness itself. We strive after Him by loving Him; we reach Him, not by becoming altogether what He is, but by coming close to Him, touching Him in a wonderfully spiritual way, and being illuminated and pervaded utterly by His truth and holiness. He is the Light itself,

whereas we receive our enlightenment from Him. The first and greatest commandment, therefore, that leads us to the happy life is: 'Thou shalt love the Lord thy God with thy whole heart, and with thy whole soul, and with thy whole mind.' For 'to those who love God all things work together unto good.' And that is why St. Paul adds a little further on: 'I am sure that neither death, nor life, nor angels, nor virtue, nor things present, nor things to come, nor height, nor depth, nor any other creature will be able to separate us from the love of God,' which is in Christ Jesus our Lord.'

If, therefore, for those who love God all things work together unto good, and if, as no one doubts, the supreme or perfect good must not only be loved but be so loved that loved more, as is indicated by the words: 'With thy whole soul, and with thy whole heart, and with thy whole mind,' who, may I ask, would doubt, since these things are all established and firmly believed, that what is best for us is God, and that we should put aside all else and hasten to reach Him? Moreover, if nothing can separate us from His love, what can be better or more certain than this good?

(19) Let us briefly consider each phrase singly. No one separates us from God in threatening us with death. For since that with which we love God cannot die except by not loving Him, death is in not loving Him, that is, in loving and seeking something else in preference to Him. No one separates us from God in promising life, for we are not drawn away from the fountain by the promise of water. No angel separates us from God, for there is no angel more powerful than our mind when it adheres to God. Virtue does not separate us from Him, for if by virtue is meant that which has a certain power in this world, the mind adhering to God is far above the whole world. If, however, by virtue is meant an upright disposition of mind, if this disposition be in someone else, it will favor our union with God, and if in us, it will itself unite us to Him. Present troubles do not separate us from God, for the closer we adhere to Him from whom they attempt to separate us, the lighter these burdens feel. The promise of future good does not separate us from Him, for His promise of future good is more certain than any other, and there is no greater good than God Himself who is already truly present to those who adhere to Him.

Height and depth do not separate us from God, for if these words are taken to mean the height and depth of knowledge, I will not be curious so as not to be separated from Him. Nor does any doctrine purporting to dispel error separate me from Him, for one errs only in separating oneself from Him. But if by height and depth are meant the upper and lower regions of the world, would anyone promise me heaven in order to separate me from the Maker of heaven? And could hell frighten me into deserting Him, when I would never have known hell had I not already deserted Him? In short, can any place isolate me from His love when He would not be wholly present everywhere were He contained in any single place?

CHAPTER 12

(20) 'No other creature' separates us, says he. 'O man of profound mysteries.' He was not content to say no creature, but says no other creature, reminding us that that with which we love God and adhere to Him, that is, our soul and mind, is itself a creature. The body, therefore, is another creature, and if the soul is something immaterial—something known only by the intelligence—this creature, the body, includes everything sensible, that is to say, everything known to us through the eyes, or ears, or through the sense of smell, or taste, or touch, and this must be inferior to what is grasped by the intelligence alone.

Now, since God can be known by deserving souls only through the intelligence, although He is far superior to the mind as its Creator and Author, there was reason to fear that the human mind, inasmuch as it, too, is counted among invisible and immaterial beings, might consider itself to be of the same nature as its Creator, thus cutting itself off by pride from Him to whom it ought to be united by love. The mind becomes like God, to the extent this is given to it, when it humbly submits itself to Him for enlightenment. And while it achieves the greatest closeness by the submission which produces likeness, of necessity it is driven far from Him by the presumptuous desire for an ever greater likeness. It is this presumption that turns the mind from obedience to the laws of God, by making it desire to be its own master, as He is.

(21) Thus, the farther the mind departs from God, not in space but in fondness and greed for things inferior to Him, the more it is filled with foolishness and misery. And it returns to God by the love in which it does not regard itself as His equal, but rather subordinates itself to Him. The more fervently and earnestly the mind does this, the happier and more exalted it will be, and when ruled by God alone, will enjoy perfect liberty. That is why the mind must recognize that it is a creature. It must also believe the truth about its Creator—that He possesses eternally the inviolable and unchangeable nature of truth and wisdom —and must confess, in view of the errors from which it seeks to deliver itself, that it can fall victim to foolishness and deceit. Moreover, it must take care that through love of that other creature, that is, the world of sensible things, it is not separated from the love of God Himself by which it is sanctified so that it may abide in perfect happiness. No

other creature, therefore, since we also are creatures, can separate us from the love of God which is in Christ Jesus our Lord.

CHAPTER 13

(22) Let Paul tell us also who Christ Jesus our Lord is. 'To those that are called,' he says, 'we preach Christ, the virtue of God and the wisdom of God.' And does not Christ Himself say: 'I am the truth'? If, then, we ask what it means to live rightly, that is, to strive for happiness by an upright life, it will most certainly mean to love virtue and wisdom and truth—to love with our whole heart and with our whole soul and with our whole mind the virtue which is inviolate and invincible, the wisdom which never gives way to folly, and the truth which is not altered but remains ever the same. It is by this that we come to see the Father Himself, for it has been said: 'No one comes to the Father but through me.' It is to this we adhere by sanctification for, when sanctified, we are inflamed with that full and perfect love which prevents us from turning away from Him and causes us to be conformed to Him rather than to the world. 'He has predestined us,' as the Apostle says, 'to become conformed to the image of His son.'

(23) It is through love, then, that we are conformed to God, and being so conformed and made like to Him and set apart from the world, we are no longer confounded with those things which should be subject to us. But this is the work of the Holy Spirit. 'Hope,' he says, 'does not confound us, because the Charity of God is poured forth in our hearts by the Holy Spirit who has been given to us.' We could not possibly be restored to perfection by the Holy Spirit, however, unless He Himself remained forever perfect and immutable, and this, of course, could not be unless He were of the very nature and substance of God, who alone is eternally immutable and, so to speak, irreversible. It is not I, but St. Paul who exclaims: 'For creation was made subject to vanity.' Now, what is subject to vanity cannot separate us from vanity and unite us to truth. But this the Holy Spirit does. He is, therefore, not a creature, for everything that exists be either God or creature.

CHAPTER 14

(24) We ought, then, to love God the Trinity in unity, Father, Son, and Holy Spirit, and this cannot be called anything other than Being Itself. For it is truly and above all else God, 'from whom and through whom and unto whom are all things.' These are the words of St. Paul. And what does he add? 'To Him be glory.' What perfect exactitude! He does not say, 'to Them be glory,' for God is one. And what does

he mean by 'to Him be glory,' if not the greatest and highest and most widespread renown. For the better and more widely God is proclaimed, the more fervently He is loved and esteemed. And when this comes about, the human race cannot but advance surely and steadfastly toward the life of perfect happiness.

In treating of human life and morality, I do not think it necessary to inquire further than this concerning the supreme good to which all else must be referred. We have shown both by reason, to the extent this is possible, and by divine authority which goes beyond reason, that the supreme good is nothing other than God Himself. For what can be a greater good for man than the possession of that in which he finds perfect happiness? And this good is God alone to whom he can adhere only by affection, love, and esteem.

CHAPTER 15

(25) If virtue leads us to the happy life, then I would not define virtue in any other way than as the perfect love of God. For in speaking of virtue as fourfold, one refers, as I understand it, to the various dispositions of love itself. Therefore, these four virtues—would that their efficacy were present in all souls as their names are on all lips—I would not hesitate to define as follows: temperance is love giving itself wholeheartedly to that which is loved, fortitude is love enduring all things willingly for the sake of that which is loved, justice is love serving alone that which is loved and thus ruling rightly, and prudence is love choosing wisely between that which helps it and that which hinders it. Now since this love, as I have said, is not love of things in general, but rather love of God, that is, of the supreme good, the supreme wisdom, and the supreme harmony, we can define the virtues thus: temperance is love preserving itself whole and unblemished for God, fortitude is love enduring all things willingly for the sake of God, justice is love serving God alone and, therefore, ruling well those things subject to man, and prudence is love discriminating rightly between those things which aid it in reaching God and those things which might hinder it.

From Augustine, **City of God**

BOOK ELEVEN

CHAPTER 1

The expression, 'City of God,' which I have been using is justified by that Scripture whose divine authority puts it above the literature of all other people and brings under its sway every type of human genius—and that, not by some casual intellectual reaction, but by a disposition of Divine Providence. For, in this Scripture, we read: 'Glorious things are said of thee, O city of God'; and, in another psalm: 'Great is the Lord, and exceedingly to be praised in the city of our God, in His holy mountain, increasing the joy of the whole earth'; and, a little later in the same psalm: 'As we have heard, so have we seen, in the city of the Lord of hosts, in the city of our God: God hath founded it for ever'; and in another text: 'The stream of the river maketh the city of God joyful: the most High hath sanctified his own tabernacle. God is in the midst thereof, it shall not be moved.'

Through these and similar passages too numerous to quote, we learn of the existence of a City of God whose Founder has inspired us with a love and longing to become its citizens. The inhabitants of the earthly city who prefer their own gods to the Founder of the holy City do not realize that He is the God of gods—though not, of course, of those false, wicked and proud gods who, because they have been deprived of that unchangeable light which was meant for all, are reduced to a pitiful power and, therefore, are eager for some sort of influence and demand divine honors from their deluded subjects. He is the God of those reverent and holy gods who prefer to obey and worship one God rather than to have many others obeying and worshiping them.

In the ten preceding Books, I have done my best, with the help of our Lord the King, to refute the enemies of this City. Now, however, realizing what is expected of me and recalling what I promised, I shall begin to discuss, as well as I can, the origin, history, and destiny of the respective cities, earthly and heavenly, which, as I have said, are at present inextricably intermingled, one with the other. First, I shall explain how these two cities originated when the angels took opposing sides.

BOOK FOURTEEN
CHAPTER 1

I have already said, in previous Books, that God had two purposes in deriving all men from one man. His first purpose was to give unity to the human race by the likeness of nature. His second purpose was to bind mankind by the bond of peace, through blood relationship, into one harmonious whole. I have said further that no member of this race would ever have died had not the first two—one created from nothing and the second from the first—merited this death by disobedience. The sin which they committed was so great that it impaired all human nature—in this sense, that the nature has been transmitted to posterity with a propensity to sin and a necessity to die. Moreover, the kingdom of death so dominated man that all would have been hurled, by a just punishment, into a second and endless death had not some been saved from this by the gratuitous grace of God. This is the reason why, for all the difference of the many and very great nations throughout the world in religion and morals, language, weapons, and dress, there exist no more than the two kinds of society, which, according to our Scriptures, we have rightly called the two cities. One city is that of men who live according to the flesh. The other is of men who live according to the spirit. Each of them chooses its own kind of peace and, when they attain what they desire, each lives in the peace of its own choosing.

CHAPTER 28

What we see, then, is that two societies have issued from two kinds of love. Worldly society has flowered from a selfish love which dared to despise even God, whereas the communion of saints is rooted in a love of God that is ready to trample on self. In a word, this latter relies on the Lord, whereas the other boasts that it can get along by itself. The city of man seeks the praise of men, whereas the height of glory for the other is to hear God in the witness of conscience. The one lifts up its head in its own boasting; the other says to God: 'Thou art my glory, thou liftest up my head.'

In the city of the world both the rulers themselves and the people they dominate are dominated by the lust for domination; whereas in the City of God all citizens serve one another in charity, whether they serve by the responsibilities of office or by the duties of obedience. The one city loves its leaders as symbols of its own strength; the other says to its God: 'I love thee, O Lord, my strength.' Hence, even the wise men in the city of man live according to man, and their only goal has been the goods of their bodies or of the mind or of both; though some of them have reached a knowledge of God, 'they did not glorify him as God or give thanks but became vain in their reasonings, and their senseless minds have been darkened. For while professing to be wise' (that is to say, while glorifying in their own wisdom, under the domination of pride), 'they have become fools, and they have changed the glory of the incorruptible God for an image made like to corruptible man and to birds and four-footed beasts and creeping things' (meaning that they either led their people, or imitated them, in adoring idols shaped like these things), 'and they worshipped and served the creature rather than the Creator who is blessed forever.' In the City of God, on the contrary, there is no merely human wisdom, but there is a piety which worships the true God as He should be worshiped and has as its goal that reward of all holiness whether in the society of saints on earth or in that of angels of heaven, which is 'that God may be all in all.'

BOOK FIFTEEN

CHAPTER 1

Regarding the Garden of Eden, the happiness that was possible there, the life of our first parents, their sin and their punishment, a great deal has been thought, said, and written. . . .

Actually, I think I have said enough on the really great and difficult problems concerning the origin of the world, the soul, and the human race. In regard to mankind I have made a division. On the one side are those who live according to man; on the other, those who live according to God. And I have said that, in a deeper sense, we may speak of two cities or two human societies, the destiny of the one being an eternal kingdom under God while the doom of the other is eternal punishment along with the Devil.

Of the final consummation of the two cities I shall have to speak later. Of their original cause among the angels whose number no one knows and then in the first two human beings, I have already spoken. For the moment, therefore, I must deal with the course of the history of the two cities from the time when children were born to the first couple until the day when men shall beget no more. By the course of their history, as distinguished from their original cause and final consummation, I mean the whole time of world history in which men are born and take the place of those who die and depart.

Now, the first man born of the two parents of the human race was Cain. He belonged to the city of man. The next born was Abel, and he was of the City of God. Notice here a parallel between the individual man and the whole race. We all experience as individuals what the Apostle says: 'It is not the spiritual that comes first, but the physical, and then the spiritual.' The fact is that every individual springs from a condemned stock and, because of Adam, must be first cankered and carnal, only later to become sound and spiritual by the process of rebirth in Christ. So, too, with the human race as a whole, as soon as human birth and death began the historical course of the two cities, the first to be born was a citizen of this world and only later came the one who was an alien in the city of men but at home in the City of God, a man predestined by grace and elected by grace. By grace an alien on earth, by grace he was a citizen of heaven. In and of himself, he springs from the common clay, all of which was under condemnation from the beginning, but which God held in His hands like a potter, to borrow the metaphor which the Apostle so wisely and deliberately uses. For, God could make 'from the same mass one vessel for honorable, another for ignoble use.' Only later was there made a vessel for honorable use. And as with the race, so, as I have said, with the individual. First comes the clay that is only fit to be thrown away, with which we must begin, but in which we need not remain. Afterwards comes what is fit for use, that into which we can be gradually molded and in which, when molded, we may remain. This does not mean that every one who is wicked is to become good, but that no one becomes good who was not once wicked. What is true is that the sooner a man makes a change in himself for the better the sooner he has a right to be called what he has become. The second name hides the first.

Now, it is recorded of Cain that he built a city, while Abel, as though he were merely a pilgrim on earth, built none. For, the true City of the saints is in heaven, though here on earth it produces citizens in whom it wanders as on a pilgrimage through time looking for the Kingdom of eternity. When that day comes it will gather together all those who, rising in their bodies, shall have that Kingdom given to them in which, along with their Prince, the King of Eternity, they shall reign for ever and ever.

CHAPTER 2

A shadow, as it were, of this eternal City has been cast on earth, a prophetic representation of something to come rather than a real presentation in time. Yet this shadow, merely symbolic as it is and not the reality that is to be, is properly called the holy City. It was of these two cities, the one, as it were, in bondage to symbolic purpose and the other free, that the Apostle writes in the Epistle to the Galatians: 'Tell me, you who desire to be under the Law, have you not read the Law? For it is written that Abraham had two sons, the one by a slave-girl and the other by a free woman. And the son of the slave-girl was born according to the flesh, but the son of the free woman in virtue of the promise. This is said by way of allegory. For these are the two covenants: one indeed from Mount Sinai, bringing forth children unto bondage, which is Agar. For Sinai is a mountain in Arabia, which corresponds to the present Jerusalem, and is in slavery with her children. But that Jerusalem which is above is free, which is our mother. For it is written, "Rejoice thou barren, that dost not bear; break forth and cry, thou that dost not travail; For many are the children of the desolate, more than of her that has a husband." Now we, brethren, are the children of promise, as Isaac was. But as then he who was born according to the flesh persecuted him who was born according to the spirit, so also it is now. But what does the Scripture say? "Cast out the slave-girl and her son, for the son of the slave-girl shall not be heir with the son of the freewoman." Therefore, Brethren, we are not children of a slave-girl, but of the free woman—in virtue of the freedom wherewith Christ has made us free.'

This exegesis, which comes to us with apostolic authority, opens up for us a way to understand much that is written in both Testaments, the Old and the New. We see that one portion of the world community became a symbol of the heavenly City and was 'in bondage' in the sense that its significance was not in itself but in serving to signify the other city. It was, in fact, founded, not for its own sake, but as the shadow of another substance, a shadow that was itself foreshadowed by a previous symbol. For, the symbol of this shadow was Sara's handmaid, Agar, with her son. It was because shadows were to cease when the light came that the free woman, Sara, symbol of the free City (to which, in turn, the shadow served as another kind of prelude), uttered the words: 'Cast out this slave-girl with her son; for the son of this slave-girl shall not be heir with my son Isaac,' or, to use the Apostle's expression, 'with the son of the free woman.'

In the world community, then, we find two forms, one being the visible appearance of the earthly city and another whose presence serves as a shadow of the heavenly city.

Notice that it is nature, flawed by sin, that begets all the citizens in the world community, whereas nothing but grace, which frees nature from sinfulness, can bring forth citizens of the heavenly City. The former are called 'vessels of wrath'; the latter, 'vessels of mercy.' This distinction was symbolized in the two sons of Abraham. One, Ishmael, was born of the slave-girl whose name was Agar and he was born according to the flesh. The other, Isaac, was born of the free woman, Sara, according to the promise. Of course, both were sons of Abraham, but he begot the one by a law suggesting the order of nature, while the other was born in virtue of a promise which pointed to the order of grace. What is clear in the one case is human action; in the other, divine favor.

CHAPTER 4

As for the city of this world, it is neither to last forever nor even to be a city, once the final doom of pain is upon it. Nevertheless, while history lasts, it has a finality of its own; it reaches such happiness by sharing a common good as is possible when there are no goods but the things of time to afford it happiness. This is not the kind of good that can give those who are content with it any freedom from fear. In fact, the city of man, for the most part, is a city of contention with opinions divided by foreign wars and domestic quarrels and by the demands for victories which either end in death or are merely momentary respites from further war. The reason is that whatever part of the city of the world raises the standard of war, it seeks to be lord of the world, when, in fact, it is enthralled in its own wickedness. Even when it conquers, its victory can be mortally poisoned by pride, and if, instead of taking pride in the success already achieved, it takes account of the nature and normal vicissitudes of life and is afraid of future failure, then the victory is merely momentary. The fact is that the power to reach domination by war is not the same as the power to remain in perpetual control.

Nevertheless, it is wrong to deny that the aims of human civilization are good, for this is the highest end that mankind of itself can achieve. For, however lowly the goods of earth, the aim, such as it is, is peace. The purpose even of war is peace. For, where victory is not followed by resistance there is a peace that was impossible so long as rivals were competing, hungrily and unhappily, for something material too little to suffice for both. This kind of peace is a product of the work of war, and its price is a so-called glorious victory; when victory goes to the side that had a juster cause it is surely a matter for human rejoicing, and the peace is one to be welcomed.

The things of earth are not merely good; they are undoubtedly gifts from God. But, of course, if those who get such goods in the city of men are reckless about the better goods of the City of God, in which there is to be the ultimate victory of an eternal, supreme, and untroubled peace, if men so love the goods of earth as to believe that these are the only goods or if they love them more than the goods they know to be better, then the consequence is inevitable; misery and more misery.

CHAPTER 10

Not even the holy faithful followers of the one true and supreme God are beyond the reach of demonic trickery and temptation in its many forms. Yet our anxiety in this matter is good for us, so long as we inhabit this frail body in this evil world, for it sends us seeking more ardently after that heavenly peace which is to be unshakeable and unending. There, all of our natural endowments—all that the Creator of all natures has given to our nature—will be both good and everlasting, where every wound in the soul is to be healed by wisdom and every weakness of body to be removed by resurrection; where our virtues will be no longer at war with passion or opposition of any kind, but are to have, as the prize of victory, an eternally imperturbable peace. This is what is meant by the consummate beatitude, the limitless perfection, that end that never ends.

On earth we are happy, after a fashion, when we enjoy the peace, little as it is, which a good life brings; but such happiness compared with the beatitude which is our end in eternity is, in point of fact, misery. When we mortal men, living amid the realities of earth, enjoy the utmost peace which life can give us, then it is the part of virtue, if we are living rightly, to make a right use of the goods we are enjoying. When, on the other hand, we do not enjoy this temporal peace, then it is the function of virtue to make a right use of the misfortunes which we are suffering. By genuine Christian virtue we mean here that we refer not only all good things which are being rightly used, and all the right use we are making of blessings and misfortunes, but our very virtue itself to that End in which there will be a peace so good that no peace could be better, a peace so great that a greater would be impossible.

CHAPTER 11

Thus, we may say of peace what we have said of eternal life—that it is our highest good; more particularly because the holy Psalmist was addressing the City of God (the nature of which I am trying, with so much difficulty, to make clear) when he said: 'Praise the Lord, O Jerusalem; praise thy God, O Sion. Because he hath strengthened the bolts of thy gates, he hath blessed thy children within thee. He hath placed peace in thy borders.' For, when the bolts of that city's gates will have been strengthened, none will enter in and none will issue forth. Hence, its borders *(fines)* must be taken to mean that peace which I am trying to show is our final good. Note, too, that Jerusalem, the mystical name which symbolizes this City, means, as I have already mentioned, 'the vision of peace.'

However, the word 'peace' is so often applied to conditions here on earth, where life is not eternal, that it is better, I think, to speak of 'eternal life' rather than of 'peace' as the end or supreme good of the City of God. It is in this sense that St. Paul says: 'But now being made free from sin, and become servants of God, you have your fruit unto sanctification, and the end life everlasting.'

It would be simplest for all concerned if we spoke of 'peace in eternal life,' or of 'eternal' or of 'eternal life in peace,' as the end or supreme good of this City. The trouble with the expression 'eternal life' is that those unfamiliar with the Scriptures might take this phrase to apply also to the eternal loss of the wicked, either because, as philosophers, they accept the immortality of the soul, or even because, as Christians, they know by faith that the punishment of the wicked has no end and, therefore, that they could not be punished forever unless their life were eternal.

The trouble with 'peace' is that, even on the level of earthly and temporal values, nothing that we can talk about, long for, or finally get, is so desirable, so welcome, so good as peace. At any rate, I feel sure that if I linger a little longer on this topic of peace I shall tire very few of my readers. After all, peace is the end of this City which is the theme of this work; besides, peace is so universally loved that its very name falls sweetly on the ear.

CHAPTER 12

Any man who has examined history and human nature will agree with me that there is no such thing as a human heart that does not crave for joy and peace. One has only to think of men who are bent on war. What they want is to win, that is to say, their battles are but bridges to glory and to peace. The whole point of victory is to bring opponents to their knees—this done, peace ensues. Peace, then, is the purpose of waging war; and this is true even of men who have a passion for the exercise of military prowess as rulers and commanders.

What, then, men want in war is that it should end in peace. Even while waging a war every man wants peace, whereas no one wants war while he is making peace. And even when men are plotting to disturb the peace, it is merely to fashion a new peace nearer to the heart's desire; it is not because they dislike peace as such. . . .

CHAPTER 13

The peace, then, of the body lies in the ordered equilibrium of all its parts; the peace of the irrational soul, in the balanced adjustment of its appetites; the peace of the reasoning soul, in the harmonious correspondence of conduct and conviction; the peace of body and soul taken together, in the well-ordered life and health of the living whole. Peace between a mortal man and his Maker consists in ordered obedience, guided by faith, under God's eternal law; peace between man and man consists in regulated fellowship. The peace of a home lies in the ordered harmony of authority and obedience between the members of a family living together. The peace of the political community is an ordered harmony of authority and obedience between citizens. The peace of the heavenly City lies in a perfectly ordered and harmonious communion of those who find their joy in God and in one another in God. Peace, in its final sense, is the calm that comes of order. Order is an arrangement of like and unlike things whereby each of them is disposed in its proper place.

This being so, those who are unhappy, in so far as they are unhappy, are not in peace, since they lack the calm of that Order which is beyond every storm; nevertheless, even in their misery they cannot escape from order, since their very misery is related to responsibility and to justice. They do not share with the blessed in their tranquility, but this very separation is the result of the law of order. Moreover, even the miserable can be momentarily free from anxiety and can reach some measure of adjustment to their surroundings and, hence, some tranquility of order and, therefore, some slender peace. However, the reason why they remain unhappy is that, although they *may* be momentarily free from worry and from pain, they are not in a condition where they *must* be free both from worry and pain. Their condition of misery is worse when such peace as they have is not in harmony with that law which governs the order of nature. Their peace can also be disturbed by pain and in proportion to their pain; yet, some peace will remain, so long as the pain is not too acute and their organism as a whole does not disintegrate.

Notice that there can be life without pain, but no pain without some kind of life. In the same way, there can be peace without any kind of war, but no war that does not suppose some kind of peace. This does not mean that war as war involves peace; but war, in so far as those who wage it or have it waged upon them are beings with organic natures, involves peace—for the simple reason that to be organic means to be ordered and, therefore, to be, in some sense, at peace.

Similarly, there can be a nature without any defect and, even, a nature in which there can be no kind of evil whatever, but there can be no nature completely devoid of good. Even the nature of the Devil, in so far as it is a nature, is not evil; it was perversity—not being true to itself—that made it bad. The Devil did not 'stand in the truth' and, therefore, did not escape the judgment of truth. He did not stand fast in the tranquility of order—nor did he, for all that, elude the power of the Ordainer. The goodness which God gave to his nature does not withdraw him from the justice of God by which that nature is subject to punishment. Yet, even in that punishment, God does not hound the good which He created, but only the evil which the Devil committed. So it is that God does not take back the whole of His original gift. He takes a part and leaves a part; He leaves a nature that can regret what God has taken back. Indeed, the very pain inflicted is evidence of both the good that is lost and the good that is left. For, if there were no good left, there would be no one to lament the good that has been lost.

A man who sins is just that much worse if he rejoices in the loss of holiness; but one who suffers pain, and does not benefit by it, laments, at least, the loss of his health. Holiness and health are both good things and, because the loss of any good is more a cause for grief than for gladness (unless there be some higher compensation— the soul's holiness, to be sure, is preferable to the body's health), it is more in accordance with nature that a sinner grieve over his punishment than that he rejoice over his offense. Consequently, just as a man's happiness in abandoning the good of wrong-doing betrays his bad will, so his sorrowing for the good he has lost when in pain bears witness to the good of his nature. For, anyone who grieves over the loss of peace to his nature does so out of some remnant of that peace wherewith his nature loves itself. This is what happens—deservedly, too—in eternal punishment. In the midst of their agonies the evil and the godless weep for the loss of their nature's goods, knowing, meanwhile, that God whose great generosity they condemned was perfectly just when He took these goods away.

God, the wise Creator and just Ordainer of all natures, has made the mortal race of man the loveliest of all lovely things on earth. He has given to men good gifts suited to their existence here below. Among these is temporal peace, according to the poor limits of mortal life, in health, security, and human fellowship; and other gifts, too, needed to preserve this peace or regain it, once lost—for instance, the blessings that lie all around us, so perfectly adapted to our senses: daylight, speech, air to breathe, water to drink, everything that goes to feed, clothe, cure, and beautify the body. These good gifts are granted, however, with the perfectly just understanding that whoever uses the goods which are meant for the mortal peace of mortal men, as these goods should be used, will receive more abundant and better goods—nothing less than immortal peace and all that goes with it, namely, the glory and honor of enjoying God and one's neighbor in God everlastingly; but that whoever misuses his gifts on earth will both lose what he has and never receive the better gifts of heaven.

CHAPTER 14

In the earthly city, then, temporal goods are to be used with a view to the enjoyment of earthly peace, whereas, in the heavenly city, they are used with a view to the enjoyment of eternal peace. Hence, if we were merely unthinking brutes, we would pursue nothing beyond the orderly interrelationship of our bodily part and the appeasing of our appetites, nothing, that is, beyond the comfort of the flesh and plenty of pleasures, so that the peace of body might contribute to peace of the soul. For, if order in the body be lacking, the peace of an irrational soul is checked, since it cannot attain the satisfaction of its appetites. Both of these forms of peace meanwhile subserve that other form of peace which the body and soul enjoy between them, the peace of life and health in good order.

For, just as brutes show that they love the peace or comfort of their bodies by shunning pain, and the peace of their souls by pursuing pleasure to satisfy their appetites, so, too, by running from death, they make clear enough how much they love the peace which keeps body and soul together.

Because, however, man has a rational soul, he makes everything he shares with brutes subserve the peace of his rational soul, so that he first measures things with his mind before he acts, in order to achieve that harmonious correspondence of conduct and conviction which I called the peace of the rational soul. His purpose in desiring not to be vexed with sin, not disturbed with desire, not disintegrated by death is that he may learn something profitable and so order his habits and way of life. However, if the infirmity of his human mind is not to bring him in his pursuit of knowledge to some deadly error, he needs divine authority to give secure guidance, and divine help so that he may be unhampered in following the guidance given.

And because, so long as man lives in his mortal body and is a pilgrim far from the Lord, he walks, not by vision, but by faith. Consequently, he refers all peace of body or soul, or their combination, to that higher peace which unites a mortal man with the immortal God and which I defined as 'ordered obedience guided by faith, under God's eternal law.'

Meanwhile, God teaches him two chief commandments, the love of God and the love of neighbor. In these precepts man finds three beings to love, namely, God, himself, and his fellow man, and knows that he is not wrong in loving himself as long as he loves God. As a result, he must help his neighbor (whom he is obliged to love as himself) to love God. Thus, he must help his wife, children, servants, and all others whom he can influence. He must wish, moreover, to be similarly helped by his fellow man, in case he himself needs such assistance. Out of all this love he will arrive at peace, as much as in him lies, with every man—at that human peace which is regulated fellowship. Right order here means, first, that he harm no one, and, second, that he help whomever he can. His fundamental duty is to look out for his own home, for both by natural and human law he has easier and readier access to their requirements.

St. Paul says: 'But if any does not take care of his own, and especially of his household, he has denied the faith and is worse than an unbeliever.' From this care arises that peace of the home which lies in the harmonious interplay of authority and obedience among those who live there. For, those who have the care of the others give the orders —a man to his wife, parents to their children, masters to their servants. And those who are cared for must obey—wives their husband, children their parents, servants their masters. In the home of a religious man, however, of a man living by faith and as yet a wayfarer from the heavenly City, those who command serve those whom they appear to rule—because, of course, they do not command out of lust to domineer, but out of a sense of duty, not out of pride like princes but out of solicitude like parents.

CHAPTER 17

While the homes of unbelieving men are intent upon acquiring temporal peace out of the possessions and comforts of this temporal life, the families which live according to faith look ahead to the good things of heaven promised as imperishable, and use material and temporal goods in the spirit of pilgrims, not as snares or obstructions to block their way to God, but simply as helps to ease and never to increase the burdens of this corruptible body which weighs down the soul. Both types of homes and their masters have this in common, that they must use things essential to this mortal life. But the respective purposes to which they put them are characteristic and very different.

So, too, the earthly city which does not live by faith seeks only an earthly peace, and limits the goal of its peace, of its harmony of authority and obedience among its citizens, to the voluntary and collective attainment of objectives necessary to mortal existence. The heavenly City, meanwhile—or, rather, that part that is on pilgrimage in mortal life and lives by faith—must use this earthly peace until such time as our mortality which needs such peace has passed away. As a consequence, so long as her life in the earthly city is that of a captive and an alien (although she has the promise of ultimate delivery and the gift of the Spirit as a pledge), she has no hesitation about keeping in step with the civil law which governs matters pertaining to our existence here below. For, as mortal life is the same for all, there ought to be common cause between the two cities in what concerns our purely human living.

Now comes the difficulty. The city of this world, to begin with, has had certain 'wise men' of its own mold, whom true religion must reject, because either out of their own daydreaming or out of demonic deception these wise men came to believe that a multiplicity of divinities was allied with human life, with different duties, in some strange arrangement, and different assignments: this one over the body, that one over the mind; in the body itself, one over the head, another over the neck, still others, one for each bodily part; in the mind, one over the intelligence, another over learning, another over temper, another over desire; in the realities, related to life, that lie about us, one over flocks and one over wheat, one over wine, one over oil, and another over forests, one over currency, another over navigation, and still another over warfare and victory, one over marriage, a different one over fecundity and childbirth, so on and so on.

The heavenly City, on the contrary, knows and, by religious faith, believes that it must adore one God alone and serve Him with that complete dedication which the Greeks call *latreia* and which belongs to Him alone. As a result, she has been unable to share with the earthly city a common religious legislation, and has had no choice but to dissent on this score and so become a nuisance to those who think otherwise. Hence, she has had to feel the weight of their anger, hatred, and violence, save in those instances when, by sheer numbers and God's help, which never fails, she has been able to scare off her opponents.

So long, then, as the heavenly City is wayfaring on earth, she invites citizens from all nations and all tongues, and unites them into a single pilgrim band. She takes no issue with that diversity of customs, laws, and traditions whereby human peace is sought and maintained. Instead of nullifying or tearing down, she preserves and appropriates whatever in the diversities of divers races is aimed at one and the same objective of human peace, provided only that they do not stand in the way of the faith and worship of the one supreme and true God.

Thus, the heavenly City, so long as it is wayfaring on earth, not only makes use of earthly peace but fosters and actively pursues along with other human beings a common platform in regard to all that concerns our purely human life and does not interfere with faith and worship. Of course, though, the City of God subordinates this earthly peace to that of heaven. For this is not merely true peace, but, strictly speaking, for any rational creature, the only real peace, since it is, as I said, 'the perfectly ordered and harmonious communion of those who find their joy in God and in one another in God.'

When this peace is reached, man will be no longer haunted by death, but plainly and perpetually endowed with life, nor will his body, which now wastes away and weighs down the soul, be any longer animal, but spiritual, in need of nothing, and completely under the control of our will.

This peace the pilgrim City already possesses by faith and it lives holily and according to this faith so long as, to attain its heavenly completion, it refers every good act done for God or for his fellow man. I say 'fellow man' because, of course, any community life must emphasize social relationships.

CHAPTER 27

The City of God, however, has a peace of its own, namely, peace with God in this world by faith and in the world to come by vision. Still, any peace we have on earth, whether the peace we share with Babylon or our own peace through faith, is more like a solace for unhappiness than the joy of beatitude. Even our virtue in this life, genuine as it is because it is referred to the true goal of every good, lies more in the pardoning of sins than in any perfection of virtues. Witness the prayer of God's whole City, wandering on earth and calling out to Him through all her members: 'Forgive us our debts as we also forgive our debtors.'

This prayer is effective, not on the lips of those whose faith without works is dead, but only on the lips of men whose faith works through charity. This prayer is necessary for the just because their reason, though submissive to God, has only imperfect mastery over their evil inclinations so long as they live in this world and in a corruptible body that 'is a load upon the soul.' Reason may give commands, but can exercise no control without a struggle. And, in this time of weakness, something will inevitably creep in to make the best of soldiers—whether in victory or still in battle with such foes—offend by some small slip of the tongue, some passing thought, if not by habitual actions. This explains why we can know no perfect peace so long as there are evil inclinations to master. Those which put up a fight are put down only in perilous conflict; those that are already overcome cannot be kept so if one relaxes, but only at the cost of vigilant control. These are the battles which Scripture sums up in the single phrase: 'The life of man upon earth is a warfare.'

Who, then, save a proud man, will presume that he can live without needing to ask God: 'Forgive us our debts'? Not a great man, you may be sure, but one blown up with the wind of self-reliance—one whom God in His justice resists while He grants His grace to the humble. For 'God resists the proud, but gives grace to the humble.'

This, then, in this world, is the life of virtue. When God commands, man obeys; when the soul commands, the body obeys; when reason rules, our passions, even when they fight back, must be conquered or resisted; man must beg God's grace to win merit and the remission of his sins and must thank God for the blessings he receives.

But, in that final peace which is the end and purpose of all virtue here on earth, our nature, made whole by immortality and incorruption, will have no vices and experience no rebellion from within or without. There will be no need for reason to govern non-existent evil inclinations. God will hold sway over man, the soul over the body; and the happiness in eternal life and law will make obedience sweet and easy. And in each and all of us this condition will be everlasting, and we shall know it to be so. That is why the peace of such blessedness or the blessedness of such peace is to be our supreme good.

CHAPTER 28

On the other hand, the doom in store for those who are not of the City of God is an unending wretchedness that is called 'the second death,' because neither the soul, cut off from the life of God, nor the body, pounded by perpetual pain, can there be said to live at all. And what will make that second death so hard to bear is that there will be no death to end it.

Now, since unhappiness is the reverse of happiness, death of life, and war of peace, one may reasonably ask: If peace is praised and proclaimed as the highest good, what kind of warfare are we to think of as the highest evil? If this inquirer will reflect, he will realize that what is hurtful and destructive in warfare is mutual clash and conflict, and, hence, that no one can imagine a war more unbearably bitter than one in which the will and passions are at such odds that neither can ever win the victory, and in which violent pain and the body's very nature will so clash that neither will ever yield. When this conflict occurs on earth, either pain wins and death puts an end to all feeling, or nature wins and health removes the pain. But, in hell, pain permanently afflicts and nature continues to feel it, for neither ever comes to term, since the punishment must never end.

However, it is through the last judgment that good men achieve that highest good (which all should seek) and evil men that highest evil (which all should shun), and so, as God helps me, I shall discuss that judgment in the Book that comes next.

BOOK TWENTY-TWO

CHAPTER 1

As I mentioned in the preceding Book, the present one is to be the last of the whole work, and is to deal with the eternal blessedness of the City of God. The word 'eternal' as here used means more than

any period, however long, of centuries upon centuries which, ultimately, must have an end. It means 'everlasting' in the sense of the
text which runs: 'Of his kingdom there shall be no end.' It does not
mean the kind of apparent perpetuity produced by successive generations which come and go by births and deaths. Such a perpetuity is
merely perennial like the color of the evergreen that seems to continue
forever because the new leaves, sprouting while the old ones wither
and fall, maintain an unchanging density of foliage. On the contrary,
in the eternal City of God, each and all of the citizens are personally
immortal with an immortality which the holy angels never lost and
which even human beings can come to share. This is to be achieved
by the supreme omnipotence of the Creator, the Founder of the City.
It is a realization which God, who cannot but keep His word, has
promised, and He has given abundant pledges of its fulfillment in the
promises which He has already kept and in the uncovenanted blessings
which He has already bestowed.

For it was this same God who, in the beginning, created the universe
and filled it with all those things that the eye can see and all those
realities which the mind can know. Of all such creations the highest
were the spirits to whom He gave the gift of intelligence and the power
to behold God and to be filled with His beatitude. These He has linked
by a common bond of love in a single society which we call the holy
and heavenly City. In this community, God is the life by which the
spirits live. He is the food on which their blessedness is fed. God gave
these spirits the gift of freedom, but it was a power of choice so rooted
in their nature, as intelligence is, that, once they used their power to
fall away from God, the Source of all their joy, misery was bound to
follow. Although God foresaw that some of these free angels would
try to lift themselves up to a level where they might find their happiness in themselves alone and so abandon God, their only good, God
did not take away their freedom. He judged it better and more in
accord with His power to bring some greater good even out of evil
than to permit no evil whatsoever.

Now, what makes such evil possible is the fact that no created
nature can be immutable. Every such nature is made, indeed, by God,
the supreme and immutable Good who made all things good, but, by
choosing to sin, such a nature brings evil upon itself. This very sinning, however, bears witness to the fact that the nature in itself, as it
comes from the hand of God, is good. For, unless the nature in itself
were a really great good—though, of course, not good in the measure
that the Creator is good—then the falling away from God into the
creature's own darkness could not be a misfortune for the nature. Sin
is to a nature what blindness is to an eye. The blindness is an evil or

defect which is a witness to the fact that the eye was created to see the light and, hence, the very lack of sight is the proof that the eye was meant, more than any other member of the body, to be the one particularly capable of seeing the light. Were it not for this capacity, there would be no reason to think of blindness as a misfortune. So is it with that nature that basked in God as an eye does in light. The very sin which deprived this nature of happiness in God and left it miserable is the best proof of how good that nature was, as it came from the hand of God.

In the case of the deliberate falling away of some of the angels, God most justly imposed the punishment of an everlasting unhappiness. The other angels remained in union with God, their supreme Good, and to these God gave, as a kind of reward for their remaining, the certain assurance that this remaining would be without end.

As for human nature, God made it likewise unfallen, but free to fall away. Man was an animal made out of earth, but not unfit for heaven, if only he would remain close to his Creator. But, as with the angels, if human nature should choose to fall away from God, misery proportionate to the offense was bound to follow. Here, too, God foresaw the fall, the disregard of His law, the desertion from Good, yet He left man's free choice unchecked because He also foresaw to what good He would turn man's evil. And, in fact, out of this mortal race of men, justly doomed by their own deserts, God gathers, by His grace, so numerous a people that out of them He fills the places and restores the ranks emptied by the fallen angels. Thus is it that the beloved City, which is above, is not deprived of the full complement of its citizens and, in fact, may even rejoice in a fuller complement than it had before the angels' fall.

CHAPTER 30

Who can measure the happiness of heaven, where no evil at all can touch us, no good will be out of reach; where life is to be one long laud extolling God, who will be all in all; where there will be no weariness to call for rest, no need to call for toil, no place for any energy but praise. Of this I am assured whenever I read or hear the sacred song: 'Blessed are they that dwell in thy house, O Lord: they shall praise thee forever and ever.' Every fiber and organ of our imperishable body will play its part in the praising of God. On earth these varied organs have each a special function, but, in heaven, function will be swallowed up in felicity, in the perfect certainty of an untroubled everlastingness of joy. Even those muted notes in the diapason of the human organ, which I mentioned earlier, will swell into a great hymn of praise to the supreme Artist who has fashioned us, within and without, in every fiber, and who, by this and every other element of a magnificent and marvelous Order, will ravish our minds with spiritual beauty.

These movements of our bodies will be of such unimaginable beauty that I dare not say more than this: There will be such poise, such grace, such beauty as become a place where nothing unbecoming can be found. Wherever the spirit wills, there, in a flash, will the body be. Nor will the spirit ever will anything unbecoming either to itself or to the body.

In heaven, all glory will be true glory, since no one could ever err in praising too little or too much. True honor will never be denied where due, never be given where undeserved, and, since none but the worthy are permitted there, no one will unworthily ambition glory. Perfect peace will reign, since nothing in ourselves or in any others could disturb this peace. The promised reward of virtue will be the best and the greatest of all possible prizes—the very Giver of virtue Himself, for that is what the Prophet meant: 'I will be your God and you shall be my people.' God will be the source of every satisfaction, more than any heart can rightly crave, more than life and health, food and wealth, glory and honor, peace and every good—so that God, as St. Paul said, 'may be all in all.' He will be the consummation of all our desiring—the object of our unending vision, of our unlessening love, or our unwearying praise. And in this gift of vision, this response of love, this paean of praise, all alike will share, as all will share in ever-lasting life.

But, now, who can imagine, let alone describe, the ranks upon ranks of rewarded saints, to be graded, undoubtedly, according to their variously merited honor and glory. Yet, there will be no envy of the lower for the higher, as there is no envy of angel for archangel—for this is one of the great blessednesses of this blessed City. The less rewarded will be linked in perfect peace with the more highly favored, but lower could not more long for higher than a finger, in the ordered integration of a body, could want to be an eye. The less endowed will have the high endowment of longing for nothing loftier than their lower gifts.

The souls in bliss will still possess the freedom of will, though sin will have no power to tempt them. They will be more free than ever—so free, in fact, from all delight in sinning as to find, in not sinning, an unfailing source of joy. By the freedom which was given to the first man, who was constituted in rectitude, he could choose either to sin or not to sin; in eternity, freedom is that more potent freedom which makes all sin impossible. Such freedom, of course, is a gift of God, beyond the power of nature to achieve. For, it is one thing to be God, another to be a sharer in the divine nature. God, by His nature, cannot sin, but a mere sharer in His nature must receive from God such immunity from sin. It was proper that, in the process of divine endowment, the first step should be a freedom not to sin, and the last a freedom even from the power to sin. The first gift made merit possible; the second is a part of man's reward. Our nature, when it was free to sin, did sin. It took a greater grace to lead us to that larger liberty which frees us from the very power to sin. Just as the immortality that Adam lost by his sin was, at first, a mere possibility of avoiding death, but, in heaven, becomes the impossibility of death, so free will was, at first, a mere possibility of avoiding sin, but, in heaven, becomes an utter inability to sin.

Our will will be as ineradicably rooted in rectitude and love as in beatitude. It is true that, with Adam's sin, we lost our right to grace and glory, but, with our right, we did not lose our longing to be happy. And, as for freedom, can we think that God Himself, who certainly cannot sin, is therefore without freedom? The conclusion is that, in the everlasting City, there will remain in each and all of us an inalienable freedom of the will, emancipating us from every evil and filling us with every good, rejoicing in the inexhaustible beatitude of everlasting happiness, unclouded by the memory of any sin or of sanction suffered, yet with no forgetfulness of our redemption nor any loss of gratitude for our Redeemer.

The memory of our previous miseries will be a matter of purely mental contemplation, with no renewal of any feelings connected with these experiences—much as learned doctors know by science many of those bodily maladies which, by suffering, they have no sensible experience. All ills, in fact, can be forgotten in the double way in which we learn them, namely notionally and experientially. It is one thing to be a philosopher, learning by ethical analysis the nature of each and every vice, and another to be a scoundrel, learning his lessons from a dissolute life. So, too, the student who becomes a doctor forgets in a way different from that of a patient who has suffered disease. The one forgets by giving up his practice; the patient, by being freed from pains. Now, it is into this second kind of oblivion that the previous miseries of the saints will fall, for not a trace of any sensible experience of suffering will remain.

However, in virtue of the vigor of their minds, they will have not merely a notional remembrance of their own past but also a knowledge of the unending torments of the damned. For, if they had no kind of memory of past miseries, how could the Psalmist have said: 'The mercies of the Lord they will sing forever'? And, surely, in all that City, nothing will be lovelier than this song in praise of the grace of Christ by whose Blood all there were saved.

Heaven, too, will be the fulfillment of that Sabbath rest foretold in the command: 'Be still and see that I am God.' This, indeed, will be that ultimate Sabbath that has no evening and which the Lord foreshadowed in the account of His creation: 'And God rested on the seventh day from all his work which he had done. And he blessed the seventh day and sanctified it: because in it he had rested from all his work which God created and made.' And we ourselves will be a 'seventh day' when we shall be filled with His blessing and remade by His sanctification. In the stillness of that rest we shall see that He is the God whose divinity we ambitioned for ourselves when we listened to the seducer's words, 'You shall be as Gods,' and so fell away from Him, the true God who would have given us a divinity by participation that could never be gained by desertion. For, where did the doing without God end but in the undoing of man through the anger of God?

Only when we are remade by God and perfected by a greater grace shall we have the eternal stillness of that rest in which we shall see that He is God. Then only shall we be filled with Him when He will be all in all. For, although our good works are, in reality, His, they will be put to our account as payment for this Sabbath peace, so long as we do not claim them as our own; but, if we do, they will be reckoned as servile and out of place on the Sabbath, as the text reminds us: 'The seventh day . . . is the rest of the Lord. . . . Thou shalt not do any work therein.' In this connection, too, God has reminded us, through the Prophet Ezechiel: 'I gave them my Sabbaths, to be a sign between me and them, that they might know that I am the Lord that sanctifies them.' It is this truth that we shall realize perfectly when we shall be perfectly at rest and shall perfectly see that it is He who is God.

There is a clear indication of this final Sabbath if we take the seven ages of world history as being 'days' and calculate in accordance with the data furnished by the Scriptures. The first age or day is that from Adam to the flood; the second, from the flood to Abraham. (These two 'days' were not identical in length of time, but in each there were ten generations.) Then follow the three ages, each consisting of fourteen generations, as recorded in the Gospel of St. Matthew: the first, from Abraham to David; the second, from David to the transmigration to Babylon; the third, from then to Christ's nativity in the flesh. Thus, we have five ages. The sixth is the one in which we now are. It is an age not to be measured by any precise number of generations, since we are told: 'It is not for you to know the times or dates which the Father has fixed by his own authority.' After this 'day,' God will rest on the 'seventh day,' in the sense that God will make us, who are to be this seventh day, rest in Him.

There is no need here to speak in detail of each of these seven 'days.'

Suffice it to say that this 'seventh day' will be our Sabbath and that it will end in no evening, but only in the Lord's day—that eighth and eternal day which dawned when Christ's resurrection heralded an eternal rest both for the spirit and for the body. On that day we shall rest and see, see and love, love and praise—for this is to be the end without the end of all our living, that Kingdom without end, the real goal of our present life.

I am done. With God's help, I have kept my promise. This, I think, is all that I promised to do when I began this huge work. From all who think that I have said either too little or too much, I beg pardon; and those who are satisfied I ask, not to thank me, but to join me in rejoicing and in thanking God. Amen.

Part Three

The Middle Ages

Introduction

The long period, *c.* 400-*c.* 1300, which followed the collapse of the Roman Empire in the West, is usually referred to as the Middle Ages, and in due time it came to have its own very different cultural unity and complexity. It was a long process of rebuilding, but eventually a civilization emerged that in its own way rivaled the cultural greatness of classical antiquity.

Rome and her empire symbolized an important and enduring cultural legacy. In the first centuries of the Christian era it seemed to most inhabitants of the Roman Empire that this great power would last forever. However, it turned out that Rome's days of greatness were numbered. What happened was what Edward Gibbon called in eloquent fashion, the *Decline and Fall of the Roman Empire.* The economic prosperity of the Roman Empire waned; the political unity crumbled and was replaced by political isolation and separatism; the ancient cultural dominance was shattered. Some have seen in these events one of the great tragedies of all time—the passing of the classical world.

What succeeded the Roman Empire was very different in many ways. Western Europe underwent a process of political fragmentation which resulted in the formation of kingdoms dominated by barbarian groups like the Visigoths, Ostrogoths, Franks, Angles, and Saxons. The economic vitality of the empire—based on the city-states with their prosperous middle class, their money economy, and their flourishing exchange of goods and services—declined until many urban units disappeared, trade and commerce slowed to a trickle, and the manor with its all-important peasant class became the focus of an almost exclusively rural economy. The Latin language, which had served as a universal medium of communication all around the Mediterranean Sea, was replaced by a bewildering variety of languages, the linguistic ancestors of the modern European languages.

The Christian tradition and Christian humanism assumed a dominant role in the process of reshaping civilization. Two new cultural forms in turn played significant roles in the development of the Christian outlook: monasticism and scholasticism. Monasticism played its most important shaping

135

role from *c.* 400-*c.* 1100, while scholasticism played the leading part from *c.* 1100-*c.* 1300.

Already in Augustine's time (354-430) the fragmentation of the Roman Empire was underway; his most famous work, *City of God,* was written to rebut the charge that desertion of the Roman gods in favor of Christianity had brought about the sack of Rome in 410. The decay of Roman institutions, particularly in the West, brought about a political and cultural vacuum. Eventually, almost by default, the Christian church became the matrix for preserving the diverse cultural traditions in the West. By the end of the sixth century the papacy replaced the old Roman imperial authority as the most significant unifying cultural institution. Not until the thirteenth century was papal leadership to become preeminent, and its rise to prominence was sometimes slow, often fitful, and not free from setbacks. Meanwhile, as the Roman Empire in the West headed for extinction, monasticism, a Christian institution of unusual strength and tenacity, began to flourish.

Monasticism was a way of life which focused on the monastery, a simple, self-contained community of people devoted to a life of work and worship. It was increasingly attractive in the fifth century and met the needs of that time and many centuries thereafter. In the early sixth century, *The Rule of St. Benedict* laid out a pattern for monastic life that seemed to combine the best of Roman practicality and legality with Christian charity and idealism. The aim of Benedict's *Rule* was simple: to follow the example of Christ as set forth in the Gospels. Reading through the *Rule* even casually, one is struck by some of its features: the importance attached to worship, the necessity of meaningful manual labor, the carefully calculated moderation of this way of life, and the guiding role of the abbot—all part of the community service of Christ. The monasteries performed a holding action for civilization; they kept alive an ideal for the Christian life which aimed at spiritual perfection, but often fell far short of it.

In Charlemagne's time (768-814) Benedictine monasticism became the standard by which religious "rules" came to be judged. From the sixth through the eleventh centuries Benedictine monasticism served to preserve much of what was best from the past. This was a time when Western civilization came through by the skin of its teeth. Preservation of the heritage of the past was a prime necessity and no mean accomplishment.

Considering the number of times monasteries needed to be reformed, it would seem that even Benedict's *Rule* was made to be broken. Through a variety of circumstances careful observance of the provisions of the *Rule* was from time to time neglected. Some monasteries through diligence and hard work became quite prosperous, and growing wealth presented a host of problems; some monasteries came under the supervision of unworthy abbots who failed to provide the kind of guidance called for by the *Rule;* some monasteries came to be so involved in worldly affairs that the affairs of the spirit suffered. Usually a need for reform was eventually perceived and measures were taken to correct at least the most flagrant abuses.

The Emperor Charlemagne and his successors in the ninth century fostered a rather thoroughgoing reform of monasteries associated with Benedict's namesake, Benedict of Aniane. The aim of this reform was simple: strict adherence to Benedict's *Rule*. Careful attention was paid to liturgy, work, and life-style.

Eventually monastic reform became necessary again, and the valiant efforts of the newly founded (910) Monastery of Cluny wrought wonders in the tenth century by making the abbot of Cluny specially responsible for monasteries founded out of Cluny.

In the late eleventh and early twelfth centuries, the Cistercians aimed to secure a permanent process of reform by formulating significant constitutional procedures involving the visitation of monasteries to insure strict adherence to the *Rule*. To a greater or lesser extent the Benedictine *Rule* was the measuring device for all Christians who chose to live some kind of religious community life. Even that religious genius, Francis of Assisi, when drawing up a rule for his followers who would belong to a religious order but would not live in a monastery, saw fit to consult Benedict's *Rule* for guidance in writing his own. Benedict's *Rule* thus remained a timeless and timely source of inspiration for the Christian life for many centuries.

During the early Middle Ages (*c.* 400-*c.* 1100), monastic schools provided almost the only opportunity for education and learning. Those intending to become monks needed to be taught reading and writing, the chant necessary for divine worship, and in some cases the copying and illuminating of manuscripts. Though Benedict himself did not leave specific instructions on how monks were to be educated, one of his contemporaries, Cassiodorus (*c.* 480-*c.* 575), caused a monastery he founded to become a center for theological studies, and this model was later followed by many Benedictine monasteries.

The curriculum studied in the monasteries was generally the liberal arts as prescribed by Augustine and sanctioned by Cassiodorus, divided into the *trivium:* grammar, rhetoric, and dialectic; and the *quadrivium:* arithmetic, geometry, astronomy, and music. These disciplines also emphasized the study of Scripture and patristic commentaries on Scripture, as Augustine had instructed. The education was rudimentary, and there was relatively little independent thought, but some sense and semblance of the past were preserved.

Important monasteries had to have some way of duplicating needed books and a place for writing documents, letters, and other books. This was known as the *scriptorium*—a kind of publishing house. Here again the influence of Cassiodorus was important, for the monastery he founded featured the *scriptorium* prominently. In the *scriptorium* were produced books for ordinary everyday use as well as magnificent volumes fit for use in divine worship. Before the time of Charlemagne, monastic handwriting took a

bewildering variety of forms. Thereafter, encouraged by the patronage of
the imperial court, a kind of standardization took place with Caroline minis-
cule, a most beautiful and legible script. Indeed, it is appropriate to claim
that the most important as well as beautiful survivals from the early Middle
Ages are the splendid illuminated books. Also produced in the monastic
scriptorium were the sumptuous volumes—psalters, Gospel books, Bibles,
sacramentaries—meant for use in divine worship. Illuminating a manuscript
was a rare privilege for a monk, and it required artistic skills of a high order.
The seventh through the tenth centuries witnessed the production of some
of the most magnificent books ever made. One has only to look at the *Book
of Kells* or the *Lorsch Gospels* to grasp the truth of that assertion.

Along with the *scriptorium* for producing books it was necessary to have
some sort of library to conserve them. By comparison with modern libraries,
those of most monasteries contained pitifully few volumes; the best library
in western Europe in the tenth century did not possess a thousand volumes.
Under the Carolingians, the imperial successors of Charlemagne, conscientious efforts to expand monastic library holdings were made. The results of
these Carolingian undertakings were astounding. Most of the literary works
from classical antiquity that have survived to the present day are now available because these enterprising Carolingians and the monasteries they patronized took pains to preserve this priceless legacy from the past—a legacy whose
contents and value they themselves only dimly perceived. Thus the medieval
monasteries, with their precious monastic libraries, rank as the most significant transmitters of the classical past to the present. All the while, the monks
kept striving to relate all the knowledge they encountered to the Bible, as
Augustine instructed, and in so doing they preserved that knowledge.

Benedict's *Rule* placed great emphasis on the importance of worship for
the monastic community. The monks prayed together eight times during the
course of a day, and as time went on, this regimen of prayer developed in
both form and content. Extensive use was made of Scripture in prayers and
readings, while the Psalms provided poetic expression that could be set to
music and sung to add variety to the worship service.

As early as the fourth century, the hymn, one of the most important as
well as one of the earliest forms of Christian Latin poetry, had come into
being. These hymns expressed the faith of the church in poetic form and
were eminently suitable for congregational singing, for which they were
frequently used. Because monastic worship required variety to enhance the
devotional life of the monks, many old hymns became part of the monastic
repertory and new ones were composed to celebrate specific occasions. Times
of day, seasons of the church year, persons of the Trinity, and mysteries of
the faith were commemorated in hymns both spiritually penetrating and
emotionally moving. Many of the best and most famous hymns from the
fourth century on owe their preservation to the fact that they became incor-

porated in the framework of monastic worship. The hymns are a sure guide for the devotional life of the church and the changing emphasis in the Christian outlook. The wonder of the cross, the cult of the Virgin, the gifts of the Spirit, and the terrors of death and damnation are all expressed in hymns of astonishing power and beauty. They constitute an enduring legacy and an incomparable treasury of Christian humanism.

In the early Middle Ages (*c.* 400-*c.* 1100), cathedrals too had schools, maintained by the local bishop for the education of his clergy. Curricula in the cathedral schools were similar to those in the monastic schools. Not until the tenth century did cathedral schools equal the best of the monastic schools. With the growth of towns and trade after the tenth century, cathedral schools began to flourish, and some like Chartres, Reims, Paris, Cologne, and Canterbury attained distinction. Although there were efforts to heed Augustine's advice about the proper place and role of secular knowledge, it proved more and more difficult not to let secular studies have an independent place. To put the matter bluntly, secular studies became separated from biblical studies.

In the late tenth century, Gerbert, a *scholasticus* at the cathedral school of Reims, lectured on the entire corpus of logical works of Boethius, the main source for what was then known in the West about ancient logic. From logic Gerbert's interest gravitated to rhetoric and then to arithmetic, astronomy, and music. Gerbert achieved considerable fame in his time as a teacher and went on to become Pope Sylvester II. Cathedral schools tended to flourish with the presence of an impressive individual like Gerbert. Perhaps the most important example of this was the cathedral school at Paris with its magnetic teacher, Peter Abelard.

After Gerbert's time there was a new and revived interest in the study of logic (dialectic). In a world as chaotic as that of the tenth century, logic exerted a fascinating power: logic could produce intellectual order. Gerbert reawakened interest in the logical corpus of Boethius who had preserved Aristotle's elementary works on logic. Aristotle was able again to inspire wide study and appreciation once his work could be digested. The task took centuries and was revolutionary. Theology was most profoundly affected, for the methodology of theological discussion underwent drastic change. Logical analysis was applied to the study of the sacraments, the persons of the Trinity, and Christ's humanity and divinity. Every branch of thought came to be affected by logic. This phenomenal growth in the study and application of logic is basic to the development of scholasticism, the methodology of the schools, whose fullest development was seen in the universities.

The monasteries of Europe were the great centers of spiritual influence in the early Middle Ages, but in the monasteries too a change in this regard came about. What was the essence of this change? It was a greater concentration on the human being and on human experience as a means of knowing

God. Here was an important element in restoring the idea of the dignity of the human being because it became an integral part of religious life to study what it meant to be human. Great figures of the twelfth century, such as Anselm of Canterbury, Bernard of Clairvaux, and Richard of St. Victor, made popular this method of introspection. In a short time friendship—the sharing of self-knowledge—came to be thought of as essential to religious life, as a treatise of Aelred of Rievaulx demonstrates. His Christian humanism is seen as he describes friendship developing in an illuminating series of steps: nature prompts; reason regulates; experience strengthens; religion perfects. No friendship was more important or eagerly sought than the friendship between God and the human being. The key to this friendship came to be the notion of the humanity of God. This idea was explored in clear, logical fashion, c. 1100, by Anselm of Canterbury (c. 1033-1109), the father of scholasticism, in a treatise entitled *Cur Deus Homo*. In a sense, Anselm, the monk and abbot, can be said to be a bridge from the soon-to-be superseded monastic culture and Christian humanist outlook of the early Middle Ages to the emerging scholastic enterprise which surged forward for two centuries thereafter. It can rightly be claimed that when scholasticism reached its apogee with Thomas Aquinas (1225-1274), medieval humanism scored its greatest triumph: to make God seem human.

The next problem was how to make a universe that for so many centuries had seemed chaotic and mysterious appear friendly, familiar, and intelligible. This task fell to the new schools, the universities, which faced the world, unlike the monasteries which faced away from it. It is also appropriate to emphasize the emancipating role of the medieval universities and scholasticism. This has come to be obscured by the trenchant, sometimes narrow-minded, criticism of later centuries. Beginning c. 1200 the medieval universities brought intellectual order into human life and did so with remarkable swiftness.

A renewal of a sense of the dignity and nobility of the human being followed, and the role of reason came to be exalted. This, of course, is why the relationship of faith and reason became so dominating an issue in medieval intellectual activities. Reason was seen as the tool whereby a human being could collaborate with God in the restoration of creation. In intellectual circles, there was a new optimism and confidence, perhaps overconfidence, in what the human being could do. The prospect for human improvement seemed to stretch forth. Christian intellectual pursuits could follow many and diverse paths. Aristotle became the dominant influence from the Greek past, but Plato was never entirely absent. It was reckoned that Arabic and Jewish learning might have much that was valuable to contribute to Christian understanding of the Bible. In a sense a dialogue between Aristotle and the Bible took place which, because of the attendant problems, challenged scholastic thinkers to the utmost. The more one knew of Aristotle, the more challenging biblical study became. It has been claimed that the paradoxes of the Bible did more for rational argument by stimulating discussion than all the reasons of Aristotle, which were swallowed whole.

Thomas Aquinas represents some of the best and most enduring intellectual effort produced during the Middle Ages. His work reflects luminously on the reputation of the University of Paris, where he taught in the thirteenth century. The task of synthesis he set for himself was nothing less than a comprehensive harmonization of Aristotelian philosophy and Christian theology. Aquinas agreed with Aristotle that the universe is orderly and rational and that the human being is important as the link between the created universe and the divine intelligence. Only the human being in the world of nature could understand nature. Only the human being in nature could understand the nature of God. Only the human being could use and perfect nature in accordance with the will of God and thus achieve full human nobility. Here was Christian humanism at its best.

Following Aquinas and using Aristotle, the supreme poet of the age, Dante Alighieri (1265-1321), gave poetic expression to some of these ideas in his *Divine Comedy.* In his *De Monarchia,* again drawing upon Aristotle, Dante explored the relationship between the human political environment and the realization of full human potential.

The brilliant achievement of Aquinas was not without its critics, even during his own lifetime. When possible he answered his critics, but his life was too short and his literary production too great for him to deal with the numerous objections raised. There were jealousies and rivalries within his own Dominican order, although the order after his death accepted his work and made its study mandatory. His boldly confident rationalism was opposed by those who followed the more mystical, traditional, and Platonic approach to the divine set forth by Augustine and strongly adhered to by the Franciscan order, especially Aquinas's great contemporary, Bonaventura (1221-1274).

The founder of the Franciscan order, Francis of Assisi (1182-1226), though impervious to most of the intellectual currents around him, provided some significant stimuli for Christian humanism. Utterly simple, touched by the conventions of courtly love, and inclined to mysticism, Francis seemed to inspire wonder and affection wherever he went. For the Christian life, he and his *Rule* called for strict apostolic poverty; neither the Franciscan order nor its members were to own anything. Francis spoke of being betrothed to Lady Poverty. He advocated preaching simply from the Bible without the encumbrance of centuries of Christian exegesis. Francis was one of those individuals who come along periodically in the history of Christianity stressing the need to return to the essentials of the Christian life and message. Another endearing quality of this spiritual genius was his respect and love for nature. It is said that Francis preached to the birds and the beasts who found what he had to say eminently worth hearing. His was not the sophisticated and inquiring respect for nature found in some of the scholastics, but rather a kind of reverence for all living things. Francis's nature had dignity. He was unique, however, and difficult to follow. Some of his followers veered toward an anti-intellectual stand and became bitter opponents of Aquinas.

It should be obvious that Aquinas and his achievements encountered opposition from many directions. Thomas also encountered hostility from officials in the papal *curia* who thought that some of his ideas veered dangerously close to heresy. Thus, great though the impact of Aquinas's work was it was not universally accepted. An important aspect of Thomas' work was his methodology with its popular appeal to reason. Scholasticism, the scholastic method, remained for centuries a dominating influence in many universities of northern Europe. Handled with subtlety and skill and put to searching purpose by an Aquinas, the scholastic method could achieve brilliant results, but when employed by a lesser mind, scholastic method could be arid and sterile, as Erasmus and Luther later claimed. Even when employed magnificently by an outstanding mind, the scholastic method had its dangerous aspects for dealing with matters theological: it was liable to a charge of being too rational, or too subtle, or too philosophical, or simply too difficult. In short, by c. 1300 scholasticism was going out of intellectual fashion.

Moreover, the advent of the fourteenth century brought sudden and unsettling changes. Almost inexplicably and without warning the intellectual climate shifted. Where the outlook had formerly been broad, confident, and forward-looking, it became narrow, tentative, and introspective. The optimism which carried forth so many intellectual efforts in the thirteenth century suddenly evaporated. Political malaise in the form of weak leadership overtook England, France, and Germany; the rapidly expanding European economy began to contract; recurrent plague, the Black Death, devastated the European population; international conflict, the Hundred Years war, was waged intermittently between England and France during the course of the fourteenth and fifteenth centuries. The universe seemed a great deal less reasonable. With this strange turn of events, the synthetic vision of an Aquinas seemed out of place.

Thus Christian humanism faced another crisis. Swept along on the scholastic tide, Christian humanism had identified human potential with human reason. When the universe and human affairs suddenly seemed less reasonable, there was bound to be a reaction. Compounding the problems, the fourteenth century brought a crisis of leadership in the church.

For centuries papal leadership had been vigorous, effective, spiritual; the spotlight remained on the papacy, but now the popes appeared self-serving, venal, worldly. Christian thought and action seemed out of harmony with the gospel; Christ's vicar did not seem to take Christ as his model. For some Christianity seemed to have lost its capacity to inspire the faithful; new sources of inspiration were being sought and were soon to be found in pagan classical antiquity. New forms of the Christian life were to bring spiritual consolation and renewal. The medieval experience demonstrated that for Christian humanism the age-old tension between Christianity and its cultural context had a new dimension: Christianity had embraced the world, and some saw Christianity crushed in the embrace.

BENEDICT

The *Rule* of Benedict of Nursia (c. 480-550) already reflects the experience of over two centuries of monastic tradition. Written in central Italy, presumably for his monastery of Monte Cassino, Benedict's *Rule* was chiefly patterned after a much longer and more authoritarian *Rule of the Master* written a generation earlier. Benedict tempered and abbreviated this rule with additions from Basil, Augustine, and Cassian as well as from his own living monastic experience. It is important to remember that the *Rule* of Benedict, like all other monastic rules, was not drawn up in abstract. Rather, this code of Christian life comes from the actual day-by-day needs and experience of a living community. Thus Benedict can be said to sum up the finest of the various ancient monastic traditions, while casting them in a new and *stable* framework which has lasted for 1,500 years.

The essence of Benedict's genius lies in his moderation and careful balance of the needs of both the *individual* monk and the *community* as a whole (cf. *Rule*, Chaps. 3, 27, 29, 34, 36, 37, 41, 55, 68). The focus of the *Rule* is clearly on *obedience* and *humility* (cf. Prol., Chap. 7). Benedict does not approach these virtues in any superficial way. He is concerned with a profound change of heart or conversion by which the monk will, "run the way of God's commandments with unspeakable sweetness of love." The chief sin in Benedict's monastery is "murmuring" or grumbling. A wise judge of human nature, Benedict condemns this dangerous, destructive, demoralizing vice throughout the *Rule*. The monk who physically obeys but yet murmurs in his heart will not be found acceptable (Chap. 5).

Benedict's monastery is a renewed, Christian society in which the Scripture is lived (cf. Chaps. 4, 33, 73) so as to permeate the life of the monk and restructure and reorient the mundane and routine objects and actions of life into a holy vision where God can be truly "all in all."

From **The Rule of Saint Benedict**
PROLOGUE

Listen carefully, my son, to the master's instructions, and attend to them with the ear of your heart. This is advice from a father who loves you; welcome it, and faithfully put it into practice. The labor of obedience will bring you back to him from whom you had drifted through the sloth of disobedience. The message of mine is for you, then, if you are ready to give up your own will, once and for all, and armed with the strong and noble weapons of obedience to do battle for the true King, Christ the Lord.

First of all, every time you begin a good work, you must pray to him most earnestly to bring it to perfection. In his goodness, he has already counted us as his sons, and therefore we should never grieve him by our evil actions. With his good gifts which are in us, we must obey him at all times that he may never become the angry father who disinherits his sons, nor the dread lord, enraged by our sins, who punishes us forever as worthless servants for refusing to follow him to glory.

Let us get up then, at long last, for the Scriptures rouse us when they say: It is high time for us to arise from sleep. Let us open our eyes to the light that comes from God, and our ears to the voice from heaven that every day calls out this charge: If you hear his voice today, do not harden your hearts. And again: You that have ears to hear, listen to what the Spirit says to the churches. And what does he say? Come and listen to me, sons; I will teach you the fear of the Lord. Run while you have the light of life, that the darkness of death may not overtake you.

Seeking his workman in a multiple of people, the Lord calls out to him and lifts his voice again: Is there anyone here who yearns for life and desires to see good days? If you hear this and your answer is "I do," God then directs these words to you: If you desire true and eternal life, keep your tongue free from vicious talk and your lips from all deceit; turn away from evil and do good; let peace be your quest and aim. Once you have done this, my eyes will be upon you and my ears will listen for your prayers; and even before you ask me, I will say to you: Here I am. What, dear brothers, is more delightful than this voice of the Lord calling to us? See how the Lord in his love shows us the way of life. Clothed then with faith and the performance of good works, let us set out on this way, with the Gospel for our guide, that we may deserve to see him who has called us to his kingdom.

If we wish to dwell in the tent of this kingdom, we will never arrive unless we run there by doing good deeds. But let us ask the Lord with the Prophet: Who will dwell in your tent, O Lord; who will find rest upon your holy mountain? After this question, brothers, let us listen well to what the Lord says in reply, for he shows us the way to his tent. One who walks without blemish, he says, and is just in all his dealings; who speaks the truth from his heart and has not practiced deceit with his tongue; who has not wronged a fellowman in any way, nor listened to slanders against his neighbor. He has foiled the evil one, the devil, at every turn, flinging both him and his promptings far from the sight of his heart. While these temptations were still young, he caught hold of them and dashed them against Christ. These people fear the Lord, and do not become elated over their good deeds; they judge it is the Lord's power, not their own, that brings about the good in them. They praise the Lord working in them, and say with the Prophet: Not to us, Lord, not to us give the glory, but to your name alone. In just this way Paul the Apostle refused to take credit for the power of his preaching. He declared: By God's grace I am what I am. And again he said: He who boasts should make his boast in the Lord. That is why the Lord says in the Gospel: Whoever hears these words of mine and does them is like a wise man who built his house upon rock; the floods came and the winds blew and beat against the house, but it did not fall: it was founded on rock.

With this conclusion, the Lord waits for us daily to translate into action, as we should, his holy teachings. Therefore our life span has been lengthened by way of a truce, that we may amend our misdeeds. As the Apostle says: Do you not know that the patience of God is leading you to repent? And indeed the Lord assures us in his love: I do not wish the death of the sinner, but that he turn back to me and live.

Brothers, now that we have asked the Lord who will dwell in his tent, we have heard the instruction for dwelling in it, but only if we fulfill the obligations of those who live there. We must, then, prepare our hearts and bodies for the battle of holy obedience to his instructions. What is not possible to us by nature, let us ask the Lord to supply by the help of his grace. If we wish to reach eternal life, even as we avoid the torments of hell, then—while there is still time, while we are in this body and have time to accomplish all these things by the light of life—we must run and do what will profit us forever.

Therefore we intend to establish a school for the Lord's service. In drawing up its regulations, we hope to set down nothing harsh, nothing burdensome. The good of all concerned, however, may prompt us to a little strictness in order to amend faults and to safeguard love.

Do not be daunted immediately by fear and run away from the road that leads to salvation. It is bound to be narrow at the outset. But as we progress in this way of life and in faith, we shall run on the path of God's commandments, our hearts overflowing with the inexpressible delight of love. Never swerving from his instructions, then, but faithfully observing his teaching in the monastery until death, we shall through patience share in the sufferings of Christ that we may deserve also to share in his kingdom. Amen.

[Here begins the text of the rule.]

[It is called a rule because it regulates the lives of those who obey it.]

Chapter 1.

THE KINDS OF MONKS

There are clearly four kinds of monks. First, there are the cenobites, that is to say, those who belong to a monastery, where they serve under a rule and an abbot.

Second, there are the anchorites or hermits, who have come through the test of living in a monastery for a long time, and have passed beyond the first fervor of monastic life. Thanks to the help and guidance of many, they are now trained to fight against the devil. They have built up their strength and go from the battle line in the ranks of their brothers to the single combat of the desert. Self-reliant now, without the support of another, they are ready with God's help to grapple single-handed with the vices of body and mind.

Third, there are the sarabaites, the most detestable kind of monks, who with no experience to guide them, no rule to try them as gold is tried in a furnace, have a character as soft as lead. Still loyal to the world by their actions, they clearly lie to God by their tonsure. Two or three together, or even alone, without a shepherd, they pen themselves up in their own sheepfolds, not the Lord's. Their law is what they like to do, whatever strikes their fancy. Anything they believe in and choose, they call holy; anything they dislike, they consider forbidden.

Fourth and finally, there are the monks called gyrovagues, who spend their entire lives drifting from region to region, staying as guests for three or four days in different monasteries. Always on the move, they never settle down, and are slaves to their own wills and gross appetites. In every way they are worse than sarabaites.

It is better to keep silent than to speak of all these and their disgraceful way of life. Let us pass them by, then, and with the help of the Lord, proceed to draw up a plan for the strong kind, the cenobites.

Chapter 2.

QUALITIES OF THE ABBOT

To be worthy of the task of governing a monastery, the abbot must always remember what his title signifies and act as a superior should. He is believed to hold the place of Christ in the monastery, since he is addressed by a title of Christ, as the Apostle indicates: You have received the spirit of adoption of sons by which we exclaim, abba, father. Therefore, the abbot must never teach or decree or command anything that would deviate from the Lord's instructions. On the contrary, everything he teaches and commands should, like the leaven of divine justice, permeate the minds of his disciples. Let the abbot always remember that at the fearful judgment of God, not only his teaching but also his disciples' obedience will come under scrutiny. The abbot must, therefore, be aware that the shepherd will bear the blame wherever the father of the household finds that the sheep have yielded no profit. Still, if he has faithfully shepherded a restive and disobedient flock, always striving to cure their unhealthy ways, it will be otherwise: the shepherd will be acquitted at the Lord's judgment. Then, like the Prophet, he may say to the Lord: I have not hidden your justice in my heart; I have proclaimed your truth and your salvation, but they spurned and rejected me. Then at last the sheep that have rebelled against his care will be punished by the overwhelming power of death.

Furthermore, anyone who receives the name of abbot is to lead his disciples by a twofold teaching: he must point out to them all that is good and holy more by example than by words, proposing the commandments of the Lord to receptive disciples with words, but demonstrating God's instructions to the stubborn and the dull by a living example. Again, if he teaches his disciples that something is not to be done, then neither must he do it, lest after preaching to others, he himself be found reprobate and God some day call to him in his sin: How is it that you repeat my just commands and mouth my covenant when you hate discipline and toss my words behind you? And also this: How is it that you can see a splinter in your brother's eye, and never notice the plank in your own?

The abbot should avoid all favoritism in the monastery. He is not to love one more than another unless he finds someone better in good actions and obedience. A man born free is not to be given higher rank than a slave who becomes a monk, except for some other good reason. But the abbot is free, if he sees fit, to change anyone's rank as justice demands. Ordinarily, everyone is to keep to his regular place, because whether slave or free, we are all one in Christ and share alike in bearing arms in the service of the one Lord, for God shows no partiality among persons. Only in this are we distinguished in his sight: if we are found better than others in good works and in humility. Therefore, the abbot is to show equal love to everyone and apply the same discipline to all according to their merits.

In his teaching, the abbot should always observe the Apostle's recommendation, in which he says: Use argument, appeal, reproof. This means that he must vary with circumstances, threatening and coaxing by turns, stern as a taskmaster, devoted and tender as only a father can be. With the undisciplined and restless, he will use firm argument; with the obedient and docile and patient, he will appeal for greater virtue; but as for the negligent and disdainful, we charge him to use reproof and rebuke. He should not gloss over the sins of those who err, but cut them out while he can, as soon as they begin to sprout, remembering the fate of Eli, priest of Shiloh. For upright and perceptive men, his first and second warnings should be verbal; but those who are evil or stubborn, arrogant or disobedient, he can curb only by blows or some other physical punishment at the first offense. It is written, The fool cannot be corrected with words; and again, Strike your son with a rod and you will free his soul from death.

The abbot must always remember what he is and remember what he is called, aware that more will be expected of a man to whom more has been entrusted. He must know what a difficult and demanding burden he has undertaken: directing souls and serving a variety of temperaments, coaxing, reproving and encouraging them as appropriate. He must so accommodate and adapt himself to each one's character and intelligence that he will not only keep the flock entrusted to his care from dwindling, but will rejoice in the increase of a good flock. Above all, he must not show too great concern for the fleeting and temporal things of this world, neglecting or treating lightly the welfare of those entrusted to him. Rather, he should keep in mind that he has undertaken the care of souls for whom he must give an account. That he may not plead lack of resources as an excuse, he is to remember what is written: Seek first the kingdom of God and his justice, and all these things will be given you as well, and again, Those who fear him lack nothing.

The abbot must know that anyone undertaking the charge of souls must be ready to account for them. Whatever the number of brothers he has in his care, let him realize that on judgment day he will surely have to submit a reckoning to the Lord for all their souls—and indeed for his own as well. In this way, while always fearful of the future examination of the shepherd about the sheep entrusted to him and careful about the state of others' accounts, he becomes concerned also about his own, and while helping others to amend by his warnings, he achieves the amendment of his own faults.

Chapter 3.
SUMMONING THE BROTHERS FOR COUNSEL

As often as anything important is to be done in the monastery, the abbot shall call the whole community together and himself explain what the business is; and after hearing the advice of the brothers, let him ponder it and follow what he judges the wiser course. The reason why we have said all should be called for counsel is that the Lord often reveals what is better to the younger. The brothers, for their part, are to express their opinions with all humility, and not presume to defend their own views obstinately. The decision is rather the abbot's to make, so that when he has determined what is more prudent, all may obey. Nevertheless, just as it is proper for disciples to obey their master, so it is becoming for the master on his part to settle everything with foresight and fairness.

Accordingly in every instance, all are to follow the teaching of the rule, and no one shall rashly deviate from it. In the monastery no one is to follow his own heart's desire, nor shall anyone presume to contend with his abbot defiantly, or outside the monastery. Should anyone presume to do so, let him be subjected to the discipline of the rule. Moreover, the abbot himself must fear God and keep the rule in everything he does; he can be sure beyond any doubt that he will have to give an account of all his judgments to God, the most just of judges.

If less important business of the monastery is to be transacted, he shall take counsel with the seniors only, as it is written: Do everything with counsel and you will not be sorry afterward.

Chapter 5.
OBEDIENCE

The first step of humility is unhesitating obedience, which comes naturally to those who cherish Christ above all. Because of the holy service they have professed, or because of dread of hell and for the glory of everlasting life, they carry out the superior's order as promptly as if the command came from God himself. The Lord says of men like this: No sooner did he hear than he obeyed me; again, he tells teachers: Whoever listens to you, listens to me. Such people as these immediately put aside their own concerns, abandon their own will, and lay down whatever they have in hand, leaving it unfinished. With the ready step of obedience, they follow the voice of authority in their actions.

Almost at the same moment, then, as the master gives the instruction the disciple quickly puts it into practice in the fear of God; and both actions together are swiftly completed as one.

It is love that impels them to pursue everlasting life; therefore, they are eager to take the narrow road of which the Lord says: Narrow is the road that leads to life. They no longer live by their own judgment, giving in to their whims and appetites; rather they walk according to another's decisions and directions, choosing to live in monasteries and to have an abbot over them. Men of this resolve unquestionably conform to the saying of the Lord: I have come not to do my own will, but the will of him who sent me.

This very obedience, however, will be acceptable to God and agreeable to men only if compliance with what is commanded is not cringing or sluggish or half-hearted, but free from any grumbling or any reaction of unwillingness. For the obedience shown to superiors is given to God, as he himself said: Whoever listens to you, listens to me. Furthermore, the disciples' obedience must be given gladly, for God loves a cheerful giver. If a disciple obeys grudgingly though he carries out the order, his action will not be accepted with favor by God, who sees that he is grumbling in his heart. He will have no reward for service of this kind; on the contrary, he will incur punishment for grumbling, unless he changes for the better and makes amends.

Chapter 7.

HUMILITY

Brothers, divine Scripture calls to us saying: Whoever exalts himself shall be humbled, and whoever humbles himself shall be exalted. In saying this, therefore, it shows us that every exaltation is a kind of pride, which the Prophet indicates he has shunned, saying: O Lord, my heart is not exalted; my eyes are not lifted up and I have not walked in the ways of the great nor gone after marvels beyond me. And why? If I had not a humble spirit, but were exalted instead, then you would treat me like a weaned child on its mother's lap.

Accordingly, brothers, if we want to reach the highest summit of humility, if we desire to attain speedily that exaltation in heaven to which we climb by the humility of this present life, then by our ascending actions we must set up that ladder on which Jacob in a dream saw angels descending and ascending. Without doubt, this descent and ascent can signifiy only that we descend by exaltation and ascend by humility. Now the ladder erected is our life on earth, and if we humble our hearts the Lord will raise it to heaven. We may call our body and soul the sides of this ladder, into which our divine vocation has fitted the various steps of humility and discipline as we ascend.

The first step of humility, then, is that a man keeps the fear of God always before his eyes and never forgets it. He must constantly remember everything God has commanded, keeping in mind that all who despise God will burn in hell for their sins, and all who fear God have everlasting life awaiting them. While he guards himself at every moment from sins and vices of thought or tongue, of hand or foot, of self-will or bodily desire, let him recall that he is always seen by God in heaven, that his actions everywhere are in God's sight and are reported by angels at every hour.

The Prophet indicates this to us when he shows that our thoughts are always present to God, saying: God searches hearts and minds; again he says: The Lord knows the thoughts of men; likewise, From afar you know my thoughts; and, The thought of man shall give you praise. That he may take care to avoid sinful thoughts, the virtuous brother must always say to himself: I shall be blameless in his sight if I guard myself from my own wickedness.

Truly, we are forbidden to do our will, for Scripture tells us: Turn away from your desires. And in the Prayer too we ask God that his will be done in us. We are rightly taught not to do our own will, since we dread what Scripture says: There are ways which men call right that in the end plunge into the depths of hell. Moreover, we fear what is said of those who ignore this: They are corrupt and have become depraved in their desires.

As for the desires of the body, we must believe that God is always with us, for all my desires are known to you, as the Prophet tells the Lord. We must then be on guard against any base desire, because death is stationed near the gateway of pleasure. For this reason Scripture warns us, Pursue not your lusts.

Accordingly, if the eyes of the Lord are watching the good and the wicked, if at all times the Lord looks down from heaven on the sons of men to see whether any understand and seek God; and if every day the angels assigned to us report our deeds to the Lord day and night, then, brothers, we must be vigilant every hour or, as the Prophet says in the psalm, God may observe us falling at some time into evil and so made worthless. After sparing us for a while because he is a loving father who waits for us to improve, he may tell us later, This you did, and I said nothing.

The second step of humility is that a man loves not his own will nor takes pleasure in the satisfaction of his desires; rather he shall imitate by his actions that saying of the Lord: I have come not to do my own will, but the will of him who sent me. Similarly we read, "Consent merits punishment; constraint wins a crown."

The third step of humility is that a man submits to his superior in all obedience for the love of God, imitating the Lord of whom the Apostle says: He became obedient even to death.

The fourth step of humility is that in his obedience under difficult, unfavorable, or even unjust conditions, his heart quietly embraces suffering and endures it without weakening or seeking escape. For Scripture has it: Anyone who perseveres to the end will be saved, and again, Be brave of heart and rely on the Lord. Another passage shows how the faithful must endure everything, even contradiction, for the Lord's sake, saying in the person of those who suffer, For your sake we are put to death continually; we are regarded as sheep marked for slaughter. They are so confident in their expectations of reward from God that they continue joyfully and say, But in all this we over-come because of him who so greatly loved us. Elsewhere Scripture says: O God, you have tested us, you have tried us as silver is tried by fire; you have led us into a snare, you have placed afflictions on our backs. Then, to show that we ought to be under a superior, it adds: You have placed men over our heads.

In truth, those who are patient amid hardships and unjust treatment are fulfilling the Lord's command: When struck on one cheek, they turn the other; when deprived of their coat, they offer their cloak also; when pressed into service for one mile, they go two. With the Apostle Paul, they bear with false brothers, endure persecution, and bless those who curse them.

The fifth step of humility is that a man does not conceal from his abbot any sinful thoughts entering his heart, or any wrongs commit-ted in secret, but rather confesses them humbly. Concerning this, Scripture exhorts us: Make known your way to the Lord and hope in him. And again, Confess to the Lord, for he is good; his mercy is forever. So too the Prophet: To you I have acknowledged my offense; my faults I have not concealed. I have said: Against myself I will report my faults to the Lord, and you have forgiven the wickedness of my heart.

The sixth step of humility is that a monk is content with the low-est and most menial treatment, and regards himself as a poor and worthless workman in whatever task he is given, saying to himself with the Prophet: I am insignificant and ignorant, no better than a beast before you, yet I am with you always.

The seventh step of humility is that a man not only admits with his tongue but is also convinced in his heart that he is inferior to all and of less value, humbling himself and saying with the Prophet: I am truly a worm, not a man, scorned by men and despised by the people. I was exalted, then I was humbled and overwhelmed with confusion. And again, It is a blessing that you have humbled me so that I can learn your commandments.

The eighth step of humility is that a monk does only what is endorsed by the common rule of the monastery and the example set by his superiors.

The ninth step of humility is that a monk controls his tongue and remains silent, not speaking unless asked a question, for Scripture warns, In a flood of words you will not avoid sinning and, A talkative man goes about aimlessly on earth.

The tenth step of humility is that he is not given to ready laughter, for it is written: Only a fool raises his voice in laughter.

The eleventh step of humility is that a monk speaks gently and without laughter, seriously and with becoming modesty, briefly and reasonably, but without raising his voice, as it is written: "A wise man is known by his few words."

The twelfth step of humility is that a monk always manifests humility in his bearing no less than in his heart, so that it is evident as the Work of God, in the oratory, the monastery or the garden, on a journey or in the field, or anywhere else. Whether he sits, walks or stands, his head must be bowed and his eyes cast down. Judging himself always guilty on account of his sins, he should consider that he is already at the fearful judgment, and constantly say in his heart what the publican in the Gospel said with downcast eyes: Lord, I am a sinner, not worthy to look up to heaven. And with the Prophet: I am bowed down and humbled in every way.

Now, therefore, after ascending all these steps of humility, the monk will quickly arrive at that perfect love of God which casts out fear. Through this love, all that he once performed with dread, he will now begin to observe without effort, as though naturally, from habit, no longer out of fear of hell, but out of love for Christ, good habit and delight in virtue. All this the Lord will by the Holy Spirit graciously manifest in his workman now cleansed of vices and sins.

Chapter 16.

THE CELEBRATION OF THE DIVINE OFFICE DURING THE DAY

The Prophet says: Seven times a day have I praised you. We will fulfill this sacred number of seven if we satisfy our obligations of service at Lauds, Prime, Terce, Sext, None, Vespers and Compline, for it was of these hours during the day that he said: Seven times a day have

I praised you. Concerning Vigils, the same Prophet says: At midnight I arose to give you praise. Therefore, we should praise our Creator for his just judgments at these times: Lauds, Prime, Terce, Sext, None, Vespers and Compline; and let us arise at night to give him praise.

Chapter 19.
THE DISCIPLINE OF PSALMODY

We believe that the divine presence is everywhere and that in every place the eyes of the Lord are watching the good and the wicked. But beyond the least doubt we should believe this to be especially true when we celebrate the divine office.

We must always remember, therefore, what the Prophet says: Serve the Lord with fear, and again, Sing praise wisely; and, In the presence of the angels I will sing to you. Let us consider, then, how we ought to behave in the presence of God and his angels, and let us stand to sing the psalms in such a way that our minds are in harmony with our voices.

Chapter 31.
QUALIFICATIONS OF THE MONASTERY CELLARER

As cellarer of the monastery, there should be chosen from the community someone who is wise, mature in conduct, temperate, not an excessive eater, not proud, excitable, offensive, dilatory or wasteful, but God-fearing, and like a father to the whole community. He will take care of everything, but will do nothing without an order from the abbot. Let him keep to his orders.

He should not annoy the brothers. If any brother happens to make an unreasonable demand of him, he should not reject him with disdain and cause him distress, but reasonably and humbly deny the improper request. Let him keep watch over his own soul, ever mindful of that saying of the Apostle: He who serves well secures a good standing for himself. He must show every care and concern for the sick, children, guests and the poor, knowing for certain that he will be held accountable for all of them on the day of judgment. He will regard all utensils and goods of the monastery as sacred vessels of the altar, aware that nothing is to be neglected. He should not be prone to greed, nor be wasteful and extravagant with the goods of the monastery, but should do everything with moderation and according to the abbot's orders.

Above all, let him be humble. If goods are not available to meet a request, he will offer a kind word in reply, for it is written: A kind word is better than the best gift. He should take care of all that the abbot entrusts to him, and not presume to do what the abbot has forbidden.

He will provide the brothers their allotted amount of food without any pride or delay, lest they be led astray. For he must remember what the Scripture says that person deserves who leads one of the little ones astray.

If the community is rather large, he should be given helpers, that with their assistance he may calmly perform the duties of his office. Necessary items are to be requested and given at the proper times, so that no one may be disquieted or distressed in the house of God.

Chapter 33.
MONKS AND PRIVATE OWNERSHIP

Above all, this evil practice must be uprooted and removed from the monastery. We mean that without an order from the abbot, no one may presume to give, receive or retain anything as his own, nothing at all—not a book, writing tablets or stylus—in short, not a single item, especially since monks may not have the free disposal even of their own bodies and wills. For their needs, they are to look to the father of the monastery, and are not allowed anything which the abbot has not given or permitted. All things should be the common possession of all, as it is written, so that no one presumes to call anything his own.

But if anyone is caught indulging in this most evil practice, he should be warned a first and a second time. If he does not amend, let him be subjected to punishment.

Chapter 34.
DISTRIBUTION OF GOODS ACCORDING TO NEED

It is written: Distribution was made to each one as he had need. By this we do not imply that there should be favoritism—God forbid—but rather consideration for weaknesses. Whoever needs less should thank God and not be distressed, but whoever needs more should feel humble because of his weakness, not self-important because of the kindness shown him. In this way all the members will be at peace. First and foremost, there must be no word or sign of the evil of grumbling, no manifestation of it for any reason at all. If, however, anyone is caught grumbling, let him undergo more severe discipline.

Chapter 35.
KITCHEN SERVERS OF THE WEEK

The brothers should serve one another. Consequently, no one will be excused from kitchen service unless he is sick or engaged in some important business of the monastery, for such service increases reward and fosters love. Let those who are not strong have help so that they may serve without distress, and let everyone receive help as the size of the community or local conditions warrant. If the community is rather large, the cellarer should be excused from kitchen service, and, as we have said, those should also be excused who are engaged in important business. Let all the rest serve one another in love.

On Saturday the brother who is completing his work will do the washing. He is to wash the towels which the brothers use to wipe their hands and feet. Both the one who is ending his service and the one who is about to begin are to wash the feet of everyone. The utensils required for the kitchen service are to be washed and returned intact to the cellarer, who in turn issues them to the one beginning his week. In this way the cellarer will know what he hands out and what he receives back.

An hour before mealtime, the kitchen workers of the week should each receive a drink and some bread over and above the regular portion, so that at mealtime, they may serve their brothers without grumbling or hardship. On solemn days, however, they should wait until after the dismissal.

On Sunday immediately after Lauds, those beginning as well as these completing their week of service should make a profound bow in the oratory before all and ask for their prayers. Let the server completing his week recite this verse: Blessed are you, Lord God, who have helped me and comforted me. After this verse has been said three times, he receives a blessing. Then the one beginning his service follows and says: God, come to my assistance; Lord, make haste to help me. And all repeat this verse three times. When he has received a blessing, he begins his service.

Chapter 36.

THE SICK BROTHERS

Care of the sick must rank above and before all else, so that they may truly be served as Christ, for he said: I was sick and you visited me, and, What you did for one of these least brothers you did for me. Let the sick on their part bear in mind that they are served out of honor for God, and let them not by their excessive demands distress their brothers who serve them. Still, sick brothers must be patiently borne with, because serving them leads to a greater reward. Consequently, the abbot should be extremely careful that they suffer no neglect.

Let a separate room be designated for the sick, and let them be served by an attendant who is God-fearing, attentive and concerned. The sick may take baths whenever it is advisable, but the healthy, and especially the young, should receive permission less readily. Moreover, to regain their strength, the sick who are very weak may eat meat, but when their health improves, they should all abstain from meat as usual.

The abbot must take the greatest care that cellarers and those who serve the sick do not neglect them, for the shortcomings of disciples are his responsibility.

Chapter 37.

THE ELDERLY AND CHILDREN

Although human nature itself is inclined to be compassionate toward the old and the young, the authority of the rule should also provide for them. Since their lack of strength must always be taken into account, they should certainly not be required to follow the strictness of the rule with regard to food, but should be treated with kindly consideration and allowed to eat before the regular hours.

Chapter 38.

THE READER FOR THE WEEK

Reading will always accompany the meals of the brothers. The reader should not be the one who just happens to pick up the book, but some-one who will read for a whole week, begininng on Sunday. After Mass and Communion, let the incoming reader ask all to pray for him so that God may shield him from the spirit of vanity. Let him begin this verse in the oratory: Lord, open my lips, and my mouth shall proclaim your praise, and let all say it three times. When he has received a blessing, he will begin this week of reading.

Let there be complete silence. No whispering, no speaking—only the reader's voice should be heard there. The brothers should by turn serve one another's needs as they eat and drink, so that no one need ask for anything. If, however, anything is required, it should be requested by an audible signal of some kind rather than by speech. No one should presume to ask a question about the reading or about anything else, lest occasion be given [to the devil]. The superior, however, may wish to say a few words of instruction.

Because of holy Communion and because the fast may be too hard for him to bear, the brother who is reader for the week is to receive some diluted wine before he begins to read. Afterward he will take his meal with the weekly kitchen servers and the attendants.

Brothers will read and sing, not according to rank, but according to their ability to benefit their hearers.

Chapter 39.
THE PROPER AMOUNT OF FOOD

For the daily meals, whether at noon or in midafternoon, it is enough, we believe, to provide all tables with two kinds of cooked food because of individual weaknesses. In this way, the person who may not be able to eat one kind of food may partake of the other. Two kinds of cooked food, therefore, should suffice for all the brothers, and if fruit or fresh vegetables are available, a third dish may also be added. A generous pound of bread is enough for a day whether for only one meal or for both dinner and supper. In the latter case the cellarer will set aside one third of this pound and give it to the brothers at supper.

Should it happen that the work is heavier than usual, the abbot may decide—and he will have the authority—to grant something additional, provided that it is appropriate, and that above all overindulgence is avoided, lest a monk experience indigestion. For nothing is so inconsistent with the life of any Christian as overindulgence. Our Lord says: Take care that your hearts are not weighed down with overindulgence.

Young boys should not receive the same amount as their elders, but less, since in all matters frugality is the rule. Let everyone, except the sick who are very weak, abstain entirely from eating the meat of four-footed animals.

Chapter 40.
THE PROPER AMOUNT OF DRINK

Everyone has his own gift from God, one this and another that. It is, therefore, with some uneasiness that we specify the amount of food and drink for others. However, with due regard for the infirmities of the sick, we believe that a half bottle of wine a day is sufficient for each. But those to whom God gives the strength to abstain must know that they will earn their own reward.

The superior will determine when local conditions, work or the summer heat indicates the need for a greater amount. He must, in any case, take great care lest excess or drunkenness creep in. We read that monks should not drink wine at all, but since the monks of our day cannot be convinced of this, let us at least agree to drink moderately, and not to the point of excess, for wine makes even wise men go astray.

However, where local circumstances dictate an amount much less than what is stipulated above, or even none at all, those who live there should bless God and not grumble. Above all else we admonish them to refrain from grumbling.

Chapter 48.

THE DAILY MANUAL LABOR

Idleness is the enemy of the soul. Therefore, the brothers should have specified periods for manual labor as well as for prayerful reading.

We believe that the times for both may be arranged as follows: From Easter to the first of October, they will spend their mornings after Prime till about the fourth hour at whatever work needs to be done. From the fourth hour until the time of Sext, they will devote themselves to reading. But after Sext and their meal, they may rest on their beds in complete silence; should a brother wish to read privately, let him do so, but without disturbing the others. They should say None a little early, about midway through the eighth hour, and then until Vespers they are to return to whatever work is necessary. They must not become distressed if local conditions or their poverty should force them to do the harvesting themselves. When they live by the labor of their hands, as our fathers and the apostles did, then they are really monks. Yet, all things are to be done with moderation on account of the fainthearted.

From the first of October to the beginning of Lent, the brothers ought to devote themselves to reading until the end of the second hour. At this time Terce is said and they are to work at their assigned tasks until None. At the first signal for the hour of None, all put aside their work to be ready for the second signal. Then after their meal they will devote themselves to their reading or to the psalms.

During the days of Lent, they should be free in the morning to read until the third hour, after which they will work at their assigned tasks until the end of the tenth hour. During this time of Lent each one is to receive a book from the library, and is to read the whole of it straight through. These books are to be distributed at the beginning of Lent.

Above all, one or two seniors must surely be deputed to make the rounds of the monastery while the brothers are reading. Their duty is to see that no brother is so apathetic as to waste time or engage in idle talk to the neglect of his reading, and so not only harm himself but also distract others. If such a monk is found—God forbid—he should be reproved a first and a second time. If he does not amend, he must be subjected to the punishment of the rule as a warning to others. Further, brothers ought not to associate with one another at inappropriate times.

On Sunday all are to be engaged in reading except those who have been assigned various duties. If anyone is so remiss and indolent that he is unwilling or unable to study or to read, he is to be given some work in order that he may not be idle.

Brothers who are sick or weak should be given a type of work or craft that will keep them busy without overwhelming them or driving them away. The abbot must take their infirmities into account.

Chapter 52.
THE ORATORY OF THE MONASTERY

The oratory ought to be what it is called, and nothing else is to be done or stored there. After the Work of God, all should leave in complete silence and with reverence for God, so that a brother who may wish to pray alone will not be disturbed by the insensitivity of another. Moreover, if at other times someone chooses to pray privately, he may simply go in and pray, not in a loud voice, but with tears and heartfelt devotion. Accordingly, anyone who does not pray in this manner is not to remain in the oratory after the Work of God, as we have said; then he will not interfere with anyone else.

Chapter 53.
THE RECEPTION OF GUESTS

All guests who present themselves are to be welcomed as Christ, for he himself will say: I was a stranger and you welcomed me. Proper honor must be shown to all, especially to those who share our faith and to pilgrims.

Once a guest has been announced, the superior and the brothers are to meet him with all the courtesy of love. First of all, they are to pray together and thus be united in peace, but prayer must always precede the kiss of peace because of the delusions of the devil.

All humility should be shown in addressing a guest on arrival or departure. By a bow of the head or by a complete prostration of the body, Christ is to be adored because he is indeed welcomed in them. After the guests have been received, they should be invited to pray; then the superior or an appointed brother will sit with them. The divine law is read to the guests for his instruction, and after that every kindness is shown to him. The superior may break his fast for the sake of a guest, unless it is a day of special fast which cannot be broken. The brothers, however, observe the usual fast. The abbot shall pour water on the hands of the guests, and the abbot with the entire community shall wash their feet. After the washing they will recite this verse: God, we have received your mercy in the midst of your temple.

Great care and concern are to be shown in receiving poor people and pilgrims, because in them more particularly Christ is received; our very awe of the rich guarantees them special respect.

The kitchen for the abbot and guests ought to be separate, so that guests—and monasteries are never without them—need not disturb the brothers when they present themselves at unpredictable hours. Each year, two brothers who can do the work competently are to be assigned to this kitchen. Additional help should be available when needed, so that they can perform this service without grumbling. On the other hand, when the work slackens, they are to go wherever other duties are assigned them. This consideration is not for them alone, but applies to all duties in the monastery; the brothers are to be given help when it is needed, and whenever they are free, they work wherever they are assigned.

The guest quarters are to be entrusted to a God-fearing brother. Adequate bedding should be available there. The house of God should be in the care of wise men who will manage it wisely.

No one is to speak or associate with guests unless he is bidden; however, if a brother meets or sees a guest, he is to greet him humbly, as we have said. He asks for a blessing and continues on his way, explaining that he is not allowed to speak with a guest.

Chapter 54.

LETTERS OR GIFTS FOR MONKS

In no circumstances is a monk allowed, unless the abbot says he may, to exchange letters, blessed tokens or small gifts of any kind, with his parents or anyone else, or with a fellow monk. He must not presume to accept gifts sent him even by his parents without previously telling the abbot. If the abbot orders acceptance, he still has the power to give the gift to whom he will; and the brother for whom it was originally sent must not be distressed, lest occasion be given to the devil. Whoever presumes to act otherwise will be subjected to the discipline of the rule.

Chapter 55.

THE CLOTHING AND FOOTWEAR OF THE BROTHERS

The clothing distributed to the brothers should vary according to local conditions and climate, because more is needed in cold regions and less in warmer. This is left to the abbot's discretion. We believe that for each monk a cowl and tunic will suffice in temperate regions; in winter a woolen cowl is necessary, in summer a thinner or worn one; also a scapular for work, and footwear—both sandals and shoes.

Monks must not complain about the color or coarseness of all these articles, but use what is available in the vicinity at a reasonable cost.

However, the abbot ought to be concerned about the measurements of these garments that they not be too short but fitted to the wearers.

Whenever new clothing is received, the old should be returned at once and stored in a wardrobe for the poor. To provide for laundering and night wear, every monk will need two cowls and two tunics, but anything more must be taken away as superfluous. When new articles are received, the worn ones—sandals or anything old—must be returned.

Brothers going on a journey should get underclothing from the wardrobe. On their return they are to wash it and give it back. Their cowls and tunics, too, ought to be somewhat better than those they ordinarily wear. Let them get these from the wardrobe before departing, and on returning put them back.

For bedding the monks will need a mat, a woolen blanket and a light covering as well as a pillow.

The beds are to be inspected frequently by the abbot, lest private possessions be found there. A monk discovered with anything not given him by the abbot must be subjected to very severe punishment. In order that this vice of private ownership may be completely uprooted, the abbot is to provide all things necessary: that is, cowl, tunic, sandals, shoes, belt, knife, stylus, needle, handkerchief and writing tablets. In this way every excuse of lacking some necessity will be taken away.

The abbot, however, must always bear in mind what is said in the Acts of the Apostles: Distribution was made to each one as he had need. In this way the abbot will take into account the weaknesses of the needy, not the evil will of the envious; yet in all his judgments he must bear in mind God's retribution.

Chapter 63.

COMMUNITY RANK

The monks keep their rank in the monastery according to the date of their entry, the virtue of their lives, and the decision of the abbot. The abbot is not to disturb the flock entrusted to him nor make any unjust arrangements, as though he had the power to do whatever he wished. He must constantly reflect that he will have to give God an account of all his decisions and actions. Therefore, when the monks come for the kiss of peace and for Communion, when they lead psalms or stand in choir, they do so in the order decided by the abbot or already existing among them. Absolutely nowhere shall age automatically determine rank. Remember that Samuel and Daniel were still boys when they judged their elders. Therefore, apart from those mentioned above whom the abbot has for some overriding consideration promoted, or for a specific reason demoted, all the rest should keep to the order of their entry. For example, someone who came to the monastery at the second hour of the day must recognize that he is junior to someone who came at the first hour, regardless of age or distinction. Boys, however, are to be disciplined in everything by everyone.

The younger monks, then, must respect their seniors, and the seniors must love their juniors. When they address one another, no one should be allowed to do so simply by name; rather, the seniors call the younger monks "brother" and the younger monks call their seniors *nonnus,* which is translated as "venerable father." But the abbot, because we believe that he holds the place of Christ, is to be called "lord" and "abbot," not for any claim of his own, but out of honor and love for Christ. He, for his part, must reflect on this, and in his behavior show himself worthy of such honor.

Wherever brothers meet, the junior asks his senior for a blessing. When an older monk comes by, the younger rises and offers him a seat, and does not presume to sit down unless the older bids him. In this way, they do what the words of Scripture say: They should each try to be the first to show respect to the other.

In the oratory and at table, small boys and youths are kept in rank and under discipline. Outside or anywhere else, they should be supervised and controlled until they are old enough to be responsible.

Chapter 64.
THE ELECTION OF AN ABBOT

In choosing an abbot, the guiding principle should always be that the man placed in office be the one selected either by the whole community acting unanimously in the fear of God, or by some part of the community, no matter how small, which possesses sounder judgment. Goodness of life and wisdom in teaching must be the criteria for choosing the one to be made abbot, even if he is the last in community rank.

May God forbid that a whole community should conspire to elect a man who goes along with its own evil ways. But if it does, and if the bishop of the diocese or the abbots or Christians in the area come to know of these evil ways to any extent, they must block the success of this wicked conspiracy, and set a worthy steward in charge of God's house. They may be sure that they will receive a generous reward for this, if they do it with pure motives and zeal for God's honor. Conversely, they may be equally sure that to neglect to do so is sinful.

Once in office, the abbot must keep constantly in mind the nature of the burden he has received, and remember to whom he will have to give an account of his stewardship. Let him recognize that his goal must be profit for the monks, not preeminence for himself. He ought, therefore, to be learned in divine law, so that he has a treasury of knowledge from which he can bring out what is new and what is old. He must be chaste, temperate and merciful. He should always let mercy triumph over judgment so that he too may win mercy. He must hate faults but love the brothers. When he must punish them, he should use prudence and avoid extremes; otherwise, by rubbing too hard to remove the rust, he may break the vessel. He is to distrust his own frailty and remember not to crush the bruised reed. By this we do not mean that he should allow faults to flourish, but rather, as we have already said, he should prune them away with prudence and love as he sees best for each individual. Let him strive to be loved rather than feared.

Excitable, anxious, extreme, obstinate, jealous or oversuspicious he must not be. Such a man is never at rest. Instead, he must show forethought and consideration in his orders, and whether the task he assigns concerns God or the world, he should be discerning and moderate, bearing in mind the discretion of holy Jacob, who said: If I drive my flocks too hard, they will all die in a single day. Therefore, drawing on this and other examples of discretion, the mother of virtues, he must so arrange everything that the strong have something to yearn for and the weak nothing to run from.

He must, above all, keep this rule in every particular, so that when he has ministered well he will hear from the Lord what that good servant heard who gave his fellow servants grain at the proper time: I tell you solemnly, he said, he sets him over all his possessions.

Chapter 71.

MUTUAL OBEDIENCE

Obedience is a blessing to be shown by all, not only to the abbot but also to one another as brothers, since we know that it is by this way of obedience that we go to God. Therefore, although orders of the abbot or of the priors appointed by him take precedence, and no unofficial order may supersede them, in every other instance younger monks should obey their seniors with all love and concern. Anyone found objecting to this should be reproved.

If a monk is reproved in any way by his abbot or by one of his seniors, even for some very small matter, or if he gets the impression that one of his seniors is angry or disturbed with him, however slightly, he must, then and there without delay, cast himself on the ground at the other's feet to make satisfaction, and lie there until the disturbance is calmed by a blessing. Anyone who refuses to do this should be subjected to corporal punishment or, if he is stubborn, should be expelled from the monastery.

Chapter 72.
THE GOOD ZEAL OF MONKS

Just as there is a wicked zeal of bitterness which separates from God and leads to hell, so there is a good zeal which separates from evil and leads to God and everlasting life. This, then, is the good zeal which monks must foster with fervent love: They should each try to be the first to show respect to the other, supporting with the greatest patience one another's weaknesses of body or behavior, and earnestly competing in obedience to one another. No one is to pursue what he judges better for himself, but instead, what he judges better for someone else. To their fellow monks they show the pure love of brothers; to God, loving fear; to their abbot, unfeigned and humble love. Let them prefer nothing whatever to Christ, and may he bring us all together to everlasting life.

Chapter 73.
THIS RULE ONLY A BEGINNING OF PERFECTION

The reason we have written this rule is that, by observing it in monasteries, we can show that we have some degree of virtue and the beginnings of monastic life. But for anyone hastening on to the perfection of monastic life, there are the teachings of the holy Fathers, the observance of which will lead him to the very heights of perfection. What page, what passage of the inspired books of the Old and New Testaments is not the truest of guides for human life? What book of the holy catholic Fathers does not resoundingly summon us along the true way to reach the Creator? Then, besides the *Conferences* of the Fathers, their *Institutes* and their *Lives*, there is also the rule of our holy father Basil. For observant and obedient monks, all these are nothing less than tools for the cultivation of virtues; but as for us, they make us blush for shame at being so slothful, so unobservant, so negligent. Are you hastening toward your heavenly home? Then with Christ's help, keep this little rule that we have written for beginners. After that, you can set out for the loftier summits of the teaching and virtues we mentioned above, and under God's protection you will reach them. Amen.

HYMNS AND SEQUENCES FROM THE MIDDLE AGES

Hymns are among the most important and earliest forms of Christian Latin poetry. The earliest hymns clearly demonstrate how poetic forms from classical antiquity were adapted for Christian uses, principally in the liturgy. The verbal contents of these hymns are expressions of the faith of the church and illustrate its changing devotional patterns.

It seems clear that the authors even of the earliest hymns intended that they be sung. Indeed Augustine provides a definition of a hymn: the praise of God in song. One of the earliest Latin writers of hymns, Ambrose, is recorded to have encouraged congregational singing of hymns at Milan where he was bishop in the late fourth century. Augustine in his *Confessions* reports that he had heard the congregational singing which Ambrose had developed. Hymns ascribed to Ambrose survive for morning and evening worship; *Aeterne rerum conditor* was meant for morning worship and was taken into monastic worship for the office of Lauds. Another very early hymn is the *Te Deum laudamus* which came to be used in the monastic office at the end of Matins; ascribed to St. Nicetas this hymn came to be recognized as particularly suitable for use as a song of thanksgiving. Many composers from the sixteenth century to the present have set the text of this hymn to celebrate great occasions of thanksgiving. The great esteem with which martyrdom was greeted in the early church is commemorated in a hymn by the celebrated Latin writer Prudentius (348-*c*. 413).

The specific occasions for which most early hymns were written are no longer known. An important exception to this is found in connection with the composition of *Vexilla Regis* by Venantius Fortunatus (530-609). A Frankish queen had received a large relic of Christ's cross and commissioned the author to write this hymn, which was to be sung when the relic was carried in procession. The hymn testifies to the growing importance of the cross as an object of religious significance and attention.

The continuing Christian fascination with light and God's creative power is seen in Gregory the Great's (540-604) fine hymn, *Lucis creator optime,* which achieved a place in the monastic office of Vespers on festive occasions.

The moving hymn, *Te lucis ante terminum,* is obviously intended for use in the evening. This anonymous seventh century composition came to be used for the monastic office at Compline.

Another anonymous seventh century hymn achieved great popularity for use during Advent where Christ's first coming as an infant babe was juxtaposed with his appearance as judge in the second coming at the end of time.

Beginning in the ninth century Christian Latin poetry in the form of hymns came to be employed more and more frequently in connection with the mass. The era of Charlemagne (768-814) ushered in a burst of activity and creativity in the production of hymns. Several of the most memorable hymns of all time were composed at this time. Theodulph of Orleans (d. 821) was the author of *Gloria, laus et honor* which was used for the mass of Palm Sunday in the procession of the palms; Rhabanus Maurus (776-856) was the author of *Veni, Creator Spiritus* which was used as a Vesper hymn during Whitsun week.

An important development in the eleventh century and for several centuries thereafter was the production of a new form, the sequence. This was a special species of hymn meant to be sung in the mass between the reading of the Epistle and the singing of the Gospel. Originally an extension of the Gradual and its following Alleluia, the sequence quickly became a separate entity, a kind of meditation on the major theme of the mass for the day. The earliest of these sequences to survive in the mass is the *Victimae paschali laudes* ascribed to Wipo (11th century) and used on Easter Sunday.

Many of the most important figures of the high Middle Ages (*c.* 1050-*c.* 1300) wrote hymns which came to be included in the liturgy. Among these Bernard of Clairvaux (1091-1153) contributed the emotional meditation on the name of Christ which came to be used as the Vesper hymn for the feast commemorating Christ's Name. Another famous figure, Pope Innocent III (1198-1216), is a likely candidate for the authorship of *Veni, Sancte Spiritus*, a sequence which came to be used for Whitsunday. Thomas Aquinas (1227-1274) succinctly sets forth the thirteenth century teaching on the Eucharist in the hymn *Pange Lingua* and the sequence, *Lauda Sion, Salvatorem*, both of which he composed specifically for the feast of Corpus Christi instituted in 1265. The *Dies irae*, perhaps the greatest of sequences, sets forth the terrors of the Last Judgment and *Stabat Mater*, a product of the "cult of the Virgin," dwells on the sufferings of the sorrowing mother of Christ.

St. Ambrose (340-397), **Aeterne rerum conditor**

Maker of all, eternal King,
Who day and night about dost bring:
Who weary mortals to relieve,
Dost in their times the seasons give:

Now the shrill cock proclaims the day,
And calls the sun's awakening ray,
The wandering pilgrim's guiding light,
That marks the watches night by night.

Roused at the note, the morning star
Heaven's dusky veil uplifts afar:

Night's vagrant bands no longer roam,
But from their dark ways hie them home.

The encouraged sailor's fears are o'er,
The foaming billows rage no more:
Lo! e'en the very Church's Rock
Melts at the crowing of the cock.

O let us then like men arise;
The cock rebukes our slumbering eyes,
Bestirs who still in sleep would lie,
And shames who would their Lord deny.

New hope his clarion note awakes,
Sickness the feeble frame forsakes,
The robber sheathes his lawless sword,
Faith to the fallen is restored.

Look on us, Jesu, when we fall,
And with Thy look our souls recall:
If Thou but look our sins are gone,
And with due tears our pardon won.

Shed through our hearts Thy piercing ray,
Our soul's dull slumber drive away:
Thy Name be first on every tongue,
To Thee our earliest praises sung.

All laud to God the Father be;
All praise, Eternal Son, to Thee;
All glory, as is ever meet,
To God the Holy Paraclete.

Venantius Fortunatus (530-609), **Vexilla regis**

Abroad the regal banners fly,
Now shines the Cross's mystery;
Upon it Life did death endure,
And yet by death did life procure.

Who, wounded with a direful spear,
Did, purposely to wash us clear

From stain of sin, pour out a flood
Of precious water mixed with blood.

That which the prophet-king of old
Hath in mysterious verse foretold,
Is now accomplished, whilst we see
God ruling nations from a Tree.

O lovely and refulgent Tree,
Adorned with purpled majesty;
Culled from a worthy stock, to bear
Those limbs which sanctified were.

Blest Tree, whose happy branches bore
The wealth that did the world restore;
The beam that did that Body weigh
Which raised up hell's expected prey.

Hail Cross, of hopes the most sublime!
Now, in this mournful Passion time;
Grant to the just increase of grace,
And every sinner's crimes efface.

Blest Trinity, salvation's spring
May every soul Thy praises sing;
To those Thou grantest conquest by
The holy Cross, rewards supply.

Anon. (7th cent.), **Creator alme siderum**

Bright Builder of the heavenly poles,
Eternal light of faithful souls,
Jesus, Redeemer of mankind,
Our humble prayers vouchsafe to mind:

Who, lest the fraud of hell's black king
Should all men to destruction bring,
Didst, by an act of generous love,
The fainting world's physician prove.

Thou, that Thou mightst our ransom pay
And wash the stains of sin away,

Didst from a Virgin's womb proceed
And on the Cross a Victim bleed.

Thy glorious power, Thy saving name
No sooner any voice can frame,
But heaven and earth and hell agree
To honor them with trembling knee.

Thee, Christ, who at the latter day
Shalt be our Judge, we humbly pray
Such arms of heavenly grace to send
As may Thy Church from foes defend.

Be glory given and honor done
To God the Father and the Son
And to the Holy Ghost on high,
From age to age eternally.

Anon. (7th cent.), **Te lucis ante terminum**

Before the ending of the day,
Creator of the world, we pray
That, with Thy wonted favor, Thou
Wouldst be our guard and keeper now.

From all ill dreams defend our eyes,
From nightly fears and fantasies;
Tread under foot our ghostly foe,
That no pollution we may know.

O Father, that we ask be done,
Through Jesus Christ, Thine only Son.
Who, with the Holy Ghost and Thee,
Doth live and reign eternally.

Theodulph of Orleans (760-821), **Gloria, laus et honor**

All glory, praise, and honor
To Thee, Redeemer, King,
To whom the lips of children
Made sweet Hosannas ring.
        All glory, etc.

Thou art the King of Israel,
Thou David's royal Son,
Who in the Lord's Name comest,
The King and blessed One.
    All glory, etc.

The company of Angels
Are praising Thee on high,
And mortal men and all things
Created make reply.
    All glory, etc.

The people of the Hebrews
With palms before Thee went;
Our praise and prayer and anthems
Before Thee we present.
    All glory, etc.

To Thee before Thy Passion
They sang their hymns of praise;
To Thee now high exalted
Our melody we raise.
    All glory, etc.

Thou didst accept their praises,
Accept the prayers we bring,
Who in all good delightest,
Thou good and gracious King.
    All glory, etc.

Rhabanus Maurus (776-856), **Veni, Creator Spiritus**

Creator-Spirit, all-divine,
Come, visit every soul of Thine,
And fill with Thy celestial flame
The hearts which Thou Thyself didst frame.

O gift of God, Thine is the sweet
Consoling name of Paraclete—
And spring of life and fire and love
And unction flowing from above.

The mystic sevenfold gifts are Thine.
Finger of God's right hand divine;
The Father's promise sent to teach
The tongue a rich and heavenly speech.

Kindle with fire brought from above
Each sense, and fill our hearts with love;
And grant our flesh, so weak and frail,
The strength of Thine which cannot fail.

Drive far away our deadly foe,
And grant us Thy true peace to know;
So we, led by Thy guidance still,
May safely pass through every ill.

To us, through Thee, the grace be shown
To know the Father and the Son;
And Spirit of Them both, may we
Forever rest our faith in Thee.

To Sire and Son be praises meet,
And to the Holy Paraclete;
And may Christ send us from above
That Holy Spirit's gift of love.

Wipo (11th cent.), **Victimae paschali**

The holy Paschal work is wrought,
The Victim's praise be told,
The loving Shepherd back hath brought
The sheep into His fold:
The Just and Innocent was slain
To reconcile to God again.

Death from the Lord of life hath fled—
The conflict strange is o'er;
Behold, He liveth that was dead,
And lives forevermore:
Mary, thou soughtest Him that day;
Tell what thou sawest on the way.

"I saw the empty cavern's gloom,
The garments of the prison,

The Angel-guardians of the tomb,
The glory of the Risen."
We know that Christ hath burst the grave,
Then, victor King, Thy people save.

Bernard of Clairvaux (1091-1153), **Jesu, dulcis memoria**

Jesu, the very thought of Thee
With sweetness fills my breast;
But sweeter far Thy face to see,
And in Thy presence rest.

Nor voice can sing, nor heart can frame,
Nor can the memory find
A sweeter sound than Thy blest Name,
O Savior of mankind!

O hope of every contrite heart,
O joy of all the meek,
To those who fall, how kind Thou art!
How good to those who seek!

But what to those who find? Ah! this
Nor tongue nor pen can show:
The love of Jesus, what it is
None but His loved ones know.

Jesu, our only joy be Thou,
As Thou our prize wilt be;
Jesu, be Thou our glory now,
And through eternity.

Thomas Aquinas (1225-1274), **Lauda, Sion, Salvatorem**

Praise, O Sion, praise thy Savior,
Shepherd, Prince, with glad behavior,
Praise in hymn and canticle:
Sing His glory without measure,
For the merit of your treasure
Never shall your praises fill.

Wondrous theme of mortal singing,
Living Bread and Bread life-bringing,

Sing we on this joyful day:
At the Lord's own table given
To the twelve as Bread from heaven,
Doubting not we firmly say.

Sing His praise with voice sonorous:
Every heart shall hear the chorus
Swell in melody sublime:
For this day the Shepherd gave us
Flesh and Blood to feed and save us,
Lasting to the end of time.

At the new King's sacred table,
The new Law's new Pasch is able
To succeed the ancient rite:
Old to new its place hath given,
Truth has far the shadows driven,
Darkness flees before the Light.

And as He hath done and planned it—
"Do this"—hear His love command it,
"For a memory of me."
Learned, Lord, in Thy own science,
Bread and wine, in sweet compliance,
As a Host we offer Thee.

Thus in faith the Christian heareth:
That Christ's Flesh as bread appeareth,
And as wine His Precious Blood:
Though we feel it not nor see it,
Living Faith that doth decree it
All defects of sense makes good.

Lo! beneath the species dual
(Signs not things), is hid a jewel
Far beyond creation's reach!
Though His Flesh as food abideth,
And His Blood as drink—He hideth
Undivided under each.

Whoso eateth It can never
Break the Body, rend or sever;

Christ entire our hearts doth fill:
Thousands eat the Bread of heaven,
Yet as much to one is given:
Christ, though eaten, bideth still.

Good and bad, they come to greet Him:
Unto life the former eat Him,
And the latter unto death;
These find death and those find heaven;
See, from the same life-seed given,
How the harvest differeth!

When at last the Bread is broken,
Doubt not what the Lord hath spoken:
In each part the same love-token,
The same Christ, our hearts adore:
For no power the Thing divideth—
'Tis the symbols He provideth,
While the Savior still abideth
Undiminished as before.

Hail, angelic Bread of heaven
Now the pilgrim's hoping-leaven,
Yea, the Bread to children given
That to dogs must not be thrown:
In the figures contemplated,
'Twas with Isaac immolated,
By the Lamb 'twas antedated.
In the Manna it was known.

O Good Shepherd, still confessing
Love, in spite of our transgressing,—
Here Thy blessed Food possessing,
Make us share Thine every blessing
In the land of life and love:
Thou, whose power hath all completed
And Thy Flesh as Food hath meted,
Make us, at Thy table seated,
By Thy Saints, as friends be greeted,
In Thy paradise above.

Thomas of Celano, **Dies irae**

That day of wrath, that dreadful day,
When heaven and earth shall pass away,
Both David and the Sibyl say.

What terror then shall us befall,
When lo, the Judge's steps appall,
About to sift the deeds of all.

The mighty trumpet's marvelous tone
Shall pierce through each sepulchral stone
And summon all before the throne.

Now Death and Nature in amaze
Behold the Lord His creatures raise,
To meet the Judge's awful gaze.

The books are opened, that the dead
May have their doom from what is read,
The record of our conscience dread.

The Lord of judgment sits Him down,
And every secret thing makes known;
No crime escapes His vengeful frown.

Ah, how shall I that day endure?
What patron's friendly voice secure,
When scarce the just themselves are sure?

O King of dreadful majesty,
Who grantest grace and mercy free,
Grant mercy now and grace to me.

Good Lord, 'twas for my sinful sake,
That Thou our suffering flesh didst take;
Then do not now my soul forsake.

In weariness Thy sheep was sought;
Upon the Cross His life was bought;
Alas, if all in vain were wrought.

O just avenging Judge, I pray,
For pity take my sins away,
Before the great accounting-day.

I groan beneath the guilt, which Thou
Canst read upon my blushing brow;
But spare, O God, Thy suppliant now.

Thou who didst Mary's sins unbind,
And mercy for the robber find,
Dost fill with hope my anxious mind.

My feeble prayers can make no claim,
Yet, gracious Lord, for Thy great Name,
Redeem me from the quenchless flame.

At Thy right hand, give me a place
Among Thy sheep, a child of grace,
Far from the goats' accursed race.

Yet, when Thy justly kindled ire
Shall sinners hurl to endless fire,
Oh, call me to Thy chosen choir.

In suppliant prayer I prostrate bend,
My contrite heart like ashes rend,
Regard, O Lord, my latter end.

Oh, on that day, that tearful day,
When man to judgment wakes from clay,
Be thou the trembling sinner's stay,

And spare him, God, we humbly pray,
Yea, grant to all, O Savior Blest,
Who die in Thee, the Saints' sweet rest.

Jacopone da Todi (d. 1306), **Stabat Mater dolorosa**

At the Cross her station keeping,
Stood the mournful Mother weeping,
Close to Jesus to the last:

Through her heart, His sorrow sharing,
All His bitter anguish bearing,
Now at length the sword had passed.

Oh, how sad and sore distressed
Was that Mother highly blest
Of the sole-begotten One!

Christ above in torment hangs;
She beneath beholds the pangs
Of her dying glorious Son.

Is there one who would not weep,
Whelmed in miseries so deep
Christ's dear Mother to behold?

Can the human heart refrain
From partaking in her pain,
In that Mother's pain untold?

Bruised, derided, cursed, defiled,
She beheld her tender Child
All with bloody scourges rent;

For the sins of His own nation,
Saw Him hang in desolation,
Till His Spirit forth He sent.

O thou Mother! fount of love!
Touch my spirit from above,
Make my heart with thine accord:

Make me feel as thou hast felt;
Make my soul to glow and melt
With the love of Christ my Lord.

Holy Mother! pierce me through:
In my heart each wound renew
Of my Savior crucified:

Let me share with thee His pain,
Who for all my sins was slain,
Who for me in torments died.

Let me mingle tears with thee,
Mourning Him who mourned for me
All the days that I may live:

By the Cross with thee to stay;
There with thee to weep and pray
Is all I ask of thee to give.

Virgin of all virgins blest!
Listen to my fond request:
Let me share thy grief divine;

Let me, to my latest breath,
In my body bear the death
Of that dying Son of thine.

Wounded with His every wound,
Steep my soul till it hath swooned
In His very Blood away;

Be to me, O Virgin, nigh,
Lest in flames I burn and die,
In His awful Judgment Day.

Christ, when Thou shalt call me hence,
By Thy Mother my defense,
By Thy Cross my victory;

While my body here decays,
May my soul Thy goodness praise,
Safe in Paradise with Thee.

STEPHEN HARDING

The Benedictine *Rule* quickly established itself after the sixth century as the standard by which monastic (and other) rules were judged. Its sensibility, common sense, and practicality made it suitable to a relatively uncomplicated society and social structure which became the norm in Europe for six centuries after the "fall of Rome."

Splendid and practical though the Benedictine *Rule* was, however, monasteries were not always the spiritual communities they were clearly meant to be. How strictly or loosely the *Rule* was interpreted made a great deal of difference. What kind of person the abbot was and how he came to be chosen for his office affected the life of the monastic community and often played a key role in guiding the spiritual and material welfare of its members. Because monasteries were often thriving economic enterprises, secular rulers wished to control them and use their wealth. This was accomplished through rulers usurping the right to choose an abbot for a given monastery. The choice of unworthy abbots for monasteries led to further corruptions of the *Rule,* and thus there arose the need to call monasteries back to the original intent of strict and careful observance of many provisions of the *Rule.*

Noteworthy examples of monastic reform occurred under Charlemagne (768-814) and under the auspices of the monastery of Cluny founded in Burgundy in 910. As almost seemed inevitable, monasteries again became corrupt, and secular interference very prominent in the tenth and eleventh centuries. The new need for reform was answered in part by the foundation of the Cistercians in 1098. Within twenty years the *Charter of Love* was issued as a plan for guiding monasteries in the strict observance of the Benedictine *Rule.* The author of the *Charter of Love* was the second abbot of the monastery of Citeaux, Stephen Harding, who seems to have finished the document *c.* 1117. Firmly grounded in the Benedictine *Rule,* the *Charter of Love* seeks to insure its strict observance in monasteries under the control of the abbot of Citeaux. In the course of the twelfth century the Cistercians became a popular and thriving religious order, fine testimony to the success of this new wave of monastic reform.

One of the consequences of the popularity of the Cistercians was the foundation of hundreds of daughter-houses throughout Europe. Perhaps the most influential of all the Cistercians, Bernard of Clairvaux (1091-1153), was abbot of Clairvaux for over thirty years. Not only did Bernard rule his own monastery, but his influence reached all over Europe. He was one of the most intense opponents of Peter Abelard, the brilliant teacher from Paris, who was so important in shaping the early course of scholasticism. Bernard went all over Europe enjoining, or commanding, a new spirituality.

From Stephen Harding, **The Charter of Love**

Before the Cistercian abbeys began to flourish, the lord abbot, Stephen, and his monks ordained that abbeys were on no account to be established in the diocese of any bishop prior to his ratification and confirmation of the decree drawn up in writing between the abbey of Citeaux and its daughter-houses, in order to avoid occasion of offence between the bishop and the monks. In this decree, therefore, the aforesaid brethren, guarding against possible dangers to their mutual peace, have made clear and established and handed down to later generations in what manner and by what agreement, nay rather, with what love the monks of their Order, though separated in body and abbeys in divers parts of the world, might be knit together inseparably in spirit. Moreover, they were of opinion that this decree should be called the "Charter of Love," because it casts off the burden of all exactions, pursues love alone and promotes the welfare of souls in things human and divine.

I. Inasmuch as we are known to be servants of the One True King, Lord and Master, albeit unprofitable, we therefore make no claim for worldly advantage or temporal gain on our abbots and brother monks, whom in divers places devotion to God shall call through us, the most wretched of men, to live under regular discipline. For, in our desire for their profit and that of all sons of holy Church, we are not disposed to lay any burden upon them or to effect anything calculated to diminish their substance, lest in striving to grow rich at their expense, we may not escape the sin of avarice, which is declared by the apostle to be servitude to idols.

II. Nevertheless we desire for love's sake to retain the cure of their souls, so that if they shall essay to swerve from their sacred purpose and the observance of the holy Rule—which God forbid—they may through our solicitude return to righteousness of life.

III. We will therefore command them to observe the Rule of St. Benedict in all things as it is observed in the new monastery. Let the monks put no other interpretation upon the holy Rule but what the holy fathers, our predecessors, namely the monks of the new minster, have understood and maintained: and as we today understand and uphold it, so let them do also.

IV. And inasmuch as we receive in our cloister all the monks of their houses who come to us, and they likewise receive ours in theirs, so it seems good to us and in accordance with our will that they should maintain the customary ceremonial, chants, and all books necessary for the canonical offices, both by day and by night, and for the Mass, after the form of the customs and books of the new minster, so that there be no discord in our worship, but that we may all dwell in one love and under one rule and with like customs.

V. No church or person of our Order shall presume to solicit from anyone a privilege contrary to the common customs of the Order, or in any wise retain it, if it has been granted.

VI. When the abbot of the new minster shall come on a visitation to one of these houses, let the abbot of the place recognize the church of the new minster as his mother-church and give place to him in all the precincts of the monastery, and let the visiting abbot take the place of the abbot of that house, so long as he remains there.

VII. Except that he shall not take his meals in the guest-room, but in the refectory with the brethren, that discipline may be preserved, unless the abbot of the house be absent. Likewise let it be done in the case of all abbots of our Order who may chance to come on a visit. But if several shall come at the same time, and the abbot of the house be absent, let the abbot senior in rank take his meals in the guest-room. An exception shall also be made that the abbot of the house shall, even when a greater abbot is present, bless his own novices after the regular term or probation.

VIII. But let the abbot of the new minster be careful not to presume in any wise to conduct or order the affairs of the house he is visiting, or meddle in them, against the will of the abbot or the brethren.

IX. But if he learn that the precepts of the Rule or of our Order are transgressed in the said house, let him be diligent to correct the brethren lovingly, and with the advice and in the presence of the abbot. Even if the abbot be absent, he shall nevertheless correct what he has found wrong therein.

X. Once a year let the abbot of the mother-church visit all the houses of his foundation either in person or through one of his co-abbots. And if he shall visit the brethren more often, let them the more rejoice.

XI. Moreover, let the abbey of Citeaux be visited by the four primary abbots, namely of La Ferte, Pontigny, Clairvaux and Morimond, together in person on such a day as they may choose, except that appointed for the holding of the annual chapter, unless perchance one of them be prevented by grievous sickness.

XII. When any abbot of our Order shall come to the new minster, let fitting reverence be shown to him; let him occupy the abbot's stall and take his meals in the guest-room if the abbot be absent. But if the abbot shall be present, let him do none of these things, but let him dine in the refectory. Let the prior of the abbey take charge of its affairs.

XIII. Between abbeys having no direct relationship with each other, this shall be the rule. Let every abbot give place to his co-abbot within the precincts of his monastery, that the saying may be fulfilled, "in honour preferring one another." If two or more abbots shall come to the monastery, the superior in rank shall take precedence of the others. But let them all take their meals together in the refectory, except the abbot of the house, as stated above. But whenever they meet on other occasions, they shall maintain their rank in accordance with the seniority of their abbeys, so that he whose church is of older foundation, shall take precedence of the others.

Whenever they take their seats together, let each humble himself before the others.

XIV. But when any of our churches has by God's grace so increased that it is able to establish a new house, let the two houses maintain the same relationship between them as obtains between us and our brethren, except that they shall not hold an annual chapter among themselves.

XV. But all the abbots of our Order shall without fail attend each year the general chapter at Citeaux, with the sole exception of those detained by bodily infirmity. The latter, however, ought to appoint a suitable delegate, by whom the reason for their absence may be reported to the chapter. An exception may also be made for those who dwell in distant lands; let them attend at the intervals appointed for them in the chapter. But if, and when, on any other occasion any abbott shall presume to absent himself from our general chapter, let him crave pardon for his fault at the chapter held in the following year; let his absence not be passed over without serious attention being paid to it.

XVI. In this general chapter let the abbots take measures for the salvation of their souls, and if anything in the observance of the holy Rule or of the Order ought to be amended or supplemented, let them ordain it and re-establish the bond of peace and charity among themselves.

XVII. But if any abbot be found remiss in keeping the Rule, or too intent upon worldly affairs or in any way corrupt or wicked, let him be charged with the offence in the chapter, albeit in all charity. Let the accused crave pardon and perform the penance laid on him for his fault. Such a charge, however, may not be brought except by an abbot.

XVIII. If perchance any dispute shall arise between certain abbots, or an offence be charged against one of them so grave as to merit suspension or deposition, the decision of the chapter shall be observed without question.

XIX. But if, by reason of a difference of opinion, the case shall result in discord, the judgment of the abbot of Citeaux and of those of sounder and more appropriate counsel shall be inflexibly upheld, precaution being taken that none of those personally involved in the case shall take part in the judgment.

XX. Should any church fall into extreme poverty, let the abbot of that house take pains to inform the whole chapter of the fact. Thereupon the abbots, one and all inflamed with an ardent fire of love, shall hasten to relieve that church from its poverty, so far as they are able, out of resources bestowed upon them by God.

XXI. If any house of our Order become bereft of its abbot, let the abbot of the house from which it sprung, take every care for its governance, until a new abbot shall be elected. Moreover, on the day appointed for the election, let the abbots of the daughter-houses of that house be summoned, and let them and the monks of that house elect an abbot with the advice and assent of the abbot of the mother-house.

XXII. When the house of Citeaux, the mother of us all, shall be bereft of its abbot, let the four primary abbots, namely those of La Ferte, Pontigny, Clairvaux and Morimond, make provision for it, and let the responsibility for the abbey rest upon them, until a new abbot be elected and appointed.

XXIII. A day having been fixed and named for the election of an abbot of Citeaux, let a summons be conveyed with at least fifteen days' notice to the abbots of the houses sprung from Citeaux and to such others as the aforesaid abbots and the monks of Citeaux shall deem suitable and, being assembled in the name of the Lord, let the abbots and the monks of Citeaux elect an abbot.

XXIV. It is permissible for any monk to be raised to the office of abbot of the mother-church of our Order, not only those of her daughter-churches, but also, in case of necessity for their abbots to be free to do so. But no member of another Order may be elected abbot, even as it is not permissible for one of us to be appointed to another monastery which is not of our Order.

XXV. Should any abbot beg leave of his father, the abbot of the house from which his own has sprung, to be relieved of the burden of his office on the pretext of his incapacity or through faint-heartedness, let the father-abbot have a care lest he assent to his request too readily and without a reasonable cause and urgent need. But if the necessity be very great, let the father-abbot do nothing in the matter of his own initiative, but let him summon certain other abbots of our Order and by their advice act in the way they have agreed upon.

XXVI. If any abbot become notorious for contempt of the holy Rule or as a transgressor of the Order or an accessory to the faults of the brethren committed to his charge, let the abbot of the mother-church, either in person or through his prior, or in whatever way is more convenient, exhort him on four occasions to mend his ways. But if he will neither suffer correction nor yield of his own accord, let a sufficient number of the abbots of our congregation be gathered together, and let them remove the transgressor of the holy Rule from his office; after which another more worthy of it may be elected by the monks of that church with the advice and goodwill of the greater abbot and in co-operation with the abbots and those who are related to it, as stated above.

XXVII. But if—which God forbid—the deposed abbot or his monks shall be contumacious and rebellious, and will not acquiesce in the sentence, let them be subject to excommunication by the abbot of the mother-church and his co-abbots, and thereafter coerced by him according as he thinks fit and is able.

XXVIII. Arising out of this, should any one of those so condemned come to himself again and desire to arise from the death of the soul and return to his mother, let him be received as a penitent son. For except for this occasion, which should always be avoided as far as possible, let no abbot retain a monk belonging to any other abbot of our Order without his assent; also let none bring his monks to dwell in the house of any other without his permission.

XXIX. In like manner if—which God forbid—the abbots of our Order shall discover that our mother-church of Citeaux is becoming luke-warm in its sacred purpose, or is departing from the observance of the holy Rule, let them admonish the abbot of that house four times through the four primary abbots, namely those of La Ferte, Pontigny, Clairvaux and Morimond, in the name of the other abbots of the Order, to amend his life and take pains to amend that of others, and let them diligently fulfil in his case the remaining precepts prescribed for the other abbots, when they are intolerant of correction. But if he will not yield of his own accord, they may neither depose him nor condemn him as contumacious, until they come to depose him from his office as an unprofitable steward, either in the general chapter or —if perchance it be already known that the chapter is not due for summons—in another assembly specially convened for the abbots of the daughter-houses of Citeaux and some of the others; whereupon both the said abbots and the monks of Citeaux shall take care to elect a suitable abbot in his place. But if the former abbot and the monks of Citeaux shall contumaciously resist, let them not forbear to strike them with the sword of excommunication.

XXX. Should any such transgressor afterwards come to his senses and, in the desire to save his soul, take refuge in one of our four primary churches, whether at La Ferte, or Pontigny, or Clairvaux, or Morimond, let him be received as an inmate and co-partner in the abbey in accordance with the Rule, until such time as he be justly reconciled with his own church, whereupon he may be restored thither. In the meantime the annual chapter of the abbots shall not be held at Citeaux, but wheresoever the above-named four abbots shall previously have appointed.

FRANCIS OF ASSISI

Francis of Assisi (1182-1226) was in the best sense of the word a thir-teenth-century phenomenon. He is a splendid example of the importance of medieval popular piety. Word of his life and deeds spread rapidly throughout Europe and made him a figure tremendously admired and loved. He was canonized within two years of his death in 1226 partly because he was a legend in his own lifetime.

This lovable, personable character was the son of a prosperous merchant who hoped to make a soldier of his son. Francis, however, was inclined to-ward poetry and song, much to the chagrin of his family, who hoped for better things for him. After a youth spent in leisure and pleasure Francis underwent a conversion. His life changed and acquired a deeply moving spirituality. Francis never lost his love for song which now came to be directed to the all-loving God. Living out the message of the gospel be-came his goal, and he took "Lady Poverty" as his bride. An intense feeling for nature, all living creatures, often filled him with a kind of ecstasy.

After living as a hermit for a time Francis turned to minister to the poor and unfortunate, especially to the lepers, that most despised group in medie-val society. At first Francis was rejected by his friends and even his family. Gradually the situation changed, however, and Francis attracted a great following, numbers so great that the pope had to take notice of Francis and his work. The great Pope Innocent III reluctantly gave his consent to recog-nize the Franciscans as a religious order with its own individual rule.

The eleventh through the thirteenth centuries saw great changes in Europe in many areas of human existence. The growth of towns and trade, the cen-tralization of monarchical authority, the development of institutional intel-lectual life culminating in the university, the great outburst of creative activ-ity in the arts, all combined to have a profound impact on the religious life of Europe. The role of the church was all-encompassing; it was part of all the aforementioned developments and went through its own growing pains. New forms of spirituality were needed to fit the changed conditions of the time. Greater wealth and improved economic conditions combined with the reappearance of a thriving town life for the first time since the fall of Rome made for increased emphasis on material existence. Chivalry and the cult of the "ideal lady" created the institution of courtly love.

Francis of Assisi rebelled against the growing materialism of his time. He achieved great popularity during his lifetime, so much so that he hardly had any other choice than to set down a rule for his followers. He delib-erately rejected the Benedictine *Rule* for himself and his followers. It is an interesting exercise to compare these two great rules.

The devotion of the following attracted by Francis is well-represented by the *Writings of Leo, Rufino, and Angelo,* three of the closest friends of the saint, who contributed reflections on his life and work to a Franciscan collection. Their work deals with Francis's composition of the famous "Canticle of the Sun"—the "Canticle" itself follows.

From St. Francis, **The Rule of St. Francis**

1. This is the Rule and way of life of the brothers minor; to observe the holy Gospel of our Lord Jesus Christ, living in obedience, without personal possessions, and in chastity. Brother Francis promises obedience and reverence to our Lord Pope Honorius, and to his canonical successors, and to the Roman Church. And the other brothers shall be bound to obey brother Francis and his successors.

2. If any wish to adopt this way of life, and shall come to our brothers, they shall send them to their provincial ministers; to whom alone, and to no others, permission is given to receive brothers. And the ministers shall carefully examine them in the Catholic faith and the sacraments of the Church. And if they believe all these, and will confess them faithfully and observe them steadfastly to the end; and if they have no wives, or if they have them and the wives have already entered a convent, or if with permission of the diocesan bishop they shall have given them permission to do so—they themselves having already taken a vow of continence, and their wives being of such age that no suspicion can arise in connection with them: the ministers shall tell them, in the words of the holy Gospel, to go and sell all that they have and carefully give it to the poor. But if they shall not be able to do this, their good will is enough. And the brothers and their ministers shall be careful not to concern themselves about their temporal goods; so that they may freely do with those goods exactly as God inspires them. But if advice is required, the ministers shall be allowed to send them to some God-fearing men by whose counsel they shall dispense their goods to the poor. After that they shall be given the garments of probation: namely two gowns without cowls and a belt, and hose and a cape down to the belt: unless to these same ministers something else may at some time seem to be preferable in the sight of God. And, when the year of probation is over, they shall be received into obedience; promising always to observe this way of life and Rule. And, according to the mandate of the lord pope, they shall never be allowed to break these bonds. For according to the holy Gospel, no one putting his hand to the plow and looking back is fit for the kingdom of God. And those who have now promised obedience shall have one gown with a cowl, and another, if they wish it, without a cowl. And those who really need them may wear shoes. And all the brothers shall wear humble garments, and may repair

them with sack cloth and other remnants, with God's blessing. And I warn and exhort them lest they despise or judge men whom they shall see clad in soft garments and in colors, enjoying delicate food and drink; but each one shall rather judge and despise himself.

3. The clerical brothers shall perform the divine service according to the order of the Holy Roman Church; excepting the psalter, of which they may have extracts. But the lay brothers shall say twenty-four Paternosters at Matins, five at Lauds, seven each at Prime, Terce, Sext and None, twelve at Vespers, seven at the Completorium; and they shall pray for the dead. And they shall fast from the feast of All Saints to the Nativity of the Lord; but as to the holy season of Lent, which begins after the Epiphany of the Lord and continues forty days, a season to the Lord consecrated by his holy fast—those who fast during this time shall be blessed of the Lord, and those who do not wish to fast shall not be bound to do so; but otherwise they shall fast until the Resurrection of the Lord. At other times the brothers shall not be bound to fast save on the sixth day (Friday); but when there is a compelling reason the brothers shall not be bound to observe a physical fast. But I advise, warn and exhort my brothers in the Lord Jesus Christ, that, when they go into the world, they shall not quarrel, nor contend with words, nor judge others. But let them be gentle, peaceable, modest, merciful and humble, with honorable conversation towards all, as is fitting. They ought not to ride, save when necessity or infirmity clearly compels them so to do. Into whatsoever house they enter let them first say, 'Peace be to this house.' And according to the holy Gospel it is lawful for them to partake of all dishes placed before them.

4. I strictly command all the brothers never to receive coin or money either directly or through an intermediary. The ministers and guardians alone shall make provision, through spiritual friends, for the needs of the infirm and for other brothers who need clothing, according to the locality, season or cold climate, at their discretion. . . .

5. Those brothers, to whom God has given the ability to work shall faithfully and devotedly and in such a way that, avoiding idleness, the enemy of the soul, they do not quench the spirit of holy prayer and devotion, to which other and temporal activities should be subordinate. As the wages of their labor they may receive corporal necessities for themselves and their brothers but not coin nor money, and this with humility, as is fitting for servants of God, and followers of holy poverty.

6. The brothers shall possess nothing, neither a house, nor a place, nor anything. But, as pilgrims and strangers in this world, serving God in poverty and humility, they shall confidently seek alms, and not be ashamed, for the Lord made Himself poor in this world for us. This is

the highest degree of that sublime poverty, which has made you, my dearly beloved brethren, heirs and kings of the Kingdom of Heaven; which has made you poor in goods but exalted in virtues. Let this be 'your portion,' which leads you to 'the land of the living' [Ps. cxlii.5]. If you cleave wholly to this, beloved, you will wish to have for ever in Heaven nothing save the name of Our Lord Jesus Christ. Wherever the brethren are, and shall meet together, they shall show themselves as members of one family; each shall with confidence unfold his needs to his brother. A mother loves and cherishes her son in the flesh; how much more eagerly should a man love and cherish his brother in the Spirit? And if any of them fall sick the other brothers are bound to minister to him as they themselves would wish to be ministered to.

7. But if any of the brethren shall commit mortal sin at the prompting of the adversary: in the case of those sins concerning which it has been laid down that recourse must be had to the provincial ministers, the aforesaid brethren must have recourse to them without delay. Those ministers, if they are priests, shall with mercy enjoin penance: if they are not priests they shall cause it to be enjoined through others, who are priests of the order, as it seems to them most expedient in the sight of God. They must beware lest they become angry and disturbed on account of the sin of any brother; for anger and indignation hinder love in ourselves and others.

8. All the brothers shall be bound always to have one of the brothers of the order as minister general and servant of the whole brotherhood, and shall be strictly bound to obey him. On his death the election of a successor shall be made by the provincial ministers and guardians in the chapter at Pentecost, at which the provincial ministers shall always be bound to assemble, wherever the minister general provides, and this once in three years or at a greater or less interval, according as is ordered by the aforesaid minister. And if at any time it shall be clear to the whole body of provincial ministers and guardians that the said minister does not suffice for the service and common advantage of the brethren, it shall be the duty of the said brethren who have the right of election to elect another as their guardian, in the name of God. But after the chapter held at Pentecost the ministers and guardians may (if they so wish and it seem expedient) call together their brethren, in their several districts, to a chapter, once in that same year.

9. The brothers shall not preach in the dioceses of any bishop who has forbidden them to do so. And none of the brothers shall dare to preach at all to the people unless he has been examined and approved by the minister general of this brotherhood and the privilege of preaching has been granted him. I also exhort these same brothers that in all their preaching their language shall be pure and careful, to the advan-

tage and edification of the people; preaching to them of vices and virtues, punishment and glory; and let their discourse be brief; for the words which the Lord spoke upon earth were brief.

10. The brothers who are the ministers and servants of the other brothers shall visit and admonish their brothers and humbly and lovingly correct them; not teaching them anything which is against their conscience and our Rule. But the brothers who are subjected to them shall remember that, before God, they have discarded their own wills. Wherefore I strictly charge them that they obey their ministers in all things which they have promised God to observe, and which are not contrary to their conscience and to our Rule. And wherever there are brothers who are conscious of their inability to observe the Rule in the spirit, they may and should have recourse to their ministers. But the ministers shall receive them lovingly and kindly, and shall exercise such familiarity towards them, that they may speak out and act towards them as masters to their servants; for so it ought to be, that the ministers should be the servants of all the brothers. I warn and exhort, moreover, in Christ Jesus the Lord, that the brothers be on their guard against all pride, vainglory, envy, avarice, care and worldly anxiety, detraction and murmuring. And they shall not be concerned to teach those who are ignorant of letters, but shall take care that they desire to have the spirit of God and its holy workings; that they pray always to God with a pure heart, that they have humility, patience, in persecution and infirmity; and that they love those who persecute, revile and attack us. For the Lord saith: 'Love your enemies, and pray for those that persecute you and speak evil against you; Blessed are they that suffer persecution for righteousness' sake, for of such is the kingdom of Heaven; He that is steadfast unto the end shall be saved.'

11. I strictly charge all the brethren not to hold conversation with women so as to arouse suspicion, nor to take counsel with them. And, with the exception of those to whom special permission has been given by the Apostolic Chair, let them not enter nunneries. Neither may they become fellow godparents with men or women, lest from this cause a scandal may arise among the brethren or concerning brethren.

12. Whoever of the brothers by divine inspiration may wish to go among the Saracens and other infidels, shall seek permission to do so from their provincial ministers. But to none shall the ministers give permission to go, save to those whom they shall see to be fit for the mission.

Furthermore, I charge the ministers on their obedience that they demand from the lord pope one of the cardinals of the Holy Roman Church, who shall be the governor, corrector and protector of the fraternity, so that, always submissive and lying at the feet of that same

Holy Church, steadfast in the Catholic faith, we may observe poverty and humility, and the holy Gospel of our Lord Jesus Christ; **as we** have firmly promised.

St. Francis, **The Song of Brother Sun**

Most High, Almighty, good Lord,
Thine be the praise, the glory, the honour,
And all blessing.

To Thee alone, Most High, are they due,
And no man is worthy
To speak Thy Name.

Praise to Thee, my Lord, for all Thy creatures,
Above all Brother Sun
Who brings us the day and lends us his light.

Lovely is he, radiant with great splendour,
And speaks to us of Thee,
O Most High.

Praise to Thee, my Lord, for Sister Moon and the stars
Which Thou hast set in the heavens,
Clear, precious, and fair.

Praise to Thee, my Lord, for Brother Wind,
For air and cloud, for calm and all weather,
By which Thou supportest life in all Thy creatures.

Praise to Thee, my Lord, for Sister Water,
Who is so useful and humble,
Precious and pure.

Praise to Thee, my Lord, for Brother Fire,
By whom Thou lightest the night;
He is lovely and pleasant, mighty, and strong.

Praise to Thee, my Lord for our sister Mother Earth
Who sustains and directs us,
And brings forth varied fruits, and coloured flowers,
  and plants.

Praise to Thee, my Lord, for those who pardon one another
For love of Thee, and endure
Sickness and tribulation.

Blessed are they who shall endure it in peace,
For they shall be crowned by Thee,
O Most High.

Praise to Thee, my Lord, for our Sister bodily Death
From whom no man living may escape:
Woe to those who die in mortal sin.

Blessed are they who are found in Thy most holy will,
For the second death cannot harm them.

Praise and bless my Lord, Thank Him and serve Him
With great humility.

ANSELM

Anselm (c. 1033-1109) was one of the key figures in the development of scholasticism. Indeed, he is often referred to as the father of scholasticism. Born at Aosta in the kingdom of Burgundy, he came north of the Alps as a young man and spent most of his life in an Anglo-Norman milieu. Many details of his life are known with precision because a personal friend of his, the monk Eadmer, wrote an estimable and often penetrating biography of him. Anselm entered the abbey of Notre Dame at Bec in Normandy where he was professed as a monk and later served as prior and abbot. There were significant stirrings of monastic reform in Anselm's time, and he gave strong support to them both at his own monastery and at others with which he had connections. Anselm was appointed archbishop of Canterbury by the king of England, William Rufus, in 1093, and held the office during a time of considerable tension between the Church and State. As a supporter of the ideals of Pope Gregory VII, Anselm late in life became a champion of ecclesiastical independence from unwarranted secular interference. Shortly after he helped to negotiate a compromise between the English Church and monarchy, Anselm died, worn out by his labors on behalf of right order in the world.

While at the abbey of Bec, Anselm wrote a great variety of works. Even in old age he again took up his pen when he felt compelled to do so. His writings achieved considerable fame in his lifetime and continued to enhance his reputation for a long time after his death. Among his most significant works and prayers and meditations are these: the *Monologion,* a treatise on the existence and essence of God, written at the request of some monks of Bec who wanted everything to be proved by reason and nothing based on scriptural authority; the *Proslogion,* a treatise which contains the famous ontological argument for the existence of God; the *Cur Deus Homo,* his greatest intellectual achievement, in which he sought to demonstrate that Christ's incarnation was a necessary fact of Christian theology; and a splendid series of letters.

One of the most original thinkers of the twelfth, or any century, Anselm asserted that the more human beings understood their faith, the closer they drew to the sight of God. One phrase from Anselm relating faith to reason is an important summary of his outlook: *credo ut intelligam*—I believe in order that I may understand. This formula was adopted by most of the scholastics who followed Anselm. Thus reason had a role complementary to that of faith. Accepting on faith those matters required by the church, the Christians could then seek to establish a rational basis for this faith. Quite simply put, faith sought understanding. Anselm was the first to attempt a thoroughly logical system of theology and in brilliant fashion launched scholasticism, the methodology of the schools.

From St. Anselm, **Cur Deus Homo**
BOOK SECOND
CHAPTER I

How man was made holy by God, so as to be happy in the enjoyment of God.

Anselm. It ought not to be disputed that rational nature was made holy by God, in order to be happy in enjoying Him. For to this end is it rational, in order to discern justice and injustice, good and evil, and between the greater and the lesser good. Otherwise it was made rational in vain. But God made it not rational in vain. Wherefore, doubtless, it was made rational for this end. In like manner is it proved that the intelligent creature received the power of discernment, since man's discretion would be useless unless he loved and avoided according to it. But it does not befit God to give such power in vain. It is, therefore, established that rational nature was created for this end, viz., to love and choose the highest good supremely, for its own sake and nothing else; for if the highest good were chosen for any other reason, then something else and not itself would be the thing loved. But intelligent nature cannot fulfil this purpose without being holy. Therefore that it might not in vain be made rational, it was made, in order to fulfil this purpose, both rational and holy. Now, if it was made holy in order to choose and love the highest good, then it was made such in order to follow sometimes what it loved and chose, or else it was not. But if it were not made holy for this end, that it might follow what it loves and chooses then in vain was it made to love and choose holiness; and there can be no reason why it should be ever bound to follow holiness. Therefore, as long as it will be holy in loving and choosing the supreme good, for which it was made, it will be miserable; because it will be impotent despite of its will, inasmuch as it does not have what it desires. But this is utterly absurd. Wherefore rational nature was made holy, in order to be happy in enjoying the supreme good, which is God. Therefore man, whose nature is rational, was made holy for this end, that he might be happy in enjoying God.

THOMAS AQUINAS

Thomas Aquinas (1225-1274) has long been recognized as the greatest of the scholastic thinkers. It is necessary, however, to see his achievement against the background of a long series of important developments. The originality of Anselm's writings, the provocative quality of Abelard's work, the labors of countless translators in recovering the lost heritage of Aristotle, and the development of the university as an institution of higher learning lie behind what Aquinas was able to achieve.

Born near Aquino, Italy, of noble parents, Thomas was educated by the monks of Monte Cassino. He attended the University of Naples and then moved on to study at the University of Paris where he met the impressive Dominican scholar, Albert the Great. Like his teacher, Aquinas became a Dominican and achieved fame for his order as well as for himself. Large of girth and reticent of manner, Thomas, as a student, was referred to as the "Dumb Ox." Shy, humble, and generous throughout his life, Aquinas became an outstanding teacher at the University of Paris and thereby enhanced its reputation as a center of learning. Though sought after by popes and kings, Thomas was not altogether comfortable in their company. He was the quintessential scholar and loved learning for its own sake in the best tradition of the liberal arts. Not yet 50 years old, Thomas died on his way to attend the church council at Lyons in 1274.

Many, including atheists and agnostics, have commented on the subtlety and brilliance of Aquinas' intellect. He was able to use effectively what was available in the tradition of scholasticism before him. Among Thomas' prolific writings perhaps the best and most important were the *Summa Theologiae*, a classic synthesis of Christian thought, and the *Summa Contra*

Gentiles, in which Thomas attempted to lead nonbelievers by the path of reason to the point of being able to make an act of faith. The *Summa Theologiae,* which remained unfinished at Thomas' death, was an exhaustive treatment of such topics as God and his attributes, creation and creatures, pure spirits and corporeal beings, man and his end, human acts, habits and virtues, sins and vices, law and grace, theological and cardinal virtues, redemption and salvation through Christ, the sacraments, and immortal life.

Aquinas owed a great debt to Aristotle. He took from Aristotle those elements which could be absorbed into Christian thought. He fitted Aristotle to Christianity. In his approach, Thomas was both orthodox and scholarly. Throughout his work, Aquinas employed scholastic method, and reason played an important part. He took care to distinguish between the proofs of faith and those of reason and in so doing delineated two separate disciplines: theology and philosophy. The feature that is most characteristically Aristotelian about Thomas is his insistence that much of human knowledge comes by way of experience. This view was contrary to the Platonic-Augustinian view of knowledge, which was the main intellectual current before Thomas, and its impact was revolutionary.

From Thomas Aquinas, **Summa Contra Gentiles**

BOOK I

CHAPTER 1.

The Office of the Wise Man

"My mouth shall meditate truth, and my lips shall hate impiety"
(Prov. 8:7).

(1) The usage of the multitude, which according to the Philosopher is to be followed in giving names to things, has commonly held that they are to be called wise who order things rightly and govern them well. Hence, among other things that men have conceived about the wise man, the Philosopher includes the notion that "it belongs to the wise man to order." Now, the rule of government and order for all things directed to an end must be taken from the end. For, since the end of each thing is its good, a thing is then best disposed when it is fittingly ordered to its end. And so we see among the arts that one functions as the governor and the ruler of another because it controls its end. Thus, the art of medicine rules and orders the art of the chemist because health, with which medicine is concerned, is the end of all the medications prepared by the art of the chemist. A similar situation obtains in the art of ship navigation in relation to shipbuilding, and in the military art with respect to the equestrian

art and the equipment of war. The arts that rule other arts are called architectonic, as being the ruling arts. That is why the artisans devoted to these arts, who are called master artisans, appropriate to themselves the name of wise men. But, since these artisans are concerned, in each case, with the ends of certain particular things, they do not reach to the universal end of all things. They are therefore said to be wise with respect to this or that thing; in which sense it is said that "as a wise architect, I have laid the foundation" (I Cor. 3:10). The name of the absolutely wise man, however, is reserved for him whose consideration is directed to the end of the universe, which is also the origin of the universe. That is why, according to the Philosopher, it belongs to the wise man to consider the highest causes.

(2) Now, the end of each thing is that which is intended by its first author or mover. But the first author and mover of the universe is an intellect, as will be later shown. The ultimate end of the universe must, therefore, be the good of an intellect. This good is truth. Truth must consequently be the ultimate end of the whole universe, and the consideration of the wise man aims principally at truth. So it is that, according to His own statement, divine Wisdom testifies that He has assumed flesh and come into the world in order to make the truth known: "For this was I born, and for this came I into the world, that I should give testimony to the truth" (John 18:37). The Philosopher himself establishes that first philosophy is the science of truth, not of any truth, but of that truth which is the origin of all truth, namely, which belongs to the first principle whereby all things are. The truth belonging to such a principle is, clearly, the source of all truth; for things have the same disposition in truth as in being.

(3) It belongs to one and the same science, however, both to pursue one of two contraries and to oppose the other. Medicine, for example, seeks to effect health and to eliminate illness. Hence, just as it belongs to the wise man to meditate especially on the truth belonging to the first principle and to teach it to others, so it belongs to him to refute the opposing falsehood.

(4) Appropriately, therefore, is the twofold office of the wise man shown from the mouth of Wisdom in our opening words: to meditate and speak forth of the divine truth, which is truth in person (Wisdom touches on this in the words *my mouth shall meditate truth*), and to refute the opposing error (which Wisdom touches on in the words *and my lips shall hate impiety*). By impiety is here meant falsehood against the divine truth. This falsehood is contrary to religion, which is likewise named piety. Hence, the falsehood contrary to it is called impiety.

CHAPTER 2

The Author's Intention in the Present Work

(1) Among all human pursuits, the pursuit of wisdom is more perfect, more noble, more useful, and more full of joy.

It is more perfect because, in so far as a man gives himself to the pursuit of wisdom, so far does he even now have some share in true beatitude. And so a wise man has said: "Blessed is the man that shall continue in wisdom" (Ecclus. 14:22).

It is more noble because through this pursuit man especially approaches to a likeness to God Who "made all things in wisdom" (Ps. 103:24). And since likeness is the cause of love, the pursuit of wisdom especially joins man to God in friendship. That is why it is said of wisdom that "she is an infinite treasure to men! which they that use become the friends of God" (Wis. 7:14).

It is more useful because through wisdom we arrive at the kingdom of immortality. For "the desire of wisdom bringeth to the everlasting kingdom" (Wis. 6:21).

It is more full of joy because "her conversation hath no bitterness, nor her company any tediousness, but joy and gladness" (Wis. 7:16).

(2) And so, in the name of the divine Mercy, I have the confidence to embark upon the work of a wise man, even though this may surpass my powers, and I have set myself the task of making known, as far as my limited powers will allow, the truth that the Catholic faith professes, and of setting aside the errors that are opposed to it. To use the words of Hilary: "I am aware that I owe this to God as the chief duty of my life, that my every word and sense may speak of Him."

(3) To proceed against individual errors, however, is a difficult business, and this for two reasons. In the first place, it is difficult because the sacrilegious remarks of individual men who have erred are not so well known to us so that we may use what they say as the basis of proceeding to a refutation of their errors. This is, indeed, the method that the ancient Doctors of the Church used in the refutation of the errors of the Gentiles. For they could know the positions taken by the Gentiles since they themselves had been Gentiles, or at least had lived among the Gentiles and had been instructed in their teaching. In the second place, it is difficult because some of them, such as the Mohammedans and the pagans, do not agree with us in accepting the authority of any Scripture, by which they may be convinced of their error. Thus, against the Jews we are able to argue by means of the Old Testament, while against heretics we are able to argue by means of the New Testament. But the Mohammedans and the pagans accept neither the one nor the other. We must, therefore,

have recourse to the natural reason, to which all men are forced to give their assent. However, it is true, in divine matters the natural reason has its failings.

(4) Now, while we are investigating some given truth, we shall also show what errors are set aside by it; and we shall likewise show how the truth that we come to know by demonstration is in accord with the Christian religion.

CHAPTER 3

On the Way in Which Divine Truth Is to Be Made Known

(1) The way of making truth known is not always the same, and, as the Philosopher has very well said, "it belongs to an educated man to seek such certitude in each thing as the nature of that thing allows." The remark is also introduced by Boethius. But, since such is the case, we must first show what way is open to us in order that we may make known the truth which is our object.

(2) There is a twofold mode of truth in what we profess about God. Some truths about God exceed all the ability of the human reason. Such is the truth that God is triune. But there are some truths which the natural reason also is able to reach. Such are that God exists, that He is one, and the like. In fact, such truths about God have been proved demonstratively by the philosophers, guided by the light of the natural reason.

(3) That there are certain truths about God that totally surpass man's ability appears with the greatest evidence. Since, indeed, the principle of all knowledge that the reason perceives about some thing is the understanding of the very substance of that being (for according to Aristotle "what a thing is" is the principle of demonstration), it is necessary that the way in which we understand the substance of a thing determines the way in which we know what belongs to it. Hence, if the human intellect comprehends the substance of some thing, for example, that of a stone or of a triangle, no intelligible characteristic belonging to that thing surpasses the grasp of the human reason. But this does not happen to us in the case of God. For the human intellect is not able to reach a comprehension of the divine substance through its natural power. For, according to its manner of knowing in the present life, the intellect depends on the sense for the origin of knowledge; and so those things that do not fall under the senses cannot be grasped by the human intellect except in so far as the knowledge of them is gathered from sensible things. Now, sensible things cannot lead the human intellect to the point of seeing in them the nature of the divine substance; for sensible things

are effects that fall short of the power of their cause. Yet, beginning with sensible things, our intellect is led to the point of knowing about God that He exists, and other such characteristics that must be attributed to the First Principle. There are, consequently, some intelligible truths about God that are open to the human reason; but there are others that absolutely surpass its power.

(4) We may easily see the same point from the gradation of intellects. Consider the case of two persons of whom one has a more penetrating grasp of a thing by his intellect than does the other. He who has the superior intellect understands many things that the other cannot grasp at all. Such is the case with a very simple person who cannot at all grasp the subtle speculations of philosophy. But the intellect of an angel surpasses the human intellect much more than the intellect of the greatest philosopher surpasses the intellect of the most uncultivated simple person; for the distance between the best philosopher and a simple person is contained within the limits of the human species, which the angelic intellect surpasses. For the angel knows God on the basis of a more noble effect than does man; and this by as much as the substance of an angel, through which the angel in his natural knowledge is led to the knowledge of God, is nobler than sensible things and even than the soul itself, through which the human intellect mounts to the knowledge of God. The divine intellect surpasses the angelic intellect much more than the angelic surpasses the human. For the divine intellect is in its capacity equal to its substance, and therefore it understands fully what it is, including all its intelligible attributes. But by his natural knowledge the angel does not know what God is, since the substance itself of the angel, through which he is led to the knowledge of God, is an effect that is not equal to the power of its cause. Hence the angel is not able, by means of his natural knowledge, to grasp all the things that God understands in Himself; nor is the human reason sufficient to grasp all the things that the angel understands through his own natural power. Just as, therefore, it would be the height of folly for a simple person to assert that what a philosopher proposes is false on the ground that he himself cannot understand it, so (and even more so) it is the acme of stupidity for a man to suspect as false what is divinely revealed through the ministry of the angels simply because it cannot be investigated by reason.

(5) The same thing, moreover, appears quite clearly from the defect that we experience every day in our knowledge of things. We do not know a great many of the properties of sensible things, and in most cases we are not able to discover fully the natures of those properties that we apprehend by the senses. Much more it is the case, therefore,

that the human reason is not equal to the task of investigating all the intelligible characteristics of that most excellent substance.

(6) The remark of Aristotle likewise agrees with this conclusion. He says that "our intellect is related to the prime beings, which are most evident in their nature, as the eye of an owl is related to the sun."

(7) Sacred Scripture also gives testimony to this truth. We read in Job: "Peradventure thou wilt comprehend the steps of God, and wilt find out the Almighty perfectly?" (11:7). And again: "Behold, God is great, exceeding our knowledge" (Job 36:26). And St. Paul: "We know in part" (I Cor. 13:9).

(8) We should not, therefore, immediately reject as false, following the opinion of the Manicheans and many unbelievers, everything that is said about God even though it cannot be investigated by reason.

CHAPTER 4

That the Truth About God to Which the Natural Reason
Reaches Is Fittingly Proposed to Men for Belief

(1) Since, therefore, there exists a twofold truth concerning the divine being, one to which the inquiry of the reason can reach, the other which surpasses the whole ability of the human reason, it is fitting that both of these truths be proposed to man divinely for belief. This point must first be shown concerning the truth that is open to the inquiry of the reason; otherwise, it might perhaps seem to someone that, since such a truth can be known by the reason, it was uselessly given to men through a supernatural inspiration as an object of belief.

(2) Yet, if this truth were left solely as a matter of inquiry for the human reason, three awkward consequences would follow.

(3) The first is that few men would possess the knowledge of God. For there are three reasons why most men are cut off from the fruit of diligent inquiry which is the discovery of truth. Some do not have the physical disposition for such work. As a result, there are many who are naturally not fitted to pursue knowledge; and so, however much they tried, they would be unable to reach the highest level of human knowledge which consists in knowing God. Others are cut off from pursuing this truth by the necessities imposed upon them by their daily lives. For some men must devote themselves to taking care of temporal matters. Such men would not be able to give so much time to the leisure of contemplative inquiry as to reach the highest peak at which human investigation can arrive, namely, the knowledge of God. Finally, there are some who are cut off by indolence. In order to know the things that the reason can investigate concerning God, a

knowledge of many things must already be possessed. For almost all of philosophy is directed towards the knowledge of God, and that is why metaphysics, which deals with divine things, is the last part of philosophy to be learned. This means that we are able to arrive at the inquiry concerning the aforementioned truth only on the basis of a great deal of labor spent in study. Now, those who wish to undergo such a labor for the mere love of knowledge are few, even though God has inserted into the minds of men a natural appetite for knowledge.

(4) The second awkward effect is that those who would come to discover the abovementioned truth would barely reach it after a great deal of time. The reasons are several. There is the profundity of this truth, which the human intellect is made capable of grasping by natural inquiry only after a long training. Then, there are many things that must be presupposed, as we have said. There is also the fact that, in youth, when the soul is swayed by the various movements of the passions, it is not in a suitable state for the knowledge of such lofty truth. On the contrary, "one becomes wise and knowing in repose," as it is said in the *Physics*. The result is this. If the only way open to us for the knowledge of God were solely that of the reason, the human race would remain in the blackest shadows of ignorance. For then the knowledge of God, which especially renders men perfect and good, would come to be possessed only by a few, and these few would require a great deal of time in order to reach it.

(5) The third awkward effect is this. The investigation of the human reason for the most part has falsity present within it, and this is due partly to the weakness of our intellect in judgment, and partly to the admixture of images. The result is that many, remaining ignorant of the power of demonstration, would hold in doubt those things that have been most truly demonstrated. This would be particularly the case since they see that, among those who are reputed to be wise men, each one teaches his own brand of doctrine. Furthermore, with the many truths that are demonstrated, there sometimes is mingled something that is false, which is not demonstrated but rather asserted on the basis of some probable or sophistical argument, which yet has the credit of being a demonstration. That is why it was necessary that the unshakeable certitude and pure truth concerning divine things should be presented to men by way of faith.

(6) Beneficially, therefore, did the divine Mercy provide that it should instruct us to hold by faith even those truths that the human reason is able to investigate. In this way, all men would easily be able to have a share in the knowledge of God, and this without uncertainty of error.

(7) Hence it is written: "Henceforward you walk not as also the Gentiles walk in the vanity of their mind, having their understanding darkened" (Eph. 4:17-18). And again: "All thy children shall be taught of the Lord" (Isa. 54:13).

CHAPTER 5

That the Truths the Human Reason Is Not Able to Investigate Are Fittingly Proposed to Men for Belief

(1) Now, perhaps some will think that men should not be asked to believe what the reason is not adequate to investigate, since the divine Wisdom provides in the case of each thing according to the mode of its nature. We must therefore prove that it is necessary for man to receive from God as objects of belief even those truths that are above the human reason.

(2) No one tends with desire and zeal towards something that is not already known to him. But, as we shall examine later on in this work, men are ordained by the divine Providence towards a higher good than human fragility can experience in the present life. That is why it was necessary for the human mind to be called to something higher than the human reason here and now can reach, so that it would thus learn to desire something and with zeal tend towards something that surpasses the whole state of the present life. This belongs especially to the Christian religion, which in a unique way promises spiritual and eternal goods. And so there are many things proposed to men in it that transcend human sense. The Old Law, on the other hand, whose promises were of a temporal character, contained very few proposals that transcended the inquiry of the human reason. Following this same direction, the philosophers themselves, in order that they might lead men from the pleasure of sensible things to virtue, were concerned to show that there were in existence other goods of a higher nature than these things of sense, and that those who gave themselves to the active or contemplative virtues would find much sweeter enjoyment in the taste of these higher goods.

(3) It is also necessary that such truth be proposed to men for belief so that they may have a truer knowledge of God. For then only do we know God truly when we believe Him to be above everything that it is possible for man to think about Him; for, as we have shown, the divine substance surpasses the natural knowledge of which man is capable. Hence, by the fact that some things about God are proposed to man that surpass his reason, there is strengthened in man the view that God is something above what he can think.

(4) Another benefit that comes from the revelation to men of

truths that exceed the reason is the curbing of presumption, which is the mother of error. For there are some who have such a presumptuous opinion of their own ability that they deem themselves able to measure the nature of everything; I mean to say that, in their estimation, everything is true that seems to them so, and everything is false that does not. So that the human mind, therefore, might be freed from this presumption and come to a humble inquiry after truth, it was necessary that some things should be proposed to man by God that would completely surpass his intellect.

(5) A still further benefit may also be seen in what Aristotle says in the *Ethics*. There was a certain Simonides who exhorted people to put aside the knowledge of divine things and to apply their talents to human occupations. He said that "he who is a man should know human things, and he who is mortal, things that are mortal." Against Simonides Aristotle says that "man should draw himself towards what is immortal and divine as much as he can." And so he says in the *De animalibus* that, although what we know of the higher substances is very little, yet that little is loved and desired more than all the knowledge that we have about less noble substances. He also says in the *De caelo et mundo* that when questions about the heavenly bodies can be given even a modest and merely plausible solution, he who hears this experiences intense joy. From all these considerations it is clear that even the most imperfect knowledge about the most noble realities brings the greatest perfection to the soul. Therefore, although the human reason cannot grasp fully the truths that are above it, yet, if it somehow holds these truths at least by faith, it acquires great perfection for itself.

(6) Therefore it is written: "For many things are shown to thee above the understanding of men" (Ecclus. 3:25). Again: "So the things that are of God no man knoweth but the Spirit of God. But to us God hath revealed them by His Spirit" (I Cor. 2:11, 10).

CHAPTER 6

That to Give Assent to the Truths of Faith Is Not Foolishness Even Though They Are Above Reason

(1) Those who place their faith in this truth, however, "for which the human reason offers no experimental evidence," do not believe foolishly, as though "following artificial fables" (II Peter 1:16). For these "secrets of divine Wisdom" (Job 11:6) the divine Wisdom itself, which knows all things to the full, has deigned to reveal to men. It reveals its own presence, as well as the truth of its teaching and inspiration, by fitting arguments; and in order to confirm those truths

that exceed natural knowledge, it gives visible manifestation to works
that surpass the ability of all nature. Thus, there are the wonderful
cures of illnesses, there is the raising of the dead, and the wonderful
immutation in the heavenly bodies; and what is more wonderful,
there is the inspiration given to human minds, so that simple and
untutored persons, filled with the gift of the Holy Spirit, come to
possess instantaneously the highest wisdom and the readiest eloquence. When these arguments were examined, through the efficacy
of the abovementioned proof, and not the violent assault of arms or
the promise of pleasures, and (what is most wonderful of all) in the
midst of the tyranny of the persecutors, an innumerable throng of
people, both simple and most learned, flocked to the Christian faith.
In this faith there are truths preached that surpass every human intellect; the pleasures of the flesh are curbed; it is taught that the
things of the world should be spurned. Now, for the minds of mortal
men to assent to these things is the greatest of miracles, just as it is a
manifest work of divine inspiration that, spurning visible things, men
should seek only what is invisible. Now, that this has happened
neither without preparation nor by chance, but as a result of the disposition of God, is clear from the fact that through many pronouncements of the ancient prophets God had foretold that He would do
this. The books of these prophets are held in veneration among us
Christians, since they give witness to our faith.

(2) The manner of this confirmation is touched on by St. Paul:
"Which," that is, human salvation, "having begun to be declared by
the Lord, was confirmed unto us by them that hear Him: God also
bearing them witness of signs, and wonders, and divers miracles, and
distributions of the Holy Ghost" (Heb. 2:3-4).

(3) This wonderful conversion of the world to the Christian faith
is the clearest witness of the signs given in the past; so that it is not
necessary that they should be further repeated, since they appear
most clearly in their effect. For it would be truly more wonderful
than all signs if the world had been led by simple and humble men
to believe such lofty truths, to accomplish such difficult actions, and
to have such high hopes. Yet it is also a fact that, even in our own
time, God does not cease to work miracles through His saints for the
confirmation of the faith.

(4) On the other hand, those who founded sects committed to
erroneous doctrines proceeded in a way that is opposite to this. The
point is clear in the case of Mohammed. He seduced the people by
promises of carnal pleasure to which the concupiscence of the flesh
goads us. His teaching also contained precepts that were in conformity with his promises, and he gave free rein to carnal pleasure. In all

this, as is not unexpected, he was obeyed by carnal men. As for proofs of the truth of his doctrine, he brought forward only such as could be grasped by the natural ability of anyone with a very modest wisdom. Indeed, the truths that he taught he mingled with many fables and with doctrines of the greatest falsity. He did not bring forth any signs produced in a supernatural way, which alone fittingly gives witness to divine inspiration; for a visible action that can be only divine reveals an invisibly inspired teacher of truth. On the contrary, Mohammed said that he was sent in the power of his arms—which are signs not lacking even to robbers and tyrants. What is more, no wise men, men trained in things divine and human, believed in him from the beginning. Those who believed in him were brutal men and desert wanderers, utterly ignorant of all divine teaching, through whose numbers Mohammed forced others to become his followers by the violence of his arms. Nor do divine pronouncements on the part of preceding prophets offer him any witness. On the contrary, he perverts almost all the testimonies of the Old and New Testaments by making them into fabrications of his own, as can be seen by anyone who examines his law. It was, therefore, a shrewd decision on his part to forbid his followers to read the Old and New Testaments, lest these books convict him of falsity. It is thus clear that those who place any faith in his words believe foolishly.

CHAPTER 7

That the Truth of Reason Is Not Opposed to the Truth of the Christian Faith

(1) Now, although the truth of the Christian faith which we have discussed surpasses the capacity of the reason, nevertheless that truth that the human reason is naturally endowed to know cannot be opposed to the truth of the Christian faith. For that with which the human reason is naturally endowed is clearly most true; so much so, that it is impossible for us to think of such truths as false. Nor is it permissible to believe as false that which we hold by faith, since this is confirmed in a way that is so clearly divine. Since, therefore, only the false is opposed to the true, as is clearly evident from an examination of their definitions, it is impossible that the truth of faith should be opposed to those principles that the human reason knows naturally.

(2) Furthermore, that which is introduced into the soul of the student by the teacher is contained in the knowledge of the teacher—unless his teaching is fictitious, which it is improper to say of God. Now, the knowledge of the principles that are known to us naturally has been implanted in us by God; for God is the Author of our nature.

These principles, therefore, are also contained by the divine Wisdom. Hence, whatever is opposed to them is opposed to the divine Wisdom, and, therefore, cannot come from God. That which we hold by faith as divinely revealed, therefore, cannot be contrary to our natural knowledge.

(3) Again. In the presence of contrary arguments our intellect is chained, so that it cannot proceed to the knowledge of the truth. If, therefore, contrary knowledges were implanted in us by God, our intellect would be hindered from knowing truth by this very fact. Now, such an effect cannot come from God.

(4) And again. What is natural cannot change as long as nature does not. Now, it is impossible that contrary opinions should exist in the same knowing subject at the same time. No opinion of belief, therefore, is implanted in man by God which is contrary to man's natural knowledge.

(5) Therefore, the Apostle says: "The word is nigh thee, even in thy mouth and in thy heart. This is the word of faith, which we preach" (Rom. 10:8). But because it overcomes reason, there are some who think that it is opposed to it: which is impossible.

(6) The authority of St. Augustine also agrees with this. He writes as follows: "That which truth will reveal cannot in any way be opposed to the sacred books of the Old and the New Testament."

(7) From this we evidently gather the following conclusion: whatever arguments are brought forward against the doctrines of faith are conclusions incorrectly derived from the first and self-evident principles imbedded in nature. Such conclusions do not have the force of demonstration; they are arguments that are either probable or sophistical. And so, there exists the possibility to answer them.

CHAPTER 8

How the Human Reason Is Related to the Truth of Faith

(1) There is also a further consideration. Sensible things, from which the human reason takes the origin of its knowledge, retain within themselves some sort of trace of a likeness to God. This is so imperfect, however, that it is absolutely inadequate to manifest the substance of God. For effects bear within themselves, in their own way, the likeness of their causes, since an agent produces its like; yet an effect does not always reach to the full likeness of its cause. Now, the human reason is related to the knowledge of the truth of faith (a truth which can be most evident only to those who see the divine substance) in such a way that it can gather certain likenesses of it, which are yet not sufficient so that the truth of faith may be comprehended

as being understood demonstratively or through itself. Yet it is useful for the human reason to exercise itself in such arguments, however weak they may be, provided only that there be present no presumption to comprehend or to demonstrate. For to be able to see something of the loftiest realities, however thin and weak the sight, may be, as our previous remarks indicate, a cause of the greatest joy.

(2) The testimony of Hilary agrees with this. Speaking of this same truth, he writes as follows in his *De Trinitate:* "Enter these truths by believing, press forward, persevere. And though I may know that you will not arrive at an end, yet I will congratulate you in your progress. For, though he who pursues the infinite with reverence will never finally reach the end, yet he will always progress by pressing onward. But do not intrude yourself into the divine secret, do not, presuming to comprehend the sum total of intelligence, plunge yourself into the mystery of the unending nativity; rather, understand that these things are incomprehensible."

CHAPTER 9

The Order and Manner of Procedure in the Present Work

(1) It is clearly apparent, from what has been said, that the intention of the wise man ought to be directed toward the twofold truth of divine things, and toward the destruction of the errors that are contrary to this truth. One kind of divine truth the investigation of the reason is competent to reach, whereas the other surpasses every effort of the reason. I am speaking of a "twofold truth of divine things," not on the part of God himself, Who is truth one and simple, but from the point of view of our knowledge, which is variously related to the knowledge of divine things.

(2) Now, to make the first kind of divine truth known, we must proceed through demonstrative arguments, by which our adversary may become convinced. However, since such arguments are not available for the second kind of divine truth, our intention should not be to convince our adversary by arguments: it should be to answer his arguments against the truth; for, as we have shown, the natural reason cannot be contrary to the truth of faith. The sole way to overcome an adversary of divine truth is from the authority of Scripture—an authority divinely confirmed by miracles. For that which is above the human reason we believe only because God has revealed it. Nevertheless, there are certain likely arguments that should be brought forth in order to make divine truth known. This should be done for the training and consolation of the faithful, and not with any idea of refuting those who are adversaries. For the very inade-

quacy of the arguments would rather strengthen them in their error, since they would imagine that our acceptance of the truth of faith was based on such weak arguments.

(3) This, then, is the manner of procedure we intend to follow. We shall first seek to make known that truth which faith professes and reason investigates. This we shall do by bringing forward both demonstrative and probable arguments, some of which were drawn from the books of the philosophers and of the saints, through which truth is strengthened and adversary overcome. Then, in order to follow a development from the more manifest to the less manifest, we shall proceed to make known that truth which surpasses reason, answering the objections of its adversaries and setting forth the truth of faith by probable arguments and by authorities, to the best of our ability.

(4) We are aiming, then, to set out following the way of the reason and to inquire into what the human reason can investigate about God. In this aim the first consideration that confronts us is of that which belongs to God in Himself. The second consideration concerns the coming forth of creatures from God. The third concerns the ordering of creatures to God as to their end.

(5) Now, among the inquiries that we must undertake concerning God in Himself, we must set down in the beginning that whereby His Existence is demonstrated, as the necessary foundation of the whole work. For, if we do not demonstrate that God exists, all consideration of divine things is necessarily suppressed.

DANTE ALIGHIERI

Dante Alighieri (1265-1321) was born into a family that had been influential in the politics of Florence for generations. His own involvement in politics was to bring about his exile from his native city. Forced to wander from city to city in Italy, Dante directed his creative energies to writing; he was an important Latin writer and an incomparable writer in the vernacular, Italian.

In addition to the political experiences in Florence which shaped his life and outlook, two individuals made a profound impression upon Dante. One was the lady Beatrice whom Dante met, but never courted or married. She married another man and died at the young age of 24. For Dante, Beatrice was the very embodiment of chaste love and in his greatest work, the *Divine Comedy*, she is used as a symbol of God's grace and serves as Dante's guide in Paradise.

The other important individual for Dante and his work was the Holy

Roman Emperor, Henry VII. It was Dante's fond hope that the Holy Roman Emperor might restore peace to a wartorn Italy.

Dante was forced out of Florence in 1302. While in exile, he wrote *De Monarchia* against the claims of the Roman papacy to temporal political power. *De Monarchia* remains one of the great statements of the Christian dream of human universalism.

Dante thought the coming of peace after 1310 might make possible his return to his beloved Florence. What Dante hoped for from Henry VII did not come to pass and his exile from the city of his birth continued. He never again returned. Though his life was marked by bitterness and disappointment, Dante remained a man of hope and compassion.

Dante's greatest work—some have called it the greatest of all poems—is the *Divine Comedy*. It achieved "divine" status only after Dante's death. The poem contains 100 cantos of verse and is the journey of a soul from spiritual misery to blessed bliss. It is called *Comedy*, not because it is humorous, but simply because the story has a happy ending. The journey takes Dante (the soul) from *Inferno* (hell) to *Purgatorio* (purgatory) and thence to *Paradiso* (paradise). Dante aimed to show how and why God punishes those who insist upon having their own way and how God rewards those who choose to do his will. Canto I of *Paradiso* gives an indication of Dante's sentiments about his poetic calling, the guidance he receives from Beatrice, the universe and its order, and man's role in the universe.

From Dante Alighieri, **De Monarchia**
BOOK ONE
III

Therefore let us see what is the ultimate end of human society as a whole; once that is grasped our task is more than half accomplished, as the Philosopher says in the *Nicomachean Ethics*.

In order to clarify the issue it may be noted that nature forms the thumb for one end and the whole hand for another, and the arm for yet another, whilst each of these ends is different from that of the family community; the village has one end, the city another and the kingdom yet another; and last of all there is the end that the eternal God has established for the whole human race by means of nature, which is the mode of his art. It is this last-mentioned end that we are looking for and that will be the guiding principle in our inquiry.

The first point to realize is that 'God and nature never do anything in vain', for whatever is brought into existence has some purpose to serve. Yet it is not the being of any creature but its proper function that is the ultimate end of the Creator in creating, and so the proper function is not instituted for the sake of the creature but the latter is created to serve its proper function. From this it follows that there must be some particular function proper to the human species as whole and for which the whole species in its multitudinous variety was created; this function is beyond the capacity of any one man or household or village, or even of any one city or kingdom. What this function is will become clear once the specific capacity of mankind as a whole is evident.

I say therefore that no property that is common to beings of different species represents the specific capacity of any one of them; because, since its ultimate capacity is what constitutes each species, it would follow that one being would be specifically constituted by several specifying factors—which is impossible. And so the specific capacity of man does not consist simply in being, since the very elements also share in being: nor does it consist in *compound being,* for this is also found in the minerals; nor in *animate being,* which the plants also enjoy; nor in the capacity to apprehend things, for this is shared by brute animals, but it consists in the capacity to apprehend by means of the *possible intellect,* and it is this that sets man apart both from inferior and from superior beings. For although there are other beings endowed with the intellect, their intellect is not *possible* like that of man, since such things are completely intellectual; in them intellect and being coincide, and their very *raison d'etre is* to perform intellectual operations without pause, otherwise they would not be eternal. From which it is evident that the specific capacity of mankind is an intellectual capacity or potentiality. And because that potentiality cannot wholly and at once be translated into action by one man, or by any one of the particular communities listed above, mankind has to be composed of a multitude through which this entire potentiality can be actualized. Similarly there needs to be a multitude of things which can be generated from prime matter if the entire potency of that matter is to be brought into action all the time. The alternative is for potentiality to exist separately; this is impossible. Averroes agrees with this opinion in his commentary on the *De Anima.*

This intellectual power of which I am speaking not only deals with universal forms or species but also extends to particulars. Hence it is commonly said that the speculative intellect becomes practical by extension, and is thereby directed toward action and making things. I am referring to action as governed by the virtue of political prudence, and to the making of things as governed by art. But both are subordinate to speculation as the highest function for the sake of which the Supreme Goodness brought mankind into being.

From all this one begins to appreciate what is meant in the *Politics* by the sentence: 'Men of superior intellect naturally rule over others.'

IV

Thus it is quite clear that the task proper to mankind considered as a whole is to fulfil the total capacity of the possible intellect all the time, primarily by speculation and secondarily, as a function and extension of speculation, by action. Now since what applies to the part applies also to the whole, and since the individual man becomes perfect in wisdom and prudence through sitting in quietude, so it is in the quietude or tranquility of peace that mankind finds the best conditions for fulfilling its proper task (almost a divine task, as we learn from the statement: 'Thou hast made him a little lower than the angels.'). Hence it is clear that the universal peace is the most excellent means of securing our happiness. This is why the message from on high to the shepherds announced neither wealth, nor pleasure, nor honour, nor long life, nor health, nor strength, nor beauty, but peace. The heavenly host, indeed, proclaims: 'Glory to God on high, and on earth peace to men of good will.' 'Peace be with you' was also the salutation given by the Saviour of men, because it was fitting that the supreme Saviour should utter the supreme salutation—a custom which, as everyone knows, his disciples and Paul sought to preserve in their own greetings.

This argument shows us what is the better, indeed the very best means available to mankind for fulfilling its proper role; and also what is the most direct means of reaching that goal to which all our doings are directed—universal peace. This will serve as the basis for our subsequent argument. Such is the common ground which we declared to be essential so as to have something axiomatic to which all our proofs and demonstrations can refer.

BOOK THREE

XVI

In the preceding chapter it has been shown, by bringing out the incongruity implicit in the argument, that the authority of the Empire is not derived from the authority of the Supreme Pontiff. But it has not been completely proved that the Imperial authority is derived immediately from God unless the consequence of our argument is stated. The consequence is that if he does not depend upon the vicar of God, then he must depend upon God himself. So in order to present a conclusive demonstration of the proposition we need to prove directly that the Emperor, or monarch of the world, stands in immediate relationship to the prince of the world, who is God.

In order to grasp this it must be realized that man is unique amongst all beings in linking corruptible with incorruptible; hence the philosophers rightly liken him to the line of the horizon which is the meeting-place of two hemispheres. For if man is considered according to his essential constituents, that is, his soul and his body, he is corruptible in respect of one, the body, but incorruptible in respect of the other, the soul. Thus in the second book of the *De Anima* the Philosopher rightly says of the incorruptible constituent of man: 'and this alone, being eternal, is capable of separating itself from the corruptible world.' Therefore man is, so to say, a middle-term between corruptible and incorruptible things, and since every middle-term participates in the nature of the extremes which it unites, man must participate in these two natures. And since every nature is ordered towards some ultimate goal, it follows that man's ultimate goal is twofold—because since man is the only being sharing in both corruptibility and incorruptibility he is the only being who is ordered towards two ultimate goals. One of these constitutes his goal in so far as he is corruptible and the other in so far as he is incorruptible.

Unerring Providence has therefore set man to attain two goals: the first is happiness in this life, which consists in the exercise of his own powers and is typified by the earthly paradise; the second is the happiness of eternal life, which consists in the enjoyment of the divine countenance (which man cannot attain to of his own power but only by the aid of divine illumination) and is typified by the heavenly paradise. These two sorts of happiness are attained by diverse means, just as one reaches different conclusions by different means. We attain to the first by means of philosophical teaching, being faithful to it by exercising our moral and intellectual virtues. We arrive at the second by means of spiritual teaching (which transcends human reason), in so far as we exercise the theological virtues of faith, hope and charity. These conclusions, and the means toward them, are revealed to us, on the one hand by human reason (in the light of which the philosophers have made one human situation perfectly clear), and on the other hand by the Holy Spirit, who has revealed the supernatural truth necessary for our salvation by means of the prophets and sacred writers, and through the Son of God, who is co-eternal with the Spirit, Jesus Christ, and through Christ's disciples. Nevertheless human cupidity would fling such aids aside if men, like horses stampeding to satisfy their bestiality, were not held to the right path by the bit and the rein. This explains why two guides have been appointed for many to lead him to his twofold goal: there is the Supreme

Pontiff who is to lead mankind to eternal life in accordance with revelation; and there is the Emperor who, in accordance with philosophical teaching, is to lead mankind to temporal happiness. None would reach this harbour—or, at least, few would do so, and only with the greatest difficulty—unless the waves of alluring cupidity were assuaged and mankind were freed from them so as to rest in the tranquility of peace; and this is the task to which that protector of the world must devote his energies who is called the Roman Prince. His office is to provide freedom and peace for men as they pass through the testing-time of this world. Furthermore, since the condition of this world has to harmonize with the movements of the heavens, it is necessary for the protector of this world to receive knowledge of the appropriate conditions directly from the one who sees the whole course of the heavens at a glance; only then can he apply the principles of liberty and peace at the appropriate times and places. But this One is none other than He who foreordained the condition of the heavens, providentially intended by Him to hold all things together in harmony. If this be so, then God alone elects and confirms the Emperor, since God has no superior. Consequently it can be seen that the title of elector should not be accorded either to those now described as electors, nor to any others; properly speaking their office is to proclaim what God has providentially decided. Failure to realize this sometimes results in discord amongst those privileged to make this proclamation, because all—or some of them—are so befogged by the mists of greed that they fail to perceive the obvious decision of divine providence. Thus it is obvious that the temporal Monarch received his authority directly and without intermediary, from the Source of all authority, which Source (though utterly indivisible in the citadel of its simplicity) flows out into manifold channels through its abounding goodness.

And now it seems to me that I have achieved the target I aimed at. For I have sifted out the truth about the three questions at issue: whether the office of Monarch is essential for the well-being of the world: whether it was by right that the Roman people obtained the Empire; and last, but not least, whether the Monarch's authority derives directly from God or comes through some intermediary. Yet the truth upon this last issue is not to be narrowly interpreted as excluding the Roman Prince from all subordination to the Roman Pontiff, since in a certain fashion our temporal happiness is subordinate to our eternal happiness. Caesar, therefore, is obliged to observe that reverence towards Peter which a firstborn son owes to his father; so that when he is enlightened by the light of paternal grace he may the more powerfully enlighten the world, at the head of which he has been placed by the One who alone is ruler of all things spiritual and temporal.

From Dante Alighieri, **Divine Comedy—Paradiso**

CANTO I

The glory of Him who moves all things soe'er
Impenetrates the universe, and bright
The splendour burns, more here and lesser there.

Within that heav'n which most receives His light
Was I, and saw such things as man nor knows
Nor skills to tell, returning from that height;

For when our intellect is drawing close
To its desire, its paths are so profound
That memory cannot follow where it goes.

Yet now, of that blest realm whate'er is found
Here in my mind still treasured and possessed
Must set the strain for all my song to sound.

Gracious Apollo! in this crowning test
Make me the conduit that thy power runs through!
Fit me to wear those bays thou lovest best.

One peak of thy Parnassus hitherto
Has well sufficed me, but henceforth I strive
In an arena where I need the two.

Breathe in me, breathe, and from my bosom drive
Music like thine, when thou didst long ago
The limbs of Marsyas from their scabbard rive.

O power divine, grant me in song to show
The blest realm's image—shadow though it be—
Stamped on my brain; thus far thyself bestow

And thou shalt see me to thy darling tree
Draw near, and twine those laurels on my brow
Which I shall merit by my theme and thee.

So seldom, Father, are they gathered now
For Caesar's triumph or the poet's meed
(Such sin, such shame or human wills allow!)

That the Peneian frond must surely breed
Joy in the joyous Delphic god, whene'er
Any aspires to make it his indeed.

From one small spark springs up a mighty flare;
If I set forth, others may come behind,
More worthy, and win Cirrha by their prayer.

Through divers portals rises on mankind
The lantern of the world, but from that part
Where the three crosses the four circles bind,

With happiest stars he comes conjunct, to start
His happiest course, and seals and tempers here
This mundane wax most after his own heart.

Nigh to that point he'd made the dawn appear
Yonder, and here the dusk; all whiteness shone
That side, and darkness veiled our hemisphere,

When Beatrice, intent upon the sun,
Turned leftward, and so stood and gazed before;
No eagle e'er so fixed his eyes thereon.

And, as the second ray doth evermore
Strike from the first and dart back up again,
Just as the peregrine will stoop and soar,

So through my eyes her gesture, pouring in
On my mind's eye, shaped mine; I stared wide-eyed
On the sun's face, beyond the wont of men.

There, much is granted which is here denied
To human senses; in that gracious spot
Made for mankind such virtue doth reside,

Short time I endured him, yet so short 'twas not
But that I saw him sparkle every way
Like iron from out the furnace drawn white-hot;

And, on a sudden, day seemed joined to day,
As though the hand that hath the power had sped
A second sun to make the skies more gay.

Beatrice stood, her eyes still riveted
On the eternal wheels; and, constantly,
Turning mine thence, I gazed on her instead;

'Twas even thus a change came over me,
As Glaucus, eating of the weed, changed race
And grew a god among the gods of sea.

Transhumanized—the fact mocks human phrase;
So let the example serve, till proof requite
Him who is called to experience this by grace.

If I was naught, O Love that rul'st the height,
Save that of me which Thou didst last create,
Thou know'st, that didst uplift me by Thy light.

The wheel Thou mak'st eternal through innate
Desire of Thee, no sooner took mine ear
With strains which Thou dost tune and modulate,

Than I saw blaze on me so vast a sphere
Fired by the sun, that never rain nor streams
Formed such a huge illimitable mere.

The unwonted sound, the bright and burning beams,
Kindled my eagerness to know their cause
Beyond the yearning of my dearest dreams;

Whence she to whom my whole self open was
As to myself, to calm my troubled fit
Stayed not my question, but without a pause

Opened her lips: "Thou dullest thine own wit
With false imagination, nor perceivest
That which thou wouldst perceive, being rid of it.

Thou art not still on earth as thou believest;
Lightning from its sphere falling never matched
The speed which thou, returning there, achievest."

But I, my first bewilderment despatched
By these few smiling words, was more perplexed
Now, by a new one which I promptly hatched.

I said: "I rest content, no longer vexed
By one great doubt; but how come I to fly
Through these light spheres? This doubt assails me next."

She turned on me, after a pitying sigh,
A look such as a mother's eyes let fall
Upon her infant, babbling feverishly.

Then she began: "All beings great and small
Are linked in order; and this orderliness
Is form, which stamps God's likeness on the All.

Herein the higher creatures see the trace
Of that Prime Excellence who is the end
For which that form was framed in the first place.

And being thus ordered, all these natures tend
Unto their source, or near or farther off,
As divers lots their divers fashions blend;

Wherefore to divers havens all these move
O'er the great sea of being, all borne on
By instinct given, to every one enough.

'Tis this that draws the fire up to the moon,
The mover this, in hearts of mortal things,
This that binds up the earth and makes it one.

Yea, and this bow's discharge by no means wings
Irrational creatures only to their goal,
But those endowed with loves and reasonings.

The Providence that integrates the whole
Keeps in perpetual stillness by its light
That heav'n wherein the swiftest heav'n doth roll;

Thither, as to our own appointed site,
That mighty string impels us now, which still
Speeds to the gold its every arrow's flight;

True, as the form fails sometimes to fulfil
The art's intention, if the lumpish clay
Prove unresponsive to the craftsman's skill,

Even so the creature that has power to stray
Out of its course, though launched by that strong thrust,
Will swerve at times, and go its wilful way,

(As lightning quits the cloud and strikes the dust),
From its first impetus and upward route
Diverted earthward by some fair false lust.

But thy ascent, if rightly I compute,
Ought no more to surprise thee than to see
A stream rush down from mountain crest to foot;

Nay, but if thou, from every hindrance free,
Shouldst hug the ground, that *would* be a surprise—
As stillness in quick flame on earth would be."

Then back again to heav'n she turned her eyes.

BONIFACE VIII

During the high Middle Ages many developments left their mark on medieval civilization. The emergence of strong feudal monarchies in France, England, and elsewhere provided a significant measure of political stability in Europe. The revival of trade and the growth of towns brought disposable wealth and economic prosperity once again to the Mediterranean world and its environs. The world of thought experienced a quickening that began inside monastery walls and soon spread outside, resulting in intellectual feats whose brilliance and originality could rival those of classical antiquity. An architectual achievement of the first magnitude was manifest when Europe was covered in a mantle of dazzling new cathedrals. The church came to exert moral and political authority over Christendom to a degree unequalled in the past. No small part of the last development, and several others as well, was due to the initiative of the papacy.

The monastic reform that had begun with the foundation of the monastery of Cluny in 910 spread throughout Europe until a century and a half later it overtook the papacy. The Hildebrandine reformation—so-called because the monk, Hildebrand, as Pope Gregory VII, assumed its leadership —sought thoroughgoing reform of the church including everyone from the pope himself to simple lay folk. Pope Gregory VII (1073-85) initiated the Investiture Controversy in which he sought to divest the clerical order of its feudal entanglements and also to purify that order of long-standing abuses. Gregory was an able and dynamic pope, only one of many during this period, who sought to reform the church and strengthen its moral authority.

This endeavor to enhance papal leadership was aided by the intellectual and administrative capabilities of such popes as Alexander III (1159-81), Innocent III (1198-1216), and Innocent IV (1243-1254); by the growth of canon law initiated by the publication of Gratian's *Decretum* in 1140; and by vigorous challenges of political and moral derelictions of secular rulers.

The saga of medieval history is punctuated by colorful clashes between popes and kings. The Investiture Controversy has the scene of the barefooted Emperor Henry IV standing in the snow beseeching the forgiveness of Pope Gregory VII; another striking panorama had Pope Alexander III leading the Lombard League against the restless Frederick Barbarossa; Pope Innocent III was the very picture of moral indignation, forcing Philip Augustus of France to accept once more his disconsolate spouse or John of England to accept Stephen Langton as archbishop of Canterbury; it was a grim landscape indeed, where wonder of the world, Frederick II, was pursued by Pope Innocent IV to remove the Emperor's menacing presence from Italy. Perhaps the most dramatic confrontation of all came at the end of the thirteenth century when Pope Boniface VIII challenged King Philip the Fair of France and lost. It was a serious and damaging loss for the papacy. *Unam Sanctam*, issued by Pope Boniface in 1302, contains an extreme claim of papal supremacy in and over the church.

From Pope Boniface VIII, **Unam Sanctam**

We are obliged by the faith to believe and to hold—and we do firmly believe and sincerely confess—that there is one Holy Catholic and Apostolic Church, and that outside this Church there is neither salvation nor remission of sins. . . . In which Church there is one Lord, one faith, one baptism. At the time of the flood there was one ark of Noah, symbolizing the one Church; this was completed in one cubit and had one, namely Noah, as helmsman and captain; outside which all things on earth, we read, were destroyed. . . . Of this one and only Church there is one body and one head—not two heads, like a monster—namely Christ, and Christ's vicar is Peter, and Peter's successor, for the Lord said to Peter himself, 'Feed My sheep.' 'My sheep' He said in general, not these or those sheep; wherefore He is understood to have committed them all to him. Therefore, if the Greeks or others say that they were not committed to Peter and his successors, they necessarily confess that they are not of Christ's sheep, for the Lord says in John, 'There is one fold and one shepherd.'

And we learn from the words of the Gospel that in this Church and in her power are two swords, the spiritual and the temporal. For when the apostles said, 'Behold, here' (that is, in the Church, since it was the apostles who spoke) 'are two swords'—the Lord did not reply, 'It is too much,' but 'It is enough.' Truly he who denies that the temporal sword is in the power of Peter, misunderstands the words of the Lord, 'Put up thy sword into the sheath.' Both are in the power of the Church, the spiritual sword and the material. But the latter is to be used for the Church, the former by her; the former by the priest, the latter by kings and captains but at the will and by the permission of the priest. The one sword, then, should be under the other, and temporal authority subject to spiritual. For when the apostle says 'there is no power but of God, and the powers that be are ordained of God they would not be so ordained were not one sword made subject to the other. . . .'

Thus, concerning the Church and her power, is the prophecy of Jeremiah fulfilled, 'See, I have this day set thee over the nations and over the kingdoms,' etc. If, therefore, the earthly power err, it shall be judged by the spiritual power; and if a lesser power err, it shall be judged by a greater. But if the supreme power err, it can only be judged by God, not by man; for the testimony of the apostle is 'The spiritual man judgeth all things, yet he himself is judged of no man.' For this authority, although given to a man and exercised by a man, is not human, but rather divine, given at God's mouth to Peter and established on a rock for him and his successors in Him whom he confessed, the Lord saying to Peter himself, 'Whatsoever thou shalt bind,' etc. Whoever therefore resists this power thus ordained of God, resists the ordinance of God. . . . Furthermore we declare, state, define and pronounce that it is altogether necessary to salvation for every human creature to be subject to the Roman pontiff.

Part Four

The Renaissance

Introduction

In the history of European civilization, the period known as the Renaissance represents the transition from the Middle Ages to modern times. The chronological framework generally assigned for this period is 1300-1600. Calling the Renaissance a transitional age in no way diminishes its importance; instead it calls attention to its key significance.

The two essential and characteristic elements that shaped medieval civilization were feudalism and the universal church. Both of these institutions affected the form and the substance of medieval civilization in many ways. Given the feudal system, social and political life were shaped by an agrarian and relatively moneyless economy. Given the universal church, intellectual and cultural pursuits followed the interests and needs of a dominant and dominating clerical elite.

During the Renaissance important changes began to be perceptible, changes which added up to an essential change in the character of European civilization. While it is true that the feudal and ecclesiastical elements remained important in the civilization of the Renaissance, they were no longer dominant. The civilization of the Renaissance is distinguished by the predominance of the urban and lay elements which gave it form and substance. Unable to find nourishment in the feudal and ecclesiastical soil of the Middle Ages, these lay citizens eagerly sought their roots in classical antiquity, which seemed to provide a congenial environment and one so like their own.

The Renaissance brought a new awareness, perhaps self-consciousness, to Western thought in the fourteenth century. What it meant to be human, what the appropriate setting for human existence might be, and what made this particular historical time unique, were topics of lively discussion. It would be amiss to claim that these topics had not attracted attention during the Middle Ages, but beginning in the fourteenth century there were new, or rediscovered sources of inspiration in the art and thought of classical antiquity (hence, *Renaissance—rebirth*). Indeed many saw classical antiquity being born again after the long slumber of the Middle Ages. For three hundred years, from 1300 to 1600, these impulses were to grow stronger until they affected virtually the whole of Europe. Thus the Renaissance is an important and discrete segment of the development of Christian humanism.

Renaissance thinkers who perceived themselves as creating a new age felt a sense of excitement and exhilaration. This Renaissance consciousness or awareness of the dawning of a new age had about it both positive and negative aspects, and both have made the Renaissance and its significance a topic of vigorous controversy ever since.

Beginning in the fourteenth century in Italy, first in Florence and later in other city-states, thinkers, mostly lay people, perceived themselves as strikingly different from, indeed better than, their predecessors. They felt they were bringing into being a new age. Italian Renaissance thinkers saw themselves creating a culture with stylistic values markedly different, often at odds with, the scholastic culture of the Middle Ages. The writers of the Italian Renaissance did not shy away from making invidious comparisons between what was being created in their own cultural golden age and what they said came before it in the preceding cultural "dark" age.

The Renaissance had its beginnings in Italy with its close proximity to many remains of classical antiquity and was associated with the urban environment of the city-state, whereas the scholastic culture of the Middle Ages focused on France, with its well-developed feudal traditions and was intimately tied up with the development of the university as an institution. These circumstances help explain the differences between the medieval and Renaissance outlook.

Ever since the time of Jakob Burckhardt, the nineteenth century scholar of the Renaissance, it has been fashionable to call Francesco Petrarch (1304-1374) the first modern man. Regarded as the father of Renaissance humanism, Petrarch formulated the idea of the Renaissance as a new age. The thousand year interval from the Emperor Constantine's conversion to Christianity in the fourth century until his own time in the mid-fourteenth century Petrarch saw as an era of such debased culture and learning that he labeled it the Dark Age. Though he himself did not specifically charge Christianity with responsibility for the debasement, others later drew that inference. It would be far from the truth to allege that Petrarch was anti-Christian, or a-Christian, for his own life and work show his deep devotion to Christianity and Christian values. Time and again Augustine's life and work come to Petrarch's mind as models for his own. At the same time his reverence for the classics, his emphasis on the importance of their revival, and his deliberate attempts to imitate their literary style, had a profound effect on his contemporaries and successors. On the one hand, his Christian values could be perceived as rather conventional, while on the other, his excitement at the rediscovery of antiquity was remarkably new and different. Petrarch's successors chose to follow the exciting path.

Throughout the Middle Ages there had been significant interest in the literature of classical antiquity. After all, the scholastics had revived interest in Aristotle, and Aquinas and Dante revered him as a master second to none. What was different about Petrarch was his new attitude toward antiquity and the zeal with which he expounded it. Petrarch was drawn to the *style* of antique writers as well as to the content of their writings. He took pains to show that form and content went closely together. His concern for classical style led Petrarch to abandon his highly successful career writing in the Italian vernacular in order to imitate the epic style of Virgil and the rhetorical eloquence of Cicero. However, the beauty of Petrarch's Latin works never equaled that of his early Italian poetry. Posterity, too, has not dealt kindly with Petrarch's epic venture, *Africa*. The fame Petrarch sought rests on his Italian love sonnets.

Petrarch's Christian humanism is frequently in evidence throughout his works. Like Augustine, Petrarch is given to self-confession and often is at his best when expressing his deep emotions: his desire for fame, his self-doubts and torments, his intensely human love, and his concern about salvation. Petrarch is ever mindful that he will be judged both in this world and in the next, and he is uncomfortable about it. To Burckhardt, what appeared modern about Petrarch was a capacity for probing introspection. Yet there is something paradoxical here, for this introspective side is clearly seen in Petrarch's model, Augustine. Like Augustine, he searches, questions his motives, searches again, and agonizes over what he has found. There were tensions in Petrarch's life and conflicts in his personality: between the active life and the contemplative life, between melancholy and optimism, and between the values of classical antiquity and the Christian life. Some striking ambiguities in Petrarch's position can be perceived in his description of his ascent of Mount Ventoux: he looks out and revels in the beauties of nature only to be struck by how much more important it is to look within himself. Here too is expressed, quite forcefully, another theme of Christian humanism, the dignity of nature. Generations of Italian humanists found inspiration in Petrarch, and his motivating influence in the classical revival remained strong for well over two centuries.

The idea that a new age was underway became accepted in Italian intellectual circles in the late fourteenth century, and in the next century Flavio Biondo set forth a periodization of European history that has since become conventional: classical antiquity, the Middle Ages, and modern times. While Petrarch favored the revival of classical letters and saw himself as the great reviver, others called for a revival of classical art and saw in the work of Giotto (*c.* 1266-1337) its beginning. This view was articulated most forcefully by Giorgio Vasari (1511-1574), pioneer art historian, who did place blame for the decay of classical art upon the Christians and gave credit to the cult of the classics for bringing about a revival in art that rivaled ancient Rome and in some instances even surpassed it. Thinking about and creating the new age was a tonic for the ego of many a Renaissance figure, and the spirit of the age seems to have done little to promote intellectual modesty.

Because of the splendor of the achievements in Renaissance art and letters and because of the esteem for their views, the legacy of Petrarch and Vasari had its unfortunate side. The characterization of the Middle Ages as a Dark Age led to misunderstanding and distortion of the nature and value of the intellectual and artistic heritage of the medieval period. Ever since, it has been difficult to put the Renaissance in proper historical perspective because its dynamism, brilliance, and originality have been promoted against the background of the Renaissance characterization of the Middle Ages as stagnant, dark, and sterile. Thinkers of the Italian Renaissance saw themselves as making a definite break with the medieval past and definitely for the better.

Following Petrarch, Italian humanism in the late fourteenth and early fifteenth centuries clearly broke with medieval thought and tradition in the area of education. Italian humanism advocated education and training in the liberal arts and the study of classical literature. The aim of this kind of education was simple: practical and worthy living. Roman and Greek writers of classical antiquity were believed to have bequeathed to posterity a treasure trove of valuable lessons for living in the world. The Greeks and the Romans possessed civilizations of surpassing importance, and both exalted the value of human activity in the world. The reverence for classical antiquity and the dependence on classical models for human existence were not perceived by the Italian humanists to be antagonistic to Christian values. Italian humanism and Christianity were not seen to be in conflict, though it might be said that Christianity was simply accepted as a given. Ideas of unity, hierarchy, and order—all of which came to be valued in the Middle Ages for the good life—were scorned by the Italian humanists. Prized as essential for the good life in the Renaissance were diversity, individuality, and practicality.

Italian humanism put human beings at the center of intellectual and artistic inquiry, but it gave them no fixed nature, no metaphysical underpinnings. In his treatise on painting, the fifteenth-century artist Leon Battista Alberti (1404-1472) instructs painters on how they are to judge the size of each object in the pictorial space: by the scale of the human figures in the painting. To emphasize his point Alberti employed a maxim used long before by Protagoras, "Man is the measure of all things." Italian humanism focused on human qualities and human potential; it offered glory in this world rather than salvation in the next. There was a concern for fame and reputation that sometimes bordered on obsession. Recognizing that human life exists in a changing temporal continuum, the Italian humanists stressed how important it is to study history. The social background of the Italian humanists is not an irrelevant consideration; the majority were from the laity, had urban connections, and by profession were lawyers, notaries, and public servants. In the Middle Ages, learning had been a prerogative of the clergy.

Given the different background, attitudes, and outlook of the Italian humanists, the course of study in the schools was bound to be different. The curriculum of Italian humanism included five interrelated disciplines: *grammar, rhetoric, poetry, history,* and *moral philosophy.* Grammar meant first, the study of Latin, and then, ambitiously, Greek. Renaissance educational theory held that for entering public service a knowledge of Latin *grammar* was necessary. The summit of grammatical study was philology, which involved a sense of the historical development of a language as well as a comprehensive grasp of its literature. *Rhetoric* involved knowing techniques of persuasion, especially those which might be useful for a career in public service where speaking well and writing elegantly might pay rich dividends. *Poetry* helped to shape what would now be called a well-rounded individual; it could broaden one's outlook. From classical poets like Horace, Vergil, even Homer, one could learn how to enrich what one had to say. *History* brought some sense of unity to Italian humanism. These writers possessed a common view that classical ideals reaffirmed their own ideals. They did not see it as important to study the ancient past just for its own sake but rather for its practical value for current affairs. *Moral philosophy* involved placing the focus of intellectual interest as much as possible on the human being. This sometimes involved a shift away from religious dimensions simply by taking God for granted and then examining some aspect of the human being, relying heavily on the support of classical texts and arguments.

The process of rediscovering classical antiquity involved the Italian humanists more and more deeply in the study of classical languages, first Latin, then Greek. Throughout the fourteenth century classical Latin writings exerted the major influence on the thought of the Italian humanists because classical Greek studies were still in their infancy. During the course of the fifteenth century there was steadily increasing interest in classical Greek literature, which was further stimulated by the arrival in Italy of many learned Greeks to attend the church council of Ferrara-Florence in 1438-1439. Some of the attendants at the council were eminent Platonic scholars who chose to stay in Italy after the conclusion of the council. Italian humanism thereupon experienced a new surge of Platonism, thus expanding the vogue for Plato which had begun with Petrarch, who had expressed a decided preference for that philosopher over Aristotle. Several features of Plato's work proved attractive to the generations of Italian humanists after 1450: its stylistic grace, its unsystematic format, and a deep vein of mysticism —all qualities seemingly lacking in Aristotle. The task of making the Platonic heritage available in its widest form to Italian humanist circles fell to a young Florentine, Marsilio Ficino.

Ficino (1433-1499) was attracted to the writings of Plato. As a very

young man he accepted the patronage of Cosimo de' Medici, the most important man in Florentine political affairs and a significant figure in intellectual
circles as well. Cosimo de' Medici provided Ficino with a comfortable living
in a villa outside Florence and gave him a splendid library of manuscripts
in order to get underway a pet project, a school devoted to the study of
Plato. Appropriately called the Platonic Academy, or Florentine Academy,
this became a center for some of the most advanced humanist thinking in a
Christian vein. As the study of Plato's works developed, Ficino hoped that
they might serve as a foundation for the spiritual renewal of Christian piety.
In his *Theologia Platonica* published in 1474, Ficino attempted to synthesize Christian and Platonic thought. Ficino used the works of Plato to provide a philosophical foundation for the idea that it is in the nature of the
human being to find the highest good in the knowledge and enjoyment of
God, who is infinite goodness, beauty, and truth. He also found in Platonic
thought a philosophical foundation for the notion of the dignity of the human
being. In the great chain of being, the human being has a central place and
serves as the ontological link between the material and the spiritual. Ficino's
own work and the intellectual circles in which he moved served to focus
attention on the dignity of the human being and on the dignity of nature
as well. Another mark of the importance of Ficino was the influence he
had on the greatest Christian humanist of the age, Erasmus of Rotterdam,
who read and absorbed what his Italian predecessor had to say.

The most famous Renaissance assertion of the dignity of the human being
was produced by a friend and pupil of Ficino, Giovanni Pico della Mirandola
(1463-1494). Pico della Mirandola was blessed with wealth, a title, good
looks, and considerable intelligence. Moreover, after a brief lifetime of just
over 30 years, he enjoyed the kind of reputation of which even Petrarch
would have been proud and one that now seems out of proportion to what
he in fact achieved.

Like Ficino, he saw the reconciliation of Christian and Platonic thought
as a worthwhile venture, but broadened the task to include Aristotelian
thought, the Hebrew cabala, and Arabic, Pythagorean, and Zoroastrian
learning. Needless to say, he was not able to bring this sprawling mass of
ideas together in any kind of system. Judging by what remains of his work,
Pico was a great borrower and combiner of ideas. His works are alternately
amazing and frustrating. There is no doubt that he was a most able student
of languages (he was fluent in Latin, Greek, Hebrew, and Arabic) and that
he possessed a ripe erudition for his intellectual life's task.

His main claim to fame, the *Oration on the Dignity of Man*, makes the
most extravagant claims for human dignity of any writing by an Italian
humanist. Going well beyond the assertions claimed for human dignity by
his master, Ficino, Pico envisions the human being not just as the central
link between the material and the spiritual in the great chain of being, but

as able to shape and control human destiny. Among all the creatures, only the human being is completely free. Human beings have the power to make themselves what they will. The human being can ascend to the divine or descend to a level of utter bestiality. This is within the power of the human being to choose. In a certain sense, the human being is outside the great chain of being.

With claims such as these, it is little wonder that Pico was sometimes thought to have gone outside the bounds of the Christian tradition! Little wonder, too, that more sober northern Europeans found some of the assertions of Italian humanism hard to swallow. For all the hopes of Ficino, Italian humanism seems to have done little to advance the renewal of Christian piety in Italy, but the seeds Ficino sowed did bear fruit in northern Europe through the efforts of Erasmus of Rotterdam.

The Renaissance had made its way throughout Italy for about a century and a half (*c.* 1350-*c.* 1500) before the ideas developed by the Italian humanists began to have a major impact on northern Europe. The reasons for the delayed impact are many: Italian humanism was more congenial to the social and political environment of the various Italian city-states than to the feudal arrangements of the northern nobility; the physical proximity of the remains of classical antiquity in Italy made the greatness and worth of classical civilization more tangible in Italy than in northern Europe, where the monuments of antiquity were fewer and less impressive; scholasticism was far more deeply imbedded in the intellectual life of northern Europe than it had ever been in Italy, and therefore it proved more difficult to supplant. Then shortly before 1500, Renaissance ideas burst out of Italy and engulfed much more of Europe, including Spain, France, England, the Low Countries, and Germany.

When Renaissance ideas flooded over Europe from out of Italy, there was a significant difference in outlook: the Christian element was to the fore. In rediscovering the ancient past the great northern humanists, almost without exception, looked to Hebrew antiquity along with Greek and Roman antiquity for inspiration. The Hebrew past, especially the Old Testament, was rediscovered. The importance of this development must not be overlooked. Though the Latin and Greek classics often cast a powerful spell over the northern imagination, a deeply religious dimension was rarely lacking. It is for this reason that the great writers of northern Europe have frequently been labeled *Christian humanists*.

Though others like Thomas More, Jacques LeFevre d'Etaples, Johann Reuchlin, labored in the vineyard, the preeminent representative of Christian humanism in northern Europe was Erasmus of Rotterdam (1469-1536). Many religious currents ran through the Low Countries in the fourteenth and fifteenth centuries, and this eminent Dutchman imbibed from several of them. The Christian element was dominant in the work and writings of

Erasmus. Prominent in his Christian humanism is the idea that the Christian religion is more a matter of ethics than of dogma; how one behaves is more important than what one believes.

Erasmus studied carefully the work of many Italian humanists, and one can see the imprint of men like Ficino, Valla, and Pico on his work. He could perceive what was noble and ennobling about antiquity and at the same time cast it in a Christian mold. His sensitivity to classical style was renowned but it never blinded him to the importance of Christian meaning. The sense of balance that was so much a part of his personality is evident in the way he unites the Christian and the classical without sacrificing either to the other.

Erasmus was the most famous and respected intellectual of his age. In an age unusually sensitive to the need for reform in religion, Erasmus appeared as a responsible and constructive critic of society. He criticized the superstition as well as the scholasticism of the late medieval church. His criticisms of the church were couched in a style both lucid and elegant, sometimes as gentle satires, sometimes as practical guides to a pious life. To the very end of his days he remained gently tolerant, though some of his contemporaries, most notably Luther, did not appreciate his gentle tolerance. The critical powers of Erasmus are perhaps best displayed in his *Praise of Folly* where the weaknesses of human nature are almost mercilessly revealed. In the *Enchiridion Militis Christiani* Erasmus sets forth his view on how the Christian life should be lived. The Christian life is meant to embody the *philosophia Christi*, a blending of ancient wisdom and Christian piety, an alliance of humanist learning and evangelical devotion. True Christian piety is a matter of the spirit, and it must find expression in the conduct of daily life. Erasmus' prescription for the Christian life is simple, yet eloquent and moving.

Erasmus magnificently demonstrated his Christian humanism in his editorial work. He carefully edited many works from the patristic age and provided commentaries that were models of their kind. Because the life of a Christian had to be modeled on that of Christ, there had to be available the best possible editions of the writings dealing with that life, the New Testament. His most important editorial service came with his Greek edition of the New Testament; in the preface, called *Paraclesis*, he assesses the importance of the Scriptures for the Christian life. With the advent of printing it was widely recognized in Europe that a text of the Bible purged of copyists' errors was highly desirable and necessary, but at the same time some scholars and churchmen feared that making the Greek text of the Bible available would throw into question the traditional Latin version, Jerome's Vulgate. In the face of considerable opposition Erasmus persisted and in the end triumphed. His version of the New Testament was soon recognized as the best available.

The reputation of Erasmus was enhanced by the way in which he took advantage of a new technology of his time, the printing press. All of his works were printed, even his letters, and eagerly sought after by an avid public. The Christian humanism of Erasmus offered a stance that for a time was widely attractive. It presented a point of view that was tolerant, humane, and deeply religious; simultaneously it provided a sophisticated perception of human beings in their precise historical settings. The qualities that made Erasmus appear to be the "Prince of Humanists" or the ideal Christian humanist were often the very qualities that made him objectionable in the age of the Reformation. His tolerance seemed like equivocation or vacillation; his humane outlook was mistaken for worldliness; and his advocacy of religious ethics smacked too much of good works. Suddenly this dear friend of Thomas More, the "man for all seasons," was himself out of season.

FRANCESCO PETRARCH

Francesco Petrarch (1304-1374), like Dante in the generation before him, came from a family associated with Florence and her complicated urban political life. Involvement in politics brought about the exile of Petrarch's father from Florence and a move to the city of Avignon, in the south of France, to which the papal court and administration had moved in the early fourteenth century. Young Francesco was encouraged to become a lawyer and actually studied to do so, but developed a distaste for legal studies, practice, and practitioners, and therefore abandoned his legal career. Instead he developed his talents as a poet, writer, and critic and was able to win fame and fortune by his efforts. He wrote in the Italian vernacular and produced love sonnets dedicated to a lady, Laura, whom he loved from afar, and showed himself to be a sensitive individual with a gift for writing sensual poetry.

Though posterity has shown great fondness for Petrarch's Italian poetry, the poet himself came to regard it as rather unworthy of his talent and referred to it slightingly. What Petrarch came to regard as far more important than his Italian writings were his Latin works. He pointedly called attention to the "barbaric" quality of medieval Latin writings and encouraged the study of ancient Roman writings. He had an interest in the Latin style of the ancients that frequently bordered on an obsession. To emphasize his disdain for the poor quality of medieval Latin writing he coined the phrase "Dark Ages" to refer to the period between the fall of Rome and his own times. The role he envisioned for himself was no small one; he saw himself as responsible for bringing about the revival of the great Latin style of classical antiquity!

Sometimes he suffered from an attack of conscience, and some deep religious sentiments overcame him. In his moments of religious crisis, Petrarch saw himself called to asceticism and Augustine, not necessarily in that order.

At times he became an almost violent critic of the church, especially the papacy in its residency at Avignon. Petrarch, like every good Christian, believed that the papacy properly should reside in Rome. Petrarch aimed to bring about reform in the church primarily by directing the popes to return to Rome, the see of Peter. Petrarch's concerns are unmistakably conveyed in the two letters included here; his gift with words is manifest in virtually every sentence.

From Francesco Petrarch, **Letter to Francesco Nelli**

I noticed in a letter of yours that you were pleased at my mixture of sacred and secular themes, and that you thought Saint Jerome would have been likewise pleased. You mention the charm of variety, the beauty of structure, the force of association. What can I reply? You must make your own judgments, and certainly you are not easily or commonly deceived, except that well-wishers readily err, and often are eager to do so.

But putting all this to one side, let me speak of myself and my new but serious enthusiasm, which turns my thoughts and my writings to sacred literature. Let the supercilious laugh, who are revolted by the austerity of holy words, as the modest garb of a chaste matron repels those who are used to the flaunting colors of light women. I think that the Muses and Apollo will not merely grant me permission, they will applaud, that after giving my youth to studies proper to that age, I should devote my riper years to more important matters. Nor am I to be criticized, if I, who so often used to rouse by night to work for empty fame and celebrate the futile lauds of men, should now arise at midnight to recite the lauds of my creator, and devote the hours proper to quiet and repose to him who shall neither slumber nor sleep while he keepeth Israel: nor is he content with universal custodianship, but he watches over me personally and is solicitous for my welfare. I am clearly conscious of this, and all men capable of gratitude must feel the same. He cares for each individual as if he were forgetful of mankind *en masse;* and so he rules the mass as if he were careless of each individual. Thus I have it firmly fixed in mind that if it be heaven's will I shall spend the rest of my life in these studies and occupations. In what state could I better die than in loving, remembering, and praising him, without whose constant love I should be nothing, or damned, which is less than nothing? And if his love for me should cease, my damnation would have no end.

I loved Cicero, I admit, and I loved Virgil. I delighted in their thought and expression so far that I thought nothing could surpass them. I loved many others also of the troop of great writers, but I loved Cicero as if he were my father, Virgil as my brother. My admiration, my familiarity with their genius, contracted in long study, inspired in me such love for their persons that you may think it hardly possible to feel a like affection for living men. Similarly I loved, of the Greeks, Plato and Homer. When I compared their genius with that of our own masters, I was often in despair of sound judgment.

But now I must think of more serious matters. My care is more for my salvation than for noble language. I used to read what gave me pleasure, now I read what may be profitable. This is my state of mind, and it has been so for some time. I am not just beginning this practice, and my white hair warns me that I began none too soon. Now my orators shall be Ambrose, Augustine, Jerome, Gregory; my philosopher shall be Paul, my poet David. You remember that years ago, in the first eclogue of my *Bucolicum carmen* I contrasted him with Homer and Virgil, and I left the victory among them undecided. But now, in spite of my old deep-rooted habit, experience and the shining revelation of truth leave me in no doubt as to the victor. But although I put the Christian writers first, I do not reject the others. (Jerome said that he did so, but it seems to me from the imitative style of his writing that he actually approved them.) I seem able to love both groups at once, provided that I consciously distinguish between those I prefer for style and those I prefer for substance. Why should I not act the prudent householder, who assigns part of his furniture for use and another for ornament, who appoints some of his slaves to guard his son, and others to provide the son with sport? Both gold and silver are kinds of money, and you must know their value and not confound them. Especially since those ancient writers demand nothing of me except that I do not let them fall into oblivion. Happy that I have spent upon them my early studies, they now let me give all my time to more important matters.

Since I had already come of myself to this conclusion, I shall now so act the more confidently, thanks to your encouragement. If circumstances require, I shall practice, for style, Virgil and Cicero, and I shall not hesitate to draw from Greece whatever Rome may seem to lack. But for the direction of life, though I know much that is useful in the Classics, I shall still use those counselors and guides to salvation, in whose faith and doctrine there can be no suspicion of error. First among them in point of merit will David always be to me, the more beautiful for his naivety, the more profound, the more vigorous for his purity. I want to have his Psalter always at hand during my waking hours where I may steal a glance at it; and I want to have it beneath my pillow when I sleep and when I come to die. I think that such an outcome will be no less glorious for me than was the act of Plato, greatest of philosophers, in keeping the *Mimes* of Sophron under his pillow.

Farewell, and remember me.

Petrarch, **Letter Describing the Ascent of Mont Ventoux**

Today I climbed the highest mountain of this region, which is not improperly called Mons Ventosus, Windy Mount. I was moved by no other purpose than a desire to see what the great height was like. I had carried this project in mind for many years, for, as you know, I had lived in these parts from childhood on, by the fate that determines human affairs. I had long planned to do what I did today. The actual impulse came when, a day or two ago, I was rereading Livy's *History of Rome*, and I happened on the passage where Philip of Macedon, who carried on the war against the Romans, climbed Mount Hemus in Thessaly. From its summit, according to report, he thought he would be able to descry two seas, the Adriatic and the Euxine. I don't know if this is true or false, for the mountain is far from our regions, and the disagreement of commentators makes it dubious. I won't assemble them all, but Pomponius Mela accepts the statement without hesitation while Livy thinks it false. I shouldn't have left the question long in doubt if the ascent of that mountain were as easy as this one. But to drop that matter, I shall come to our own mountain. I thought it proper for a young private person to attempt what no one criticizes in an aged king.

Thinking about a companion, I found hardly any of my friends entirely suitable, remarkable to state, for even among one's intimates a perfect concord of character and purpose is very rare. One was too phlegmatic, another too eager; one too slow, another too quick; one too gloomy, one too gay; one too dull, another more prudent than I should like. I was frightened by the muteness of one, the talkativeness of another, by the overweight of one, by another's leanness and weakness. The cold incuriosity of one, the officiousness of another discouraged me. Those are the defects that are tolerable enough at home (for charity suffers all things and friendship rejects no burdens), but they are much too serious on a journey. Thus fastidiously, with only my pleasure in view, I cast about, weighing my friends in the balance without doing any injury to friendship; and I silently condemned whatever characteristics might prove a hindrance to my proposed journey. What do you suppose? Finally I looked for aid to my own family. I broached the matter to my younger brother Gherardo, whom you know.

He jumped at the idea. He was much pleased to act at the same time as friend and brother.

On the appointed day we left home and by evening reached Malaucene, at the base of the mountain, on the north side. We stayed there a day, and finally today we made the ascent with two servants, not without difficulty, for the mountain is very steep, an almost inaccessible mass of rock. But the poet well said: "Dogged labor conquers all." The long daylight, the inspiriting air, our high hearts and stout bodies, and all the circumstances helped us on our way. Our obstacle was the nature of the place.

Among the mountain's ridges we met an old shepherd, who tried to discourage us from the ascent with much talk. He said that fifty years before, with an ardent youthful purpose like ours, he had climbed to the very summit and that he had got nothing from it but toil and repentance and torn clothes and scratches from the rocks and briars. Never, he said, had he heard that anyone else either before or after had ventured to do the same. His shouted discouragements merely increased our eagerness, as young men's minds are naturally incredulous of good counselors. So the old man, recognizing that his efforts were useless, went with us a little way among the rocks and pointed out to us a steep course, crying many recommendations and warnings to our retreating backs. We had left with him our extra baggage and other encumbrances and kept only what was necessary for the climb. And so we mounted eagerly upward.

But, as often happens, fatigue soon followed our strenuous effort. So before long we sat down on a rock. Then we went on more slowly, I especially taking the rocky way at a more modest pace. My brother chose the shortest and steepest course, directly up the ridges. Softer than he, I kept turning along the slopes, and when he called to me and pointed to the shorter way, I kept answering that I would find an easier approach on another side, and I didn't mind a longer course that would not be so steep. But this was merely an excuse for laziness. While the others kept to the high ridge, I wandered in the hollows without finding any gentler upward path, and I just lengthened my journey and increased my useless labor. After this floundering vainly and tediously I decided to climb straight up. Exhausted and anxious, I found my brother seated, refreshed by his long wait for me. For a while we kept together. But hardly had we left that rise than what do I do but forget my previous digression and again tend to take a downward course! And again, rounding the hollows and looking for an easy way, I landed in much difficulty. Thus I kept putting off the trouble of climbing; but man's wit can't alter the nature of things, and there is no way for anyone to reach the heights by going downward.

In short, to my brother's great amusement and to my fury, the same thing happened to me three or four times within a few hours. Being so befooled, I sat down in a hollow. My thought quickly turned from the material to the spiritual, and I said to myself in approximately these words: "What you have experienced so often today in the ascent of this mountain certainly happens to you and to many who are striving for the blessed life. But the spiritual straying is not so easily to be perceived, for the movements of the body are in the open, whereas those of the soul are hidden and invisible. The life that we call blessed is situated on a high place; and narrow, we are told, is the way that leads to it; and many hills stand in the way, and we must advance from virtue to virtue up shining steps. The summit is the ultimate goal, the terminus of the road on which we journey. Everyone wishes to arrive there, but, as Ovid says: 'To wish is not enough; to gain your end you must ardently yearn.' You, certainly, both wish and ardently yearn, unless you are fooling yourself, as you so often do. What then holds you back? Surely nothing but the level road that seems at first sight easier, amid base earthly pleasures. But after much wandering you will either have to climb upward eventually, with labors long shirked, to the heights of the blessed life, or lie sluggishly in the valley of your sins. And if—I shudder at the thought!—the darkness and the shadows of death find you there, you will spend an eternal night in perpetual torture."

These thoughts, remarkably enough, spurred my mind and body to accomplish what remained to be done. God grant that my soul may follow the road for which I long night and day, as today I journeyed with my corporeal feet, conquering all difficulties! And why not? The agile, immortal soul can gain its goal in a twinkling, with no intermediate stages. That should be much easier than today's journey, step by step, through the compliance of my feeble, mortal body, burdened by its members.

One hill dominates the others. It is called by the mountaineers Filiolus, or Little Son; why, I don't know, unless by antiphrasis, as is often the case, for it seems the father of all the mountains round about. There is a small level space at the top. There, exhausted, we came to rest.

And now, my dear Father, since you have heard the troubles mounting in the heart of the mounting man, do please hear the rest, and give an hour to reading the events of my day.

At first, affected by the rare quality of the air and by the widespreading view, I stand as if stunned. I look about. Clouds lie far below. The tales of Athos and Olympus seem less incredible, when what I had read of them comes true on this less famous mountain. I look toward

Italy, whither most my soul inclines. The noble snow-topped Alps seem close by, far away though they are. (Through them that fierce enemy of the Roman name once made his way, splitting the rocks with vinegar, if we can believe the story.) I admit that I sighed for the Italian skies, evident more to my thought than to my eyes, and an unspeakable longing invaded me to see again my friend [Giacomo Colonna] and my native land, although I reproached myself for this somewhat unmanly weakness. (Yet there might be excuse for both my desires, and excellent authorities could be alleged in support.)

Then a new thought came to me, rather of time than of space. I said to myself: "Today ten years have passed since you finished your youthful studies and left Bologna. Oh immortal God! Oh immutable Wisdom! What changes in your character have these years seen!" I suppress much, for I have not yet reached a safe harbor from which to look back on the storms of the past. The time will perhaps come when I shall review all my past deeds in their order, prefacing them with the words of St. Augustine: "I wish to recall the filth of my past and the carnal corruptions of my soul, not that I love them, but that I may love thee, O my God!" Indeed, a heavy, a dubious burden still lies upon me. What I used to love, I love no longer. No, I am lying. I love it still, but more moderately. No, again I have lied. I love, but with more shame, more sadness; and now at last I have told the truth. This is the fact: I love, but i love what I long not to love, what I should like to hate. I love nonetheless, but unwillingly, under compulsion, with sadness and mourning. I feel in myself, wretchedly, the sense of Ovid's famous line: "I shall hate if I can; otherwise I shall love in my own despite."

Less than three years have passed since that perverse and guilty desire that totally possessed me, reigning without opposition in my heart's chambers, began to find a champion struggling against it. Between the two impulses a grueling battle has long been fought in my mind by the two men within me, and the outcome is still uncertain.

Thus my thoughts ran back over the previous ten years. Then I transported my distresses to the future, and I asked myself: "If you should by chance prolong this transitory life for ten years more, and continue approaching virtue, substituting new dispositions for old, as you have in the past two years, breaking down your old obstinacy, could you not then, with luck, encounter death at forty and calmly renounce that residuum of life that dwindles into old age?" Such thoughts as these, Father, ran through my mind. I was happy at my progress, I wept for my imperfections, and I took pity on the common inconstancy of human actions; and I forgot what the place was, why I had come there, and how I must have looked to the others.

Then, dismissing my troubles to some more suitable occasion, I looked about me and saw what I had come to see. It was already time to think of starting back, for the sun was descending and the great shadow of the mountain was extending below. Roused and warned, I looked back to the west. The Pyrenean range, boundary of France and Spain, was not visible, not because of any intervening obstacle, but because of the weakness of human vision. On the other hand I could clearly see the Cevennes to the right, and to the left the sea beyond Marseilles and Aigues-Mortes, all several days' journey distant. The Rhone itself lay under our eyes.

While I was admiring all these features, now recognizing some earthly object, now uplifting my soul, like my body, it occurred to me to look at the *Confessions* of Augustine, the gift of your love. (I keep it always with me, for the sake of the author and of the donor. It's of pocket size, but its small volume contains infinite sweetness.) I opened it to read whatever might start forth; what but pious and devout words could start forth? Now by chance it opened to the tenth book. My brother stood intently by, waiting to hear what Augustine would say through my lips. I call God to witness, and my brother too, that the first words on which my eyes fell were these: "Men go to admire the high mountains and the great flood of the seas and the wide-rolling rivers and the ring of Ocean and the movements of the stars; and they abandon themselves!"

I was stunned, I admit. Asking my brother, who was eager to hear more, not to bother me, I shut the book. I was angry with myself for admiring the things of this world, when I should have learned long since from the pagan philosophers themselves that nothing is admirable except the soul, beside the greatness of which nothing is great.

Then, sated with sight of the mountain, I turned my inward eye upon myself, and from that time no one heard me utter a word until we got to the bottom. That quotation had given me enough food for thought, and I couldn't conceive that it had emerged by chance. I was sure that what I read had been written for me and for no one else. I was reminded that Augustine had thought the same when, as he himself tells, he was reading the Epistles and first happened on the passage: "Not in rioting and drunkenness, not in chambering and impurities, not in contention and envy; but put ye on the Lord Jesus Christ, and make not provision for the flesh in its concupiscences." The same thing happened earlier to St. Anthony when he was listening to the Gospel, where it is written: "If thou wilt be perfect, go sell that thou hast, and give to the poor, and thou shalt have treasure in heaven; and come, follow me." As if this Scriptural passage had been uttered for him alone, he drew the kingdom of Heaven to himself, as his biographer Athanasius says. And as Anthony, on hearing these words, asked nothing further, and as Augustine, after reading the significant words, stopped short, so did I, after the few words I have recorded, put an end to my reading.

I thought in silence of the vanity of men's purposes. Neglecting the nobler part of themselves, they disperse themselves in a multitude of trifles and waste themselves in vain shows, and look abroad for what they could find within. I wondered also at the nobility of the human spirit—unless, degenerate, it has wandered from its primitive origins and has turned to shame what God gave it for honor. How often, on the descent, I turned around and looked back at the mountain peak! It seemed hardly more than a cubit high, in comparison with the height of human thought, unless this is plunged in the filth of earth! This thought possessed me for a time: if we were willing to endure so much labor and sweat to raise our bodies a little closer to Heaven, what cross, what prison, what rack should terrify the soul in its approach to God, treading down upthrusting pride and all man's mortal lot? How few are they who are not tempted from this path by fear of hardship or by desire of ease! How happy is such a man, if there be any such! It is he, I think the poet had in mind:

> Happy the man who is skilled to understand
> Nature's hid causes; who beneath his feet
> All terrors casts, and death's relentless doom,
> And the loud roar of greedy Acheron.

How eagerly we should strive to tread beneath our feet, not the world's heights, but the appetites that spring from earthy impulses!

Amid these surging emotions, with no consciousness of the rough and stony way, I came back in deep night to the little country inn from which I had set forth before daybreak. The full moon gave us welcome assistance as we descended. Then, while the servants were busy getting a meal, I retired to a private room to write all this to you hastily and extemporaneously. I was afraid that if I should put it off and go to another place my mood might change and I would lose my eagerness to write you.

Observe then, loving Father, that I wish to keep nothing of myself secret from you. I display to you not only the course of my life but also my various thoughts. And I ask your prayers that these vague, wandering thoughts may some day gain coherence. Now so vainly dispersed, may they be turned to the one good, true, certain, stable end! Farewell.

MARSILIO FICINO

Marsilio Ficino (1433-99), an important figure in Florentine intellectual circles during the Renaissance, was the son of a physician who served Cosimo de' Medici. The Medici had been leading citizens of Florence for several generations and had come to be thought of as generous and discerning patrons of arts and letters. By the time Marsilio came to be educated, Florentine leadership in the revival of classical antiquity was widely recognized and appreciated. Cosimo de' Medici was eager to enhance the reputation of his family and city, and sought projects which would accomplish his goal. Thus it was important that he search out talented young people and see to it that they were well educated so as to become intellectual ornaments for Florence. Upon the urging of a scholar attending the Council of Florence in 1439, Cosimo de' Medici decided to found an academy to foster Greek studies and chose the young Ficino, when he would be educated, to be its head. It was a noble destiny, and Cosimo chose well.

There was considerable debate in Florence about the relative merits of Plato and Aristotle; Cosimo de' Medici made his position on the issue clear when he decreed that his was to be a Platonic Academy. In his late teens, Ficino served as a member of the Medici household and became an avid student of Greek. His rapid progress endeared him to Cosimo who saw his future academician quickly master philosophy in addition to Greek. When Ficino was 23, he presented to Cosimo a work entitled *Outlines of Platonic Thought*. A few years later Cosimo repaid Marsilio handsomely by presenting him with a villa, Careggi, which became the site of Ficino's Academy. In the course of his studies, Ficino became more and more devoted to Christian thought. Eventually, when he was 40, he became a priest.

Ficino remained a student of Greek thought for the remainder of his life. He was inspired by Cosimo de' Medici, nourished by the translations of the master's dialogues he undertook, and fed almost to overflowing by the many scholars with whom he came in contact. His love for Plato was the dominating influence in his life. Completely dedicated to philosophy and shunning the usual amusements of his time, he worked day and night with Plato's texts to penetrate the truths they contained. He often gathered with fellow-lovers of Plato around the bust of the master to discuss and analyze his works. To the end of his life Ficino remained convinced that the thought of Plato was in fundamental accord with Christianity. His most famous work, *Theologia Platonica*, attempted to synthesize Platonic philosophy and Christian theology. This work encompasses all existence but focuses on the human being. Ficino's concern for morality permeates much of his work, and he emphasizes that piety and learning are mutually supportive. At the end of his life his enthusiasm for moral education led Ficino and his academy to support the reforming friar Savonarola. However, as often happens, the reformer's zeal became excessive, and Ficino became disillusioned with his efforts.

From Marsilio Ficino, **Platonic Theology**

Man is really the vicar of God, since he inhabits and cultivates all elements and is present on earth without being absent from the ether. He uses not only the elements, but also all the animals which belong to the elements, the animals of the earth, of the water, and of the air, for food, convenience, and pleasure, and the higher, celestial beings for knowledge and the miracles of magic. Not only does he make use of the animals, he also rules them. It is true, with the weapons received from nature some animals may at times attack man or escape his control. But with the weapons he has invented himself man avoids the attacks of wild animals, puts them to flight, and tames them. Who has ever seen any human beings kept under the control of animals, in such a way as we see everywhere herds of both wild and domesticated animals obeying men throughout their lives? Man not only rules the animals by force, he also governs, keeps, and teaches them. Universal providence belongs to God, who is the universal cause. Hence man who provides generally for all things, both living and lifeless, is a *kind* of god. Certainly he is the god of the animals, for he makes use of them all, rules them all, and instructs many of them. It is also obvious that he is the god of the elements, for he inhabits and cultivates all of them. Finally, he is the god of all materials, for he handles, changes, and shapes all of them. He who governs the *body* in so many and so important ways, and is the vicar of the immortal God, he is no doubt immortal.

But these arts, although they shape the material of the world, rule the animals, and thus imitate God the artisan of nature, are yet inferior to those arts which imitating the divine rule, take care of human government. Individual animals are hardly capable of taking care of themselves or their young. Man alone abounds in such a perfection that he first rules himself, something that no animals do, and thereafter rules the family, administers the state, governs nations, and rules the whole world. As if he were born to rule, he is unable to endure any kind of slavery. Moreover, he undergoes death for the common weal, a thing which no animal does. For man despises these mortal blessings, being confident in the firmness of the common and eternal good.

Some may think that these arts pertain to the present life, and that so much care is not necessary for the present life but should be devoted to the imitation of the divine providence. Let us therefore consider those arts which are not only unnecessary for bodily life, but are most harmful to it, such as all the liberal arts, the study of which weakens the body and impedes the comfort of life: the subtle reckoning of numbers, the curious drawing of figures, the obscure movements of lines and the awe-inspiring consonance of music, the long-continued observation of the stars, the inquiry into natural causes, the investigation of things long past, the eloquence of orators and the madness of poets. In all these arts the mind of man despises the service of the body, since the mind is able at times, and can even now begin, to live without the help of the body.

One point above all should be noted, that not every man can understand how and in what manner the skillful work of a clever artisan is constructed, but only he who possesses a like artistic genius. Certainly no one could understand how Archimedes constructed his brazen spheres and gave them motions like the heavenly motions unless he were endowed with a similar genius. He who can understand it because he has a like genius could doubtless, as soon as he has understood it, also construct another, provided he did not lack the proper material. Now, since man has observed the order of the heavens, when they move, whither they proceed and with what measures, and what they produce, who could deny that man possesses as it were almost the same genius as the Author of the heavens? And who could deny that man could somehow also make the heavens, could he only obtain the instruments and the heavenly material, since even now he makes them, though of a different material, but still with a very similar order?

We have shown that our soul in all its acts is trying with all its power to attain the first gift of God, that is, the possession of all truth and all goodness. Does it also seek His second attribute? Does not the soul try to become everything just as God is everything? It does in a wonderful way; for the soul lives the life of a plant when it serves the body in feeding it; the life of an animal, when it flatters the senses; the life of a man when it deliberates through reason on human affairs; the life of the heroes, when it instigates natural things; the life of the daemons, when it speculates on mathematics; the life of the angels, when it inquires into the divine mysteries; the life of God, when it does everything for God's sake. Every man's soul experiences all these things in itself in some way, although different souls do it in different ways, and thus the human species strives to become all things by living the lives of all things. This is what Hermes Trismegistus was admiring when he said: Man is a great miracle, a living creature worthy of reverence and adoration, for he knows the genus of the daemons as if he were by nature related to them, and he transforms himself into God as if he were God himself.

Moreover, all things that exist, insofar as they exist, are true; and insofar as they possess some force, order and purpose they are good.

We have already shown that the soul seeks all true and all good things. Hence it seeks all things.

What else does the soul seek except to know all things through the intellect and to enjoy them all through the will? In both ways it tries to become all things. One of the senses, for instance, sight, cannot perceive colours unless it assumes the forms of those colours, and unless a single thing is produced from the power of seeing and the actualizing of the visible form, just as a single thing is produced from air and light. In the same way the intellect does not know things themselves unless it is clothed with the forms of the things to be known, and unless a single thing results from the power of thinking and the actualizing of the intelligible form, and their union is accompanied by a single action. . . .

Finally, since the mind is more excellent than matter, it also receives and unites to itself the desired form much more effectively than does matter. We must not believe that the mind is less able to unite to itself what it takes in than is the body. For the body transforms the most diverse foods, the soul digesting them. The mind also transforms into itself what it receives or conceives, and much more so. For corporeal extension prevents a mutual union in bodies, whereas spiritual things are much more adapted to union. Hence, according to Plotinus, the ideas *(rationes)* of things intellectually known pass into the substance of the intellect much more than do foods into the substance of the body. . . .

To conclude, our soul by means of the intellect and will, as by those twin Platonic wings, flies toward God, since by means of them it flies toward all things. By means of the intellect it attaches all things to itself; by means of the will, it attaches itself to all things. Thus the soul desires, endeavours, and begins to become God, and makes progress every day. Every movement directed towards a definite end first begins, then proceeds, then gradually increases and makes progress, and is finally perfected. It is increased through the same power through which it was increased; and finally, it is perfected through the same power through which it made progress. Hence our soul will sometime be able to become in a sense all things; and even to become a god.

PICO DELLA MIRANDOLA

Pico della Mirandola (1463-1494) belongs to the intellectual and cultural movement known as the Italian Renaissance. This movement had its beginnings in the Italian city-state of Florence, and the influential scholar and writer, Petrarch, has often been suggested as its father. Petrarch's respect and admiration for classical antiquity was imparted to the generations of scholars and writers who followed him in Florence and became the dominant intellectual current in Italy in the fifteenth century. The exploration of the various strands of antique culture eventually called attention to Hebrew antiquity and, of course, the Bible. The more that was discovered, the more some scholars sought to blend, harmonize, and finally synthesize the various traditions.

One of the most audacious synthesizers was Pico della Mirandola. A precocious lad, Pico studied at several Italian universities, the University of Paris, and finally came to Florence in 1484. Known for his fabulous memory, he was fluent in Latin and Greek at the age of 16. His studies at the Academy in Florence embraced both the thought of classical antiquity and Christian thought. He decided to learn Hebrew in order to become more profoundly acquainted with Scripture and came to harbor the conviction that he could arrive at a synthesis of Christian and Platonic thought. In 1486, he published in Rome nine hundred *conclusiones,* theses which he offered to defend publicly against all comers. He even offered to pay the traveling expenses of any challenger! Pico's most famous publication, *On the Dignity of Man,* exalts the creative potentialities of man well beyond the usual Christian notions of Pico's time. Religious sensitivity was prominent in Pico's nature, and his ideas are not without traces of extravagance. When he died in 1494, at the untimely age of 31, he devoutly believed that Christ, Plato, Aristotle, Moses, and Mohammed were in basic agreement, and that all truth and knowledge are one!

Pico della Mirandola, **Oration on the Dignity of Man**

I have read in the records of the Arabians, reverend Fathers, that Abdala the Saracen, when questioned as to what on this stage of the world, as it were, could be seen most worthy of wonder, replied: "There is nothing to be seen more wonderful than man." In agreement with this opinion is the saying of Hermes Trismegistus: "A great miracle, Asclepius, is man." But when I weighed the reason for these maxims, the many grounds for the excellence of human nature reported by many men failed to satisfy me—that man is the intermediary between the creatures, the intimate of the gods, the king of the lower beings, by the acuteness of his senses, by the discernment of his reason, and by the light of his intelligence and the interpreter of nature, the interval between fixed eternity and fleeting time, and (as the Persians say) the bond, nay, rather, the marriage song of the world, on David's testimony but little lower than the angels. Admittedly great though these reasons be, they are not the principal grounds, that is, those which may rightfully claim for themselves the privilege of the highest admiration. For why should we not admire more the angels themselves and the blessed choir of heaven? At least it seems to me I have come to understand why man is the most fortunate of creatures and consequently worthy of all admiration and what precisely is that rank which is his lot in the universal chain of Being—a rank to be envied not only by brutes but even by the stars and by minds beyond this world. It is a matter past faith and a wondrous one. Why should it not be? For it is on this very account that man is rightly called and judged a great miracle and a wonderful creature indeed.

2. But hear, Fathers, exactly what this rank is and, as friendly auditors, conformably to your kindness, do me this favor. God the Father, the supreme Architect, had already built this cosmic home we behold, the most sacred temple of His godhead, by the laws of His mysterious wisdom. The region above the heavens He had adorned with Intelligence, the heavenly spheres He had quickened with eternal souls, and the excrementary and filthy parts of the lower world He had filled with a multitude of animals of every kind. But, when the work was finished, the Craftsman kept wishing that there were someone to ponder the plan of so great a work, to love its beauty, and to wonder at its vastness. Therefore, when everything was done (as Moses and Timaeus bear witness), He finally took thought concerning the creation of man. But there was not among His archetypes that from which He could fashion a new offspring, nor was there in His treasurehouses anything which He might bestow on His new son as an inheritance, nor was there in the seats of all the world a place where the latter might set to contemplate the universe. All was now complete; all things had been assigned to the highest, the middle, and the lowest orders. But in its final creation it was not the part of the Father's power to fail as though exhausted. It was not the part of His wisdom to waver in a needful matter through poverty of counsel. It was not the part of His kindly love that he who was to praise God's divine generosity in regard to others should be compelled to condemn it in regard to himself.

3. At last the best artisans ordained that that creature to whom He had been able to give nothing proper to himself should have joint possession of whatever had been peculiar to each of the different kinds of being. He therefore took man as a creature of indeterminate nature and, assigning him a place in the middle of the world, addressed him thus: "Neither a fixed abode nor a form that is thine alone nor any function peculiar to thyself have we given thee, Adam, to the end that according to thy longing and according to thy judgment thou mayest have and possess what abode, what form, and what functions thou thyself shall desire. The nature of all other beings is limited and constrained within the bounds of laws prescribed by Us. Thou, constrained by no limits, in accordance with thine own free will, in whose hand

We have placed thee, shalt ordain for thyself the limits of thy nature. We have set thee at the world's center that thou mayest from thence more easily observe whatever is in the world. We have made thee neither of heaven nor of earth, neither mortal nor immortal, so that with freedom of choice and with honor, as though the maker and molder of thyself, thou mayest fashion thyself in whatever shape thou shalt prefer. Thou shalt have the power to degenerate into the lower forms of life, which are brutish. Thou shalt have the power, out of thy soul's judgment, to be reborn into the higher forms, which are divine."

4. O supreme generosity of God the Father, O highest and most marvelous felicity of man! To him it is granted to have whatever he chooses, to be whatever he wills. Beasts as soon as they are born (so says Lucilius) bring with them from their mother's womb all they will ever possess. Spiritual beings, either from the beginning or soon thereafter, become what they are to be for ever and ever. On man when he came into life the Father conferred the seeds of all kinds and the germs of every way of life. Whatever seeds each man cultivates will grow to maturity and bear in him their own fruit. If they be vegetative, he will be like a plant. If sensitive, he will become brutish. If rational, he will grow into a heavenly being. If intellectual, he will be an angel and the son of God. And if, happy in the lot of no created thing, he withdraws into the center of his own unity, his spirit, made one with God, in the solitary darkness of God, who is set above all things, shall surpass them all. Who would not admire this our chameleon? Or who could more greatly admire aught else whatever? It is man who Asclepius of Athens, arguing from his mutability of character and from his self-transforming nature, on just grounds says was symbolized by Proteus in the mysteries. Hence those metamorphoses renowned among the Hebrews and the Pythagoreans.

10. Then let us fill our well-prepared and purified soul with the light of natural philosophy, so that we may at last perfect her in the knowledge of things divine. And lest we be satisfied with those of our faith, let us consult the patriarch Jacob, whose form gleams carved on the throne of glory. Sleeping in the lower world but keeping watch in the upper, the wisest of fathers will advise us. But he will advise us through a figure (on this way everything was wont to come to those men) that there is a ladder extending from the lowest earth to the highest heaven, divided in a series of many steps, with the Lord seated at the top, and angels in contemplation ascending and descending over them alternately by turns.

13. Surely, Fathers, there is in us a discord many times as great; we have at hand wars grievous and more than civil, wars of the spirit which, if we dislike them, if we aspire to that peace which may so

raise us to the sublime that we shall be established among the exalted of the Lord, only philosophy will entirely allay and subdue in us. In the first place, if our man but ask a truce of his enemies, moral philosophy will check the unbridled inroads of the many-sided beast and the leonine passions of wrath and violence. If we then take wiser counsel with ourselves and learn to desire the security of everlasting peace, it will be at hand and will generously fulfill our prayers. After both beasts are felled into a sacrificed sow, it will confirm an inviolable compact of holiest peace between flesh and spirit. Dialectic will appease the tumults of reason made confused and anxious by inconsistencies of statement and sophisms of syllogisms. Natural philosophy will allay the strife and differences of opinion which vex, distract, and wound the spirit from all sides. But she will so assuage them as to compel us to remember that, according to Heraclitus, nature was begotten from war, that it was on this account repeatedly called "strife" by Homer, and that it is not, therefore, in the power of natural philosophy to give us in nature a true quiet and unshaken peace but that this is the function and privilege of her mistress, that is, of holiest theology. She will show us the way and as comrade lead us to her who, seeing us hastening from afar, will exclaim "Come to me, ye who have labored. Come and I will restore you. Come to me, and I will give you peace, which the world and nature cannot give you."

17. If anyone investigates the holy names of Apollo, their meanings and hidden mysteries, these amply show that god is no less a philosopher than a seer; but, since Ammonius has sufficiently examined this subject, there is no reason why I should now treat it otherwise. But, Fathers, three Delphic precepts may suggest themselves to your minds, which are very necessary to those who are to go into the most sacred and revered temple, not of the false but of the true Apollo, who lights every soul as it enters this world. You will see that they give us no other advice than that we should with all our strength embrace this threefold philosophy which is the concern of our present debate. For the saying *mēden agan*, that is, "Nothing too much," prescribes a standard and rule for all the virtues through the doctrine of the Mean, with which moral philosophy deals. Then the saying *gnōthi seauton*, that is, "Know thyself," urges and encourages us to the investigation of all nature, of which the nature of man is both the connecting link and, so to speak, the "mixed bowl." For he who knows himself in himself knows all things, as Zoroaster first wrote, and then Plato in his *Alcibiades*. When we are finally lighted in this knowledge by natural philosophy, and nearest to God are uttering the theological greeting, *ei*, that is, "Thou Art," we shall likewise in bliss be addressing the true Apollo on intimate terms.

[Note: Pico goes on to discuss the views of Pythagoras, Zoroaster, and the "Chaldeans" and others. Finally, he turns to the Jewish cabala, a medieval occult interpretation of the Bible too complex to attempt to describe further here.]

ERASMUS

Erasmus of Rotterdam (1469-1536) is regarded by many as the pre-eminent Christian humanist of the Renaissance. That view was widely held even by many contemporaries of Erasmus. Born in the Low Countries, Erasmus spent his youth in the care of the Brethren of the Common Life, from whom he learned much. He seemed destined for the monastery but developed a strong dislike for monks and the monastic learning of his time. He became one of the most severe critics of monasticism and remained so for most of the rest of his life.

His studies put him in contact with the writings of the ancients, and he developed a taste for pagan Latin writings. He quickly learned the value of a good literary style and all of his writings demonstrate his concern to develop a lucid, elegant Latin literary style. In this there is no doubt that he succeeded.

For his time he was a man who traveled rather widely. He sampled scholasticism at the University of Paris and found it arid and unprofitable; he visited England and made many friends at Oxford, including the young Thomas More.

During his travels Erasmus worked on his publications, most of which achieved considerable fame during his lifetime. In 1500, he published his *Adages,* a collection of sayings culled from Latin writers; this work went through many editions during his lifetime. In 1503 Erasmus published his *Handbook of a Militant Christian (Enchiridion Militis Christiani)* in praise of Christian ideals; the work was warmly received all over Europe and achieved great influence in the sixteenth century. When he published his most famous and popular work, *Praise of Folly,* in 1511, he was already a man of considerable renown. This satire proved to be a devastating attack on human foibles: folly is at the root of every human action. A continual stream of letters flowed from his pen, each a minor literary masterpiece. In 1516 Erasmus published what he considered the highlight of his schol-arly work, a new edition of the Greek text of the New Testament. This too was warmly received throughout Europe.

Late in his life Erasmus tangled with the great Martin Luther. Though both men strongly criticized the church, they took divergent paths toward reform. By temperament, Erasmus was inclined to moderation and compromise, traits many of his contemporaries, including Luther, did not appreciate.

The subject over which Erasmus fought with Luther was the freedom of the will. In 1520 Luther published *The Freedom of the Christian* which declared that good works, if done with an eye to gaining credit with God, are "damnable sins." Erasmus disputed these assertions in *Concerning the Freedom of the Will*. Erasmus was willing to speak of human cooperation with God in salvation.

From Erasmus, **Handbook of a Militant Christian**

I

You have requested, my dearly beloved in Christ, that I compose for you a kind of compendium, or guide for spiritual living, so that being instructed by it you may attain those virtues of mind that should characterize him who is truly Christian. In this request you have also indicated that your preoccupation with mundane affairs has forced you to perceive the need you have of abandoning worldly pursuits and turning your efforts rather to the attainment of virtue. Our own close friendship only adds to the joy with which I undertake this proposal, and I sincerely hope that He who is solely responsible for your decision will aid me in this endeavor. So that what I have to write will not in the end prove fruitless, let us begin by calling upon the kindly spirit of Jesus so that He will fill my mind with words of salvation, and that what I write will be for you a source of strength and determination.

1. *In this life it is necessary that we be on guard.*

To begin with we must be constantly aware of the fact that life here below is best described as being a type of continual warfare. This is a fact that Job, that undefeated soldier of vast experience, tells us so plainly. Yet in this matter the great majority of mankind is often deceived, for the world, like some deceitful magician, captivates their minds with seductive blandishments, and as a result most individuals behave as if there had been a cessation of hostilities. They celebrate as if they were assured of victory when, as a matter of fact, genuine peace could never be further away. It is amazing to see in what false security these people live and in what a complacent manner they close their minds to reality. In the meantime the vices, our armored enemies, attack us unceasingly; we are entrapped by their espionage and assaulted by their endless deceptions. If you but look around, you will see that regardless of where you go they are observing you. They are prepared to attack us with a thousand stratagems and, evil demons that they are, they concentrate on wounding our minds with inflammable and poisonous weapons. Unless we ward them off with the impenetrable shield of faith, they will prove to wield weapons of certain death. Nor is there any slackening in the manner of their attack, as it comes from all sides.

This is that world that St. John describes so well as being constituted entirely of vice. It is a world that is both contrary and hateful to Christ. It must be pointed out that the type of warfare it wages is anything but simple and straightforward. From time to time, especially in adverse circumstances, this raging world shakes the very walls of the mind. At other times it incites the mind to betrayal with vain promises. Or again, whenever it finds us unaware, in idle and false security, it unexpectedly and with secret contrivances captures the mind. Most important of all, that slimy snake, the first betrayer of our peace and the father of restlessness, never ceases to watch and lie in wait beneath the heel of woman, whom he once poisoned. By "woman" we mean, of course, the carnal or sensual part of man. For this is our Eve, through whom the crafty serpent entices and lures our mind to deadly pleasures. And yet, as if it were not enough that he threatens us from all directions on the outside, he also penetrates into the inner recesses of our minds. This is the ancient and earthly Adam, more intimate than our closest companions and more zealous than our deadliest enemy, since he cannot be contained by entrenchment or expelled with an army. He must be watched, then, with a hundred eyes, lest he expose God's fortress to demons.

Since it is quite plain that all of us are engaged in a major and difficult effort against an enemy who is numerically superior, better armed and more experienced than we are, are we not insane if we fail to take up arms against him? Are we not extremely foolish if we do not stand continually on our guard and hold all things suspect? The fact of the matter is, however, that we slumber complacently through the whole siege. Indulgence in pleasure rather than hard work seems to be the norm. The self-interest we display would convince one that we are living in peaceful times. It seems that life is a drinking bout rather than a war. We clothe ourselves with boudoir trappings rather than armor. Ease and self-indulgence are everywhere preferred to the rigors of military preparedness. We practice on the peaceful harp rather than on the weapons of warfare, unaware that this sort of peace is the most terrible of all wars.

Anyone who concludes a treaty with vice violates the agreement made with God in baptism. You foolishly cry, "peace, peace," and at the same time treat as an enemy God, who alone is peace and the author of peace. He Himself has made it quite plain through His prophet:

"There is no peace for the wicked." The condition that He lays down for peace is that we fight in the garrison of the body against all of our vices. If we compromise, if we consort with vice, we will make a foe of Him who alone, as a friend, is able to bless us, but who as an enemy will surely damn us. He will be our enemy for two reasons. First of all we will be siding with those vices that are diametrically opposed to the divine, for how can light and darkness be in agreement? In the second place, in so doing we ungratefully fail to abide by the pledge that we have made to Him, violating what we have solemnized with sacred ceremonies. Perhaps you are not aware, O Christian soldier, that when you were initiated into the mysteries of life-giving Baptism, you gave yourself by name to Christ as your leader. That is the reason you are doubly indebted to Him. He not only gave you life in the first place but He also restored it. You owe Him more than you could ever owe to yourself. If you break this contract, does it not occur to you that you are violating a pledge to such a kindly leader? Does it become quite plain to you that you have dedicated yourself in this sacrament to His most noble cause? Why did He see to it that you were anointed with sacred oils except to take up arms in this struggle against vice? What could be more shameful, more degrading, than to separate yourself from this princely leader? Is there any reason why you should hold Christ the King in derision? Does not the fact that He is God at least instill you with fear? Are you not moved by the love of Him who for your sake became man? Has no one ever warned you of the promise you once laid before Him? Will you actually betray Him who once redeemed you with the price of His blood?

Certainly you show the greatest impudence if you dare raise a hostile standard against a King who gave His life for your sake. He Himself has told us clearly that he who does not stand for Him stands against Him, and he who does not gather with Him, scatters. Not only do you fight under a disgraceful banner, but consider for a moment what your reward will be. St. Paul, the standard-bearer of Christian warfare, tells us "the wages of sin is death." Would anyone engage in warfare if death were the only reward? Death of the soul is hardly a reward. Look at the actual condition of misery that accompanies human warfare. What motivates the soldiers to endure such hardships and deprivation? Is it not the promise of booty, the dread of loss, and the fear of being accused of cowardice? If all they get is the praise of their officers or the hope of a little more pay, that is not much of a reward. Our motives can be neither the fear of shame nor the hope of reward. The same Person witnesses our struggle who will one day reward us. Our reward is that which "neither eye has seen, nor ear heard, nor has entered into the heart of man." I think this in itself ought to be of great consolation as we carry on the battle, for it is eternal happiness that will be ours.

In all earthly engagements a reputation for bravery is the goal, and even the material rewards are handed out by lot. With us in our struggle against vice the case is not quite the same. We do not fight for praise but for Life itself. And the very highest reward will go to him who perseveres, just as the most severe punishment will be meted out to him who deserts. Heaven itself is the promise we seek, and certainly the very hope of such a prize ought to encourage our efforts, especially when it is promised by Him who can neither deceive nor be deceived. Then, too, our struggle takes place before the all-seeing eye of God and is witnessed by the entire populace of heaven. The shame of defeat in the presence of such an audience ought at least to help inspire us to bravery. He will praise our effort whose mere approval alone is the equivalent of the greatest happiness. If the tepid mind is not aroused by the prospect of reward, it must be admitted that fear of punishment can awaken even the most indolent.

In ancient times it was customary in war to violate the corpses of the enemy. It was considered a great calamity if the body were separated by the sword from the soul. This enemy of ours is not only determined to destroy the body but he intends to cast both the body and the soul into hell. For this is actually what occurs when life, which is God Himself, is taken away from the soul. We know well enough that it is the nature of the body eventually to perish because, even though no one attempts to kill it, it cannot live on forever. But for the soul to die is another matter, one of extreme misfortune. I do not have to point out to you the great care and solicitude we exercise in caring for the wounds of the body; we doctor them with the greatest of concern. And yet at the same time we woefully neglect the wounds of the soul. All of us are horrified at the sight of a dying boy because we are able to witness it with our bodily eyes. Yet, since the death of the soul is something we cannot witness, there are very few who believe in it and even fewer who are actually frightened at the thought of it. I might point out that the death of the soul is certainly more frightful than the death of the body. This is evident from the fact that the soul is something far greater than the body, and God, whose loss it entails, is greater than the soul.

Let me give you some signs, some evidence, whereby you can determine whether or not your soul is diseased or perhaps even dead. If you are troubled with indigestion, if it is difficult to retain food, it is quite apparent that there is something physically wrong with your body. Now the Word of God has been referred to as the food of the soul. If it is unpalatable, if it nauseates you, there can be little doubt that

the palate of your soul is infected with disease. If the food is not retained, if it does not proceed along the digestive tract, it is pretty clear
that your soul is sick. When your knees totter and it is only with difficulty that you drag your ailing limbs about, it is quite evident that you
have an ailing body. Now you must certainly have a disease of the soul
when the performance of an act of piety is done with great reluctance
and hesitancy, when you have no strength to bear up under a slight
rebuke, or when the loss of a few pennies makes you troubled and
angry. There can be no doubt that after the sight leaves the body, when
the ears fail to hear and the whole body loses its sensitivity, then the
soul has departed. When the eyes of the heart are so obscured that you
cannot perceive the brightest light (that is, truth), when you are no
longer aware with your inner ears of the divine voice, do you think
your soul is really alive? You see your brother suffering indignities.
Provided your own affairs are not endangered, your mind is not in
the least moved. Why at this point does your soul feel absolutely
nothing? It certainly must be because it is dead. Why dead? Because
God, its very life, is not present. Where God is, there is charity, for
God is charity. Otherwise, if you are a living member, how can any
part of the body be in pain without your feeling anything?

Let me give you another sign that is even more certain. Supposing
that you have deceived a friend, or that you have committed adultery;
in other words, you should have received a major wound, and yet not
only are you unaware of any pain, but you actually take pleasure in
recalling your wickedness. Can there be any doubt that your soul is
dead? We generally assume that the body is not alive if it is insen-
sible to the prick of a pin. Can a soul be considered alive if it is unfeeling in this matter? Let us take another example. You happen to be
in the company of someone who is using filthy language, who is raging in anger against his neighbor. If you think that his soul is alive,
you are deceiving yourself. It is more like a stinking corpse whose
foulness infects all who come near it. Christ referred to the Pharisees
as whitened sepulchers. Why? Because they carried their dead souls
about within themselves. The bodies of holy people are temples of the
Holy Spirit. The bodies of evil men are sepulchers of dead corpses.
No cadaver is so dead as that soul that has been abandoned by God.
And certainly no corpse offends the nostrils of men to the extent that
the evil odor of the buried soul offends the sensibility of the heavenly
court. When dying words proceed from the heart, we can assume that
a dead soul lies within. For, according to the saying of the Gospel, "the
mouth speaks from the abundance of the heart," and if God, the life of
the soul, is present, the soul will speak divine words.

If we read the Gospel, we find that the disciples once asked our Lord,

"Whither shall we go? You have the words of life." Why "words of life"? The only answer to be found is the fact that these words flowed from a soul that was never for a moment separated from the divinity and that alone restores us to everlasting life. It is not a rare thing that pious men have recalled a dead body to life. But we must never forget that God does not revive a dead soul except by an extraordinary and gratuitous power, and certainly He does not resuscitate it if it is already dead when it leaves the body. I think that we can agree that the sensation of death in the body is very slight or, at least, very brief. The sensation of death in the case of the soul is entirely different; it is more than death itself, because it is everlasting.

With these remarks in mind need I point out further the tremendous powers of our adversary? It would be sheer stupidity not to be aroused to this fearful danger and to take the necessary precautions against it. On the other hand you must avoid the pitfalls of losing courage or feeling unable to cope with the situation. For we must never forget that regardless of the strength of the enemy we have an ever-present and an all-powerful auxiliary. "If God is for us, who is against us?" If He sustains us, what can be lacking? We must be ever inflamed with the hope and conviction of final victory. Let us not forget that our encounter is not with an undefeated enemy but with one who was once broken and who many years ago was overthrown, despoiled, and led captive by Christ our Head. This same Christ will unquestionably subdue him again in us. If we but remember to whose Body we belong, we will triumph in the strength of our Head. No man is strong in his own strength. In Him alone will we find our real worth.

This is the reason why I reiterate that the outcome of this war is not in the least to be doubted. Victory is not something that depends upon chance; it is entirely in the hands of God and, through Him, also in our hands. Anyone who has failed in this struggle was simply lacking in a will to conquer. The kindness of our Leader has never failed anyone. If you but listen to His call and do your part, you will be assured of victory, for not only will He fight alongside you, but His very liberality will be imputed to you as merit. At the same time you must thank Him alone for the victory. He alone is immune from sin and He alone first oppressed its tyranny. Yet this victory will not come without your own effort and diligence, for He who said, "Have confidence, I have conquered the world," does not want your confidence to be a matter of complacency. Profiting by His example, we will fight as He fought. We must steer a middle course between Scylla and Charybdis, neither acting too presumptuously because we rely too much on divine grace, nor surrendering in despair because we are disheartened by the difficulties of the war.

2. The weapons of Christian warfare.

I think we can truthfully say that nothing is more important in military training than a thorough knowledge of the weapons to be employed and the nature of the enemy to be encountered. I would add to this that the need for preparedness, of having the weapons close at hand, is also of the utmost importance. In ordinary warfare it is customary that leave of absence or actual retirement to winter quarters brings about a cessation of hostilities from time to time. This is certainly not the case in the kind of warfare we are describing. We can never permit ourselves to be even a finger's length from our weapons. Since our enemy is incessant in his attacks, we must be constantly on the battle line, constantly in a state of preparedness. As a matter of fact, our enemy, when he appears peaceful, when he feigns flight or a truce, can at that very moment be assumed to be preparing for an attack. He is most dangerous when he appears peaceful, and it is during his violent attacks that we can actually feel most secure. It is for this reason that our primary concern must be to keep the mind armed. Our enemies are armed for no other purpose than to destroy us; surely we should not be ashamed to take up arms so as not to perish.

We will speak about Christian armor more in detail when we treat that subject later on. Meanwhile I would like to point out briefly two weapons that we should prepare to use in combating the chief vices. These weapons are prayer and knowledge. St. Paul clearly expresses the desire that men be continually armed when he commands us to pray without ceasing. Pure prayer directed to heaven is able to subdue passion, for it is, as it were, a citadel inaccessible to the enemy. Knowledge, or learning, fortifies the mind with salutary precepts and keeps virtue ever before us. These two are inseparable, the former imploring but the latter suggesting what should be prayed for. St. James tells us that we should pray always for faith and hope, seeking the things of salvation in Jesus' name. We may recall that Christ asked the sons of Zebedee if they really knew what they were praying for. We must always emphasize the dual necessity of both prayer and knowledge. In your flight from sin imitate Aaron as a model of prayer and Moses as an example of knowledge of the law. Neither allow your knowledge to lessen nor your prayer to become sterile.

Listen for a moment to what Christ has to say in Matthew's Gospel: "But in praying, do not multiply words, as the Gentiles do; for they think that by saying a great deal, they will be heard. So do not be like them; for your Father knows what you need before you ask Him." And St. Paul condemns ten thousand words spoken with the lips in favor of five uttered in understanding. Moses spoke nothing yet he

heard the words, "Why do you call after me?" It is not the loud sound
of the mouth, but rather the pleas of an ardent soul that reach the
divine ear. Try to let this be a practice with you: When the enemy
assaults you and the other vices give you trouble, lift up your mind to
heaven and in your faith do not fail to raise up your hands also. Perhaps the best remedy in this matter is to be continually occupied with
works of piety so that you will revert, not to worldly affairs, but
to Christ.

You must believe me when I say that there is really no attack from
the enemy, no temptation so violent, that a sincere resort to Holy Writ
will not easily get rid of it. There is no misfortune so sad that a reading
of the Scriptures does not render bearable. Therefore, if you will but
dedicate yourself entirely to the study of the Scriptures, if you meditate
day and night on the divine law, nothing will ever terrorize you and
you will be prepared against any attack of the enemy.

I might also add that a sensible reading of the pagan poets and philosophers is a good preparation for the Christian life. We have the
example of St. Basil, who recommends the ancient poets for their
natural goodness. Both St. Augustine and St. Jerome followed this
method. St. Cyprian has worked wonders in adorning the Scriptures
with the literary beauty of the ancients. Of course it is not my intention
that you imbibe the bad morals of the pagans along with their literary
excellence. I am sure that you will nonetheless find many examples in
the classics that are conducive to right living. Many of these writers
were, of course, very good teachers of ethics. We have the example of
Moses, who did not spurn the advice of Jethro. These readings mature
us and constitute a wonderful preparation for an understanding of the
Scriptures. I feel this is quite important, because to break in upon these
sacred writings without this preparation is almost sacrilegious. St.
Jerome assails the presumption of those who, even though they may be
learned in other fields, presume to expatiate on the Bible. You can
imagine the audacity of those who, having no preparation whatsoever,
try to do the same thing.

We must not persist in clinging to the letter, and the reading of
Homer and Virgil will be of no use unless we look to its allegorical
side. If you like the classics, then you will understand what I mean.
If the obscene passages in the ancients bother you, then by all means
refrain from reading them. Of all the philosophical writings I would
recommend the Platonists most highly. For not only their ideas but
their very mode of expression approaches that of the Gospels. Of course
they should be read in a cursory manner, and whatever is of real value
in them should be applied and referred to Christ. If to the pure of heart

all things are clean, then to the impure everything appears to be unclean. Whenever the reading of secular selections arouses your baser appetites, then leave them alone.

Reading the Scriptures with a clean heart is a basic rule. It prevents what is intended to be medicinal from becoming noxious. You must maintain at all times a high regard for the revealed word. It is genuine because it has its origin in the very mind of God. If you approach the Scriptures in all humility and with regulated caution, you will perceive that you have been breathed upon by the Holy Will. It will bring about a transformation that is impossible to describe. You will perceive the delights of the Blessed Bridegroom; you will see the riches of Solomon. The hidden treasures of eternal wisdom will be yours. Yet I would caution you. The entrance to this abode of wisdom is narrow. The doorway is low, and there is danger in not stooping when you enter. There is nothing that you can believe with greater certitude than what you read in these writings. The senses themselves cannot offer greater certainty. Divine revelation has made it clear that heaven and earth will not pass away before all that is contained therein is fulfilled. Man may lie and make mistakes; the truth of God neither deceives nor is deceived.

Let me mention another requirement for a better understanding of Holy Scripture. I would suggest that you read those commentators who do not stick so closely to the literal sense. The ones I would recommend most highly after St. Paul himself are Origen, Ambrose, Jerome, and Augustine. Too many of our modern theologians are prone to a literal interpretation, which they subtly misconstrue. They do not delve into the mysteries, and they act as if St. Paul were not speaking the truth when he says that our law is spiritual. There are some of these theologians who are so completely taken up with these human commentators that they relegate what the Fathers had to say to the realm of dreams. They are so entranced with the writings of Duns Scotus that, without ever having read the Scriptures, they believe themselves to be competent theologians. I care not how subtle their distinctions are; they are certainly not the final word on what pertains to the Holy Spirit.

If your interest in sacred doctrine revolves more about what is vital and dynamic rather than merely dialectical, if you incline more toward what moves the inner man than to what leads to empty arguments, then read the Fathers. Their deep piety has withstood the test of time. Their very thoughts constitute a prayerful meditation, and they penetrate into the very depths of the mysteries they propound. I do not mean to condemn modern theologians; I am merely pointing out that in view of our purpose, namely, a more practical piety, they are hardly to be recommended. Let us not forget that the Divine Spirit has its own

manner of speaking and its own figures of speech. Learn these from the
very outset. The Divine Wisdom speaks to us and, like an attentive
mother, adjusts Her language to our infancy. For the tiny infants she
provides milk and for the sick, herbs. To receive solid food you must
grow up spiritually. She lowers Herself to your humility. You must
raise yourself to Her sublimity. To remain like an infant is unfortunate.
Unending illness is reprehensible. Pluck the marrow from the broken
bone: meditation upon a single verse gives more nourishment, brings
more wisdom, than continued verbal repetition of the whole psalm.

I warn you with the more diligence because I know that this error
has confused, not merely the crowd, but also those who in name and
in garb claim perfect religion. These people believe the greatest piety
is repeating as many psalms as possible every day, though they scarcely
understand them. On every side monastic piety grows cold, languishes,
and disappears because the monks grow old and gray in the letter of
the Scriptures rather than maturing to a spiritual understanding. They
fail to hear Christ proclaiming in the Gospel, "The flesh profits nothing,
it is the spirit that gives life." We know the law is spiritual. Spiritual
things should not be made carnal. In times past the Father was worshipped in the mountains. Now He wants to be worshipped in the spirit.

I do not want to be misunderstood. I by no means despise the weakness of those who, from feebleness of mind, do the only things they are
able to do. Certain words in magic rituals are thought efficacious even
when those who pronounce them do so without understanding them.
Likewise, divine words, though little understood, should be believed
beneficial for those who speak or hear them in sincere faith and pure
affection. The angels who are present bring assistance. Nor, indeed,
does Paul condemn those who sing in the spirit or those who speak in
tongues. But he does urge a fuller use of graces. Of course there is no
shame for those prevented from better things by vice, not of the mind,
but of nature. As St. Paul has said, "Let not him who eats despise
him who does not eat; and let not him who does not eat judge him
who eats."

However, I do not want you who are better endowed to remain content with the barren letter. Rather, I want you to pass on to the more
profound mysteries. Strengthen yourselves with frequent prayer, until
He who holds the key of David, who closes and no one opens, will open
for you the book sealed with the seven seals—the secrets of the Father,
which no one knows except the Son and he to whom the Son deigns to
reveal them.

But how should you pray? I intended to describe a way of life, not
a method of learning. Yet I deviated a bit to point out an arsenal of

weapons that you could profitably use in this new type of warfare. So pick out from pagan books whatever is best. In studying the ancients follow the example of the bee flying about the garden. Like the bee, suck out only what is wholesome and sweet; reject what is useless and poisonous. Follow this rule, and your mind will be better clothed. Then you will enter into the battle of daily life better armed. Nonetheless, whenever you find truth and virtue, refer it to Christ. If you wish to consult the treasure house of Paul, that valiant captain, there you will discover "that the weapons of our warfare are not of the flesh, but are mighty before God for the destruction of fortifications, destroying counsels and every height that tends to bar the knowledge of God." You will find the weapons of God by which you can endure an evil day. On your right you will find the arms of justice, on your left the armor of truth, the breastplate of justice, and the shield of faith, a shield with which you can ward off the fiery darts of the devil. You will find also the helmet of salvation and the sword of the spirit, which is the word of God. Carefully fortified with these weapons, a man can fearlessly utter those courageous words of Paul: "Who shall separate us from the love of Christ? Shall tribulation, or distress, or famine, or peril, or persecution, or the sword?" See the many enemies the devil directs and how frightened they are at everything. But hear something stronger. Paul adds, "But in all these things we conquer because of Him who has loved us. For I am sure that neither death, nor life, nor angels, nor principalities, nor powers, nor things present, nor any other creatures shall be able to separate us from the love of God which is in Christ Jesus." What a happy confidence the arms of light give to Paul, an insignificant man who called himself a castoff of the world!

But to return to our original purpose. We must forge a handy weapon, an enchiridion, a dagger, that you can always carry with you. You must be on guard when you eat or sleep, even when you travel in the course of worldly concerns and perhaps become weary of bearing this righteous armor. Never allow yourself to be totally disarmed, even for a moment, lest your wily foe oppress you. Do not be ashamed to carry this little sword with you. For it is neither a hardship to bear nor useless in defending yourself. Though it is a small weapon, it will enable you, if you use it skillfully, to withstand the enemy's tumultuous assaults quite easily and avoid a deadly wound. Now is the time for us to teach ourselves a kind of "manual of arms." I promise that, if you diligently train yourself in it, our sovereign Lord, Jesus Christ, will transfer you, rejoicing and victorious, from this garrison to the city of Jerusalem, where there is neither tumult nor war at all, but everlasting peace and perfect tranquillity. Meanwhile all hope of safety should be placed in your arms and your armor.

3. *The crown of wisdom is that you know yourself; and of the two sorts of wisdom, false and true.*

Peace is the highest good to which even the lovers of the world turn all their efforts. As has been said, however, their peace is a false one. It is this same sort of peace that the philosophers promise to those who follow their teachings. Christ alone grants that peace that the world cannot give. There is but one way to attain it; we must wage war with ourselves. We must contend fiercely with our vices. God, our peace, is separated from these enemies by an implacable hatred. His nature is virtue itself. He is the parent and author of all virtue. The dregs drawn from every kind of vice are called folly by the staunchest defenders of virtue, the Stoics. Scripture labels this folly malice. Among all these writers absolute probity is called wisdom. Does not the oracle of the wise man say "wisdom conquers malice"? The father and prince of malice is that ruler of darkness, Belial. Anyone who follows his leadership, walking in the night, hastens to eternal night. On the contrary, the author of wisdom, and Himself Wisdom, Christ Jesus, who is the true Light, alone shatters the night of earthly folly. He is the Splendor of paternal glory, who, as He was made the redemption and justification for us reborn in Him, so also was made Wisdom, as Paul testifies: "We preach Christ crucified, to the Jews a stumbling block, and to the Gentiles foolishness; but to them that are called, both Jews and Greeks, Christ is the Power of God and the Wisdom of God." Through this Wisdom, by His example, we are able to triumph over the malice of the enemy. If we are wise in Him, in Him also shall we conquer. Make the most of this Wisdom. Embrace it! You must set at naught the wisdom of the world, which bears a false title and shows itself only to fools. For St. Paul there is no greater foolishness in the sight of God than worldly wisdom; it must be forgotten by him who would be truly wise. If any man among you seems to be wise in this world, let him be known as a fool, for the wisdom of this world is foolishness with God. It is written, "I will destroy the wisdom of the wise, and the prudence of the prudent I will reprove." Where is the wise man, where is the subtle lawyer, where is the searcher of this world? Has not God made the wisdom of this world foolishness?

I doubt not that these wise fools now trouble you hatefully. These blind leaders of the blind shout that you are raving mad. They become hysterical because you are preparing to go over to Christ's side. Merely in name are they Christians. In all other respects they are first mockers and then attackers of Christ's teachings. Beware lest you be swayed by the blindness of those whose blindness ought to be pitied and deplored rather than imitated. For what is this preposterous kind of wisdom that is so cautious and skillful in worthless things and nothingness? Indeed, it is employed for wicked ends. Furthermore, it is no wiser than a dumb beast in those things that alone pertain to our salvation. Paul wishes us to be wise, but in what is good; simple in what is evil. These are wise that they may act evilly; they know not how to be good.

The eloquent Greek poet Hesiod judges those who, though they lack wisdom themselves, still refuse to accept good advice to be useless. In what class must we place those who, despite the fact that they are perniciously foolish themselves, never cease to disturb, to mock, and to hinder those who have recovered their senses? But shall not the mockers be mocked? He who dwells in the heavens shall mock them, and our Lord shall laugh them to scorn. We read in the Book of Wisdom, "They shall see and shall despise him; but God shall mock them." To be mocked by evil men, is, as it were, to be praised. Their worldly wisdom leads inevitably to false presumption, which is followed by blindness of the mind, slavery to base appetites, and all other species of vice. The bad habits developed in this manner produce a dullness or insensibility of the mind, and the victim no longer considers himself a sinner. The climax of this gradual process of degradation is a sudden and unprovided-for death, which is followed by death everlasting.

But of the wisdom of Christ, which the world considers foolishness, we read, "All good things came to me together with her, and innumerable honors came to me through her hands. And I rejoiced in all of these for this wisdom went before me and I knew not that she was the mother of them all." She brings as her companions modesty and gentleness. Gentleness enables you to receive the divine Spirit, for the Spirit rejoices to rest upon a humble and gentle person. While there, it will imbue your minds with its sevenfold grace; it will produce an abundant crop of virtues that will bear blessed fruits—especially that inner or secret joy that is known only to those who have experienced it and that, in the end, neither vanishes nor is destroyed, but is gathered up into eternal joy. My brother, you ought, in accordance with James' admonition, to seek this wisdom from God with the most ardent intentions and, according to a certain wise man, to "dig it out" from the veins of Divine Scripture "like treasures."

The crown of this God-given wisdom is to know yourself, a maxim that the ancients believed sent from heaven and in which the great authors took enormous delight, holding it to epitomize the fullness of wisdom. However, let even this have little weight among you if it does not agree with Scripture. The mystical lover in Canticles threatens his bride, ordering her to depart unless she know herself: "If you know not yourself, O beautiful among women, go forth and follow after the sheep of your flock." No one should hold the fantastic opinion that he knows himself well enough. Might I not also question whether anyone knows his body completely, or, indeed, whether anyone will truly recognize a habit of mind: Even Paul, whom God so loved that He revealed to him the mysteries of the third heaven, dared not judge himself. He would undoubtedly have done so had he known himself well enough. If such a man, a man so spiritual that he could judge all things without himself being judged by anyone, knew himself so little, in what are we carnal folk to put our faith? Surely a soldier who knows neither his own forces nor those of the enemy is quite useless. Yet our war is not between man and man, but within ourselves: The hostile battle lines spring forth in opposition to us from our very flesh itself. A friend is distinguished from an enemy by such a fine line that there is great danger of inadvertently defending an enemy as a friend, or attacking a friend thinking him to be an enemy. Our notorious enemy always takes on the appearance of an angel of light. We need always ask, "Are you one of ours or one of our adversaries?" Since you must war with yourself and since the first hope of victory lies in whether you know yourself as much as possible, I shall now put before you a kind of likeness of yourself so that you may plainly know what is within and what is merely skin-deep.

4. Of the outer and inner man.

Man is a very complex creature composed of several contending parts: a soul, which may be likened to a sort of divine will, and a body, comparable to a dumb beast. Insofar as the body is concerned we do not surpass the dumb beasts; indeed, we are inferior to them in every bodily endowment. In regard to the soul we are capable of divinity, that is, we may climb in flight above the minds of the very angels themselves and become one with God. If you did not possess a body, you would be but a beast. The greatest craftsman of all has joined together in happy concord these two diverse natures, but the serpent, hating peace, has split them in unhappy discord. Now they can neither be separated without the greatest suffering nor live together without constant war. Either of these natures might well say to the other, "I cannot live either with you or without you." They contend with one another to such an extent that one would think that they were utterly incompatible, but they are, in reality, one. Inasmuch as the body is itself visible, it delights in things visible; inasmuch as it is mortal, it follows things temporal; inasmuch as it is heavy, it sinks downward. On the contrary, the soul, mindful of its celestial nature, struggles strenuously against the weight of the earthly body to press upward. It distrusts things seen because it knows such things to be transient.

It seeks only those things that are true and everlasting. The immortal loves things immortal; the heavenly, things heavenly. Like takes to like unless it be too deeply immersed in the sordid things of the body. The resulting contagion may cause it to lose its natural gentleness. Neither the fabled Prometheus nor nature itself has implanted this discord, but sin, evilly corrupting what has been well founded, has sown the poisonous seeds of dissension between these two natures that formerly dwelt together in peace. In the past the mind commanded the body without trouble, and the body obeyed freely and willingly. Now, with the natural order of things disturbed, the passions of the body seek to override the reason, and reason is compelled, in a sense, to forsake its direction.

Man, hampered as he is by this perplexing division, may be compared to an unruly state. Such a state is composed of various sorts of men whose dissensions create frequent disturbances and factions. To prevent strife the greatest power must be given to one supreme authority, and this authority must be of such a nature that it commands nothing that is not for the welfare of the state. To this end it is necessary for him who is wiser to govern, while he who is less wise ought to obey. No one is more lacking in sense than the lower classes, and for this reason they should obey the magistrate and not hold office themselves. The king, it is true, should consult the nobility, or the greater by birth, but the final decision must remain in his hands. He should sometimes be warned, but he should never allow himself to be forced or led.

In man, reason discharges the office of king. His nobles may be considered to be certain bodily, but not brute, affections. These include: true piety toward parents, charity toward brothers, benevolence toward friends, compassion for those who are afflicted, fear of dishonor, desire for an honest reputation, and like qualities. Consider the dregs of the lower classes to be those affections or passions that dissent as much as possible from the decrees of reason and that are least humble. These are lust, lechery, envy, and similar diseases of the mind, which we ought to resist as overseers restrain dirty, vile slaves so as to ensure that they perform the tasks assigned them by the master, or, at least, so as to prevent them from doing harm. The divinely inspired Plato wrote of all these things in his *Timaeus*.

The proper endowments of kings are: first, that they be as wise as possible so that they do not go amiss through error or lack of knowledge; then, that they do only those things they know to be good and right and that they do not will, falsely and corruptly, anything contrary to the dictates of reason. Whoever lacks either of these two qualities judge to be not a king but a usurper.

5. *Of the diversity of passions.*

Though our king, reason, may at times be oppressed, he cannot be corrupted without protesting. He will be able to recover because of the eternal law that has been divinely engraven upon him. If the rest of the common people will obey him, he will do nothing either pernicious or that should be repented. He will do all things with the greatest moderation and the greatest calmness. While the Stoics and the Peripatetics disagree on the subject of the affections, they both agree that we should be guided by reason rather than by passion. The Stoics believe that, when those passions that are most closely connected with the senses have educated you to the point of being able to discriminate between what is to be avoided and what is to be sought, then those passions are to be discarded. They not only regard them as useless for the further pursuit of knowledge, but they consider them to be actually pernicious. For this reason they contend that the truly wise man must be free of all passions of this sort as diseases of the mind. Indeed, they scarcely wish to concede to the perfectly wise man those primary and more human impulses which precede the reason and which they call fantasies. On this point the Peripatetics disagree: they teach that the passions are not to be completely destroyed but merely subdued, for they consider them to be of value as incentives to virtue. Thus they regard anger as the incentive to fortitude and envy as the incentive to industry. Socrates, in the *Phaedo* of Plato, appears to agree with the Stoics when he says that philosophy is nothing more than a meditation upon death, that is, a withdrawal of the mind, as much as possible, from corporal and sensible things, and a dedication to those things that can be perceived only by reason.

Therefore, it is fitting, first, that we come to recognize the inclinations of the mind, and then that we realize that none of them is so violent that it cannot be restrained by reason or redirected toward virtue. Everywhere I hear the harmful opinion that men are compelled to vice. And there are others who, because of their ignorance of their own natures, follow those passions believing them to be the precepts of reason. Because anger or envy has prompted them, they think they have acted from zeal for God. As one state is more strife-ridden than another, so, too, is one person more prone to virtue than another. However, this difference proceeds, not from any mental differences, but from their ancestors, or from their upbringing, or from the complexion of the body itself. Socrates' fable of the good and bad charioteers and the good and bad horses is no old wives' tale. There are some who are born with such a moderate temper and who are so easy to get along with that they incline toward virtue without any virtue at all. They even seem to hurry on of their own accord without any prodding whatsoever. For others the rebellious body can scarcely be subdued with the roughest rein, goad, or spur, so like to a ferocious, untamed, bucking horse is it. If such happens to be your lot, do not immediately abandon the struggle, but persevere with greater determination. Convince yourself, not that the path of virtue is closed to you, but that a richer means of virtue has been offered you. If, instead, you are endowed with a gentle mind, do not consider yourself to be better than another. You are merely more fortunate, and more fortunate in such a way that you are under greater obligation. Furthermore, who is so fortunate in disposition that there are not a great many things in which he needs to struggle?

Therefore, reason must especially guard that in which one feels most vulnerable. Certain vices appear to be most characteristic of certain nations. Thus deceit is a common vice among some people, gluttony among others, and lechery among still others. These vices accompany certain bodily habits, as for example, effeminacy and love of pleasure with the sanguine; anger, ferocity, and evil tongues with the quick-tempered; inactivity and sluggishness with the phlegmatic; envy, sadness and bitterness with the melancholic. Some of these passions either slacken or increase with age. For example, in youth there is lust, prodigality, and rashness, while in old age there is niggardliness, moroseness, and avarice. There are also passions that seem to be related to sex. For example, men are characterized by ferocity; women by vanity and desire for revenge. Meanwhile, nature, as if to make amends, compensates certain diseases of the mind with certain virtues. Thus this person is prone to pleasure, but at the same time he is not at all irascible or envious; another person is of uncorrupted modesty, but is prouder, more irascible, and more worldly. Nor is there any lack of those who are troubled by such great and fatal vices as theft, sacrilege, and homicide. Every effort must be made to combat these, and a firm wall of definite purpose must be built against their exertions. On the other hand there are certain passions that are so similar to virtue that there is danger lest we be deceived by the doubtful distinction between them. These ought to be corrected in such a manner as to turn them toward the nearby virtue. To give an example, a person who is quite irascible should throw a rein over his mind, and he will be eager, not the least bit sluggish, and he will walk erect. He will be free and simple. Another person is somewhat grasping; let him exercise his reason and he will be frugal. Let him who is inflexible become constant. Let him who is sad become serious-minded. Let him who is tactless become courteous. Other light diseases of the mind should be directed to similar ends. We must be on our guard, however, lest we cloak a vice of nature with the name of a virtue, calling sadness gravity, harshness justice, envy zeal, niggardliness thrift, adulation friendship, scurrility urbanity.

This then is the only road to happiness: first, know yourself; do not allow yourself to be led by the passions, but submit all things to the judgment of the reason. Be sane and let reason be wise, that is, let it gaze upon decent things.

You say that it is difficult to put this advice into practice. Who denies it? Plato has a fitting saying: "Those things which are beautiful are also difficult." Nothing is harder than for a man to conquer himself, but there is no greater reward or blessing. St. Jerome expresses this thought very clearly, just as he does all others. No one is happier than the Christian to whom is promised the Kingdom of Heaven. No one is more burdened than he who must fear for his life every day. No one is stronger than he who conquers the devil. No one is weaker than he who is overcome by the desires of the flesh. If you carefully weigh your own strength, you will say that there is nothing more difficult than to subject the flesh to the spirit; but if you are mindful of God as your helper, there is nothing easier. Assume a perfect life as your goal; having done so, pursue it in a spirit of determination. The human mind has never strongly commanded itself to do anything it has failed to accomplish. One of the most essential elements of Christianity is a willingness to be and to act as a Christian. This rule of conduct may appear to be too difficult to accomplish at first, but in the process of time it will become easy and, with persistence, actually a pleasure. As the poet Hesiod declares, "The way of virtue is difficult at first, but after you have arrived at the summit there is perfect tranquillity." There is no beast so ferocious that he cannot be tamed by human effort. Can it be that there is no power to tame that agent that is the tamer of all things? In order to train the body you are able to abstain from overindulgence in drink and to give up the company of women for certain periods of time. Why, then, can you not sacrifice a few months to gain control of your evil inclinations? You must do all things necessary to save your body, as well as your soul, from eternal death.

   6. *Of the inner and outer man and his two parts as found in Holy Scripture.*

It is always a great source of embarrassment to me to realize that the great majority of those who bear the name Christian act for the most part as if they were dumb beasts. Most of them are such slaves to their baser appetites that in this spiritual combat they are unable to distinguish between the dictates of reason and the promptings of passion. They actually believe that they are behaving in a reasonable manner so long as they act upon what they feel or see. In fact, they consider that alone to have existence which is perceptible to the senses. Their only criterion for right or wrong is that which appeals to their desires. What they mean by peace is in reality a deplorable state of servitude. Entirely bereft of reason, they follow heedlessly wherever their selfish interests lead. This is that false and unhappy peace that Christ, the Author of peace, who will one day reward us, has come to do away with. He accomplishes this by stirring up a wholesome war between father and son, husband and wife, and between those things that weak arguments have attempted to reconcile.

I think it is agreed that the authority of the philosophers rests upon the fact that they state what is contained in a different manner in the Scriptures. What the philosophers term "reason" St. Paul calls either "the spirit" or "the inner man" or occasionally the "law of the mind." What they refer to as the "passions" he calls "the flesh," "the body," "the outer man," or "the law of the members." He says, for example, "Walk in the Spirit, and you shall not fulfill the lusts of the flesh. For the flesh lusts against the Spirit, and the Spirit against the flesh . . . so that you do not the things you would." And again: "If you live accordingly to the flesh you will die; if, however, you mortify the flesh by the spirit, you will live." Certainly this is a new order of things; to seek peace in war, war in peace, life in death, death in life, freedom in slavery, slavery in freedom. Listen to what Paul says of freedom: "But if you are led by the Spirit, you are not under the law. We have not received the spirit of bondage in fear, but you have received the spirit of adoption, as sons of God." We read also in St. Paul concerning "the outer man who is corrupt and the inner man who is renewed from day to day." Plato distinguished two souls in one man. In the same way, Paul describes two men so joined in one that both of them will be together in eternal glory or eternal damnation. They cannot be separated. The death of one cannot be the life of the other. What Paul writes to the Corinthians is, I believe, also pertinent. "The first came from the earth and is terrestrial. The second came from heaven and is celestial." And to make this even more clear he applies this duality not only to Christ and to Adam but to ourselves as well. "As was the earthy man, such also are the earthy; and as is the heavenly man, such also are the heavenly. Therefore, even as we have borne the likeness of the earthy, let us bear also the likeness of the heavenly. This I say, brethren, because flesh and blood can obtain no part of the kingdom of God, neither will corruption have any part in incorruption."

I think you can see how evident it is that Paul, who elsewhere spoke of the "flesh" and the "outer or corruptible man," here calls him the "earthy Adam." This is certainly the "body of death" about which Paul so frequently speaks. "Unhappy man that I am, who will deliver me

from the body of this death?" Pointing out a far different fruit of the
flesh and the spirit, he writes elsewhere: "For he who sows in the flesh
will also reap corruption but he who sows in the Spirit will reap life
everlasting." We know that a messenger of Satan came to trouble Paul
in the flesh. When the tempter refused to leave him, God gave him
this answer: "Paul, my grace is sufficient for thee." For strength is
made perfect in weakness. This certainly is a new sort of remedy. Lest
Paul be proud, he is tempted by pride. That he might be made firm
in Christ, he is forced to be infirm. For he carried the treasure of
heavenly revelations in a vessel of clay, that the sublimity might reflect
the power of God, and not his own power. There are, of course, many
other examples in the writings of St. Paul that indicate how we are
to overcome temptation. Our first recourse in any kind of temptation
is to implore the assistance of Almighty God. In fact, those who are
well advanced on the road to perfection will actually welcome these
temptations, for they guard virtue and, especially, form a bulwark
against the danger of vanity that often lurks in the midst of the virtues.
We might compare this vanity to the Herculean hydra because it is
so difficult to destroy. Let us follow the example of the holy patriarch
Jacob in this struggle against sin. He teaches us to persevere during
the dark night of struggle until the dawn of divine assistance shines
forth. Like him, let us say to God, "I will not let go until you bless
me. . . ." The reward that this great wrestler with evil obtained contains
a message for all of us. In the first place God blessed him on the very
spot. This shows that after we overcome a temptation graces are immediately granted us so that we can resist the next attack. Furthermore,
we read that God and the angel then smote Jacob so that henceforth
he was lame in one foot. This was, of course, to show that God curses
those who attempt to serve two masters. From that time Jacob walked
only on the right foot, that is to say, he walked in the spirit. Even his
name was changed, and from a highly active person he was transformed into a contemplative. In like manner, after you have overcome
temptation and crucified your flesh with its evil desires, you will find
true peace and tranquillity, and you will see that the Lord is sweet.
God is never perceived in the midst of temptation, but once the tempest
subsides, we will bask in the sunshine of spiritual consolation. Examine
yourself in all honesty. If you are flesh alone, you will not see God, you
will not be saved. Make it your determined effort, then, to become
spiritual.

7. Of the three parts of man: spirit, soul, and flesh.

In order to carry this comparison a bit further and to investigate it
more fully, let us briefly refer to Origen and his treatment of the nature

of man. Following St. Paul and those prophets of the Old Testament, Isaiah and Daniel, Origen speaks of a threefold division in man. The body or flesh is our lowest. Because of the original transgression Satan has, as it were, inscribed upon this part the law of sin whereby we are inclined to evil. Failure to overcome this inclination brings us completely under his control. The spirit, on the other hand, may be said to represent us as a reflection of the divine nature of our Creator. Here we find the original pattern of the divine mind wherein the eternal law is engraved by the finger of God, the Holy Spirit. This is that part of us that binds us to God and makes us one with Him. Finally, there is the third part, resting between the other two, which makes us sensual and subject to the terrible fate of those who live according to the flesh.

Let us sum up how we distinguish these various components of man. The spirit has the capacity of making us divine; the flesh tends to bring out our animal nature; the soul is what really constitutes us as human beings. It is the spirit that gives us the qualities of religion, obedience, kindness, and mercy. The flesh makes us despisers of God, disobedient, and cruel. The soul, on the other hand, is indifferent, neither good nor bad in itself. Let me show you how this threefold tendency operates in actual life. You respect your parents, you love members of your own family, your friends. Certainly we cannot honestly say that there is any real virtue in this. Yet not to do so would immediately be condemned as evil. Even those who are not Christians are expected to love those who are near and dear to them. This is found in the very nature of things and can hardly be imputed to meritorious action. But take a situation where reverence toward parents, or love of children, must be sacrificed for the love of God. Here the soul finds itself torn in two directions. The flesh beckons in one direction, the spirit cries out in the other. The spirit argues that you must obey God as you owe Him all you have. The flesh will answer, "If you disobey your father, he will disinherit you, you will be accused of disrespect and lose your good name. Besides, God will not notice this, and if He does, you can be later reconciled with Him." The soul begins to waver. If, holding the spirit in contempt, she turns to the harlot, that is, to the flesh, she will be one body with it. On the other hand, if, spurning the flesh, she rises to the spirit, she will be transformed into the spirit alone. How would you act in like circumstances?

I think it is a great mistake, indeed, to call virtuous those actions that proceed entirely from natural inclinations. There are even certain passions that some mistake for virtue. Take a judge, for example, who condemns a felon simply because this gives him a feeling of self-righteousness. Can you say that he cares in a virtuous way? If he upholds the law for his own evil purposes, for financial gain or personal reputation, his condemnation of the prisoner is tantamount to murder. If, on the other hand, his treatment of the criminal is motivated by personal concern and genuine equity, he acts according to the spirit. I feel that entirely too many people confuse what are really natural gifts or endowments with virtues. You will find that certain individuals are not in the least bothered by temptations of the flesh. Actually, this is an indifferent matter. We can speak of virtue in this regard only in the overcoming of an evil inclination. There are some people, too, who get a great deal of consolation out of attending divine services, Mass, vespers, and novenas. If they do this merely because they find pleasure in the ceremonies, because it is emotionally pleasurable or because it enhances their reputation, then they ought to examine their motives. They are in great danger of deceiving themselves. How many there are who, while in the very act of praying, pass judgment on those who are not naturally prayerful. Or again, in the matter of fast and abstinence, what virtue is there if, while you fast, you mentally condemn someone who fails to observe this regulation?

Too many feel that whoever does not carry out the same religious practices as they do is spiritually inferior. Take, for example, a case where your brother is in dire need of your help, and yet you go on mumbling your prayers, pretending not to notice his predicament. God will actually despise that kind of prayer. For how can He possibly listen to your petition while you cannot find it in your heart to help a fellow man? Take another example: You say that you love your wife simply because she is your spouse. There is really no merit in this. Even the pagans do this, and the love can be based upon physical pleasure alone. But, on the other hand, if you love her because in her you see the image of Christ, because you perceive in her His reverence, modesty, and purity, then you do not love her in herself but in Christ. You love Christ in her. This is what we mean by spiritual love, and we will say more about it later on.

II

SOME GENERAL RULES FOR LIVING
A CHRISTIAN LIFE

Since we now have a general idea of what is to be accomplished by this little treatise, let us proceed lest this become a voluminous tome rather than a manual. It is my plan to propose a number of fundamental rules or norms that will guide us through the labyrinth of this world into the pure light of the spiritual life. If every other science has its own rules, then certainly the art of pious living must have some basic regulations. Leading a virtuous life is accompanied by a certain discipline that the Holy Spirit breathes into those who sincerely aim at godliness. Yet I feel that a certain predisposition is necessary, for a refusal to be willing to accept direction is a refusal of God's mercy.

The rules that I will suggest will be garnered from several sources, partly from the Person of God Himself, partly from the devil, and partly from ourselves. They will consist in an enumeration of both virtues and vices as well as components of these. They will be directed for the most part against the evil vestiges of original sin. For it is plain enough that although baptism has taken away the original stain, yet the remnants of this former disease remain. They are still with us so that our humility might be preserved and so that they might occasion the increase of virtue. We will call them blindness, the flesh, and infirmity or weakness. It is this blindness that dims our reason, resulting in ignorance. For there is very little of that divine light of God's countenance remaining in us. It was partially obscured by the sin of our first parents, and what remains has been completely enveloped through corrupt upbringing, evil companionship, and sinful habits. It is this blindness that drives us to seek after the worst instead of the best. It is this blindness that clouds our judgment, leading us to a false standard of values. It is the flesh that, through our passions, prompts us to cherish what is wrong, even though we know better. Weakness causes us either through tediousness or temptation to lose what virtue we may have already acquired. Blindness harms the judgment, the flesh weakens our will, and weakness destroys our constancy.

To counteract these three vestiges of original sin I would propose the following: First of all, to combat blindness we must develop a fine sense of discernment by investigating those things that are to be avoided. The flesh will be overcome if we immediately reject evil thoughts and desires and turn our thoughts to what is of God. Finally, we must acquire the habit of perseverance, so that abandoning the pursuit of virtue may appear to us more evil than never having pursued it. Ignorance must be remedied to give us a proper perspective. The flesh must be subdued lest it lead us from the straight and narrow into the alluring path of vice. And last of all, our weakness must be ever strengthened, so that, once putting our hand to the plow we refrain from looking back and advance like a giant, rejoicing until we receive the crown promised to those who persevere.

FIRST RULE

Now since faith is the only gateway to Christ, the first rule I would lay down is that we ought to place great reliance on the Scriptures.

This belief should not be, as is the case with most Christians, something cold, careless, and calculated, but rather should come from a fullness of heart. Be convinced that there is not a single item contained in Holy Writ that does not pertain to your salvation. The fact that the majority of mankind considers heaven and hell as some kind of legend or old wives' tale ought not to disturb you. Even if the entire world appear mad, even though the angels revolt and the very elements change, the truth cannot lie. What God has foretold must inevitably take place.

If you believe God exists, then you must believe that He speaks the truth. Convince yourself that nothing you perceive with your senses is as true as what you read in the Scriptures. The will of heaven, Truth Itself, has inspired it; the prophets of old have made it known; the blood of martyrs has proven it; and the constant belief of countless generations has testified to it. Christ Himself in His life here below has exemplified its pervading truth. Even the demons have confessed its veracity since they believe in it just as much as they fear it. Certainly the very beauty of the message it contains should in itself convince anyone who reads it. If such be the case, would it not be sheer madness not to believe? Take, for example, the many incredible things that were foretold by the prophets concerning Christ. Not one of them has not taken place. Do you think for a moment that He who did not deceive them would try to deceive others. If these prophets did not lie, certainly Christ, the greatest of all prophets, did not deceive us.

If, convinced of these truths, you ask God to increase your faith, it will indeed amaze me if you do not recoil from an evil life. I think anyone would change his life if he saw the eternal punishment and the torture of a guilty conscience that followed upon sin. Who could possibly exchange the joys of a clear conscience and the anticipation of an eternal reward for a moment of fleeting pleasure?

SECOND RULE

If our first rule demands that we doubt nothing in the divine promises, the second is that we act upon these promises without delay and hesitation. With resolute purpose we must be prepared to undergo loss of everything—property, life itself—for Christ's sake. The kingdom of heaven does not belong to the lazy; it suffers violence, and "the violent bear it away." As you advance on the path to perfection, you must determine not to turn back. Neither the affection of your loved ones, the allurements of the world, nor the cares of domestic life should stand in your way. Whenever you cannot disentangle yourself from the affairs and business of the world, you must knife your way through them. The fleshpots of Egypt must be forsaken once and for all. We know what took place when Sodom was not forgotten at once. The woman looked back and was turned to a block of salt; Lot went on into the hills and was saved.

Looking back in this flight from the world will spell immediate defeat. I do not have to point out to you how many there are who delay in their flight from vice. They feel that if they immediately free themselves from this or that business they will not be able to finish it. Let them recall the words: "What if today I should require your soul from you?" I think it is apparent to all that business merely begets more business. One vice merely gives way to another. It is for this reason that I would advise haste in abandoning the world. Do it now—even a little recklessness would not be out of place. Forget about how much you are giving up or what you could have otherwise accomplished and realize that in Christ is the fulfillment of all things. Dedicate yourself to Him with your whole heart. Trust yourself no longer but rather cast yourself entirely into His care. Remember what the prophet said? "The Lord is my Shepherd and I shall not want." You must dare to believe in Him with your whole heart and to distrust yourself entirely. In other words get out of your own self and let Him support you. Give up this idea of trying to divide yourself between the world and Christ. "You cannot serve two masters." There is no compromise between God and Belial. Never forget for a moment that our God is a jealous lover of souls. He wants all for Himself. And rightly so, for did He not purchase all of us with His blood? Fellowship with Satan is out of the question, as Christ has completely conquered him by His death.

There are only two paths open to you: the one through gratification of the passions leads to perdition; the other, through mortification of the flesh, leads to life. Which one of these do you choose? There is no third way, and sooner or later you will have to make up your mind about one or the other of these. Yet let me remind you that this is a path upon which few men walk and that you yourself can walk only by exercising the greatest skill. Yet to say that it is beyond our capacities is ridiculous. Christ has trodden this same path, and since the beginning of time men pleasing to God have traveled it. You know well enough that if you desire to live with Christ, you must be crucified to this world. Then why delude yourself like a fool? Why, in such an all-important matter, are you so prone to self-deception?

There are all kinds of excuses, of course. Some will say, "I am a secular priest; I am obliged to live in the world." Some will reason, "Even though I am a priest, I have not joined a monastic order, I am no monk." They are in for a shock. And of course the monks easily

delude themselves. "We do not belong to a strict order. This message
is for others." The young, the rich, the generous, those in high positions
reply that what was said to the Apostles can have no possible application to them. What a terrible delusion! Does the idea of living in Christ
have any meaning at all? If you are in the world, you are not in Christ.
Of course, if you mean by the world the earth, the sea, the atmosphere,
the heavens, then obviously all of us are in the world. But if the world
is for your ambition, desire for honor, promotion, or authority, if the
world consists of pleasure and lust, then I doubt if you are even a
Christian. Christ spoke indifferently to all men, that whoever would
not take up His cross and follow Him would not and could not be His
disciple. If living by His Spirit means nothing to you, then certainly
to die with Christ means even less. If to be crucified to this world, to
live for God alone, to be buried with Christ, to rise in His glory, have
no meaning, then what does? If His humility, poverty, disregard of
self, and incessant labors have no meaning, then neither does His
kingdom.

It seems to me that nothing could be more lacking in justice than to
offer the same reward to everyone while requiring a few to carry out
the mandates upon which the reward is based. What could be more
ridiculous than to desire to rule jointly with our Head and yet to refuse
to suffer with Him? Consequently, stop looking about you and trying
to flatter yourself by comparison with others. I will grant that to die
to sin is a difficult accomplishment. Even few monks ever actually
achieve this. And yet at the same time we must agree that this is
something that all of us without exception are sworn to do. When you
were baptized, you took an oath to do just that. To my way of thinking there is no vow or no promise that is more religious or sacred than
this. All of us, princes or paupers, are going to stand or fall on this one
promise. There is really no other way of salvation. Even though all of
us cannot reach this goal, cannot attain the perfect imitation of the
Head, all of us must aim for this goal with all our efforts. The honest
decision to become a Christian implies that one has already chosen
the better part of Christianity.

THIRD RULE

I feel that fear is one of the real obstacles to the pursuit of virtue.
This pursuit seems difficult because it involves relinquishing so many
things we have come to love and because it demands incessant struggle against those three really formidable elements, the flesh, the devil,
and the world. With that in mind I would like to propose a third rule.
We must analyze these unfounded fears; when we do, we will find that

they are not as bad as they appear. Even if we prescind from the notion of reward, the way of Christ is the most sensible and logical one to follow.

If you take a little time to think it over, it becomes quite apparent that there is no manner of life in this world that is not crowded with difficulties and hardships. Take a man in high political position. No one in his right mind would aspire to such a position if he were aware of the difficulties that beset such an office. What an endless parade of scraping and bowing to woo the good will of those above you! What an interminable suppression of disdain and concealment of despite for those with whom you must work! Need I mention the vicissitudes of the military life? The risks and dangers encountered by merchants and businessmen are well enough known. Take the state of matrimony. The cares and miseries flowing from domestic difficulties are incredible. Only those who are married can really appreciate and understand how real they are. Regardless of the vocation you may have chosen, there are difficulties on all sides. The life of man is filled from beginning to end with tribulation, and besides, the virtuous suffer right along with the guilty. If these are the difficulties you fear, you will find that they actually serve to increase your merit. Without virtue, you will have to put up with them anyway, and with greater trouble and no reward at all.

Let us take a look at those who have decided to fight for the world. In the first place, for how many years do they not endure all kinds of hardships and privations? And for what? For fleeting nothings, mainly. And is there any time during this relentless pursuit of pleasure that they can really be said to be hopeful of the outcome? The miseries that they incur are of such a nature that the longer they pursue false goals the greater is the pain. And what is the end of all this toil and anxiety? Eternal punishment! Now compare this with the life of virtue. To begin with, it becomes less and less tedious as we advance, and this increased pleasantness is further advanced by the hope we have of eternal happiness. In other words the proportionately greater efforts of the wicked lead only to interminable labor, whereas the lightest efforts of the good culminate in eternal rest. The divine assistance offered to those who labor for God not only lightens the load but changes gall to honey. In the way of the world one care only adds to another, one sorrow gives rise to a second, and there is no peace whatever. Christ sums this all up, "Take my yoke upon you and you will find rest for your souls. For my yoke is easy and my burden light." To put it quite briefly, nothing is more pleasurable than a peaceful conscience, nothing more wretched than to have the mind tormented with a bad conscience.

Yet I would like to add that even were the rewards the same and the toil equal in this comparison, would it not be much nobler to fight and work under the banner of Christ than that of Satan? I think that it is quite obviously preferable to suffer awhile with Christ than to consort with the devil. No man in his right senses would take up arms, regardless of the reward, for so deceitful a leader. The rigors of the campaign are hardly worth such a fleeting recompense. Besides, can Satan be trusted to pay what he promises? The worry and concern resulting from this distrust would nullify any real anticipation of gain. If you lose in this gamble, you will be doubly miserable, since you were tricked out of what you hoped for, and your whole effort will be a miserable failure. Remember that Christ neither mocks nor is He mocked. When you abandon the world for Christ you do not give anything up—rather, you exchange it for something far better. You change silver into gold and rocks into precious gems.

Granted, your friends will be disappointed. Yet you will soon find more pleasant and reliable ones. You will have to give up some of the pleasures of the body, but they are not in the least comparable to those more certain and purer pleasures of the mind. This change will also bring about diminution of your material possessions, but here again what you will gain will be immune from moths and thieves. If your reputation in the world is not what it was, the friendship of Christ will more than make up for this. You will gradually come to realize the transparency of what you once cherished. Even those things that are of themselves quite harmless and licit you will come to regard with indifference. Good fortune usually comes to those who are not looking for it, and certainly if you are attached to absolutely nothing at all, what comes your way will be beneficial. Do not hesitate, then, to give up the devil and seek after Christ. For, regardless of how you estimate the situation, there is absolutely no comparison between the two.

FOURTH RULE

In order to help you expedite this decision I am going to lay down a fourth rule: Make Christ the only goal of your life. Dedicate to Him all your enthusiasm, all your effort, your leisure as well as your business. And don't look upon Christ as a mere word, an empty expression, but rather as charity, simplicity, patience, and purity—in short, in terms of everything He has taught us. Consider as the devil, on the other hand, anything that deters us from Christ and His teaching. "When your eye is single, your whole body will be filled with light." Direct your gaze toward Christ alone to the extent that you love nothing, or desire nothing, unless it be either Christ or because of

Christ. This way whatever you do, whether you sleep or wake, or eat or drink, or take your leisure, you will increase your reward.

Now since there are many situations where we have to decide whether or not a seemingly indifferent act leads toward or away from Christ, I am going to prescribe a threefold norm to determine our action in just such a situation. There are certain actions that can at no time be considered as other than intrinsically evil. To avenge a wrong, or to desire to injure your neighbor, are of this type. These must be shunned at all costs. There are other actions that by their very nature are so virtuous that they can never be really wicked—for example, wishing well to all men, helping friends with honest aid, hating vices, and participating in godly conversation. There are other things that of their very nature are indifferent, morally speaking. Among these we might list health, beauty, strength, eloquence, learning, and the like. Now none of these attributes should be used other than to aim at Christ. They should be evaluated in terms of how adequately they lead to this goal. This should be the criterion upon which we accept or reject them. I would say that among these things knowledge is the most to be valued. I would prefer it to beauty, strength of body, and riches. And although all learning is of great value, there is here again a certain priority. If you are interested in learning, certainly this is a fine quality, provided you turn your knowledge to Christ. If, on the other hand, you love letters only for the sake of knowledge, you have not gone far enough. You should go a step further. Let your study bring you to a clearer perception of Christ so that your love for Him will increase and you will in turn be able to communicate this knowledge of Him to others. However, I would admonish you to know your own limitations in this matter.

On the other attributes I have mentioned, I would urge you to use them as the occasion presents, but in such a way that they do not form a hindrance to your spiritual progress. Suppose you come into money. If this does not harm your personal integrity, then by all means use it. But if you feel that it may be an occasion for dishonesty, then imitate Crates of old and throw your wealth away. You can do this rather easily if you accustom yourself to admiring nothing that is outside yourself, namely, things that do not pertain to the inner man. This way you will neither grow arrogant if fortune does smile on you, nor will you be greatly troubled if your wealth is taken away. It will help you in your conviction that Christ alone is the measure of happiness. If you feel that good fortune might be a real hindrance to your progress, then imitate Prometheus and leave the box alone. Anyone who actually admires money as the most precious thing in life and rests his security on it to the extent of believing that, as long as he possesses it, he will be happy, has fashioned too many false gods for himself. Too many people put money in the place of Christ, as if it alone has the key to their happiness or unhappiness.

What I say about money also applies to honors, pleasures, health—in fact, to the life of the body itself. Our determination to imitate Christ should be of such a nature that we have no time for these matters. St. Paul tells us, "The time is short; it remains that they who enjoy this world be as if not enjoying it." There is no doubt that this sort of reasoning is the object of scorn and derision in the world. Yet this is precisely the type of foolishness with which it has pleased God to protect those who believe. "For the foolishness of God is wiser than men." Let this saying be a guide for your every action. If you are a breadwinner engaged in supporting your family, then this is a noble end in itself. But do not forget that your household must be won over for Christ. Suppose you decide to fast. Certainly this has all the appearance of a virtuous act. But what is the motive for your fasting; to what do you refer it? Is it not perhaps that you might conserve food? Is it because others will then think you more pious? Most likely you fast in order to preserve your health. And why are you fearful of overeating? For the simple reason that this can interfere with your pursuit of pleasure. Perhaps you are concerned about your health so that you can continue your studies. And why, might I ask, are you so concerned about studies? In order to obtain the easy living of a clergyman, living that is for your own pleasure and not for Christ's. You have really missed the target toward which every Christian ought to aim. If you eat sufficiently and take care of your health so that you can take part in religious exercises, then you are hitting the mark. If your concern for health and gracious living is only to enable you to be more vigorous in lustful pursuits, you have fallen away from Christ and have made a god out of yourself.

Now there are not a few who are given over to the veneration of the saints, with elaborate ceremonies. Some, for example, have a great devotion to St. Christopher. Provided his statue is in sight, they pray to him almost every day. Why do they do this? It is because they wish to be preserved from a sudden and unprovided-for death that day. There are others who have a great devotion to St. Roch. Why? Because they believe that Roch can immunize them against certain physical ailments. Others mumble certain prayers to St. Barbara or St. George so they will not fall into the hands of the enemy. Still others fast in honor of St. Apollo so that they will not be troubled with toothaches. Others visit the image of holy Job to prevent boils. There are certain merchants who assign a portion of their profits to the poor so that they will not suffer a loss of merchandise in shipwreck. A candle is burned in honor of St. Jerome so that lost goods might be recovered. In short, for everything we fear or desire we set up a corresponding deity. This has gone to the extent that each nation has its own. Among the French St. Paul is esteemed, among us Germans St. Jerome has a special place. Certain areas hold St. James or St. John in lesser or greater esteem. This kind of piety, since it does not refer either our fears or our desires to Christ, is hardly a Christian practice. As a matter of fact, it is not a great deal different from the superstitions of the ancients. They pledged a tenth of their goods to Hercules that they might get rich, or a cock to Aesculapius to regain their health. A bull was sacrificed to Neptune to avoid mishap at sea. The names may have been changed, but the purpose and intentions are the same.

You pray that you may not be overtaken by a premature death. Would it not be more Christian to pray that you might be of such a virtuous mind that wherever death overtakes you, it will not find you unprepared? You have absolutely no intention of changing your way in life, and yet you ask God that you may not die. Certainly the only reason you pray is that you may continue your life of sin as long as possible. You pray for the material things of this world and have not the slightest idea of how to use divine things. Are you not actually praying for your own ruin? You pray for good health and yet you continue to abuse it. Is not this rather a dishonoring than an honoring of Almighty God?

I am sure that these remarks will be disturbing to certain so-called saintly men who identify the worship of God with financial gain and who, with their sweet benedictions, deceive the minds of the innocent, serving their own bellies rather than Christ. They will protest that I am forbidding the veneration of the saints in whom God is also honored. I do not damn those who do these things with a simple and childish sort of superstition so much as I do those who, for their own advantage, magnify these practices completely out of proportion. They encourage these devotions, which of themselves are tolerable, for their own profit and thereby capitalize on the ignorance of the masses. What I utterly condemn is the fact that they esteem the indifferent in place of the highest, the nonessentials to the complete neglect of what is essential. What is of the smallest value spiritually they make the greatest. I will certainly praise them for seeking a healthy body from St. Roch, provided they consecrate their life to Christ. But I will praise them still more if they pray for nothing else than a love of virtue and of hatred for vice. As for dying or living, let them leave such matters in the hands of God, and let them say with Paul, "Whether we live, we live unto the Lord; and whether we die, we die unto the Lord." What would be ideal is that they desire to be dissolved from the body and be with Christ. It would be perfect if they, in disease and misfortune, make their real joy consist in this, that they have conformed their lives to Christ their Head. Accordingly, to practice these devotions is not so much to be condemned as is the danger inherent in them, namely, that of relying entirely or too much on them. I suffer from infirmity and weakness, but with St. Paul I show forth a more excellent way. Examine yourself in the light of these rules and you will not be content with these indifferent actions until all of them are referred to Christ; you will not stop midway but will continue so that all is aimed at serving and honoring God.

FIFTH RULE

I am now going to add a fifth, subsidiary rule. You will find that you can best maintain this piety if, turning away from visible things, which are for the most part either imperfect or of themselves indifferent, you seek the invisible. We will follow the divisions we mentioned previously in discussing the nature of man. I am going to stress the difference between the visible and invisible because I find so many Christians, either out of neglect or sheer ignorance, as superstitious as the pagans. Let us suppose that there are two worlds, the one intelligible, the other visible. The intelligible or angelic world is that in which God dwells with the blessed. The visible world embraces the circle of heaven, the planets, the stars, and all that is included in them.

Now let us imagine that man is a third world participating in both of the others, the visible referring to his corporeal part, the invisible to his soul. In the visible world, since we are, as it were, mere sojourners, we ought to consider all that we perceive through our senses in terms of its relationship to the intelligent world. The sun, for example, in the visible world might be compared to the divine mind. The moon might be thought of in terms of the whole assembly of the angelic hosts and of the elect whom we call the Church Triumphant. These celestial bodies operate in relation to the earth as God does in relation to our soul. It is the sun that quickens, produces, matures, purges, softens, illuminates, brightens, and gladdens. When you are delighted by the beauty of the rising sun, consider the joy of those in heaven upon whom the divine light shines eternally. Paul tells us, "For God who commanded light to shine out of darkness, has shone in our hearts, to give enlightenment concerning the knowledge of the glory of God, shining on the face of Christ Jesus." I suggest that you repeat over and over those passages from Holy Scripture in which grace is compared to the rays of the sun. If the darkness of night is oppressive to you, then think of how destitute is the soul without the light of God. If you find any darkness within your soul, then pray that the Sun of righteousness may shine upon you.

The things that we can see with our physical eyes are mere shadows of reality. If they appear ugly and ill formed, then what must be the ugliness of the soul in sin, deprived of all light? The soul, like the body, can undergo transformation in appearance. In sin it appears as completely ugly to the beholder. In virtue it shines resplendently before God. Like the body the soul can be healthy, youthful, and so on. It can undergo pain, thirst, and hunger. In this physical life, that is, in the visible world, we avoid whatever would defile or deform the body; how much more, then, ought we to avoid that which would tarnish the soul? I feel that the entire spiritual life consists in this: That we gradually turn from those things whose appearance is deceptive to those things that are real . . . from the pleasures of the flesh, the honors of the world that are so transitory, to those things that are immutable and everlasting. Socrates had this in mind when he said that the soul will leave the body at the time of death with little fear if, during life, it has rehearsed death by despising material things.

Now the cross to which Christ calls us and the death in which St. Paul urges us to die with our Head are of this earth. Once we have tasted the sweetness of what is spiritual, the pleasures of the world will have no attraction for us. If we disregard the shadows of things, then we will penetrate their inner substance. Sickness, for example, can be a means of advancing in spirituality. In fact, a little less care for physical well-being will give us more time to devote to the mind. If you fear the death of the body, then certainly you should fear the death of the soul. If lightning terrifies you, then think of that invisible lightning that is the wrath of God saying, "Depart ye cursed persons into eternal fire." Are you attracted by what is beautiful in the human figure? Think rather of the beauty of the soul that it conceals. You worry whether the drought will end. It is far better that you pray that God may water your mind lest virtue wither away in it. You are greatly concerned with money that is lost or being wasted, or you worry about the advance of old age. I think it much to be desired that you provide first of all for the needs of your soul.

Now this distinction that we make of body and soul can be applied also to what we read in Holy Scripture. Everything that is written has both an external, or, as it were, corporeal, meaning as well as a mysterious, or spiritual, significance. The Old Testament is filled with the accounts of events that would in no way edify us if we did not understand them in allegorical manner, that is, by searching out the spiritual meaning. St. Paul, following the example of our Lord Himself, has used allegory as a means of better understanding the Scriptures.

Origen, of course, is also a great advocate of the allegorical approach. Yet I think you will have to admit that our modern theologians either despise this method of interpretation or are completely ignorant of it. As a matter of fact they surpass the pagans of antiquity in the subtlety of their distinctions.

I find that in comparison with the Fathers of the Church our present-day theologians are a pathetic group. Most of them lack the elegance, the charm of language, and the style of the Fathers. Content with Aristotle, they treat the mysteries of revelation in the tangled fashion of the logician. Excluding the Platonists from their commentaries, they strangle the beauty of revelation. Yet no less an authority than St. Augustine prefers to express himself in the flowing style that so enhanced the lovely writings of this Platonist school. He prefers them not only because they have so many ideas that are appropriate to our religion but also because the figurative language that they use, abounding in allegories, very closely approaches the language of Scripture itself. The great Christian writers of the past were able to treat even the most arid subjects with a beautiful prose. They enriched and colored their sermons and commentaries with the constant use of allegory. Almost all of them were at home with the writings of Plato and the poets, and they used this literary training to the very best advantage in interpreting the words of Scripture.

It is for this reason that I would recommend that you familiarize yourself with the Fathers. They will lead you to an inner penetration of the word of God, to an understanding of the spiritual worth it contains. This is certainly to be preferred to the scholastic method that invariably ends up in useless disputation. In getting closer to the inner spiritual meaning you will find what is really most important— a hope for the unknown. We have already referred to the Old Testament as abounding in this sort of figurative writing. It is also to be found in the Gospel. For the New Testament has its flesh and its spirit. Paul tells us that we see not the thing itself, but that we see in an obscure manner. We see as through a mirror. We see but an image or a representation of the real object. Christ Himself tells us, "The flesh profits nothing; it is the spirit that gives life." He actually goes beyond what I am saying. As Truth Itself, he says that the flesh profits nothing. St. Paul reiterates the same point when he says that the flesh is actually fatal if it does not lead to the spirit. We have already explained that the body cannot even exist without the spirit. Yet the spirit is completely independent of the body.

If, then, the spirit is that alone which gives life, then it is obvious enough that our every action should tend toward the spirit. Time and time again in his Epistles St. Paul exhorts us not to place our trust in the flesh but in the spirit. Here alone is life, liberty, adoption. Everywhere he belittles and condemns the flesh. This is even more evident in the case of our Lord. By giving sight to the blind, by allowing men to eat with unwashed hands and, on the Sabbath, to lift the ass from the pit and to pick grain from the fields, He shows his disdain for the flesh. The parable of the Pharisee and the publican, the boastings of the Jews, the bringing of gifts to the altar, are all examples of His condemning the flesh of the law and the superstition of those who preferred to be Jews in public rather than in their secret selves.

He makes this very plain in the case of the Samaritan woman: "Woman, believe me, the hour is coming, when you shall neither on this mountain nor in Jerusalem adore the Father. But the hour is coming, and now is, when the true adorer shall adore the Father in spirit and truth." He meant the same thing when at the marriage feast He turned the water of the cold and insipid letter into the wine of the spirit. And just in case you feel that this was the limit of His disdain for those who seek the flesh and not the spirit, recall to mind what contempt He had for those who eat His flesh and drink His blood in other than a spiritual manner. To whom do you suppose He directed those words? It was certainly to none other than those who think their salvation consists in wearing a blessed medal or carrying an indulgenced relic. If receiving the sacrament of His Body is nothing unless done in a spiritual manner, then I think it is plain enough that all other material things are useless unless they are spiritualized.

Perhaps you celebrate Mass daily. Yet if you live as if this were only for your own welfare and have no concern for the difficulties and needs of your neighbor, you are still in the flesh of the sacrament. The sacrifice of the Mass in this spiritual sense really means that we are of one body with the Body of Christ, we are living members of the Church. If you love nothing except in Christ, if you hold that all of your possessions are the common property of all men, if you make the difficulties and privations of your neighbor your very own, then you may say Mass with great fruit because you do so in a spiritual manner. I think there are far too many who count up how many times they attend Mass and rely almost entirely upon this for their salvation. They are convinced that they owe nothing further to Christ. Leaving church, they immediately turn to their former habits. I certainly do not hesitate to praise them for getting to Mass but I am forced to condemn them for stopping at this point. They have failed to let what takes place at Mass also take place in their hearts; the death of our Head that is there represented does not take place in their souls. Examine yourself and see if attendance at divine services renders you dead to the world. If you are filled with ambition and envy, even though you offer the sacrifice yourself, you are far from the real significance of the Mass. Christ was slain for you. Sacrifice yourself, then, to Him who sacrificed Himself to the Father. If you believe in what takes place at the altar but fail to enter into the spiritual meaning of it, God will despise your flabby display of religion.

Let us consider a moment the matter of baptism. Do you really think that the ceremony of itself makes you a Christian? If your mind is preoccupied with the affairs of the world, you may be a Christian on the surface, but inwardly you are a Gentile of the Gentiles. Why is this? It is simply because you have grasped the body of the sacrament, not the spirit. The ceremony consists of washing the body with water, but for you this is not a cleansing of the soul. Salt is placed upon your tongue, but your mind remains uncured. The body is anointed with oil, but the soul remains unanointed. You have been sprinkled with holy water, but this accomplishes nothing unless you cleanse the inner filth of your mind.

Perhaps you are wont to venerate the relics of the saints, yet at the same time you condemn their greatest legacy, the example of their lives. No veneration of Mary is more beautiful than the imitation of her humility. No devotion to the saints is more acceptable to God than the imitation of their virtues. Say you have a great devotion to St. Peter and St. Paul. Then by all means imitate the faith of the former and the charity of the latter. This will certainly be more rewarding than a dozen trips to Rome. Do you really want to honor St. Francis? Then why not give away your wealth to the poor, restrain your evil inclinations, and see in everyone you meet the image of Christ? By avoiding contentions and overcoming evil with good, you will shine forth brighter in the sight of God than a hundred lighted candles. Do you value being buried in the Franciscan habit? The cowl of St. Francis will not benefit you after death if during your life you did not imitate his personal integrity. I have continually emphasized that the only complete example of perfect piety is to be found in the imitation of Christ. Yet I do not condemn the imitation of His saints; emulate them in such a way that each of them prompts you to eradicate one or another vice, and practice their particular virtues.

You may have a great veneration for the remains of St. Paul. If your religion conforms to this, then I cannot say that there is really anything wrong with it. But if you merely venerate the ashes of his remains and fail to imitate the resplendent image of him portrayed in his writings, you make your religion a ridiculous thing. You worship his bones hidden away and preserved in nooks and niches, but you fail to worship the great mind of Paul hidden in the Scriptures. A little fragment of his body seen through a glass covering evokes your admiration; why not marvel at his wonderful personality? The ashes you venerate are the very thing that vice will lead to. Let them evoke a feeling of sorrow. Our bodies will all one day be reduced to ashes. When you venerate the image of Christ in the paintings and other works of art that portray Him, think how much more you ought to revere that portrait of His mind that the inspiration of the Holy Spirit has placed in Holy Writ. No artist could possibly have reproduced those words and prayers of Christ that represent Him so exactly in the Gospel. If our Father in heaven finds His perfect reflection in His divine Son, so the words of His Son are the closest image of His divine personality. No relic of our Blessed Lord can possibly approach the strength and beauty of His very self. You may gaze in silent amazement at the tunic that reputedly belonged to Christ, yet you read the wonderful sayings of that same Christ half asleep. You are convinced that it is advantageous to have a small particle of the true Cross in your home, yet this is nothing compared with carrying the mystery of the Cross fixed in your mind. If these external things were the true source of holiness, then certainly there could never have been any people more religious than the Jews. They lived with Him, listened to His words, touched Him—yet most of them rejected him. What could be more envied than what Judas did, to press the divine mouth with his own? Even our Blessed Lady would not have been the great beneficiary of what Christ did unless she had conceived Him in the Spirit.

Let us carry this idea a bit further. The Apostles are a fine example of this failure of spirit. Even after all the miracles of Christ, after having listened to His teachings for so many years, after so many proofs of His resurrection, what does He say to them? As He is about to leave them He reproves them for their unbelief. Why was this? Surely it was because the flesh of Christ stood in their way. He tells them "If I go not, the Paraclete will not come to you; it is necessary that I go." If the very physical presence of Christ is useless to salvation, how can you put your trust in corporeal things? St. Paul actually saw Christ in the flesh. Yet he says, "And if we have known Christ according to the flesh, now we know Him no longer." He meant by this that, in the spirit, he had advanced beyond this kind of knowledge.

Perhaps I am arguing with more verbosity than He who taught the rules. I have a reason for doing so. The attitudes I am talking about are, in my opinion, the worst plague of Christianity. This false set of values brings more ruin than any other because in appearance it is very close to godliness. There are no vices that are more dangerous than those that have the veneer of virtue. And it is precisely because of this fact that so many good people easily fall into this deception and

that the uneducated faithful are led astray. Violent objections are made
to anyone who attempts to point out these things. I care very little
about objections to my criticisms so long as they have been approved
by ecclesiastical authority. They are signs, supports of piety. And
they are quite necessary for children in Christ, at least until they have
become a little more mature. Even those more advanced in perfection
should not scorn them, lest their scorn work great harm among the
simple and uninstructed. My approval rests on the assumption that
they are steps, or gradations, that lead to more appropriate means of
salvation.

But to place the whole of religion in external ceremonies is sublime
stupidity. This amounts to revolt against the spirit of the Gospel and
is a reversion to the superstitions of Judaism. St. Paul was incessant in
his attempt to remove the Jews from their faith in external works.
I feel that the vast majority of Christians have sunk once again into
this unhealthy situation. . . .

Charity does not consist in many visits to churches, in many pros-
trations before the statues of saints, in the lighting of candles, or in
the repetition of a number of designated prayers. Of all these things
God has no need. Paul declares charity to be the edification of one's
neighbor, the attempt to integrate all men into one body so that all
men may become one in Christ, the loving of one's neighbor as one's
self. Charity for Paul has many facets; he is charitable who rebukes
the erring, who teaches the ignorant, who lifts up the fallen, who
consoles the downhearted, who supports the needy. If a man is truly
charitable, he will devote, if needs be, all his wealth, all his zeal, and
all his care to the benefit of others.

Just as Christ gave Himself completely for us, so also should we
give ourselves for our neighbor. If the attitude of the religious were
comparable to the attitude of Christ, the life of the religious would be
much easier and much happier than we now know it to be. No longer
would the religious be sad, weary, superstitious, and prone to many
temptations; no longer would he fall a victim to the vices of the laity.
You who are religious claim to be followers of the rule of Augustine;
were he now to return to this life, I wonder if he would recognize as
disciples you who turn not to the rule of the Apostles as Augustine
desired, but to the superstitions of the Jews. Some among you attempt
to justify the emphasis you place on little things by claiming that unless you are faithful in the less important matters you are opening
the door to greater vices. This view deserves some commendation,
but there is also a danger that in emphasizing the less you may forget
the more.

In short, you must avoid the horns of the dilemma. To observe these unimportant things is, of course, wholesome, but to make them the whole object of your devotions is extremely dangerous. St. Paul recommends ceremonies but he does not bind us to the law, since we are free in Christ. He is not opposed to good works (without them it would be impossible to be a good Christian), yet they do not make the Christian. Paul does not put great worth in the works of Abraham; why should you trust so in your works: Did not God chide the Jews of old for their empty sacrifices and fasts? He tells us that not every man who says "Lord, Lord" is saved and points out that the practice of charity is more important than empty ceremonies. Help him who is oppressed, aid the fatherless, the motherless, the friendless, defend the widow. He recommends that instead of fasting we cancel the debt of him who owes us, that we lighten the burden of him who labors, that we share our bread with the hungry, that we house the homeless and clothe the naked.

I am not advocating that you neglect the mandates of the Church or that you despise honorable traditions and godly customs. If, however, you consider yourselves to be good religious striving for perfection, let your acts be those of one who sincerely desires perfection. If there is a question as to what works should come first, there should be no doubt in your minds. I am not condemning manual works, but I am trying to impress upon you that such works are of little value unless they are accompanied by internal piety. God is a Spirit and is appeased by spiritual sacrifices. A little known poet once wrote, "If God is mind, in poems he's revealed; with a pure mind, then, you ought to worship him." Each one of us should meditate upon these words. While it is true that the author is a pagan and that he has no place of prominence in the world of letters, yet his message, which is read by few and understood by fewer, should not be despised. His advice is worthy of a great theologian. God is mind, the most pure and most simple mind of all; therefore, he must be worshipped with a pure mind.

You believe God to be greatly touched by such material things as a slain bull or the smell of incense; you think that burned wax is a sacrifice. Why, then, did David say, "An afflicted spirit is a sacrifice to God"? If God despised the blood of goats and bulls, he will not despise a contrite and humble heart. If you attend fervently to these things that men expect you to do, spend much more time on those things that God expects of you. Of what advantage to you is a body covered by a religious habit if that same body possesses a mind that is worldly? If your habit is white, should not your mind be white, too? If your tongue is at rest in public, should not your mind be also at rest? What does it profit you when you kneel to venerate the wood of the Cross and forget the mystery of the Cross? You fast and abstain from those things that do not pollute men, yet you do not refrain from obscene conversations, which are a cause of pollution not only to yourself but also to those to whom you speak.

Why do you feed the body and starve the soul? You keep the Sabbath outwardly, but in the secret recesses of your mind you permit all kinds of vices to run rampant. Your body does not commit adultery, but you make your soul to be an adulterer by your greediness. You sing psalms, but your thoughts do not keep pace with your tongue. You bless with the mouth and curse with the heart. You hear the word of God spoken to you, but you refuse it entrance to your heart. Listen closely to the words of the prophet: "Unless you hear within, your soul will weep." And again: "You hear, but you do not understand." Blessed are they who hear the words of God internally. Happy are they to whom the Lord speaks inwardly, for their salvation is assured. Do you wonder why the daughter of the king, she who was goodness itself, was ordered by David to listen within for the voice of God?

Finally, what does it mean if you do not do the evil things that your mind lusts after? What does it mean if you perform good deeds in public but allow evil deeds to dominate your mind? Where is the profit if you have the appearance of a Jerusalem but the character of a Sodom, an Egypt, or a Babylon? If it is to a man's credit that his body walks in Christ's footsteps, it is more to his credit that his mind has followed the way of Christ. If it is a wonderful thing to have touched the Lord's sepulcher, it is more wonderful to have learned the lesson of the mystery of the sepulcher. You who reproach yourselves when you confess your sins to a priest, how will you feel when God accuses you of the same sins? Perhaps you believe that by wax seals, by sums of money, or by pilgrimages your sins are washed away immediately. If you are confident that these are the ways of forgiveness, you are sadly mistaken. If you wish to be forgiven, you, who have loved what you should have hated and who have hated what you should have loved, must attack the enemy within.

Perhaps I am devoting too much time to discussing your external actions, but I will not be convinced of your sanctity until you begin to hate and to flee those things that you used to love. Mary Magdalene loved much, and many sins were forgiven her. The more you love Christ the more you will hate your vices, for just as the shadow follows the body, the hatred of sin follows the love of godliness. I would prefer that you really hate your evil deeds internally rather than enumerate them ten times before a priest.

Therefore, my brethren, put on Christ. Take as your rule that you no longer wish to crawl upon the ground with the beasts, but to rise upon those wings that sprout in the minds of those who love. Advance from the body to the Spirit, from the visible world to the invisible, from things sensible to things intelligible, from things compound to things simple. If you come near to the Lord, He will come near to you; if you make a sincere effort to escape from the chains of blindness with which the love of sensible things has bound you, He will come to you, and you, no longer chained to the things of earth, will be enveloped in the silence of God.

SIXTH RULE

From among the many thoughts that have entered my mind since I began this letter to you, I think it would be fitting to choose a sixth rule—a rule that, incidentally, is observed by too few of those who claim to be followers of Christ. If we would be holy, we must go to the sole archetype of godliness, Christ Himself. Anyone who refuses to do this is outside the pale. Plato in his *Republic* points out that no man can defend virtue unless he has trained his mind in opinions regarding the true nature of good and evil. We can see then how dangerous it is if false opinions of those things that pertain to wellbeing should sink deeply into the mind.

A man's actions are mere expressions of his inner convictions; for a man to live so as to always act well, he must be taught even from infancy the things that are of Christ. Since nothing takes root more deeply in a man's mind than that which is taught to him in his earliest years, children should always be protected from any vestige of evil example. A child, being what he is, is most susceptible to example; therefore let good example be given always so that no sinful errors may creep into the child's mind and so that salutary habits may take firm root. He who has such salutary habits will follow virtue of his own accord, and he will judge those who do wrong to be deserving of pity, and not of imitation. Socrates might be mentioned here, as he points out that virtue is nothing other than the knowledge of things that are to be sought after or of things that are to be avoided, with a distinction made between knowledge of goodness and love of it. Vice, then, can proceed from no other source than wrong opinions. Both he who loves Christ and follows Him and he who loves evil pleasures think that they seek something that is good for themselves. The world has never advanced in goodness to the point where common opinion does not still give its approval to what is basically evil. . . .

True pleasure consists in this, that out of love of Christ we are never moved by false pleasures. Take for example how the world abuses the expressions love and hate. When a foolish young man is completely

out of his mind for the affection of a common wench, the common folk
call this love. There is in fact no truer form of hate. True love looks
primarily to the benefit of another. Whoever seeks after his own pleasure does not really love the object of his affections but rather himself. No man can hate except he first hate himself. Nonetheless, there
are occasions when to truly love is to hate well, and to hate well is to
love well. In the case of a young man about to seduce a girl with flat-
tery and gifts, is this love or hate? What is more hateful than the action
of those parents who, neglecting to discipline their children, pamper
them to the point that they inculcate false values that will be detrimental to their eternal welfare? If you kill the sinner, you save the man.
If you destroy what man has made, you will restore what God has
fashioned.

Take, for example, power and weakness, courage and cowardice:
What does popular error think them to be? Do they not call him powerful who can easily harm whomever he will? Although to be able to do
harm, to inflict evil, is a power excessively hateful, it is common to
cowardice, along with flies and scorpions, and the devil himself.

God alone is truly powerful, who could neither do harm if He wished
nor want to do it if He could, for His very nature is to do good. But
how, then, does this powerful One harm man? Will He snatch money
away, will He strike the body, will He take away life? If he does this
to a pious man, He has given good for evildoing; if He does it to a
wicked man, He has but furnished the occasion—the man has harmed
himself. For no one is harmed except by himself. No one prepares to
harm another unless he has already far more gravely harmed himself.
You prepare to cause me a loss of money, but since you have already
lost charity, you have suffered the gravest loss of all. You cannot inflict a wound upon me unless you have already received at your own
hands a much more frightful hurt. You will not deprive men of the
body unless you have already safely slain your own soul. Yet does
not Paul boast that he can do all things in Christ, for he is feeble in
inflicting injury but exceedingly strong in bearing it? The crowd
considers him strong and courageous who is fierce and of weak mind,
who boils over with anger at any injury, however slight, who returns
reproach for reproach, evil deed for evil deed. On the other hand
they call him who disregards or conceals an injury that he has sustained cowardly, pusillanimous, spiritless. What is more foreign to
greatness of mind than to be driven by a mere word from peace of
mind, hence not to be able to condemn folly as alien, so that you do
not think yourself to be a man unless you heap curse upon curse?
Yet how much more manly, with full and lofty purpose, is it to be
able to ignore an injury and, besides that, to return good for evil. . . .

From Erasmus, **Paraclesis**

The illustrious Lactantius Firmianus, good reader, whose eloquence Jerome especially admires, as he begins to defend the Christian religion against the pagans, desires especially an eloquence second only to Cicero's be given him, thinking it wrong, I believe, to want an equal eloquence. But I indeed might heartily wish, if anything is to be gained by wishes of this kind, so long as I exhort all men to the most holy and wholesome study of Christian philosophy and summon them as if with the blast of a trumpet, that an eloquence far different than Cicero's be given me: an eloquence certainly much more efficacious, if less ornate than his. Or rather [I might wish for that kind of eloquence], if such power of speech was ever granted anyone, as the tales of the ancient poets not entirely without cause attributed to Mercury, who as if with a magic wand and a divine lyre induces sleep when he wishes and likewise snatches sleep away, plunging whom he wished into hell and again calling them forth from hell; or as the ancient tales assigned to Amphion and Orpheus, one of whom is supposed to have moved hard rocks, the other to have attracted oaks and ashes with a lyre; or as the Gauls ascribed to their Ogmius, leading about whither he wished all men by little chains fastened to their ears from his tongue; or as fabled antiquity attributed to Marsyas; or really, lest we linger too long on fables, as Alcibiades imputed to Socrates and old comedy to Pericles, an eloquence which not only captivates the ear with its fleeting delight but which leaves a lasting sting in the minds of its hearers, which grips, which transforms, which sends away a far different listener than it had received. One reads that the noble musician Timotheus, singing Doric melodies, was wont to rouse Alexander the Great to a desire for war. Nor were they lacking in former times who considered nothing more effective than the entreaties which the Greeks call epodes. But if there were any such kind of incantation anywhere, if there were any power of song which truly could inspire, if any Pytho truly swayed the heart, I would desire that it be at hand for me so that I might convince all of the most wholesome truth of all. However, it is more desirable that Christ Himself, whose business we are about, so guide the strings of our lyre that this song might deeply affect and move the minds of all, and, in fact, to accomplish this there is no need for syllogisms and exclamations of the orators. What we desire is that nothing may stand forth with greater certainty than the truth itself, whose expression is the more powerful the simpler it is.

And in the first place it is not pleasing to renew at the present time this complaint, not entirely new but, alas, only too just—and perhaps never more just than in these days—that when men are devoting them-

selves with such ardent spirit to all their studies, this philosophy of
Christ alone is derided by some, even Christians, is neglected by many,
and is discussed by a few, but in a cold manner. (I shall not say insin-
cerely.) Moreover, in all branches of learning which human industry
has brought forth, nothing is so hidden and obscure which the keenness of genius has not explored, nothing is so difficult which tremendous
exertion has not overcome. Yet how is it that even those of us who
profess to be Christian fail to embrace with the proper spirit this philosophy alone? Platonists, Pythagoreans, Academics, Stoics, Cynics,
Peripatetics, Epicureans not only have a deep understanding of the
doctrines of their respective sects, but they commit them to memory,
and they fight fiercely in their behalf, willing even to die rather than
abandon the defense of their author. Then why do not we evince far
greater spirit for Christ, our Author and Prince? Who does not judge
it very shameful for one professing Aristotle's philosophy not to know
that man's opinion about the causes of lightning, about prime matter,
about the infinite? And neither does this knowledge render a man
happy, nor does the lack of it render him unhappy. And do not we,
initiated in so many ways, drawn by so many sacraments to Christ,
think it shameful and base to know nothing of His doctrines, which
offer the most certain happiness to all? But what purpose is served
to exaggerate the matter by controversy since it is what I might call
a kind of wicked madness to wish to compare Christ with Zeno or
Aristotle and His teaching with, to put it mildly, the paltry precepts
of those men? Let them magnify the leaders of their sect as much as
they can or wish. Certainly He alone was a teacher who came forth
from heaven, He alone could teach certain doctrine, since it is eternal
wisdom, He alone, the sole author of human salvation, taught what
pertains to salvation, He alone fully vouches for whatsoever He
taught, He alone is able to grant whatsoever He has promised. If anything is brought to us from the Chaldeans or Egyptians, we desire
more eagerly to examine it because of the fact that it comes from a
strange world, and part of its value is to have come from far off; and
oftentimes we are anxiously tormented by the fancies of an insignificant man, not to say an imposter, not only to no avail but with great
loss of time (I am not adding a more serious note, for the matter as
it stands is most serious). But why does not such a desire also excite
Christian minds who are convinced—and it is a fact— that this teaching
has come not from Egypt or Syria but from heaven itself? Why do
not all of us ponder within ourselves that this must be a new and
wonderful kind of philosophy since, in order to transmit it to mortals,
He who was God became man, He who was immortal became mortal,
He who was in the heart of the Father descended to earth? It must

be a great matter, and in no sense a commonplace one, whatever it is, because that wondrous Author came to teach after so many families of distinguished philosophers, after so many remarkable prophets. Why, then, out of pious curiosity do we not investigate, examine, explore each tenet? Especially since this kind of wisdom, so extraordinary that once for all it renders foolish the entire wisdom of this world, may be drawn from its few books as from the most limpid springs with far less labor than Aristotle's doctrine is extracted from so many obscure volumes, from those huge commentaries of the interpreters at odds with one another—and I shall not add with how much greater reward. Indeed, here there is no requirement that you approach equipped with so many troublesome sciences. The journey is simple, and it is ready for anyone. Only bring a pious and open mind, possessed above all with a pure and simple faith. Only be docile, and you have advanced far in this philosophy. It itself supplies inspiration as a teacher which communicates itself to no one more gladly than to minds that are without guile. The teachings of the others, besides the fact that they give hope of a false happiness, drive off the natural talents of many by the very difficulty, it is clear, of their precepts. This doctrine in an equal degree accommodates itself to all, lowers itself to the little ones, adjusts itself to their measure, nourishing them with milk, bearing, fostering, sustaining them, doing everything until we grow in Christ. Again, not only does it serve the lowliest, but it is also an object of wonder to those at the top. And the more you shall have progressed in its riches, the more you shall have withdrawn it from the shadow of the power of any other. It is a small affair to the little ones and more than the highest affair to the great. It casts aside no age, no sex, no fortune or position in life. The sun itself is not as common and accessible to all as is Christ's teaching. It keeps no one at a distance, unless a person, begrudging himself, keeps himself away.

Indeed, I disagree very much with those who are unwilling that Holy Scripture, translated into the vulgar tongue, be read by the uneducated, as if Christ taught such intricate doctrines that they could scarcely be understood by very few theologians, or as if the strength of the Christian religion consisted in men's ignorance of it. The mysteries of kings, perhaps, are better concealed, but Christ wishes his mysteries published as openly as possible. I would that even the lowliest women read the Gospels and the Pauline Epistles. And I would that they were translated into all languages so that they could be read and understood not only by Scots and Irish but also by Turks and Saracens. Surely the first step is to understand in one way or another. It may be that many will ridicule, but some may be taken captive. Would that, as a result, the farmer sing some portion

of them at the plow, the weaver hum some parts of them to the movement of his shuttle, the traveller lighten the weariness of the journey
with stories of this kind! Let all the conversations of every Christian
be drawn from this source. For in general our daily conversations
reveal what we are. Let each one comprehend what he can, let him
express what he can. Whoever lags behind, let him not envy him
who is ahead; whoever is in the front rank, let him encourage him who
follows, not despair of him. Why do we restrict a profession common
to all to a few? For it is not fitting, since Baptism is common in an
equal degree to all Christians, wherein there is the first profession
of Christian philosophy, and since the other sacraments and at length
the reward of immortality belong equally to all, that doctrines alone
should be reserved for those very few whom today the crowd call
theologians or monks, the very persons whom, although they comprise
one of the smallest parts of the Christian populace, yet I might wish
to be in greater measure what they are styled. For I fear that one may
find among the theologians men who are far removed from the title
they bear, that is, men who discuss earthly matters, not divine, and
that among the monks who profess the poverty of Christ and the
contempt of the world you may find something more than worldliness.
To me he is truly a theologian who teaches not by skill with intricate
syllogisms but by a disposition of mind, by the very expression and
the eyes, by his very life that riches should be disdained, that the
Christian should not put his trust in the supports of this world but
must rely entirely on heaven, that a wrong should not be avenged,
that a good should be wished for those wishing ill, that we should
deserve well of those deserving ill, that all good men should be loved
and cherished equally as members of the same body, that the evil
should be tolerated if they cannot be corrected, that those who are
stripped of their goods, those who are turned away from possessions,
those who mourn are blessed and should not be deplored, and that
death should even be desired by the devout, since it is nothing other
than a passage to immortality. And if anyone under the inspiration
of the spirit of Christ preaches this kind of doctrine, indicates it,
exhorts, incites, and encourages men to it, he indeed is truly a theologian, even if he should be a common laborer or weaver. And if
anyone exemplifies this doctrine in his life itself, he is in fact a great
doctor. Another, perhaps, even a non-Christian, may discuss more
subtly how the angels understand, but to persuade us to lead here an
angelic life, free from every stain, this indeed is the duty of the
Christian theologian.

But if anyone objects that these notions are somewhat stupid and
vulgar, I should respond to him only that Christ particularly taught

these rude doctrines, that the Apostles inculcated them, that however vulgar they are, they have brought forth for us so many sincerely Christian and so great a throng of illustrious martyrs. This philosophy, unlettered as it appears to these very objectors, has drawn the highest princes of the world and so many kingdoms and peoples to its laws, an achievement which the power of tyrants and the erudition of philosophers cannot claim. Indeed I do not object to having that latter wisdom, if it seems worthwhile, discussed among the educated. But let the lowly mass of Christians console themselves certainly with this title because, whether the Apostles knew or other Fathers understood these subtleties or not, they surely didn't teach them. If princes in the execution of their duties would manifest what I have referred to as a vulgar doctrine, if priests would inculcate it in sermons, if schoolmasters would instill it in students rather than that erudition which they draw from the fonts of Aristotle and Averroes, Christendom would not be so disturbed on all sides by almost continuous war, everything would not be boiling over with such a mad desire to heap up riches by fair means or foul, every subject, sacred as well as profane, would not be made to resound everywhere with so much noisy disputation, and finally, we would not differ from those who do not profess the philosophy of Christ merely in name and ceremonial. For upon these three ranks of men principally the task of either renewing or advancing the Christian religion has been placed: on the princes and the magistrates who serve in their place, on the bishops and their delegated priests, and on those who instruct the young eager for all knowledge. If it happen that they, having laid aside their own affairs, should sincerely cooperate in Christ, we would certainly see in not so many years a true and, as Paul says, a genuine race of Christians everywhere emerge, a people who would restore the philosophy of Christ not in ceremonies alone and in syllogistic propositions but in the heart itself and in the whole life. The enemies of the Christian name will far more quickly be drawn to the faith of Christ by these weapons than by threats or arms. In the conquest of every citadel nothing is more powerful than the truth itself. He is not a Platonist who has not read the works of Plato; and is he a theologian, let alone a Christian, who has not read the literature of Christ? Who loves me, Christ says, keeps my word, a distinguishing mark which He himself prescribed. Therefore, if we are truly and sincerely Christian, if we truly believe in Him who has been sent from Heaven to teach us that which the wisdom of the philosophers could not do, if we truly expect from Him what no prince, however powerful, can give, why is anything more important to us than His literature? Why indeed does anything seem learned that is not in harmony with His decrees?

Why in the case of this literature that should be revered do we also allow ourselves, and I shall say almost to a greater extent than do the secular interpreters in the case of the imperial laws or the books of the physicians, to speak what ever comes to mind, to distort, to obscure? We drag heavenly doctrines down to the level of our own life as if it were a Lydian rule, and while we seek to avoid by every means appearing to be ignorant and for this reason gather in whatever is of account in secular literature, that which is of special value in Christian philosophy I shall not say we corrupt, but—and no one can deny it— we restrict to a few, although Christ wished nothing to be more public. In this kind of philosophy, located as it is more truly in the disposition of the mind than in syllogisms, life means more than debate, inspiration is preferable to erudition, transformation is a more important matter than intellectual comprehension. Only a very few can be learned, but all can be Christian, all can be devout, and—I shall boldly add—all can be theologians.

Indeed, this philosophy easily penetrates into the minds of all, an action in especial accord with human nature. Moreover, what else is the philosophy of Christ, which He himself calls a rebirth, than the restoration of human nature originally well formed? By the same token, although no one has taught this more perfectly and more effectively than Christ, nevertheless one may find in the books of the pagans very much which does agree with His teaching. There was never so coarse a school of philosophy that taught that money rendered a man happy. Nor has there ever been one so shameless that fixed the chief good in those vulgar honors and pleasures. The Stoics understood that no one was wise unless he was good; they understood that nothing was truly good or noble save real virtue and nothing fearful or evil save baseness alone. According to Plato, Socrates teaches in many different ways that a wrong must not be repaid with a wrong, and also that since the soul is immortal, those should not be lamented who depart this life for a happier one with the assurance of having led an upright life. In addition, he teaches that the soul must be drawn away from the inclinations of the body and led to those which are its real objectives although they are not seen. Aristotle has written in the *Politics* that nothing can be a delight to us, even though it is not in any way despised, except virtue alone. Epicurus also acknowledges that nothing in man's life can bring delight unless the mind is conscious of no evil from which awareness true pleasure gushes forth as from a spring. What shall we say of this, that many—notably Socrates, Diogenes, and Epictetus—have presented a good portion of His teaching? But since Christ both taught and presented the same doctrine so much more fully, is it not a monstrous thing that Christians either disregard or neglect or even ridicule it? If there are things that belong particularly to Christianity in these ancient writers, let us follow them. But if these alone can truly make a Christian, why do we consider them as almost more obsolete and replaced than the Mosaic books? The first step, however, is to know what He taught; the next is to carry it into effect. Therefore, I believe, anyone should not think himself to be Christian if he disputes about instances, relations, quiddities, and formalities with an obscure and irksome confusion of words, but rather if he holds and exhibits what Christ taught and showed forth. Not that I condemn the industry of those who not without merit employ their native intellectual powers in such subtle discourse, for I do not wish anyone to be offended, but that I think, and rightly so, unless I am mistaken, that that pure and genuine philosophy of Christ is not to be drawn from any source more abundantly than from the evangelical books and from the Apostolic Letters, about which, if anyone should devoutly philosophize, praying more than arguing and seeking to be transformed rather than armed for battle, he would without a doubt find that there is nothing pertaining to the happiness of man and the living of his life which is not taught, examined, and unraveled in these works. If we desire to learn, why is another author more pleasing than Christ himself? If we seek a model for life, why does another example take precedence for us over that of Christ himself? If we wish some medicine against the troublesome desires of the soul, why do we think the remedy to be more at hand somewhere else? If we want to arouse a soul that is idle and growing listless by reading, where, I ask, will you find sparks equally alive and efficacious? If the soul seems distracted by the vexations of this life, why are other delights more pleasing? Why have we steadfastly preferred to learn the wisdom of Christ from the writings of men than from Christ himself? And He, since He promised to be with us all days, even unto the consummation of the world, stands forth especially in this literature, in which He lives for us even at this time, breathes and speaks, I should say almost more effectively than when He dwelt among men. The Jews saw and heard less than you see and hear in the books of the Gospels, to the extent that you make use of your eyes and ears, whereby this can be perceived and heard.

And what kind of a situation is this, I ask? We preserve the letters written by a dear friend, we kiss them fondly, we carry them about, we read them again and again, yet there are many thousands of Christians who, although they are learned in other respects, never read, however, the evangelical and apostolic books in an entire lifetime. The Mohammedans hold fast to their doctrines, the Jews also today from the very cradle study the books of Moses. Why do not we in

the same way distinguish ourselves in Christ? Those who profess the
way of life of Benedict hold, study, absorb a rule written by man, and
by one nearly uneducated for the uneducated. Those who are in the
Augustinian order are well versed in the rule of their founder. The
Franciscans reverence and love the little traditions of their Francis,
and to whatever corner of the earth they go, they carry them with
them; they do not feel safe unless the little book is on their person.
Why do these men attribute more to a rule written by man than does
the Christian world to its rule, which Christ delivered to all and which
all have been equally professed in baptism? Finally, although you
may even cite a thousand rules, can anything be holier than this? And
I wish that this may come to pass: just as Paul wrote that the law of
Moses was not full of glory compared with the glory of the Gospel
succeeding it, so may all Christians hold the Gospels and Letters of
the Apostles as so holy that in comparison with them these other writings do not seem holy. What others may wish to concede to Albert
the Great, to Alexander, to Thomas, to Egidio, to Richard, to Occam,
they will certainly be free, as far as I am concerned, to do, for I do
not want to diminish the fame of anyone or contend with the studies
of men that are now of long standing. However learned these may
be, however subtle, however seraphic, if they like, yet they must
admit that the former are the most tried and true. Paul wishes that
the spirits of those prophesying be judged whether they are of God.
Augustine, reading every kind of book with discretion, asks nothing
more than a just hearing also for his own works. But in this literature
alone [i.e., Holy Scripture] what I do not comprehend, I nevertheless
revere. It is no school of theologians who has attested to this Author
for us but the Heavenly Father Himself through the testimony of
the divine voice, and He has done this on two occasions: first at the
Jordan at the time of the Baptism, then on Mount Tabor at the Transfiguration. "This is my beloved Son" He says, "in whom I am well
pleased; hear Him." O solid and truly irrefragable authority, as the
theologians say! What is this phrase, "Hear Him"? Certainly He is
the one and only teacher, let us be the disciples of Him alone. Let
each one extol in his studies his own author as much as he will wish,
this utterance has been said without exception of Christ alone. A dove
first descended on Him, the confirmation of the Father's testimony.
Peter next bears His spirit, to whom the highest Pastor three times
entrusted the feeding of his sheep, feeding them without a doubt,
however, on the food of Christian doctrine. This spirit was born again,
as it were, in Paul, whom He himself called a "chosen vessel" and an
extraordinary herald of His name. What John had drawn from that
sacred font of His heart, he expressed in his own writings. What, I

pray, is like this in Scotus (I do not wish that this remark be taken as a pretext for abuse), what is like this in Thomas? Nevertheless, I admire the talents of the one, and I also revere the sanctity of the other. But why do not all of us apply ourselves to philosophy in these authors of such great value? Why do we not carry them about on our persons, have them ever in our hands? Why do we not hunt through these authors, thoroughly examine them, assiduously investigate them? Why devote the greater part of life to Averroes rather than to the Gospels? Why spend nearly all of life on the ordinances of men and on opinions in contradiction with themselves? The latter, in fact, may now be the views of the more eminent theologians, if you please; but certainly the first steps of the great theologian in the days to come will be in these authors [of Holy Scripture].

Let all those of us who have pledged in baptism in the words prescribed by Christ, if we have pledged sincerely, be directly imbued with the teachings of Christ in the midst of the very embraces of parents and caresses of nurses. For that which the new earthen pot of the soul first imbibes settles most deeply and clings most tenaciously. Let the first lispings utter Christ, let earliest childhood be formed by the Gospels of Him whom I would wish particularly presented in such a way that children also might love Him. For as the severity of some teachers causes children to hate literature before they come to know it, so there are those who make the philosophy of Christ sad and morose, although nothing is more sweet than it. In these studies, then, let them engage themselves until at length in silent growth they mature into strong manhood in Christ. The literature of others is such that many have greatly repented the effort expended upon it, and it happens again and again that those who have fought through all their life up to death to defend the principles of that literature, free themselves from the faction of their author at the very hour of death. But happy is that man whom death takes as he meditates upon this literaure [of Christ]. Let us all, therefore, with our whole heart covet this literature, let us embrace it, let us continually occupy ourselves with it, let us fondly kiss it, at length let us die in its embrace, let us be transformed in it, since indeed studies are transmuted into morals. As for him who cannot pursue this course (but who cannot do it, if only he wishes?), let him at least reverence this literature enveloping, as it were, His divine heart. If anyone shows us the footprints of Christ, in what manner, as Christians, do we prostrate ourselves, how we adore them! But why do we not venerate instead the living and breathing likeness of Him in these books? If anyone displays the tunic of Christ, to what corner of the earth shall we not hasten so that we may kiss it? Yet were you to bring forth His entire wardrobe, it would not manifest Christ more clearly and truly than the Gospel writings. We embellish a wooden or stone statue with gems and gold for the love of Christ. Why not, rather, mark with gold and gems and with ornaments of greater value than these, if such there be, these writings which bring Christ to us so much more effectively than any paltry image? The latter represents only the form of the body—if indeed it represents anything of Him—but these writings bring you the living image of His holy mind and the speaking, healing, dying, rising Christ himself, and thus they render Him so fully present that you would see less if you gazed upon Him with your very eyes.

From Erasmus, **A Diatribe or Sermon Concerning Free Will**

Among the many difficulties encountered in Holy Scripture—and there are many of them—none presents a more perplexed labyrinth than the problem of the freedom of the will. In ancient and more recent times philosophers and theologians have been vexed by it to an astonishing degree, but, as it seems to me, with more exertion than success on their part. Recently, Carlstadt and Eck restored interest in the problem, debating it, however, with moderation. Soon thereafter, Martin Luther took up the whole controversy once more—and in a rather heated fashion—with his formal *Assertion* concerning the freedom of the will. And although more than one has answered his *Assertion*, I, too, encouraged by my friends, am going to try to see whether, by the following brief discussion, the truth might not become more visible. . . .

I have not yet formed a definite opinion on any of the numerous traditional views regarding the freedom of the will; all I am willing to assert is that the will enjoys some power of freedom. . . .

Holy Scripture contains secrets into which God does not want us to penetrate too deeply, because if we attempt to do so, increasing darkness envelopes us, so that we might come to recognize in this manner both the unfathomable majesty of divine wisdom and the feebleness of the human mind. . . .

6) *Man's Limited Capacity to Know*

Men were not wont to intrude upon these concealed, even superfluous questions with irreligious curiosity, namely, whether God's foreknowledge is contingent; whether our will can contribute anything to our eternal salvation, or whether it simply undergoes the action of operative grace; whether everything we do, good or evil, is done out of mere necessity, or whether we are rather in a state of passive acceptance. Some things God wishes to remain totally unknown to us, such as the day of our death and the day of the last judgment. . . .

Other things He wanted us to know with utmost clarity, as for example, the precepts for a morally good life. . . .

There are certain kinds of truth which, even though they could be known, would nonetheless be unwisely offered for indiscriminate consideration. . . .

7) *Unsuitableness of Luther's Teachings*

Let us assume the truth of what Wycliffe has taught and Luther has asserted, namely, that everything we do happens not on account of our free will, but out of sheer necessity. What could be more useless than to publish this paradox to the world? Secondly, let us assume that it is true, as Augustine has written somewhere, that God causes both good and evil in us, and that he rewards us for his good works wrought in us and punishes us for the evil deeds done in us. What a loophole the publication of this opinion would open to godlessness among innumerable people? In particular, mankind is lazy, indolent, malicious, and in addition, incorrigibly prone to every impious outrage. How many weak ones would continue in their perpetual and laborious battle against their own flesh? What wicked fellow would henceforth try to better his conduct? Who could love with all his heart a God who fires a hell with eternal pain, in order to punish there poor mankind for his own evil deeds, as if God enjoyed human distress? Most people would react as they are sketched above. People are universally ignorant and carnal-minded. They tend toward unbelief, wickedness and blasphemy. There is no sense in pouring oil upon the fire.

Thus Paul, the prudent disburser of the divine word, frequently consults charity and prefers to pursue what serves the neighbor, rather than what is permissible. . . .

Since Luther recognizes no authority of any author, however approved, except that of the canonical books, I gladly accept this diminution of labor.

I admit that it is right that the sole authority of Holy Scripture surpasses the voices of all mortals.

But we are not involved in a controversy regarding Scripture. The same Scripture is being loved and revered by both parties. Our battle concerns the sense of Scripture. . . .

Nobody can deny that Sacred Scripture contains many passages stating the obvious freedom of the human will. On the other hand, there are some passages which seem to deny the former. Yet, it is certain that Scripture cannot contradict itself, since all passages are inspired by the same Spirit. Therefore, we shall first examine those passages which confirm our view and then we shall try to dispose of those that seem to be opposed.

By freedom of the will we understand in this connection the power of the human will whereby man can apply to or turn away from that which leads unto eternal salvation. . . .

52) *Some Reformer's Views Justified*

Evidently these people considered it quite apt for the simple obedience of a Christian that man depend completely on the will of God when he places his entire trust and all his hopes in his promises; when he, conscious of his own wretchedness, admires and loves his immense mercy which he gives us plentifully without charge; when he, furthermore, subjects himself completely to his will, no matter whether he wants to save or destroy him; when he accepts no praise whatsoever for his good works, and rather ascribes all glory to his grace, thinking that man is nothing else but a living tool of the divine Spirit. . . .

These utterances are also very praiseworthy to me, because they agree with Holy Scripture. . . .

56) *Exaggerating and Underrating*

But care should be taken not to deny the freedom of the will, while praising faith. For if this happens, there is no telling how the problem of divine justice and mercy could be solved. . . .

Here we could state, in order to assuage those who permit man no possibility for any good unless indebted to God, that we owe our entire life work to God, without whom we could accomplish nothing, furthermore, that the free will contributes very little to an effect; finally, that it is also a work of divine grace that we can turn our heart to the things of salvation and co-operate with grace. . . .

57) *Human Nature and Salvation*

In my opinion the free will could have been so defined as to avoid overconfidence in our merits and the other disadvantages which Luther shuns, as well as to avoid such as we recited above, and still not lose the advantages which Luther admires. This, it seems to me, is accomplished by those who attribute everything to the pulling by grace which is the first to excite our spirit, and attribute only something to human will in its effort to continue and not withdraw from divine grace. But since all things have three parts, a beginning, a continuation and an end, grace is attributed to the two extremities, and only in continuation does the free will effect something. Two causes meet in this same work, the grace of God and the human will, grace being the principal cause and will a secondary, since it is impotent without the principal cause, while the latter has sufficient strength by itself. Thus, while the fire burns through its natural strength, the principal cause is still God, who acts through the fire. God alone would indeed suffice, and without Him fire could not burn. Due to this combination, man must ascribe his total salvation to divine grace, since it is very little that the free will can effect, and even that comes from divine grace which has at first created free will and then redeemed and healed it. . . .

59) *Addressed to Luther*

Those who deny any freedom of the will and affirm absolute necessity, admit that God works in man not only the good works, but also evil ones. It seems to follow that inasmuch as man can never be the author of good works, he can also never be called the author of evil ones. This opinion seems obviously to attribute cruelty and injustice to God, something religious ears abhor vehemently. (He would no longer be God if anything vicious and imperfect were met in him). Nonetheless those holding such an implausible view have an answer: He is God; He is able to do only the best and most beautiful. If you observe the fittingness of the universe, even what is evil in itself, is good in it and illustrates the glory of God. No creature can adjudge the Creator's intentions. Man must subject himself completely to them. . . .

60) *Further Exaggeration and Difficulties*

But let us cease reasoning with those devoid of reason. We began our disputation with man, created in the image and likeness of God, and for whose pleasure He created all things. We note that some are born with healthy bodies and good minds, as though born for virtue, again others with monstrous bodies and horrible sickness, others so stupid that they almost have fallen to the level of brute animals, some even more brutish than the brutes, others so disposed toward disgraceful passion, that it seems a strong fate is impelling them, others insane and possessed by the devils. How will we explain the question of God's justice and mercy in such cases? Shall we say with Paul: "O the depth . . ." (Romans 11:33)? I think this would be better than to judge with impious rashness God's decisions, which man cannot explore. And truly, it is even more difficult to explain how God crowns his favors in some with immortal life, and punishes his misdeeds in others with eternal suffering. In order to defend such a paradox they resort to other paradoxes and to maintain the battle against their adversary. They immensely exaggerate original sin which supposedly has corrupted even the most excellent faculties of human nature, makes man incapable of anything, save only ignoring and hating God, and not even after grace and justification by faith can he effect any work which wouldn't be sin. They make that inclination to sin in us, remaining after the sin of our first parents, an invincible sin in itself, so that not one divine precept exists which even a man justified by faith could possibly keep. All the commandments of God have supposed no other purpose than to amplify the grace of God, which, irrespective of merit, grants salvation. . . .

I like the sentiments of those who attribute a little to the freedom of the will, the most, however, to grace. One must not avoid the Scylla of arrogance by going into the Charybdis of desperation and indolence. In resetting a disjointed limb, one must not dislocate it in the opposite direction, but put it back in its place. One must not fight with an enemy in such a manner that turning the face, you are caught off guard.

According to this moderation man can do a good, albeit imperfect work; man should not boast about it; there will be some merit, but man owes it completely to God. The life of us mortals abounds in many infirmities, imperfections and vices. Whoever wishes to contemplate himself, will easily lower his head. But we do not assume that even a justified man is capable of nothing but sin, especially because Christ speaks of rebirth and Paul of a new creature.

Why, you ask, is anything attributed to the freedom of the will, then? It is in order to justify blaming the godless ones who resist spitefully the grace of God; to prevent calumnies attributing cruelty and injustice to God; to prevent despair in us; to prevent a false sense of security; to stimulate our efforts. For these reasons the freedom of the will is asserted by all. Yet it is, however, ineffectual without the continuous grace of God, in order not to arrogate anything in ourselves. Someone says, what's the good of the freedom of the will, if it does not effect anything? I answer, what's the good of the entire man, if God treats him like the potter his clay, or as he can deal with a pebble? . . .

Part Five

The Reformation

Introduction

There seems to be a peculiar dynamic in the lives of human beings and of their institutions: from time to time they stray so far from their ideals as to require reform. To this rule the Christian church is no exception. While it believes itself to be guided by the Holy Spirit, it is at the same time composed of fallible, indeed sinful, members. The ancient church fathers had recognized the need for continual reform in the church. During the Middle Ages the monastic communities had been the principal centers of reform. From the monasteries reform sometimes spread throughout the church, as in the case of Hildebrand, the monk who became pope as Gregory VII in the 11th century. General councils also carried out reforms, such as the fourth Lateran Council of 1215.

In the sixteenth century dramatic changes were under way in many aspects of life. Feudalism was breaking down. Unified nations such as England, France, and Spain were emerging, under strong monarchs. A capitalist economy was beginning to develop. There was social ferment. The peasants were restless and sometimes rebellious. The invention of movable type had made it possible to publish new ideas more easily and more broadly than ever before.

With these changes came a widespread clamor for reform in the church. A number of statesmen, humanistic scholars, and churchmen recognized the need. Generally speaking, the impetus originated from below, though in time the hierarchy also caught the spirit. But several questions arose, to which varying answers were given: On the basis of what authority was the reform to be carried out? What was to be reformed? To what extent? By whom?

Italian humanists, northern humanists, and biblical reformers all had one thing in common: they all sought to "return to the sources" of ancient times. But they disagreed on *what* sources. The Renaissance humanists had rediscovered many ancient texts, pagan and Christian, and had championed their study. In order to do this, it was of course necessary to learn the an-

307

cient languages, Greek and Hebrew as well as classical Latin. The humanists' greatest contribution to reform was the impetus they gave to renewed
study of the Bible and the ancient Greek and Latin fathers.

From ancient times the Christian humanist tradition had forged a synthesis
of the Greek philosophical and the biblical streams of thought. In the Renaissance and Reformation this synthesis broke down. The reform in the church
took two very different forms, Protestant and Catholic. Institutionally, the
Western church was splintered. But even more important, it was divided
religiously and theologically. The Italian humanists of the Renaissance,
while not anti-Christian or ignoring the Bible and the Fathers, sought their
inspiration primarily in the classical pagan literature, with its emphasis on
the dignity and freedom of mankind. The northern humanists emphasized
the biblical tradition, though they drew from pagan sources as well. They
rejected the scholastic theology. This was the theology, definitively formulated by Thomas Aquinas, which expressed Christian belief in the logic
and terminology of Aristotle. The Protestant reformers also rejected this
tradition. Although more or less influenced by humanism and retaining
remnants of Greek philosophy, they were more radical in their insistence
on the Bible as the ultimate norm for Christian faith and life. They took a
position sharply opposed to the Italian humanists, especially in their
assessment of the human condition. The Roman church, pope, and council
reaffirmed the medieval scholastic synthesis. On the concept of man, it
took a middle-of-the-road position. While admitting that mankind was
corrupted by original sin, Catholicism denied that human free will had
been entirely lost with regard to salvation, and asserted that it could and
must cooperate with divine grace in justification.

It was generally agreed that there were a number of practical abuses in
the church which required reform: simony, pluralism, absenteeism, nepo-
tism, an uneducated clergy, and the indulgence traffic. Monasticism was
more or less decadent, weighed down by too much wealth and too little
discipline. This emphasis on practical and moral reform characterized
Erasmus, for example, and many loyal Catholics.

Martin Luther (1483-1546), a German Augustinian monk, and the various Protestants who followed him, were more radical. They believed that
the church had gone astray not only morally but theologically. They believed that the church had obscured the gospel itself. While the Protestants took for granted the dogmatic decisions of the ancient councils with
regard to the triune God and the two natures of Christ, they raised a number of theological issues. Foremost was the question of how a sinful human
being is justified before God, or the relative role of God and of man in
eternal salvation. In their concept of human nature, the Protestants believed that they were following the theology of Paul and of Augustine.
On this issue, whether to stress the human abilities or the human limitations,

the dialectic of Christian humanist anthropology, the decisive break came. When Luther's standpoint was condemned as heretical and he himself was excommunicated, other issues arose, such as the question of authority in the church. The result was increasingly vehement attacks on the papacy on the part of Protestants.

Luther's reform grew out of his personal religious experience. Suffering under severe conviction of sin, and failing to find relief for his conscience in the monastic life, he became convinced that the church was not seeing the problem of human sinfulness in sufficient depth. As a teacher and preacher of the Bible, he found his answer in the Pauline doctrine of justification by grace received through faith. The indulgence traffic was the catalyst for the famous 95 Theses, published in 1517 and usually regarded as marking the beginning of the Protestant Reformation. The corollary of the belief that salvation was entirely the work of divine grace was that in the matter of salvation, human beings have no free will. The ancient church, led by Augustine, had condemned as heretical the teaching of the Pelagians on the ground that it ascribed too much to human free will. Both sides reaffirmed this condemnation in the sixteenth century. But Luther regarded the standpoint of the medieval church as semi-Pelagian. This was the point at issue in his controversy with Erasmus.

Luther was not a humanist in the strict sense. He was acquainted with some of the classical authors, but he much preferred to quote the Bible and the church fathers, especially Augustine. What he took from humanism was primarily the study of the biblical languages as tools for exposition and the humanists' sponsorship of education. He also took a positive view generally of culture, in contrast to the "enthusiasts" or Anabaptists. He was culturally as well as politically conservative. Luther's scheme of social ethics was his so-called doctrine of the two kingdoms. On this view, the one God rules over two realms, which must be distinguished though not separated. Their relationship is a dialectical one. The kingdom on the right is his proper, eternal kingdom, the communion of saints, the sum total of believers, "hidden" within the institutional church. Here God rules primarily through the gospel. The kingdom on the left includes the various "orders of creation" (family, political order, economic order). Here God rules primarily through the law. Christians belong to both kingdoms and take active part in the affairs of the world. Christians serve as the conscience of the orders of creation. They act out of love, received from God, and by means of reason. The kingdom on the left is temporal and serves the kingdom on the right chiefly by maintaining order so that the gospel may be freely proclaimed in Word and sacrament.

This scheme has broad implications. It must above all be kept in mind that God rules over both kingdoms. Therefore, Christians must take a positive view also of the kingdom on the left and human nature. The secular authority is derived from God, as opposed to the medieval church's claim that the chain of command runs from God through the papacy to the kings. Secular authority thus rules over the body, but it can never rule over the soul and conscience. (Luther was the first, even before the Baptists, to promote freedom of conscience in religion.)

Moreover, "secular" authorities are responsible to God for their actions. This is closely related to Luther's doctrine of the priesthood of all believers and his concept of vocation. All Christians have direct access to God, but they are also obligated to serve as priests to their neighbors. Every honorable occupation can be a Christian calling. This is the basis of Luther's criticism of clericalism and monasticism, that it divides Christians into two classes, the "religious" or spiritual athletes, and the common horde. His view did not preclude the idea of a divine call to some Christians to the ministry, but this was a distinction of function rather than of spiritual status. One result was that monasticism became a victim of the Protestant reformation. Virtually all the monastic communities in Protestant territory were disbanded.

Liturgically, Luther was conservative. With the exception of the Eucharistic canon, with its emphasis upon sacrifice, Luther retained the form of the mass. Paintings and sculpture were preserved in the churches. Although there were a few Lutheran painters, Lutheranism's chief contribution to the arts was in the area of music. Luther and his followers supplied excellent hymns for congregational singing. Later, Lutheran church musicians developed more complex forms, culminating in the great choral and organ works of Johann Sebastian Bach. Luther's translation of the Bible had a powerful impact on German language and literature.

Luther's closest and most influential collaborator was Philip Melanchthon (1497-1560), a brilliant scholar with a thoroughly humanistic education and an irenic temperament. He became the first systematizer of Lutheran theology with his *Loci Communes* (1521), which became the basic textbook of Lutheran theology for more than a century. Although Luther first appealed to the councilmen of the cities of Germany to establish Christian schools, it was Melanchthon who organized the school system in the Lutheran states. He is often referred to as "the preceptor of Germany." He was also the author (after consultation with the outlawed Luther) of the Augsburg Confession of 1530 and the much longer Apology to the Augsburg Confession. Although he was highly regarded by Luther, his later years were marred by charges that he was too conciliatory toward both Catholicism and Calvinism, and his standpoint has continued to provoke controversy among scholars.

John Calvin (1509-1564), the Frenchman who led the Swiss reform after the early death of Ulrich Zwingli, is generally regarded as the most brilliant and learned of the Protestant reformers. Calvinism spread to

Holland and Britain, and eventually became a dominant force in North America. Calvin was deeply influenced by Luther's writings, and Calvinism and Lutheranism are closer to one another than either is to any other branch of the church. Calvin also taught justification by grace and the supreme authority of Scripture. He too was a strong disciple of Augustine. However, there were differences. Calvin was more humanistically and more broadly educated than Luther. He knew the classical pagan writers better, and quoted them more often, along with the Bible and the fathers. Educated both in the law and in theology, he possessed the kind of logical mind which produced the most thorough and most learned systematic theology of the Protestant reformation, the *Institutes of the Christian Religion* (1535). This work had enormous influence. Calvin's theology had a different emphasis from that of Luther. Though not lacking in warmth of piety, his starting point was not in the experience of forgiveness but in the idea of the absolute sovereignty of God. From this he proceeded to expound the doctrines of Christianity, following the order of the ancient creeds. His logic led him to go beyond Luther's doctrine of election to posit a "double" predestination. Whereas Luther followed the Pauline usage of this term (Rom. 8:29-30) to refer only to salvation, and refused to speculate about those who were being damned, regarding this as a mystery which only God understood, Calvin reasoned that if God had predestined some to salvation, he must have predestined the rest to damnation.

Calvin also tended to use Scripture more as a code of law and to find in it a blueprint for organization of church and society. Though the use of the term has been debated, Calvin's ideal form of society was the Hebrew theocracy. He carried out this scheme in the city of Geneva. Hundreds of other reformers like the Scotsman John Knox and the English Puritans, temporarily feeling Catholic reaction, came to Geneva, and later brought Calvinism back to their homelands. H. Richard Niebuhr correctly describes the attitude of Calvinism to culture as one of Christ transforming culture. Although, like Luther, Calvin made a distinction between the spiritual and the civil realms, he also asserted that the civil magistrates were responsible for enforcing both tables of the law. In the Calvinist theocracy, which was temporarily realized in sixteenth century Geneva and colonial America, the saints governed; only professed Christians could hold office or vote, though all were taxed to support the church.

It might be supposed that the doctrine of double predestination would lead to moral laxity. It did not. On the contrary, it lead to moral rigor. While on Calvin's view it was impossible to be certain that you were elected to salvation, there were certain signs of election in the lives of Christians. These included works of piety, such as prayer, Bible reading, and participation in worship. They also included such moral virtues as sobriety, industry, thrift, and the shunning of frivolous amusements so commonly associated with "the Protestant work ethic" and with Puritanism. These were in their way culturally creative.

Calvinism, like Lutheranism, gave great impetus to education. On the other hand, it was not creative in the fine arts. In worship, simplicity, even austerity, prevailed. The churches were stripped of their works of art. Only the Old Testament psalms were sung, because they were biblical, and original hymns were not introduced until two centuries later. Even the term "altar" was replaced by the expression "communion table." The outstanding exception in the fine arts was the great painter of biblical themes, Rembrandt van Rijn (1606-1669) who came out of Calvinist Holland, although he was not in favor with the Calvinist establishment.

The Roman Church undertook its own reform. It had begun in Spain before Luther, when Cardinal Ximenes founded the University of Alcala in 1499 and published the Polygot Bible (Hebrew, Greek, and Latin). Translation of the Gospels and Epistles into Spanish also appeared in 1512. Abuses in churches and monasteries were corrected. Spurred by humanists like Erasmus and by the Protestant revolt, Catholic reform gathered strength as the 16th century progressed. Eventually the worldly Renaissance popes gave way to men of spirituality. The most important single event in what is often called the "counter-reformation" was the Council of Trent (1545-1563), which set the apologetic tone and defined Catholic doctrine and standards of practice that became normative for the ensuing four centuries. The Council formulated Catholic theology in conscious reaction to Protestant beliefs. While reaffirming predestination, it took a position diametrically opposed to Luther and Calvin on free will. Sanctification and the necessity of good works for salvation were stressed. The greater part of the decrees of the Council involved a reaffirmation of the seven sacraments and reform of abuses connected with them. The church was defined as a sacramental community with a hierarchical structure. The power of the papacy and the bishops was enhanced. Canon law was tightened, and various practical abuses were condemned. One of the chief aims of the Council was to improve the education and to enhance the piety of the clergy. This was accomplished by the decree that at least one seminary was to be established in each diocese. The Council's decrees were approved by Pope Pius IV, and with the aid of the Inquisition, he and later popes (notably Pius V) carried out the reform.

Trent can be seen as both a victory and a defeat. On the one hand, it reformed and solidified Roman Catholicism. It created what the older generation today calls "the old (pre-Vatican II) church." Three centuries would pass before another council was called, and it continued the Romanizing tendency by promulgating the dogma of papal infallibility. On the other hand, Trent represents the recognition that the Western church was no longer one, and by its decrees it helped to make permanent the division.

A powerful instrument in the hands of the reforming popes were the new religious orders, particularly the Society of Jesus, founded by Ignatius Loyola (1491-1556). This order, destined to become the largest in the church, did herculean work, especially in education. The Jesuits soon became teachers and confessors to the Catholic nobility of Europe, and thus came to exert considerable political influence. The Jesuits, more than any other group, combined the piety and morality of the Catholic reform with classical humanistic learning. They went further than Trent in proclaiming human free will, a teaching which contributed to the protests of Jansenism in 17th century France.

Cultural life was strongly affected by the Catholic reform. Worship was made uniform: local variations of the liturgy gave way to the Roman rite, and the continued use of Latin in the mass was made mandatory. Among reforms of Pope Pius V were the issuance of a new breviary (1568) and a new missal (1570). The fine arts entered a new era, in which they flourished but were made to serve the church more strictly than in the Renaissance. For a generation after Trent, they were made to express Catholic orthodoxy, as opposed to both Renaissance humanism and Protestantism. Their subjects were restricted to persons like Christ, Mary, and the other saints. Suffering and martyrdom were often depicted. A new mood of religious seriousness set in. Nothing heretical, profane, or indecent was to be portrayed, and nudes from an earlier period were clothed. The medieval ideal that art was to be "the Bible of the illiterate" was revived. The arts were to serve as incitements to piety, to arouse the emotions as well as the intellect. As the 17th century dawned, more and more emphasis was placed on the emotional, under the influence of the popes and the Jesuits. The result was a new era in art, the exuberant Baroque. The reform of church music is best typified by the dignified and spare polyphony of Palestrina, whose influence spread far and wide from his Roman base. The simplicity of his music aimed to serve the text and thus to emphasize the importance of the words of the mass.

The reformation of the sixteenth century was the most traumatic event in the history of the Western church. The results were mixed. On the one hand, it shattered the unity of the church. Protestants and Catholics took up entrenched positions, and mutual polemic drove them farther and farther apart, until the dramatic change brought about by the ecumenical movement of the twentieth century. Catholics, Lutherans, and Calvinists all solidified their theologies in a new scholasticism which appeared strong but which sometimes proved to be a brittle weapon as it was confronted by the revolutions of succeeding centuries. The ideal of uniformity in religion which had prevailed since the fourth century died hard. It was only after savage persecution and devastating wars failed to maintain it that the exhausted adversaries began to accept a measure of pluralism.

On the other hand, there were many positive results. The church was reformed, and the church experienced a quickening of spiritual life in all its branches. Diversity had its positive aspects: new forms of Christianity emerged, and events eventually forced the acceptance of religious liberty. Tremendous impetus was given to education at all levels. In particular, the 16th century was one of the great creative periods in Christian theology. But the renewal and innovation in education, under Christian humanist auspices, went far beyond theology. Liberal educators, both Catholic and Protestant, struggled to create a new synthesis of learning after the decline and dissolution of the monastic schools. Men like Melanchthon, Calvin, and Knox, and the Catholic orders (chiefly the Jesuits) organized new systems of vernacular elementary schools, humanistic secondary schools ("Latin Schools" or *gymnasia*), and universities. They established an educational tradition which, despite the nationalistic and secularizing tendencies and the great broadening of curriculum of modern times, persists to the present day. The arts flourished, and their greatest patron was the church. It could even be argued that the Christian thought of this period gave rise to the new scientific, philosophical, and economic currents which in the succeeding period appeared to challenge the Christian life view.

MARTIN LUTHER

Psychologists have described two types of religious personalities: the "once born" whose religious life is one of harmonious development, and the "twice born," for whom religion involves discontinuity and at least one major crisis. Martin Luther (1483-1546) was of the latter type. His life was a stormy one, internally and externally. A serious-minded young man, he was guilt-ridden over his sins. Caught in a violent thunderstorm, he vowed to become a monk if his life should be spared. Failing to find peace of soul in the monastery, he was led through his biblical studies to an experience which he called his discovery of the gospel; in theological terms, it was the doctrine of justification by grace alone received through faith.

From his pulpit and lectern in the little town of Wittenberg in Saxony, he began his effort to reform the church. When negotiation and debate failed to silence Luther, he was excommunicated in 1520, and at the Diet of Worms the following year he was outlawed by the emperor.

He spent the rest of his life largely confined to Saxony, but his ideas spread rapidly and broadly through his writings. A blunt, plain-spoken, earthy person, Luther could sound harsh; he could also display a childlike faith and a deep compassion in a pastoral role. In 1520 he published among other occasional writings the *Treatise on Christian Liberty* or *The Freedom of a Christian*, which offers a good summary of his basic theology. The chief point is that human beings are justified solely by God's grace, and that good works follow spontaneously from a Spirit-led life devoted to the service of others. After he was placed under the Imperial ban, Luther in seclusion translated the New Testament into German and later the Old Testament. Luther's German Bible was a literary masterpiece; his version of high German became the national literary language. He undertook two reforms of the liturgy, the first retaining the Latin, the second (1525) using the German language. He wrote two catechisms (the Small and the Large) for religious instruction. He was soon engaged in controversy on two fronts: against Rome and against the radical Protestant "enthusiasts." The Peasants' Revolt of 1524-25 was led by the latter. Though he sympathized with many of the demands of the peasants, he eventually came down strongly against them because he feared that their confusing law and gospel, their use of force for religious aims, their attempt to rule the secular realm by the gospel were not only wrong but would lead to anarchy.

Simultaneously, he became embroiled in a controversy with the learned Erasmus over the question of whether the human will is free to contribute anything toward the salvation of the individual. Luther's theology here is consistent with what he had written in *The Freedom of the Christian.* Erasmus, on the other hand, takes a moderate Catholic position. The controversy further reveals the considerable difference in the personalities of these two great figures of the 16th century.

From Luther, **The Freedom of a Christian**

Many people have considered Christian faith an easy thing, and not a few have given it a place among the virtues. They do this because they have not experienced it and have never tasted the great strength there is in faith. It is impossible to write well about it or to understand what has been written about it unless one has at one time or another experienced the courage which faith gives a man when trials oppress him. But he who has had even a faint taste of it can never write, speak, meditate, or hear enough concerning it. . . .

To make the way smoother for the unlearned—for only them do I serve—I shall set down the following two propositions concerning the freedom and the bondage of the spirit:

A Christian is a perfectly free lord of all, subject to none.

A Christian is a perfectly dutiful servant of all, subject to all.

These two theses seem to contradict each other. If, however, they should be found to fit together they would serve our purpose beautifully. Both are Paul's own statements, who says in I Cor. 9 [:19], "For though I am free from all men, I have made myself a slave to all," and in Rom. 13 [:8], "Owe no one anything, except to love one another."

Love by its very nature is ready to serve and be subject to him who is loved. So Christ, although he was Lord of all, was "born of woman, born under the law" [Gal. 4:4], and therefore was at the same time a free man and a servant, "in the form of God" and "of a servant" [Phil. 2:6-7].

Let us start, however, with something more remote from our subject, but more obvious. Man has a twofold nature, a spiritual and a bodily one. According to the spiritual nature, which men refer to as the soul, he is called a spiritual, inner, or new man. According to the bodily nature, which men refer to as flesh, he is called a carnal, or old man, of whom the Apostle writes in 2 Cor. 4 [:16], "Though our outer nature is wasting away, our inner nature is being renewed every day." Because of this diversity of nature the Scriptures assert contradictory things concerning the same man, since these two men in the same man contradict each other, "for the desires of the flesh are against the Spirit, and the desires of the Spirit are against the flesh," according to Gal. 5 [:17].

First, let us consider the inner man to see how a righteous, free, and pious Christian, that is, a spiritual, new and inner man, becomes what he is. It is evident that no external thing has any influence in producing Christian righteousness or freedom, or in producing unrighteousness or servitude. . . .

Furthermore, to put aside all kinds of works, even contemplation, meditation, and all that the soul can do, does not help. One thing, and only one thing, is necessary for Christian life, righteousness and freedom. That one thing is the most holy Word of God, the gospel of Christ, as Christ says, John 11 [:25], "I am the resurrection and the life; he who believes in me, though he die, yet shall he live"; and John 8 [:36], "So if the Son makes you free, you will be free indeed"; and Matt. 4 [:4], "Man shall not live by bread alone, but by every word that proceeds from the mouth of God." Let us then consider it certain and firmly established that the soul can do without anything except the Word of God and that where the Word of God is missing there is no help at all for the soul. If it has the Word of God it is rich and lacks nothing since it is the word of life, truth, light, peace, righteousness, salvation, joy, liberty, wisdom, power, grace, glory, and of every calculable blessing. This is why the prophet in the entire Psalm [119] and in many other places yearns and sighs for the Word of God and uses so many names to describe it.

On the other hand, there is no more terrible disaster with which the wrath of God can afflict men than a famine of the hearing of his Word. . . .

You may ask, "What then is the Word of God, and how shall it be used, since there are so many words of God?" I answer: The Apostle explains this in Romans 1. The Word is the gospel of God concerning His Son, who was made flesh, suffered, rose from the dead, and was glorified through the Spirit who sanctifies. To preach Christ means to feed the soul, make it righteous, set it free, and save it, provided it believes the preaching. Faith alone is the saving and efficacious use of the Word of God, according to Rom. 10 [:9]: "If you confess with your lips that Jesus is Lord and believe in your heart that God raised him from the dead, you will be saved." Furthermore, "Christ is the end of the law, that every one who has faith may be justified" [Rom. 10:4]. Again, in Rom. 1 [:17], "He who through faith is righteous shall live." The Word of God cannot be received and cherished by any works whatever but only by faith. Therefore it is clear that, as the soul needs only the Word of God for its life and righteousness, so it is justified by faith alone and not any works; for if it could be justified by anything else, it would not need the Word, and consequently it would not need faith. . . .

Here we must point out that the entire Scripture of God is divided into two parts: commandments and promises. Although the commandments teach things that are good, the things taught are not done as soon as they are taught, for the commandments show us what we ought to do but do not give us the power to do it. They are intended to teach man to know himself, that through them he may recognize his inability to do good and may despair of his own ability. That is why they are called the Old Testament and constitute the Old Testament. For example, the commandment, "You shall not covet" [Exod. 20:17], is a command which proves us all to be sinners, for no one can avoid coveting no matter how much he may struggle against it. Therefore, in order not to covet and to fulfil the commandment, a man is compelled to despair of himself, to seek the help which he does not find in himself elsewhere and from someone else. . . .

Now when a man has learned through the commandments to recognize his helplessness and is distressed about how he might satisfy the law—since the law must be fulfilled so that not a jot or tittle shall be lost, otherwise man will be condemned without hope—then, being truly humbled and reduced to nothing in his own eyes, he finds in himself nothing whereby he may be justified and saved. Here the second part of Scripture comes to our aid, namely, the promises of God which declare the glory of God, saying, "If you wish to fulfil the law and not covet, as the law demands, come, believe in Christ in whom grace, righteousness, peace, liberty, and all things are promised you. If you believe, you shall have all things; if you do not believe, you shall lack all things." That which is impossible for you to accomplish by trying to fulfil all the works of the law—many and useless as they all are—you will accomplish quickly and easily through faith. God our Father has made all things depend on faith so that whoever has faith will have everything, and whoever does not have faith will have nothing. "For God has consigned all men to disobedience, that he may have mercy upon all," as it is stated in Rom. 11 [:32]. Thus, the promises of God give what the commandments of God demand and fulfil what the law prescribes so that all things may be God's alone, both the commandments and the fulfilling of the commandments. He alone commands, he alone fulfils. Therefore the promises of God belong to the New Testament. Indeed, they are the New Testament. . . .

From what has been said it is easy to see from what source faith derives such great power and why a good work or all good works together cannot equal it. No good work can rely upon the word of God or live in the soul, for faith alone and the word of God rule in the soul. Just as the heated iron glows like fire because of the union of fire with it, so the word imparts its qualities to the soul. It is clear, then, that a Christian has all that he needs in faith and needs no works to justify him; and if he has no need of works, he has no need of the law; and if he has no need of the law, surely he is free from the law. It is true that "the law is not laid down for the just" [1 Tim. 1:9]. This is that Christian liberty, our faith, which does not induce us to live in idleness or wickedness but makes the law and works unnecessary for any man's righteousness and salvation.

This is the first power of faith. Let us now examine also the second. It is a further function of faith that it honors him whom it trusts with the most reverent and highest regard since it considers him truthful and trustworthy. There is no other honor equal to the estimate of truthfulness and righteousness with which we honor him whom we trust. Could we ascribe to a man anything greater than truthfulness and righteousness and perfect goodness? On the other hand, there is no way in which we can show greater contempt for a man than to regard him as false and wicked and to be suspicious of him, as we do when we do not trust him. So when the soul firmly trusts God's promises, it regards Him as truthful and righteous. Nothing more excellent than this can be ascribed to God. The very highest worship of God is this that we ascribe to Him truthfulness, righteousness, and whatever else should be ascribed to one who is trusted. When this is done, the soul consents to his will. . . .

The third incomparable benefit of faith is that it unites the soul with Christ as a bride is united with her bridegroom. By this mystery, as the Apostle teaches, Christ and the soul become one flesh [Eph. 5:31-32]. And if they are one flesh and there is between them a true marriage—indeed the most perfect of all marriages, since human marriages are but poor examples of this one true marriage—it follows that everything they have they hold in common, the good as well as the evil. Accordingly the believing soul can boast of and glory in whatever Christ has as though it were its own, and whatever the soul has Christ claims as his own. . . .

Thus the believing soul by means of the pledge of its faith is free in Christ, its bridegroom, free from all sins, secure against death and hell, and is endowed with the eternal righteousness, life, and salvation of Christ its bridegroom. . . .

From this you once more see that much is ascribed to faith, namely, that it alone can fulfil the law and justify without works. You see that the first commandment, which says, "You shall worship one God," is fulfilled by faith alone. . . .

But works, being inanimate things, cannot glorify God, although they can, if faith is present, be done to the glory of God. Here, however, we are not inquiring what works and what kind of works are done, but who it is that does them, who glorifies God and brings forth the works. This is done by faith which dwells in the heart and is the source and substance of all our righteousness. Therefore it is a blind and dangerous doctrine which teaches that the commandments must be fulfilled by works. The commandments must be fulfilled before any works can be done, and the works proceed from the fulfillment of the commandments [Rom. 13:10], as we shall hear. . . .

Hence all of us who believe in Christ are priests and kings in Christ, as 1 Pet. 2 [:9] says: "You are a chosen race, God's own people, a royal priesthood, a priestly kingdom, that you may declare the wonderful deeds of him who called you out of darkness into his marvelous light." . . .

From this anyone can clearly see how a Christian is free from all things and over all things so that he needs no works to make him righteous and save him, since faith alone abundantly confers all these things. Should he grow so foolish, however, as to presume to become righteous, free, saved, and a Christian by means of some good work, he would instantly lose faith and all its benefits, a foolishness aptly illustrated in the fable of the dog who runs along a stream with a piece of meat in his mouth and, deceived by the reflection of the meat in the water, opens his mouth to snap at it and so loses both the meat and the reflection. . . .

Let this suffice concerning the inner man, his liberty, and the source of his liberty, the righteousness of faith. He needs neither laws nor good works but, on the contrary, is injured by them if he believes that he is justified by them.

Now let us turn to the second part, the outer man. Here we shall answer all those who, offended by the word "faith" and by all that has been said, now ask, "If faith does all things and is alone sufficient unto righteousness, why then are good works commanded? We will take our ease and do no works and be content with faith." I answer: not so, you wicked men, not so. That would indeed be proper if we were wholly inner and perfectly spiritual men. But such we shall be only at the last day, the day of the resurrection of the dead. As long as we live in the flesh we only begin to make some progress in that which shall be perfected in the future life. For this reason the Apostle in Rom. 8 [:23], calls all that we attain in this life "the first fruits of the Spirit" because we shall indeed receive the greater portion, even the fulness of the Spirit, in the future. This is the place to assert that which was said above, namely, that a Christian is the servant of all and made subject to all. Insofar as he is free he does no works, but insofar as he is a servant, he does all kinds of works. How this is possible we shall see.

Although, as I have said, a man is abundantly and sufficiently justified by faith inwardly, in his spirit, and so he has all that he needs, except insofar as this faith and these riches must grow from day to day even to the future life; yet he remains in this mortal life on earth. In this life he must control his own body and have dealings with men. Here the works begin; here a man cannot enjoy leisure; here he must indeed take care to discipline his body by fastings, watchings, labors, and other reasonable discipline and to subject it to the Spirit so that it will obey and conform to the inner man and faith and not revolt against faith and hinder the inner man, as it is the nature of the body to do if it is not held in check. . . . In doing these works, however, we must not think that a man is justified before God by them, for faith, which alone is righteousness before God cannot endure that erroneous opinion. . . .

The following statements are therefore true: "Good works do not make a good man, but a good man does good works; evil works do not make a wicked man, but a wicked man does evil works." Consequently, it is always necessary that the substance or person himself be good before there can be any good works, and that good works follow and proceed from the good person, as Christ also says, "A good tree cannot bear evil fruit, nor can a bad tree bear good fruit" [Matt. 7:18]. . . .

We do not, therefore, reject good works; on the contrary, we cherish and teach them as much as possible. We do not condemn them for their own sake but on account of this godless addition to them and the perverse idea that righteousness is to be sought through them; for that makes them appear good outwardly, when in truth they are not good.

They deceive men and lead them to deceive one another like ravening wolves in sheep's clothing [Matt. 7:15]. . . .

Lastly we shall also speak of the things which he does toward his neighbor. A man does not live for himself alone in this mortal body to work for it alone, but he lives also for all men on earth; rather he lives only for others and not for himself. To this end he brings his body into subjection that he may the more sincerely and freely serve others, as Paul says in Rom. 14 [:7-8], "None of us lives to himself, and none of us dies to himself. If we live, we live to the Lord, and if we die, we die to the Lord." He cannot ever in this life be idle and without works toward his neighbors, for he will necessarily speak, deal with, and exchange views with men, as Christ also, being made in the likeness of men [Phil. 2:7], was found in form as a man and conversed with men, as Baruch 3[:38] says.

Man, however, needs none of these things for his righteousness and salvation. Therefore he should be guided in all his works by this thought and contemplate this one thing alone, that he may serve and benefit others in all that he does, considering nothing except the need and the advantage of his neighbor. Accordingly, the Apostle commands us to work with our hands so that we may give to the needy, although he might have said that we should work to support ourselves. He says, however, "that he may be able to give to those in need" [Eph. 4:28]. This is what makes caring for the body a Christian work, that through its health and comfort we may be able to work, to acquire, and lay by funds with which to aid those who are in need, that in this way the strong member may serve the weaker, and we may be sons of God, each caring for and working for the other, bearing one another's burdens and so fulfilling the law of Christ [Gal. 6:2]. This is truly a Christian life. Here faith is truly active through love [Gal. 5:6], that is, it finds expression in works of the freest service, cheerfully and lovingly done, with which a man willingly serves another without hope of reward; and for himself he is satisfied with the fulness and wealth of his faith. . . .

He ought to think: "Although I am an unworthy and condemned man, my God has given me in Christ all the riches of righteousness and salvation without any merit on my part, out of pure, free mercy, so that from now on I need nothing except faith which believes that this is true. Why should I not therefore freely, joyfully, with all my heart, and with an eager will do all things which I know are pleasing and acceptable to such a Father who has overwhelmed me with his inestimable riches? I will therefore give myself as a Christ to my neighbor, just as Christ offered himself to me; I will do nothing in this life except what I see is necessary, profitable, and salutary to my neighbor, since through faith I have an abundance of all good things in Christ." . . .

Behold, from faith thus flow forth love and joy in the Lord, and from love a joyful, willing, and free mind that serves one's neighbor willingly and takes no account of gratitude or ingratitude, of praise or blame, of gain or loss. For a man does not serve that he may put men under obligations. He does not distinguish between friends and enemies or anticipate their thankfulness or unthankfulness, but he most freely and most willingly spends himself and all that he has, whether he wastes all on the thankless or whether he gains a reward. As his Father does, distributing all things to all men richly and freely, making "his sun rise on the evil and on the good" [Matt. 5:45], so also the son does all things and suffers all things with that freely bestowing joy which is his delight when through Christ he sees it in God, the dispenser of such great benefits. . . .

Who then can comprehend the riches and glory of the Christian life? It can do all things and has all things and lacks nothing. It is lord over sin, death and hell, and yet at the same time it serves, ministers to, and benefits all men. . . .

We conclude, therefore, that a Christian lives not in himself, but in Christ and in his neighbor. Otherwise he is not a Christian. He lives in Christ through faith, in his neighbor through love. By faith he is caught up beyond himself into God. By love he descends beneath himself into his neighbor.

From Luther, **To the Councilmen of All Cities in Germany That They Establish and Maintain Christian Schools**

I beg of you now, all my dear sirs and friends, to receive this letter kindly and take to heart my admonition.

First of all, we are today experiencing in all the German lands how schools are everywhere being left to go to wrack and ruin. The universities are growing weak, and monasteries are declining.

Therefore, I beg all of you, my dear sirs and friends, for the sake of God and our poor young people, not to treat this matter as lightly as many do, who fail to realize what the ruler of this world [John 14:30] is up to. For it is a grave and important matter, and one which is of vital concern both to Christ and the world at large, that we take steps to help the youth. By so doing we will be taking steps to help also ourselves and everybody else. Bear in mind that such insidious, subtle, and crafty attacks of the devil must be met with great Christian determination. My dear sirs, if we have to spend such large sums every year on guns, roads, bridges, dams, and countless similar items to insure the temporal peace and prosperity of a city, why should not much more be devoted to the poor neglected youth—at least enough to engage one or two competent men to teach school?

Moreover, every citizen should be influenced by the following consideration. Formerly he was obliged to waste a great deal of money and property on indulgences, masses, vigils, endowments, bequests, anniversaries, mendicant friars, brotherhoods, pilgrimages, and similar nonsense. Now that he is, by the grace of God, rid of such pillage and compulsory giving, he ought henceforth, out of gratitude to God and for his glory, to contribute a part of that amount toward schools for the training of the poor children. That would be an excellent investment. If the light of the gospel had not dawned and set him free, he would have had to continue indefinitely giving up to the above-mentioned robbers ten times that sum and more, without hope of return. Know also that where there arise hindrances, objections, impediments, and opposition to this proposal, there the devil is surely at work, the devil who voiced no such objection when men gave their money for monasteries and masses, pouring it out in a veritable stream; for he senses that this kind of giving is not to his advantage. Let this, then, my dear sirs and friends, be the first consideration to influence you, namely, that herein we are fighting against the devil as the most dangerous and subtle enemy of all.

A second consideration is, as St. Paul says in II Corinthians 6[:1-2], that we should not accept the grace of God in vain and neglect the time of salvation. Almighty God has indeed graciously visited us Germans and proclaimed a true year of jubilee. We have today the finest and most learned group of men, adorned with languages and all the arts, who could also render real service if only we would make use of them as instructors of the young people. Is it not evident that we are now able to prepare a boy in three years, so that at the age of fifteen or eighteen he will know more than all the universities and monasteries have known before? Indeed, what have men been learning till now in the universities and monasteries except to become asses, blockheads, and numbskulls? For twenty, even forty, years they pored over their books, and still failed to master either Latin or German, to say nothing of the scandalous and immoral life there in which many a fine young fellow was shamefully corrupted. . . .

The third consideration is by far the most important of all, namely, the command of God. . . .

Ah, you say, but all that is spoken to the parents; what business is it of councilmen and the authorities? Yes, that is true; but what if the parents fail to do their duty? Who then is to do it? Is it for this reason to be left undone, and the children neglected? How will the authorities and council then justify their position, that such matters are not their responsibility?

There are various reasons why parents neglect this duty. In the first place, there are some who lack the goodness and decency to do it, even if they had the ability. . . .

In the second place, the great majority of parents unfortunately are wholly unfitted for this task. They do not know how children should be brought up and taught, for they themselves have learned nothing but how to care for their bellies. It takes extraordinary people to bring children up right and teach them well.

In the third place, even if parents had the ability and desire to do it themselves, they have neither the time nor the opportunity for it, what with their other duties and the care of the household. . . .

It therefore behooves the council and the authorities to devote the greatest care and attention to the young. Since the property, honor, and life of the whole city have been committed to their faithful keeping, they would be remiss in their duty before God and man if they did not seek its welfare and improvement day and night with all the means at their command. Now the welfare of a city does not consist solely in accumulating vast treasures, building mighty walls and magnificent buildings, and producing a goodly supply of guns and armor. Indeed, where such things are plentiful, and reckless fools get control of them, it is so much the worse for the city suffers even greater loss. A city's best and greatest welfare, safety, and strength consist rather in its having many able, learned, wise, honorable, and well-educated citizens. They can then readily gather, protect, and properly use treasure and all manner of property. . . .

After all, temporal government has to continue. Are we then to permit none but louts and boors to rule, when we can do better than that? That would certainly be a crude and senseless policy. We might as well make lords out of swine and wolves, and set them to rule over those who refuse to give any thought to how they are ruled by men. Moreover, it is barbarous wickedness to think no further than this: We will rule now; what concern is it of ours how they will fare who come after us? Not over human beings, but over swine and dogs should such persons rule who in ruling seek only their own profit or glory. Even if we took the utmost pains for positions in government, there would still be plenty of labor and anxious care involved in seeing that things went well. What then is to happen if we take no pains at all?

"All right," you say again, "suppose we do have to have schools; what is the use of teaching Latin, Greek, and Hebrew, and the other liberal arts? We could just as well use German for teaching the Bible and God's word, which is enough for our salvation. I reply: Alas! I am only too well aware that we Germans must always be and remain brutes and stupid beasts, as the neighboring nations call us, epithets which we richly deserve. But I wonder why we never ask, "What is the use of silks, wine, spices, and other strange foreign wares when we ourselves have in Germany wine, grain, wool, flax, wood, and stone not only in quantities sufficient for our needs, but also of the best and choicest quality for our glory and ornament?" Languages and the arts, which can do us no harm, but are actually a greater ornament, profit, glory, and benefit, both for the understanding of Holy Scripture and the conduct of temporal government—these we despise. But foreign wares which are neither necessary nor useful, and in addition strip us down to a mere skeleton—these we cannot do without. Are not we Germans justly dubbed fools and beasts? . . .

Yes, you say, but many of the fathers were saved and even became teachers without the languages. That is true. But how do you account for the fact that they so often erred in the Scriptures? How often does not St. Augustine err in the Psalms and in his other expositions, and Hilary too—in fact, all those who have undertaken to expound Scripture without a knowledge of the languages? Even though what they said about a subject at times was perfectly true, they were never quite sure whether it really was present there in the passage where by their interpretation they thought to find it. Let me give yon an example: It is rightly said that Christ is the Son of God; but how ridiculous it must have sounded to the ears of their adversaries when they attempted to prove this by citing from Psalm 110: "*Tecum principium in die virtutis tuae,*" though in the Hebrew there is not a word about the Deity in this passage! When men attempt to defend the faith with such uncertain arguments and mistaken proof texts, are not Christians put to shame and made a laughingstock in the eyes of adversaries who know the language? The adversaries only become more stiff-necked in their error and have an excellent pretext for regarding our faith as a mere human delusion.

When our faith is thus held up to ridicule,where does the fault lie? It lies in our ignorance of the languages; and there is no other way out than to learn the languages. Was not St. Jerome compelled to translate the Psalter anew from the Hebrew because, when we quoted our [Latin] Psalter in disputes with the Jews, they sneered at us, pointing out that our texts did not read that way in the original Hebrew? Now the expositions of all the early fathers who dealt with Scripture apart from a knowledge of the languages (even when their teaching is not in error) are such that they often employ uncertain, indefensible, and inappropriate expressions. They grope their way like a blind man

along the wall, frequently missing the sense of the text and twisting it
to suit their fancy, as in the case of the verse mentioned above, "*Tecum
principium,*" etc. Even St. Augustine himself is obliged to confess, as he
does in his *Christian Instruction,* that a Christian teacher who is to
expound the Scriptures must know Greek and Hebrew in addition to
Latin. Otherwise, it is impossible to avoid constant stumbling; indeed,
there are plenty of problems to work out even when one is well versed
in languages.

There is a vast difference therefore between a simple preacher of the
faith and a person who expounds Scripture, or, as St. Paul puts it
[I Cor. 12:28-30; 14:26-32], a prophet. A simple preacher (it is true)
has so many clear passages and texts available through translations
that he can know and teach Christ, lead a holy life, and preach to
others. But when it comes to interpreting Scripture, and working with
it on your own, and disputing with those who cite it incorrectly, he is
unequal to the task; that cannot be done without languages. Now there
must always be such prophets in the Christian church who can dig into
Scripture, expound it, and carry on disputations. A saintly life and right
doctrine are not enough. Hence, languages are absolutely and altogether necessary in the Christian church, as are the prophets or interpreters;
although it is not necessary that every Christian or every preacher be
such a prophet, as St. Paul points out in I Corinthians 12 [:4-30] and
Ephesians 4 [:11]. . . .

We should not be led astray because some boast of the Spirit and
consider Scripture of little worth, and others, such as the Waldensian
Brethren, think the languages are unnecessary. Dear friend, say what
you will about the Spirit, I too have been in the Spirit and have seen
the Spirit, perhaps even more of it (if it comes to boasting of one's
own flesh) than those fellows with all their boasting will see in a
year. Moreover, my spirit has given some account of itself, while theirs
sits quietly in its corner and does little more than brag about itself.
I know full well that while it is the Spirit alone who accomplishes
everything, I would surely have never flushed a covey if the languages
had not helped me and given me a sure and certain knowledge of
Scripture. . . .

To this point we have been speaking about the necessity and value of
languages and Christian schools for the spiritual realm and the salvation of souls. Now let us consider also the body. . . .

It is not necessary to repeat here that the temporal government is
a divinely ordained estate (I have elsewhere treated this subject so
fully that I trust no one has any doubt about it). The question is
rather: How are we to get good and capable men into it? Here we
are excelled and put to shame by the pagans of old, especially the

Romans and the Greeks. Although they had no idea of whether this estate were pleasing to God or not, they were so earnest and diligent in educating and training their young boys and girls to fit them for the task, that when I call it to mind I am forced to blush for us Christians, and especially for us Germans. We are such utter blockheads and beasts that we dare to say, "Pray, why have schools for people who are not going to become spiritual?" Yet we know, or at least we ought to know, how essential and beneficial it is—and pleasing to God—that a prince, lord, councilman, or other person in a position of authority be educated and qualified to perform the functions of his office as a Christian should.

Now if (as we have assumed) there were no souls, and there were no need at all of schools and languages for the sake of the Scriptures and of God, this one consideration alone would be sufficient to justify the establishment everywhere of the very best schools for both boys and girls, namely, that in order to maintain its temporal estate outwardly the world must have good and capable men and women. . . .

The exceptional pupils, who give promise of becoming skilled teachers, or holders of other ecclesiastical positions, should be allowed to continue in school longer, or even be dedicated to a life of study, as we read of [those who trained] the holy martyrs SS. Agnes, Agatha, Lucy, and others. That is how the monasteries and foundations originated; they have since been wholly perverted to a different and damnable use. There is great need of such advanced study. . . .

Finally, one thing more merits serious consideration by all those who earnestly desire to have such schools and languages established and maintained in Germany. It is this: no effort or expense should be spared to provide good libraries or book repositories, especially in the larger cities which can well afford it. For if the gospel and all the arts are to be preserved, they must be set down and held fast in books and writings (as was done by the prophets and apostles themselves, as I have said above). This is essential, not only that those who are to be our spiritual and temporal leaders may have books to read and study, but also that the good books may be preserved and not lost.

From Luther, **The Bondage of the Will**
ASSERTIONS IN CHRISTIANITY

To begin with, I would like to review some parts of your Preface in which you attempt to disparage our case and to embellish your own.

First, I notice that, as in your other works, you censure me for obstinacy of assertion. Here in this book you say your "dislike of assertions is so great that you prefer the views of the sceptics wherever the inviolable authority of Scripture and the decisions the Church permit; though you gladly submit your opinion whether you comprehend what she prescribes or not." . . .

NO LIBERTY TO BE A SCEPTIC

[604] . . . What a Proteus is the man talking about "inviolable authority of Scriptures and the decisions of the Church"!—as if you had the greatest respect for the Scriptures and the church, when in the same breath you explain that you wish you had the liberty to be a sceptic! What Christian could talk like this? . . .

[605] In short, your words amount to this, that it matters little to you what anyone believes anywhere, as long as the peace of the world is undisturbed. . . .

CLARITY OF SCRIPTURES

[606] . . . I hope you credit Luther with some acquaintance with and judgment in the sacred writings. . . .

God and the Scriptures are two things, just like God and creation are two things. Nobody doubts that in God many things are hidden of which we know nothing. . . . But that there are in Scriptures some things abstruse and not quite plain, was spread by the godless Sophists, whom you echo, Erasmus. . . .

THE CRUCIAL ISSUE: KNOWING FREE WILL

[610] If, as you say, it be irreligious, curious, superfluous to know whether God's foreknowledge is contingent; whether our will can contribute anything pertinent to our eternal salvation, or whether it simply endures operative grace; whether everything we do, good or evil, is done out of mere necessity, or whether we are rather enduring, what then, I ask, is religious, serious and useful knowledge? This is weak stuff, Erasmus. *Das ist zu viel!* . . .

The essence of Christianity which you describe . . . is without Christ, without the Spirit, and chillier than ice. . . . You plainly assert that the will is effective in things pertaining to eternal salvation, when you speak of its striving. And again you assert that it is passive, when saying that without the mercy of God it is ineffective. But you fail to define the limits within which we should think of the will as acting and as being acted upon. Thus you keep us in ignorance as to how far the mercy of God extends, and how far our own will extends; what man's will and God's mercy really do effect. . . .

[613] It is not irreligious, curious or superfluous, but extremely wholesome and necessary for a Christian to know whether or not his will has anything to do in matters pertaining to salvation. This, let me tell you, is the very hinge upon which our disputation turns. It is the crucial issue between you and me. . . .

SPONTANEITY OF NECESSITATED ACTS

[632] You say: Who will endeavor to reform his life? I answer: Nobody! No man can! God has no time for your self-reformers, for they are hypocrites. The elect who hear God will be reformed by the Holy Spirit. The rest will perish unreformed. . . .

You say, by our doctrine a floodgate of iniquity is opened. Be it so. Ungodly men are part of that evil leprosy spoken of before. Nevertheless, these are the same doctrines which throw open to the elect, who fear God, a gateway to righteousness, an entrance into heaven, a way unto God. . . . These truths are published for the sake of the elect. . . .

[634] . . . As to the other paradox you mention, that whatever is done by us, is not done by free will, but of mere necessity, let us briefly consider it. . . .

By necessity I do not mean compulsion. I meant what they term the necessity of immutability. That is to say, a man void of the Spirit of God does not do evil against his will, under pressure, as though taken by the neck and forced into it, . . . but he does it spontaneously and willingly. And this willingness and desire of doing evil he cannot, by his own strength, eliminate, restrain or change. . . .

This would not be the case if it were free or had a free will.

[635] On the other hand, when God works in us, the will is changed under the sweet influence of the Spirit of God. It desires and acts not from compulsion, but responsively of its own desire and inclination. It cannot be altered by any opposition. It cannot be compelled or overcome even by the gates of hell. It still goes on to desire, crave after and love that which is good, just as once it desired, craved after and loved evil. . . . Thus the human will is like a beast of burden. If God rides it, it wills and goes whence God wills; as the psalm says, "I was as a beast of burden before thee" (Psalm 72:22). If Satan rides, it wills and goes where Satan wills. Nor may it choose to which rider it will run, nor which it will seek. But the riders themselves contend who shall have and hold it.

GRACE AND FREE WILL

[636] And now, what if I prove from your own words, in which you assert the freedom of the will, that there is no such thing as free will

at all? What, if I should show that you unwittingly deny what you labor with so much sagacity to affirm? If I fail here, I promise to revoke all that I wrote against you in this book; and all that your Diatribe advances against me shall be confirmed!

You make the power of free will small and utterly ineffective apart from the grace of God. Acknowledged? Now then, I ask you: If God's grace is wanting, or if it be taken away from that certain small degree of power, what can it do for itself? You say it is ineffective and can do nothing good. Therefore it will not do what God or His grace wills. And why? Because we have now taken God's grace away from it, and what the grace of God does not do is not good. Hence it follows that free will without the grace of God is not free at all, but is the permanent bond-slave and servant of evil, since it cannot turn itself unto good. . . .

[638] But, if we do not want to drop this term altogether (which would be the safest and most Christian thing to do), we may still use it in good faith denoting free will in respect not of what is above him, but of what is below him. This is to say, man should know in regard to his goods and possessions the right to use them, to do or to leave undone, according to his free will. Although at the same time, that same free will is overruled by the free will of God alone, just as He pleases. However, with regard to God, and in all things pertaining to salvation or damnation, man has no free will, but is a captive, servant and bondslave, either to the will of God, or to the will of Satan. . . .

DOCTRINE OF SALVATION BY FAITH IN CHRIST DISPROVES FREE WILL

[767] . . . Paul now proclaims with full confidence and authority: "But now the righteousness of God has been made manifest independently of the Law, being attested by the Law and the Prophets; the righteousness of God through faith in Jesus Christ upon all who believe. For there is no distinction, as all have sinned and have need of the glory of God. They are justified freely by his grace through the redemption which is in Christ Jesus, whom God has set forth as a propitiation by his blood through faith, etc." (Romans 3:21-25). Here Paul utters very thunderbolts against free will. . . .

This saying, "without the law" can mean nothing else, but that Christian righteousness exists without the works of the law. . . .

From all this it is clearly manifest that the endeavor and effect of free will are simply nothing. For if the righteousness of God exists without the law, and without the works of the law, how shall it not much more exist without free will? The supreme concern of free will is to exercise itself in moral righteousness. . . .

And though I should grant that free will by its endeavors can advance in some direction, namely, unto good works, or unto the righteousness of the civil or moral law, it does not yet advance towards God's righteousness, nor does God in any respect allow its devoted efforts to be worthy unto gaining His righteousness; for He says that His righteousness stands without the law. . . .

PERSONAL COMFORT IN THE DOCTRINE OF BONDAGE

[738] . . . As for myself, I frankly confess, that I should not want free will to be given me, even if it could be, nor anything else be left in my own hands to enable me to strive after my salvation. And that, not merely, because in the face of so many dangers, adversities and onslaughts of devils, I could not stand my ground and hold fast my free will—for one devil is stronger than all men, and on these terms no man could be saved—but because, even though there were no dangers, adversities or devils, I should still be forced to labor with no guarantee of success and to beat the air only. If I lived and worked to all eternity, my conscience would never reach comfortable certainty as to how much it must do to satisfy God. Whatever work it had done, there would still remain a scrupling as to whether or not it pleased God, or whether He required something more. The experience of all who seek righteousness by works proves that. I learned it by bitter experience over a period of many years. But now that God has put my salvation out of the control of my own will and put it under the control of His, and has promised to save me, not according to my effort or running, but . . . according to His own grace and mercy, I rest fully assured that He is faithful and will not lie to me, and that moreover He is great and powerful, so that no devils and no adversities can destroy Him or pluck me out of His hand. . . . I am certain that I please God, not by the merit of my works, but by reason of His merciful favor promised to me. So that, if I work too little or badly, He does not impute it to me, but, like a father, pardons me and makes me better. This is the glorying which all the saints have in their God. . . .

And now, my friend Erasmus, I entreat you for Christ's sake to keep your promise. You promised that you would willingly yield to him who taught better than yourself. . . . I confess that you are a great man, adorned with many of God's noblest gifts, with talent, learning and an almost miraculous eloquence, whereas I have and am nothing, except to glory in being a Christian.

Moreover, I give you hearty praise: alone, in contrast to all others, you have discussed the real thing, i.e., the essential point. You have not wearied me with those irrelevant points about the Papacy, purgatory, indulgences and such trifles. . . . For that I heartily thank you.

JOHN CALVIN

John Calvin (1509-1564), unlike Luther, seems to have had a relatively uneventful youth and adolescence. In the 1520s he studied at the University of Paris. In his student days he was greatly affected by the Roman writers and their concern for morality. He looked rather carefully into Augustine and came to have profound respect and admiration for that father of the church. About 1533 he underwent a conversion, and his theological standpoint changed dramatically. Where hitherto he had embraced the notions of free will and human greatness, he now abandoned them in favor of God's omnipotence and sovereignty. By the time of Calvin's conversion much of Europe was in the throes of religious reformation, even revolution, and Calvin was forced to leave France where Protestantism was unpopular. He found his way to Geneva, a city convulsed with religious tension, to which Calvin himself made a noteworthy contribution. Though on occasion he himself was expelled from Geneva, this city was to be the primary scene of Calvin's labors for the rest of his life. He left an indelible mark on the city and its culture.

Calvin's major work, the *Institutes of the Christian Religion,* was first published in 1536 and underwent continual revision until the last edition of 1559. Calvin was fluent in both Latin and French, and the various editions of the work were published in both languages. Calvin's influence on the French language constitutes no small part of his total achievement. The changes made in the later editions of the *Institutes* were aimed at emphasizing differences from Lutheran positions. The basic concept of the *Institutes* is the majesty of God. According to Calvin, God so transcends humankind that his nature is totally beyond the normal course of human experience. The corollary of the idea of God's majesty is the idea of man's depravity. Man's depravity was not, however, to be a call to despair. There is justification and there is predestination; it is God who justifies and predestines some to be saved. All men, however, are on earth to lead lives which glorify God through obedience to his commandments. This is best done through a well-regulated, socially useful life on earth. Calvin emphasizes that membership in the church is important and not optional. The goal of the church is to embrace all human beings, who are consequently obliged to work for God's glory.

From Calvin, **Institutes of the Christian Religion**
BOOK ONE
THE KNOWLEDGE OF GOD THE CREATOR
CHAPTER I
The Knowledge of God and That of Ourselves Are Connected.
How Are They Interrelated?

1. *Without knowledge of self there is no knowledge of God*

Nearly all the wisdom we possess, that is to say, true and sound wisdom, consists of two parts: the knowledge of God and of ourselves. But, while joined by many bonds, which one precedes and brings forth the other is not easy to discern. In the first place, no one can look upon himself without immediately turning his thoughts to the contemplation of God, in whom he "lives and moves" [Acts 17:28]. For, quite clearly, the mighty gifts with which we are endowed are hardly from ourselves; indeed, our very being is nothing but subsistence in the one God. Then, by these benefits shed like dew from heaven upon us, we are led as by rivulets to the spring itself. Indeed, our very poverty better discloses the infinitude of benefits reposing in God. The miserable ruin, into which the rebellion of the first man cast us, especially compels us to look upward. Thus, not only will we, in fasting and hungering, seek thence what we lack; but, in being aroused by fear, we shall learn humility. For, as a veritable world of miseries is to be found in mankind, and we are thereby despoiled of divine raiment, our shameful nakedness exposes a teeming horde of infamies. Each of us must, then, be so stung by the consciousness of his own unhappiness as to attain at least some knowledge of God. Thus, from the feeling of our own ignorance, vanity, poverty, infirmity, and—what is more—depravity and corruption, we recognize that the true light of wisdom, sound virtue, full abundance of every good, and purity of righteousness rest in the Lord alone. To this extent we are prompted by our own ills to contemplate the good things of God; and we cannot seriously aspire to him before we begin to become displeased with ourselves. For what man in all the world would not gladly remain as he is—what man does not remain as he is—so long as he does not know himself, that is, while content with his own gifts, and either ignorant or unmindful of his own misery? Accordingly, the knowledge of ourselves not only arouses us to seek God, but also, as it were, leads us by the hand to find him.

2. *Without knowledge of God there is no knowledge of self*

Again, it is certain that man never achieves a clear knowledge of himself unless he has first looked upon God's face, and then descends from contemplating him to scrutinize himself. For we always seem to ourselves righteous and upright and wise and holy—this pride is innate in all of us—unless by clear proofs we stand convinced of our own unrighteousness, foulness, folly, and impurity. Moreover, we are not thus convinced if we look merely to ourselves and not also to the Lord, who is the sole standard by which this judgment must be measured. For, because all of us are inclined by nature to hypocrisy, a kind of empty image of righteousness in place of righteousness itself abundantly satisfies us. And because nothing appears within or around us that has not been contaminated by great immorality, what is a little less vile pleases us as a thing most pure—so long as we confine our minds within the limits of human corruption. Just so, an eye to which nothing is shown but black objects judges something dirty white or even rather darkly mottled to be whiteness itself. Indeed, we can discern still more clearly from the bodily senses how much we are deluded in estimating the powers of the soul. For if in broad daylight we either look down upon the ground or survey whatever meets our view round about, we seem to ourselves endowed with the strongest and keenest sight; yet when we look up to the sun and gaze straight at it, that power of sight which was particularly strong on earth is at once blunted and confused by a great brilliance, and thus we are compelled to admit that our keenness in looking upon things earthly is sheer dullness when it comes to the sun. So it happens in estimating our spiritual goods. As long as we do not look beyond the earth, being quite content with our own righteousness, wisdom, and virtue, we flatter ourselves most sweetly, and fancy ourselves all but demigods. Suppose we but once begin to raise our thoughts to God, and to ponder his nature, and how completely perfect are his righteousness, wisdom, and power—the straightedge to which we must be shaped. Then, what masquerading earlier as righteousness was pleasing in us will soon grow filthy in its consummate wickedness. What wonderfully impressed us under the name of wisdom will stink in its very foolishness. What wore the face of power will prove itself the most miserable weakness. That is, what in us seems perfection itself corresponds ill to the purity of God.

3. Man before God's majesty

Hence, that dread and wonder with which Scripture commonly represents the saints as stricken and overcome whenever they felt the presence of God. . . .

CHAPTER VI

Scripture Is Needed as Guide and Teacher for Anyone Who Would Come to God the Creator

1. *God bestows the actual knowledge of himself upon us only in the Scriptures*

That brightness which is borne in upon the eyes of all men both in heaven and on earth is more than enough to withdraw all support from men's ingratitude—just as God, to involve the human race in the same guilt, sets forth to all without exception his presence portrayed in his creatures. Despite this, it is needful that another and better help be added to direct us aright to the very Creator of the universe. It was not in vain, then, that he added the light of his Word by which to become known unto salvation; and he regarded as worthy of this privilege those whom he pleased to gather more closely and intimately to himself. For because he saw the minds of all men tossed and agitated, after he chose the Jews as his very own flock, he fenced them about that they might not sink into oblivion as others had. With good reason he holds us by the same means in the pure knowledge of himself, since otherwise even those who seem to stand firm before all others would soon melt away. Just as old or bleary-eyed men and those with weak vision, if you thrust before them a most beautiful volume, even if they recognize it to be some sort of writing, yet can scarcely construe two words, but with the aid of spectacles will begin to read distinctly; so Scripture, gathering up the otherwise confused knowledge of God in our minds, having dispersed our dullness, clearly shows us the true God. This, therefore, is a special gift, where God, to instruct the church, not merely uses mute teachers but also opens his own most hallowed lips. Not only does he teach the elect to look upon a god, but also shows himself as the God upon whom they are to look. He has from the beginning maintained this plan for his church, so that besides these common proofs he also put forth his Word, which is a more direct and more certain mark whereby he is to be recognized. . . .

CHAPTER VII

Scripture Must Be Confirmed by the Witness of the Spirit

4. *The witness of the Holy Spirit: this is stronger than all proof*

We ought to remember what I said a bit ago: credibility of doctrine is not established until we are persuaded beyond doubt that God is its Author. Thus, the highest proof of Scripture derives in general from the fact that God in person speaks in it. The prophets and apostles do not boast either of their keenness or of anything that obtains credit for them as they speak; nor do they dwell upon rational proofs. Rather, they bring forward God's holy name, that by it the whole world may be brought into obedience to him. Now we ought to see how apparent it is not only by plausible opinion but by clear truth that they do not call upon God's name heedlessly or falsely. If we desire to provide in the best way for our consciences—that they may not be perpetually beset by the instability of doubt or vacillation, and that they may not also boggle at the smallest quibbles—we ought to seek our conviction in a higher place than human reasons, judgments, or conjectures, that is, in the secret testimony of the Spirit. True, if we wished to proceed by arguments, we might advance many things that would easily prove —if there is any god in heaven—that the law, the prophets, and the gospel come from him. Indeed, ever so learned men, endowed with the highest judgment, rise up in opposition and bring to bear and display all their mental powers in this debate. Yet, unless they become hardened to the point of hopeless impudence, this confession will be wrested from them: that they see manifest signs of God speaking in Scripture. From this it is clear that the teaching of Scripture is from heaven. And a little later we shall see that all the books of Sacred Scripture far surpass all other writings. Yes, if we turn pure eyes and upright senses toward it, the majesty of God will immediately come to view, subdue our bold rejection, and compel us to obey. . . .

BOOK TWO

THE KNOWLEDGE OF GOD THE REDEEMER
IN CHRIST . . .

CHAPTER I

By the Fall and Revolt of Adam, the Whole Human Race was delivered to the Curse and Degenerated from its Original Condition

8. *The nature of original sin*

So that these remarks may not be made concerning an uncertain and unknown matter, let us define original sin. It is not my intention to investigate the several definitions proposed by various writers, but simply to bring forward the one that appears to me most in accordance with truth. Original sin, therefore, seems to be a hereditary depravity and corruption of our nature, diffused into all parts of the soul, which first makes us liable to God's wrath, then also brings forth in us those works which Scripture calls "works of the flesh" [Gal. 5:19]. And that is properly what Paul often calls sin. The works that come forth from it—such as adulteries, fornication, thefts, hatreds, murders, carousings —he accordingly calls "fruits of sin" [Gal. 5:19-21], although they are also commonly called "sins" in Scripture, and even by Paul himself.

We must, therefore, distinctly note these two things. First, we are so vitiated and perverted in every part of our nature that by this great corruption we stand justly condemned and convicted before God, to whom nothing is acceptable but righteousness, innocence, and purity. And this is not liability for another's transgression. For, since it is said that we become subject to God's judgment through Adam's sin, we are to understand it not as if we, guiltless and undeserving, bore the guilt of his offense but in the sense that, since we through his transgression have become entangled in the curse, he is said to have made us guilty. Yet not only has punishment fallen upon us from Adam, but a contagion imparted by him resides in us, which justly deserves punishment. For this reason, Augustine, though he often calls sin "another's" to show more clearly that it is distributed among us through propagation, nevertheless declares at the same time that it is peculiar to each. And the apostle himself most eloquently testifies that "death has spread to all because all have sinned" [Rom. 5:12]. That is, they have been enveloped in original sin and defiled by its stains. For that reason, even infants themselves, while they carry their condemnation along with them from the mother's womb, are guilty not of another's fault but of their own. For, even though the fruits of their iniquity have not yet come forth, they have the seed enclosed within them. Indeed, their whole nature is a seed of sin; hence it can be only hateful and abhorrent to God. From this it follows that it is rightly considered sin in God's sight, for without guilt there would be no accusation.

Then comes the second consideration: that this perversity never ceases in us, but continually bears new fruits—the works of the flesh that we have already described—just as a burning furnace gives forth flame and sparks, or water ceaselessly bubbles up from a spring. Thus those who have defined original sin as "the lack of the original righteousness, which ought to reside in us," although they comprehend in this definition the whole meaning of the term, have still not expressed effectively enough its power and energy. For our nature is not only destitute and empty of good, but so fertile and fruitful of every evil that it cannot be idle. Those who have said that original sin is "concupiscence" have used an appropriate word, if only it be added—something that most will by no means concede—that whatever is in man, from the understanding to the will, from the soul even to the flesh, has been defiled and crammed with this concupiscence. Or, to put it more briefly, the whole man is of himself nothing but concupiscence. . . .

CHAPTER II

*Man Has Now Been Deprived of Freedom of Choice and Bound
Over to Miserable Servitude*

12. *Supernatural gifts destroyed; natural gifts corrupted; but enough of
reason remains to distinguish man from brute beasts*

And, indeed, that common opinion which they have taken from
Augustine pleases me: that the natural gifts were corrupted in man
through sin, but that his supernatural gifts were stripped from him.
For by the latter clause they understand the light of faith as well as
righteousness, which would be sufficient to attain heavenly life and
eternal bliss. Therefore, withdrawing from the Kingdom of God, he is
at the same time deprived of spiritual gifts, with which he had been
furnished for the hope of eternal salvation. From this it follows that
he is so banished from the Kingdom of God that all qualities belonging
to the blessed life of the soul have been extinguished in him, until he
recovers them through the grace of regeneration. Among these are
faith, love of God, charity toward neighbor, zeal for holiness and for
righteousness. All these, since Christ restores them in us, are considered adventitious, and beyond nature: and for this reason we infer
that they were taken away. On the other hand, soundness of mind and
uprightness of heart were withdrawn at the same time. This is the corruption of the natural gifts. For even though something of understanding and judgment remains as a residue along with the will, yet we shall
not call a mind whole and sound that is both weak and plunged into
deep darkness. And depravity of the will is all too well known.

Since reason, therefore, by which man distinguishes between good
and evil, and by which he understands and judges, is a natural gift, it
could not be completely wiped out; but it was partly weakened and
partly corrupted, so that its misshapen ruins appear. John speaks in
this sense: "The light still shines in the darkness, but the darkness
comprehends it not" [John 1:5]. In these words both facts are clearly
expressed. First, in man's perverted and degenerate nature some sparks
still gleam. These show he is endowed with understanding. Yet, secondly, they show this light choked with dense ignorance, so that it
cannot come forth effectively.

Similarly the will, because it is inseparable from man's nature, did
not perish, but was so bound to wicked desires that it cannot strive
after the right. This is, indeed, a complete definition, but one needing
a fuller explanation. . . .

14. *Understanding as regards art and science*

Then follow the arts, both liberal and manual. The power of human acuteness also appears in learning these because all of us have a certain aptitude. But although not all the arts are suitable for everyone to learn, yet it is a certain enough indication of the common energy that hardly anyone is to be found who does not manifest talent in some art. There are at hand energy and ability not only to learn but also to devise something new in each art or to perfect and polish what one has learned from a predecessor. This prompted Plato to teach wrongly that such apprehension is nothing but recollection. Hence, with good reason we are compelled to confess that its beginning is inborn in human nature. Therefore this evidence clearly testifies to a universal apprehension of reason and understanding by nature implanted in men. Yet so universal is this good that every man ought to recognize for himself in it the peculiar grace of God. The Creator of nature himself abundantly arouses this gratitude in us when he creates imbeciles. Through them he shows the endowments that the human soul would enjoy unpervaded by his light, a light so natural to all that it is certainly a free gift of his beneficence to each! Now the discovery or systematic transmission of the arts, or the inner and more excellent knowledge of them, which is characteristic of few, is not a sufficient proof of common discernment. Yet because it is bestowed indiscriminately upon pious and impious, it is rightly counted among natural gifts.

15. *Science as God's gift*

Whenever we come upon these matters in secular writers, let that admirable light of truth shining in them teach us that the mind of man, though fallen and perverted from its wholeness, is nevertheless clothed and ornamented with God's excellent gifts. If we regard the Spirit of God as the sole fountain of truth, we shall neither reject the truth itself, nor despise it wherever it shall appear, unless we wish to dishonor the Spirit of God. For by holding the gifts of the Spirit in slight esteem, we contemn and reproach the Spirit himself. What then? Shall we deny that the truth shone upon the ancient jurists who established civic order and discipline with such great equity? Shall we say that the philosophers were blind in their fine observation and artful description of nature? Shall we say that those men were devoid of understanding who conceived the art of disputation and taught us to speak reasonably? Shall we say that they are insane who developed medicine, devoting their labor to our benefit? What shall we say of all the mathematical sciences? Shall we consider them the ravings of madmen? No, we cannot read the writings of the ancients on these subjects without great admiration. We marvel at them because we are compelled to recognize how preeminent they are. But shall we count anything praiseworthy or noble without recognizing at the same time that it comes from God?

Let us be ashamed of such ingratitude, into which not even the pagan poets fell, for they confessed that the gods had invented philosophy, laws, and all useful arts. Those men whom Scripture [I Cor. 2:14] calls "natural men" were, indeed, sharp and penetrating in their investigation of inferior things. Let us, accordingly, learn by their example how many gifts the Lord left to human nature even after it was despoiled of its true good.

16. *Human competence in art and science also derives from the Spirit of God*

Meanwhile, we ought not to forget those most excellent benefits of the divine Spirit, which he distributes to whomever he wills, for the common good of mankind. . . .

CHAPTER III

Only Damnable Things Come Forth From Man's Corrupt Nature

5. *Man sins of necessity, but without compulsion*

Because of the bondage of sin by which the will is held bound, it cannot move toward good, much less apply itself thereto; for a movement of this sort is the beginning of conversion to God, which in Scripture is ascribed entirely to God's grace. So Jeremiah prayed to the Lord to be "converted" if it were his will to "convert him" [Jer. 31:18, cf. Vg.]. Hence the prophet in the same chapter, describing the spiritual redemption of the believing folk, speaks of them as "redeemed from the hand of one stronger than they" [v. 11 passim]. By this he surely means the tight fetters with which the sinner is bound so long as, forsaken by the Lord, he lives under the devil's yoke. Nonetheless the will remains, with the most eager inclination disposed and hastening to sin. For man, when he gave himself over to this necessity, was not deprived of will, but of soundness of will. Not inappropriately Bernard teaches that to will is in us all: but to will good is gain: to will evil, loss. Therefore simply to will is of man; to will ill, of a corrupt nature; to will well, of grace.

Now when I say that the will bereft of freedom is of necessity either drawn or led into evil, it is a wonder if this seems a hard saying to anyone, since it has nothing incongruous or alien to the usage of holy men. But it offends those who know not how to distinguish between necessity and compulsion. . . .

The chief point of this distinction, then, must be that man as he was corrupted by the Fall, sinned willingly, not unwillingly or by compulsion; by the most eager inclination of his heart, not by forced compulsion; by the prompting of his own lust, not by compulsion from without. Yet so depraved is his nature that he can be moved or impelled only to evil. But if this is true, then it is clearly expressed that man is surely subject to the necessity of sinning. . . .

BOOK THREE
THE WAY IN WHICH WE RECEIVE THE GRACE OF CHRIST . . .

CHAPTER XXI

Eternal Election, by Which God Has Predestined Some to Salvation, Others to Destruction

Summary survey of the doctrine of election

As Scripture, then, clearly shows, we say that God once established by his eternal and unchangeable plan those whom he long before determined once for all to receive into salvation, and those whom, on the other hand, he would devote to destruction. We assert that, with respect to the elect, this plan was founded upon his freely given mercy, without regard to human worth; but by his just and irreprehensible but incomprehensible judgment he has barred the door of life to those whom he has given over to damnation. Now among the elect we regard the call as a testimony of election. Then we hold justification another sign of its manifestation, until they come into the glory in which the fulfillment of that election lies. But as the Lord seals his elect by call and justification, so, by shutting off the reprobate from knowledge of his name or from the sanctification of his Spirit, he, as it were, reveals by these marks what sort of judgment awaits them. Here I shall pass over many fictions that stupid men have invented to overthrow predestination. They need no refutation, for as soon as they are brought forth they abundantly prove their own falsity. I shall pause only over those which either are being argued by the learned or may raise difficulty for the simple, or which impiety speciously sets forth in order to assail God's righteousness. . . .

BOOK FOUR
THE EXTERNAL MEANS OR AIDS BY WHICH GOD INVITES US INTO THE SOCIETY OF CHRIST AND HOLDS US THEREIN

CHAPTER XX
Civil Government

1. *Differences between spiritual and civil government*

Now, since we have established above that man is under a twofold government, and since we have elsewhere discussed at sufficient length the kind that resides in the soul or inner man and pertains to eternal life, this is the place to say something also about the other kind, which pertains only to the establishment of civil justice and outward morality.

For although this topic seems by nature alien to the spiritual doctrine of faith which I have undertaken to discuss, what follows will show that I am right in joining them, in fact, that necessity compels me to do so. This is especially true since, from one side, insane and barbarous men furiously strive to overturn this divinely established order; while on the other side, the flatterers of princes, immoderately praising their power, do not hesitate to set them against the Rule of God himself. Unless both these evils are checked, purity of faith will perish. Besides, it is of no slight importance for us to know how lovingly God has provided in this respect for mankind, that greater zeal for piety may flourish in us to attest our gratefulness.

First, before we enter into the matter itself, we must keep in mind that distinction which we previously laid down so that we do not (as commonly happens) unwisely mingle these two, which have a completely different nature. For certain men, when they hear that the gospel promises a freedom that acknowledges no king and no magistrate among men, but looks to Christ alone, think that they cannot benefit by their freedom as long as they see any power set up over them. They therefore think that nothing will be safe unless the whole world is reshaped to a new form, where there are neither courts, nor laws, nor magistrates, nor anything in their opinion restricts their freedom. But whoever knows how to distinguish between body and soul, between this present fleeting life and that future eternal life, will without difficulty know that Christ's spiritual Kingdom and the civil jurisdiction are things completely distinct. . . .

2. The two "governments" are not antithetical

Yet this distinction does not lead us to consider the whole nature of government a thing polluted, which has nothing to do with Christian men. . . .

4. The magistracy is ordained by God

The Lord has not only testified that the office of magistrate is approved by and acceptable to him, but he also sets out its dignity with the most honorable titles and marvelously commends it to us. . . .

10. The magistrates' exercise of force is compatible with piety

But here a seemingly hard and difficult question arises: if the law of God forbids all Christians to kill [Ex. 20:13; Deut. 5:17; Matt. 5:21], and the prophet prophesies concerning God's holy mountain (the church) that in it men shall not afflict or hurt [Is. 11:9; 65:25]—how can magistrates be pious men and shedders of blood at the same time?

Yet if we understand that the magistrate in administering punishments does nothing by himself, but carries out the very judgments of God, we shall not be hampered by this scruple. . . .

31. Constitutional defenders of the people's freedom

But however these deeds of men are judged in themselves, still the Lord accomplished his work through them alike when he broke the bloody scepters of arrogant kings and when he overturned intolerable governments. Let the princes hear and be afraid.

But we must, in the meantime, be very careful not to despise or violate that authority of magistrates, full of venerable majesty, which God has established by the weightiest decrees, even though it may reside with the most unworthy men, who defile it as much as they can with their own wickedness. For, if the correction of unbridled despotism is the Lord's to avenge, let us not at once think that it is entrusted to us, to whom no command has been given except to obey and suffer.

I am speaking all the while of private individuals. For if there are now any magistrates of the people, appointed to restrain the willfulness of kings (as in ancient times the ephors were set against the Spartan kings, or the tribunes of the people against the Roman consuls, or the demarchs against the senate of the Athenians; and perhaps, as things now are, such power as the three estates exercise in every realm when they hold their chief assemblies), I am so far from forbidding them to withstand, in accordance with their duty, the fierce licentiousness of kings, that, if they wink at kings who violently fall upon and assault the lowly common folk, I declare that their dissimulation involves nefarious perfidy, because they dishonestly betray the freedom of the people, of which they know that they have been appointed protectors by God's ordinance.

32. Obedience to man must not become disobedience to God

But in that obedience which we have shown to be due the authority of rulers, we are always to make this exception, indeed, to observe it as primary, that such obedience is never to lead us away from obedience to him, to whose will the desires of all kings ought to be subject, to whose decrees all their commands ought to yield, to whose majesty their scepters ought to be submitted.

THE COUNCIL OF TRENT

The Council of Trent, which met from 1545 to 1563, is generally regarded as the definitive Catholic response to the Protestant Reformation and the foundation of Rome's subsequent efforts for internal reform. Roman Catholics recognize Trent as the 19th ecumenical council of the church.

The need for an ecumenical council to reform the Western church had long been felt. In fact, two councils were called in rapid succession early in the 1400s. The Council of Constance went so far as to depose two claimants to the papal throne and to elect a new pope. Conciliarism was clearly riding high at this time. However, it and the Council of Basel failed to carry out other reforms. Subsequent popes generally resisted demands for a council, fearing loss of their power to both councils and European monarchs.

By the 16th century the problems became acute. Demands for a council came from various quarters, including the University of Paris and the Protestant reformers. The German emperor, desperate for peace in his lands, hoped that a compromise could be reached whereby Protestants would accept papal authority in return for a program of reform and the concessions of communion under both species and a married clergy. In Rome, the cardinals were split into two camps, one favoring compromise, the other allowing no concessions whatsoever. Finally, Paul III, seeing that the disorder and turmoil of the church far outweighed the dangers of a council, summoned the meeting at the town of Trent, accessible to Italian bishops and within the boundaries of the German Empire.

When the council met, the bishops had the Augsburg Confession before them and, by the end of their meetings, the Anglican 39 Articles as well. Most of the bishops came from lands largely unaffected by the Reformation, and the decrees of the council, as the following document shows, were framed in a polemical tone in response to the Protestant confessions. Recent scholarship has shown that these decrees were not necessarily foregone conclusions. A wide diversity of opinion was expressed. One Italian bishop proclaimed his belief in the sufficiency of Scripture alone for salvation and asserted his right to believe so until the council should define otherwise. This points to the wide diversity in theology during the Middle Ages. It was not until Trent that many points of doctrine were defined. Even the canon of Scripture was not determined for Catholics until, in response to Protestant claims, the Council of Trent was forced to make a decision. The minutes of the council show that many bishops interpreted the meaning of decrees differently from the stringent interpretations later made by both Catholics and Protestants and that the decrees were carefully framed to allow for this latitude. Historically, however, the stringent interpretation prevailed and the council effectively ended any hopes for reconciliation, despite the presence, at the insistence of the emperor, of Lutheran representatives in 1551.

The decrees of the council more clearly defined certain doctrines and, of equal importance, reformed discipline. The office of indulgence-seller was abolished, specific pastoral demands were enjoined upon bishops and priests, and bishops were given more effective powers of supervision over their dioceses. Because of Protestant influence, a new emphasis was placed on preaching and personal devotion. New editions of the catechism, breviary, and missal were requested of the Pope, which laid the groundwork for a greater, though frequently abused, unity in doctrine and worship.

From **The Canons and Decrees of the Council of Trent**

DECREE CONCERNING THE EDITION AND THE USE OF THE SACRED BOOKS

Furthermore, in order to restrain petulant spirits, It decrees, that no one, relying on his own skill, shall, in matters of faith, and of morals pertaining to the edification of Christian doctrine, wresting the sacred Scripture to his own senses, dare to interpret the said sacred Scripture contrary to that sense which holy mother Church, whose it is to judge of the true sense and interpretation of the holy scriptures, hath held and doth hold; or even contrary to the unanimous consent of the Fathers; even though suchlike interpretations were never (intended) to be at any time published.

DECREE CONCERNING ORIGINAL SIN

That our Catholic *faith, without which it is impossible to please God,* may, errors being cleared away, continue in its own perfect and undefiled integrity, and that the Christian people may not *be carried about with every wind of doctrine;* whereas that old serpent, the perpetual enemy of the human race, amongst the very many evils by which the Church of God is in these our times disturbed, has also stirred up not only new, but even old dissensions touching original sin, and the remedy thereof; the sacred and holy, ecumenical and general Synod of Trent, lawfully assembled in the Holy Ghost, the three same legates of the Apostolic See presiding therein,—wishing now to come to the recalling of the erring, and the confirming of the wavering, following the testimonies of the sacred Scriptures, and of the holy fathers, and of the most approved councils, and the judgment and consent of the Church itself, ordains, confesses, and declares these things touching the said original sin:—

1. If any one does not confess that the first man, Adam, when he

had transgressed the commandment of God in Paradise, immediately lost the holiness and justice in which he had been constituted; and that he incurred, through the offence of such prevarication, the wrath and indignation of God, and consequently death, which God had previously threatened to him, and, together with death, captivity under the power of him who thenceforth *had the empire of death, that is to say, the devil,* and that the entire Adam, through that offence of prevarication, was changed as respects the body and soul, for the worse; let him be anathema.

2. If any one asserts, that the prevarication of Adam injured himself alone, and not his posterity; and that he lost for himself alone, and not for us also, the holiness and justice, received of God, which he lost; or that he, defiled by the sin of disobedience, has only transfused death, and pains of the body, into the whole human race, but not sin also, which is the death of the soul, let him be anathema; inasmuch as he contradicts the apostle, who says: *By one man sin entered into the world, and by sin death, and so death passed upon all men, in whom all have sinned.*

3. If any one asserts that this sin of Adam, which in its origin is one, and being transfused into all by propagation, not by imitation, is in each one as his own, is taken away either by the powers of human nature, or by any other remedy than the merit of the *one mediator, our Lord Jesus Christ, who has reconciled us to God in his own blood, made unto us righteousness, sanctification, and redemption,* or, if he denies that the same merit of Jesus Christ is applied both to adults and to infants, by the sacrament of baptism rightly administered in the form of the Church; let him be anathema: *For there is no other name under heaven given to men, whereby we must be saved.* Whence that voice: *Behold the lamb of God, behold him who taketh away the sins of the world;* and that other,—*As many of you as have been baptized have put on Christ.*

On the Necessity of Preparation for Justification, in the Case of Adults, and Whence It Proceeds

(This synod) furthermore declares, that, in adults, the beginning of the said Justification is to be taken from the prevenient grace of God, through Jesus Christ, that is to say, from His vocation, by which, without the existence of any merits on their parts, they are called; that so they, who through sins were turned away from God, may, through His quickening and assisting grace, be disposed to turn themselves unto their own justification, by freely assenting to, and co-operating with that said grace: so that, while God toucheth the heart of man by the illumination of the Holy Ghost, neither is man himself utterly inactive while he receives that inspiration, inasmuch as he is also able to reject it; yet is he not able, without the grace of God, by his own free will to move himself unto justice in His sight. Whence, when it is said in the sacred writings: *Turn ye unto me, and I will turn unto you,* we are admonished of our liberty: when we answer; *Turn thou us, O Lord, unto thee, and we shall be turned,* we confess that we are prevented by the grace of God.

On Justification

Canon I. If any one shall say, that man may be justified before God by his own works, whether done through the strength of human nature, or through the teaching of the law, without the divine grace through Jesus Christ; let him be anathema.

Canon IV. If any one shall say, that the free will of man moved and excited by God, by assenting to God exciting and calling, nowise co-operates to the end that it should dispose and prepare itself for obtaining the grace of justification; and that it cannot refuse consent, if it would, but that, like something inanimate, it does nothing whatever, and is merely in a passive state; let him be anathema.

Canon V. If any one shall say, that, since Adam's sin, the free will of man is lost and extinguished; or, that it is a thing with a name only, yea, a title without a reality, a figment, in fine, brought into the Church by Satan; let him be anathema.

Canon IX. If any one shall say, that by faith alone the impious is justified; so as to mean that nothing else is required to co-operate in order unto the obtaining the grace of justification, and that it is not in any respect necessary that he be prepared and disposed by the movement of his own will; let him be anathema.

Canon XVIII. If any one shall say, that the commandments of God are, even for a man that is justified and constituted in grace, impossible to keep; let him be anathema.

Canon XXIV. If any one shall say, that the justice received is not preserved, and also increased in the sight of God through good works; but that the said works are merely the fruits and signs of justification received, but not a cause of the increase thereof; let him be anathema.

THAT A RASH PRESUMPTION IN REGARD TO PREDESTINATION IS TO BE AVOIDED

No one, moreover, so long as he exists in this mortal state, ought so far to presume concerning the secret mystery of divine predestination, as to determine for certain that he is assuredly in the number of the predestined; as if it were true, that he who is justified, either cannot sin any more, or if he do sin, that he ought to promise himself a certain repentance; for except by a special revelation, it cannot be known whom God has chosen unto himself.

DECREE CONCERNING THE SACRAMENTS
PREFACE

For the consummation of the salutary doctrine of Justification, it hath seemed fitting to treat of the most holy sacraments of the Church, through which all true justice either begins, or being begun is increased, or being lost is repaired. Wherefore, the sacred and holy, ecumenical and general Council of Trent, has thought fit to establish and decree these present canons.

Canon I. If any one shall say, that the sacraments of the New Law were not all instituted by Jesus Christ, our Lord; or, that they are more, or less than seven, to wit, Baptism, Confirmation, the Eucharist, Penance, Extreme Unction, Orders, and Matrimony; or even that any one of these seven is not truly and properly a sacrament; let him be anathema.

Canon IV. If any one shall say, that the sacraments of the New Law are not necessary unto salvation, but superfluous, and that without them, and without the desire thereof, men, through faith alone, obtain of God the grace of justification; though all [the sacraments] be not necessary for every individual; let him be anathema.

Canon VII. If any one shall say, that grace, as far as concerneth God's part, is not given through the said sacraments, always, and to all men, even though they rightly receive them, but [only] sometimes, and to some persons; let him be anathema.

Canon VIII. If any one shall say, that by the said sacraments of the New Law grace is not conferred through the act performed, but that faith alone in the divine promise suffices for obtaining grace; let him be anathema. . . .

DECREE TOUCHING THE MOST HOLY SACRAMENT OF THE EUCHARIST
CHAPTER I

On the Real Presence of our Lord Jesus Christ in the most holy Sacrament of the Eucharist

In the first place, the holy synod teaches, and openly and simply professes, that, in the sacred sacrament of the holy Eucharist, after the consecration of the bread and wine, our Lord Jesus Christ, true God and man, is truly, really, and substantially contained under the species of those sensible things. . . .

CHAPTER II

On the Reason of the Institution of this most Holy Sacrament

Our Saviour, therefore, when about to depart from this world unto the Father, instituted this Sacrament, in which He, as it were, poured forth the riches of His divine love towards man, *making a remembrance of his wonderful* memory, and to *show his death until He come* to judge the world. And He also willed that this sacrament should be received as the spiritual food of souls, whereby may be nourished and strengthened those who live with His life, who said, *He that eateth me, he also shall live by me,* and as an antidote, by the which we may be freed from daily faults, and preserved from mortal sins. He willed, furthermore, that it should be a pledge of our glory to come, and of everlasting happiness, and thus be a symbol of that one body of which He would fain have us, as members, be united by the closest bond of faith, hope, and charity, *that we might all speak the same thing, and there might* be no schisms among us. . . .

CHAPTER V

On the Ceremonies and Rites of the Mass

And whereas such is the nature of man, that, without external helps, he cannot be easily upraised to the meditation of divine things; on this account has holy Mother Church instituted certain rites, to wit that certain things be pronounced in the mass in a softened, and others in a raised tone. She has likewise made use of ceremonies, such as mystic benedictions, lights, fumigations of incense, vestments, and many other things of this kind, derived from an apostolic discipline and tradition, whereby both the majesty of so great a sacrifice might be recommended, and the minds of the faithful be excited, by these visible signs of religion and piety, to the contemplation of those most sublime things which lie hidden in this sacrifice. . . .

DECREE TOUCHING THE THINGS TO BE OBSERVED AND TO BE AVOIDED IN THE CELEBRATION OF THE MASS

How great care is to be taken, that the sacred and holy sacrifice of the mass be celebrated with all religious service and veneration, each one may easily make an estimate, who considers, that, in holy writ, he is called *accursed, who doth the work of God negligently.* And if we must needs confess, that no other work can be performed by the faithful so holy and divine as this tremendous mystery itself, wherein that life-giving victim, by which we were reconciled unto God the Father, is daily immolated on the altar by the priests; it is also sufficiently clear, that all industry and diligence is to be applied to this end, that it be performed with the greatest possible inward cleanness and purity of heart, and outward show of devotion and piety. Whereas, therefore, either through the wickedness of the times, or through the carelessness and unworthiness of men, many things already seem to have crept in, which are alien from the dignity of so great a sacrifice; to the end that the honour and worship due thereunto may be restored, unto the glory of God and the edification of the faithful people; the holy synod decrees, that the ordinary bishops of places shall diligently take care, and be bound to prohibit and abolish all those things which either *covetousness, which is a serving of idols,* or irreverence, which can scarcely be separated from impiety; or superstition, the false imitatress of true piety, have introduced. . . .

They shall also keep from the churches all those kinds of music, in which, whether by the organ, or in the singing, there is mixed up anything lascivious or impure; as also all secular actions; vain and therefore profane conversations, all walking about, noise, and clamour; that so the house of God may truly seem to be, and may be called, *a house of prayer.* . . .

THE TRUE AND CATHOLIC DOCTRINE, TOUCHING THE SACRAMENT OF ORDERS, IN CONDEMNATION OF THE ERRORS OF OUR TIME, DECREED AND PUBLISHED BY THE HOLY SYNOD OF TRENT, IN THE SEVENTH SESSION.

DECREE CONCERNING REFORMATION

Chapter XVIII.   Method of Erecting a Seminary

Whereas the age of youth, unless it be rightly trained, is prone to pursue the pleasures of the world, and unless it be formed, from its tender years, unto piety and religion, before habits of vice have wholly taken possession of men, it never will perfectly, and without the greatest, and almost singular, help of Almighty God, persevere in ecclesiastical discipline; the holy synod ordains, that all cathedral, metropolitan, and other churches greater than these, shall be bound, each according to the measure of its means and the extent of the diocese, to maintain, to educate religiously, and to instruct in ecclesiastical discipline, a certain number of youths of their city and diocese, or, if (that number) cannot be found, of that province, in a college to be chosen by the bishop for this purpose near the said churches, or in some other convenient place. And into this college shall be received such as are at least twelve years old, born in lawful wedlock, and who know how to read and write competently, and whose disposition and inclination afford a hope that they will always serve in the ecclesiastical ministries. And it wishes that the children of the poor be principally selected; though it does not however exclude those of the more wealthy, provided they be maintained at their own expense, and carry before them a desire of serving God and the Church. The bishop, having divided these youths into as many classes as shall seem fit to him, according to their number, age, and progress in ecclesiastical discipline, shall, when it seems convenient to him, assign some of them to the ministry of the churches, (and) keep the others in the college to be instructed; and shall supply the place of those who have been withdrawn, by others; that so this college may be a perpetual seminary of ministers of God. And to the end that the youths may be the more conveniently trained in the aforesaid ecclesiastical discipline, they shall always at once wear the tonsure and the clerical dress; they shall learn grammar, singing, ecclesiastical computation, and the other liberal arts; they shall be instructed in sacred Scripture; ecclesiastical books; the homilies of the saints; the manner of administering the sacraments, especially those things which shall seem suited unto hearing confessions; and the forms of the rites and ceremonies. The bishop shall take care that they be every day present at the sacrifice of the mass, and that they confess their sins at least once a month; and receive the body of our Lord Jesus Christ, according to the judgment of their confessor; and on festivals serve in the cathedral and other churches of the place. All which, and other things advantageous and needful unto this object, all bishops shall ordain, with the advice of two of the senior and most discreet canons whom themselves have chosen, as the Holy Spirit shall have suggested; and shall make it their care, by frequent visitation, that the same be always observed. . . .

Touching the Invocation, Veneration, and on Relics of Saints, and Sacred Images

The holy synod enjoins on all bishops, and others sustaining the office and charge of teaching, that, according to the usage of the Catholic and Apostolic Church, received from the primitive times of the Christian religion, and according to the consent of the holy fathers, and to the decrees of sacred councils, they especially instruct the faithful diligently touching the intercession and invocation of the saints; the honour paid to relics; and the lawful use of images; teaching them, that the saints, who reign together with Christ, offer up their own prayers, aid, and help, for obtaining benefits from God, through His Son, Jesus Christ our Lord, who alone is our Redeemer and Saviour; . . .

Moreover, that the images of Christ, of the Virgin Mother of God, and of the other saints, are to be had and retained particularly in temples, and that due honour and veneration are to be awarded them; not that any divinity or virtue is believed to be in them, on account of which they are to be worshipped; or that anything is to be asked of them; or that confidence is to be reposed in images, as was of old done by the Gentiles, who placed their hope in idols, but because the honour which is shown unto them is referred to the prototypes which they represent; in such wise that by the images which we kiss, and before which we uncover the head, and prostrate ourselves, we adore Christ, and venerate the saints, whose similitude they bear. And this, by the decrees of councils, and especially of the second synod of Nicaea, has been ordained against the opponents of images.

And the bishops shall carefully teach this; that, by means of histories of the mysteries of our Redemption, depicted by paintings or other representations, the people are instructed, and strengthened in remembering, and continually reflecting on the miracles of faith; as also that great profit is derived from all sacred images, not only because the people are thereby admonished of the benefits and gifts which have been bestowed upon them by Christ, but also because the miracles of God through the means of the saints, and their salutary examples, are set before the eyes of the faithful; that so for those things they may give God thanks; may order their own life and manners in imitation of the saints; and may be excited to adore and love God, and to cultivate piety. But if any one shall teach or think contrary to these decrees; let him be anathema. And if any abuses have crept in amongst these holy and salutary observances, the holy synod earnestly desires that they be utterly abolished; in such wise that no images conducive to false doctrine, and furnishing occasion of dangerous error to the uneducated, be set up. And if at times, when it shall be expedient for the unlearned people; it happen that the histories and narratives of holy scripture are portrayed and represented; the people shall be taught, that not thereby is the Divinity represented, as though it could be perceived by the eyes of the body, or be depicted by colours or figures. Moreover, in the invocation of the saints, the veneration of relics, and the sacred use of images, every superstition shall be removed, all filthy lucre be abolished, finally, all lasciviousness be avoided; in such wise that figures shall not be painted or adorned with a wantonness of beauty; nor shall men also pervert the celebration of the saints, and the visitation of relics, into revellings and drunkenness; as if festivals are celebrated to the honour of the saints by luxury and wantonness. Finally, let so great care and diligence be used by bishops touching these matters, as that there appear nothing disorderly, or unbecomingly or confusedly arranged, nothing profane, nothing indecorous; *since holiness becometh the house of God.*

THE SOCIETY OF JESUS

Roman Catholics, Lutherans, and Calvinists defined their theological standpoints over against one another in the sixteenth century. As a result, all parties sought to counteract the variety of popular, folk religion with a carefully defined set of beliefs. This required a system of education, and it is remarkable how similar the systems created in this period were. All shared the Christian humanist ideal of combining the Renaissance emphasis upon the classical languages and literature with orthodox belief and piety. This synthesis remained normative in Western education until the nineteenth century.

Typical of this ideal and most influential within the Roman Catholic communion was the work of the Society of Jesus. Ignatius Loyola (1491-1556) had imbibed the humanistic influence at the University of Paris and combined this with a profound piety. It was clear to him that education was a prime necessity in combating Protestantism. The *First Sketch of the Institute of the Society of Jesus* drawn up in 1539 begins:

> Whoever wishes to be a soldier of God under the standard of the cross and serve the Lord alone and His vicar on earth in our Society . . . should . . . bear in mind that he is part of a community founded principally for the advancement of souls in Christian life and doctrine and for the propagation of the faith by the ministry of the Word, by spiritual exercises, by works of charity, and expressly by the instruction in Christianity of children and the uneducated.

The Society offered itself to the Pope for these purposes, grew very rapidly, and became highly successful. Its members were not only dedicated but also very able, and they developed a curriculum for secondary and higher education which stood unchanged for nearly two and a half centuries. This was the *Ratio Studiorum*, drawn up in 1599 on the basis of the experience of half a century. Heavy emphasis was placed on the classical languages. Together with biblical studies, Latin and Greek grammar, rhetoric, and literature made up the bulk of the curriculum of the faculty of letters. From this "college" education, the student would continue his professional studies in law, medicine, philosophy, or theology at the university level. Thus, all educated men were products of a classical education.

The aim of the *Ratio* was to mold young men both morally and intellectually. It was to teach them to write Latin like Cicero and to think like Aristotle and Thomas Aquinas. Its most distinctive feature was the deliberate attempt to subject both teacher and student to the authority of the order and the church. But the Jesuit system was not harsh. It utilized the carrot rather than the stick, with ample opportunity for a change of pace in games and dramatic productions.

The success of the Jesuits was due to many factors: careful preparation of the teachers, their dedication, a graded system, and the fact that they charged no tuition. By the time of the death of Ignatius, the Society administered a hundred colleges and houses, and by the time the *Ratio* was introduced, it controlled a very large part of Catholic education.

Since the nineteenth century, the curriculum has been broadened, and more flexibility has been permitted.

From the Society of Jesus, **Ratio Studiorum**

SYSTEM AND PLAN OF STUDIES OF THE SOCIETY OF JESUS

Since it is one of the weightiest duties of our society to teach men all the branches of knowledge in keeping with our organization in such a manner, that they may be moved thereby to a knowledge and love of our Creator and Redeemer, let the Provincial hold it as his duty, to provide with all zeal, that the results, which the grace of our vocation demands, abundantly answer to our manifold labors in education. . . .

In order to preserve a knowledge of classical literature and to establish a sort of nursery for gymnasium teachers, let him [the Provincial] endeavor to have in his province at least two or three men distinguished in these services and in eloquence. To this end, from the number of those who are capable and inclined to these studies, he shall set apart for that work alone a few who are sufficiently instructed in the other departments, in order that through their efforts and activity a body of good teachers may be maintained and provided for the future. . . .

Furthermore, care must be exercised that where there are too few schools, always the higher classes, so far as possible, must be retained, and the lower classes given up. . . .

The subject matter of tragedies and comedies, which however, shall be only in Latin and seldom acted, shall be of a sacred and pious character; the interludes also shall be in Latin and of due decorum; female roles and costumes are prohibited. . . .

The special aim of the teacher, in his lectures on suitable occasion and elsewhere, should be to inspire his pupils to the service and love of God and to the exercise of the virtues through which we may please him, and to lead them to recognize this as the sole end of their studies. . . .

Let him [the professor of Holy Scripture] recognize it as his principal duty, piously, learnedly, and thoroughly to explain the books given of God, according to their genuine and liberal sense, which confirms the right faith in God and the principles of good morals. Among other ends which he is to pursue, let this stand as chief, that he is to defend the translation (Vulgate) approved by the Church. . . .

When the canons of the popes or councils, especially the general councils, indicate the literal sense of a passage of Scripture as the true one, let him also by all means defend it and adduce no other literal sense, except where special reasons exist. When they employ a text expressly as proof of an article of faith, let him teach likewise that this is the indubitable sense, whether literal or mystical. . . .

When he comes upon a text, over which we are in controversy with heretics, or which is quoted on both sides in theological discussions, let him expound it simply, yet thoroughly and vigorously, especially against heretics, and point out what weight is in the passage for deciding the question at issue; all the rest let him lay aside, in order that he, mindful of his vocation, may be simply an expounder of the Holy Scriptures. . . .

In teaching, confirmation of faith and growth in piety must above all be considered. Therefore in questions, which St. Thomas has not expressly handled, no one shall teach anything that does not well harmonize with the views of the Church and the generally received traditions, and that in any way disturbs the foundation of genuine piety. . . .

Let him [the professor of Church history] treat the history of the Church with the view and with such skill, that he may render the study of theology more easy for his students, and more deeply impress upon their minds the dogmas of faith and the canons.

Let him clearly demonstrate that the rights of the Church and of its head rest upon antiquity, and let him show that the statements of innovators about the late origin of such rights are pure inventions. . . .

In all important questions he must not deviate from the teaching everywhere accepted in the academies. Let him defend the orthodox faith with his might, and seek thoroughly to refute the philosophical systems and arguments directed against it. Finally let him not forget in the choice of different opinions that theology must light the way. . . .

From the beginning of logic on, the students shall be so instructed that in their disputations they may be ashamed of nothing more than of a departure from syllogistic form. . . .

Christian doctrine must be learned by heart in all the classes; and in the three grammar classes, and if necessary, in the other classes, it must be repeated Fridays or Saturdays. According to the grade of each class more ample explanations shall be given and required.

On Friday or Saturday let him [the Professor of the lower classes] deliver for half an hour a pious exhortation or explanation of the catechism; but especially let him exhort to daily prayer to God, to a daily reciting of the rosary or office of the Blessed Virgin, to an examination of the conscience every evening, to a frequent and worthy reception of the sacraments of penance and the altar, to an avoidance of evil habits, to a detestation of vice, and finally to a practice of all the virtues becoming a Christian. . . .

Especial care must be exercised that the students acquire the habit of speaking Latin. Therefore the teacher, at least from the upper grammar grade, must speak in Latin, and require also that the students speak Latin, especially in the explanation of rules, the correction of Latin exercises, in disputations, and in their daily intercourse. In the translation of authors he must himself have great regard for the purity and correct pronunciation of the mother tongue, and strictly require the same from the students.

Part Six

Christian Humanism
after the Reformation:

The Humanism of the Incarnation

Introduction

Modern Christian humanism is more than a continuation of a movement of the Renaissance or of the Reformation. It is a deeply rooted influence, a strong reaffirmation of the central incarnational tradition of the church fathers amid the new circumstances of science, political revolution, and industrialization.

To a self-confident society of scientific facts, industrial matter, and revolutionary individualism, Christian humanists from 1615 on recalled human limits: of the need for knowledge which transcends human experience, of the need for a spiritual dimension to culture, of the need for life in community. A divided Christendom was recalled from imbalanced faith: from authoritarian structures, from worldly power, from emotional appeal, from biblical inerrancy, from obsession with salvation in the hereafter.

In Jesus the true character of human life becomes clear to Christian humanists. It is in the substantial likeness of the earth's population to Christ that they find the possibility for existence which strikes a balance between the material and the spiritual, the individual and the community, and freedom and limits. Christian humanists assert that Jesus continues to be encountered in modern times above all in the church, in baptism, and at the Lord's Supper, rather than around campfires, in football stadiums, or before the television. Most take the authority of the church and sacraments seriously. The physical dimension of sacraments implies that the new life of kingdom, church, baptism, and Supper must be realized in worthy temporal conditions.

The early texts of the humanism of the incarnation appear in Parts Two, Three, and Four of *Readings in Christian Humanism*. In the New Testament the atoning work of Jesus is placed in a far wider context than the salvation of a collection of self-contained individuals. Atonement is placed in the context of the re-creation and re-assembly of the entire ruined and scattered human race. The cosmic significance of the atonement is suggested in Colossians 1:20, where it is God's intention through Christ to draw all things unto himself. Far from damning the material realm, the incarnation is perceived as an ecological link to the fulfillment of the physical universe.

The apostle Paul broadened the doctrine of the incarnation to suggest in Ephesians that the totality of Christ's body consists not just of Jesus, but of Jesus and his church. The particular note of Paul is the universality of this body, that the church of Christ embraces all people and is the institution commissioned to restore the lost unity of humankind.

This great Pauline theme was taken up and developed by St. Irenaeus of Lyons, the first significant thinker in the Christian church after the time of the apostles. For Irenaeus creation and redemption are parts of a single plan: "He who feeds our bodies with his flesh and blood in the Eucharist is also he who makes provision for the earthly needs of those same bodies in the order of creation.'"

The conviction that all of civilization is caught up into one whole with sacraments and church permeated Christian teaching from Justin to Augustine. On this basis in the second century Justin defended the synthesis of pagan learning with the Bible. The irenic Christianity reached great heights in Augustine's *City of God* in 410, in the monumental endorsement of the goodness of human civilization which helped to fashion a climate favorable to the scientific study of the material world and saved Christendom from a completely otherworldly outlook.

The *Rule* of Benedict reminds us further how little early Christianity was a religion of "private experience." The *Rule* calls persons to transform themselves and one another "into the likeness of Christ" within a shared life. Early monasteries were practical models of patristic moderation, striking a balance between the needs of the individual monk and the community as a whole. Benedict's monastery is a renewed earthly society in which mundane and routine objects and actions have an honored role in perfecting a locale where God can be "all in all." Thus in the monastic tradition the sacramental aura of the incarnation is extended to the world of work in the great importance given to formal, liturgical prayer (termed "the work of God") and in the religious significance conferred upon meaningful manual labor.

The worldly content of the incarnation was no less central to the enterprise of the medieval scholastics, for whom the whole earth was a bodily and visible gospel of the Word. We have already seen that in the *Cur Deus Homo* Anselm regarded reason as the tool whereby human beings could collaborate with Christ in the restoration of creation. Every department of the material world found a place in the ecclesiastical summas, universal histories, and cycles of legends of the Middle Ages, not as incongruous accessories but filled with religious content and invested with spiritual character.

John Ruskin observed the same syncretism in art: "Christianity was professed in art, but paganism was practiced. They put the madonna and Aphrodite in the same procession." Too much has been made of the inquisitional attitude of the medieval church. When on the eve of the Reformation Cesare Borgia wished to set up a strict censorship in Rome, his father Alexander VI, not the most zealous of popes, answered that at Rome everyone had always said just what he thought, and the Pope could not stop it, even if he wanted to.

New Secular Forces

From the sixteenth century on a number of the Christian humanists presented here perceived a schism between the sacred and the secular in Western civilization. The churches came to apply Christ's atonement primarily to individuals. The incarnation receded into the background. New secular forces in science, politics, and industry were not generally embraced in the cosmic scheme of salvation. Censorship rather than integration became the response of the church to the world. A fragmented image of man appeared, as described by Romano Guardini: "There came a human type cut adrift from the ties which make man's physical and mental life organic. [Man] has fallen away on the one hand into a world of abstraction, on the other into the purely physical sphere; from union with nature into the purely scholastic and artificial; from the community into isolation."

Science

Science is held to be the first of the "schismatic forces" which mark the modern world. The scientific achievements of the century and a half between the publication of Copernicus's *De Revolutionibus Orbium Caelestium* (1543) and Newton's *Principia* (1687) opened a new period of intellectual and cultural ferment. This was to continue through the publication of Darwin's theory of evolution in 1859 and the upheavals in physics and in psychology of the twentieth century. What distinguished this age from its predecessors was that knowledge came to be based on physical experiments and natural observation. Science made the world of the Spirit dim. It became increasingly difficult to agree with the sixteenth-century Anglican Richard Hooker that the laws governing the Book of Nature "are an original draught written in the bosom of God himself."

Newton's seventeenth century *Principia* pictured the universe as a machine whose fundamental features were numbers and invariable laws. Copernicus's heliocentric theory had made the human no longer the physical center of the cosmos. But in Charles Darwin's *Descent of Man* (1871) the origin of man appeared to lie in the operation of the impersonal forces of natural selection instead of in the direct personal action of God.

The progressive animalization of the image of the human species begun in Darwin was carried forward by modern psychology. All seemingly spiritual feelings and activities, poetic creation, pity and devotion, or contemplative love became the sublimation of sexual libido in Sigmund Freud (1856-1939) or the outgrowth of conditioned behavior in B. F. Skinner (1904-).

For growing numbers in the eighteenth century revealed religion was driven out of the physical universe into the region of private morals. The scheme of Christian salvation, which was based on the supposition that Adam had all at once been created with a fully formed capacity for communion with God, was thrown into disarray for the faithful of the nineteenth century by Darwin's theory that higher animals and man had evolved from lower forms of life as a result of the struggle for existence. Twentieth-century psychological man no longer sought recourse to Christian revelation for the justification of his moral code. The popular impression was conveyed that religion itself had been discredited and that the substitution of ancient world-views by those of modern science made it unnecessary any longer to trouble about the Christian estimate of man.

Philosophy

Philosophical revolution accompanied the rise of science with a gradual secularization of mind. The French philosopher René Descartes (1596-1650) sought to reconcile science and religion in the seventeenth century by saving the best features of both. But Descartes advanced the schism of the sacred and the secular. He kept God on as a First Cause "very well skilled in mechanics," but he eliminated religious purposes from nature. Descartes left religion only in control of private belief and morals. There is a great concentration on the individual in Descartes, with his fundamental philosophical formula "I think, therefore I am." Descartes concludes that the mind is a thinking thing, quite independent of natural substances, and likewise, independent of any human community. Cartesian individualism grew in the eighteenth century into a faith in human omnipotence. The limits of creaturehood tended to be forgotten.

The message of the eighteenth century Enlightenment may be summed up in the phrase "Use your brains!" The human mind became the measure of all things. The eighteenth-century *philosophes* of the Enlightenment extended to society the methods and laws of the natural scientists. The *philosophes* divested political and economic thinking of religion. Public institutions could do without the sanctions of the church. "Let us recognize the plain truth," wrote the *philosophe* Holbach, "that it is these supernatural ideas that have obscured morality, corrupted politics, hindered the advance of the sciences, and extinguished happiness and peace in the very heart of man."

Antipathy to revealed religion was ingrained in the intellectual presuppositions of the Enlightenment. In his discussion of miracles in the patristic church, the Englishman Edward Gibbon remarked in the *Decline and Fall of the Roman Empire* (1776) that "in modern times, a latent and even involuntary skepticism adheres to the most pious dispositions. Our reason is not sufficiently prepared to sustain the visible action of the Deity." Gibbon testifies to the declining sense of the miraculous in the eighteenth century. The *philosophes* rejected all divine intervention in nature. Voltaire (1694-1778) subjected the Bible to merciless criticism, thus laying the foundations for the scientific "higher criticism" of the Bible of the nineteenth century.

For revealed religion Voltaire and many other *philosophes* substituted their own brand of natural religion, called deism. Deism was watered-down theism, and it represented an attempt to construct a religion in keeping with modern science. God remained, but he was hardly a God to whom you could pray.

In *Christianity and Civilization* Emil Brunner describes how the two contrasting ideals of nineteenth-century philosophy, individualism and collectivism, maintained the schismatic character of Western culture. In France the Enlightenment was continued as a completely secularist interpretation of human nature in Auguste Comte's *The Positive Philosophy* (1839-1842) with its negation of all metaphysics and its proclamation of a natural religion of humanity. In England a similar school of thought led by John Stuart Mill (1806-1873) was influenced by Comte to interpret man from merely immanent presuppositions. From the Enlightenment Mill inherited the goal of emancipating the human personality from ecclesiastical or political collectives. Mill's works, which summon the individual to freedom and independent dignity, are the classic definitions of democratic liberalism. *On Liberty* (1859) is the finest secular defense ever written of individual freedom, a defense grounded not in religion or abstract rights, but in the practical argument that a clash of opinions is necessary to the attainment of truth. Individualism reached a totalitarian level in the German Friedrich Nietzsche's (1844-1900) proclamation that the "death of God" has liberated a higher type of man. Nietzsche's free man overcomes the harsh and cruel realities of a godless world through aggressive self-reliance and will to power.

Brunner's collectivist nineteenth century philosophy is idealist humanism. Idealist humanism begins in Immanuel Kant's (1724-1804) critique of the Enlightenment and leads on in the German philosophies of Fichte and Hegel to an idealization of the Prussian State. The idealist humanism of G. W. F. Hegel (1770-1831) separates spirit and nature. Man is divided in two: into an animal or sensual, and a spiritual or divine part. As idealist humanism evolved from Hegel to Marx the principle of human reason was more and more divested of its spiritual content. The half-transcendental reason of Hegel becomes completely lost in the fierce collectivist reaction of Karl Marx (1818-1883) against the rampant individualism of nineteenth-century Europe. In Marx the economic element becomes the center of human life. Ideas and spiritual values are dependents and superstructures of economic processes. Depersonalized mass-man forms a particle of the social structure of the collective state. Thus by 1900 the West was divided by camps of extreme collectivism, as well as by extreme individualism.

By the 1930s the schism in philosophy had become almost complete, with continental European philosophers speculating about ethics and metaphysics, and the British and Americans analyzing narrow problems that were compatible with the scientific methods of logical empiricism. Continental philosophers were either existentialists or phenomenologists. Both of these traditions remained true to the early idealist doctrine that ultimate reality lay in the world of ideas and spirit rather than in sense experience. Existentialism and phenomenology shared a confidence in the power of human intuition to pierce behind the surface appearances of the physical world.

Nineteenth-century positivism, stripped of its historical optimism, emerged as the contrasting Anglo-American doctrine of logical positivism or logical empiricism, which reduced to nonsense the traditional concerns of ethics and metaphysics. According to the analytical philosophers, nothing that could not be talked about without ambiguity in the language of mathematical symbols or of ordinary speech deserved to be treated as philosophy. The cleavage was so great that logical positivists found it impossible to have meaningful exchange with existentialists or phenomenologists.

Political Change

Politicians also repudiated the old synthesis of the sacred and the secular. Authoritarian collectivism subjected religious life to state control. Democratic liberalism excluded the church from public affairs.

The English Civil War (1641-1649) and the Puritan Commonwealth and Protectorate (1649-1660) demonstrated that a nation could get on not only without a king, but without bishops and ecclesiastical courts. In England after 1660 bishops never again controlled the national bureaucracy and the Clarendon Code (1661-1665) could not destroy the variety of Nonconformist sects. The common law triumphed over the prerogative of church courts. Although the union of church and state survived, the public influence of the Church of England waned through the eighteenth and nineteenth centuries. In the 1820s Anglicans lost their monopoly in English and Irish politics. In 1833 the British government was able to abolish unilaterally 12 Irish dioceses of the United Church of England and Ireland. In 1836 a government Ecclesiastical Commission redistributed the incomes of English bishops. Parliament removed religious tests from entrance and taking of degrees at Oxford and Cambridge in 1854 and 1856.

By the end of the nineteenth century in most areas of English life the Church of England had been reduced to a tangential formality.

The effect of the French Revolution of 1789 and of Napoleon was more extreme. Ecclesiastical reforms of 1789-1790 abolished the Roman Catholic Church in France. Monastic communities were destroyed by legislation of 1791. Although Napoleon signed a concordat with Rome in 1801, the French state retained the right to redraw the boundaries of the ancient dioceses of France whenever political whim dictated. The Napoleonic Organic Articles of 1802 severely restricted public church activity. Christmas, Ascension, and All Saints were the only feasts which could be celebrated on days other than Sunday. The faithful were forbidden to leave work for weekday celebrations of the Eucharist.

After the Napoleonic regime had been planted in the western German states, the *Reichsdeputationshauptschluss* of 1803 enacted a thorough secularization of all church lands, territories, and institutions. The political and economic, the spiritual and outer ecclesiastical existence of the Roman Church as it had developed its own forms in Germany was destroyed. Foundations of secular and regular canons, monasteries, universities, cathedral chapters, all disappeared with one Napoleonic stroke. Twenty-two ecclesiastical states which had so recently produced Mozart at Salzburg and an architectural flowering at Würzburg were wiped from the map. The historic German church in all its rich spiritual and worldly form vanished. The result of these changes for one religious order may be measured: in 1790 in western Europe there were over 1000 monasteries for Benedictine men and over 500 for women. Fourteen years later less than two percent of these houses remained, and by 1845 only five percent had been restored. These were woefully reduced in size and despoiled of their libraries and other possessions.

In the nineteenth century Berlin stood at the center of a society in which the church was totally dominated by the bureaucracy of the state. In 1837 the Prussians incarcerated a Rhineland Archbishop, Klemens August von Droste-Vischering and in 1838 a Polish Archbishop, Robert Dunin, because both refused to sanction cabinet orders decreeing that mixed marriages should be blessed by the clergy. After 1848 the liturgical and catechetical affairs of Protestant and Catholic churches were controlled by the Prussian ministry of Public Worship and Education.

The high tide of anticlerical nationalism reached Rome in November 1848 when a mob inspired by the romantic nationalism of Mazzini's Young Italy declared the city to be a democratic republic, assassinated the papal prime minister Count Pellegrino Rossi, abolished the temporal power of the Pope, and drove Pope Pius IX into exile in the Kingdom of Naples. This was a short, symbolic success of a national liberation movement which in the 1860s would permanently deprive the papacy of the Italian Marches and Umbria, then of the Romagna, and finally, in 1870, of Rome itself.

In the twentieth century nationalist hostility to the churches was advanced to supreme heights by the Hitler regime in Germany (1933-1945). Hitler launched vicious propaganda campaigns against members of religious communities, accusing monks and nuns of smuggling and sexual immorality. By 1937 he had effectively destroyed the influence of Catholic education. Nearly all church schools were closed. Hitler tried to unify and to Nazify the Protestants by forcing church organizations into a single Reich church under the rule of a Nazi *Reichsbishop*. By 1937 Protestant dissidents who refused submission to the *Reichskirche* and constituted themselves as the "Confessional Church" were being dispatched to concentration camps.

The Bolshevik victors of the Russian revolution moved toward the establishment of a completely secular society in Russia after 1917 and in eastern Europe after 1945. In January 1918 the separation of church and state and the secularization of education were decreed throughout the Soviet Union. The property of the church was confiscated without compensation. The church was deprived of juridical existence. Worship was allowed only at the sufferance of state authority. The Metropolitan of St. Petersburg was shot. The Patriarch of Moscow was imprisoned. In Yugoslavia Marshal Tito brought to trial the spiritual leader of the Croats, Archbishop Alois Stepinac, who was condemned in 1946 to a long prison term. A similar fate befell the primate of Hungary, Cardinal Joseph Mindszenty, whose trial in 1949 recalled the early Soviet purges of the church, and Archbishop Beran of Prague, who was deported from his see in 1951. By the early 1950s the churches in Croatia, Czechoslovakia, and Hungary had been terrified into submission to the state.

Industrialization

To many, industrialization completed the alienation of matter and spirit and individual and community in the West. The industrial revolution was essentially a replacement by machines of human and animal labor, and it included the organization of machine work into the factory system. It began in England in the eighteenth century and had spread by the 1850s to the northern United States and by the 1870s to the German Rhineland. Patterns of life were transformed in every industrialized society. Ancient crafts were replaced by machines. The majority of Europeans and Americans ceased to be farmers and became city dwellers.

In preindustrial Europe life spent on the job was lived at a slower pace, accompanied by a variety of convivial social practices (singing and drinking). The factory created a new notion of work. Work was to be a limited segment of life and not necessarily a pleasant one. Factory workers had to be on time and stand at their machine six days a week. They had to keep up with the machine for endless hours. The factory forced upon women and men a new rigorous discipline which removed them from their families, from parish communities, from easygoing preindustrial habits. Workers complained that they were a mere number manipulated by a faceless bureaucracy, toiling for the profit of an unknown millionaire. A survey by Adolf Levenstein in Europe in 1900 revealed these reactions: 60% of miners, 75% textile workers, 57% metal workers found no joy in their work. In 1917 J. L. and Barbara Hammond described the relation of the industrial revolution to humanism in *The Town Labourer:* "The depreciation of human life was the leading fact about the new system for the working class. The human material was used up rapidly . . . . at the end the working class, which was now contributing not only the men but the entire family, seemed to be what it was at the beginning, a mere part of the machinery without a share in the increased wealth or the increased power over life that machinery had brought."

Individualism and materialism were keystones of the industrial revolution. Nineteenth-century capitalists extolled individual prowess. They prided themselves on the creation of a new "acquisitive man" for an economically focused society. The literature of the times brims over with "will power," "the gospel of work," "self-help," "self-reliance," "useful knowledge," "captains of industry." The leader of the Manchester School of Economics, Richard Cobden (1804-1865), was as much a materialist as Karl Marx. He talked about "economic man" freed to pursue his own self-interest. He preached "free enterprise," "free trade," "free contracts," as the end of human problems. Cobden was suspicious of general ideas especially when they involved some mystical, collective, or common good. "Mine is that masculine species of charity," he wrote, "which would lead me to inculcate in the minds of the laboring classes the love of independence, the privilege of self-respect, the disdain of being patronized or petted, the desire to accumulate, and the ambition to rise."

Individualism and materialism show through the culture of the industrial age in a hundred different places: in the nineteenth-century love of biographies and autobiographies; in the predominance of the Victorian novel of character; in the ascendancy of the factory materials concrete, steel, and glass in modern architecture; in the industrial city where hundreds of thousands of all classes crowded by one another as though they had nothing in common but the brutal indifference, the unfeeling isolation of each in his own private interest and narrow self-seeking.

A chorus of secular protest arose about this world. We hear it in the *Stones of Venice* of John Ruskin in 1851: "The great cry that rises from all our manufacturing cities, louder than their furnace blast—is that we manufacture everything there except men . . . to brighten, to strengthen, to refine or to form a single living spirit, never enters into our estimate of advantages." It is still there in the 1920s in the German Bauhaus of Walter Gropius: "Only work which is the product of an inner compulsion can have spiritual meaning. Mechanized work is lifeless, proper only to the lifeless machine . . . . the solution depends on a change in the individual's attitude toward his work." But to the modern Christian humanists the weakness and collapse of the churches in urbanized and industrial areas was so great that little protest arose within them. In London the churches had room for only one-tenth of the population. St. George's-in-the-East in London had 30,000 parishioners in 1838 with an average Sunday attendance of 100. In the second half of the nineteenth century some Berlin churches like Zum Heilig Kreuz had 100,000 parishioners and felt the need for only one worship service a week. The Christian humanist would have to criticize the churches for their paralysis before the new science and philosophy, for unrealistic political stances, for fomenting Christian alienation of the individual and the community.

The Churches: Forced Retreat or Subservience

The churches themselves advanced the fragmentation of Western culture. Some Christians maintained a forced retreat from the modern world. Others demonstrated excessive subservience before the conclusions of science, the authoritarianism of the state, or the modern ideology of individualism.

The Roman Catholic Church took a stand against that which was to become modern science and against any philosophy associated with the scientific revolution. This attitude stemmed from the Counter-Reformation pontificate of Pope Paul IV (1555-1558) who published the first *Index of Prohibited Books*. All the works of Erasmus, King Henry VIII, Machiavelli, Rabelais, and even two editions of the Koran were found on the *Index*. Though modified, the *Index* and the Roman Inquisition were continued by the Council of Trent in 1564, and both institutions continued to be a disaster for Catholic scientists and philosophers. In the early seventeenth century the Roman Inquisition declared the Copernican heliocentric theory to be heretical and ordered the Italian scientist Galileo not to teach or defend the proposition that the earth moves around the sun. In 1632 in open and flagrant violation of this injunction Galileo published his *Dialogue on the Great World Systems*. The *Dialogue* was soon put on the *Index*. The Inquisition made Galileo appear for examination under threat of torture. Though Galileo recanted, he was condemned to protective custody.

In 1864 Pius IX once again set the Roman Catholic Church squarely against contemporary science in the encyclical *Quanta Cura* and the *Syllabus of Errors*. The encyclical summed up the teaching of the pontificate of Pius IX against rationalism, socialism, communism, naturalism, and freemasonry. The *Syllabus* culminates in the famous denial "that the Roman pontiff can and ought to reconcile himself and reach agreement with progress, liberalism, and modern civilization."

In the decree *Lamentabili* of 1910, Pope Pius X condemned a number of propositions which made even a moderately conservative use of scientific criticism impossible for Catholic biblical scholars and theologians. In the encyclical *Pascendi* Pius X condemned as heretical the teaching of Catholic Modernists, who had endorsed the scientific method. Throughout the world, councils of vigilance were appointed in every diocese, and an anti-Modernist oath was imposed upon all Roman clergy. Pius X stacked the Roman Biblical Commission with conservatives who proceeded in the twentieth century to oblige Roman Catholics not to call into question the Mosaic authorship of the Pentateuch, the unity of the Book of Isaiah, or the Pauline authorship of Hebrews—opinions which had been abandoned by nearly all liberal Protestant scholars.

Though hostility to science was exhibited by some conservative Protestants and fundamentalists, Liberal Protestants were ready to bend Christian revelation to match the insights of modern science and philosophy. Liberal Protestantism is a wide tradition, going by many names: "New Theology," "Progressive Orthodoxy," "Modernism." On the European continent liberals traced their ancestry from Erasmus, through Poland, to the eighteenth-century German University of Halle, and in the nineteenth century through D. F. Strauss, Ritschl, Harnack, and Albert Schweitzer. In English Christianity liberalism is traced through Locke and Paley to American Unitarianism, the Oxford Noetics, and the Broad Church in Anglicanism. Liberals appealed to their own intellects and the methods of science in religious matters. Science was used as an implement of faith in order to fashion a Christianity adaptable to the needs of modern times. Jesus and the Bible had authority to the liberals only if approved by science, philosophy, or history.

There were many German liberal Protestants at the University of Halle. There in the middle of the eighteenth century Jacob Baumgarten was preaching, "My words are intended for those who are at once Christians and men of reason." Baumgarten's students, Johann David Michaelis at Göttingen and Johann August Ernesti at Leipzig argued that the same rules of criticism which were applied to profane authors should be put to the authors of Scripture. In the nineteenth century D. F. Strauss (1809-1874) completely rejected the supernatural element of the biblical record in his *Life of Jesus* of 1835 and portrayed Christ as a purely human person who came to believe himself to be the Messiah. To the principal exponent of liberal Protestantism in Germany at the end of the 19th century, Adolf von Harnack (1851-1930), the essence of Christianity was Harnack's short definition of what he regarded as the essence of Christ's teaching: individual trust in the divine fatherhood of God and the brotherhood of man. This was the religion *of* Jesus. Harnack rejected supernatural religion *about* Jesus. To Harnack, traditional Christianity, with the institutional church, christological dogmas, and Catholic liturgy, was a perversion of the gospel.

Similar attitudes were prevalent in the Church of England. In the 1820s the Noetics of Oriel College at Oxford called historical aspects of the church into question. The Provost of Oriel, Edward Copleston (1776-1849), rejected any sacramental characteristics of the church bestowed by historical connection. His successor, Edward Hawkins, brought all doctrine before the bar of reason. By 1860 the widening of Anglican liberalism into an entire school in the church, known as the "Broad Church," was signaled by the publication of a volume entitled *Essays and Reviews*. Benjamin Jowett (1817-1893), the Master of Balliol College, Oxford, wound up the series with a careful argument for the use of reason in the interpretation of Scripture. Jowett suggested that the time had come when students of the Bible could no longer possibly ignore the results of the scientific criticism of the biblical record.

The greatest development of liberal Protestantism took place in America. No better description of American liberal Protestantism as it appeared to its critics at the turn of the century has been written than these words of H. Richard Niebuhr:

> In ethics Liberal Protestantism reconciled the interests of the individual with those of society by means of faith in a natural identity of interests or in the benevolent altruistic character of man. In politics and economics it slurred over national and class divisions, seeing only the growth of unity and ignoring the increase of self-assertion and exploitation. In religion it reconciled God and man by deifying the latter and humanizing the former. . . . A God without wrath brought men without sin into a kingdom without judgment through the ministrations of a Christ without a cross.

The Churches: Prey to the State

In the seventeenth and eighteenth centuries, and in some countries until quite recently, there was a movement to ally Roman and non-Roman churches with political authority and to oppose the churches to intellectual freedom. The attitude of bishops of the Church of England to the Puritans and to Parliamentary democracy from 1601 to 1649 and the stance of the Church of France in regard to the Jansenists from 1640 to 1750 illustrates this tendency toward ecclesiastical authoritarianism abhorred by Christian humanists.

Throughout the controversy over political power and freedom of religion in England in the seventeenth century the bishops gave monarchy unquestioned allegiance. Seventeenth-century bishops thought of themselves more as civil servants than as servants of the church. It was common before 1649 to speak of "Kings, Bishops, and other State Officers." Churchmen depended on the crown for protection and promotion. Bishops elevated the theory of the divine right of kings to an important doctrine of the church. The High Commission of the Church of England was used to censor political as well as religious tracts, and excommunication was wielded against opponents of the monarchy, both great and small. William Laud, the Archbishop of Canterbury after 1633, denied opponents of monarchy the right to publish or to preach in churches. Even in the early nineteenth century, the political orientation of the higher clergy continued to be the single most important requisite for the appointment of bishops in England and Ireland.

At the same time in France the church allowed itself to become a willing tool in a campaign for domestic political conformity. To that end the Catholic Jansenists were crushed. Faced with the revolt of the Fronde (1649-1652), a series of rebellions by segments of the French nobility to preserve local autonomy, Louis XIV moved to centralize the French state within his own hands. The Jesuits and a majority of the French bishops proved to be willing agents of his policy of state uniformity. The king's Jesuit tutor Bishop Jacques-Bénigne Bossuet (1627-1704) even provided a theological justification of Louis's policy in his own reworking of the theory of the divine right of kings.

The Jansenists opposed the theology and the political influence of the Jesuits. The Jansenists were Catholics who adhered to the Augustinian tradition which had done much to shape the Lutheran and the Calvinist confessions. In 1640, the Arnaulds, a Parisian family prominent in the Gallican opposition to the Jesuits, had imported from the Low Countries into France a book *Augustinus* by Bishop Cornelius Jansen, which assailed Jesuit teaching on sin and grace. During the 1640s Cistercian communities at Port-Royal and Paris were dominated by the Arnaulds and became centers of religious nonconformity and political opposition.

The 1650s saw this incipient religious pluralism crushed and replaced by the closed Catholic state of Louis XIV. The papacy and the Jesuits cooperated in imposing throughout France the motto of Louis XIV: "One King, One Law, One Faith." In 1653 Jansenism was declared a heresy by Pope Innocent X. In 1656 the Sorbonne censured the Arnaulds. After 1660 Louis XIV closed down Port-Royal and systematically drove the Jansenists underground.

Beginning in 1713 the crown and the Jesuits embarked on an even more thorough purge of Jansenist sentiment in France, using the bull *Unigenitus* as a test of obedience to royal and papal decrees. Cardinal de Noailles,

Archbishop of Paris, led the opposition to *Unigenitus*, for which he was excommunicated in 1718. Charles Coffin, author of "Oh, come, all ye faithful," was compelled to die without the last sacraments in 1749 because he would not sign *Unigenitus.*

The churches became easy prey for state control because after the sixteenth century religious life tended increasingly away from the objective sphere towards the individual. Religion was considered as something within a man. The church came to be seen as a legal entity for clergy, or an invisible society. Communal religious experience was not primary. In divine worship the faithful were particularly unaware of themselves as a community.

The anticommunal spirit in modern Christianity may be seen in two guises: in the Reformation churches with their pew boxes, prominent pulpits, and scriptural exercises; and the Counter-Reformation churches, with their confessional boxes, baroque pulpits, and extraliturgical cults. Protestant worship stressed preaching, instruction, hearing, understanding—activities of individual minds and hearts. Even as it evolved through the Evangelical Awakening and revivalism, Protestant worship was concerned with the individual soul, which was to be called to repentance and conversion and assured of forgiveness by the emotional instruments of personal religion: stirring sermons, the singing of newly-composed hymns, dramatic testimonies and conversions. At the same time, Protestant worship was a highly clericalized function, with nearly all action, speaking, and prayers performed by ordained ministers, while the laity were present simply as recipients of the spiritual benefits to be bestowed.

Because of the sixteenth century controversy with Protestants, the whole stress of Roman Catholic thought on the Eucharist and worship was clerical and individualistic. Divine service was celebrated in an unknown tongue, and the cup was denied the laity. Baroque piety greeted Christ as the divine king within the monstrance or visited him as the suffering prisoner of the tabernacle. The mass liturgy was understood as a collection of rubrics. Liturgical texts were smothered under polyphony. Baroque celebrants were surrounded with operatic lights, jewels, singers, and pageantry.

When a change in this state of affairs was suggested in 1845, Bishop Jean-Jacques Fayet of Orleans, one of the leading churchmen of France, endorsed popular Catholic refrains: religion is moral virtue, private and individualistic. Worship is, at best, the preserve of the clergy. "The Christian people are not obliged to understand or even be acquainted with liturgical rites," he wrote. "When we have saved religion, which is perishing, then it will be time to talk about worship." Fayet was not perturbed that throughout France the laity had no idea of what happened at a high mass, did not sing at mass, avoided the divine office. A nineteenth-century cardinal was asked the position of the layman in church. "The layman has two positions," answered the cardinal. "He kneels before the altar; that is one. And he sits below the pulpit; that is another." Then the cardinal added that there is a third: "The layman also puts his hand into his pocket."

Science and Christian Humanism

We turn now to Christian humanists who sought a middle way between these contending forces. Galileo, Pascal, Lyman Abbott, and Walker Percy all wrote on science and religion.

Galileo

Galileo Galilei (1564-1642), the Italian scientist, is one of those giants whose achievements are even now surprising in their scope. Galileo's scientific discoveries exerted an almost incalculable effect on the seventeenth century. He proved the factual basis of Copernicus's heliocentric theory in a number of works, the most famous being the *Dialogues on the Two Chief Systems of the World* (1632) which brought down upon him the condemnation of the Roman Catholic Church in 1633. Galileo perfected the telescope and observed a number of astronomical facts which once and for all destroyed ancient conceptions about the universe. As a literary force Galileo is also not to be ignored. He was a master of clear Italian prose. His books and pamphlets were in strong contrast to the verbose and convoluted arguments of Italian academics. Galileo's clarity of expression was something that caught on among the growing scientific fraternity.

In most minds Galileo's image is that of a martyr, the oppressed scientist, the symbol of Christian persecution of science. The facts are well known: In 1611 Galileo came under attack by certain churchmen for championing the Copernican theory. In 1633 he was condemned in a closed session of the Inquisition. In 1633 he was dragged publicly before the Inquisition. He recanted and promised to abandon all thoughts of a moving earth. It is often forgotten, however, that Galileo himself was a sincerely religious man and a loyal churchman. He sought to reconcile the new science and traditional faith in two important documents. The first is a letter of December 1613 to Benedetto Castelli, a Benedictine scientist who may be considered the father of modern hydrostatics. The second is a revised version of this letter sent in 1615 to the Grand Duchess Christina of Lorraine, mother of his patron the Duke of Tuscany. Excerpts are reprinted here as *Letter to the Grand Duchess Christina*. The two letters reveal a deep understanding of the Scriptures and a broad reading of the church fathers (particularly Augustine), rare among the Italian laity of the seventeenth century. Believing God to be the author of both nature and the Bible, Galileo refused to regard any apparent disagreement be-

tween the two as more than a shortcoming due to limited human understanding. Galileo looked upon scientific evidence as only one aspect of divine
wisdom. At the same time he warned his contemporaries of fallibility in
interpreting ancient biblical writings. He urged tolerant confidence in the
fact that "two truths cannot contradict each other." Galileo fought with
every weapon to make Christians accept the new Copernican universe
because he could not tolerate separate secular and theological cosmologies.

Pascal

Blaise Pascal (1623-1662) was similar to Galileo in standing as the
greatest scientific figure of his nation (France), in finding himself at the
center of a famous seventeenth-century ecclesiastical controversy (the
battle of the Jansenists with Louis XIV and the Jesuits), and in being a
master of his vernacular tongue. Contemporaries compared Pascal with
Aristotle. He laid the foundation of modern hydraulics. He designed a
Machine Arithmetique along the same lines as the modern computer. He
was a great pioneer in pure mathematics. Even after an ecstatic conversion experience of 1654 which led to permanent retreat at the comfortably
austere Jansenist community of Port-Royal, Pascal continued with scientific studies and researches. As late as the last year of his life Pascal began
the first public transportation system in Paris.

The duality of the seventeenth-century world of scientific rationalism,
on the one hand, and the Christian tradition, on the other, was tragically
felt by Pascal. Pascal did not denounce the methods of science. On points
of fact he agreed that the testimony of the senses must be yielded to and
reason be regarded as the proper instrument for determining unrevealed
truth. Quoting St. Augustine, Pascal proclaimed that any other position
"would render our religion contemptible." But he did abhor the pretensions
of science. He was a great intellectual who wrote of how little the intellect
can do: "If physicians did not have cassocks and mules and professors did
not have square hats and robes four sizes too large, they would never have
been able to fool people." Human nature for Pascal bears the characteristics
of fraud and fragmentation. In dealing with humanity, rational analysis can
not prevail, only the reasons of the heart.

Pascal was convinced that belief in God improves life psychologically
and disciplines it morally. His only access to God is Christ. "Not only do
we know God only through Jesus Christ, but only through Jesus Christ do
we know ourselves. . . . Outside of Jesus Christ, we know neither what
our life is, nor our death, nor God, nor ourselves." Christ is the point of
convergence of human elements, which taken without him, stand in contradiction. Christ is the solution to the riddle of human limitation. His personality, his life, his way of thinking, are the canon of the humanity intended
for man. To believe means to enter with one's own existence into the

sphere of this incarnational canon: "For by virtue of his glory as God, He is all that is great, and by virtue of his mortal life He is all that is poor and wretched. His purpose in assuming this unhappy state was to enable Himself to be present in all persons and the model for all conditions of mankind."

Pascal's religion was no private affair between himself and God. It had both a sacramental base and a social outreach. The church for Pascal is "a body composed of thinking members . . . . to be a member is to have life, being, and movement only through the Spirit of the body and for the sake of the body." The all-embracing corporate life of the church accommodates a scientific universe. Pascal's conception of the church is far removed from the organizational and doctrinal conformity enforced by worldly sanctions and authorities. Instead of the Jesuit word "obedience," Pascal used the more spiritual word "submission" to signify discipleship to Christ.

Pascal was buried in 1662 in a common pauper's grave. He had sold all his books, keeping only the Bible and Augustine's *Confessions*. This greatest and proudest of scientists had himself sought the experience of human limitation.

Lyman Abbott

After the publication of *The Origin of the Species* in 1859, Charles Darwin's theory of evolution was so pervasive an idea that it was more than a fact or a doctrine—it was an atmosphere which even theologians breathed. Darwin's work led some religious thinkers to reject revealed theology and adopt a materialistic philosophy. It caused others to spurn modern science and set up a fortress of religious conservatism. A third group sought to reconcile science and religion. Lyman Abbott (1835-1922) was an important representative of this middle position.

Abbott was an American Congregationalist minister who acquired a national reputation as a preacher, theologian, and editor. In 1888 he succeeded Henry Ward Beecher as a pastor of Plymouth Church in Brooklyn, a vast red-brick meeting house which had 1600 members and one of the most influential pulpits in America. At the same time Abbott was editor of the significant New York religious weekly *Outlook*, which had 125,000 readers. Abbott once remarked that "I get my recreation by going from the editor's chair to the pulpit and from the pulpit to the editor's chair." Because of his moderation and mediation, Abbott was successful in persuading many Americans that the theory of evolution, far from demolishing Christianity, actually purified and strengthened it.

Lyman Abbott would not separate himself from the past, nor anchor to it. Thus, he translated old concepts into new language. The Bible he considered to be the product of centuries of growth. The church was "a tree, rooted and grounded in Christ." A Christian social order was the "one far-off divine event to which the whole creation moves." Christ came "to evolve the latent

divinity which he has implanted in us." Redemption was not heavenly restoration but an earthly process of intellectual and spiritual development.

Abbott repudiated distinctions between the natural and the supernatural.
The opinion that God had manifested himself in unusual ways was not inconsistent with belief that he was always manifesting himself in all conceivable
ways in the ordinary processes of life. Human life is central to Abbott's
Christian evolutionism. Its goal is the kingdom of God on earth—a cooperative society based on self-sacrifice. In 1921 Abbott summarized his Christian
humanism in *What Christianity Means to Me:* "A new spirit of love, service,
and sacrifice in humanity. . . . Faith in a Leader who both sets our tasks and
shares it with us; . . . Faith in a companionable God whom we cannot understand, still less define, but with whom we can be acquainted."

Walker Percy

Walker Percy (1916-   ) was born in Alabama and at age 14 was adopted
by William Alexander Percy, a planter, lawyer, and author of hymns and
essays, who struggled all his life to reconcile cosmopolitan interests with his
love of the Mississippi Delta. Walker Percy studied chemistry, biology, and
physics at the University of North Carolina and medicine at Columbia College of Physicians. From 1942 to 1947 he was confined to bed with tubercu-
losis. In 1947 he moved to New Orleans, living first in the Pontchatrain Hotel
and then across Lake Pontchatrain in the village of Covington. From 1954
to 1961 he published philosophical articles; after 1961 five novels, including
The Moviegoer (which won the National Book Award), *Love in the Ruins*
(1971), and *The Second Coming* (1980).

Percy is a physician and philosopher who has heard and come to believe
the Christian message, which is, in his description, "the sacramental and
historico-incarnational nature of Christianity . . . all that business about God,
the Jews, Christ, and the Church." After being immersed in the scientific
enterprise for the first part of his life, he came to see that there is room for
other ways of thinking. In his articles and novels Percy does not attack "the
objective-empirical methods" of science with all its "truth and beauty and
fruitfulness." But Robert Coles summarizes Percy's hunt for knowledge
which transcends science in this way: "I have something to search for outside the laboratory or the seminar room, and without hard feelings I am
going to do so." Science has its limits. Human nature defies scientific label-
ing. Social scientists must not be allowed to claim complete victory over the
mystery of man's station in the universe.

In novels and essays Percy argues that there are some questions science
was never meant to answer. These questions are answered by "news." The
human condition generates a hunger for news. News has its own importance.
It cannot be evaluated by the criteria of science. It speaks of the depths of
being. Percy conceives the most significant news from across the border of

sense experience to be "this little advertisement, this *nota bene* on a page of universal history—'we have believed that in such and such a year God appeared among us in the humble figure of a servant, that he lived and taught in our community, and finally died.' " Christ's "good news" is "the message in the bottle" which is most responsive to the human condition.

Christian Humanism in English Christianity

Six authors stand amid the evolution of English history. John Milton and John Bunyan relate Christian humanism to the epoch of the Civil War; John Wesley relates it to the Enlightenment and to incipient industrialization; John Henry Newman, to nineteenth century liberalism; *Lux Mundi*, to Darwinism; and Dorothy Sayers, to totalitarianism.

John Milton

John Milton (1608-1674) was the son of a devout Puritan father. At Christ's College, Cambridge, he became a devoted student of the Christian and pagan classics, and in 1638 he traveled to Italy, where the lingering Renaissance atmosphere was congenial to him. In 1639 Milton joined the struggle against Charles I, Archbishop Laud, and the bishops of the Church of England. He used his literary talents to attack the episcopal role in government and to support parliamentary reforms. Milton wanted the Church of England dissolved in favor of the local authority of individual congregations. He defended the execution of Charles I by Parliament in 1649 on religious grounds and later served as secretary to the executive committee of Parliament during Oliver Cromwell's Protectorate.

Milton's *Paradise Lost* is a masterpiece of English blank verse. It was completed during the Restoration of the monarchy and published in 1667. In *Paradise Lost* Milton sought to produce for the English a national epic similar to that given Greece in Homer's *Iliad* and Rome in Vergil's *Aeneid*, but with a Christian subject matter.

Milton made use of the doctrine of the incarnation to strengthen his political and ecclesiastical positions. He placed the regeneration of England within a cosmic scheme of salvation. In political pamphlets in the 1640s and 1650s Milton argued that in taking on man's form, Christ had ennobled human beings and made them worthy of freedom: of spiritual freedom in the church and of political freedom in the state. There is no Christian defense for ecclesiastical or state servitude. Freedom has already been purchased by Christ. A prominent image in *Of Reformation* (1641), Milton's divorce pamphlets (1643), and the *Likeliest Means* is that of Christ the physician healing his body, the church. In *A Treatise of Civil Power in Ecclesiastical Causes* (1659) the definition of the church as the mystical body of Christ is used as an argument against fines and corporal punishments, and against any

external compulsions to enforce church discipline. Milton adopts the image
of the humility of the Son of God to censor the worldliness of English
bishops. In the *Tenure of Kings and Magistrates* (1649), Milton mentions
the honorable station of man as the image of God in order to point up privileges and liberties rightfully belonging to the English people as a whole.
Christ as Universal Reason or Logos justifies intellectual liberty and educational pursuits in *Areopagitica* (1644) and *Of Education* (1644): "The
end, then, of learning is to repair the ruins of our first parents by regaining
to know God aright, and out of that knowledge . . . to imitate him . . . which
being united to the heavenly grace of faith makes up the highest perfection."

John Bunyan

John Bunyan (1628-1688), a second Christian humanist scion of the
Puritan party of the Church of England, produced two classics of seven-
teenth-century spirituality: *Grace Abounding* (1666) and *The Pilgrim's
Progress* (1678, 1684). If *Paradise Lost* was the poetic epic of the English
intellectuals, *Pilgrim's Progress* was the prose epic of the common folk.
Bunyan's life was spent at the opposite end of the social scale from that of
Milton. Of humble origin, Bunyan lived through the Commonwealth and
Protectorate as one of the ordinary men whose aspirations innovators like
Milton articulated. After the restoration of the monarchy in 1660 Bunyan
was arrested for Nonconformist preaching and put in Bedford jail for
twelve years. Had he been willing to alter his views, he might have been
released. But Puritans considered the compromise of one's beliefs with secular authority a tragic flaw, and Bunyan steadfastly refused all such suggestions.

Bunyan's questing for salvation came to expression in *Pilgrim's Progress*,
a work which contributed much to modern Western religious symbolism
and has been a perennial favorite with English-speaking people. Though
the imagery is extracted from Bunyan's experience in the Civil War, *Pilgrim's
Progress* is an allegory of the journey of Christian and his friends Hopeful
and Faithful to the Celestial City. It teaches that one must deny earthly
security and go in search of "life, life eternal life." During the long journey
the travelers must resist the temptations of Worldly-wisemen and Vanity
Fair, pass through the Slough of Despond, and endure a long dark night in
Doubting Castle, their faith being tested at every turn. The real temptation
of the journeying Christian in Bunyan's eyes is conforming to the legalistic
arguments and practices of worldly religion. In Part I it is the apprehension
of Christ's love when Christian sees the cross that suddenly relieves him of
the burden of sin and clothes him with a new identity. Christian is transformed into a man who knows what life is about and where he is going.

Part II of *Pilgrim's Progress* describes the journey of a woman Christiana,
her friend Mercy, and four children. These six are joined by a whole group

waiting to cross the Final River. The theme is again pilgrimage, but the distinctive note is that of a family party making a multiple quest. In Part II this "people of God" do not think it necessary to ban from life the human arts. They take an extraordinary sense of pleasure in the body and its delights. The characters dance, eat, drink to the point of being "merry," and stay up all night talking. Bunyan shows compassion and respect for those not cast in the heroic mold of Part I: Mr. Dispondencie and his daughter Much-afraid, Mr. Fearing, Mr. Ready-to-halt, and the children, who get tired, lose their shoes, make embarrassing remarks about others' hospitality, and behave, not as Puritans, but as real children. It is the joining of opposites within the Christian life which Bunyan demonstrates in Part II. The crippled Mr. Ready-to-halt dies with the words "Welcome Life" on his lips. It seems to have been a balanced life that Bunyan himself had finally succeeded in finding.

John Wesley

Puritanism continued to exercise a strong influence in English church life into the eighteenth century. John Wesley (1703-1791) had roots in the Puritan tradition. However, he revolted against the doctrine of predestination in orthodox Puritanism and followed instead the "Arminian" theology imported from Holland. This asserted that Christ died for all people, and not only for the elect. It also claimed that, while divine grace was necessary for salvation, those who hear the gospel have sufficient free will to respond by accepting it. While strongly asserting the authority of Scripture as Word of God, Wesley placed even greater emphasis upon the internal testimony of the Holy Spirit, in the mystical tradition. While teaching that people are justified by faith, he also placed perhaps greater emphasis upon sanctification, holy living, and moral improvement. This led to his most controversial teaching, that of "Christian perfection" or "entire sanctification."

Thus, the founder of Methodism combined a number of contradictory emphases within the Christian tradition. A high-church priest of the Church of England, he became one of the pioneers of modern revivalism. Influenced by Catholic mystical writers, he carried out a highly activist ministry which included preaching over 40,000 sermons in a lifetime of traveling over 200,000 miles within the British Isles. He and his brother Charles (later to become the most prolific hymn-writer of Methodism) formed the "Holy Club" at Oxford in 1729 to advance systematic, liturgical piety (hence "Method") and attendance at the Eucharist. They brilliantly organized the Methodist movement to make full use of lay abilities. After an unsuccessful experience as a missionary in Georgia, John Wesley passed through a conversion experience in 1738 which impelled him upon his great revivalist mission. Censoring the riches, worldliness, and latitude of the Church of England, denied access to its parish churches, Wesley took to preaching to the poor wherever he could find them, particularly in the new industrial cities of northern England. He held services in the open air. "The devil hates field-preaching," he once remarked. While he lived, he struggled to keep his movement within the Church of England, but in the nineteenth century Methodism became a separate denomination in England and America, where it was to have its greatest success.

The humanism of the Methodists had practical results. Wesley and his followers fought from the beginning for the abolition of slavery in the British Empire, which was realized in 1833. Their freer evangelism and more flexible attitudes to the church were better adapted to the industrial conditions of England and frontier life in America than those of the established church. Wesley's sermons appealed particularly to those whose lives were bleak and inadequate. To many working people and artisans Wesley brought color, solace, and hope. The sole influence to counteract early industrial degradation in parts of Britain was to be found in the Methodists. It was in the mining areas around Bristol and Newcastle that the preaching of Wesley gained its first triumphs. From 1740 until 1800 Methodism was the one civilizing influence at work among miners, whether in Durham or in Cornwall, or in the half-tribal principality of Wales. There is no doubt that the Methodist movement was one of the great cultural phenomena of the eighteenth century.

John Henry Newman

John Henry Newman (1801-1890) grew up in the evangelical revival launched by Wesley's preaching, but an understanding of Newman's life and thought is impossible without knowledge of his career at Oxford and as a leader of the Oxford Movement (1833-1845). The Oxford Movement began as an association of university men (Pusey, Keble, Froude, Newman) to prevent the destruction of the influence of church in society by the forces of political and religious liberalism. The crisis of government reform of the Church of England (1833) was at once a foretaste of assaults on the church to be anticipated from liberalism as well as a stimulus to Christian action. Newman's instruments for combating liberalism were the *Tracts for the Times* (1833-1841) and the *Parochial and Plain Sermons* (1834-1839). These are devastating analyses of the nationalistic and individualistic attitudes which were sapping the spiritual strength of the Church of England. Newman presents the argument that there need be no dichotomy between vital religion and revealed dogma, and that a religion unnourished by the realities of dogmatic truth could not maintain vital spiritual life in a revolutionary age.

After joining the Roman Catholic Church in 1845 Newman wrote and preached in England as a priest of the Oratory of St. Philip Neri. In the 1850s he was asked by the Irish bishops to found a Catholic University in

Dublin. It was an opportunity to provide for the higher education of the laity. Newman hoped that the Catholic University would be a meeting place for clergy and laity and would enable them to work together. But his proposed university ended in failure, and in the 1860s and 1870s a suspicion of heresy hung over Newman's head, and his influence was undermined, particularly by the Archbishop of Westminster, Henry Manning, and the London Oratorians. Since Newman's death in 1890 his influence has spread wide and deep in the Catholic church and beyond.

Newman was dangerous in the nineteenth century because he described the church not as a clerical hierarchy, but as the people of God. It is the body of Christ as a whole which exercises the functions of Christ as prophet, priest, and king. This conception required that an end be brought to the division of the church into two cultures—clerical and lay—with their separate systems of education and ways of life. Newman defined the laity's function in positive terms, a vocation to "make the church present and operative in those places and circumstances where only through them [the laity] can it become the salt of the earth."

Newman wrote against those who claimed that the church fulfills its function by committing its members to specific social and political programs. The church's function is to form and deepen persons—persons so formed will bear upon their society. Through them the church works to humanize existing social, political, and industrial institutions.

The Lux Mundi School

The majority of the adherents to the Oxford Movement stayed within the Church of England and evolved into the Anglo-Catholic party which flowed into another stream of Christian humanism from 1860 to 1900. The Anglo-Catholics conveyed two impressions. One was that they were a persecuted minority fighting secular civilization in the face of the disdainful frowns of Evangelicals and the sneers of Erastians. They were upholding the Catholic tradition and reintroducing the people of England to their forgotten heritage. The other impression conveyed was that the future lay with them. Anglo-Catholics pointed to parish after parish in industrial districts in which church life had been dull, formal, and stagnant before the arrival of some human, warmhearted priest who knew exactly why he had come to the parish: to teach certain definite truths and to gather around him a compact body of believers in sacramental worship who regarded themselves as builders of the Catholic Church of England. These two aspects of the movement were balanced with great skill until the turn of the twentieth century.

Pusey House was opened at Oxford in 1884 to be the intellectual center of Anglo-Catholicism. Its first principal was Charles Gore (1853-1932). Gore and his friends Aubrey Moore, Arthur Lyttleton, H. S. Holland, J. R. Illingworth, E. S. Talbot, and R. C. Moberly addressed the conflict of the Bible and science, particularly the implications of the theory of evolution, in 1889 in *Lux Mundi: A Series of Studies in the Religion of the Incarnation. Lux Mundi* exhibited the conclusions of a generation brought up on the Catholic liturgy of Anglo-Catholic parishes: the Scriptures must be understood as the book of a worshiping community. "The Bible thus ought to be viewed not as a revelation itself," wrote Gore in the introduction to *Lux Mundi*, "but a record of the proclaiming and receiving of a revelation by a body which is still existent and which propounds revelation to us, namely the body of Christians commonly called the Church." *Lux Mundi* argued that the theory of evolution restored the Catholic truth of divine immanence in the incarnation which the deism of the eighteenth century had denied.

A variety of Anglo-Catholic socialism grew up based upon the concept that concrete Christian fellowship had evolved from the incarnation. To Gore and his followers, sacraments were thus both social ceremonies and means for the sanctification of society, symbols of Christ's immanence in nature: "Baptism is our regeneration or our incorporation into the new manhood by the Spirit, and involves a deep break with the past." The Eucharist is the means "to bind into an indissoluble unity our fellowship with God and our fellowship with our brother members in the Church."

Dorothy Sayers

Dorothy Leigh Sayers (1893-1957) is popular again today as a writer of detective fiction. In 1923 she created the learned and urbane gentleman—private eye Lord Peter Wimsey in *Whose Body*, and she wrote 10 more novels and 21 stories about Wimsey and his friend Harriett Vane until 1937. Many of these intricate and sophisticated novels approach the level of serious fiction. They made Dorothy Sayers independently wealthy and famous.

It is less well known that Dorothy Sayers was a lay theologian of considerable knowledge and skill. She is to be classed with other humanists like T. S. Eliot and Charles Williams who were associated with Anglo-Catholicism. Unlike many Christian intellectuals, Sayers did not have an adult conversion experience. She never left the Church of England to rejoin it later. Nor did she join the Church of Rome, though her views of doctrine made her a spokesman for Roman Catholics as well as Anglo-Catholics. She did work her way through an adolescent mistrust of an emotionally pious and sentimental Christianity which paid no attention to the historic creeds. Under the influence of G. K. Chesterton, Sayers became convinced that "dogma is the drama of Christianity." Of Chesterton's influence she later wrote, "He blew out of the Church a quantity of stained glass of a very poor period and let in gusts of fresh air, in which the dead leaves of doctrine danced."

Beginning in 1937 and particularly during World War II, Dorothy Sayers turned almost exclusively to religious apologetic. She attended conferences, spoke on the radio, and published articles, books, and plays. Following Chesterton's model, she sought to convey the church's concern over a possible breakdown of civilization, "Western, Mediterranean, and Christian," under the onslaught of Nazi and Soviet totalitarianism. Many of her essays and her book *The Mind of the Maker* deal with the Christian concept of creation, divine and human. Interpreting the creative action of the Holy Trinity in terms of "Idea," "Energy," and "Power," she draws an analogy between the creative activity of God and human artistic (particularly literary) creativity. Her first play, *The Zeal of Thy House* (1937), deals with the construction of Canterbury Cathedral, and her last play, *The Emperor Constantine* (1951), is about political vocation. Dorothy Sayer's Christian humanist doctrine of work is summarized in a Psalm verse from her memorial plaque in the chapel of Somerville College, Oxford: "Praise Him that He hath made man in His own image, a maker and craftsman like Himself."

Christian Humanism on the Continent and in America

Schleiermacher

Six Christian humanists included here are from Continental or American Protestant traditions. Friedrich Schleiermacher (1768-1834) was one of those giants of thought who opened an entirely new era of Protestant theology. The day after he died someone said, "From him a new period in the history of the Church will one day take its origin." The prophecy was accurate. Schleiermacher moved theology to a fresh stage beyond the hardening positions of scholastic orthodoxy and eighteenth century rationalism. He saw religion as a universal human experience, not a set of dogmas. Yet he was committed to the uniqueness of redemption in Jesus Christ, the God-man. Within his theological horizons he found room for the warmhearted piety of his Moravian education and the historical-critical examination of the Christian tradition.

Schleiermacher was educated among Moravian pietists. Later he taught at the University of Halle, a center of German rationalism, and he was one of the founders of the University of Berlin in 1806. His fame as a theologian rested primarily on two works, *Speeches on Religion to Its Cultured Despisers* (1799) and *The Christian Faith* (1821-22). His thought in the *Speeches* represents a reaction against both those who stressed adherence to the dogmas of Christianity and those who reduced Christianity to moralism. Schleiermacher sought to demonstrate that the essence of religion lies in neither intellectual assent nor morality. Rather, he defined it as the inner experience of oneness with God. His word *Gefühl* had a broader meaning than our word "feeling," and included something like intuition. It could be interpreted to mean the relationship of love and trust which informs the concept of faith of the Protestant reformers.

Schleiermacher interpreted redemption as a corporate process. Sin is social as well as individual. Its operation in one individual produces evil in others. Through the fellowship that Jesus founded, the church, fellowship with God is communicated and sustained. Schleiermacher taught that the church is the body of Christ, an organism animated by the Holy Spirit, but that it is also human and mutable. Though he strongly supported the Prussian Union, a union of Lutherans and Calvinists forced upon the churches by the king, his conviction that belief should be free made him an opponent in principle of the union of church and state.

Schleiermacher's theology came under sharp criticism from some twentieth-century theologians. Yet Karl Barth tells the interesting story that on his deathbed Schleiermacher celebrated Holy Communion with his family, using water instead of wine. "Was this a parable of his theology?" Barth asks. "But there can be no doubt of the fact that Schleiermacher . . . wanted in his Christology, whose content might perhaps be compared with the water, to proclaim Christ."

N. F. S. Grundtvig

Nikolai Grundtvig (1783-1872) was what in biblical language is termed a "ten-talent" man. Grundtvig was an active statesman who helped to write a new liberal constitution for his native Denmark in 1849. He was a theologian and churchman whose activity led to the formation of a high church party within the Danish church which still lives on. Although he had charge of no diocese, he was given the honorary title of bishop by the Danish king. He was a leader in the educational, social, and economic life of his country, and a proponent of the Christian Cooperative Movement. He was a scholar of literature, a poet, and a hymn writer of the first rank.

In the realm of education, Grundtvig reacted strongly against both the content and the rote methods of the classical education he had received in the Latin School and the University. While recognizing the need for scholarship in the learned professions, he originated the concept of the folk high school, an institution for the humanistic education of young adults, and launched an effort to create schools all over Denmark where the atmosphere would be free and subjects like history, literature, and the arts of his native country would be emphasized.

When Grundtvig emerged upon the religious scene, Danish theology was dominated by Enlightenment thought. He first became known as "the Bible's lone defender" against the historical critics of the Bible. He discovered that his opponents no longer interpreted Scripture in such a way as to teach traditional Christian doctrine. At this point, he made what he called his "unparalleled discovery." It was that true Christianity had been founded and preserved not by Biblicism, but by the "living word" from God and the "living word" of the Christian community in the sacraments and the creeds of the church. Grundtvigianism was thus a movement paralleling the Oxford Movement in the Church of England.

Although Grundtvig recognized the fallen nature of humankind, his Christian humanism was clearly evident in his insistence that human beings did not lose their human dignity on this account. Despite the fact that he suffered no fewer than three nervous breakdowns in his life, or perhaps because of it, he urged upon his followers a "happy Christianity" in contrast to the rather gloomy piety which prevailed among other Danish Christians. Grundtvig was a person of large heart and broad vision, with a deep appreciation for the Greek and Hebrew traditions and a dream of uniting them with the Nordic.

Walter Rauschenbusch

Walter Rauschenbusch (1861-1918) was the chief theologian of the Social Gospel movement in American Protestantism. A second generation German-American, he was descended from seven generations of clergymen. His immigrant father converted from the Lutheran to the Baptist church, and in significant ways Rauschenbusch represented certain emphases of the continental Anabaptist tradition in his dislike of state churches, his critique of Luther's standpoint in the Peasants' Rebellion, and his sympathy with the poor. However, he learned the latter also as pastor of a small church of poor German immigrants for 11 years in "Hell's Kitchen" on the lower east side of Manhattan.

Rauschenbusch was appointed professor at the Rochester Theological Seminary in 1902. His most productive period coincided with the Progressive Era in American political history. In a series of popular books, beginning with *Christianity and the Social Crisis* (1907), he worked out the Christian Socialist ideas which have led some to call him the most influential Christian of his age. The key phrase in his books is "kingdom of God." Social progress, which for Rauschenbusch meant socialism, was progress toward the kingdom of God, though Rauschenbusch stopped just short of identifying the two.

This new understanding of the kingdom had come to him in New York and continued through the years to inform his understanding of both religion and society. "The kingdom of God is the first and most essential dogma of the Christian faith," Rauschenbusch insisted at the end of his life. "It is the lost social ideal of Christendom. No man is a Christian in the full sense of original discipleship until he has made the kingdom of God the controlling purpose of his life." The notion shaped Rauschenbusch's Christology. He understood Jesus as one who lived close to the Father and therefore is the inaugurator of a new humanity, the first whole man, the initiator of the new kingdom.

Emil Brunner

After World War I the synthesis of personal religion and social concern which had been central to Rauschenbusch proved difficult to maintain. The Social Gospel tended toward secular humanism. The Swiss theologians Karl Barth (1886-1968) and Emil Brunner (1889-1966) made the theological foundations of Rauschenbusch's Christian humanism less acceptable to many Protestants. Brunner, whose major contributions to theology were made between 1927 and 1960, is an excellent guide for the modern student who wants to understand the distinctive ways in which the Christian faith supports a full-bodied humanism, and why Christianity cannot be uncritical over against the assumptions that lie behind secular forms of humanism. Brunner maintains that the Christian faith is the only sure basis for a true humanism. At the same time, he was constantly critical of the church of his time.

The names Brunner and Barth are associated with the "dialectical theology" or the "theology of crisis." "Theology of crisis" points to the grave turning point Western civilization had come to in the 1920s and 1930s with economic depression and the threat of Soviet and Nazi totalitarianism hanging over Europe. "Theology of crisis" also calls attention to the perpetual *krisis* or judgment under which women and men fall when they seek to solve the problems of their destiny with their own power. The judgment of God is operative always on earth, Brunner and Barth maintained, not just at the end of time. Over every institution, every culture, every church stands God's judgment. He constantly intersects the horizontal line of human existence.

From this position the paradoxical character of all that men say or do or create is revealed, hence the "dialectical" character of the Barth-Brunner school. If we claim that God was revealed in Jesus Christ, it must also be said that he was hidden and unknown. If we argue that the church is the body of Christ, it is also a wretched company of sinful men. Ambiguity is present in all human things, including redeemed humanity. A dialectical theology recognizes this paradox and matches this condition. A church whose theology is dialectical will always realize that it stands in need of constant reformation. There will be no claim that the form of the church or the pattern of Christian life has been once and for all set in the past.

Emil Brunner has always had more influence among Anglo-Saxon Christians than Karl Barth, partly because his works have been less hefty than Barth's and also because he has made a number of lecture tours in England, Scotland, and the United States. *The Mediator* (1927), *The Divine Imperative* (1932), *The Divine-Human Encounter* (1937), *Revelation and Reason* (1942), and *Christianity and Civilization* (1948-49), have been appealing to those who have considered themselves the "neo-orthodox."

Reinhold Niebuhr

Reinhold Niebuhr (1892-1971) has been the most profound American theologian of neo-orthodoxy. Like Rauschenbusch, his theology was strongly tempered by world events and by 13 years' service as pastor of a working class church in Detroit. In 1928 he became professor in the Union Seminary in New York, and together with his brother H. Richard Niebuhr of Yale, he became a leader in the neo-orthodox movement in American Protestant theology.

Niebuhr's neo-orthodoxy was typical in its acceptance of the scientific historical-critical approach to the Bible, while at the same time reaffirming the authority of the Bible as divine revelation. He also ascribed crucial importance to the traditional incarnational view of Christ as God and man. His concept of the human, set forth with profundity and power in his most extensive work, *The Nature and Destiny of Man,* was paradoxical: men and women are creatures capable of both great nobility and great depravity.

Niebuhr's special field of interest was Christian social ethics, on which he wrote prolifically. The depression of the 1930s convinced him that capitalism was bankrupt and should be replaced by socialism. The rise of Nazism made him an early and powerful advocate of American intervention against it. He and his colleagues at Union founded the small but influential journal *Christianity and Crisis* to counteract American isolationism and pacifism. His basic standpoint was that while perfection in this world is impossible, improvement is always possible. While love must always represent the ideal in Christian ethics, a measure of justice might be the best that could be hoped for in the complex realm of modern society. Thus, Niebuhr's theology was sometimes called "Christian Realism." He managed to combine the traditional gospel of eternal salvation with active social concern in the present world. A powerful preacher, he exercised a prophetic critique of American life, and in his later years he was as persistent a critic of the abuse of United States power as he had been in favor of its use in World War II.

Dietrich Bonhoeffer

Dietrich Bonhoeffer (1906-1945) is perhaps the most famous Christian martyr of World War II. His fragmentary writings, struggles against Nazism, and martyr's death inspired a post-World War II generation questing for new directions in a disturbing world divided by Communist and capitalist power. During his own lifetime, Bonhoeffer's influence was mainly felt in Germany and in ecumenical circles. But since his death in 1945, he has become widely known and enormously influential because of the wide circulation of his *Cost of Discipleship,* his *Ethics* and *Letters and Papers from Prison,* both of which are fragmentary.

Bonhoeffer was born in Breslau, Germany. His father was a noted psychiatrist and professor at Berlin University, where Bonhoeffer studied under the great liberal theologian Adolf von Harnack. But he was most strongly influenced by the "theology of crisis" as set forth by Barth and Brunner. Bonhoeffer also studied for a year at Union Seminary in New York, and he served as a pastor in London and Berlin. He returned briefly to America in 1939, and Reinhold Niebuhr urged him to stay, since he was already known as an opponent of the National Socialists.

But Bonhoeffer returned to Germany, determined to take part in the church's struggle against Nazism and to share in the sufferings which he foresaw for his people. He became the leader of a seminary training pastors for the "Confessing Church," a dissident group opposed to the statist idolatry and the anti-Semitism of the Nazis. Though outlawed by the Gestapo, the seminary continued underground during World War II.

Bonhoeffer became active in the German resistance movement, went on secret negotiating missions abroad, was arrested by the Gestapo, imprisoned for two years and finally hanged in Flossenburg Concentration Camp only days before it was liberated by the American Army. While in prison, he corresponded secretly with his family, friends, and fiancee, who preserved his letters, later published as *Letters and Papers from Prison*. The circumstances of Bonhoeffer's life and death contributed to the impact of his first published work, *The Cost of Discipleship* (1937), in which he launches an attack on the "cheap grace" being dispensed by the church ostensibly based upon Luther's principle of "justification by grace alone." Cheap grace offered Christians an excuse for avoiding the costly obligations of discipleship.

Bonhoeffer's theological position, like that of "crisis theology," was strongly Christological. He made the closest identification of Christ and the church. He argued that Christ exists today as the church or, in his words, the church is "Christ existing as community." For Bonhoeffer, since Christ is not merely Lord of the church but of the entire world, the church cannot be something apart from the world as an enclave within it, but, like its Lord, the church is there in and for the world.

Bonhoeffer was a relentless opponent of all dualisms or "two-sphere thinking" which permitted what Luther called the "two kingdoms" to be separated. Such separation resulted in a claim of autonomy by the state and denied to the church any voice in political matters. Over and over Bonhoeffer stressed that God's presence is not to be found only at the periphery of existence and knowledge, where human resources run out, but at the center of human existence, in strength and in knowledge, not in weakness and ignorance and negation. Bonhoeffer's theology reasserts the strongly humanistic potential of classic Christian theology as a basis for Christians to deal creatively and redemptively with the secular world.

Roman Catholics

Four of the documents in Part Six are Roman Catholic. Two are the work of German theologians. Two are official pronouncements of the Roman Catholic Church. Two are from the nineteenth century; two are from the twentieth century.

J. A. Möhler

Johann Adam Möhler (1796-1838) was one of a circle of young Catholic theologians at the University of Tübingen in southwestern Germany who sought to do for German Catholicism what Schleiermacher had done for German Protestantism. After growing up in southern Germany amid the ruins of church and state which were the aftermath of the Napoleonic regime, Möhler traveled to Berlin to hear Schleiermacher and to study with Schleiermacher's disciple, the patristic historian Augustus Neander, in 1822. Möhler returned to Tübingen in 1825 and published two of the most important books of nineteenth-century Catholic ecclesiology: *The Unity in the Church* (1825) and *Symbolism* (1832). In 1833 Möhler was forced out of Tübingen by the Protestant government of Württemberg, and he died in 1838, while teaching at the University of Munich.

Möhler knew of the Young Hegelians in Germany who described religion as the destroyer of community. But the Catholic theologian defended religious institutions. To him the church was the architect of social cohesion. Möhler looked to the past and found the Christian fathers. Around the fathers there had been unity. Around Möhler there was atomization. In the early church spiritual authority dispensed solicitous paternalism. Now it fostered compulsory exploitation. In the early church there were sympathetic relationships. Now the attitude of the businessman prevailed.

Möhler argued that Christian unity could once again be the source of social stability in Europe. Its ground was not the clergy or the state but the communal life of all believers. To Möhler the essence of the church was the people, not the hierarchy. The collective life of the Christian people was the only medium through which Spirit could break into the world. Spirit is present in the church because the church is the continuation of the incarnation. Möhler's definition of the church as a corporate unity with a mystical Spirit, rather than as a legal entity, is based on the incarnation. The people themselves are the body of Christ, participators in divinity. The goal of the incarnation, the uniting of matter and spirit, is continually carried out in the assembly of Christians.

Like many of his German contemporaries, Möhler found freedom only in the imposition of external bonds. He wrote that the individual controlled by the will of the community was freed from personal aberration and made healthy and normal. A social body is thus necessary for the survival of civilization, and the Christian church alone can be that body. By the end of his career Möhler proclaimed that Christianity could transform daily existence if the faithful would but see that religion is not concepts and dogmas, but a life lived in common.

Leo XIII

Throughout the nineteenth century the papacy suffered a severe loss of power, wealth, and prestige. Paradoxically, however, the Vatican experienced a remarkable spiritual revival. A movement called Ultramontanism induced Roman Catholics to look beyond the Alps to Rome for authoritative guidance. Two Popes, Pius IX and Leo XIII, provided strong leadership during lengthy reigns. Leo XIII reigned from 1878 to 1903 and published a number of important encyclicals. For Christian humanism the most influential papal pronouncement of the nineteenth century is Leo's encyclical *Rerum novarum* (1891).

Rerum novarum was a milestone because in it for the first time the Roman Catholic Church expressed sympathy with the laboring class. While reaffirming the traditional right of private property and rejecting the inevitability of class conflict as asserted by the Marxists, *Rerum novarum* asserted the right of labor to a living wage and decent working conditions. An organic model of society is favored, stressing cooperation between classes. It was especially significant that in 1891 for the first time the Pope sanctioned labor unions. The Pope also encouraged state intervention to prevent exploitation of labor.

Leo's encyclical turned out to be a Janus-faced document which served as an endorsement for milder forms of fascist rule and as a summons to almost revolutionary Catholic action. Later Catholic social teaching, such as Pius XI's *Quadragesimo Anno* (1931), built on the foundation of Leo's *Rerum novarum*. During World War II its principles inspired the Christian Democrats of France, Italy, and Germany, who played a militant role in Resistance movements. These same principles stimulated widespread Catholic support of the welfare state.

Romano Guardini

Romano Guardini (1885-1968) was the pivotal figure in the revival of the Catholic Church in Germany which opened the way for the radical reforms of Vatican II. Guardini is a symbolic early twentieth-century intellectual who was drawn to the church as much by secular as by ecclesiastical influences. He was born in Italy, educated at a number of German universities, including Tübingen, and profoundly influenced by the Benedictine liturgical revival at the German abbeys of Beuron and Maria Laach. Guardini preached to large student audiences at the University of Berlin in the 1920s and '30s. From a castle above the Main River he led the Catholic Youth

Movement (Quickborn) until the S.S. arrived in 1939. At Burg Rothenfels he experimented with facing the people during the celebration of the Eucharist in the round and revived ancient vigil services. At Rothenfels he preached that solidarity based on a youthful Christianity would redeem mankind from an eternal slavery to soulless technology.

Above all, Guardini told his contemporaries that humankind would escape the cleavage of modern life through Christian worship. His conception of how to achieve community stood between two disparate European political groups. National Socialists taught that the good life of the past had been destroyed by modernization. The only solution for meaningful existence lay in a rejection of the present and no accommodation with industrial or urban society. Totalitarian order would return to Europe through escape into art, or the mystery of a nationalistic religion, or abandonment of the values of the West. Intellectuals of the left countered with the argument that communistic order could be restored out of the chaos of industrialism by embracing the materialism of the technical world.

Balancing right and left, Guardini urged that the community must not reject existence in the contemporary world. But the choking life of materialism would be transcended only if men adopted a system of values whose end was not man himself but reached beyond man and mere concern with the standard of living. The community is formed by that act of reaching beyond. That act is the liturgy of the mass. The liturgy expresses the authenticity, austerity, simplicity, dignity, and "other-ness," which overcomes the industrial world.

Vatican II

The rediscovery of the communal dimension of the Roman Church begun in Möhler, the renewal of social mission in the pontificate of Leo XIII, and the revival of liturgical worship all culminated in the Second Vatican Council (1961-1964). The documents of Vatican II are a milestone of Christian humanism and a summation of the themes of the 300 years of Christian thought outlined here. The Vatican II documents point out how profoundly Christianity is a communion of people together with God. To the Council, social conscience reflects the communal dimension of human beings that is only brought to fulfillment in the body of Christ. To insist upon an individual experience of God and a secular commitment to man makes Christianity the enemy of integral human life. To the Council such a dichotomy contradicts the command of Jesus that we love one another as he loves us, and it contradicts the New Testament description of the church as a *koinonia,* a community.

GALILEO GALILEI

The Letter to the Grand Duchess Christina is Galileo's most carefully considered expression of his opinions on the proper relation of scientific revolution to religion. It was written in 1615 as the culmination of controversies with churchmen which had simmered for four years.

Galileo (1564-1642) begins the letter with a review of the violent opposition which his discoveries had brought down upon him. He asks why Copernicus's book *De Revolutionibus* should be condemned by those who have never read it. The next section of the *Letter* concerns the relation of the Bible to science. Galileo points out that the Scriptures never err when the true meaning is understood. He warns, however, that the biblical exegete who confines himself to unadorned grammatical meanings may find himself in trouble, because many Bible verses are abstruse and mean something different from what the bare words signify. Galileo closes the *Letter* with a warning about proper authority in science and religion. In physical matters one should begin looking for the truth not from the authority of Scripture passages but from "sense experience and necessary demonstrations." Christians should look not to Bible teachers who "gain a reputation for wisdom without effort or study" but to the teaching magisterium of the church for interpretation of Scripture.

The *Letter to Christina* was not printed until many years later because of Galileo's condemnation by the Inquisition. The *Letter* was finally published at Strasbourg in 1635 with Galileo's Italian and Latin texts on facing pages. The edition was small, and the book was rigorously suppressed in Roman Catholic countries.

From Galileo, Letter to the Grand Duchess Christina

Some years ago, as Your Serene Highness well knows, I discovered in the heavens many things that had not been seen before our own age. The novelty of these things, as well as some consequences which followed from them in contradiction to the physical notions commonly held among academic philosophers, stirred up against me no small number of professors—as if I had placed these things in the sky with my own hands in order to upset nature and overturn the sciences. They seemed to forget that the increase of known truths stimulates the investigation, establishment, and growth of the arts; not their diminution or destruction.

Showing a greater fondness for their own opinions than for truth, they sought to deny and disprove the new things which, if they had cared to look for themselves, their own senses would have demonstrated to them. To this end they hurled various charges and published numerous writings filled with vain arguments, and they made the grave mistake of sprinkling these with passages taken from places in the Bible which they had failed to understand properly, and which were ill suited to their purposes.

These men would perhaps not have fallen into such error had they but paid attention to a most useful doctrine of St. Augustine's, relative to our making positive statements about things which are obscure and hard to understand by means of reason alone. Speaking of a certain physical conclusion about the heavenly bodies, he wrote: "Now keeping always our respect for moderation in grave piety, we ought not to believe anything inadvisedly on a dubious point, lest in favor to our error we conceive a prejudice against something that truth hereafter may reveal to be not contrary in any way to the sacred books of either the Old or the New Testament."

Well, the passage of time has revealed to everyone the truths that I previously set forth; and, together with the truth of the facts, there has come to light the great difference in attitude between those who simply and dispassionately refused to admit the discoveries to be true, and those who combined with their incredulity some reckless passion of their own. . . .

Persisting in their original resolve to destroy me and everything mine by any means they can think of, these men are aware of my views in astronomy and philosophy. They know that as to the arrangement of the parts of the universe, I hold the sun to be situated motionless in the center of the revolution of the celestial orbs while the earth rotates on its axis and revolves about the sun. They know also that I support this position not only by refuting the arguments of Ptolemy and Aristotle, but by producing many counter-effects whose causes can perhaps be assigned in no other way. In addition there are astronomical arguments derived from many things in my new celestial discoveries that plainly confute the Ptolemaic system while admirably agreeing with and confirming the contrary hypothesis. Possibly because they are disturbed by the known truth of other propositions of mine which differ from those commonly held, and therefore mistrusting their defense so long as they confine themselves to the field of philosophy, these men have resolved to fabricate a shield for their fallacies out of the mantle of pretended religion and the authority of the Bible. These they apply, with little judgment, to the refutation of arguments that they do not understand and have not even listened to.

First they have endeavored to spread the opinion that such propositions in general are contrary to the Bible and are consequently damnable and heretical. They know that it is human nature to take up causes whereby a man may oppress his neighbor, no matter how unjustly, rather than those from which a man may receive some just encouragement. Hence they have had no trouble in finding men who would preach the damnability and heresy of the new doctrine from their very pulpits with unwonted confidence, thus doing impious and inconsiderate injury not only to that doctrine and its followers but to all mathematics and mathematicians in general. Next, becoming bolder, and hoping (though vainly) that this seed which first took root in their hypocritical minds would send out branches and ascend to heaven, they began scattering rumors among the people that before long this doctrine would be condemned by the supreme authority. They know, too, that official condemnation would not only suppress the two propositions which I have mentioned, but would render damnable all other astronomical and physical statements and observations that have any necessary relation or connection with these. . . .

I think in the first place that it is very pious to say and prudent to affirm that the holy Bible can never speak untruth—whenever its true meaning is understood. But I believe nobody will deny that it is often very abstruse, and may say things which are quite different from what its bare words signify. Hence in expounding the Bible if one were always to confine oneself to the unadorned grammatical meaning, one might fall into error. Not only contradictions and propositions far from true might thus be made to appear in the Bible, but even grave heresies and follies. Thus it would be necessary to assign to God feet, hands, and eyes, as well as corporeal and human affections, such as anger, repentance, hatred, and sometimes even the forgetting of things past and ignorance of those to come. These propositions uttered by the Holy Ghost were set down in that manner by the sacred scribes in order to accommodate them to the capacities of the common people, who are rude and unlearned. For the sake of those who deserve to be separated from the herd, it is necessary that wise expositors should produce the true senses of such passages, together with the special reasons for which they were set down in these words. This doctrine is so widespread and so definite with all theologians that it would be superfluous to adduce evidence for it.

Hence I think that I may reasonably conclude that whenever the Bible has occasion to speak of any physical conclusion (especially those which are very abstruse and hard to understand), the rule has been observed of avoiding confusion in the minds of the common people which would render them contumacious toward the higher mysteries. Now the Bible, merely to condescend to popular capacity, has not hesitated to obscure some very important pronouncements, attributing to God himself some qualities extremely remote from (and even contrary to) His essence. Who, then, would positively declare that this principle has been set aside, and the Bible has confined itself rigorously to the bare and restricted sense of its words, when speaking but casually of the earth, of water, of the sun, or of any other created thing? Especially in view of the fact that these things in no way concern the primary purpose of the sacred writings, which is the service of God and the salvation of souls—matters infinitely beyond the comprehension of the common people.

This being granted, I think that in discussions of physical problems we ought to begin not from the authority of scriptural passages, but from sense-experiences and necessary demonstrations; for the holy Bible and the phenomena of nature proceed alike from the divine Word, the former as the dictate of the Holy Ghost and the latter as the observant executrix of God's commands. It is necessary for the Bible, in order to be accommodated to the understanding of every man, to speak many things which appear to differ from the absolute truth so far as the bare meaning of the words is concerned. But Nature, on the other hand, is inexorable and immutable; she never transgresses the laws imposed upon her, or cares a whit whether her abstruse reasons and methods of operation are understandable to men. For that reason it appears that nothing physical which sense-experience sets before our eyes, or which necessary demonstrations prove to us, ought to be called in question (much less condemned) upon the testimony of biblical passages which may have some different meaning beneath their words. For the Bible is not chained in every expression to conditions as strict as those which govern all physical effects; nor is God any less excellently revealed in Nature's actions than in the sacred statements of the Bible. Perhaps this is what Tertullian meant by these words:

"We conclude that God is known first through Nature, and then again, more particularly, by doctrine; by Nature in His works, and by doctrine in His revealed word." . . . If I may speak my opinion freely, I should say further that it would perhaps fit in better with the decorum and majesty of the sacred writings to take measures for preventing every shallow and vulgar writer from giving to his compositions (often grounded upon foolish fancies) an air of authority by inserting in them passages from the Bible, interpreted (or rather distorted) into senses as far from the right meaning of Scripture as those authors are near to absurdity who thus ostentatiously adorn their writings. Of such abuses many examples might be produced, but for the present I shall confine myself to two which are germane to these astronomical matters. The first concerns those writings which were published against the existence of the Medicean planets recently discovered by me, in which many passages of holy Scripture were cited. Now that everyone has seen these planets, I should like to know what new interpretations those same antagonists employ in expounding the Scripture and excusing their own simplicity. My other example is that of a man who has lately published, in defiance of astronomers and philosophers, the opinion that the moon does not receive its light from the sun but is brilliant by its own nature. He supports this fancy (or rather thinks he does) by sundry texts of Scripture which he believes cannot be explained unless his theory is true; yet that the moon is inherently dark is surely as plain as daylight.

It is obvious that such authors, not having penetrated the true senses of the Scripture, would impose upon others an obligation to subscribe to conclusions that are repugnant to manifest reason and sense, if they had any authority to do so. God forbid that this sort of abuse should gain countenance and authority, for then in a short time it would be necessary to proscribe all the contemplative sciences. People who are unable to understand perfectly both the Bible and the sciences far outnumber those who do understand. The former, glancing super-ficially through the Bible, would arrogate to themselves the authority to decree upon every question of physics on the strength of some word which they have misunderstood, and which was employed by the sacred authors for some different purpose. And the smaller number of understanding men could not dam up the furious torrent of such people who would gain the majority of followers simply because it is much more pleasant to gain a reputation for wisdom without effort or study than to consume oneself tirelessly in the most laborious disci-plines. Let us therefore render thanks to Almighty God, who in His beneficence protects us from this danger by depriving such persons of all authority, reposing the power of consultation, decision, and decree on such important matters in the high wisdom and benevolence of most prudent Fathers, and in the supreme authority of those who cannot fail to order matters properly under the guidance of the Holy Ghost. Hence we need not concern ourselves with the shallowness of those men whom grave and holy authors rightly reproach, and of whom in particular St. Jerome said, in reference to the Bible:

"This is ventured upon, lacerated, and taught by the garrulous old woman, the doting old man, and the prattling sophist before they have learned it. Others, led on by pride, weigh heavy words and philoso-phize amongst women concerning holy Scripture. Others—oh, shame! —learn from women what they teach to men, and (as if that were not enough) glibly expound to others that which they themselves do not understand. I forbear to speak of those of my own profession who, attaining a knowledge of the holy Scriptures after mundane learning, tickle the ears of the people with affected and studied expressions, and declare that everything they say is to be taken as the law of God. Not bothering to learn what the prophets and the apostles have maintained, they wrest incongruous testimonies into their own senses—as if distorting passages and twisting the Bible to their individual and contradictory whims were the genuine way of teaching, and not a corrupt one." . . .

Let us grant then that theology is conversant with the loftiest divine contemplation, and occupies the regal throne among sciences by dignity. But acquiring the highest authority in this way, if she does not descend to the lower and humbler speculations of the subordinate sciences and has no regard for them because they are not concerned with blessedness, then her professors should not arrogate to themselves the authority to decide on controversies in professions which they have neither studied nor practiced. Why, this would be as if an absolute despot, being neither a physician nor an architect but knowing himself free to command, should undertake to administer medicines and erect buildings according to his whim—at grave peril of his poor patients' lives, and the speedy collapse of his edifices.

Again, to command that the very professors of astronomy themselves see to the refutation of their own observations and proofs as mere fallacies and sophisms is to enjoin something that lies beyond any possibility of accomplishment. For this would amount to commanding that they must not see what they see and must not understand what they know, and that in searching they must find the opposite of what they actually encounter. Before this could be done they would have to be taught how to make one mental faculty command another, and the inferior powers the superior, so that the imagination and the will might be forced to believe the opposite of what the intellect understands. I am referring at all times to merely physical propositions, and not to supernatural things which are matters of faith.

I entreat those wise and prudent Fathers to consider with great care the difference that exists between doctrines subject to proof and those subject to opinion. Considering the force exerted by logical deductions, they may ascertain that it is not in the power of the professors of demonstrative sciences to change their opinions at will and apply themselves first to one side and then to the other. There is a great difference between commanding a mathematician or a philosopher and influencing a lawyer or a merchant, for demonstrated conclusions about things in nature or in the heavens cannot be changed with the same facility as opinions about what is or is not lawful in a contract, bargain, or bill of exchange. This difference was well understood by the learned and holy Fathers, as proven by their having taken great pains in refuting philosophical fallacies. This may be found expressly in some of them; in particular, we find the following words of St. Augustine: "It is to be held as an unquestionable truth that whatever the sages of this world have demonstrated concerning physical matters is in no way contrary to our Bibles; hence whatever the sages teach in their books that is contrary to the holy Scriptures may be concluded without any hesitation to be quite false. And according to our ability let us make this evident, and let us keep the faith of our Lord, in whom are hidden all the treasures of wisdom, so that we neither become seduced by the verbiage of false philosophy nor frightened by the superstition of counterfeit religion."

From the above words I conceive that I may deduce this doctrine: That in the books of the sages of this world there are contained some physical truths which are soundly demonstrated, and others that are merely stated; as to the former, it is the office of wise divines to show that they do not contradict the holy Scriptures. And as to propositions which are stated but not rigorously demonstrated, anything contrary to the Bible involved by them must be held undoubtedly false and should be proved so by every possible means.

BLAISE PASCAL

Toward the end of his life Pascal (1623-1662) was known to be engaged upon an "Apology" for Christianity, which was to be an antidote to the Jesuits on the one hand and to the emerging freethinkers on the other. By 1658 the work was sufficiently advanced to enable Pascal to give an outline of his scheme in a lecture at Port-Royal. At his death in 1662 the "Apology" was still incomplete, and the materials consisted of a mass of papers of all sorts and sizes, gathered together in bundles, but in no order. In 1670 Pascal's executors published the notes as an anthology of random *Thoughts on Religion and Other Topics* (in French, *Les Pensées*).

Some hearers had not forgotten Pascal's 1658 lecture, and later editions arranged the *Thoughts* according to the arguments of Pascal's projected "Apology." After a preface in which Pascal affirms his intention of appealing to the heart as well as to the understanding in the duty of seeking God and loving him, the plan of the "Apology" is unfolded. There are two parts dealing with man—without God, and with God. Pascal concludes that man without God is a jumble of incompatible elements. In relation to the universe, humans are all out of proportion; in relation to themselves, they are a mixture of misery, feebleness, and corruption.

The theme of Part II is human happiness with God. Pascal reviews secular philosophies and non-Christian religions and is disgusted at their triviality. A close study of the Bible proves it to be the only document that accurately portrays man and reveals God, solves the contradictions of human existence, and promises a remedy for human ills. Christ is the fulfillment of the Bible. He is the Center of all history, the Redeemer, Chief in the Order of Creation, which is the theme of all Scripture. His life and death have set before humankind an ideal. His followers form his body, the church, being members both of him and of one another.

In the *Pensées* we behold the threefold Pascal: the scientist putting forward Christianity as a solution to the problem of human destiny; the man of the world showing the hollowness of non-Christian life; and the Christian putting forward his own experience that others might partake of his joy.

From Pascal, **Pensées**

43. . . . Let man then contemplate Nature in her full and lofty majesty, and turn his eyes away from the mean objects which surround him. Let him look at that dazzling light hung aloft as an eternal lamp to lighten the universe; let him behold the earth, a mere dot compared with the vast circuit which that orb describes, and stand amazed to find that the vast circuit itself is but a very fine point compared with the orbit traced by the stars as they roll their course on high.

But if our vision halts there, let imagination pass beyond; it will fail to form a conception long before Nature fails to supply material. The whole visible world is but an imperceptible speck in the ample bosom of Nature. No notion comes near it. Though we may extend our thought beyond imaginable space, yet compared with reality we bring to birth mere atoms. Nature is an infinite sphere whereof the centre is everywhere, the circumference nowhere. In short, imagination is brought to silence at the thought, and that is the most perceptible sign of the all-power of God.

Let man reawake and consider what he is compared with the reality of things; regard himself lost in this remote corner of Nature; and from the tiny cell where he lodges, to wit the Universe, weigh at their true worth earth, kingdoms, towns, himself. What is man face to face with infinity? . . .

Let us then know our limits. We are something, but we are not all; such existence as we have deprives us of the knowledge of first principles whose source is the Nothing; and the pettiness of our existence hides from our sight the Infinite.

Our intelligence stands in the order of Intelligibles just where our body does in the vast realm of Nature. Confined as we are in every way, this middle state between two extremes figures in all our faculties. Our senses perceive nothing extreme; too much noise deafens us, too much light blinds, too great distance or too great nearness hampers vision, too many words, or too few, obscure speech, too much truth baffles us

(I know some men who cannot understand that four from nought leaves nothing), first principles are too plain for us, too much pleasure is a bore, too many concords in music are unpleasing, too many benefits are an annoyance. We desire means to overpay the debt: *"Benefits bestowed are welcome so long as they seem capable of repayment; after that, gratitude turns to resentment."* We feel neither extreme heat nor extreme cold. Qualities in excess are hostile to us and imperceptible, we do not feel them—we suffer them.

Extreme youth, and extreme age block the mind, like too much or too little instruction. In short, extremes are for us non-existent, and we are nothing to them. They escape us or we escape them.

Such is a true condition, rendering us incapable of certain knowledge or of absolute ignorance. We sail over a vast expanse, ever uncertain, ever adrift, carried to and fro. To whatever point we think to fix and fasten ourselves it shifts and leaves us; and if we pursue it it escapes our grasp, slips away, fleeing in eternal flight. Nothing stays for us. That is our condition, natural, yet most contrary to our inclination; we have a burning desire to find a sure resting place and a final fixed basis whereon to build a tower rising to the Infinite; but our whole foundation cracks, and the earth yawns to the abyss. Let us then cease to look for security and stability. Our reason is ever cheated by misleading appearances: nothing can fix the finite between the two Infinites which enclose it and fly from it. . . .

And what completes our incapacity to know things is the fact that they are simple in themselves, whereas we are composed of two natures, opposite and different in kind, viz. soul and body. For it is impossible that the reasoning part in us should be other than spiritual; and, though it were claimed that we are simply corporeal, that would far more exclude us from the knowledge of things, there being nothing so inconceivable as to say that matter knows itself; we cannot possibly know how it should know itself.

And so, if we are simply material, we can know nothing at all, and if we are composed of spirit and matter we cannot know perfectly things that are simple, whether spiritual or corporeal.

Hence it comes that almost all philosophers confound ideas, and speak of corporeal things in terms of spirit, and of spiritual things in terms of matter. For they say boldly that bodies tend to fall, seek their centre, fly from destruction, fear the void; that the thing possesses inclinations, sympathies, antipathies, which are all attributes that belong to mind alone. And, speaking of spirits, they regard them as possessing locality, and they assign to them movement from place to place, qualities belonging to body alone.

Instead of accepting these things in their pure simplicity, we tinge them with our own qualities, and we set the stamp of our composite being upon the simple things that lie before us.

You would surely think, when you see how we form everything of mind and body, that the resulting blend would be quite intelligible to us. Yet that is what we comprehend least of all. Man is to himself the most abnormal object in Nature, for he cannot conceive what body is, still less what is mind, and least of all how a body can be united to a mind. This is man's crowning difficulty, and yet it is his essential being. *"How the spirit is attached to the body is incomprehensible to man, and yet this is what man is."* Finally, to complete the proof of our weakness, I shall conclude by the two following considerations. . . .

44. Two infinites, the mean: Reading too fast or too gently you are unintelligible.

45. Too much and too little wine: give him none, he cannot find truth; similarly if you give him too much. . . .

193. It is not good to be too free. It is not good to have all one wants. . . .

240. Other religions, such as heathenism, are more popular, for they are all external; but they are not for men of ability. A purely intellectual religion would better suit *them;* but it would not help the commonalty. Christianity alone, with its blend of external and internal, is suited to all. It uplifts the commonalty inwardly, and humbles the proud outwardly; to be perfect it needs both; the commonalty must understand the spirit of the letter, the able submit their spirit to the letter. . . .

310. Between us and hell or heaven there is only life, and that is the most fragile thing in the world. . . .

558. . . . *Jesus Christ. Duties*

He had, alone, to bring forth a great people, elect, holy, and chosen; lead them, feed them, bring them to a place of rest and holiness; consecrate them to God, save them from the wrath of God, deliver them from the bondage of sin which reigneth visibly in man; give this people laws, grave them upon their hearts, offer Himself to God on their behalf, sacrifice Himself for them, be a victim without blemish and Himself the sacrificing priest: having to offer Himself, His Body and His Blood, and yet to offer bread and wine to God. . . .

564. I contemplate Jesus Christ in all individuals and in ourselves: Jesus Christ as father in His Father, Jesus Christ as brother in His brethren, Jesus Christ as poor in the poor, Jesus Christ as rich in the rich, Jesus Christ as doctor and priest in the priests, Jesus Christ as sovran in princes, etc. For by His glory, being God, He is all that is great, and by His mortal life all that is mean and abject. For this cause He has taken this state of misery that He might be in all individuals, and the pattern for all conditions. . . .

569. As Jesus Christ dwelt among men, unknown, so His truth lies hidden among common opinions with no apparent difference. So the Eucharist amid ordinary bread. . . .

585. Not only do we not know God save through Jesus Christ, but we know not ourselves save through Jesus Christ. We know neither life nor death save through Jesus Christ. Apart from Jesus Christ we know not what our life is, nor our death, nor God, nor ourselves.

Thus without Scripture, whose sole object is Jesus Christ, we know nothing, we see nothing but darkness and confusion in God's nature and our own.

615. To be a member is to have no life, being, or movement save by the spirit of the body and for the sake of the body. A severed member, failing to see the body to which it belongs, has henceforth but a decaying and dying existence. Yet it fancies itself to be a whole and, seeing no body upon which it depends, it fancies that it depends upon itself, and tries to make itself its own centre and body. But, having in itself no vital principle, it is lost in bewildered uncertainty as to its own being, for it feels that it is not a body, and yet does not see that it is a member of a body. At length, when it comes to know itself, it is, so to speak, at home again, and it loves itself for the sake of the body alone. It laments its past errors. Its nature forbids its loving another thing, save for its own self, and in order to master that thing, for each thing loves itself above all else. But in loving the body it loves itself, because it has no existence save in the body, through it and for it: "He who is joined to God is one spirit." . . .

The body loves the hand; and the hand, did it possess a will, should love itself, just as it is loved by the soul. Any love going beyond this is wrong.

"He who is joined to God is one spirit." I love myself because I am a member of Jesus Christ. I love Jesus Christ because He is the body of which I am a member. All is one, the one is in the other, as in the Trinity of persons. . . .

625. . . . So I open my arms to my Liberator who, after 4,000 years of being foretold, came to suffer and die for me on earth, at the time and under the circumstances foretold; and by His Grace I await death in peace, in the hope of eternal union with Him; and meanwhile I live happy, whether amid the blessings which He vouchsafes to bestow, or amid the woes which He sends for my welfare and which by His example He has taught me to bear.

626. The heart has its own reasons which Reason does not know; a thousand things declare it. I say that the heart loves the universal Being naturally, and itself naturally, according to its obedience to either; and it hardens against one or the other, as it pleases. You have cast away the one and kept the other; do you love by reason?

JOHN MILTON

Paradise Regained was published in 1671 and is a sequel to *Paradise Lost.* The poem is a further witness to the incarnation as central to understanding the ways of God with man. Not Christ's atonement, but his life, his successful resistance to Satan, provides the appropriate symbol of humanity's potential.

John Milton (1608-1674) presents here almost a Christian Platonic dialogue between Christ and Satan. The poem's subject is the temptation of the Son of God in the wilderness. Satan attempts to seduce Jesus with earthly power and classical learning. By withstanding Satan's wiles Jesus comes to understand his own nature, gains a paradise of inward peace, and demonstrates that trust and obedience belong to God alone.

The poet emphasizes that the Son's obedience and suffering are an ethical pattern opposed to the egoistic, conquering secular hero. The glory of true heroism is not of ambition, war, or violence.

From John Milton, **Paradise Regained**

THE FOURTH BOOK

Perplex'd and troubl'd at his bad success
The Tempter stood, nor had what to reply,
Discover'd in his fraud, thrown from his hope,
So oft, and the persuasive Rhetoric
That sleek't his tongue, and won so much on *Eve*,   5
So little here, nay lost; but *Eve* was *Eve*,
This far his over-match, who self-deceiv'd
And rash, beforehand had no better weigh'd

The strength he was to cope with, or his own:
But as a man who had been matchless held   10
In cunning, overreach't where least he thought,
To salve his credit, and for very spite
Still will be tempting him who foils him still,
And never cease, though to his shame the more;
Or as a swarm of flies in vintage time,   15
About the wine-press where sweet must is pour'd,
Beat off, returns as oft with humming sound;
Or surging waves against a solid rock,
Though all to shivers dash't, th'assault renew,
Vain batt'ry, and in froth or bubbles end;   20
So Satan, whom repulse upon repulse
Met ever, and to shameful silence brought,
Yet gives not o'er though desperate of success,
And his vain importunity pursues.
He brought our Savior to the western side
Of that high mountain, whence he might behold   25
Another plain, long but in breadth not wide;
Wash'd by the Southern Sea, and on the North
To equal length back'd with a ridge of hills
That screen'd the fruits of th'earth and seats of men
From cold *Septentrion* blasts, thence in the midst   30
Divided by a river, of whose banks
On each side an Imperial City stood,
With Towers and Temples proudly elevate
On seven small Hills, with Palaces adorn'd,   35
Porches and Theaters, Baths, Aqueducts,
Statues and Trophies, and Triumphal Arcs,
Gardens and Groves presented to his eyes,
Above the height of Mountains interpos'd:
By what strange Parallax or Optic skill   40
Of vision multiplied through air, or glass
Of telescope, were curious to inquire:
And now the Tempter thus his silence broke.
    The City which thou seest no other deem
Than great and glorious *Rome*, Queen of the Earth   45
So far renown'd, and with the spoils enrich't
Of Nations; there the Capitol thou seest,
Above the rest lifting his stately head
On the *Tarpeian rock*, her Citadel
Impregnable, and there Mount *Palatine*
Th'Imperial Palace, compass huge, and high   50

The Structure, skill of noblest Architects,
With gilded battlements, conspicuous far,
Turrets and Terraces, and glittering Spires.
Many a fair Edifice besides, more like   55
Houses of Gods (so well I have dispos'd
My Airy Microscope) thou may'st behold
Outside and inside both, pillars and roofs
Carv'd work, the hand of fam'd Artificers
In Cedar, Marble, Ivory or Gold.   60
Thence to the gates cast round thine eye, and see
What conflux issuing forth or ent'ring in,
Praetors, Proconsuls to thir Provinces
Hasting or on return, in robes of State;
Lictors and rods, the ensigns of thir power,   65
Legions and Cohorts, turms of horse and wings:
Of Embassies from Regions far remote
In various habits on the *Appian* road,
Or on th'*Aemilian*, some from farthest South,
Syene, and where the shadow both way falls   70
Meroe, Nilotic Isle, and more to West,
The Realm of *Bocchus* to the Blackmoor Sea;
From the *Asian* Kings and *Parthian* among these,
From *India* and the golden *Chersonese,*
And utmost *Indian* Isle *Taprobane,*   75
Dusk faces with white silken Turbans wreath'd;
From *Gallia, Gades,* and the *British* West,
Germans and *Scythians,* and *Sarmatians* North
Beyond *Danubius* to the *Tauric* Pool.
All Nations now to *Rome* obedience pay,   80
To *Rome's* great Emperor, whose wide domain
In ample Territory, wealth and power,
Civility of Manners, Arts, and Arms,
And long Renown thou justly mayst prefer
Before the *Parthian;* these two Thrones except,   85
The rest are barbarous, and scarce worth the sight,
Shar'd among petty Kings too far remov'd;
These having shown thee, I have shown thee all
The Kingdoms of the world, and all thir glory.
This Emperor hath no Son, and now is old,   90
Old and lascivious, and from *Rome* retir'd
To *Capreae,* an Island small but strong
On the *Campanian* shore, with purpose there
His horrid lusts in private to enjoy,

Committing to a wicked Favorite   95
All public cares, and yet of him suspicious,
Hated of all, and hating. With what ease,
Endu'd with Regal Virtues as thou art,
Appearing, and beginning noble deeds,
Might'st thou expel this monster from his Throne   100
Now made a sty, and in his place ascending
A victor people free from servile yoke?
And with my help thou mayst; to me the power
Is given, and by that right I give it thee.
Aim therefore at no less than all the world,   105
Aim at the highest, without the highest attain'd
Will be for thee no sitting, or not long
On David's Throne, be prophesi'd what will.
   To whom the Son of God unmov'd replied.
Nor doth this grandeur and majestic show   110
Of luxury, though call'd magnificence,
More than of arms before, allure mine eye,
Much less my mind; though thou should'st add to tell
Thir sumptuous gluttonies, and gorgeous feasts
On *Citron* tables or *Atlantic* stone,   115
(For I have heard, perhaps have read)
Their wines of *Setia*, *Cales*, and *Falerne*,
Chios and *Crete*, and how they quaff in Gold,
Crystal and Murrhine cups emboss'd with Gems
And studs of Pearl, to me should'st tell who thirst   120
And hunger still: then Embassies thou show'st
From Nations far and nigh; what honor that,
But tedious waste of time to sit and hear
So many hollow compliments and lies,
Outlandish flatteries? then proceed'st to talk   125
Of the Emperor, how easily subdu'd,
How gloriously; I shall, thou say'st, expel
A brutish monster; what if I withal
Expel a Devil who first made him such?
Let his tormentor Conscience find him out;   130
For him I was not sent, nor yet to free
That people victor once, now vile and base
Deservedly made vassal, who once just,
Frugal, and mild, and temperate, conquer'd well,
But govern ill the Nations under yoke   135
Peeling thir Provinces, exhausted all
By lust and rapine; first ambitious grown

Of triumph, that insulting vanity;
Then cruel, by thir sports to blood inur'd
Of fighting beasts, and men to beasts expos'd,   140
Luxurious by thir wealth, and greedier still,
And from the daily Scene effeminate.
What wise and valiant man would seek to free
These thus degenerate, by themselves enslav'd,
Or could of inward slaves make outward free?   145
Know therefore when my season comes to sit
on *David's* Throne, it shall be like a tree
Spreading and overshadowing all the Earth,
Or as a stone that shall to pieces dash
All Monarchies besides throughout the world,   150
And of my Kingdom there shall be no end:
Means there shall be to this, but what the means,
Is not for thee to know, nor me to tell.
     To whom the Tempter impudent replied.
I see all offers made by me how slight   155
Thou valu'st, because offer'd, and reject'st:
Nothing will please the difficult and nice,
Or nothing more than still to contradict:
On th'other side know also thou, that I
On what I offer set as high esteem,   160
Nor what I part with mean to give for naught;
All these which in a moment thou behold'st,
The Kingdoms of the world to thee I give;
For giv'n to me, I give to whom I please
No trifle; yet with this reserve, not else,   165
On this condition, if thou wilt fall down,
And worship me as thy superior Lord.
Easily done, and hold them all of me;
For what can less so great a gift deserve?
     Whom thus our Savior answer'd with disdain.   170
I never lik'd thy talk, thy offers less,
Now both abhor, since thou hast dar'd to utter
Th'abominable terms, impious condition;
But I endure the time, till which expir'd,
Thou hast permission on me. It is written   175
The first of all Commandments, Thou shalt worship
The Lord thy God, and only him shalt serve;
And dar'st thou to the Son of God propound
To worship thee accurst, now more accurst
For this attempt bolder than that on *Eve*,   180

And more blasphémous? which expect to rue.
The Kingdoms of the world to thee were giv'n,
Permitted rather, and by thee usurp't,
Other donation none thou canst produce:
If given, by whom but by the King of Kings,   185
God over all supreme? If giv'n to thee,
By thee how fairly is the Giver now
Repaid? But gratitude in thee is lost
Long since. Wert thou so void of fear or shame,
As offer them to me the Son of God,   190
To me my own, on such abhorred pact,
That I fall down and worship thee as God?
Get thee behind me; plain thou now appear'st
That Evil one, Satan for ever damn'd.
   To whom the Fiend with fear abasht replied.   195
Be not so sore offended, Son of God,
Though Sons of God both Angels are and Men;
If I to try whether in higher sort
Than these thou bear'st that title, have propos'd
What both from Men and Angels I receive,   200
Tetrarchs of fire, air, flood, and on earth
Nations besides from all the quarter'd winds,
God of this world invok't and world beneath;
Who then thou art, whose coming is foretold
To me so fatal, me it most concerns.   205
The trial hath indamag'd thee no way,
Rather more honor left and more esteem;
Mee naught advantag'd, missing what I aim'd.
Therefore let pass, as they are transitory,
The Kingdoms of this world; I shall no more   210
Advise thee, gain them as thou canst, or not.
And thou thyself seem'st otherwise inclin'd
Than to a worldly Crown, addicted more
To contemplation and profound dispute,
As by that early action may be judg'd.   215
When slipping from thy Mother's eye thou went'st
Alone into the Temple; there wast found
Among the gravest Rabbis disputant
On points and questions fitting *Moses'* Chair,
Teaching not taught; the childhood shows the man,   220
As morning shows the day. Be famous then
by wisdom; as thy Empire must extend,
So let extend thy mind o'er all the world,

In knowledge, all things in it comprehend.
All knowledge is not couch't in *Moses'* Law,   225
The *Pentateuch* or what the Prophets wrote;
The *Gentiles* also know, and write, and teach
To admiration, led by Nature's light;
And with the *Gentiles* much thou must converse,
Ruling them by persuasion as thou mean'st,   230
Without thir learning how wilt thou with them,
Or they with thee hold conversation meet?
How wilt thou reason with them, how refute
Thir Idolisms, Traditions, Paradoxes?
Error by his own arms is best evinc't.   235
Look once more ere we leave this specular Mount
Westward, much nearer by Southwest, behold
Where on the *Aegean* shore a City stands
Built nobly, pure the air, and light the soil
Athens, the eye of *Greece,* Mother of Arts   240
and Eloquence, native to famous wits
Or hospitable, in her sweet recess,
City or Suburban, studious walks and shades;
See there the Olive Grove of *Academe,*
Plato's retirement, where the *Attic* Bird   245
Trills her thick-warbl'd notes the summer long;
There flow'ry hill *Hymettus* with the sound
Of Bees' industrious murmur oft invites
To studious musing; there *Ilissus* rolls
His whispering stream; within the walls then view   250
The schools of ancient Sages; his who bred
Great *Alexander* to subdue the world;
Lyceum there, and painted *Stoa* next;
There thou shalt hear and learn the secret power
Of harmony in tones and numbers hit   255
By voice or hand, and various-measur'd verse,
Aeolian charms and *Dorian Lyric* Odes.
And his who gave them breath, but higher sung,
Blind *Melesigenes* thence *Homer* call'd,
Whose Poem *Phoebus* challeng'd for his own.   260
Thus what the lofty grave Tragedians taught
In *Chorus* or *Iambic,* teachers best
Of moral prudence, with delight received
In brief sententious precepts, while they treat
Of fate, and chance, and change in human life,   265
High actions, and high passions best describing:

Thence to the famous Orators repair,
Those ancients, whose resistless eloquence
Wielded at will that fierce Democracy,
Shook the Arsenal and fulmin'd over to *Greece,*   270
To *Macedon,* and *Artaxerxes'* Throne;
To sage Philosophy next lend thine ear,
From Heaven descended to the low-rooft house
Of *Socrates,* see there his Tenement,
Whom well inspir'd the Oracle pronounc'd   275
Wisest of men; from whose mouth issu'd forth
Mellifluous streams that water'd all the schools
Of Academics old and new, with those
Surnam'd *Peripatetics,* and the Sect
Epicurean, and the *Stoic* severe,   280
These here revolve, or, as thou lik'st, at home
Till time mature thee to a Kingdom's weight;
These rules will render thee a King complete
Within thyself, much more with Empire join'd.
    To whom our Savior sagely thus replied.   285
Think not but that I know these things; or think
I know them not; not therefore am I short
Of knowing what I ought: he who receives
Light from above, from the fountain of light,
No other doctrine needs, though granted true;   290
But these are false, or little else but dreams,
Conjectures, fancies, built on nothing firm.
The first and wisest of them all profess'd
To know this only, that he nothing knew;
The next to fabling fell and smooth conceits   295
A third sort doubted all things, though plain sense;
Others in virtue plac'd felicity,
But virtue join'd with riches and long life;
In corporal pleasure he, and careless ease;
The Stoic last in Philosophic pride,   300
By him call'd virtue; and his virtuous man
Wise, perfect in himself, and all possessing
Equal to God, oft shames not to prefer,
As fearing God nor man, contemning all
Wealth, pleasure, pain or torment, death and life,   305
Which when he lists, he leaves, or boasts he can,
For all his tedious talk is but vain boast,
Or subtle shifts conviction to evade.
Alas! what can they teach, and not mislead;

Ignorant of themselves, of God much more, 310
And how the world began, and how man fell
Degraded by himself, on grace depending?
Much of the Soul they talk, but all awry,
And in themselves seek virtue, and to themselves
All glory arrogate, to God give none, 315
Rather accuse him under usual names,
Fortune and Fate, as one regardless quite
Of mortal things. Who therefore seeks in these
True wisdom, finds her not, or by delusion
Far worse, her false resemblance only meets, 320
An empty cloud. However, many books
Wise men have said are wearisome; who reads
Incessantly, and to his reading brings not
A spirit and judgment equal or superior
(And what he brings, what needs he elsewhere seek) 325
Uncertain and unsettl'd still remains,
Deep verst in books and shallow in himself,
Crude or intoxicate, collecting toys,
And trifles for choice matters, worth a sponge;
As Children gathering pebbles on the shore. 330
Or if I would delight my private hours
With Music or with Poem, where so soon
As in our native Language can I find
That solace? All our Law and Story strew'd
With Hymns, our Psalms with artful terms inscrib'd 335
Our Hebrew Songs and Harps in *Babylon,*
That pleas'd so well our Victors' ear, declare
That rather *Greece* from us these Arts deriv'd;
Ill imitated, while they loudest sing
The vices of thir Deities, and thir own 340
In Fable, Hymn, or Song, so personating
Thir Gods ridiculous, and themselves past shame.
Remove their swelling Epithets thick laid
As varnish on a Harlot's cheek, the rest,
Thin sown with aught of profit or delight, 345
Will far be found unworthy to compare
With *Sion's* songs, to all true tastes excelling,
Where God is prais'd aright, and Godlike men,
The Holiest of Holies, and his Saints;
Such are from God inspir'd, not such from thee; 350
Unless where moral virtue is express'd
By light of Nature, not in all quite lost.

Thir Orators thou then extoll'st, as those
The top of Eloquence, Statists indeed,
And lovers of thir Country, as may seem;   355
But herein to our Prophets far beneath,
As men divinely taught, and better teaching
The solid rules of Civil Government
In thir majestic unaffected style
Than all the Oratory of *Greece* and *Rome*.   360
In them is plainest taught, and easiest learnt,
What makes a Nation happy, and keeps it so,
What ruins Kingdoms, and lays Cities flat;
These only, with our Law, best form a King.
  So spake the Son of God; but Satan now   365
Quite at a loss, for all his darts were spent,
Thus to our Savior with stern brow replied.
  Since neither wealth, nor honor, arms nor arts,
Kingdom nor Empire pleases thee, nor aught
By me propos'd in life contemplative,   370
Or active, tended on by glory, or fame,
What dost thou in this World? The Wilderness
For thee is fittest place; I found thee there,
And thither will return thee; yet remember
What I foretell thee; soon thou shalt have cause   375
To wish thou never hadst rejected thus
Nicely or cautiously my offer'd aid,
Which would have set thee in short time with ease
On *David's* Throne, or Throne of all the world,
Now at full age, fulness of time, thy season   380
When Prophecies of thee are best fulfill'd.
Now contrary, if I read aught in Heaven,
Or Heav'n write aught of Fate, by what the Stars
Voluminous, or single characters
In their conjunction met, give me to spell,   385
Sorrows, and labors, opposition, hate,
Attends thee, scorns, reproaches, injuries,
Violence and stripes, and lastly cruel death.
A Kingdom they portend thee, but what Kingdom,
Real or Allegoric I discern not,   390
Nor when, eternal sure, as without end,
Without beginning; for no date prefixt
Directs me in the Starry Rubric set.
  So saying he took (for still he knew his power
Not yet expir'd) and to the Wilderness   395

Brought back the Son of God, and left him there,
Feigning to disappear. Darkness now rose,
As daylight sunk, and brought in louring night,
Her shadowy offspring, unsubstantial both,
Privation mere of light and absent day.   400
Our Savior meek and with untroubl'd mind
After his airy jaunt, though hurried sore,
Hungry and cold betook him to his rest,
Wherever, under some concourse of shades
Whose branching arms thick intertwin'd might shield   405
Few dews and damps of night his shelter'd head;
But shelter'd slept in vain, for at his head
The Tempter watch'd, and soon with ugly dreams
Disturb'd his sleep; and either Tropic now
'Gan thunder, and both ends of Heav'n; the Clouds   410
From many a horrid rift abortive pour'd
Fierce rain with lightning mixt, water with fire
In ruin reconcil'd: nor slept the winds
Within their stony caves, but rush'd abroad
From the four hinges of the world, and fell   415
On the vext Wilderness, whose tallest Pines,
Though rooted deep as high, and sturdiest Oaks
Bow'd thir Stiff necks, loaden with stormy blasts,
Or torn up sheer: ill wast thou shrouded then,
O patient Son of God, yet only stood'st   420
Unshaken; nor yet stay'd the terror there.
Infernal Ghosts, and Hellish Furies, round
Environ'd thee, some howl'd, some yell'd, some shriek'd,
Some bent at thee thir fiery darts, while thou
Satt'st unappall'd in calm and sinless peace.   425
Thus pass'd the night so foul till morning fair
Came forth with Pilgrim steps in amice gray;
Who with her radiant finger still'd the roar
Of thunder, chas'd the clouds, and laid the winds,
And grisly Specters, which the Fiend had rais'd   430
To tempt the Son of God with terrors dire.
And now the Sun with more effectual beams
Had cheer'd the face of Earth, and dried the wet
From drooping plant, or dropping tree; the birds
Who all things now behold more fresh and green,   435
After a night of storm so ruinous,
Clear'd up their choicest notes in bush and spray
To gratulate the sweet return of morn.

Nor yet amidst this joy and brightest morn
Was absent, after all his mischief done,   440
The Prince of darkness; glad would also seem
Of this fair change, and to our Savior came,
Yet with no new device, they all were spent;
Rather by this his last affront resolv'd,
Desperate of better course, to vent his rage   445
And mad despite to be so oft repell'd.
Him walking on a Sunny hill he found,
Back'd on the North and West by a thick wood;
Out of the wood he starts in wonted shape,
And in a careless mood thus to him said.   450
    Fair morning yet betides thee, Son of God.
After a dismal night; I heard the rack
As Earth and Sky would mingle, but myself
Was distant; and these flaws, though mortals fear them
As dangerous to the pillar'd frame of Heaven,   455
Or to the Earth's dark basis underneath,
Are to the main as inconsiderable
And harmless, if not wholesome, as a sneeze
To man's less universe, and soon are gone;
Yet as being oftimes noxious where they light   460
On man, beast, plant, wasteful and turbulent,
Like turbulencies in the affairs of men,
Over whose heads they roar, and seem to point,
They oft fore-signify and threaten ill:
This Tempest at this Desert most was bent;   465
Of men at thee, for only thou here dwell'st.
Did I not tell thee, if thou didst reject
The perfect season offer'd with my aid
To win thy destin'd seat, but wilt prolong
All to the push of Fate, pursue thy way   470
Of gaining *David's* Throne no man knows when,
for both the when and how is nowhere told,
Thou shalt be what thou art ordain'd, no doubt;
For angels have proclaim'd it, but concealing
The time and means: each act is rightliest done,   475
Not when it must, but when it may be best.
If thou observe not this, be sure to find,
What I foretold thee, many a hard assay
Of dangers, and adversities and pains,
Ere thou of *Israel's* Scepter get fast hold;   480
Whereof this ominous night that clos'd thee round,

So many terrors, voices, prodigies
May warn thee, as a sure foregoing sign.
   So talk'd he, while the Son of God went on
And stay'd not, but in brief him answer'd thus.   485
   Mee worse than wet thou find'st not; other harm
Those terrors which thou speak'st of, did me none;
I never fear'd they could, though noising loud
And threat'ning nigh; what they can do as signs
Betok'ning or ill-boding I contemn   490
As false portents, not sent from God, but thee;
Who, knowing I shall reign past thy preventing,
Obtrud'st thy offer'd aid, that I accepting
At least might seem to hold all power of thee,
Ambitious spirit, and wouldst be thought my God,   495
And storm'st refus'd, thinking to terrify
Mee to thy will; desist, thou art discern'd
And toil'st in vain, nor me in vain molest.
   To whom the Fiend now swoln with rage replied:
Then hear, O Son of *David*, Virgin-born;   500
For Son of God to me is yet in doubt:
Of the Messiah I have heard foretold
By all the Prophets; of thy birth at length
Announc't by *Gabriel*, with the first I knew,
And of the Angelic Song in *Bethlehem* field,   505
On thy Birth-night, that sung thee Savior born.
From that time seldom I have ceas'd to eye
Thy infancy, thy childhood, and thy youth,
Thy manhood last, though yet in private bred;
Till at the Ford of *Jordan* whither all   510
Flocked to the Baptist, I among the rest,
Though not to be Baptiz'd, by voice from Heav'n
Heard thee pronounc'd the Son of God belov'd.
Thenceforth I thought thee worth my nearer view
And narrower Scrutiny, that I might learn   515
In what degree or meaning thou art call'd
The Son of God, which bears no single sense;
The Son of God I also am, or was,
And if I was, I am; relation stands;
All men are Sons of God; yet thee I thought   520
In some respect far higher so declar'd.
Therefore I watch'd thy footsteps from that hour,
And follow'd thee still on to this waste wild,
Where by all best conjectures I collect

Thou art to be my fatal enemy.   525
Good reason then, if I beforehand seek
To understand my Adversary, who
And what he is; his wisdom, power, intent,
By parle, or composition, truce, or league
To win him, or win from him what I can.   530
And opportunity I here have had
To try thee, sift thee, and confess have found thee
Proof against all temptation as a rock
Of Adamant, and as a Center, firm;
To th'utmost of mere man both wise and good,   535
Not more; for Honors, Riches, Kingdoms, Glory
Have been before contemn'd, and may again:
Therefore to know what more thou art than man,
Worth naming Son of God by voice from Heav'n,
Another method I must now begin.   540
    So saying he caught him up, and without wing
Of *Hippogrif* bore through the Air sublime
Over the Wilderness and O'er the Plain;
Till underneath them fair *Jerusalem,*
The holy City, lifted high her Towers,   545
And higher yet the glorious Temple rear'd
Her pile, far off appearing like a Mount
Of Alabaster, top't with golden Spires:
There on the highest Pinnacle he set
The Son of God, and added thus in scorn.   550
    There stand, if thou wilt stand; to stand upright
Will ask thee skill; I to thy Father's house
Have brought thee, and highest plac't, highest is best,
Now show thy Progeny; if not to stand,
Cast thyself down; safely if Son of God: 555
For it is written, He will give command
Concerning thee to his Angels, in thir hands
They shall up lift thee, lest at any time
Thou chance to dash thy foot against a stone.
    To whom thus Jesus. Also it is written   560
Tempt not the Lord thy God; he said and stood.
But Satan smitten with amazement fell
As when Earth's Son *Antaeus* (to compare
Small things with greatest) in *Irassa* strove
With *Jove's Alcides,* and oft foil'd still rose,   565
Receiving from his mother Earth new strength,
Fresh from his fall, and fiercer grapple join'd,

Throttl'd at length in th'Air, expir'd and fell;
So after many a foil the Tempter proud,
Renewing fresh assaults, amidst his pride   570
Fell whence he stood to see his Victor fall.
And as that *Theban* Monster that propos'd
Her riddle, and him who solv'd it not, devour'd
That once found out and solv'd, for grief and spite
Cast herself headlong from th'*Ismenian* steep,   575
So struck with dread and anguish fell, the Fiend,
And to his crew, that sat consulting, brought
Joyless triumphs of his hop't success,
Ruin, and desperation, and dismay,
Who durst so proudly tempt the Son of God.   580
So Satan fell; and straight a fiery Globe
Of Angels on full sail of wing flew nigh,
Who on their plumy Vans receiv'd him soft
From his uneasy station, and upbore
As on a floating couch through the blithe Air,   585
Then in a flow'ry valley set him down
On a green bank, and set before him spread.
A table of Celestial Food, Divine,
Ambrosial, Fruits fetcht from the tree of life,
And from the fount of life Ambrosial drink,   590
That soon refresh'd him wearied, and repair'd
What hunger, if aught hunger had impair'd,
Or thirst; and as he fed, Angelic Choirs
Sung Heavenly Anthems of his victory
Over temptation and the Tempter proud.   595
   True Image of the Father, whether thron'd
In the bosom of bliss, and light of light
Conceiving, or remote from Heaven, enshrin'd
In fleshly Tabernacle, and human form,
Wand'ring the Wilderness, whatever place,   600
Habit, or state, or motion, still expressing
The Son of God, with Godlike force endu'd
Against th' Attempter of thy Father's Throne,
And Thief of Paradise; him long of old
Thou didst debel, and down from Heav'n cast   605
With all his Army; now thou hast aveng'd
Supplanted *Adam*, and by vanquishing
Temptation, hast regain'd lost Paradise,
And frustrated the conquest fraudulent:
He never more henceforth will dare set foot   610

In Paradise to tempt; his snares are broke:
For though that seat of earthly bliss be fail'd,
A fairer Paradise is founded now
For *Adam* and his chosen Sons, whom thou
A Savior art come down to reinstall   615
Where they shall dwell secure, when time shall be
Of Tempter and Temptation without fear.
But thou, Infernal Serpent, shalt not long
Rule in the Clouds; like an Autumnal Star
Or Lightning thou shalt fall from Heav'n trod down   620
Under his feet: for proof, ere this thou feel'st
Thy wound, yet not thy last and deadliest wound
By this repulse receiv'd, and hold'st in Hell
No triumph; in all her gates *Abaddon* rues
Thy bold attempt; hereafter learn with awe   625
To dread the Son of God: hee all unarm'd
Shall chase thee with the terror of his voice
From thy Demoniac holds, possession foul,
Thee and thy Legions; yelling they shall fly,
And beg to hide them in a herd of Swine,   630
Lest he command them down into the deep,
Bound, and to torment sent before thir time.
Hail Son of the most High, heir of both worlds,
Queller of Satan, on thy glorious work
Now enter, and begin to save mankind.   635
    Thus they the Son of God our Savior meek
Sung Victor, and from Heavenly Feast refresht
Brought on his way with joy; hee unobserv'd
Home to his Mother's house private return'd.

The End

JOHN BUNYAN

    The religious activity of John Bunyan (1628-1688) brought him repeated imprisonment. He began *The Pilgrim's Progress* in Bedford jail. Part I was published in 1678 and won instant and enormous popularity. Part II followed in 1684.

    Part II describes the pilgrimage of Christiana, Mercy, four children, and then a whole group who wait together to cross the Final River. Along the way they meet Mr. Valiant-for-truth, bloody and scarred from the terrible battles he has fought. They wash his wounds, give him food, and he, too, joins the pilgrimage. He sings them a song about the constancy of the pilgrim "who would true valour see," which became one of the most popular of all English hymns. Together the party crosses the Enchanted Ground. The children lose their shoes in the mud and others get caught in bushes. They meet Mr. Standfast who is thanking God for his deliverance from the harlot, Madam Bubble, "Mistress of the World," who has offered him her bed, body, and purse. He too joins the company. Finally they emerge into the beauty of the Land of Beulah and wait to cross the river to the Celestial City. There in one of the most famous passages of the *Pilgrim's Progress* Mr. Valiant-for-truth makes his will.

Within four years of writing these lines John Bunyan himself was dead. They serve perhaps as the best of epitaphs for him.

From John Bunyan, **The Pilgrim's Progress**

VALIANT. "I am of Dark-land, for there I was born, and there my father and mother are still."

GREATH. "Darkland," said the guide. "Doth not that lie upon the same coast with the City of Destruction?"

VALIANT. "Yes, it doth. Now that which caused me to come on pilgrimage was this: we had one Mr. Tell-true came into our parts, and he told about what Christian had done that went from the City of Destruction, namely, how he had forsaken his wife and children and had betaken himself to a pilgrim's life. It was also confidently reported how he had killed a serpent that did come out to resist him in his journey, and how he got through to whither he intended. It was also told what welcome he had at all his Lord's lodgings, especially when he came to the gates of the Celestial City. 'For there,' said the man, 'he was received with sound of trumpet, by a company of Shining Ones.' He told it also how all the bells in the city did ring for joy at his reception, and what golden garments he was clothed with, with many other things that I shall forbear to relate. In a word, that man so told the story of Christian and his travels that my heart fell into a burning haste to be gone after him, nor could father nor mother stay me. So I got from them and am come thus far on my way."

GREATH. "You came in at the gate, did you not?"

VALIANT. "Yes, yes. For the same man also told us that all would be nothing if we did not begin to enter this way at the gate."

GREATH. "Look you," said the guide to Christiana, "the pilgrimage of your husband, and what he has gotten thereby, is spread abroad far and near."

VALIANT. "Why, is this Christian's wife?"

GREATH. "Yes, that it is, and these are also her four sons."

Valiant.   "What, and going on pilgrimage too?"

Greath.   "Yes, verily, they are following after."

Valiant.   "It glads me at the heart! Good man, how joyful will he be when he shall see them that would not go with him yet to enter after him at the gates into the city."

Greath.   "Without doubt it will be a comfort to him. For next to the joy of seeing himself there, it will be a joy to meet there his wife and his children."

Valiant.   "But now you are upon that, pray, let me see your opinion about it. Some make a question whether we shall know one another when we are there."

Greath.   "Do they think they shall know themselves then? Or that they shall rejoice to see themselves in that bliss? And if they think they shall know and do these, why not know others and rejoice in their welfare also?

"Again, since relations are our second self though that state will be dissolved there, yet why may it not be rationally concluded that we shall be more glad to see them there than to see they are wanting?"

Valiant.   "Well, I perceive whereabout you are as to this. Have you any more things to ask me about my beginning to come on pilgrimage?"

Greath.   "Yes, was your father and mother willing that you should become a pilgrim?"

Valiant.   "Oh, no. They used all means imaginable to persuade me to stay at home."

Greath.   "Why, what could they say against it?"

Valiant.   "They said it was an idle life, and if I myself were not inclined to sloth and laziness I would never countenance a pilgrim's condition."

Greath.   "And what did they say else?"

Valiant.   "Why, they told me that it was a dangerous way. 'Yea, the most dangerous way in the world,' said they, 'is that which the pilgrims go.'"

Greath.   "Did they show wherein this way is so dangerous?"

Valiant.   "Yes, and that in many particulars."

Greath.   "Name some of them."

Valiant.   "They told me of the Slough of Despond where Christian was well nigh smothered. They told me that there were archers standing ready in Beelzebub's Castle to shoot them that should knock at the wicket-gate for entrance. They told me also of the wood and dark mountains, of the Hill Difficulty, of the lions, and also of the three giants, Bloodyman, Maul and Slaygood. They said, moreover, that there was a foul fiend haunted the Valley of Humiliation, and that

Christian was, by him, almost bereft of life. 'Besides,' said they, 'you must go over the Valley of the Shadow of Death, where the hobgoblins are, where the light is darkness, where the way is full of snares, pits, traps, and gins.' They told me also of Giant Despair, of Doubting Castle, and of the ruins that the pilgrims met with there. Further, they said, I must go over the Enchanted Ground, which was dangerous, and that after all this I should find a river, over which I should find no bridge, and that that river did lie betwixt me and the Celestial Country."

GREATH. "And was this all?"

VALIANT. "No, they also told me that this way was full of deceivers and of persons that laid await there to turn good men out of the path."

GREATH. "But how did they make that out?"

VALIANT. "They told me that Mr. Worldly Wiseman did there lie in wait to deceive. They also said that there was Formality and Hypocrisy continually on the road. They said also that By-ends, Talkative, or Demas, would go near to gather me up; that the Flatterer would catch me in his net; or that with greenheaded Ignorance I would presume to go on to the gate, from whence he always was sent back to the hole that was in the side of the hill, and made to go the by-way to hell."

GREATH. "I promise you this was enough to discourage. But did they make an end here?"

VALIANT. "No, stay. They told me also of many that had tried that way of old, and that had gone a great way therein, to see if they could find something of the glory there that so many had so much talked of from time to time; and how they came back again and befooled themselves for setting a foot out-of-doors in that path to the satisfaction of all the country. And they named several that did so, as Obstinate and Pliable, Mistrust and Timorous, Turnaway and old Atheist, with several more, who, they said, had, some of them, gone far to see if they could find. But not one of them found so much advantage by going, as amounted to the weight of a feather."

GREATH. "Said they anything more to discourage you?"

VALIANT. "Yes, they told me of one Mr. Fearing, who was a pilgrim, and how he found this way so solitary that he never had comfortable hour therein; also that Mr. Despondency had like to been starved therein. Yea, and also, which I had almost forgot, that Christian himself, about whom there has been such a noise after all his ventures for a celestial crown, was certainly drowned in the black river, and never went foot further, however it was smothered up."

GREATH. "And did none of these things discourage you?"

VALIANT. "No, they seemed but as so many nothings to me."

GREATH. "How came that about?"

VALIANT. "Why, I still believed what Mr. Tell-true had said, and that carried me beyond them all."

GREATH. "Then this was your victory, even your faith?"

VALIANT. "It was so. I believed and therefore came out, got into the way, fought all that set themselves against me, and by believing am come to this place."

> Who would true valour see,
> Let him come hither;
> One here will constant be,
> Come wind, come weather.
> There's no discouragement
> Shall make him once relent
> His first avowed intent
> To be a pilgrim.
>
> Who so beset him round
> With dismal stories,
> Do but themselves confound;
> His strength the more is.
> No lion can him fright,
> He'll with a giant fight
> But he will have a right
> To be a pilgrim.
>
> Hobgoblin, nor foul fiend
> Can daunt his spirit;
> He knows, he at the end
> Shall life inherit.
> Then fancies fly away,
> He'll fear not what men say;
> He'll labour night and day
> To be a pilgrim.

By this time, they were got to the Enchanted Ground, where the air naturally tended to make one drowsy. And that place was all grown over with briers and thorns, excepting here and there, where was an enchanted arbour, upon which, if a man sits, or in which if a man sleeps, 'tis a question, say some, whether ever they shall rise or wake again in this world. Over this forest therefore they went, both one with another. And Mr. Great-heart went before, for that he was the guide; and Mr. Valiant-for-truth, he came behind, being there a guard, for fear least peradventure some fiend, or dragon, or giant, or thief, should fall upon their rear, and so do mischief. They went on here, each man with his sword drawn in his hand; for they knew it was a dangerous place. Also they cheered up one another as well as they could. Feeble-mind, Mr. Great-heart commanded, should come up after him, and Mr. Despondency was under the eye of Mr. Valiant.

Now they had not gone far, but a great mist and a darkness fell upon them all; so that they could scarce, for a great while, see the one the other. Wherefore they were forced, for some time, to feel for one another by words, for they walked not by sight. . . .

After this it was noised abroad that Mr. Valiant-for-truth was taken with a summons by the same post as the other, and had this for a token that the summons was true, "That his pitcher was broken at the fountain." When he understood it, he called for his friends and told them of it. Then said he, "I am going to my Father's, and though with great difficulty I am got hither, yet now I do not repent me of all the trouble I have been at to arrive where I am. My sword I give to him that shall succeed me in my pilgrimage, and my courage and skill to him that can get it. My marks and scars I carry with me to be a witness for me that I have fought his battles who now will be my rewarder." When the day that he must go hence was come, many accompanied him to the river-side, into which, as he went, he said, "Death, where is thy sting?" And as he went down deeper he said, "Grave, where is thy victory?" [I Corinthians 15:55] So he passed over, and the trumpets sounded for him on the other side.

JOHN WESLEY

"Free Grace" (1740) is the first of the great sermons of John Wesley (1703-1791) to appear after the city of Bristol had become the center of his activity in March 1739. At Bristol Wesley's converts were being repelled from the Lord's Table by the Anglican clergy, and a separate gathering place for the community had been built. To these "New Rooms" thronged the rough coal miners of the Bristol region, who had been neglected by the established church. At these services there were strange breakdowns of the human spirit which puzzled Wesley. He was not an emotional preacher. In cold print his sermons are judicious and rational. Yet apparently his passionate sincerity conferred an almost hypnotic power. "Free Grace" gives some inkling of the power of Wesley's preaching at its best.

The purpose of the sermon is to refute predestination. This idea that God has foredoomed some to Heaven and others to Hell, says Wesley, flatly contradicts Scripture, the whole tenor of which is that God is love. Predestination removes all motives for holiness. It destroys the happiness of Christianity. It removes any reason for good works and makes God a liar.

In "Free Grace" there is little theological speculation about the nature of Christ. But the love of Christ in bestowing saving grace is alluded to countless times. This love is basic to an understanding of Christian life. It is poured out on all persons who will be made whole by its power. It is the high calling of all persons who are in Christ.

The sermon has particular significance when seen against the prevailing deistic conceptions of God and his relation to the world. For Wesley, Christ's personal concern for the world is constant in creation and in the redemption of all persons.

From John Wesley, **Sermon CXXVIII, "Free Grace"**

1. How freely does God love the world! While we were yet sinners, "Christ died for the ungodly." While we were "dead in sin," God "spared not his own Son, but delivered him up for us all." And how freely with him does he "give us all things!" Verily, FREE GRACE is all in all!

2. The grace or love of God, whence cometh our salvation, is FREE IN ALL, AND FREE FOR ALL.

3. First. It is free IN ALL to whom it is given. It does not depend on any power or merit in man; no, not in any degree, neither in whole, nor in part. It does not in anywise depend either on the good works or righteousness of the receiver; not on anything he has done, or anything he is. It does not depend on his endeavours. It does not depend on his good tempers, or good desires, or good purposes and intentions; for all these flow from the free grace of God; they are the streams only, not the fountain. They are the fruits of free grace, and not the root. They are not the cause, but the effects of it. Whatsoever good is in man, or is done by man, God is the author and doer of it. Thus is his grace free in all; that is, no way depending on any power or merit in man, but on God alone, who freely gave us his own Son, and "with him freely giveth us all things."

4. But is it free FOR ALL, as well as IN ALL? To this some have answered, "No: It is free only for those whom God hath ordained to life; and they are but a little flock. The greater part of mankind God hath ordained to death; and it is not free for them. Them God hateth; and, therefore, before they were born, decreed they should die eternally. And this he absolutely decreed; because so was his good pleasure; because it was his sovereign will. Accordingly, they are born for this,— to be destroyed body and soul in hell. And they grow up under the irrevocable curse of God, without any possibility of redemption; for

what grace God gives, he gives only for this, to increase, not prevent, their damnation."

5. This is that decree of predestination. But methinks I hear one say, "This is not the predestination which I hold: I hold only the election of grace. What I believe is no more than this,—that God, before the foundation of the world, did elect a certain number of men to be justified, sanctified, and glorified. Now, all these will be saved, and none else; for the rest of mankind God leaves to themselves: So they follow the imaginations of their own hearts, which are only evil continually, and waxing worse and worse, are at length justly punished with everlasting destruction."

6. Is this all the predestination which you hold? Consider; perhaps this is not all. Do not you believe God ordained them to this very thing? If so, you believe the whole decree; you hold predestination in the full sense which has been above described. But it may be you think you do not. Do not you then believe, God hardens the hearts of them that perish? Do not you believe, he (literally) hardened Pharaoh's heart; and that for this end he raised him up, or created him? Why, this amounts to just the same thing. If you believe Pharaoh, or any one man upon earth, was created for this end,—to be damned,—you hold all that has been said of predestination. And there is no need you should add, that God seconds his decree, which is supposed unchangeable and irresistible, by hardening the hearts of those vessels of wrath whom that decree had before fitted for destruction.

7. Well, but it may be you do not believe even this; you do not hold any decree of reprobation; you do not think God decrees any man to be damned, nor hardens, irresistibly fits him, for damnation; you only say, "God eternally decreed, that all being dead in sin, he would say to some of the dry bones, Live, and to others he would not; that consequently, these should be made alive, and those abide in death,—these should glorify God by their salvation, and those by their destruction."

8. Is not this what you mean by the election of grace? If it be, I would ask one or two questions: Are any who are not thus elected saved? or were any, from the foundation of the world? Is it possible any man should be saved unless he be thus elected? If you say, "No," you are but where you was; you are not got one hair's breadth farther; you still believe, that, in consequence of an unchangeable, irresistible decree of God, the greater part of mankind abide in death, without any possibility of redemption; inasmuch as none can save them but God, and he will not save them. You believe he hath absolutely decreed not to save them; and what is this but decreeing to damn them? It is, in effect, neither more nor less; it comes to the same

thing; for if you are dead, and altogether unable to make yourself alive, then, if God has absolutely decreed he will make only others alive, and not you, he hath absolutely decreed your everlasting death; you are absolutely consigned to damnation. So then, though you use softer words than some, you mean the self-same thing; and God's decree concerning the election of grace, according to your account of it, amounts to neither more nor less than what others call God's decree of reprobation.

9. Call it therefore by whatever name you please, election, preterition, predestination, or reprobation, it comes in the end to the same thing. The sense of all is plainly this,—by virtue of an eternal, unchangeable, irresistible decree of God, one part of mankind are infallibly saved, and the rest infallibly damned; it being impossible that any of the former should be damned, or that any of the latter should be saved.

10. But if this be so, then is all preaching vain. It is needless to them that are elected; for they, whether with preaching or without, will infallibly be saved. Therefore, the end of preaching—to save souls—is void with regard to them; and it is useless to them that are not elected, for they cannot possibly be saved: They, whether with preaching or without, will infallibly be damned. The end of preaching is therefore void with regard to them likewise; so that in either case our preaching is vain, as your hearing is also vain.

11. This, then, is a plain proof that the doctrine of predestination is not a doctrine of God, because it makes void the ordinance of God; and God is not divided against himself. A Second, is, that it directly tends to destroy that holiness which is the end of all the ordinances of God. I do not say, none who hold it are holy; (for God is of tender mercy to those who are unavoidably entangled in errors of any kind;) but that the doctrine itself,—that every man is either elected or not elected from eternity, and that one must inevitably be saved, and the other inevitably damned,—has a manifest tendency to destroy holiness in general; for it wholly takes away those first motives to follow after it, so frequently proposed in Scripture, the hope of future reward and fear of punishment, the hope of heaven and fear of hell. That these shall go away into everlasting punishment, and those into life eternal, is no motive to him to struggle for life who believes his lot is cast already; it is not reasonable for him so to do, if he thinks he is unalterably adjudged either to life or death. You will say, "But he knows not whether it is life or death." What then?—this helps not the matter; for if a sick man knows that he must unavoidably die, or unavoidably recover, though he knows not which, it is unreasonable for him to take any physic at all. He might justly say, (and so I have

heard some speak, both in bodily sickness and in spiritual,) "If I am ordained to life, I shall live; if to death, I shall die; so I need not trouble myself about it." So directly does this doctrine tend to shut the very gate of holiness in general,—to hinder unholy men from every approach thereto, or striving to enter thereat.

12. As directly does this doctrine tend to destroy several particular branches of holiness. Such are meekness and love,—love, I mean, of our enemies,—of the evil and unthankful. I say not, that none who hold it have meekness and love; (for as is the power of God, so is his mercy;) but that it naturally tends to inspire, or increase, a sharpness or eagerness of temper, which is quite contrary to the meekness of Christ; as then especially appears, when they are opposed on this head. And it as naturally inspires contempt or coldness towards those whom we suppose outcasts from God. "O but," you say, "I suppose no particular man a reprobate." You mean you would not if you could help it: But you cannot help sometimes applying your general doctrine to particular persons: The enemy of souls will apply it for you. You know how often he has done so. But you rejected the thought with abhorrence. True; as soon as you could; but how did it sour and sharpen your spirit in the mean time! You well know it was not the spirit of love which you then felt towards that poor sinner, whom you supposed or suspected, whether you would or no, to have been hated of God from eternity.

13. Thirdly. This doctrine tends to destroy the comfort of religion, the happiness of Christianity. This is evident as to all those who believe themselves to be reprobated, or who only suspect or fear it. All the great and precious promises are lost to them; they afford them no ray of comfort: For they are not the elect of God; therefore they have neither lot nor portion in them. This is an effectual bar to their finding any comfort or happiness, even in that religion whose ways are designed to be "ways of pleasantness, and all her paths peace."

14. And as to you who believe yourselves the elect of God, what is your happiness? I hope, not a notion, a speculative belief, a bare opinion of any kind; but a feeling possession of God in your heart, wrought in you by the Holy Ghost, or, the witness of God's Spirit with your spirit that you are a child of God. This, otherwise termed "the full assurance of faith," is the true ground of a Christian's happiness. And it does indeed imply a full assurance that all your past sins are forgiven, and that you are *now* a child of God. But it does not necessarily imply a full assurance of our future perseverance. I do not say this is never joined to it, but that it is not necessarily implied therein; for many have the one who have not the other.

15. Now, this witness of the Spirit experience shows to be much

obstructed by this doctrine; and not only in those who, believing themselves reprobated, by this belief thrust it far from them, but even in them that have tasted of that good gift, who yet have soon lost it again, and fallen back into doubts, and fear, and darkness,—horrible darkness, that might be felt! And I appeal to any of you who hold this doctrine, to say, between God and your own hearts, whether you have not often a return of doubts and fears concerning your election or perseverance! If you ask, "Who has not?" I answer, Very few of those that hold this doctrine; but many, very many, of those that hold it not, in all parts of the earth;—many of those who know and feel they are in Christ to-day, and "take no thought for the morrow;" who "abide in him" by faith from hour to hour, or, rather, from moment to moment;—many of these have enjoyed the uninterrupted witness of his Spirit, the continual light of his countenance, from the moment wherein they first believed, for many months or years, to this day.

16. That assurance of faith which these enjoy excludes all doubt and fear. It excludes all kinds of doubt and fear concerning their future perseverance; though it is not properly, as was said before, an assurance of what is future, but only of what *now* is. And this needs not for its support a speculative belief, that whoever is once ordained to life must live; for it is wrought from hour to hour, by the mighty power of God, "by the Holy Ghost which is given unto them." And therefore that doctrine is not of God, because it tends to obstruct, if not destroy, this great work of the Holy Ghost, whence flows the chief comfort of religion, the happiness of Christianity.

17. Again: How uncomfortable a thought is this, that thousands and millions of men, without any preceding offence or fault of theirs, were unchangeably doomed to everlasting burnings! How peculiarly uncomfortable must it be to those who have put on Christ! to those who, being filled with bowels of mercy, tenderness, and compassion, could even "wish themselves accursed for their brethren's sake!"

18. Fourthly. This uncomfortable doctrine directly tends to destroy our zeal for good works. And this it does, First, as it naturally tends (according to what was observed before) to destroy our love to the greater part of mankind, namely, the evil and unthankful. For whatever lessens our love, must so far lessen our desire to do them good. This it does, Secondly, as it cuts off one of the strongest motives to all acts of bodily mercy, such as feeding the hungry, clothing the naked, and the like,—viz., the hope of saving their souls from death. For what avails it to relieve their temporal wants, who are just dropping into eternal fire? "Well; but run and snatch them as brands out of the fire." Nay, this you suppose impossible. They were appointed thereunto, you say, from eternity, before they had done either good or evil. You

believe it is the will of God they should die. And "who hath resisted his will?" But you say you do not know whether these are elected or not. What then? If you know they are the one or the other,—that they are either elected or not elected,—all your labour is void and vain. In either case, your advice, reproof, or exhortation is as needless and useless as our preaching. It is needless to them that are elected; for they will infallibly be saved without it. It is useless to them that are not elected; for with or without it they will infallibly be damned; therefore you cannot consistently with your principles take any pains about their salvation. Consequently, those principles directly tend to destroy your zeal for good works; for all good works; but particularly for the greatest of all, the saving of souls from death.

19. But, Fifthly, this doctrine not only tends to destroy Christian holiness, happiness, and good works, but hath also a direct and manifest tendency to overthrow the whole Christian Revelation. The point which the wisest of the modern unbelievers most industriously labour to prove, is, that the Christian Revelation is not necessary. They well know, could they once show this, the conclusion would be too plain to be denied, "If it be not necessary, it is not true." Now, this fundamental point you give up. For supposing that eternal, unchangeable decree, one part of mankind must be saved, though the Christian Revelation were not in being, and the other part of mankind must be damned, notwithstanding that Revelation. And what would an infidel desire more? You allow him all he asks. In making the gospel thus unnecessary to all sorts of them, you give up the whole Christian cause. "O tell it not in Gath! Publish it not in the streets of Askelon! lest the daughters of the uncircumcised rejoice; lest the sons of unbelief triumph!"

20. And as this doctrine manifestly and directly tends to overthrow the whole Christian Revelation, so it does the same thing, by plain consequence, in making that Revelation contradict itself. For it is grounded on such an interpretation of some texts (more or fewer it matters not) as flatly contradicts all the other texts, and indeed the whole scope and tenor of Scripture. For instance: The assertors of this doctrine interpret that text of Scripture, "Jacob have I loved, but Esau have I hated," as implying that God in a literal sense hated Esau, and all the reprobated, from eternity. Now, what can possibly be a more flat contradiction than this, not only to the whole scope and tenor of Scripture, but also to all those particular texts which expressly declare, "God is love"? Again: They infer from that text, "I will have mercy on whom I will have mercy," (Rom. ix. 15.) that God is love only to some men, viz., the elect, and that he hath mercy for those only: flatly contrary to which is the whole tenor of Scripture, as is that express declaration in particular, "The Lord is loving unto every man; and his

mercy is over all his works." (Psalm cxlv. 9.) Again: They infer from that and the like texts, "It is not of him that willeth, nor of him that runneth, but of God that showeth mercy," that he showeth mercy only to those to whom he had respect from all eternity. Nay, but who replieth against God now? You now contradict the whole oracles of God, which declare throughout, "God is no respecter of persons:" (Acts x. 34:) "There is no respect of persons with him." (Rom. ii. 11.) Again: from that text, "The children being not yet born, neither having done any good or evil, that the purpose of God according to election might stand, not of works, but of him that calleth; it was said unto her," unto Rebecca, "The elder shall serve the younger;" you infer, that our being predestined, or elect, no way depends on the foreknowledge of God. Flatly contrary to this are all the scriptures; and those in particular, "Elect according to the foreknowledge of God;" (1 Peter i. 2;) "Whom he did foreknow, he also did predestinate." (Rom. viii. 29.)

21. And "the same Lord over all is rich" in mercy "to all that call upon him:" (Rom. x. 12.) But you say, "No; he is such only to those for whom Christ died. And those are not all, but only a few, whom God hath chosen out of the world; for he died not for all, but only for those who were 'chosen in him before the foundation of the world.' " (Eph. i. 4.) Flatly contrary to your interpretation of these scriptures, also, is the whole tenor of the New Testament; as are in particular those texts: —"Destroy not him with thy meat, for whom Christ died," (Rom. xiv. 15.)—a clear proof that Christ died, not only for those that are saved, but also for them that perish: He is "the Saviour of the world;" (John iv. 42;) He is "the Lamb of God that taketh away the sins of the world;" (i. 29;) "He is the propitiation, not for our sins only, but also for the sins of the whole world;" (1 John ii. 2;) "He," the living God, "is the Saviour of all men;" (1 Tim. iv. 10;) "He gave himself a ransom for all;" (ii. 6;) "He tasted death for every man." (Heb. ii. 9.)

22. If you ask, "Why then are not all men saved?" the whole law and the testimony answer, First, Not because of any decree of God; not because it is his pleasure they should die; for, "As I live, saith the Lord God," "I have no pleasure in the death of him that dieth." (Ezek. xviii 3, 32.) Whatever be the cause of their perishing, it cannot be his will, if the oracles of God are true; for they declare, "He is not willing that any should perish, but that all should come to repentance;" (2 Pet. iii. 9;) He willeth that all men should be saved, And they, Secondly, declare what is the cause why all men are not saved, namely, that they will not be saved: So our Lord expressly, "Ye will not come unto me that ye may have life." (John v. 40.) "The power of the Lord is present to heal" them, but they will not be healed. "They reject the counsel,"

the merciful counsel, "of God against themselves," as did their stiff-necked forefathers. And therefore are they without excuse; because God would save them, but they will not be saved: This is a condemnation, "How often would I have gathered you together, and ye would not!" (Matt. xxiii. 37.)

23. Thus manifestly does this doctrine tend to overthrow the whole Christian Revelation, by making it contradict itself; by giving such an interpretation of some texts, as flatly contradicts all the other texts, and indeed the whole scope and tenor of Scripture;—an abundant proof that it is not of God. But neither is this all: For, Seventhly, it is a doctrine full of blasphemy; of such blasphemy as I should dread to mention, but will not suffer me to be silent. In the cause of God, then, and from a sincere concern for the glory of his great name, I will mention a few of the horrible blasphemies contained in this horrible doctrine. But first, I must warn every one of you that hears, as ye will answer it at the great day, not to charge me (as some have done) with blaspheming, because I mention the blasphemy of others. And the more you are grieved with them that do thus blaspheme, see that ye "confirm your love towards them" the more, and that our heart's desire, and continual prayer to God be, "Father, forgive them; for they know not what they do!"

24. This premised, let it be observed, that this doctrine represents our blessed Lord, "Jesus Christ the righteous," "the only begotten Son of the Father, full of grace and truth," as an hypocrite, a deceiver of the people, a man void of common sincerity. For it cannot be denied, that he everywhere speaks as if he was willing that all men should be saved. Therefore, to say that he was not willing that all men should be saved, is to represent him as a mere hypocrite and dissembler. It cannot be denied that the gracious words which came out of his mouth are full of invitations to all sinners. To say, then, he did not intend to save all sinners, is to represent him as a gross deceiver of the people. You cannot deny that he says, "Come unto me, all ye that are weary and heavy laden." If, then you say he calls those that cannot come; those whom he knows to be unable to come; those whom he can make able to come, but will not; how is it possible to describe greater insincerity? You represent him as mocking his helpless creatures, by offering what he never intends to give. You describe him as saying one thing, and meaning another; as pretending the love which he had not. Him, in "whose mouth was not guile," you make full of deceit, void of common sincerity;—then especially, when, drawing nigh the city, He wept over it, and said, "O Jerusalem, Jerusalem, thou that killest the prophets, and stonest them that are sent unto thee; how often *would I* have gathered thy children together,—and *ye would not;*" *ēthelēsa—kai ouch ēthelēsate.*

Now, if you say, *they would,* but *he would not,* you represent him (which who could hear?) as weeping crocodiles' tears; weeping over the prey which himself had doomed to destruction!

25. Such blasphemy this, as one would think might make the ears of a Christian to tingle! But there is yet more behind; for just as it honours the Son, so doth this doctrine honour the Father. It destroys all his attributes at once: It overturns both his justice, mercy, and truth; yea, it represents the most holy God as worse than the devil, as both more false, more cruel, and more unjust. More *false;* because the devil, liar as he is, hath never said, "He willeth all men to be saved:" More *unjust;* because the devil cannot, if he would, be guilty of such injustice as you ascribe to God, when you say that God condemned millions of souls to everlasting fire, prepared for the devil and his angels, for continuing in sin, which for want of that grace *he will not* give them, they cannot avoid: And more *cruel;* because that unhappy spirit "seeketh rest and findeth none;" so that his own restless misery is a kind of temptation to him to tempt others. But God resteth in his high and holy place; so that to suppose him, of his own mere motion, of his pure will and pleasure, happy as he is, to doom his creatures, whether they will or no, to endless misery, is to impute such cruelty to him as we cannot impute even to the great enemy of God and man. It is to represent the most high God (he that hath ears to hear let him hear!) as more cruel, false, and unjust than the devil!

26. This is the blasphemy clearly contained in *the horrible decree* of predestination! And here I fix my foot. On this I join issue with every assertor of it. You represent God as worse than the devil; more false, more cruel, more unjust. But you say you will prove it by Scripture. Hold! What will you prove by Scripture? that God is worse than the devil? It cannot be. Whatever that Scripture proves, it never can prove this; whatever its true meaning be, this cannot be its true meaning. Do you ask, "What is its true meaning then?" If I say, "I know not," you have gained nothing; for there are many scriptures the true sense whereof neither you nor I shall know till death is swallowed up in victory. But this I know, better it were to say it had no sense at all, than to say it had such a sense as this. It cannot mean, whatever it mean besides, that the God of truth is a liar. Let it mean what it will, it cannot mean that the judge of all the world is unjust. No scripture can mean that God is not love, or that his mercy is not over all his works; that is, whatever it prove beside, no scripture can prove predestination.

27. This is the blasphemy for which (however I love the persons who assert it) I abhor the doctrine of predestination, a doctrine, upon the supposition of which, if one could possibly suppose it for a mo-

ment, (call it election, reprobation, or what you please, for all comes to the same thing,) one might say to our adversary, the devil, "Thou fool, why dost thou roar about any longer? Thy lying in wait for souls is as needless and useless as our preaching. Hearest thou not, that God hath taken thy work out of thy hands; and that he doeth it much more effectively? Thou, with all thy principalities and powers, canst only so assault that we may resist thee; but he can irresistibly destroy both body and soul in hell! Thou canst only entice; but his unchangeable decree, to leave thousands of souls in death, compels them to continue in sin, till they drop into everlasting burnings. Thou temptest; He forceth us to be damned; for we cannot resist his will. Thou fool, why goest thou about any longer, seeking whom thou mayest devour? Hearest thou not that God is the devouring lion, the destroyer of souls, the murderer of men? Moloch caused only children to pass through the fire; and that fire was soon quenched; or, the incorruptible body being consumed, its torment was at an end; but God, thou art told, by his eternal decree, fixed before they had done good or evil, causes, not only children of a span long, but the parents also, to pass through the fire of hell, the 'fire which never shall be quenched;' and the body which is cast thereinto, being now incorruptible and immortal, will be ever consuming and never consumed, but 'the smoke of their torment,' because it is God's good pleasure, 'ascendeth up for ever and ever.' "

28. O how would the enemy of God and man rejoice to hear these things were so! How would he cry aloud and spare not! How would he lift up his voice and say, "To your tents, O Israel! Flee from the face of this God, or ye shall utterly perish! But whether will ye flee? Into heaven? He is there. Down to hell? He is there also. Ye cannot flee from an omnipresent, almighty tyrant. And whether ye flee or stay, I call heaven, his throne, and earth, his footstool, to witness against you, ye shall perish, ye shall die eternally. Sing, O hell, and rejoice, ye that are under the earth! For God, even the mighty God, hath spoken, and devoted to death thousands of souls, from the rising of the sun unto the going down thereof! Here, O death, is thy sting! They shall not, cannot escape; for the mouth of the Lord hath spoken it. Here, O grave, is thy victory! Nations yet unborn, or ever they have done good or evil, are doomed never to see the light of life, but thou shalt gnaw upon them for ever and ever! Let all those morning stars sing together, who fell with Lucifer, son of the morning. Let all the sons of hell shout for joy! For the decree is past, and who shall disannul it?"

29. Yea, the decree is past; and so it was before the foundation of the world. But what decree? Even this: "I will set before the sons of men 'life and death, blessing and cursing.' And the soul that chooseth

life shall live, as the soul that chooseth death shall die." This decree, whereby "whom God did foreknow, he did predestinate," was indeed from everlasting; this, whereby all who suffer Christ to make them alive are "elect according to the foreknowledge of God," now standeth fast, even as the moon, and as the faithful witnesses in heaven; and when heaven and earth shall pass away, yet this shall not pass away; for it is as unchangeable and eternal as the being of God that gave it. This decree yields the strongest encouragement to abound in all good works, and in all holiness; and it is a well-spring of joy, of happiness also, to our great and endless comfort. This is worthy of God; it is every way consistent with all the perfections of his nature. It gives us the noblest view both of his justice, mercy, and truth. To this agrees the whole scope of the Christian Revelation, as well as all the parts thereof. To this Moses and all the Prophets bear witness, and our blessed Lord and all his Apostles. Thus Moses, in the name of his Lord: "as I call heaven and earth to record against you this day, that I have set before you life and death, blessing and cursing; therefore choose life, that thou and thy seed may live." Thus Ezekiel: (To cite one Prophet for all:) "The soul that sinneth, it shall die; the son shall not bear" eternally "the iniquity of the father. The righteousness of the righteous shall be upon him, and the wickedness of the wicked shall be upon him." (xviii. 20) Thus our blessed Lord: "If any man thirst, let him come unto me and drink." (John vii. 37.) Thus his great Apostle, St. Paul: (Acts xvii. 30:) "God commandeth all men everywhere to repent;"—"all men everywhere;" every man in every place, without any exception either of place or person. Thus St. James: "If any of you lack wisdom, let him ask of God, who giveth to all men liberally, and upbraideth not, and it shall be given him." (James i. 5.) Thus St. Peter: (2 Pet. iii. 9:) "The Lord is not willing that any should perish, but that all should come to repentance." And thus St. John: "If any man sin, we have an Advocate with the Father; and he is the propitiation for our sins; and not for ours only, but for the sins of the whole world." (1 John ii. 1, 2.)

30. O hear ye this, ye that forget God! Ye cannot charge your death upon him! "Have I any pleasure at all that the wicked should die? saith the Lord God." (Ezek. xviii. 23, etc.) Repent, and turn from all your transgressions; so iniquity shall not be your ruin. Cast away from you all your transgressions whereby ye have transgressed,—for why will ye die, O house of Israel? "For I have no pleasure in the death of him that dieth, saith the Lord God. Wherefore turn yourselves, and live ye." "As I live, saith the Lord God, I have no pleasure in the death of the wicked.—Turn ye, turn ye from your evil ways; for why will ye die, O house of Israel?" (Ezek. xxxiii. 11.)

FRIEDRICH SCHLEIERMACHER

Walking home from a flute concert on the evening of December 2, 1805, a 37-year-old bachelor professor at the University of Halle, Germany, was inspired to write *Christmas Eve: Dialogue on the Incarnation.* Friedrich Schleiermacher (1768-1834) called "the church father of the nineteenth century," wrote the book in three weeks' time, finishing just before Christmas. As a translator of Plato's dialogues, Schleiermacher was familiar with the dialogue form.

The selection "On the Meaning of Christmas" strikes the modern reader as a bit heavy, but it should be noted that the discourses offered by Leonhardt, Ernst, and Edward are preceded and followed by the simple, unaffected joys of a family's Christmas Eve festivities. This arrangement tells us something important about Schleiermacher's approach to Christian reality: theological reflection stems from and is surrounded by the experience of religious faith.

The speakers at the Christmas party reveal the range of Schleiermacher's responses to the birth of Christ. Leonhardt, the young lawyer, muses on how the festival observance keeps the meaning of Christmas alive. Ernst talks about the joyful effects of Christmas. Edward is attracted to the Word becoming flesh, the union of eternal being and human being coming into being. But Josef doesn't want to make a speech; he is content to be glad and sing, to celebrate Christmas.

From Friedrich Schleiermacher, **Christmas Eve: Dialogue on the Incarnation**

IV. ON THE MEANING OF CHRISTMAS

When the visitors had departed, Ernst said: "Well, since it has been decided that we should wait the evening out in conversation and refreshment, I think we men owe the ladies something in return, so that they may be the more willing to stay by us. Story-telling is not the gift of men, however. At any rate, I know how very little I should be expected to produce myself. But what would you think if we were to follow the English fashion, not to say the Greek, of selecting a topic upon which each person is obliged to say something? Indeed, this custom is not altogether strange among us either. And we could choose a subject, and mode of discussing it, by which we would not be led to forget the ladies' presence but would consider it our finest achievement to be understood and approved by them." All agreed, and the women expressed special pleasure since they had not heard the like for a long time.

"All right, then," Leonhardt insisted, "since you ladies are taking such an interest in the proposal you must also give us the topic upon which we are to speak. Otherwise we may clumsily lay hold of something all too farfetched or indifferent to your taste."

"If the others are of the same mind," answered Friederike, "and if it wouldn't be too annoying to you, Leonhardt, I should like to propose Christmas itself as your topic, for it is this which holds us together here tonight. It has so many aspects to it that each person can easily extol it as he likes best."

No one made any objection to this. Ernestine remarked that any other subject would have been strange indeed and would in a way have disrupted the entire evening.

"Very well, then," said Leonhardt, "in accordance with our custom, as the youngest present I cannot refuse to be the first speaker. And I assent to this all the more gladly in part because my inadequate attempt can be most readily supplanted by a better one and partly because I shall most surely enjoy the pleasure of anticipating someone else's first thoughts. I must also note," he smiled, "that your arrangement invisibly doubles the number of speakers. For you will hardly fail to attend church services tomorrow, and it would indeed redound more to our annoyance than to the joy of the preachers if you had to hear the same thing in church all over again—and to you it would perhaps bring boredom at the very most! Therefore I will withdraw as far as possible from their line of thinking and start off my discourse as follows.

"One can extol and praise a thing in either of two ways: first in commending it, by which I mean acknowledging and representing its kind and its inner nature as something good; but then also in honoring it, that is, giving prominence to its comparative excellence and perfection in its kind. Now the first may be set aside, or it may be left to others to give a general commendation of the Christmas festival, as such, however much a good it may be that the remembrance of great events should be secured and furthered by certain rites and traditions repeated at appointed seasons. If there are to be such festivals, however, and if the very earliest beginning of Christianity is to be regarded as something of primary importance, then no one can deny that this festival of Christmas is an admirable one. Look how completely it effects its purpose, and under such difficult conditions too!

"Now consider: if a person wanted to say that the remembrance of the Redeemer's birth is far better preserved through Bible study and general instruction in Christianity than through this festival, I should deny it. Why? Because while it might suffice for us who are well educated, as I think, such would by no means be true for the great mass of uneducated folk. Suppose we leave out the Roman church, where the Scriptures are seldom if ever put into their hands, but stick to our own people; it is manifest how little inclined even they are to read the Bible or prepared even to understand it in proper perspective. What does instruction leave imprinted on their memory? Far more the proofs for particular teachings than the story of the Redeemer. And what do they get out of his story by this method? The death of the Redeemer is far more prominently recalled than his first entrance into the world—and out of his life the details which an instructor can readily pass on and which lend themselves to imitation.

"In relation to the life of the Redeemer, I would contend that the very ease with which we believe in the miracles presumably performed by him chiefly arises from our festival and the impressions it brings to the fore. I think it's obvious that belief in the miraculous rather arises in this way than through outright witness or doctrine. Otherwise how does it happen that the ordinary Roman Catholic Christian believes so much in the miraculous doings of his saints, even though they border on the absurd, yet would not bring himself to believe in anything similar, however alike it may be represented to him to be, of personages belonging to an alien religious or historical circle? And why does he believe in them even though the miracles of his saints have no connection at all with the truths and requirements of Christian faith? Clearly he believes all this because of the holy days set up to honor the saints. Through such festivals, attitudes which would have no persuasive power in the sheer telling take hold when they are tied up with something forcefully presented to the senses, and their hold is continually strengthened in the same way.

"It's exactly what we find in antiquity, when all sorts of strange things from the dim past were chiefly preserved in this fashion. Festivals instigated belief, even in such things as historians and poets say little or nothing of. Indeed, rites so much more effectively serve this purpose than words that not infrequently it was for the sake of festive rites and traditions, after their true signification had been lost to view, that false histories were fabricated and even came to be believed. And we have analogies in the Christian church itself for the converse procedure, in which fables have been devised to augment the miraculous still more and only really come to be believed when holy days are consecrated to them. The festival of the so-called Assumption of the Virgin Mary is such a one.

"If, then, the common folk hold so much more to rites and customs than to narratives and doctrines, we have every reason to believe that in our society belief in the supposedly miraculous events connected with the appearance of the Redeemer is very largely due to our festival and its popular conventions. And in the Catholic church all that relates to Mary aids and abets this, since she is always hailed as the Virgin. So, this consideration, and all that it implies, is the merit for which I honor and praise the festival of Christmas.

"Now I must explain what I meant by saying that the remembrance of Christmas has been especially difficult to preserve and that the merit of the Christmas festival is all the greater because of this. The more that is known of a subject the more definitely and meaningfully can its representation be made; and the more necessarily it fits together with present experience, the more simply can every provision for its recollection be established. But all that pertains to the first appearance of Christ seems to me to lack this entirely. For I'll grant, without hesitation, that Christianity is a vigorous contemporary force. But the personal activity of Christ on earth seems to me to have far less a connection with it than most people believe. I think that, in fact, they rather more suppose than believe in this connection anyway.

"Specifically, what concerns the atonement or reconciliation of the human race through him we all connect with his death first off. But that event turns more upon an eternal decree of God than upon one particular fact, as I think, and we are thus rather obliged not to tie these ideas to a distinct moment but to extend them beyond the temporal history of the Redeemer and to hold them as symbolic. And yet it is natural that the notion of remembering both the death of Christ, as the sign of reconciliation fully accomplished, and his resurrection, as the pledge of it, must be forever fortified among the faithful. Thus the resurrection was also the chief subject of the earliest proclamation and the foundation upon which the church was built, so that it perhaps wouldn't even have been necessary to have a continual repetition of its remembrance by making Sunday a fixed celebration of it.

"Irrespective of the notion of atonement, however, if we consider the human activity of Christ, whose substance is to be sought in the proclamation of his teaching and in the founding of the Christian community, it is astounding how small a part one can rightly ascribe to him within the present configuration of Christianity. Only think of how little of its doctrine or of its institutions can be traced back to Christ himself. By far the most of it is of some later origin. Suppose we arrange all these in a series: John the forerunner of the Messiah, Christ, the apostles (including the apostle Paul), then the early fathers. Surely one must admit that Christ does not stand just midway between the first and the third but that he is much closer to John the Baptist than to Paul. Indeed it remains doubtful whether it was at all in accordance with Christ's will that such an exclusive and tightly organized church should be formed, without which Christianity as we know it—and consequently our festival as well, the subject to which I am to address myself—would be inconceivable.

"For this reason the life of Christ receded far to the background of early proclamation, and as most people now believe, was only told fragmentarily and by persons removed from the actual events, subordinates. Indeed, if one notes the zealous attempt of these early accounts to attach Christ to the old line of Jewish kings—which is nevertheless entirely unimportant, whether the relation holds or not, for the founder of a world religion—then it must be admitted that his life was told only in a subordinate fashion. Christ's supernatural birth, however, seems to have been broadcast through narratives still less; otherwise there could not have been so many Christians at the time who took him to be a man begotten naturally. And thus the truth only appears to have been saved from the rubbish heap and to have retained importance by our festival. For of itself the narration would never have sufficed, because of conflicting views. If the narrators took no notice of these differences, they couldn't have got the story straight; if they did take notice, then to a certain extent they would have become party to the different views rather than witnesses and reporters. For the divergence of accounts is so great that however we may designate it every claim or report undoes the others. Or can anyone claim the resurrection occurred without having to leave it open for anyone to explain the death of Christ as having never happened?—which can mean nothing else than that a later fact declares a view which has been drawn from earlier facts to be false. Similarly, the ascension of Christ to a certain degree throws suspicion upon the truth of his life. For his life belongs to this planet, and what can be divorced from the same cannot have stood in any vital connection with it.

"Just as little remains if one takes the view of those who deny Christ a true body or of those who deny him a true human soul together with the view of people who, on the contrary, will not attribute true deity or even superhumanity to him. Indeed, if one considers the dispute over whether he is still present on earth only in a spiritual and divine way or in that way and in a bodily, sensible way as well, both parties can easily be carried to the point where the common, hidden meaning in their positions is that Christ was never present back then, or lived an earthly existence among his followers, in any different or more distinctive manner than he does now. In short, since what might be experienced and historically valid regarding the personal existence of Christ has become so precarious because of the diversity of views and doctrines, therefore if our festival is primarily to be seen as the basis of a continuing common faith in Christ, it is thereby all the more to be extolled. Moreover, a power is demonstrated within it which borders on what I have already mentioned, namely, that sometimes only through such traditions does history itself come to be made.

"But something else is most to be wondered at in all this—and can serve as an example and reproach with respect to much else. It is that the festival itself evidently owes its prevalence, to a great extent, to the fact that it has been brought into the homes and is celebrated among the children. There is where we ought to fasten down what is valuable and sacred to us, much more than we do. And we should look upon it as a bad sign and a discredit to us that we do not follow this practice.

"This tradition, therefore, we shall want to maintain as it has been handed down to us; and the less surely we can explain wherein its marvelous power lies, the less eager we will be to change even the least detail in it. For me, at least, even the smallest features are full of meaning. Just as a child is the main object of our celebration, so it is also the children above all who elevate the festival and carry it forth—and through it Christianity itself. Just as night is the historic cradle of Christianity, so the birthday celebration of Christianity is begun at nighttime; and the candles with which it sparkles are, as it were, the star above the inn and the halo without which the child would not be discerned in the darkness of the manger or in the otherwise starless night of history. Finally, just as it is dark and doubtful what we have received in the person of Christ and from whom we have received the gift, so that custom which I learned of through Karoline's narrative is also the finest way of giving presents at Christmastime, and the most aptly symbolic. This is my honest opinion, upon which I suggest we touch our glasses and empty them in a toast—a toast to an unending continuation of the Christmas festival! And I am all the more certain of your compliance that I hope thereby to make up for and to wash away everything that may have seemed offensive to you in what I have said."

"Now I understand," said Friederike, "why he made so little objection to our proposal. The unbelieving rascal had in mind speaking completely against its actual meaning! I should like to make him pay plenty for this, especially since I proposed the task and it could well be said that he has made fun of me by the way he chose to carry it out."

"Perhaps you are right," nodded Eduard. "But it would be hard to get at him; for he has taken care, true attorney that he is, to cover himself by prior explanation and by the way he has fused his disparaging remarks with the intention of exalting the Christmas festival, as indeed he had to."

"There is certainly nothing wrong with proceeding like an advocate," Leonhardt rejoined. "And why shouldn't I take every opportunity to exercise such portions of my craft as may be fitting and legitimate?

Besides, I wouldn't dare to say no to the ladies, and they couldn't have provided anything more appropriate to that manner of reflection, to which I openly confess, or for that matter anything which could have avoided it. Only in a way I haven't proceeded as an advocate at all, for nowhere in my discourse have I introduced the slightest appeal for the favor of our fair judges."

"We must also bear you witness," said Ernst, "that you have spared us much that might have been mentioned—whether because you didn't have it in hand or because you forbore it to save time and so as not to speak too learnedly and unintelligibly before the ladies."

"For my part," Ernestine said, "I should like to give him credit for so honorably keeping his promise to stay away, as much as possible, from what we might hear in places of worship tomorrow."

"All right, then," yielded Karoline, "if it is not possible to bring him to judgment straightway, then our first recourse is to refute him. And if I am not mistaken it depends on you, Ernst, to speak up and preserve the honor of our proposal."

Ernst responded: "I do intend to tackle the latter request, but without any refutation—for my part I should not care to have the two joined together. To speak against Leonhardt's notions would distract me from other topics, and then I might become liable to penalty myself. Moreover, for one who is unaccustomed to organized extemporaneous speaking, nothing is more difficult in undertaking it than trying to follow upon another's train of thought."

Ernst began: "Before you spoke, Leonhardt, I should not have known whether what I want to say should be labeled 'commending' or 'honoring.' But now I know that, in its own way it is a kind of honoring. For I too want to praise the Christmas festival as excellent in its kind. Unlike you, I shall not, however, leave up in the air whether the specific idea of the festival and its kind are to be commended as something good, but will rather presuppose this. There is one qualification. Your definition of a festival does not suffice for me. It was onesided, on the whole adapted only to your own requirements. My definition is different and proceeds from another direction. That is, while you only took the point of view that every festival is a commemoration of something, what concerns me is the question of what it commemorates. Accordingly I propose that a festival is founded only to commemorate that through the representation of which a certain mood and disposition can be aroused within men; and I propose, further, that the excellence of any festival consists in the fact that such an effect is realized within its entire scope, and vividly so.

"The mood which our festival is meant to incite is joy. That this mood is very widely and vividly aroused through the Christmas festival is so obvious that nothing more need be said on that score. Everyone can see for himself. Only there is one difficulty which might be mentioned, and I shall have to remove it. One might say that it is in no way distinctive of the Christmas festival or essential to it that it should produce this effect, which is only incidental like the particular presents that are given and received. Now this is plainly false, as I will try to show. Look, if you give children the same gifts at another time, you won't evoke even the semblance of Christmas delight—not unless you come to the corresponding point in their own lives, namely, the celebration of their birthdays. I believe I am right in calling this a corresponding point, and certainly no one will deny that the joy at a birthday has quite a different character from that at Christmastime. One's mood on his birthday has all the intimacy of being confined within a particular set of personal circumstances, while that at Christmastime bears all the fire, the rapid stirring, of a widespread, general feeling. From this we see that it is not the presents in themselves which bring out the joy, but that they are given only because there is already great cause for rejoicing. And the distinctiveness of Christmas, which consists precisely in this great universality, also extends itself to the presents, so that throughout a great part of Christendom—as far as this fine old custom is still observed—everyone is occupied in preparing a gift, and in this awareness lies a great part of its all-pervasive charm.

"Think what it would be like if only a single family held to this observance while all the others in their area had given it up. The impression would no longer be the same—not by a long shot. But the fact that people are planning together for it, working to outdo each other in preparing for the special hours of celebration—and then out-of-doors the Christmas markets, open to all and intended for the whole populace, their lights reflecting off each gift just as sparkling little stars gleam from earth in the snowy winter night as if the reflection of heaven were cast upon it—all this gives the presents their special value.

"Nor can what is so all-inclusive have been arbitrarily devised or agreed upon. Some common inner cause must underlie it, otherwise it cannot have produced so similar an effect or survived as it has, as can be seen quite satisfactorily in contrast with many recent attempts which lacked these conditions. And this inner ground cannot be other than the appearance of the Redeemer as the source of all other joy in the Christian world; and for this reason nothing else can deserve to be so celebrated as this event.

"Some, to be sure, have attempted to transfer the widespread enjoyment of the Christmas season to the New Year, the day on which the changes and contrasts of time are pre-eminent. I cannot draw attention to this view without lodging a complaint against it, and for the reason

I have just stated. Many people, of course, have followed this practice without thinking, and it would be unfair to claim that wherever gifts are exchanged at New Year's instead of at Christmas people are giving little place to the distinctively Christian element in their lives. Yet this divergent custom is connected plainly enough with just such a neglect. New Year's is devoted to the renewal of what is only transitory. Therefore is it especially appropriate that those who, lacking stability of character, live only from year to year should make a special holiday of it.

"All men are subject to the shifts of time. That goes without saying. But some of the rest of us do not desire to have our life in what is only transitory. For us the birth of the Redeemer is the uniquely universal festival of joy, precisely because we believe there is no other principle of joy than redemption. In its progress the birth of the divine Child is the first bright spot. We cannot postpone our joy by waiting for another. Thus, too, no other festival has such a kinship to this universal festival as that of baptism, through which the principle of joy in the divine Child is appropriated to the little ones. And this explains the particular fascination of Agnes' charming account, in which the two were joined.

"Yes, Leonhardt, look at it as we may there is no escaping the fact that the original, natural state of vitality and joy in which there are no opposites of appearance and being, time and eternity, is not ours to possess. And if we think these to exist in one person then we must think of him as Redeemer, and as one who must start out as a divine Child. By contrast, we ourselves begin with the cleavage between time and eternity, appearance and being; and we only attain to harmony through redemption, which is nothing other than the overcoming of these oppositions and which on this account can only proceed from one for whom they have not had to be overcome.

"Certainly no one can deny that. It is the distinctive nature of this festival that through it we should become conscious of an innermost ground out of which a new, untrammeled life emerges, and of its inexhaustible power, that in its very first germ we should already discern its finest maturity, even its highest perfection. However, unconsciously it may reside in many people, our feeling of marvel can achieve resolution only in this concentrated vision of a new world, and in no other way. This vision may grip anyone, and he who brought it into being may thus be represented in a thousand images and in the most varied ways—as the rising, e'er returning sun, as the springtime of the spirit, as king of a better realm, as the most faithful emissary of the gods, as the prince of peace.

"And so I have come to the point of refuting you after all, Leonhardt, even in noting where we agree and in comparing the different viewpoints from which we have started. However unsatisfactory the historical traces of his life may be when one examines it critically—in a lower sense—nevertheless the festival does not depend on this. It rests on the necessity of a Redeemer, and hence upon the experience of a heightened existence, which can be derived from no other beginning than him. Often you yourself find less of a trace than I in particles upon which some crystallization of truth has been formed, but even the smallest elements have sufficed to convince you that a trace was present. So it is actually Christ to whose powers of attraction this new world owes its formation. And whoever acknowledges Christianity to be a powerful contemporary force, the great pattern of man's new life—as you are inclined to do—hallows this festival. He does so not as one who dares not impugn what he cannot understand, but in that he fully understands all its particulars—the gifts and the children, the night and the light.

"With this slight improvement, which I wish might also win your favor, I give your proposal for a toast once more. I trust, then, or rather prophesy, that the marvelous festival of Christmas will ever preserve the happy childlike mood with which it returns to us ever and again. And to all who celebrate it I wish and foresee that true joy in finding the higher life once more, from which alone all its blessings spring."

"I must beg your pardon, Ernst," said Agnes. "I had feared that I would not understand you at all; but this has not happened, and you have very nicely confirmed that the religious element is in truth the essence of the festival. Only it would certainly appear, from what has been said previously, as if we women should have less share in the joy because less of that disorder you spoke of is revealed in us. But I can account for that well enough for myself."

"Very easily," Leonhardt jumped in. "One could simply say right off—and it is as plain as can be—that women bear everything lightly regarding themselves and strive after little self-gratification, but that just as their innermost suffering is literally suffering-with, sympathy, so their joy too is shared joy. You must see to it, however, that you square accounts with the sacred authority of Scripture, to which you would ever remain faithful and which so clearly points to the women as the first cause of all cleavages and of all need of redemption! But if I were Friederike, I would declare war on Ernst for having so thoughtlessly, and without the slightest consideration of his situation, given baptism prominence over betrothal, which, I hope, is also to be regarded as a lovely and joyful sacrament."

"Don't answer him, Ernst," piped Friederike. "He has already answered himself."

"How so?" inquired Leonhardt.

"Why obviously," countered Ernestine, "in that you spoke of your own situation! But people like you never notice when you mix in your own dear egos. Ernst, however, has set up the distinction very well, and would no doubt say to you that a betrothal is closer to the enjoyment of a birthday than to the joy of Christmas."

"Or," added Ernst, "if you would have something specifically Christian at this point—that it is more like Good Friday and Easter than Christmas! Now, though, let's put aside all that has preceded and listen to what Eduard has to say to us."

In response, Eduard began his discourse, as follows: "It has already been remarked on a similar occasion, by a better man than I," he said, "that the last one to speak on a topic this way, no matter what its nature, is in the worst position. That is the situation in which I find myself. For one thing, earlier speakers take the words out of one's mouth; and in this respect you two have certainly not taken much trouble to leave any particulars of the festival to me. The main difficulty, however, is that peculiar echos continue to resound from each discourse in the minds of their listeners, and this forms an increasing resistance to new ideas, which the final speaker has the greatest difficulty in surpassing. Thus I must look about for aid, and let what I want to say rest on something you already know well and appreciate, so that my thoughts may find entrance into yours more easily.

"Now Leonhardt has mostly had the more external biographers of Christ in mind, seeking out the historical truth in them. In contrast, I shall turn to the more mystical among the four evangelists, whose account offers very little in the way of particular events. The Gospel according to John hasn't any Christmas event, recounted as an external event. But in his heart prevails an everlasting childlike Christmas joy. He gives us the higher, spiritual view of our festival. And so he begins, as you know: 'In the beginning was the Word, and the Word was with God, and the Word was God. . . . In him was life, and the life was the light of men. . . . And the Word became flesh and dwelt among us . . . and we have beheld his glory, glory as of the only Son from the Father.'

"This is how I prefer to regard the object of this festival: not a child of such and such an appearance, born of this or that parent, here or there, but the Word become flesh, which was God and was with God. The flesh, however, is, as we know, nothing other than our finite, limited, sensible nature, while the Word is thinking, coming to know; and the Word's becoming flesh is therefore the appearing of this original and divine wisdom in that form. Accordingly, what we celebrate is nothing other than ourselves as whole beings—that is, human nature, or whatever else you want to call it, viewed and known from the perspective of the divine. Why we must raise up one person alone in whom human nature permits of being represented in this way, and why this union of the divine and the earthly is placed in precisely this one person, and already even at his birth—all this can be clarified from this point of view.

"In himself what else is man than the very spirit of earth, or life's coming to know in its eternal being and in its ever-changing process of becoming? In such a state there is no corruption in man, no fall, and no need of redemption. But when the individual fastens upon other formations of this earthly environment and seeks his knowledge in them, for the process of coming to know them dwells in him alone: this is only a state of becoming. Then he exists in a fallen and corrupt condition, in discord and confusion, and he can find his redemption only through man-in-himself. He finds redemption, that is, in that the same union of eternal being and of the coming into being of the human spirit, such as it can be manifested on this planet, arises in each person and thus each contemplates and learns to love all becoming, including himself, only in eternal being. And insofar as he appears as a process of becoming, he wills to be nothing other than a thought of eternal being; nor will he have his foundations in any other expression of eternal being than in that which is united with the ever-changing, ever-recurrent process of becoming. In fact, the union of being of the human spirit, such as it can be manifested on this planet, arises in each person and thus each contemplates and learns to love all becoming, including himself, only in eternal being. And insofar as he appears as a process of becoming, he wills to be nothing other than a thought of eternal being; nor will he have his foundations in any other expression of eternal being than in that which is united with the ever-changing, ever-recurrent process of becoming. In fact, the union of being and becoming is found in humanity not incidentally but eternally; and this is because that union exists and comes into being as man-in-himself does. In the individual person, however, this union—as it has reality in his own life—must come into being both as his own thinking and as the thinking which arises within a common life and activity with other men; for it is in community that that knowledge which is proper to our planet not only exists but develops. Only when a person sees humanity as a living community of individuals, cultivates humanity as a community, bears its spirit and consciousness in his life, and within that community both loses his isolated existence and finds it again in a new way —only then does that person have the higher life and peace of God within himself.

"Now this community, or fellowship, by which man-in-himself is thus exhibited or restored is the church. The church, by virtue of this relation, relates itself to all other human life around it and without, somewhat as the individual's own consciousness of humanity relates to what lacks consciousness. Everyone, therefore, in whom this genuine self-consciousness of humanity arises enters within the bounds of the church. This is why no one can truly and vitally possess the fruits of science who is not himself within the church, and why such an outsider can only externally deny the church but not deep within himself. On the other hand, there may very well be those within the church who do not possess science for themselves; for these can own that higher self-consciousness in immediate experience, if not in conceptual awareness as well. This is exactly the case with women, and likewise provides the reason why they are so much more fervently and unreservedly attached to the church.

"This community, furthermore, is not only something which is coming into being but also something which has come into being. And it is also, as a community of individual persons, something which has come into being through communication of persons with each other. We also seek, therefore for a single starting point from which this communication can proceed—although we recognize that it must further proceed from each person out of his own self-activity—so that man-in-himself may also be born and formed in each one. But the man who is regarded as the starting-point of the church, its originating conception, must already be the man-in-himself, the God-man, from birth— he must bear that self-knowledge in himself and be the light of men from the very beginning. Analogously one may as it were call the first free, spontaneous outbreak of fellowship at Pentecost, where people were joined in a common and immediate experience, the birth of the church. For it is, in fact, through the Spirit of the church that we are born again. The Spirit itself, however, proceeds only from the Son, and the Son needs no rebirth but is born of God originally. He is the Son of Man without qualification. Until he enters history, all else is presage: all human life is related to his life, and only through this relation does it partake of goodness and divinity. And now that he has come, in him we celebrate not only ourselves but all who are yet to come as well as all who have been before us, for they only were something insofar as he was in them and they in him.

"In Christ, then, we see the Spirit, according to the nature and means of our world, originating contact with us and forming his presence within the genuine self-consciousness of individual persons. In him, the Father and the brethren dwell in conformity and are one. Devotion and love are his essence. Thus it is that every mother who, profoundly feeling what she has done in bearing a human being, knows as it were by an annunciation from heaven that the Spirit of the church, the Holy Spirit, dwells within her. As a result, she forthwith presents her child to the church with all her heart, and claims this as her right. Such a woman also sees Christ in her child—and this is that inexpressible feeling a mother has which compensates for all else. And in like manner each one of us beholds in the birth of Christ his own higher birth whereby nothing lives in him but devotion and love; and in him too the eternal Son of God appears. Thus it is that the festival breaks forth like a heavenly light out of the darkness. Thus it is that a pulse of joy spreads out over the whole reborn world, a pulse which only those who are long ill or maimed of spirit do not feel. And this is the very glory of the festival, which you wished also to hear me praise.

"Ah! but I see I shall not be the last. For our long-awaited friend has come, and must have his say as well."

Josef had come in while he was talking and, although he had very quietly entered and taken a seat, Eduard had noticed him. "By no means," he replied when Eduard addressed him. "You shall certainly be the last. I have not come to deliver a speech but to enjoy myself with you; and I must quite honestly say that it seems to me odd, almost folly even, that you should be carrying on with such exercises, however nicely you may have done them. Aha! but I already get the drift. Your evil principle is among you again: this Leonhardt, this contriving, reflective, dialectical, superintellectual man. No doubt you have been addressing yourselves to him; for your own selves you would surely not have needed such goings on and wouldn't have fallen into them. Yet they couldn't have been to any avail with him! And the poor women must have had to go along with it. Now just think what lovely music they could have sung for you, in which all the piety of your discourse could have dwelt far more profoundly. Or think how charmingly they might have conversed with you, out of hearts full of love and joy. Such would have eased and refreshed you differently, and better too, than you could possibly have been affected by these celebratory addresses of yours!

"For my part, today I am of no use for such things at all. For me, all forms are too rigid, all speech-making too tedious and cold. Itself unbounded by speech, the subject of Christmas claims, indeed creates in me a speechless joy, and I cannot but laugh and exult like a child. Today all men are children to me, and are all the dearer on that account. The solemn wrinkles are for once smoothed away, the years and cares do not stand written on the brow. Eyes sparkle and dance again, the sign of a beautiful and serene existence within. To my good fortune, I too have become just like a child again. As a child stifles his childish pain, suppressing his sighs and holding back his tears, when something is done to arouse his childish joy, so it is with me today. The long, deep, irrepressible pain in my life is soothed as never before.

I feel at home, as if born anew into the better world, in which pain and grieving have no meaning and no room any more. I look upon all things with a gladsome eye, even what has most deeply wounded me. As Christ had no bride but the church, no children but his friends, no household but the temple and the world, and yet his heart was full of heavenly love and joy, so I too seem to be born to endeavor after such a life.

"And so I have roamed about the whole evening, everywhere taking part most heartily in every little happening and amusement I have come across. I have laughed, and I have loved it all. It was one long affectionate kiss which I have given to the world, and now my enjoyment with you shall be the last impress of my lips. For you know that you are the dearest of all to me.

"Come, then, and above all bring the child if she is not yet asleep, and let me see your glories, and let us be glad and sing something religious and joyful."

JOHANN ADAM MÖHLER

The subtitle of the *Symbolism* of Johann Adam Möhler (1796-1838) explains its purpose: *Exposition of the Doctrinal Differences Between Catholics and Protestants as Evidenced by Their Symbolical Writings.* There were two goals of Möhler's exposition: (1) education: to correct the ignorance of parish clergy regarding the basic tenets of the Creeds, and (2) ecumenism: "[Symbolic study] is the point at which Catholics and Protestants will one day meet and stretch a friendly hand," Möhler wrote. "Both, conscious of guilt, must exclaim, 'We all have erred.' "

Möhler's *Symbolism* is a great attack on subjective religion. Institutional visibility protects the objectivity of Christianity, Möhler maintains. The church must be understood as a community because to no single individual has religious truth been transmitted. Möhler defends the communal nature of the church on the basis of an incarnational ecclesiology. Thus, the *Symbolism* is one of the pioneering documents which stand behind the radical rethinking of the role of the laity in modern Roman Catholicism. Möhler is also *avant garde* in his description of Eucharistic worship as more important than any other activity of the church, and in encouraging lay participation in the Eucharist.

Symbolism does not hesitate to point to the secular benefits of communal Christianity: the protection of Western civilization, the promotion of international solidarity, and the amelioration of individual lives.

From Johann Adam Möhler, **Symbolism**

. . . By the Church on earth, Catholics understand the visible community of believers founded by Christ, in which, by means of an enduring apostleship, established by him, and appointed to conduct all nations, in the course of ages, back to God, the works wrought by him during his earthly life, for the redemption and sanctification of mankind, are, under the guidance of his spirit, continued to the end of the world.

Thus, to *a visible society of men*, is this great, important, and mysterious work entrusted. The ultimate reason of the visibility of the Church is to be found in the *incarnation* of the Divine Word. Had that Word descended into the hearts of men, without taking the form of a servant, and accordingly without appearing in a corporeal shape, then only an internal, invisible Church would have been established. But since the word became *flesh*, it expressed itself in an outward, perceptible, and human manner; it spoke as man to man, and suffered, and worked after the fashion of men, in order to win them to the kingdom of God; so that the means selected for the attainment of this object, fully corresponded to the general method of instruction and education determined by the nature and the wants of man. This decided the nature of those means, whereby the Son of God, even after He had withdrawn himself from the eyes of the world, wished still to work in the world, and for the world. The Deity having manifested its action in Christ according to an *ordinary human fashion*, the form also in which His work was to be continued, was thereby traced out. The preaching of his doctrine needed now a *visible, human* medium, and must be entrusted to visible envoys, teaching and instructing after the wonted method; men must speak to men, and hold intercourse with them, in order to convey to them the word of God. And as in the world nothing can attain to greatness but in society; so Christ established a community; and his divine word, his living will, and the love emanating from him, exerted an internal, binding power upon his followers; so that an inclination implanted by him in the hearts of believers, corresponded to his outward institution. And thus a living, well-connected, visible association of the faithful sprang up, whereof it might be said,— there they are, there is his Church, his institution, wherein he continueth to live, his spirit continueth to work, and the word uttered by him eternally resounds. Thus, the visible Church, from the point of view here taken, is the Son of God himself, everlastingly manifesting himself among men in a human form, perpetually renovated, and eternally young—the permanent incarnation of the same, as in Holy Writ, even the faithful are called "the body of Christ." Hence it is evident that the Church, though composed of men, is yet not purely human. Nay, as in Christ, the divinity and the humanity are to be clearly distinguished, though both are bound in unity; so is he in undivided entireness perpetuated in the Church. The Church, his permanent manifestation, is at once divine and human—she is the union of both. He it is who, concealed under earthly and human forms, works in the Church: and this is wherefore she has a divine and a human part in an undivided mode, so that the divine cannot be separated from the human, nor the human from the divine. Hence these two parts change their predicates. If the divine—the living Christ and his spirit—constitute undoubtedly that which is infallible, and eternally inerrable in the Church; so also the human is infallible and inerrable in the same way, because the divine without the human has no existence for us: yet the human is not inerrable in itself, but only as the organ, and as the manifestation of the divine. Hence, we are enabled to conceive, *how* so great, important and mysterious a charge *could* have been entrusted to men.

In and through the Church the redemption, announced by Christ, hath obtained, through the medium of his spirit, a reality; for in her his truths are believed and his institutions are observed, and thereby have become living. Accordingly, we can say of the Church, that she is the Christian religion in its objective form—its living exposition. Since the word of Christ (taken in its widest signification) found, together with his spirit, its way into a circle of men, and was received by them, it has taken shape, put on flesh and blood; and this shape is the Church, which accordingly is regarded by Catholics as the essential form of the Christian Religion itself. As the Redeemer by his word and his spirit founded a community, wherein his word should ever be living, he intrusted the same to this society, that it might be preserved and propagated. He deposited it in the Church, that it might spring out of her ever the same, and yet eternally new, and young in energy; that it might grow up, and spread on all sides. His word can never more be separated from the Church, nor the Church from his word. . . .

Hence, it is with the profoundest love, reverence, and devotion, that the Catholic embraces the Church. The very thought of resisting her, of setting himself up in opposition to her will, is one against which his inmost feelings revolt, to which his whole nature is abhorrent: and to bring about a schism—to destory unity—is a crime, before whose heinousness his bosom trembles, and from which his soul recoils. On the other hand, the idea of community, in the first place, satisfies his feelings and his imagination, and, in the second place, is equally agreeable to his reason; while, in the third place, the living appropriation of this idea by his will, appears to him to concur with the highest reli-

gious and ethical duty of humanity. Let us now consider the first of
these reasons. No more beautiful object presents itself to the imagination of the Catholic—none more agreeably captivates his feelings, than
the image of the harmonious inter-workings of countless spirits, who,
though scattered over the whole globe, endowed with freedom, and
possessing the power to strike off into every deviation to the right or
to the left; yet, preserving still their various peculiarities, constitute
one great brotherhood for the advancement of each other's spiritual
existence,—representing one idea, that of the reconciliation of men
with God, who on that account have been reconciled with one another,
and are become one body. (Eph. iv. 11-16.) If the state be such a wonderful work of art, that we account it, if not a pardonable, yet a conceivable act, for the ancients to have made it an object of divine
worship, and almost everywhere considered the duties of the citizen
as the most important;—if the state be something so sacred and venerable, that the thought of the criminal, who lays on it a destroying and
desecrating hand, fills us with detestation;—what a subject of admiration must the Church be, which, with the tenderest bonds, unites such
an infinite variety; and this unimpeded by every obstacle, by rivers and
mountains, deserts and seas, by languages, national manners, customs,
and peculiarities of every kind, whose stubborn, unyielding nature
defies the power of the mightiest conquerors? Her peace, which cometh
down from Heaven, strikes deeper roots into the human breast, than
the spirit of earthly contention. Out of all nations, often so deeply
divided by political interests and temporal considerations, the Church
builds up the house of God, in which all join in one hymn of praise;
as, in the temple of the harmless village, all petty foes and adversaries
gather round the one sanctuary with one mind. And as often here, on
a small scale, the peace of God will bring about earthly peace, so there,
on a larger scale, the same result will frequently ensue. But who can
deem it a matter of astonishment, that Catholics should be filled with
joy and hope, and, enraptured at the view of the beautiful construction
of their Church, should contemplate with delight, that grand corpora-
tion which they form, since the philosophers of art declare, that the
beautiful is only *truth manifested and embodied?* Christ, the eternal
truth, hath built the Church: in the communion of the faithful, truth
transformed by his spirit into love, is become living among men: how
could then the Church fail in the highest degree of beauty? Hence,
we can comprehend that indescribable joy, which hath ever filled the
Church, when existing contests have been allayed, and schisms have
been terminated. In the primitive ages, we may adduce the reunion of
the Novatian communities with the Catholic Church, so movingly
described by Dionysius of Alexandria, and Cyprian of Carthage; the

termination of the Meletian schism, and the rest. From a later period, we may cite the event of the reunion of the Western and Eastern Churches, which occurred at the Council of Florence. Pope Eugenius IV expresses what feelings then overflowed all hearts, when he says, "Rejoice ye heavens, and exult, O earth: the wall of separation is pulled down, which divided the Eastern and Western Churches; peace and concord have returned; for Christ, the corner-stone, who, out of two, hath made one, unites with the strongest bands of love both walls, and holds them together in the covenant of eternal unity; and so after long and melancholy evils, after the dense, cloudy darkness of a protracted schism, the light of long-desired union beams once more upon all. Let our mother, the Church, rejoice, to whom it hath been granted to see her hitherto contending sons return to unity and peace: let her, who, during their division, shed such bitter tears, now thank Almighty God for their beautiful concord. All believers over the face of the earth, all who are called after Christ, may now congratulate their mother, the Catholic Church, and rejoice with her," etc. . . .

III. The third point in which the Catholic finds his view of the church so commendable, is, the influence which it has exerted on the cultivation and direction of the will, on the religious and moral amelioration of the whole man. We speak here no longer of the influence of a clear and firm belief, of the truth on the will—a firmness of belief which only the recognition of an outward and permanent teaching authority can produce—(of this we have already spoken)—but of a direction given to the will by a living membership, with an all-embracing, religious society. An ancient philosopher has, with reason, defined man to be a social animal. However little the peculiarity of man's nature is here defined (for his peculiar kind of sociability is not pointed out,) yet, a deep trait of what determines the civilization of man by means of man, is, in this definition, undoubtedly indicated. They are only races which, groaning under the destiny of some heavy curse, have sunk into the savage state, that become from the loss of their civilization seclusive, and with the most limited foresight fall back on their own resources, feel no want of an intercourse with other nations, or of an exchange of ideas, of which they possess nothing more, or of a communication of the products of their industry and art, that having entirely disappeared. These productions, which are already in themselves symbols of the intellectual character of their authors, flow into foreign countries, dressed, as it were, in the mental habits and characteristics of their home. Traces of the spirit of all the nations through which these productions pass are impressed upon them in their course; so that they always arrive at the place of their destination, with a wealth of a far higher kind, than that which they intrinsically possess. From all these currents of civilization is the savage withdrawn; for, because he is all-sufficient to himself, is he a savage, and because he is a savage, he suffices for himself. When the foreigner (hostis) was synonymous with the enemy; when one's country, (Iran,) included all that was absolutely good, and abroad, (Turan,) all that was absolutely evil; when the gods in the east and the west, in the land of the Colchians, the Cretans, and the Egyptians, rejoiced in the blood of foreigners, what a gloomy, ferocious existence must have circumscribed nations, in this their seclusion and mutual independence! For the divinity of the nation was regaled with such blood, only because the nation itself found therein a horrible gratification, and made its own delight a standard for the joys of its deity. *The maintenance of intercourse and communion with foreigners and accordingly, the voluntary establishment of relation of dependence on them,* is thus an absolute condition to the general civilization of man; so that the more this communion and mutual dependence is extended, that is to say, the more the notion of what is foreign disappears, the more is humanity exalted. With this general relation of dependence, the dependence of man on the domestic relations of law and government keeps equal pace. The more polished and civilized the members of a state, the more are they bound together by wise ordinances, holy laws, venerable customs and manners, which wisely determine the mutual relations of rights and duties; so that, in fact, with every higher degree of internal freedom, the outward bonds are proportionably straitened. On the other hand, the greater the state of barbarism, the greater is the external independence; so that the wildest savage is, in a material point of view, the most free.

What do these facts import, but a wonderful, mysterious, inexplicable, connexion of the individual man with the human race; so that he comprehends himself better, the more he seems to be absorbed in his kind, and it is only in humanity that man is understood? Yet, this internal emancipation by means of outward restraints, of which we have hitherto spoken, is not that which is the most interior; and serves only as a similitude or illustration of something higher. The true emancipation from low-mindedness and self-seeking, is a problem, which, as is avowed, religion alone can solve. In the same way as civilization is determined by political life, and by obedience to the institutions of the state, yea, even by the dependence, though naturally looser, on other nations; so is true religiousness promoted by subjection to the Church. For it is an incontrovertible maxim of experience, that the individual who is unconnected with any ecclesiastical community, has either no religion, or a very meagre and scanty one, or is given up to a distempered fancy, and a wild fanaticism; so that in none of the three cases, can religion exert her blessed influences. On the other hand, the more stable the ecclesiastical community to which we belong, the more will the true, interior qualities of man expand, and bloom forth in freedom; so that he who will lead a righteous life in the Catholic Church, whereof the very principle is the real unity and vital communion of all believers, he, we say, will attain to the highest degree of moral and religious perfection. It is no insane conception—no idle phantom—no illusion of a distempered mind, which he embraces, and to which he surrenders his obedience; but it is a reality, and a holy reality, wherein true faith, and love manifesting itself in deeds, coupled with *humility* and *self-denial* in the strongest and most comprehensive sense of the words, are nurtured. The more widely diffused the community, to which the Catholic belongs, the more defined and the more manifold are the relations wherein he stands, the more multiplied the bonds wherewith he is encompassed. But, as we said above, those very bonds, which exhibit the reality of the community, produce a result the very reverse of restraint, and establish the internal freedom of man, or promote the purest *humanity;* for this expression may be used, since God became man. Without external bonds, there is no true spiritual association, so that the idea of a mere invisible, universal community, to which we should belong, is an idle, unprofitable phantom of the imagination and of distempered feelings, destitute of all influence on mankind. In proportion only as a religious society approximates to the Catholic Church, doth it exert a more efficacious influence on spiritual life. Here, indeed, we may observe, as shall be afterwards proved, that it is only according to Catholic principles, that a Church can be consistently formed; and, where out of her pale anything of the kind exists, the truth of what we assert is confirmed, to wit, that where a ray of true Christian light doth fall, it will have the effect of binding and uniting, whereby all the doctrines tending to schism and division are, practically at least refuted. . . .

It is now evident to all, that the belief in the real presence of Christ in the Eucharist, forms the basis of our whole conception of the mass. Without that presence, the solemnity of the Lord's Supper is a mere reminiscence of the sacrifice of Christ, exactly in the same way as the celebration by any society of the anniversary of some esteemed individual, whose image it exhibits to view, or some other symbol, recalls to mind his beneficent actions. On the other hand, with faith in the real existence of Christ in the Eucharist, the past becomes the present —all that Christ hath merited for us, and whereby he hath so merited it, is henceforth never separated from his person: He is present as that which He absolutely is, and in the whole extent of His actions, to wit, as the real victim. Hence the effects of this faith on the mind, the heart, and the will of man, are quite other than if, by the mere stretch of the human faculty of memory, Christ be called back from the distance of eighteen hundred years. He Himself manifests His love, His benevolence, His devotedness to us: He is ever in the midst of us, full of grace and truth.

Accordingly, the Catholic mass, considered as a sacrifice, is a solemnization of the blessings imparted to humanity by God in Christ Jesus, and is destined, by the offering up of Christ, partly to express in praise, thanksgiving, and adoration, the joyous feelings of redemption on the part of the faithful; partly to make the merits of Christ the subject of their perpetual appropriation. It is also clear, why this sacrifice is of personal utility to the believer; namely, because, thereby, pious sentiments, such as faith, hope, love, humility, contrition, obedience, and devotion to Christ, are excited, promoted, and cherished. The sacrifice presented to God, which, as we have often said, is not separated from the work of Christ, merits internal grace for the culture of these sentiments, which are psychologically excited from without, by faith in the present Saviour, whose entire actions and sufferings are brought before the mind. As, according to Catholic doctrine, forgiveness of sins cannot take place without sanctification, and a fitting state of the human soul is required for the reception of grace, as well as an active concurrence towards the fructification of grace, the reflecting observer may already infer, that it is not by a mere outward or bodily participation, on the part of the community, that the mass produces any vague indeterminate effects.

The sacrifice of the mass is likewise offered up for the living and the dead; that is to say, God is implored, for the sake of Christ's oblation, to grant to all those who are dear to us, whatever may conduce to their salvation. With the mass, accordingly, the faithful join the prayer, that the merits of Christ, which are considered as concentrated in the Eucharistic sacrifice, should be applied to all needing them and susceptible of them. To consider merely himself is a matter of impossibility to the Christian, how much less in so sacred a solemnity can he think only of himself and omit his supplication, that the merits of Christ, which outweigh the sins of the whole world, may likewise be appropriated by all? The communion, with the happy and perfect spirits in Christ is also renewed; for they are one with Christ, and His work cannot be contemplated without its effects. Lastly, all the concerns in inward and outward life,—sad and joyful events, good and ill fortune,—are brought in connexion with this sacrifice; and at this commemoration in Christ, to whom we are indebted for the highest gifts, we pour out to God our thanksgivings and lamentations, and in Him, and before Him, we implore consolation, and courage, and strength, under sufferings; self-denial, clemency, and meekness, in prosperity.

Hitherto, however, we have considered the mass merely as a sacrificial oblation; but this view by no means embraces its whole purport. The assembled congregation declares, from what we have stated, that *in itself, without Christ,* it discovers nothing—absolutely nothing—which can be agreeable to God: nay, nothing but what is inadequate, earthly, and sinful. Renouncing itself, it gives itself up to Christ, full of confidence, hoping for His sake forgiveness of sins and eternal life, and every grace. In this act of self-renunciation, and of entire self-abandonment to God in Christ, the believer has, as it were, thrown off himself, excommunicated himself, if I may so speak, in his existence, as separated from Christ, in order to live only by Him, and in Him. Hence he is in a state to enter into the most intimate fellowship with Christ, to commune with Him, and with his whole being to be entirely absorbed in Him. For the unseemliness of the congregation no longer communicating every Sunday (as was the case in the primitive Church,) and of the priest in the mass usually receiving alone the body of the Lord, is not to be laid to the blame of the Church (for all the prayers in the holy sacrifice presuppose the sacramental communion of the entire congregation,) but is to be ascribed solely to the tepidity of the greater part of the faithful. Yet are the latter earnestly exhorted to participate, at least spiritually, in the communion of the priest, and, in this way, to enter into the fellowship of Christ.

Who will not name such a worship most Christian, most pious, and real:—a worship wherein God is adored in spirit and in truth? Indeed, how can a carnal-minded man, who will not believe in the incarnation of the Son of God,—for the most powerful obstacle to this belief is in the fact that man clearly perceives that he must be of a godly way of thinking, so soon as he avows that God has become man—how can such a man look upon the mass as other than mere foolishness? The mass comprises an ever-recurring invitation to the confession of our sins, of our own weakness and helplessness. It is a living representation of the infinite love and compassion of God towards us, which he hath revealed, and daily still reveals, in the delivering up of His only begotten Son: and therefore it contains the most urgent exhortation to endless thanksgiving, to effective mutual love, and to our heavenly glorification. Hence an adversary to such a worship must be one whose thoughts creep exclusively on the earth, or of the whole act understands nought else, but that the priest turns sometimes to the right, sometimes to the left, and is clothed in a motley-coloured garment. On the other hand, he who misapprehends the wants of man, and the high objects of our Divine Redeemer, in the establishment of the sacraments; he who, like the Manicheans, rejects the sacraments as coarse, sensual institutions, and follows the track of a false spirituality, will regard the Catholic dogma as incomprehensible. In the opinion of such a man, a worship is in the same degree spiritual, as it is untrue. He lays before his God the lofty conceptions that have sprung out of the fulness of his intellectual powers, his holy feelings and inflexible resolves; these have no reference to the outward historical Christ, but only to the ideal one, which is merged in the subjectivity of these feelings and ideas; while yet, by the fact of the external revelation of the Logos, internal worship must needs obtain a perpetual outward basis, and, in truth, one representing the Word delivered up to suffering, because it was under the form of a self-sacrifice for the sins of the world that this manifestation occurred. How, on the other hand, any one who has once apprehended the full meaning of the incarnation of the Deity, and who with joy confesses that his duty is the reverse—namely, to pass from seeming to real and divine existence, and has accordingly attained to the perception that the doctrine of a forgiveness of sins in Christ Jesus, of an exaltation of man unto God, and of a communication of divine life to him, through our Lord, must remain unprofitable until it be brought before us in concrete forms, and be made to bear on our most individual relations—how any one, I say, who clearly perceives all this, can refuse to revere in the Catholic mass a divine institution, I am utterly at a loss to conceive.

JOHN HENRY NEWMAN

After his conversion to Roman Catholicism in 1845, John Henry Newman (1801-1890) acted for a time as rector of a proposed Catholic University in Dublin and prepared a series of discourses on university education. Newman delivered five *Discourses* in Dublin in May, 1852, and they are the heart of *The Idea of a University*. Three points are argued throughout: (1) that a university is meant to cover a wide circle of knowledge, and so must not exclude religion; (2) that university education must involve "enlargement of mind"; and that (3) knowledge is something valuable in itself; it is its own end.

What Newman most feared in the modern society he saw evolving around him was not the defeat of religion in open debate, but the closing up of intellectual debate in the universities in the interests of more useful social and professional programs. Newman feared that theology would be banished from the Catholic university because it was not immediately practical.

In Newman's *The Idea of a University* we find the model of the university as an instrument for the transformation of the church into one people of

God. To produce intellectual laypeople who are religious, and devout clergy who are intellectual would heal rifts in the church. Newman envisages a common Christian education as a seed which will flower into institutional forms appropriate to the modern world, preserving life-giving diversity, but at the same time making all one in Christ.

From John Henry Newman, **The Idea of a University**
BEARING OF THEOLOGY ON OTHER KNOWLEDGE
7.

Now what is theology? First, I will tell you what it is not. And here, in the first place (though of course I speak on the subject as a Catholic), observe that, strictly speaking, I am not assuming that Catholicism is true, while I make myself the champion of theology. Catholicism has not formally entered into my argument hitherto, nor shall I just now assume any principle peculiar to it, for reasons which will appear in the sequel, though of course I shall use Catholic language. Neither, secondly, will I fall into the fashion of the day, of identifying natural theology with physical theology, which said physical theology is mostly jejune study, considered as a science, and really is no science at all, for it is ordinarily nothing more than a series of pious or polemical remarks upon the physical world viewed religiously, whereas the word "natural" properly comprehends man and society and all that is involved therein, as the great Protestant writer Dr. Butler shows us. Nor, in the third place, do I mean by theology polemics of any kind; for instance, what are called "the Evidences of Religion," or "the Christian Evidences"; for, though these constitute a science supplemental to theology and are necessary in their place, they are not theology itself, unless an army is synonymous with the body politic. Nor, fourthly, do I mean by theology that vague thing called "Christianity," or "our common Christianity," or "Christianity the law of the land," if there is any man alive who can tell what it is. I discard it for the very reason that it cannot throw itself into a proposition. Lastly, I do not understand by theology acquaintance with the Scriptures; for though no person of religious feelings can read Scripture but he will find those feelings roused, and gain much knowledge of history into the bargain, yet historical reading and religious feeling are not science. I mean none of these things by theology; I simply mean the science of God, or the truths we know about God put into system; just as we have a science of the stars, and call it astronomy, or of the crust of the earth, and call it geology.

For instance, I mean, for this is the main point, that, as in the human frame there is a living principle, acting upon it and through it by means of volition, so, behind the veil of the visible universe, there is an invisible, intelligent Being, acting on and through it, as and when He will. Further, I mean that this invisible Agent is in no sense a soul of the world, after the analogy of human nature, but, on the contrary, is absolutely distinct from the world, as being its Creator, Upholder, Governor, and Sovereign Lord. Here we are at once brought into the circle of doctrines which the idea of God embodies. I mean then by the Supreme Being one who is simply self-dependent, and the only Being who is such; moreover, that He is without beginning or Eternal, and the only Eternal; that in consequence He has lived a whole eternity by Himself; and hence that He is all-sufficient, sufficient for His own blessedness, and all-blessed, and ever-blessed. Further, I mean a Being, who having these prerogatives, has the Supreme Good, or rather is the Supreme Good, or has all the attributes of Good in infinite intenseness; all wisdom, all truth, all justice, all love, all holiness, all beautifulness; who is omnipotent, omniscient, omnipresent; ineffably one; absolutely perfect; and such, that what we do not know and cannot even imagine of Him, is far more wonderful than what we do and can. I mean One who is sovereign over His own will and actions, though always according to the eternal Rule of right and wrong, which is Himself. I mean, moreover, that He created all things out of nothing, and preserves them every moment, and could destroy them as easily as He made them; and that, in consequence, He is separated from them by an abyss, and is incommunicable in all His attributes. And further, He has stamped upon all things, in the hour of their creation, their respective natures, and has given them their work and mission and their length of days, greater or less, in their appointed place. I mean, too, that He is ever present with His works, one by one, and confronts everything He has made by His particular and most loving Providence, and manifests Himself to each according to its needs; and has on rational beings imprinted the moral law, and given them power to obey it, imposing on them the duty of worship and service, searching and scanning them through and through with His omniscient eye, and putting before them a present trial and a judgment to come.

Such is what theology teaches about God, a doctrine, as the very idea of its subject matter presupposes, so mysterious as in its fulness to lie beyond any system, and in particular aspects to be simply external to nature, and to seem in parts even to be irreconcilable with itself, the imagination being unable to embrace what the reason determines. It teaches of a Being infinite, yet personal; all-blessed, yet ever operative; absolutely separate from the creature, yet in every part of the creation at every moment; above all things, yet under everything. It teaches of a Being who, though the highest, yet in the work of creation, conservation, government, retribution, makes Himself, as it were, the minister and servant of all; who, though inhabiting eternity, allows Himself to take an interest, and to have a sympathy, in the matters of space and time. His are all beings, visible and invisible, the noblest and the vilest of them. His are the substance, and the operation, and the results of that system of physical nature into which we are born. His too are the powers and achievements of the intellectual essences, on which He has bestowed an independent action and the gift of origination. The laws of the universe, the principles of truth, the relation of one thing to another, their qualities and virtues, the order and harmony of the whole, all that exists, is from Him; and, if evil is not from Him, as assuredly it is not, this is because evil has no substance of its own, but is only the defect, excess, perversion, or corruption of that which has substance. All we see, hear, and touch, the remote sidereal firmament, as well as our own sea and land, and the elements which compose them, and the ordinances they obey, are His. The primary atoms of matter, their properties, their mutual action, their disposition and collocation, electricity, magnetism, gravitation, light and whatever other subtle principles or operations the wit of man is detecting or shall detect, are the work of His hands. From Him has been every movement which has convulsed and refashioned the surface of the earth. The most insignificant or unsightly insect is from Him, and good in its kind; the ever teeming, inexhaustible swarms of animalculae, the myriads of living motes invisible to the naked eye, the restless, ever-spreading vegetation which creeps like a garment over the whole earth, the lofty cedar, the umbrageous banana, are His. His are the tribes and families of birds and beasts, their graceful forms, their wild gestures, and their passionate cries.

And so in the intellectual, moral, social, and political world. Man, with his motives and works, his languages, his propagation, his diffusion, is from Him. Agriculture, medicine, and the arts of life are His gifts. Society, laws, government, He is their sanction. The pageant of earthly royalty has the semblance and the benediction of the Eternal King. Peace and civilization, commerce and adventure, wars when just, conquest when humane and necessary, have His co-operation, and His blessing upon them. The course of events, the revolution of empires, the rise and fall of states, the periods and eras, the progresses and the retrogressions of the world's history, not indeed the incidental sin, overabundant as it is, but the great outlines and the results of human affairs, are from His disposition. The elements and types and seminal principles and constructive powers of the moral world, in ruins though it be, are to be referred to Him. He "enlighteneth every man that cometh into this world." His are the dictates of the moral sense, and the retributive reproaches of conscience. To Him must be ascribed the rich endowments of the intellect, the irradiation of genius, the imagination of the poet, the sagacity of the politician, the wisdom (as Scripture calls it), which now rears and decorates the Temple, now manifests itself in proverb or in parable. The old saws of nations, the majestic precepts of philosophy, the luminous maxims of law, the oracles of individual wisdom, the traditionary rules of truth, justice, and religion, even though imbedded in the corruption, or alloyed with the pride, of the world, betoken His original agency, and His long-suffering presence. Even where there is habitual rebellion against Him, or profound far-spreading social depravity, still the undercurrent, or the heroic outburst, of natural virtue, as well as the yearnings of the heart after what it has not, and its presentiment of its true remedies, are to be ascribed to the Author of all good. Anticipations or reminiscences of His glory haunt the mind of the self-sufficient sage, and of the pagan devotee; His writing is upon the wall, whether of the Indian fane or of the porticoes of Greece. He introduces Himself, He all but concurs, according to His good pleasure, and in His selected season, in the issues of unbelief, superstition, and false worship, and He changes the character of acts by His overruling operation. He condescends, though He gives no sanction, to the altars and shrines of imposture, and He makes His own fiat the substitute for its sorceries. He speaks amid the incantations of Balaam, raises Samuel's spirit in the witch's cavern, prophesies of the Messias by the tongue of the Sibyl, forces Python to recognize His ministers, and baptizes by the hand of the misbeliever. He is with the heathen dramatist in his denunciations of injustice and tyranny, and his auguries of divine vengeance upon crime. Even on the unseemly legends of a popular mythology He casts His shadow, and is dimly discerned in the ode or the epic, as in troubled water or in fantastic dreams. All that is good, all that is true, all that is beautiful, all that is beneficent, be it great or small, be it perfect or fragmentary, natural as well as supernatural, moral as well as material, comes from Him.

9

And here I am led to another and most important point in the argument in its behalf—I mean its wide reception. Theology, as I have described it, is no accident of particular minds, as are certain systems, for instance, of prophetical interpretation. It is not the sudden birth of a crisis, as the Lutheran or Wesleyan doctrine. It is not the splendid development of some uprising philosophy, as the Cartesian or Platonic. It is not the fashion of a season, as certain medical treatments may be considered. It has had a place, if not possession, in the intellectual world from time immemorial; it has been received by minds the most various, and in systems of religion the most hostile to each other. It has prima-facie claims upon us, so imposing that it can only be rejected on the ground of those claims being nothing more than imposing, that is, being false. As to our own countries, it occupies our language, it meets us at every turn in our literature, it is the secret assumption, too axiomatic to be distinctly professed, of all our writers; nor can we help assuming it ourselves, except by the most unnatural vigilance. Whoever philosophizes, starts with it, and introduces it, when he will, without any apology. Bacon, Hooker, Taylor, Cudworth, Locke, Newton, Clarke, Berkeley, and Butler, and it would be easy to find more, as difficult to find greater names among English authors, inculcate or comment upon it. Men the most opposed, in creed or cast of mind, Addison and Johnson, Shakespeare and Milton, Lord Herbert and Baxter, herald it forth. Nor is it an English or a Protestant notion only; you track it across the Continent, you pursue it into former ages. When was the world without it? Have the systems of atheism or pantheism, as sciences, prevailed in the literature of nations, or received a formation or attained a completeness such as monotheism? We find it in old Greece, and even in Rome, as well as in Judea and the East. We find it in popular literature, in philosophy, in poetry, as a positive and settled teaching, differing not at all in the appearance it presents, whether in Protestant England, or in schismatical Russia, or in the Mohammedan populations, or in the Catholic Church. If ever there was a subject of thought which had earned by prescription to be received among the studies of a university, and which could not be rejected except on the score of convicted imposture, as astrology or alchemy; if there be a science anywhere which at least could claim not to be ignored, but to be entertained, and either distinctly accepted or distinctly reprobated, or rather, which cannot be passed over in a scheme of universal instruction, without involving a positive denial of its truth, it is this ancient, this far-spreading philosophy.

10

And now, Gentlemen, I may bring a somewhat tedious discussion to a close. It will not take many words to sum up what I have been urging. I say then, if the various branches of knowledge, which are the matter of teaching in a university, so hang together that none can be neglected without prejudice to the perfection of the rest, and if theology be a branch of knowledge, of wide reception, of philosophical structure, of unutterable importance, and of supreme influence, to what conclusion are we brought from these two premises but this: that to withdraw theology from the public schools is to impair the completeness and to invalidate the trustworthiness of all that is actually taught in them.

But I have been insisting simply on natural theology, and that because I wished to carry along with me those who were not Catholics, and, again, as being confident that no one can really set himself to master and to teach the doctrine of an intelligent Creator in its fulness without going on a great deal farther than he at present dreams. I say, then, secondly: if this science, even as human reason may attain to it, has such claims on the regard, and enters so variously into the objects, of the professor of universal knowledge, how can any Catholic imagine that it is possible for him to cultivate philosophy and science with due attention to their ultimate end, which is truth, supposing that system of revealed facts and principles, which constitutes the Catholic faith, which goes so far beyond nature, and which he knows to be most true, be omitted from among the subjects of his teaching?

In a word, religious truth is not only a portion but a condition of general knowledge. To blot it out is nothing short, if I may so speak, of unravelling the web of university teaching. It is, according to the Greek proverb, to take the spring from out of the year; it is to imitate the preposterous proceeding of those tragedians who represent a drama with the omission of its principal part.

BEARING OF OTHER BRANCHES OF KNOWLEDGE ON THEOLOGY

14.

And now to sum up what I have been saying in a few words. My object, it is plain, has been—not to show that secular Science in its various departments may take up a position hostile to theology—this is rather the basis of the objection with which I opened this discourse; but to point out the cause of a hostility to which all parties will bear witness. I have been insisting then on this, that the hostility in question, when it occurs, is coincident with an evident deflection or exorbitance of science from its proper course; and that this exorbitance is sure to take place, almost from the necessity of the case, if theology be not present to defend its own boundaries and to hinder the encroachment. The human mind cannot keep from speculating and systematizing; and if theology is not allowed to occupy its own territory, adjacent sciences, nay, sciences which are quite foreign to theology, will take possession of it. And this occupation is proved to be a usurpation by this circumstance that these foreign sciences will assume certain principles as true, and act upon them, which they neither have authority to lay down themselves, nor appeal to any other higher science to lay down for them. For example, it is a mere unwarranted assumption if the antiquarian says, "Nothing has ever taken place but is to be found in historical documents"; or if the philosophic historian says, "There is nothing in Judaism different from other political institutions"; or if the anatomist, "There is no soul beyond the brain"; or if the political economist, "Easy circumstances make men virtuous." These are enunciations, not of science, but of private judgment; and it is private judgment that infects every science which it touches with a hostility to theology, a hostility which properly attaches to no science in itself whatever.

If then, Gentlemen, I now resist such a course of acting as unphilosophical, what is this but to do as men of science do when the interests of their own respective pursuits are at stake? If they certainly would resist the divine who determined the orbit of Jupiter by the Pentateuch, why am I to be accused of cowardice or illiberality because I will not tolerate their attempt in turn to theologize by means of astronomy? And if experimentalists would be sure to cry out, did I attempt to install the Thomist philosophy in the schools of astronomy and medicine, why may not I, when Divine Science is ostracized, and Laplace, or Buffon, or Humboldt, sits down in its chair, why may not I fairly protest against their exclusiveness, and demand the emancipation of theology?

15.

And now I consider I have said enough in proof of the first point which I undertook to maintain, viz., the claim of theology to be represented among the chairs of a university. I have shown, I think, that exclusiveness really attaches, not to those who support that claim, but to those who dispute it. I have argued in its behalf, first, from the consideration that, whereas it is the very profession of a university to teach all sciences, on this account it cannot exclude theology without being untrue to its profession. Next, I have said that all sciences being connected together, and having bearings one on another, it is impossible to teach them all thoroughly unless they all are taken into account, and theology among them. Moreover, I have insisted on the important influence which theology in matter of fact does and must exercise over a great variety of sciences, completing and correcting them; so that, granting it to be a real science occupied upon truth, it cannot be omitted without great prejudice to the teaching of the rest. And lastly, I have urged that, supposing theology be not taught, its provinces will not simply be neglected, but will be actually usurped by other sciences, which will teach, without warrant, conclusions of their own in a subject matter which needs its own proper principles for its due formation and disposition.

Abstract statements are always unsatisfactory; these, as I have already observed, could be illustrated at far greater length than the time allotted to me for the purpose has allowed. Let me hope that I have said enough upon the subject to suggest thoughts, which those who take an interest in it may pursue for themselves.

KNOWLEDGE VIEWED IN RELATION TO RELIGIOUS DUTY

3.

Now, on opening the subject, we see at once a momentous benefit which the philosopher is likely to confer on the pastors of the Church. It is obvious that the first step which they have to effect in the conversion of man and the renovation of his nature is his rescue from that fearful subjection to sense which is his ordinary state. To be able to break through the meshes of that thraldom, and to disentangle and to disengage its ten thousand holds upon the heart, is to bring it, I might almost say, halfway to Heaven. Here, even divine grace, to speak of things according to their appearances, is ordinarily baffled, and retires, without expedient or resource, before this giant fascination. Religion seems too high and unearthly to be able to exert a continued influence upon us: its effort to rouse the soul, and the soul's effort to co-operate, are too violent to last. It is like holding out the arm at full length, or supporting some great weight, which we manage to do for a time, but soon are exhausted and succumb. Nothing can act beyond its own nature; when then we are called to what is supernatural, though those extraordinary aids from Heaven are given us, with which obedience becomes possible, yet even with them it is of transcendent difficulty. We are drawn down to earth every moment with the ease and certainty of a natural gravitation, and it is only by sudden impulses and, as it were, forcible plunges that we attempt to mount upwards. Religion indeed enlightens, terrifies, subdues; it gives faith, it inflicts remorse, it inspires resolutions, it draws tears, it inflames devotion, but only for the occasion. I repeat, it imparts an inward power which ought to effect more than this; I am not forgetting either the real sufficiency of its aids, nor the responsibility of those in whom they fail. I am not discussing theological questions at all. I am looking at phenomena as they lie before me, and I say that, in matter of fact, the sinful spirit repents, and protests it will never sin again, and for a while is protected by disgust and abhorrence from the malice of its foe. But that foe knows too well that such seasons of repentance are wont to have their end: he patiently waits, till nature faints with the effort of resistance, and lies passive and hopeless under the next access of temptation. What we need then is some expedient or instrument, which at least will obstruct and stave off the approach of our spiritual enemy, and which is sufficiently congenial and level with our nature to maintain as firm a hold upon us as the inducements of sensual gratification. It will be our wisdom to employ nature against itself. Thus sorrow, sickness, and care are providential antagonists in our inward disorders; they come upon us as years pass on, and generally produce their natural effects on us, in proportion as we are subjected to their influence. These, however, are God's instruments, not ours; we need a similar remedy, which we can make our own, the object of some legitimate faculty, or the aim of some natural affection, which is capable of resting on the mind, and taking up its familiar lodging with it, and engrossing it, and which thus becomes a match for the besetting power of sensuality, and a sort of homoeopathic medicine for the disease. Here then I think is the important aid which intellectual cultivation furnishes to us in rescuing the victims of passion and self-will. It does not supply religious motives; it is not the cause or proper antecedent of anything supernatural; it is not meritorious of heavenly aid or reward; but it does a work, at least *materially* good (as theologians speak), whatever be its real and formal character. It expels the excitement of sense by the introduction of those of the intellect.

This then is the prima-facie advantage of the pursuit of knowledge; it is the drawing the mind off from things which will harm it to subjects which are worthy a rational being; and, though it does not raise it above nature, nor has any tendency to make us pleasing to our Maker, yet is it nothing to substitute what is in itself harmless for what is, to say the least, inexpressibly dangerous? Is it a little thing to exchange a circle of ideas which are certainly sinful, for others which are certainly not so? You will say, perhaps, in the words of the Apostle, "Knowledge puffeth up": and doubtless this mental cultivation, even when it is successful for the purpose for which I am applying it, may be from the first nothing more than the substitution of pride for sensuality. I grant it, I think I shall have something to say on this point presently; but this is not a necessary result, it is but an incidental evil, a danger which may be realized or may be averted, whereas we may in most cases predicate guilt, and guilt of a heinous kind, where the mind is suffered to run wild and indulge its thoughts without training or law of any kind; and surely to turn away a soul from mortal sin is a good and a gain so far, whatever comes of it. And therefore, if a friend in need is twice a friend, I conceive that intellectual employments, though they do no more than occupy the mind with objects naturally noble or innocent, have a special claim upon our consideration and gratitude.

10.

Hence it is that it is almost a definition of a gentleman to say he is one who never inflicts pain. This description is both refined and, as far as it goes, accurate. He is mainly occupied in merely removing the obstacles which hinder the free and unembarrassed action of those about him; and he concurs with their movements rather than takes the initiative himself. His benefits may be considered as parallel to what are called comforts or conveniences in arrangements of a personal nature like an easy chair or a good fire, which do their part in dispelling cold and fatigue, though nature provides both means of rest and animal heat without them. The true gentleman in like manner carefully avoids whatever may cause a jar or a jolt in the minds of those with whom he is cast—all clashing of opinion, or collision of feeling, all restraint, or suspicion, or gloom, or resentment; his great concern being to make every one at their ease and at home. He has his eyes on all his company; he is tender towards the bashful, gentle towards the distant, and merciful towards the absurd; he can recollect to whom he is speaking; he guards against unseasonable allusions, or topics which may irritate; he is seldom prominent in conversation, and never wearisome. He makes light of favours while he does them, and seems to be receiving when he is conferring. He never speaks of himself except when compelled, never defends himself by a mere retort, he has no ears for slander or gossip, is scrupulous in imputing motives to those who interfere with him, and interprets everything for the best. He is never mean or little in his disputes, never takes unfair advantage, never mistakes personalities or sharp sayings for arguments, or insinuates evil which he dare not say out. From a long-sighted prudence, he observes the maxim of the ancient sage that we should ever conduct ourselves toward our enemy as if he were one day to be our friend. He has too much good sense to be affronted at insults, he is too well employed to remember injuries, and too indolent to bear malice. He is patient, forbearing, and resigned, on philosophical principles; he submits to pain, because it is inevitable, to bereavement, because it is irreparable, and to death, because it is his destiny. If he engages in controversy of any kind, his disciplined intellect preserves him from the blundering discourtesy of better, perhaps, but less educated minds; who like blunt weapons, tear and hack instead of cutting clean, who mistake the point in argument, waste their strength on trifles, misconceive their adversary, and leave the question more involved than they find it. He may be right or wrong in his opinion, but he is too clear-headed to be unjust; he is as simple as he is forcible, and as brief as he is decisive. Nowhere shall we find greater candour, consideration, indulgence: he throws himself into the minds of his opponents, he accounts for their mistakes. He knows the weakness of human reason as well as its strength, its province and its limits. If he be an unbeliever, he will be too profound and large-minded to ridicule religion or to act against it; he is too wise to be a dogmatist or fanatic in his infidelity. He respects piety and devotion; he even supports institutions as venerable, beautiful, or useful, to which he does not assent; he honours the ministers of religion, and it contents him to decline its mysteries without assailing or denouncing them. He is a friend of religious toleration, and that, not only because his philosophy has taught him to look on all forms of faith with an impartial eye, but also from the gentleness and effeminancy of feeling, which is the attendant on civilization.

Not that he may not hold a religion too, in his own way, even when he is not a Christian. In that case his religion is one of imagination and sentiment; it is the embodiment of those ideas of the sublime, majestic, and beautiful, without which there can be no large philosophy. Sometimes he acknowledges the being of God, sometimes he invests an unknown principle or quality with the attributes of perfection. And this deduction of his reason, or creation of his fancy, he makes the occasion of such excellent thoughts, and the starting point of so varied and systematic a teaching that he even seems like a disciple of Christianity itself. From the very accuracy and steadiness of his logical powers, he is able to see what sentiments are consistent in those who hold any religious doctrine at all, and he appears to others to feel and to hold a whole circle of theological truths, which exist in his mind no otherwise than as a number of deductions.

Such are some of the lineaments of the ethical character which the cultivated intellect will form, apart from religious principle. They are seen within the pale of the Church and without it, in holy men, and in profligate; they form the *beau ideal* of the world; they partly assist and partly distort the development of the Catholic. They may subserve the education of a St. Francis de Sales or a Cardinal Pole; they may be the limits of the contemplation of a Shaftesbury or a Gibbon. Basil and Julian were fellow students at the schools of Athens; and one became the saint and doctor of the Church, the other her scoffing and relentless foe.

DUTIES OF THE CHURCH TOWARDS KNOWLEDGE

2.

I say then, that, even though the case could be so that the whole system of Catholicism was recognized and professed, without the direct presence of the Church, still this would not at once make such a university a Catholic institution, nor be sufficient to secure the due weight

of religious considerations in its philosophical studies. For it may easily happen that a particular bias or drift may characterize an institution, which no rules can reach, nor officers remedy, nor professions or
promises counteract. We have an instance of such a case in the Spanish
Inquisition—here was a purely Catholic establishment, devoted to the
maintenance, or rather the ascendancy of Catholicism, keenly zealous
for theological truth, the stern foe of every anti-Catholic idea, and administered by Catholic theologians; yet it in no proper sense belonged
to the Church. It was simply and entirely a state institution, it was an
expression of that very Church-and-King spirit which has prevailed in
these islands; nay, it was an instrument of the State, according to the
confession of the acutest Protestant historians, in its warfare against
the Holy See. Considered *"materially,"* it was nothing but Catholic;
but its spirit and form were earthly and secular, in spite of whatever
faith and zeal and sanctity and charity were to be found in the individuals who from time to time had a share in its administration. And in
like manner, it is no sufficient security for the Catholicity of a university, even that the whole of Catholic theology should be professed in it,
unless the Church breathes her own pure and unearthly spirit into it,
and fashions and moulds its organization, and watches over its teaching, and knits together its pupils, and superintends its action. The Spanish Inquisition came into collision with the supreme Catholic authority,
and that, from the fact that its immediate end was of a secular character; and for the same reason, whereas academical institutions (as I
have been so long engaged in showing) are in their very nature directed to social, national, temporal objects in the first instance, and since
they are living and energizing bodies, if they deserve the name of
university at all, and of necessity have some one formal and definite
ethical character, good or bad, and do of a certainty imprint that character on the individuals who direct and who frequent them, it cannot
but be that, if left to themselves, they will, in spite of their profession of
Catholic truth, work out results more or less prejudicial to its interests.

Nor is this all: such institutions may become hostile to revealed
truth in consequence of the circumstances of their teaching as well as
of their end. They are employed in the pursuit of liberal knowledge,
and liberal knowledge has a special tendency, not necessary or right-
ful, but—a tendency in fact, when cultivated by beings such as we
are, to impress us with a mere philosophical theory of life and conduct, in the place of Revelation. I have said much on this subject already. Truth has two attributes—beauty and power; and while useful
knowledge is the possession of truth as powerful, liberal knowledge is
the apprehension of it as beautiful. Pursue it, either as beauty or as
power, to its furthest extent and its true limit, and you are led by

either road to the Eternal and Infinite, to the intimations of conscience and the announcements of the Church. Satisfy yourself with what is only visibly or intelligibly excellent, as you are likely to do, and you will make present utility and natural beauty the practical test of truth, and the sufficient object of the intellect. It is not that you will at once reject Catholicism, but you will measure and proportion it by an earthly standard. You will throw its highest and most momentous disclosures into the background, you will deny its principles, explain away its doctrines, rearrange its precepts, and make light of its practices, even while you profess it. Knowledge, viewed as knowledge, exerts a subtle influence in throwing us back on ourselves, and making us our own centre, and our minds the measure of all things. This then is the tendency of that liberal education, of which a university is the school, viz., to view revealed religion from an aspect of its own—to fuse and recast it, to tune it, as it were, to a different key, and to reset its harmonies, to circumscribe it by a circle which unwarrantably amputates here, and unduly develops there; and all under the notion, conscious or unconscious, that the human intellect, self-educated and self-supported, is more true and perfect in its ideas and judgments than that of Prophets and Apostles, to whom the sights and sounds of Heaven were immediately conveyed. A sense of propriety, order, consistency, and completeness gives birth to a rebellious stirring against miracle and mystery, against the severe and the terrible.

This intellectualism first and chiefly comes into collision with precept, then with doctrine, then with the very principle of dogmatism— a perception of the beautiful becomes the substitute for faith. In a country which does not profess the faith, it at once runs, if allowed, into scepticism or infidelity; but even within the pale of the Church, and with the most unqualified profession of her Creed, it acts, if left to itself, as an element of corruption and debility. Catholicism, as it has come down to us from the first, seems to be mean and illiberal; it is a mere popular religion; it is the religion of illiterate ages or servile populations or barbarian warriors; it must be treated with discrimination and delicacy, corrected, softened, improved, if it is to satisfy an enlightened generation. It must be stereotyped as the patron of arts, or the pupil of speculation, or the protégé of science; it must play the literary academician, or the empirical philanthropist, or the political partisan; it must keep up with the age; some or other expedient it must devise, in order to explain away, or to hide, tenets under which the intellect labours and of which it is ashamed—its doctrine, for instance, of grace, its mystery of the Godhead, its preaching of the Cross, its devotion to the Queen of Saints, or its loyalty to the Apostolic See. Let this spirit be freely evolved out of the philosophical condition of mind, which in former discourses I have so highly, so justly extolled, and it is impossible but, first indifference, then laxity of belief, then even heresy will be the successive results.

Here then are two injuries which Revelation is likely to sustain at the hands of the masters of human reason unless the Church, as in duty bound, protects the sacred treasure which is in jeopardy. The first is a simple ignoring of theological truth altogether, under the pretence of not recognizing differences of religious opinion; which will only take place in countries or under governments which have abjured Catholicism. The second, which is of a more subtle character, is a recognition indeed of Catholicism, but (as if in pretended mercy to it) an adulteration of its spirit. I will now proceed to describe the dangers I speak of more distinctly, by a reference to the general subject matter of instruction which a university undertakes.

There are three great subjects on which human reason employs itself; God, nature, and man: and theology being put aside in the present argument, the physical and social worlds remain. These, when respectively subjected to human reason, form two books: the book of nature is called science, the book of man is called literature. Literature and science, thus considered, nearly constitute the subject matter of liberal education; and, while science is made to subserve the former of the two injuries, which revealed truth sustains—its exclusion, literature subserves the latter—its corruption. Let us consider the influence of each upon religion separately.

ELEMENTARY STUDIES

3.

. . . It is to be considered that our students are to go into the world, and a world not of professed Catholics, but of inveterate, often bitter, commonly contemptuous, Protestants; nay, of Protestants who, so far as they come from Protestant universities and public schools, do know their own system, do know, in proportion to their general attainments, the doctrines and arguments of Protestantism. I should desire, then, to encourage in our students an intelligent apprehension of the relations, as I may call them, between the Church and society at large; for instance, the difference between the Church and a religious sect; the respective prerogatives of the Church and the civil power, what the Church claims of necessity, what it cannot dispense with, what it can; what it can grant, what it cannot. A Catholic hears the celibacy of the clergy discussed in general society; is that usage a matter of faith, or is it not of faith? He hears the Pope accused of interfering with the prerogatives of her Majesty, because he appoints a hierarchy. What is he to answer? What principle is to guide him in the remarks which he cannot escape from the necessity of making? He fills a station of importance, and he is addressed by some friend who has political reasons for wishing to know what is the difference between canon and civil law, whether the Council of Trent has been received in France, whether a priest cannot in certain cases absolve prospectively, what is meant by his *intention,* what by the *opus operatum;* whether, and in what sense, we consider Protestants to be heretics; whether anyone can be saved without sacramental confession; whether we deny the reality of natural virtue, or what worth we assign to it?

Questions may be multiplied without limit, which occur in conversation between friends, in social intercourse, or in the business of life, when no argument is needed, no subtle and delicate disquisition, but a few direct words stating the fact, and when perhaps a few words may even hinder most serious inconveniences to the Catholic body. Half the controversies which go on in the world arise from ignorance of the facts of the case; half the prejudices against Catholicity lie in the misinformation of the prejudiced parties. Candid persons are set right, and enemies silenced, by the mere statement of what it is that we believe. It will not answer the purpose for a Catholic to say, "I leave it to theologians," "I will ask my priest"; but it will commonly give him a triumph, as easy as it is complete, if he can then and there lay down the law. I say "lay down the law"; for remarkable it is that even those who speak against Catholicism like to hear about it, and will excuse its advocate from alleging arguments if he can gratify their curiosity by giving them information. Generally speaking, however, as I have said, what is given as information will really be an argument as well as information. I recollect, some twenty-five years ago, as they then were, clergymen of the Establishment, making a tour through Ireland. In the west or south they had occasion to become pedestrians for the day; and they took a boy of thirteen to be their guide. They amused themselves with putting questions to him on the subject of his religion; and one of them confessed to me on his return that that poor child put them all to silence. How? Not, of course, by any train of arguments, or refined theological disquisition, but merely by knowing and understanding the answers in his catechism.

4.

Nor will argument itself be out of place in the hands of laymen mixing with the world. As secular power, influence, or resources are never more suitably placed than when they are in the hands of Catholics, so secular knowledge and secular gifts are then best employed when they minister to Divine Revelation. Theologians inculcate the matter,

and determine the details of that Revelation; they view it from within; philosophers view it from without, and this external view may be
called the philosophy of religion, and the office of delineating it externally is most gracefully performed by laymen. In the first age laymen
were most commonly the Apologists. Such were Justin, Tatian, Athe-
nagoras, Aristides, Hermias, Minucius Felix, Arnobius, and Lactantius. In like manner in this age some of the most prominent defences of
the Church are from laymen: as De Maistre, Chateaubriand, Nicolas,
Montalembert, and others. If laymen may write, lay students may
read; they surely may read what their fathers may have written. They
might surely study other works too, ancient and modern, written
whether by ecclesiastics or laymen, which, although they do contain
theology, nevertheless, in their structure and drift, are polemical. Such
is Origen's great work against Celsus; and Tertullian's *Apology;* such
some of the controversial treatises of Eusebius and Theodoret; or St.
Augustine's *City of God;* or the tract of Vincentius Lirinensis. And I
confess that I should not even object to portions of Bellarmine's *Controversies,* or to the work of Suarez on laws, or to Melchoir Canus's
treatises on the *Loci Theologici.* On these questions in detail, however
—which are I readily acknowledge, very delicate—opinions may differ,
even where the general principle is admitted; but, even if we confine
ourselves strictly to the philosophy, that is, the external contemplation,
of religion, we shall have a range of reading sufficiently wide, and as
valuable in its practical application as it is liberal in its character. In it
will be included what are commonly called the Evidences; and what
is a subject of special interest at this day, the Notes of the Church.

But I have said enough in general illustrations of the rule which I
am recommending. One more remark I make, though it is implied in
what I have been saying: Whatever students read in the province of
religion, they read, and would read from the very nature of the case,
under the superintendence, and with the explanations, of those who
are older and more experienced than themselves.

DISCIPLINE OF MIND
8.

But I should be transgressing the limits assigned to an address of
this nature were I to proceed. I have not said anything, Gentlemen,
on the religious duties which become the members of a Catholic University, because we are directly concerned here with your studies
only. It is my consolation to know that so many of you belong to a
society or association, which the zeal of some excellent priests, one
especially, has been so instrumental in establishing in your great towns.
You do not come to us to have the foundation laid in your breasts of

that knowledge which is highest of all: it has been laid already. You have begun your mental training with faith and devotion; and then you come to us to add the education of the intellect to the education of the heart. Go on as you have begun, and you will be one of the proudest achievements of our great undertaking. We shall be able to point to you in proof that zeal for knowledge may thrive even under the pressure of secular callings; that mother wit does not necessarily make a man idle, nor inquisitiveness of mind irreverent; that shrewdness and cleverness are not incompatible with firm faith in the mysteries of Revelation; that attainment in literature and science need not make men conceited, nor above their station, nor restless, nor self-willed. We shall be able to point to you in proof of the power of Catholicism to make out of the staple of great towns exemplary and enlightened Christians—of those classes which, external to Ireland, are the problem and perplexity of patriotic statesmen, and the natural opponents of the teachers of every kind of religion.

As to myself, I wish I could by actual service and hard work of my own respond to your zeal, as so many of my dear and excellent friends, the professors of the University, have done and do. They have a merit, they have a claim on you, Gentlemen, in which I have no part. If I admire the energy and bravery with which you have undertaken the work of self-improvement, be sure I do not forget their public spirit and noble free devotion to the university any more than you do. I know I should not satisfy you with any praise of the supplement of our academical arrangements which did not include those who give to it its life. It is a very pleasant and encouraging sight to see both parties, the teachers and the taught, co-operating with a pure *espirit de corps* voluntarily—they as fully as you can do—for a great object; and I offer up my earnest prayers to the Author of all good, that He will ever bestow on you all, on professors and on students, as I feel sure He will bestow, rulers and superiors, who, by their zeal and diligence in their own place, shall prove themselves worthy both of your cause and of yourselves.

N. F. S. GRUNDTVIG

In January 1854 Bishop Mynster of the Danish church died in Copenhagen. At his funeral Mynster was spoken of as a "true witness to the truth," as one in the chain of witnesses to the truth that reached back to the apostles. The idea that Mynster had been a witness to the truth was monstrous to Søren Kierkegaard, the Danish theologian and philosopher. Kierkegaard launched a tremendous attack on the Church of Denmark: the Christianity preached in the state church was an apostasy from the Christianity of the

New Testament. New Testament Christianity was no longer to be found anywhere in the world. The history of the church was a history of increasing degeneracy.

N. F. S. Grundtvig (1783-1872) prudently waited until the end of his life to answer Kierkegaard's attack. From 1868 to 1872 Grundtvig wrote a series of essays which summed up his own views of Christianity and the church. These were collected as *The Christian Childhood Teachings* or *Basic Christian Teachings*.

Grundtvig argues that the signs of the Christian life are the confession of faith, the proclamation of the gospel, and the songs of praise. These have always been with the church. He refuses to include the personal appropriation of faith that was so central for Kierkegaard. Grundtvig stresses that redemption is a "word from the mouth of the Lord" at baptism and communion. The claim that the confession of faith by the congregation at baptism is a word from God himself is central to Grundtvig's view of the church. In public acts of worship the community returns God's Word to him with mutual participation in the covenant.

From N. F. S. Grundtvig, **Basic Christian Teachings**
THE INNATE AND THE REBORN HUMANITY

A monkey needs only to rise on its hind legs when it is dressed up and taught to imitate our human ways. Then it is said that the monkey is as human as many people we know. As long as this is true, it is futile to speak or write about the real humanity, be it the childlike innate life from our mother's womb or the childlike reborn life to which we are given birth in the Lord's baptism, the baptism of water and the Spirit. Even when we become aware that the difference between mankind and dumb creatures lies in words and speech, the true nature of man is yet obscured if we regard words to be only sounds. These would not differ from roars and barks or even from imitations such as can be taught to magpies and parrots.

Only when we become aware that human speech on our tongue and lips can and must be a marvelous something, a matchless gift which no bird or animal can be taught to imitate, only then are we qualified to consider humanity and the various stages in which this life is revealed to us. We must call this life created and divine, for this is our common bond and therefore our bond with our common and invisible creator, God. Then we discover with ease that human words and human speech have a threefold character which is peculiar to them. They have three qualities which separate them from cackling and parroting, namely, power, truth, and love. These qualities may vary, but some degree of each must be found in speech which is called human.

When we find no force, vigor, or willfulness in so-called speech, we call it empty and dead; when we find no truth, we call it false and dishonest; and when we find no love, we call it inhuman and heartless.

When we have established that humanity has its only forceful expression, its certain goals, its clear image in human speech with a higher invisible power, a profound truth, and an unlimited love, then we have the standpoint from which it can and must be judged. It will then be evident, of course, that innate and reborn humanity are as far apart as the quality, the width, and the degree of those higher life-powers called truth and love and goodness with which humanity expresses itself in speech. On the other hand, it is always the same humanity which we consider, with the same laws, the same original character, the same vital powers and criteria. Human life in its most obscure, most poverty-stricken and uncleanest form is nevertheless of the same kind of human life in its richest, purest, and most clarified shape. In one word, the malefactor on the cross had the same humanity as the only-begotten Son of God, our Lord Jesus Christ, to whom he cried, "Lord, remember me when you come in your kingdom!" and from whom he received the honest, forceful, and loving answer, "Verily I say to you, today you shall be with me in paradise."

If this were not so, the possibility of God's only Son becoming a real, human child, born of a woman, would be no greater than the possibility of a woman-born human child becoming a child of God, born of water and the Spirit. Then divinity would have excluded humanity and in return humanity would have excluded divinity. There could then have been no talk of a hearty, spiritual mutuality, inclination, and interaction. It is therefore awkwardly true when Mohammedan theologians deny the incarnation and the fusion of two natures in the personality of our Lord Jesus Christ, for they have always agreed with Mohammed and the Koran in declaring that the divine and the human natures are so different that no contact was possible. Consequently, they also reject the possibility of the work of redemption. They ultimately reject divine revelation to mankind and any response to human prayer. The minor falsehoods flow from the primary one. If man is not created in the image of God, he could not have fallen into sin and could not have been reborn. He could not even think truly and in a living manner about God, his Word, and his kingdom.

It is evidently inconsistent, argumentative, and extremely boring when so-called Catholic or Protestant theologians, evangelical or biblical, admit and insist on the creation of man in the image of God and the renewal in the same image by faith in the Son of God and the Son of man, our Lord Jesus Christ, when with equal vigor they insist that "the Fall," which occurred between creation and renewal and which makes the reconciliation or renewal indispensable for salvation, has distorted, or rather erased, the life in God's image and destroyed mankind, so that there is nothing left of the created glory or the relation to God. Consequently, all that Mohammedan theologians say about fallen man as well as about the entire nature of mankind would be true. Then the story of revelation and the whole work of reconciliation become a series of impossibilities which must be surmounted by the dead and powerless written word that whatever is impossible for man is possible for God.

I call this written word dead and powerless because it is only in its dead and powerless literalness that it seems to surmount the impossibilities. As soon as this Word of the Lord becomes spirit and life for us, we see immediately that what this word means and what it can and will eliminate are only the essential impossibilities *(adynata),* for these are impossibilities only when omnipotence is absent. In no way, however, can or will this word eliminate the alleged impossibilities, which should really be called impracticabilities or unmentionables, which neither God nor man can perform without self-contradiction. If, in regard to this matter, we still insist that God should perform what was impossible for man, we would mock both God and the truth; the voice of God and consciousness of truth, which we call our conscience, would have to revolt. The word which is in our mouth and in our heart would then obviously be denied all facility for expressing spiritual and eternal truths, unless the only accessible truth for man would be that there was no spiritual and eternal truth, or that truth was not true to itself, so that falsehood was truth. . . .

All of the so-called Bible history can be true as a divine history of revelation only when we assume that humanity is similar and the same before and after the Fall as well as before and after the rebirth. If Adam's humanity in the image of God had been destroyed by the Fall, God could not address the fallen Adam nor could Adam answer him. Still less could Abraham, the child of Adam, be called the friend of God; nor could God speak to Moses, a child of Adam, as a man speaks to his neighbor; nor could the spirit of God rest on other children of Adam, such as Samuel, David, the prophets, and John the Baptist. God could not use the voice of man to speak to men or touch their hearts. Adam's kin would be bewitched or demonized and would be made into an animal or a demon, an unnatural changeling composed of animality and demonism, who could neither be saved from anything nor to anything. As the children of the devil have always claimed, this makes sense only when one assumes that human existence was part of the hellish punishment and confinement placed upon the fallen angels. The Egyptians told us this when they claimed that the gods, fearing Typhon and his thunder, sought refuge among the animals.

If we then assume, as Holy Writ and our Savior Jesus Christ, born of woman, assumed, that it is the life of Adam and Eve in the image of God that was transplanted to the Savior as the "seed of the woman," despite the Fall and its awful consequences, and if we assume that he is the Second Adam and the New Man, cleansed, reconciled to God, and resurrected to a new and justified life, then we must also consider the new Christian, human life in the congregation of our Lord as the same humanity, originating in Adam, propagated through Eve, fallen, plundered, ill-treated, and corrupted by the Evil One in all of us, but raised from the Fall, saved, made whole, and divinely equipped in Christ. In baptism this life is continuously reborn in the Christian congregation, so that the Christian rebirth and renewal of humanity in all of us presupposes the Holy Spirit and originates through him out of the old humanity. This old humanity is the only human womb for new life, and, like Eve, it could not decline so far nor be so impoverished or corrupted that it could not find the grace of God and give birth to the children of the most high. As it is spoken by the prophet: "Shall I, who cause to bring forth, shut the womb?" [Isa. 66:9]

This plan of God, which necessarily seems obscure to us, has a new light cast upon it when we consider the Word, which is with God and with man, to be not only a means of revelation but also the exclusive expression of spiritual life. The Word is the light of life, even as Scripture says that "whatsoever doth make manifest is light" [Eph. 5:13 KJV], and that the Word "that enlightens every man was coming into the world" [John 1:9], but the Word which is with man is both the divine image of life and the divine image of light in which God created man.

From this insight it follows that in the human word about the invisible, the spiritual, and the eternal life we can trace the involvement and development of man. We can trace the Fall with all its sad and corrupted fruits and we can trace the resurrection of life with all its joyful and blessed fruits. We are never tempted to underrate the corruption of life in the sign and the perdition of death, but neither are we tempted to underrate the value of the Word as the unifying and continuing factor of life. Light is thus shed upon the tongues of all peoples in their relation to the new Christian life, and new tongues as of fire will rest upon them as the spirit gives them utterance to proclaim the great acts of God each in his own native language [see Acts 2.]

This is an important insight into the fact that humanity and the human word are inseparable. It is the necessary presupposition for all sound consideration of a Word of God as an impingement upon human life. When we speak as human beings about divine revelation, its impression upon the human heart and its expression in human speech, we are speaking about an insight that is more human than it is actually Christian. This insight is concerned about the relation between God and man, or between spirit and dust, and it can be considered to precede Christianity. Inasmuch, however, as the Christian revelation is actually the "incarnation of the Word," and inasmuch as Christian worship in spirit and truth is the Christian yet physical acceptance and utterance of the word (hearing through the ear and confessing with the mouth), the insight into the nature of the Word must necessarily come from the Christian life of human beings, and it is completely indispensable for the full development, growth, and explanation of humanity.

Insight into the nature of the Word has been investigated and exhausted in the ancient Greek church and it has been expressed as a Logos-science or a Christo-logy. This is an obscure and complicated matter, hard to explain and therefore without much benefit. It is invaluable, however, in the knowledge and clarification of the matter, to consider historically the life of the Word in relation to the languages of God's people, particularly of our own people, and I will therefore direct the attention of all enlightened Christians to this.

It would be too elaborate to consider both the Hebrew and the Danish languages in this connection and to compare their facility for expressing "spiritual things with spiritual" [1 Cor. 2:13 KJV], and I shall postpone this to another time. I would like in closing, however, in a general way, to give information about the grossly misunderstood connection between folk-life and Christianity by calling attention to the inseparable relation between the language of a people and its inner nature, its mode of expression and its development. . . .

It would be unspiritual and awkward to banish or even eradicate the old, original humanity in order to give room to a new Christian humanity, but it would be just as unspiritual and awkward to banish and eradicate folk-life and replace it with Christianity. If we should say to the spirit of a people: Depart, thou unclean spirit and give room to the Holy Spirit!, then we could be rid of the folk spirit, but this would be no guarantee that it would be replaced by the Holy Spirit. It might exclude all spirits in this people, all spiritual influence and intuition, all spiritual and profound understanding and insight.

THE WORD OF ETERNAL LIFE FROM THE
MOUTH OF THE LORD TO THE CHURCH

The fact that the Word from the mouth of the Lord is spoken to all of us at baptism and Communion is the one true foundation for the faith of all Christians, old and young, wise and uninformed. This Word from the mouth of the Lord is the foundation for light and life; it is the rock and the sun, enlightening and enlivening in the spirit of the Lord, which never deviates from what he has said. The Holy Scriptures are means of information. The Scriptures are not mentioned by the Lord and they do not contain the confession of faith which the church uses at baptism. They are the tools of the Spirit and the scholars, and they are given freedom of influence on the condition that the scholars use them in a Christian manner, in accord with the Christian faith that is obvious to all. There must be a free interchange between the emancipated congregation of the Lord and the scholars, and the latter may never present their insights as articles of faith. . . .

I have always only toyed with the scraps of paper which dignified scholars place on the scales to counteract the unanimous witness of the church of baptism in continuous succession from generation to generation, from baptism to baptism. Even the writings of Irenaeus or Eusebius do not weigh more than a goose quill in comparison with the ancient and solemn testimony of the free congregation at baptism in regard to the faith. In the churches of compulsion, however, with their priesthoods and their ritual, this basic relationship has been so concealed, overlooked, and obscured that in my lifelong career I have not been able to make even professors understand that when I refer to the confession of faith at baptism of the ancient church I am referring to the audible "Yes—Amen!" of the congregation. I am not, as Lessing does, referring to ancient recordings of the so-called *Symbolum Apostolicum* or other utterances about the confession in the writings of the so-called fathers. . . .

Christian enlightenment proceeds from the proposition that the entire creation and temporal existence has its origin in the eternal "Word of God," which was with God and was God and which is the light of man. Similarly, the Christian enlightenment as well as the Christian life and history proceed from the spiritual fact that the "Word of God" became flesh in the fullness of time in order to gather a faithful congregation which lives in a hearty fellowship with him. This congregation derives its spirit from his spirit, its flesh from his flesh, and it must therefore be the aim of all Christian enlightenment to show how all temporal things have their original coherence in the Word of God from eternity, and to show how, in the course of time, all things have cohered in Christ Jesus and how they live and move in his congregation [John 1; Eph. 4; Col. 1.]

THE CHRISTIAN, THE SPIRITUAL,
AND THE ETERNAL LIFE

In our day it is so difficult to be understood when one speaks about
the real life, as it is lived daily among us and before our very eyes, that
everyone who writes about it can surely expect to be grossly misunderstood by most readers. If we are not believed when we write about
earthly things, how can we be believed when we write about the
heavenly? It is therefore almost miraculous that some people still speak
and write about the Christian, the spiritual, and the eternal life. Apparently no one practices it; and from the time of creation until now only
one person has carried it through, namely, the only-begotten, the
unequaled, "Jesus Christ," who was crucified under Pontius Pilate and
is now seated in heaven at the right hand of God, whence he shall
come on the final day to judge the living and the dead.

It was therefore no trick for Søren Kierkegaard, as he was applauded
by the world, to describe our so-called Christian preaching, Bible-read-
ing, worship, infant baptism, and Communion as an immense tom-
foolery and a merry farce. But this became tragicomical, yea, not only
greatly tragic but even mockery, when many people come to believe
that we so-called ministers, we "black-gowns," were deceiving them.
We were telling them that if they would just listen to us with approval,
let their infants be baptized and go to Communion on occasion, then
they were participating in a secret and incomprehensible manner, yet
in a real sense, in the Christian, the spiritual, and the eternal life, as
our Lord Jesus Christ had lived it on earth and promised it eternally
to his faithful followers.

This was no trick, and Søren Kierkegaard was careful not to write
that he, either by his own insight or out of the New Testament, had
gained a light and a power to live a real Christian, spiritual, and eternal
life which he could transmit to others. On the contrary, he writes that
out of his own experience and out of the New Testament he has learned
and can clearly demonstrate that everything which today claims to be
a truly Christian, spiritual and eternal life is a coarse lie and a monstrous delusion, even an enormous blasphemy compared to the way it
is described in the New Testament which he accepted as the true,
infallible teaching and life history of Jesus Christ. By this he has obviously pledged his own honor and the New Testament to the Danish
readers in the contention that no Christian, spiritual, and eternal life
exists on earth. It is therefore not only up to us but up to that Jesus
Christ, whom we confess, and to that Spirit which guides and comforts
us, to show the world that such a life does exist, even though it has long
been hidden and is hard to recognize.

It is quite evident that the solution to this unequaled task of living can be given only to a small degree by the pen. It is obvious that we cannot by our pens create such a Christian life, when even the Lord's apostles could not to the slightest degree transplant it or communicate it by their pens, even though we assume that their hand was guided by Christ's spirit. It is also clear as daylight that when we claim that the apostolic writings themselves did not possess or lead a Christian, spiritual, and eternal life we cannot without contradiction ascribe to these writings the ability to transplant or communicate the Christian life which they themselves did not possess or lead. We cannot without blasphemy or ridiculous pride ascribe to our own writings that divine power of living and transfer of life which we deny to the apostolic writings.

The apostolic writings, however, by being a true description of the life of Jesus Christ and of the Christian life as it was found in those who wrote and those who lived it in the Christian congregation, and by being a prophecy of the growth of Christian life in the congregation until it reaches the goal and pattern set by Jesus' own life, can be useful and illuminating for those who believe in Jesus Christ and participate in the Christian life. In the same manner our writings can be useful and illuminating for living Christians, in part when they give a truthful description of the ways and means whereby the present weak, vague, and obscure Christian life has been transmitted to us, and in part when they are a prophecy of how the Christian life will grow in the history of the church until it reaches the fullness, strength, and clarity of the Lord.

To this end I have devoted a lifetime of writing, seeking as well as I might and with great diligence to give the information that it is by the Word of the Lord's own mouth, as it is spoken at baptism and Communion and by nothing else, that his Spirit and his power of living are communicated. His spiritual life disappears where we reject or falsify this Word spoken by the Lord, and the Christian life will be untraceable, where we might maintain this Word unaltered but only half believe it, and expect spirit, life, and growth by other channels as well.

From the perplexity in the days of Søren Kierkegaard as well as the confusion that existed during the recent polemics about "altar-book baptism," it is obvious that the usefulness of my writings has not been as great as I might desire. I had not expected much else, as long as the Christian life, which cannot emerge or grow through book-writing, has not been more widespread or more clearly developed through "the Word and the Faith" at baptism and Communion than all signs show it to be. I hope, however, that my brief description of "The Christian Signs of Life" may have prepared a growing information about the cause of Christian living which we have missed up to now.

It is a Christian insight, which will shed light on the matter even though it does not completely clarify it, that we must and shall sum up the signs of Christian life in "Confession, Proclamation, and Praise" in the language of the people. I have strongly felt the absence of this when I searched for the Christian life in myself and in the congregation, and when I had to defend the Lord Jesus Christ against the dishonoring accusation that he had permitted his life to die in the church or had been unable, with the exception of a brief apostolic period, to bring it out of its swaddling clothes or to nurture it to youthful flowering or adult maturity.

According to the apostolic scriptures we assume that "faith, hope, and love" are the spiritual and eternal content of the Christian life, but as long as we cannot differentiate between "these three" according to heathen, Jewish, or Christian speech, nor distinguish between everyday and Sunday understanding, we cannot demonstrate clear expressions of life and clear signs of life, which are peculiar to Christianity. All postulates about Christian life therefore seem to be arbitrary. They seem to involve us in a confused polemic about what is spiritual and what is physical in human life, and about the relationship which Christianity, according to the witness of experience, has to that which the human spirit calls spiritual.

We must discover the Christian expressions of the life of faith in the three ways: in the confession of faith at baptism, in the Christian hope as we have it in the Lord's Prayer at baptism as well as at Communion, and in the love expressed in Christ's word of submission to his faithful or his declaration of love to his bride, the church, in Communion. Only then can we, in our congregational life, show a Christian confession, proclamation, and praise which are the peculiar and unmistakable signs of the Christian faith, the Christian hope, and the Christian love. Then we can speak clearly and judge thoroughly about their relation to faith, hope, and love.

The Christian life in itself will undoubtedly continue to be a profound mystery to us, but the same is true of our total human life, which is separate from that of animals, for no one can make the Christian life known except through comparable spiritual expressions. If someone should object that the Christian signs of life, such as confession, proclamation, and praise, are only words and not action, then we rightly answer that the invisible spirit of man as well as of God can demonstrate its life only through that invisible word which can be heard by the ear and felt in the heart. Every action, by the hand and by all visible things, is vaguely related to the invisible spirit, and we can only glimpse the relationship through a word of enlightenment. Even then we will see darkly in a vague and ambiguous way. The perfect Christian love will seek to express itself in a marvelous generosity and bodily sacrifice, but even the apostolic letter gives testimony that we can give all we own to the poor and we can give our body to be burned and still not have Christian love. It is also evident that many people have done these things without calling themselves Christian or desiring even to be Christians. Even the most dedicated works of love can only be signs of Christian love when they are clearly related to the Christian confession and the Christian song of praise.

This is the outward significance of enlightenment about "the Christian signs of life"; the significance inward and upward is even more important for all of us. We seek in vain to probe the mysteries of the Christian life, whether it be the mystery of the call in preaching the gospel (the cry of the Christmas message), or the mystery of nurture in the Supper. But the Christian way of life does become brighter and easier for us when we discover the company in which we can seek and expect the Christian faith, the Christian hope, and the Christian love, so that faith is strengthened, hope expanded, and love increased. By this we are furthermore comforted about the gap between the shape of the Christian life in the congregation of the present day and the shape in which it is described by the apostles, in part in themselves and the first fruits of the congregation, but especially in Jesus Christ with fullness and purity. We are comforted not as bookworms who depend on the perfection of an alien life whose description they devour but as a bright boy is comforted about the distance between himself and his adult brother or his aging father. When we are turned aright in our living consideration of the Christian life as a spiritual human life, which is just as real and a lot more human than our physical life, then, like the apostle Paul, we are not anxious about our distance from the goal. Then we see that the Christian life begins with a real conception according to the will of the Spirit, and as the Lord says, with a real birth by water and the Spirit. Then it continues, as did the Lord himself, to grow in age and wisdom and favor with God and man. Then, like Paul, we will strive to forget what is behind us in favor of what is ahead, and by living progress we will reach for the wreath and the crown.

When we regard the Christian life, as also the human life, the mind tells us that there is light behind us but darkness ahead. We can understand no more of life than what we have experienced. On the Christian life-way, however, there is an unusual and even superhuman light. The Lord has said that whosoever follows after him shall never be in darkness, for he is the true light of the world. The lantern that guides us through the darkness is, as the apostle writes, a sure word of prophecy, which is known by the fact that it corresponds to the Rule of Faith and mankind's sure foundation.

It is a necessary consequence of the covenant of baptism that the spiritual life to which we are born in baptism can in no way be demonic. In every way that spiritual life has to be divine. Christianity presupposes very clearly that human life in the image of God can only be reborn and renewed by a wondrous separation from devildom. How much of humanity is devildom and how much a person has to contribute during his lifetime to the release from deviltry and to the growth of divinity is a puzzle for the mind that can be solved only by experience, and it is no wonder that independent efforts to analyze and determine this matter have led to confusion. The more we listen to the description of the scribes of what is called the "order of salvation," how Scripture calls for us to shed the old man and put on the new, the less we understand the matter. We experience a boundless confusion where it seems as if all of human life must be eradicated as deviltry, or contrariwise, as if there was no deviltry, so that man should either direct the new Christian life or stand beside it as an idle observer.

When a person is a living Christian, even when he has not come of age, he realizes that none of the alternatives is true. If there were no devil, no Satan, no Father of Lies, no man of darkness, no murdering angel, if he had no power over man, there would be no word of truth in the gospel of Christ, not an iota of truth in the message about the Son of God as the savior of the world from the power of sin, darkness and death. For this power can exist and be active only in an unclean spirit of the world. If, on the other hand, all of human nature had become demonic at the Fall, the Son of God could have become a real human being as little as he could have become a devil. Then the new man could not have been wrought in God's image through a rebirth and a renewal of the old man but only by a brand new creation entirely independent of the old man. How the very complicated matter of sanctification and salvation can take place in fallen and sinful humanity, corporately as well as individually, is hidden from our eyes. The Son of God became man in all respects; he was like us but without sin. His life as man cannot demonstrate for us how the new man, who grows up, is liberated from sin and Satan by being cleansed from the "defilement of body and spirit" [2 Cor. 7:1]. If we are to know this, the spirit of truth as the spirit of our Lord Jesus Christ must reveal it for us. But, inasmuch as we, during the growth of the new man, cannot dispense with the tentative knowledge of the growth of life, the spirit of the Lord will also inform us about this when we pray. For it is written about this same spirit: "He will declare to you the things that are to come" [John 16:13]. When it still does not happen the reason must be that the church's faith in the Holy Spirit is either so shaky or so vague that he cannot be called upon or distinguished from the spirits of delusion. Inasmuch as we have only recently gained a sure and definite belief in the Holy Spirit as a divine part of the Trinity, and inasmuch as we have thereby discovered the nature of that "confession" of the incarnate Jesus Christ upon which the spirit of truth can and shall be distinguished from the spirit of delusion, we have only now received the revelation of the Spirit concerning the usefulness for the whole congregation that we keep the faith, fight, and win the crown. This happened when we placed our trust in the confession of faith at baptism as a word to us from the mouth of the Lord. . . .

It is furthermore a very ordinary bit of human information that the human life which is to be raised is the same life which is under the Fall. The same prodigal son who was lost was the one who was found. He who was dead became alive. The same sheep that was lost was carried home on the shoulder of the shepherd. In the same manner the new man is, strictly speaking, not any other man than the old man. He is only another person in the same sense that Saul became another person when he was anointed and the Spirit came upon him. It is quite clear that God's Son acquired the old mankind when he came to earth as the offspring of a woman, of Abraham's seed and David's seed. Even the new human body of the resurrection was basically the same as the body that was nailed to the cross. Yet, all the scribes who stressed the Christian life as that of our Lord Jesus Christ and no one else have more or less cut the so-called new human life in Christ and his church off from the old human life, as if the latter was a physical life of sin which had to be destroyed and eradicated in order that the new and entirely different human life could succeed it. This basic error led not only to all the monastic rules but also to all the orthodox dogmatics books, in which the total and basic depravity and spiritual incompetence for doing good was made the foundation for the work of reconciliation. This was claimed, even though it was clearly evident that the human life which was in the need of salvation, of reconciliation, of rebirth and renewal according to the image of the creator would be destroyed. The consequences were that the old human life, which was given up, daily went to the devil, while the new life either was nothing at all or had no power or was utterly useless except for the purpose of writing dogmatics and memorizing them. Or else the new spiritual life became inhuman, a demonic life, which battled against humanity and, under all sorts of aliases, raised to the skies that opinionated self-righteousness which always had been characteristic of Satan, the murderer of human life. . . .

It is finally a common human and even evangelical truth that God
and his Spirit treat us the same way they want us to treat our neighbor.
This means that we must conquer evil by good, and this is, even by
human experience, the only way in which evil is profoundly overcome,
driven out, and replaced. Even the law of God, which can crush the
proudest human being with thunder and lightning, cannot eradicate
evil desire and lust. These yield only to the desires of goodness, of
which evil desire is a distorted image. Pride is driven out of the heart
only by humility; sensuality, which is impure love, only by pure love;
and the desire for the glories of this world only by the desire for the
glories of God's kingdom. But I know of no Christian moralist since
the days of the apostles who has described the Holy Spirit in this light
and spirit. Such moralists began like the mystics, in the heart, and thus
they began in the darkness of the old man which was to be reborn and
was to nurture himself with his own love to God and the neighbor.
The result was a false and unreal Christianity from beginning to end.
Or they began with the law, not as a mirror but as a living force and
power which was to demolish the pagan temple and out of its ruins
erect the temple of the Holy Spirit. This was done despite the testimony of the Lord that when sanctification begins from without the
result will be a tomb filled with filth and dead bones. This was done
despite the fact of human experience that when sanctification begins
from within we can put on the whole armor of the law and combat the
tiniest evil desire until doomsday without moving it one whit. Christian
life in the world is always a life of faith and thereby spiritual and
invisible, but inasmuch as our physical conduct is open and visible,
the Christian church and all its members must, as the apostle writes,
use the compulsion of the law, be it the law of Moses or Danish law, to
regulate its conduct. If we wish to live a Christian life, we must guard
against a sanctification of our legal conduct. We must also guard
against the temptation to change the gospel to a new Christian law,
which is to compel the soul to a Christian way of thinking and the
heart to a Christian life of love. When we try to do this, we either know
nothing about Christian living or we squander it, for we can neither be
saved nor sanctified by the law without falling from grace.

The tangled knot of Christian living as a life of faith is seen already
in all of the letters of Paul. From the very beginning this knot has if
not strangled the Christian life among non-Jewish Chistians then
stunted its growth. It has caused that malady which has been obvious
since the days of the apostles. Inasmuch as this knot can be untied only
at the resurrection of the body from the dead or by a transformation
of the body of the living people who wait for the visible return of the
Lord, it is important not to try to cut the knot but to live with it in

faith as a thorn in the flesh and to be content with the grace of God whose "power is made perfect in weakness" [2 Cor. 12:9.]

Even when we hold fast to the faith that the Christian spiritual life, to which we are reborn in baptism and in which we are nurtured at the Supper, is truly an eternal life, we must yet give up the idea that we can become clearly aware of the Christian life's eternal nature in this world. This is so, because it is only in perfect unity with the Lord and his church that this clear awareness can arise, but also because the awareness is impossible except when "the inner becomes outward," when all the senses and the body functions become as spiritual as the Word of faith, hope, and love is spiritual on our lips and in our hearts. Our whole body must become an eternally pleasing habitation, a perfect tool, and a clear, unblemished mirror of the spirit, the divine power which came from the Father in order to begin and complete the good works in all of our Lord's church. This work will be completed only on the Day of our Lord Jesus Christ, and it will work toward this end in us only when we really denounce ourselves, give up spiritual independence, and willingly let the Holy Spirit, as a divine person, guide our heart and our tongue. Then we may have the renewed, divine power of living, which alone can create, maintain, and nurture the new humanity in the divine image of Jesus Christ.

LUX MUNDI

After Charles Gore (1853-1932) had been appointed first principal of Pusey House in 1884, he gathered about him like-minded Anglo-Catholics at Oxford. Aubrey Moore, Arthur Lyttleton, H. S. Holland, J. R. Illingworth, E. S. Talbot, R. C. Moberly, and William Locke founded a "holy society" with Gore. It was yet another in that long series of Oxford religious clubs stretching from Wycliffe's "Lollards" in the fourteenth century down through the Wesleyan "Methodists" to Newman's "Tractarians," all creating ecclesiastical sound and fury of one sort or another. In 1889 the young priests published a collection of essays entitled *Lux Mundi: A Series of Studies in the Religion of the Incarnation. Lux Mundi* signaled a positive rather than a negative impact of science upon theology. For Gore, *Lux Mundi* was part of the "process in which the Church, standing firm in her old truths, enters into the apprehension of the new social and intellectual movements of each age, and because 'the truth makes her free,' is able to assimilate all new material, to welcome and give its place to all new knowledge."

In the *Lux Mundi* essay reprinted here, "The Incarnation in Relation to Development," J. R. Illingworth (1848-1915) argues that the central con-

cept of the ancient church is the Logos doctrine of the Word of God operative in the world of material nature, everywhere and in all things, not only
in the incarnate Lord. He employs evolutionary concepts to support and
illuminate the doctrine of the incarnation. The essay maintains that divine
self-disclosure has not been confined only to the biblical record. God discloses himself in nature, art, history, and science.

To Illingworth Darwin's theory shows not only how God works naturally
in creation, but how he works in revelation: "God is as truly, though not
as fully, found in the disclosures of science as in Jesus Christ. It is really
rebellion against the word to shut our ears to scientific revelation." All
that comes before Christ, the Lux Mundi, even the Old Testament, is imperfect and infirm. The church which comes after Christ is the continuation
of his incarnate body and must interpret the eternal truth of that incarnation in the light of the knowledge of each age.

From Lux Mundi, "The Incarnation and Development"

I. The last few years have witnessed the gradual acceptance by
Christian thinkers of the great scientific generalization of our age,
which is briefly, if somewhat vaguely, described as the Theory of Evolution. History has repeated itself, and another of the 'oppositions of
science' to theology has proved upon inquiry to be no opposition at
all. Such oppositions and reconciliations are older than Christianity,
and are part of what is often called the dialectical movement; the
movement, that is to say, by question and answer, out of which all
progress comes. But the result of such a process is something more
than the mere repetition of a twice-told tale. It is an advance in our
theological thinking; a definite increase of insight; a fresh and fuller
appreciation of those 'many ways' in which 'God fulfils Himself.' For
great scientific discoveries, like the heliocentric astronomy, are not
merely new facts to be assimilated; they involve new ways of looking
at things. And this has been pre-eminently the case with the law of
evolution; which, once observed, has rapidly extended to every department of thought and history, and altered our attitude towards all
knowledge. Organisms, nations, languages, institutions, customs, creeds,
have all come to be regarded in the light of their development, and
we feel that to understand what a thing really is, we must examine how
it came to be. Evolution is in the air. It is the category of the age; a
partus temporis; a necessary consequence of our wider field of comparison. We cannot place ourselves outside it, or limit the scope of its
operation. And our religious opinions, like all things else that have
come down on the current of development, must justify their existence
by an appeal to the past.

It is the object of the following pages to consider what popular misconceptions of the central doctrine of our religion, the Incarnation, have been remedied; what more or less forgotten aspects of it have been restored to their due place; what new lights have been thrown upon the fulness of its meaning, in the course of our discussion of the various views of evolution.

In face of the historical spirit of the age, the study of past theology can never again be regarded as merely a piece of religious antiquarianism. And there are two classes of mind to which it should be of especial service. Many an earnest worker in the Christian cause, conscious how little the refinements of philosophy can influence for good or evil the majority of men, and generously impatient of all labour wasted, when the labourers are so few, is apt to underestimate what he considers the less practical departments of theology; forgetful that there are souls, and those among the noblest, to whom the primary avenue of access is the intellect, and who can only be led homeward by the illuminative way. The Christian of this type may be materially helped towards welcoming wider views, by being convinced that what he has been too easily apt to regard as metaphysical subtleties, or as dangerous innovations, or as questionable accommodations of the Gospel to the exigencies of passing controversy, are after all an integral part of the great Catholic tradition. On the other hand, many plausible attacks upon the Christian creed are due to the inadequate methods of its professed interpreters. Fragments of doctrine, torn from their context and deprived of their due proportions, are brandished in the eyes of men by well-meaning but ignorant apologists as containing the sum total of the Christian faith, with the lamentable consequence that even earnest seekers after truth, and much more its unearnest and merely factious adversaries, mislead themselves and others into thinking Christianity discredited, when in reality they have all along been only criticising its caricature. Such men need reminding that Christianity is greater than its isolated interpreters or misinterpreters in any age; that in the course of its long history it has accumulated answers to many an objection which they in their ignorance think new; and that, in the confidence of its universal mission and the memory of its many victories, it still claims to be sympathetic, adequate, adaptable to the problems and perplexities of each successive age.

The general tendency of thought since the Reformation has been in the direction of these partial presentations of Christianity. The Reformers, from various causes, were so occupied with what is now called Soteriology, or the scheme of salvation, that they paid but scant attention to the other aspects of the Gospel. And the consequence was that a whole side of the great Christian tradition, and one on which many of its greatest thinkers had lavished the labours of a lifetime, was allowed almost unconsciously to lapse into comparative oblivion; and the religion of the Incarnation was narrowed into the religion of the Atonement. Men's views of the faith dwindled and became subjective and self-regarding, while the gulf was daily widened between things sacred and things secular; among which latter, art and science, and the whole political and social order, gradually came to be classed.

Far otherwise was it with the great thinkers of the early Church; and that not from an underestimate of the saving power of the Cross, which was bearing daily fruit around them, of penitence, and sanctity, and martyrdom; but from their regarding Christian salvation in its context. They realized that redemption was a means to an end, and that end the reconsecration of the whole universe to God. And so the very completeness of their grasp on the Atonement led them to dwell upon the cosmical significance of the Incarnation, its purpose to 'gather together all things in one.' For it was an age in which the problems of the universe were keenly felt. Philosophical thinking, if less mature, was not less exuberant than now, and had already a great past behind it. And the natural world, though its structural secrets were little understood, fascinated the imagination and strained the heart with its appealing beauty. Spiritualism, superstition, scepticism, were tried in turn but could not satisfy. The questionings of the intellect still pressed for a solution. And the souls of Christians were stirred to proclaim that the new power which they felt within them, restoring, quickening, harmonizing the whole of their inner life, would also prove the key to all these mysteries of matter and of mind.

So it was that the theology of the Incarnation was gradually drawn out, from the teaching of S. Paul and of S. John. The identity of Him Who was made man and dwelt among us, with Him by Whom all things were made and by Whom all things consist; His eternal pre-existence as the reason and word of God, the Logos; His indwelling presence in the universe as the source and condition of all its life, and in man as the light of His intellectual being; His Resurrection, His Ascension,—all these thoughts were woven into one magnificent picture, wherein creation was viewed as the embodiment of the Divine ideas, and therefore the revelation of the Divine character; manifesting its Maker with increasing clearness at each successive stage in the great scale of being, till in the fulness of time He Himself became man, and thereby lifted human nature, and with it the material universe to which man is so intimately linked; and triumphing over the sin and death under which creation groaned and travailed, opened by His Resurrection and then by His Ascension vistas of the glorious destiny purposed for His creatures before the world was. . . .

Such is the view of the Incarnation in what may be called its intellectual aspect, which we find gradually expressed with increasing clearness by the Fathers, from Justin to Athanasius. And with all its deep suggestiveness, it is still a severely simple picture, drawn in but few outlines, and those strictly scriptural. It was born of no abstract love of metaphysic, and stands in striking contrast to the wild speculations of the time. Its motive and its method were both intensely practical; its motive being to present Christianity to the mind as well as to the heart; and its method no more than to connect and interpret and explain the definite statements of S. Paul and S. John. Passing over the dark ages, when thought was in comparative abeyance, and the energies of the Church absorbed in the work of conversion and organization, we come, in the twelfth and following centuries, to a second period of intellectual ferment, less brilliant than that which characterized the decadence of the old civilization, but instinct with all the fire and restlessness of youth. Unsobered as yet by experience, and unsupplied with adequate material from without, thought preyed upon itself and revelled in its new-found powers of speculation. Fragments of the various heresies which the Fathers had answered and outlived reappeared with all the halo of novelty around them. Religions were crudely compared and sceptical inferences drawn. Popular unbelief, checked in a measure by authority, avenged itself by ridicule of all things sacred. It was a period of intense intellectual unrest, too many-sided and inconsequent to be easily described. But as far as the anti-Christian influences of the time can be summarized they were mainly two:—the Arabic pantheism, and the materialism which was fostered in the medical schools; kindred errors, both concerned with an undue estimate of matter. And how did Christian theology meet them? Not by laying stress, like the later Deists, upon God's infinite distance from the world, but upon the closeness of His intimacy with it; by reviving, that is, with increased emphasis the Patristic doctrine of the Incarnation, as the climax and the keystone of the whole visible creation. There is a greater divergence of opinion, perhaps, among the Schoolmen than among the Fathers; and a far greater amount of that unprofitable subtlety for which they are apt to be somewhat too unintelligently ridiculed. But on the point before us, as on all others of primary importance, they are substantially unanimous, and never fail in dignity:

'As the thought of the Divine mind is called the Word, Who is the Son, so the unfolding of that thought in external action *(per opera extiora)* is named the word of the Word.'

'The whole world is a kind of bodily and visible Gospel of that Word by which it was created.'

'Every creature is a theophany.'

'Every creature is a Divine word, for it tells of God.'

'The wisdom of God, when first it issued in creation, came not to us naked, but clothed in the apparel of created things. And then when the same wisdom would manifest Himself to us as the Son of God, He took upon Him a garment of flesh and so was seen of men.'

'The Incarnation is the exaltation of human nature and consummation of the Universe.'

Such quotations might be multiplied indefinitely from the pages of the Schoolmen and scholastic theologians. And the line of thought which they indicate seems to lead us by a natural sequence to view the Incarnation as being the predestined climax of creation, independently of human sin. The thought is of course a mere speculation, 'beyond that which is written,' but from its first appearance in the twelfth century it has been regarded with increasing favour; for it is full of rich suggestiveness, and seems to throw a deeper meaning into all our investigations of the world's gradual development.

Again, from the relation of the Word to the universe follows His relation to the human mind. For 'that life was the light of men.'

'The created intellect is the imparted likeness of God,' says S. Thomas; and again, 'Every intellectual process has its origin in the Word of God Who is the Divine Reason.' 'The light of intellect is imprinted upon us by God Himself *(immediate a Deo).*' 'God continually works in the mind, as being both the cause and the guide of its natural light.' 'In every object of sensitive or rational experience God Himself lies hid.' 'All intelligences know God implicitly, in every object of their knowledge.' 'Christ is our internal teacher, and no truth of any kind is known but through Him; though He speaks not in language as we do, but by interior illumination.' 'The philosophers have taught us the sciences, for God revealed them to them.'

II. The point to be noticed in the teaching of which such passages are scattered samples, is that the Schoolmen and orthodox mystics of the middle age, with Pantheism, materialism, rationalism surging all around them, and perfectly conscious of the fact, met these errors, not by denying the reality of matter, or the capacity of reason, as later apologists have often done, but by claiming for both a place in the Theology of the Word. And this Theology of the Word was, in reality, quite independent of, and unaffected by, the subtleties and fallacies and false opinions of the age, cobwebs of the unfurnished intellect which time has swept away. It was a magnificent framework, outside and above the limited knowledge of the day and the peculiarities of individual thinkers; an inheritance from the Patristic tradition, which the Fathers, in their turn, had not invented, but received as Apostolic doctrine from Apostolic men, and only made more explicit by gradual definition, during centuries when, it has been fairly said, 'the highest reason, as independently exercised by the wise of the world, was entirely coincident with the highest reason as inspiring the Church.' We have now to consider whether this view of the Incarnation, which, though in the countries most influenced by the Reformation it has dropped too much out of sight, has yet never really died out of the Church at large, is in any way incompatible with the results of modern science; or whether, on the contrary, it does not provide an outline to which science is slowly but surely giving reality and content.

And at the outset we must bear in mind one truth which is now recognised on all sides as final—viz. that the finite intellect cannot transcend the conditions of finitude, and cannot therefore reach, or even conceive itself as reaching, an absolute, or, in Kantian phraseology, a speculative knowledge of the beginning of things. Whatever strides science may make in time to come towards decomposing atoms and forces into simpler and yet simpler elements, those elements will still have issued from a secret laboratory into which science cannot enter, and the human mind will be as far as ever from knowing what they really are. Further, this initial limitation must of necessity qualify our knowledge in its every stage. If we cannot know the secret of the elements in their simplicity, neither can we know the secret of their successive combinations. Before the beginning of our present system, and behind the whole course of its continuous development, there is a vast region of possibility, which lies wholly and for ever beyond the power of science to affirm or to deny. It is in this region that Christian theology claims to have its roots, and of this region that it professes to give its adherents certitude, under conditions and methods it fearlessly asserts that they are nowise inconsistent with any ascertained or ascertainable result of secular philosophy.

As regards the origin of things, this is obvious. Science may resolve the complicated life of the material universe into a few elementary forces, light and heat and electricity, and these perhaps into modifications of some still simpler energy; but of the origin of energy *(to prōton kinoun)* it knows no more than did the Greeks of old. Theology asserts that in the beginning was the Word, and in Him was life, the life of all things created: in other words, that He is the source of all that energy, whose persistent, irresistible versatility of action is for ever at work moulding and clothing and peopling worlds. The two conceptions are complementary, and cannot contradict each other.

But to pass from the origin to the development of things: the new way of looking at nature was thought at first both by its adherents and opponents alike to be inimical to the doctrine of final causes. And here was a direct issue joined with Theology at once: for the presence of final causes or design in the universe has not only been in all ages one of the strongest supports for natural religion; it is contained in the very notion of a rational creation, a creation by an Eternal Reason. And this was supposed to be directly negatived by the doctrine of the survival of the fittest through natural selection: for if of a thousand forms, which came by chance into existence, the one which happened to correspond best with its environment survived, while the remainder disappeared, the adaptation of the survivor to its circumstances would have all the appearance of design, while in reality due to accident. If, therefore, this principle acted exclusively throughout the universe, the result would be a semblance of design without any of its reality, from which no theological inference could be drawn. But this consequence of natural selection obviously depends upon the exclusiveness of its action. If it is only one factor among many in the world's development; while there are instances of adaptation in nature, and those the more numerous, for which it fails to account, what has been called its dysteleological significance is at an end. Now its own author soon saw and admitted the inadequacy of the theory of natural selection, even in biology, the field of its first observation, to account for all the facts: while countless phenomena in other regions, such as the mechanical principles involved in the structure of the universe, the laws of crystallography and chemical combination, the beauty of nature taken in connection with its effect upon the mind, irresistibly suggest design, and render the alternative hypothesis, from its mere mathematical improbability, almost inconceivable. And there is now, therefore, a general disposition to admit that the force of this particular attack upon the doctrine of final causes has been considerably overstated. . . .

All this is in perfect harmony with our Christian creed, that all things were made by the Eternal Reason; but more than this, it illustrates and is illustrated by the further doctrine of His indwelling presence in the things of His creation; rendering each of them at once a revelation and a prophecy, a thing of beauty and finished workmanship, worthy to exist for its own sake, and yet a step to higher purposes, an instrument for grander work.

> God tastes an infinite joy
> In infinite ways—one everlasting bliss,
> From whom all being emanates, all power
> Proceeds: in whom is life for evermore,
> Yet whom existence in its lowest form
> Includes; where dwells enjoyment, there is He:

With still a flying point of bliss remote,
A happiness in store afar, a sphere
Of distant glory in full view.

And science has done us good service in recalling this doctrine to
mind. For it has a religious as well as a theological importance, con-
stituting, as it does, the element of truth in that higher Pantheism
which is so common in the present day. . . .

To sum up then, the reopening of the teleological question has not
only led to its fuller and more final answer, but has incidentally contributed to revive among us an important aspect of the Theology of
the Word.

The next point upon which the theory of evolution came in contact
with received opinion, was its account of the origin of man. Man, it
was maintained, in certain quarters, was only the latest and most complex product of a purely material process of development. His reason,
with all its functions of imagination, conscience, will, was only a result
of his sensibility, and that of his nervous tissue, and that again of matter
less and less finely organized, till at last a primitive protoplasm was
reached; while what had been called his fall was in reality his rise,
being due to the fact that with the birth of reason came self-consciousness; or the feeling of a distinction between self and the outer world,
ripening into a sense, and strictly speaking an illusory sense of discord
between the two. . . .

If we believe, as we have seen that Christian Theology has always
believed, in a Divine Creator not only present behind the beginning
of matter but immanent in its every phase, and cooperating with its
every phenomenon, the method of His working, though full of speculative interest, will be of no controversial importance. Time was when
the different kinds of created things were thought to be severed by
impassable barriers. But many of these barriers have already given
way before science, and species are seen to be no more independent
than the individuals that compose them. If the remaining barriers
between unreason and reason, or between lifelessness and life should
in like manner one day vanish, we shall need to readjust the focus of
our spiritual eye to the enlarged vision, but nothing more. Our Creator
will be known to have worked otherwise indeed than we had thought,
but in a way quite as conceivable, and to the imagination more magnificent. And all is alike covered by the words 'without Him was not
anything made that was made: and in Him was life.' In fact the evolutionary origin of man is a far less serious question than the attack
upon final causes. Its biblical aspect has grown insignificant in proportion as we have learned to regard the Hebrew cosmology in a true

light. And the popular outcry which it raised was largely due to sentiment, and sentiment not altogether untinged by human pride. . . .

But the attack thus diverted from our religion glances off on our
theology. The Christian religion, it is granted, was founded by Jesus
Christ; but its theological interpretation is viewed as a misinterpreta-
tion, a malign legacy from the dying philosophies of Greece. This
objection is as old as the second century, and has been revived at intervals in various forms, and with varying degrees of success. Modern
historical criticism has only fortified it with fresh instances. But it has
no force whatever if we believe that the Divine Word was for ever
working in the world in cooperation with human reason; inspiring the
higher minds among the Jews with their thirst for holiness, and so
making ready for the coming of the Holy One in Jewish flesh: but
inspiring the Greeks also with their intellectual eagerness, and preparing them to recognise Him as the Eternal Reason, the Word, the Truth;
and to define and defend, and demonstrate that Truth to the outer
world. The fact that Greek philosophy had passed its zenith and was
declining did not make its influence upon Christianity an evil one, a
corruption of the living by the dead. It was only dying to be incorporated in a larger life. The food that supports our existence owes its
power of nutrition to the fact, that it too once lived with an inferior
life of its own. And so the Greek philosophy was capable of assimilation
by the Christian organism, from the fact that it too had once been
vitally inspired by the life that is the light of men. And the true successors of Plato and Aristotle were the men of progress who realized this
fact; not Celsus, Lucian, Porphyry, but the Fathers of the Church. . . .

But when all this has been said, there is a lingering suspicion in
many minds, that even if the details of the doctrine of development
are not inconsistent with Christianity, its whole drift is incompatible
with any system of opinion which claims to possess finality. And if
Christianity were only a system of opinion, the objection might be
plausible enough. But its claim to possess finality rests upon its further
claim to be much more than a system of opinion. The doctrine of development or evolution, we must remember, is not a doctrine of limitless
change, like the old Greek notion of perpetual flux. Species once developed are seen to be persistent, in proportion to their versatility, their
power, i.e., of adapting themselves to the changes of the world around
them. And because man, through his mental capacity, possesses this
power to an almost unlimited extent, the human species is virtually
permanent. Now in scientific language, the Incarnation may be said to
have introduced a new species into the world—a Divine man transcend-
ing past humanity, as humanity transcended the rest of the animal creation, and communicating His vital energy by a spiritual process to

subsequent generations of men. And thus viewed, there is nothing unreasonable in the claim of Christianity to be at least as permanent as the race which it has raised to a higher power, and endued with a novel strength.

III. But in saying this we touch new ground. As long as we confine ourselves to speaking of the Eternal Word as operating in the mysterious region which lies behind phenomena, we are safe it may be said from refutation, because we are dealing with the unknown. But when we go on to assert that He has flashed through our atmosphere, and been seen of men, scintillating signs and wonders in His path, we are at once open to critical attack. And this brings us to the real point at issue between Christianity and its modern opponents. It is not the substantive body of our knowledge, but the critical faculty which has been sharpened in its acquisition that really comes in conflict with our creed. Assuming Christianity to be true, there is, as we have seen, nothing in it inconsistent with any ascertained scientific fact. But what is called the negative criticism assumes that it cannot be true, because the miraculous element in it contradicts experience. Still criticism is a very different thing from science, a subjective thing into which imagination and personal idiosyncrasy enter largely, and which needs therefore in its turn to be rigorously criticised. And the statement that Christianity contradicts experience suggests two reflections, *in limine.*

In the first place the origin of all things is mysterious, the origin of matter, the origin of energy, the origin of life, the origin of thought. And present experience is no criterion of any of these things. What were their birth throes, what were their accompanying signs and wonders, when the morning stars sang together in the dawn of their appearing, we do not and cannot know. If therefore the Incarnation was, as Christians believe, another instance of a new beginning, present experience will neither enable us to assert or deny, what its attendant circumstances may or may not have been. The logical impossibility of proving a negative is proverbial. And on a subject, whose conditions are unknown to us, the very attempt becomes ridiculous. And secondly, it is a mistake to suppose that as a matter of strict evidence, the Christian Church has ever rested its claims upon its miracles. A confirmatory factor indeed, in a complication of converging arguments, they have been, and still are to many minds. But to others, who in the present day are probably the larger class, it is not so easy to believe Christianity on account of miracles, as miracles on account of Christianity. For now, as ever, the real burden of the proof of Christianity is to be sought in our present experience.

There is a fact of experience as old as history, as widely spread as is the human race, and more intensely, irresistibly, importunately real than all the gathered experience of art and policy and science,—the fact which philosophers call moral evil, and Christians sin. It rests upon no questionable interpretation of an Eastern allegory. We breathe it, we feel it, we commit it, we see its havoc all around us. It is no dogma, but a sad, solemn, inevitable fact. The animal creation has a law of its being, a condition of its perfection, which it instinctively and invariably pursues. Man has a law of his being, a condition of his perfection, which he instinctively tends to disobey. And what he does to-day, he has been doing from the first record of his existence.

> *Video meliora proboque,*
> *Deteriora sequor.*

Philosophers have from time to time attempted to explain this dark experience away, and here and there men of happy temperament, living among calm surroundings, have been comparatively unconscious of the evil in the world. But the common conscience is alike unaffected by the ingenuity of the one class, or the apathy of the other; while it thrills to the voices of men like S. Paul or S. Augustine, Dante or John Bunyan, Loyola or Luther; recognising in their sighs and tears and lamentations, the echo of its own unutterable sorrow made articulate. Nor is sin confined to one department of our being. It poisons the very springs of life, and taints its every action. It corrupts art; it hampers science; it paralyses the efforts of the politician and the patriot; and diseased bodies, and broken hearts, and mental and spiritual agony, are amongst its daily, its hourly results. It would seem indeed superfluous to insist upon these things, if their importance were not so often ignored in the course of anti-Christian argument. But when we are met by an appeal to experience, it is necessary to insist that no element of experience be left out.

And moral evil, independently of any theory of its nature or its origin, is a plain palpable fact, and a fact of such stupendous magnitude as to constitute by far the most serious problem of our life.

Now it is also a fact of present experience that there are scattered throughout Christendom, men of every age, temperament, character, and antecedents, for whom this problem is practically solved: men who have a personal conviction that their own past sins are done away with, and the whole grasp of evil upon them loosened, and who in consequence rise to heights of character and conduct, which they know that they would never have otherwise attained. And all this they agree to attribute, in however varying phrases, to the personal influence upon them of Jesus Christ. Further, these men had a spiritual ancestry.

Others in the last generation believed and felt, and acted as they now act and feel and believe. And so their lineage can be traced backward, age by age, swelling into a great multitude whom no man can number, till we come to the historic records of Him whom they all look back to, and find that He claimed the power on earth to forgive sins. And there the phenomenon ceases. Pre-Christian antiquity contains nothing analogous to it. Consciousness of sin, and prayers for pardon, and purgatorial penances, and sacrifices, and incantations, and magic formulae are there in abundance; and hopes among certain races, of the coming of a great deliverer. But never the same sense of sin forgiven, nor the consequent rebound of the enfranchised soul. Yet neither a code of morality which was not essentially new, nor the example of a life receding with every age into a dimmer past, would have been adequate to produce this result. It has all the appearance of being, what it historically has claimed to be, the entrance of an essentially new life into the world, quickening its palsied energies, as with an electric touch. And the more we realize in the bitterness of our own experience, or that of others, the essential malignity of moral evil, the more strictly supernatural does this energy appear. When, therefore, we are told that miracles contradict experience, we point to the daily occurrence of this spiritual miracle and ask 'whether is it easier to say thy sins be forgiven thee, or to say arise and walk?' We meet experience with experience, the negative experience that miracles have not happened with the positive experience that they are happening now: an old argument, which so far from weakening, modern science has immensely strengthened, by its insistence on the intimate union between material and spiritual things. For spirit and matter, as we call them, are now known to intermingle, and blend, and fringe off, and fade into each other, in a way that daily justifies us more in our belief that the possessor of the key to one must be the possessor of the key to both, and that He who can save the soul can raise the dead.

Here then is our answer to the negative criticism, or rather to the negative hypothesis, by which many critics are misled. Of course we do not expect for it unanimous assent. It is founded on a specific experience; and strangers to that experience are naturally unable to appreciate its force. But neither should they claim to judge it. For the critic of an experience must be its expert. And the accumulated verdict of the spiritual experts of all ages, should at least meet with grave respect from the very men who are most familiar with the importance of the maxim, *Cuique in sua arte credendum.* Christianity distinctly declines to be proved first, and practised afterwards. Its practice and its proof go hand in hand. And its real evidence is its power.

We now see why the Atonement has often assumed such exclusive prominence in the minds of Christian men. They have felt that it was the secret of their own regenerate life, their best intellectual apology, their most attractive missionary appeal; and so have come to think that the other aspects of the Incarnation might be banished from the pulpit and the market-place, to the seclusion of the schools. But this has proved to be a fatal mistake. Truth cannot be mutilated with impunity. And this gradual substitution of a detached doctrine for a catholic creed, has led directly to the charge which is now so common, that Christianity is inadequate to life; with no message to ordinary men, in their ordinary moments, no bearing upon the aims, occupations, interests, enthusiasms, amusements, which are human nature's daily food.

But we have already seen what a misconception this implies of the Incarnation. The Incarnation opened heaven, for it was the revelation of the Word; but it also reconsecrated earth, for the Word was made Flesh and dwelt among us. And it is impossible to read history without feeling how profoundly the religion of the Incarnation has been a religion of humanity. The human body itself, which heathendom had so degraded, that noble minds could only view it as the enemy and prison of the soul, acquired a new meaning, exhibited new graces, shone with a new lustre in the light of the Word made Flesh; and thence, in widening circles, the family, society, the state, felt in their turn the impulse of the Christian spirit, with its

> touches of things common,
> Till they rose to touch the spheres.

Literature revived; art flamed into fuller life; even science in its early days owed more than men often think, to the Christian temper and the Christian reverence for things once called common or unclean. While the optimism, the belief in the future, the atmosphere of hopefulness, which has made our progress and achievements possible, and which, when all counter currents have been allowed for, so deeply differentiates the modern from the ancient world, dates, as a fact of history, from those buoyant days of the early church, when the creed of suicide was vanquished before the creed of martyrdom, Seneca before St. Paul. It is true that secular civilization has co-operated with Christianity to produce the modern world. But secular civilization is, as we have seen, in the Christian view, nothing less than the providential correlative and counterpart of the Incarnation. For the Word did not desert the rest of His creation to become Incarnate. Natural religion, and natural morality, and the natural play of intellect have their function in the Christian as they had in the pre-Christian ages; and are still kindled by the light that lighteth every man coming into the world. And hence it is that secular thought has so often corrected and counteracted the evil of a Christianity grown professional, and false, and foul.

Still when all allowance for other influence has been made; and all the ill done in its name admitted to the full; Christianity remains, the only power which has regenerated personal life, and that beyond the circle even of its professed adherents, the light of it far outshining the lamp which has held its flame. And personal life is after all the battle-ground, on which the progress of the race must be decided. Nor ever indeed should this be more apparent than in the present day. For materialism, that old enemy alike of the Christian and the human cause, has passed from the study to the street. No one indeed may regret this more than the high-souled scientific thinker, whose life belies the inevitable consequences of his creed. But the ruthless logic of human passion is drawing out those consequences fiercely; and the luxury of the rich, and the communistic cry of the poor, and the dese-cration of marriage, and the disintegration of society, and selfishness in policy, and earthliness in art, are plausibly pleading science in their favour. And with all this Christianity claims, as of old, to cope, because it is the religion of the Incarnation. For the real strength of materialism lies in the justice which it does to the material side of nature—the love-liness of earth and sea and sky and sun and star; the wonder of the mechanism which controls alike the rushing comet and the falling leaf; the human body crowning both, at once earth's fairest flower and most marvellous machine. And Christianity is the only religion which does equal justice to this truth, while precluding its illegitimate perversion. It includes the truth, by the essential importance which it assigns to the human body, and therefore to the whole material order, with which that body is so intimately one; while it excludes its perversion, by shewing the cause of that importance to lie in its connection, com-munion, union with the spirit, and consequent capacity for endless degrees of glory.

And though its own first vocation is to seek and save souls one by one, it consecrates in passing every field of thought and action, wherein the quickened energies of souls may find their scope. It welcomes the discoveries of science, as ultimately due to Divine revelation, and part of the providential education of the world. It recalls to art the days when, in catacomb and cloister, she learned her noblest mission to be the service of the Word made Flesh. It appeals to democracy as the religion of the fishermen who gathered round the carpenter's Son. It points the social reformer to the pattern of a perfect man, laying down His life alike for enemy and friend. While it crowns all earthly aims with a hope full of immortality, as prophetic of eternal occupations otherwhere. And however many a new meaning may yet be found in the Incarnation, however many a misconception of it fade before fuller light; we can conceive no phase of progress which has not the Incarnation for its guiding star; no age which cannot make the prayer of the fifth century its own—

'O God of unchangeable power and eternal light, look favourably upon Thy whole Church, that wonderful and sacred mystery; and by the tranquil operation of Thy perpetual Providence, carry out the work of man's salvation; and let the whole world feel and see that things which were cast down are being raised up, and things which had grown old are being made new, and all things are returning to perfection through Him, from whom they took their origin, even through our Lord Jesus Christ.'

LYMAN ABBOTT

The Theology of an Evolutionist originated as a series of lectures given at Plymouth Church, Brooklyn, in 1897. In the lectures Lyman Abbott (1835-1922) repudiates the traditional view of creation by manufacture and proclaims his position of creation by evolution. This is God's way of doing things. Abbott speaks not of the *descent* of man but of his *ascent*. Human hope is grounded "in the power that shall lift him up and out of his lower self into his higher, truer, nobler self, until he shall be no longer the son of the animal, but in very truth a son of God."

Here Abbott expresses the hope that by a new theology Christians might be able to hold fast to their faith in God, to their fellowship with Christ, and to hope of eternal life. He argues that he has merely put the old wine into new bottles. But to traditionalists *The Theology of an Evolutionist* was a "dreadful book" and Abbott "neither a clear-headed nor a sober-minded man."

From Lyman Abbott, **The Theology of an Evolutionist**

Religion is the life of God in the soul of man. Belief in the reality of religion involves belief that God is, and that He stands in some personal relation to man. But it is not an opinion respecting God, nor an opinion respecting His influence in the world of men. It is a personal consciousness of God. It is a human experience, but an experience of relationship with One who transcends humanity. The creed is not religion; the creed is a statement of what certain men think about religion. Worship is not religion; worship is a method of expressing religion. The church is not religion; the church is an organization of men and women, formed for the purpose of promoting religion. Religion precedes creeds, worship, church; that is, the life precedes men's thoughts about the life, men's expression of life, men's organizations formed to promote the life. Religion may be personal or social; that is, it may be the consciousness of God in the individual soul, or it may be the concurrent consciousness of God in a great number of individuals, producing a social or communal life. In either case it is a life, not an opinion about life. It is not a definition of God, it is fellowship with Him; not a definition of forgiveness, but relief from remorse: not a definition of redemption, but a new and divine life.

Theology is the science of religion. It is the result of an attempt made by men to state in an orderly and systematic manner the facts respecting the life of God in the soul of man. It involves intellectual definition of the various forms of consciousness which constitute the religious life. Its relation to religion is the relation of other sciences to the vital phenomena which they endeavor to explain. With the growth of the human intellect there comes a wiser study of life, a better understanding of it, a new definition of its terms, and a new classification of its phenomena. The life does not change, but man's understanding of it changes. There is a new astronomy, though the stars are old: a new botany, though vegetable life is unchanged; a new chemistry, though the constituent elements of the universe are the same. So there is a new theology, though not a new religion. God, sin, repentance, forgiveness, love, remain essentially unchanged, but the definitions of God, sin, repentance, forgiveness, and love are changed from generation to generation. There is as little danger of undermining religion by new definitions of theology as there is of blotting out the stars from the heavens by a new astronomy. But as religion is the life of God in the soul of man, definitions which give to man a clearer and a more intelligible understanding of that life will promote it, and definitions which are, or seem to be, irrational, will tend to impede or impair it. To this extent theology affects the religious life as other sciences do not affect the life with which they have to deal.

Evolution is described by John Fiske as "God's way of doing things." Theology also may be described as an attempt to explain God's way of doing things. Thus, to a certain extent the science of evolution and the science of theology have the same ultimate end. Both attempt to furnish an orderly, rational, and self-consistent account of phenomena. The supposed inconsistency between science and religion is really an inconsistency between two sciences. The theologian and the scientist have given different, and to some extent inconsistent, accounts of God's way of doing things. It is important for us to know which account is correct. It is even religiously desirable that we should know, since our understanding of God's influence upon the human soul affects that influence. . . .

It is true that I am an evolutionist, and inclined to be a radical evolutionist. It is perhaps proper to indicate in a paragraph the reasons for my change of opinion,—a change which has taken place gradually and almost unconsciously.

In the first place, all biologists are evolutionists, probably without a single exception. They are not all Darwinians,—that is, they do not all regard "struggle for existence and survival of the fittest" as an adequate statement of the process of evolution. Indeed, it may be said that this is no longer by any one regarded as a complete summary of the process, even if it were so regarded by Darwin himself, which is doubtful. I am not an expert biologist; few ministers are. We are not competent to pass any independent judgment of value on the question, What is the process of life in its earliest forms? We have not the scientific habit of mind which enables us to sift the evidence and reach a conclusion. How many of those who read this chapter could pass a creditable examination on the question at issue between the Ptolemaic and the Copernican theories of astronomy, or the atomic and undulatory theory of light? Probably but few. We accept the testimony of the experts when they have reached a conclusion. Practically all scientists, I believe absolutely all biologists, are evolutionists. They have proved themselves careful, painstaking, assiduous students of life. I assume the correctness of their conclusion. I have studied, it is true, the writing of Darwin, Huxley, Haeckel, Tyndall, and the later epitomes of Le Conte, Drummond, and Tyler, and have read the more important of the criticisms on the other side,—enough to see that the hypothesis of evolution has a groundwork of fact and reason. But I accept evolution, as a statement of the process of physical life, not from a personal scientific investigation, which I have not the training to conduct, but upon the substantially unanimous testimony of those who have such training.

On the other hand, the minister ought to be a special student of the moral life. He ought to know man as a moral actor, literature as the expression of his moral consciousness, history as the record of his moral progress, society as a moral organism. He ought to be able to pass something approximating an expert judgment on the question whether and how far evolution explains "the history of the process" by which the individual man, his literature, his history, his social and political organisms, have come to be what they are. To this subject I have given years of study, sometimes systematic, sometimes desultory, sometimes in theoretical investigations, sometimes in practical applications. The result of this study has been a conclusion, very gradually formed, that the history of that process is best expressed by the word "evolution,"—

that is, that the process has been one of continuous progressive growth, from a lower to a higher, from a simpler to a more complex organization, under the influence of resident forces, and in accordance with law. And this opinion has been confirmed by Bible study. It appears to me to harmonize better with the general spirit of Biblical teaching than does the anti-evolutionary conception of life. These two reasons, the substantially unanimous judgment of experts in a department with which I am not familiar, and my own independent judgment in a department with which I have some familiarity, have led me to accept evolution as a history of the process of life, or as "God's way of doing things."

I acknowledge myself, then, a radical evolutionist.—it is hardly necessary to say a theistic evolutionist. I reverently and heartily accept the axiom of theology that a personal God is the foundation of all life: but I also believe that God has but one way of doing things; that His way may be described in one word as the way of growth, or development, or evolution, terms which are substantially synonymous; that He resides in the world of nature and in the world of men; that there are no laws of nature which are not the laws of God's own being; that there are no forces of nature, that there is only one divine, infinite force, always proceeding from, always subject to the will of God: that there are not occasional or exceptional theophanies, but that all nature and all life is one great theophany; that there are not occasional interventions in the order of life which bear witness to the presence of God, but that life is itself a perpetual witness to His presence: that He transcends all phenomena, and yet is the creative, controlling, directing force in all phenomena. In so far as the theologian and the evolutionist differ in their interpretation of the history of life—that is, upon the question whether God's way of doing things is a way of successive interventions or a continuous and unbroken progress—I agree with the evolutionists, not with the theologian. My object in this volume is to show that religion—that is, the life of God in the soul of man—is better comprehended, and will better be promoted, by the philosophy which regards all life as divine, and God's way of doing things as the way of a continuous, progressive change, according to certain laws and by means of one resident force, than by the philosophy which supposes that some things are done by natural forces and according to natural laws, and others by special interventions of a Divine Will, acting from without, for the purpose of correcting errors or filling gaps. . . .

. . . I believe that the theology of the future will frankly and gladly accept these conclusions, instead of resisting them and endeavoring to discover some evidences of interventions constantly lessening in number if not in magnitude. It, too, will affirm that there is only one force, the "Infinite and Eternal Energy from which all things proceed." It will affirm that this Infinite and Eternal Energy is never increased or diminished; that, in other words, God, who varies infinitely in His manifestations, varies in no whit in His real life. It will affirm that there are and can be no interventions in this resident force, this Infinite and Eternal Energy, for if there were there would be a second God, superior to the God who resides in the universe and controlling Him. And finally, it will affirm that this Infinite and Eternal Energy is itself intelligent and beneficent,—an infinitely wise and holy Spirit, dwelling within the universe and shaping it from within, much as the human spirit dwells within the human body and forms and controls it from within. Scientifically this is the affirmation that the forces of nature are one vital force; theologically it is the affirmation that God is an Immanent God. "Resident forces" and "Divine Immanence" are different forms of the same statement. According to this view, it is not correct to say that "God, the one Force, did somehow bring into being the earliest forms of matter with resident forces." It is correct to say that from the earliest time we know anything about, God, the one Resident Force, has been shaping matter into its various forms. . . . It is correct to say that all later forms of existence, including life and consciousness, reason and conscience, are the manifestations of His power, and the revelations of His presence who is God, "the all in all." Nor is this inconsistent with the belief that the heaven of heavens cannot contain Him. The Divine Spirit which resides in Nature transcends Nature, as the human spirit which resides in the body transcends the body. The Divine Spirit which is manifested in all phenomena is more than the sum of all phenomena, as the human spirit which is manifested in all activities of a life is more than the sum of those activities. The belief that the Divine Spirit resides *in* the universe is no more pantheism than belief that the human spirit resides *in* the body is materialism. This faith in the Divine Immanence, in an Intelligent and Beneficent Will working in the so-called forces of Nature, is neither atheistic nor pantheistic. Belief that all energies are vital is not belief that there are no vital energies. Belief that all resident forces are Divine is not belief that there is no true Divinity.

It seemed necessary to make this explanation to guard, if possible, against the common misapprehension of the evolutionist's position, as that of one whose faith in "resident forces" implies no faith in God. The theistic evolutionist believes that God is the one Resident Force, that He is in His world; that His method of work in the history of the world, whether it be the history of creation, of providence, or of redemption, whether the history of redemption in the race or of redemption in the individual soul, is the history of a growth in accordance with the great law interpreted and uttered in that one word evolution. . . .

Evolution, then,—let us understand this at the outset,—is the history of a process, not the explanation of a cause. The evolutionist believes that God's processes are the processes of growth, not of manufacture. . . .

The radical evolutionist believes that all divine processes, so far as we are able to understand them, are processes of growth; that as God makes the oak out of the acorn, and the rose out of the cutting, and the man out of the babe, and the nation of the colony, and the literature out of the alphabet, so God made all things by the development of higher from lower forms. He believes that, so far as he can see, God is never a manufacturer, but always does His work by growth processes. . . .

Over against this conception of creation by manufacture, we are coming to accept the conception of creation by evolution. It would require one far more familiar with scientific detail than I am to give the process with scientific accuracy; but it is possible to indicate the broad outlines, and I am facilitated in doing this by a somewhat vague recollection of an experiment which I saw performed by Dr. R. Ogden Doremus many years ago. On the platform where the chemist was performing his experiments was a great glass box, and in that box a colorless liquid, into which he poured a colored liquid,—red, if my memory serves me right; and running through this box, with little arms extending from it, was a cylinder, with a crank at the top. While we sat there this colored material gathered itself together in a globular form before our eyes. It was of precisely the same specific density as the colorless liquid in which it had been plunged, so that there was no attraction of gravitation to carry it to the bottom. Then gradually, very slowly at first, the lecturer began a movement with this crank, and the globe, following the cylinder which he revolved, began revolving itself very slowly, and gradually more and more rapidly, and, as it revolved, flattened at the poles, and presently, as the cylinder became more and more rapid, flung out from itself, I forget now whether a ring or a single globe.

So we saw, before our eyes, the nebular hypothesis illustrated. In some far-off epoch, misty matter hung nebulous in the universe. It came together as a globe under the law of attraction of gravitation. It began its revolution, set in motion by that infinite and eternal energy which is an infinite and eternal mystery, and which I believe is God. As it revolved, by the very process of revolution it flattened at the poles. As it revolved it cooled, the mist turned to water, the water to solid. From this revolving globe a ring, like the ring of Saturn, was

flung off, and the revolving ring itself was broken by the very process
of revolution into separate luminaries. So grew moons, so the planetary
system. In this globe was, as still there is, life,—that is, an infinite and
eternal energy which is an infinite and eternal mystery, that is, God.
Out of this life, manifesting this God, grew, as the rose grows from its
seed, the lower forms, and, by successive processes from lower forms,
other higher forms, and from these forms others still higher, until at
last the world came to be what it is to-day. There never was a time
when the world was done. It is not done to-day. It is in the making.
In the belief of the evolutionists, the same processes that were going
on in the creative days are going on here and now. Still the nebulae
are gathering together in globes; still globes are beginning their revolution; still they are flattening at the poles; still they are cooling and
becoming solid; still in them are springing up the forms of life. In our
own globe the same forces that were operative in the past to make the
world what it is are springing the plants; still the mountains are being
pushed up by volcanic forces below; still chasms are being made by
the earthquake; all the methods and all the processes that went on in
those first great days are still proceeding. Creative days! Every day is
a creative day. Every spring is a creative spring. God is always creating. Such, briefly and imperfectly outlined, is the doctrine of creation
by evolution.

Does this doctrine deny, or imply a denial, that there is intelligence
in the universe? Is my correspondent right who thinks that Spencer
and Huxley and Tyndall imagine that matter makes itself and governs
itself? Is it true that the evolutionist believes, or if he be logical must
believe, that there is no intelligence that plans, no wisdom that directs?
Paley's famous illustration suggests that a man going along the road
finds a watch; picks it up; examines it; sees that it will keep time;
knows that there was some intelligence that devised this watch. Suppose this watch which he picks up and carries in his pocket drops from
itself in a year's time a little egg, and out of that egg there comes a
perfect watch a year later; does that show less intelligence, or more?
Is the natural rose, with all its forces within itself, less wonderful than
the artificial rose, which the man makes in imitation of it out of wax?
The processes of growth are infinitely more wonderful than the processes of manufacture. It is easier by far to comprehend the intelligence
that makes the cuckoo which springs from the cuckoo clock to note the
time, than to comprehend the intelligence that makes the living bird
which springs from his nest and sings his song to the morning sun.
Growth is more wonderful than manufacture. Growth has in it more
evidence of marvelous intelligence than any manufacture. . . .

Does this doctrine of creation by evolution take God away from the world? It seems to me that it brings Him a great deal nearer. The Hindu believed that God was too great to stoop to the making of the world, so He hatched out an egg from which issued a number of little gods, and the little gods made the world. Something like that has been our past philosophy. A great First Cause in the remote past set secondary causes at work, and we stand only in the presence of secondary causes. But Herbert Spencer, the typical agnostic evolutionist, affirms that we are ever *in the presence* of an Infinite and Eternal Energy from which all things proceed. True, Herbert Spencer says that He is the Unknown; but the theist who believes with Matthew Arnold that this Infinite and Eternal Energy is an energy that makes for righteousness in human history, and the Christian theist who believes that this Infinite and Eternal Energy has manifested Himself in Jesus Christ, and has purpose and will and love and intelligence, believes no less certainly than Herbert Spencer that we are ever in His presence. There is no chasm of six thousand years between the evolutionist and his Creator. The evolutionist lives in the creative processes taking place before him.

LEO XIII

The encyclical *Rerum novarum* of Pope Leo XIII (1878-1903) states the Christian case against the existing industrial order. It severely criticizes the capitalist class for its heartlessness and its exploitation of the working classes. It endorses the intervention of the state to correct intolerable abuses and the association of working men in unions for their mutual protection and improvement. In ideological terms, the papal encyclical maintains the tradition of the "creative middle" characteristic of Christian humanism. *Rerum novarum* (1891) steers carefully between individualism and collectivism, between liberal capitalism—which "had already shown its utter impotence"—and socialism—which was called "a remedy much more disastrous than the evil it was designed to cure." As a substitute for both of these, the papacy advocated harmony between classes.

From Leo XIII, **Rerum Novarum**

It is not surprising that the spirit of revolutionary change, which has long been predominant in the nations of the world, should have passed beyond politics and made its influence felt in the cognate field of practical economy. The elements of a conflict are unmistakable: the growth of industry, and the surprising discoveries of science; the changed relations of masters and workmen; the enormous fortunes of individuals and the poverty of the masses; the working population; and, finally, a general moral deterioration. . . .

THE CONDITION OF LABOR

. . . in this Letter the responsibility of the Apostolic office urges Us to treat the question expressly and at length, in order that there may be no mistake as to the principles which truth and justice dictate for its settlement. The discussion is not easy, nor is it free from danger. . . .

But all agree, and there can be no question whatever, that some remedy must be found, and quickly found, for the misery and wretchedness which press so heavily at this moment on the large majority of the very poor. The ancient workmen's Guilds were destroyed in the last century, and no other organization took their place. Public institutions and the laws have repudiated the ancient religion. Hence by degrees it has come to pass that Working Men have been given over, isolated and defenseless, to the callousness of employers and the greed of unrestrained competition.

PRIVATE OWNERSHIP

It is surely undeniable that, when a man engages in remunerative labor, the very reason and motive of his work is to obtain property, and to hold it as his own private possession. . . .

. . . to say that God has given the earth to the use and enjoyment of the universal human race is not to deny that there can be private property. For God has granted the earth to mankind in general; not in the sense that all without distinction can deal with it as they please, but rather that no part of it has been assigned to any one in particular, and that the limits of private possession have been left to be fixed by man's own industry and the laws of individual peoples. . . .

A FAMILY RIGHT

. . . A family, no less than a State, is, as we have said, a true society, governed by a power within itself, that is to say, by the father. Wherefore, provided the limits be not transgressed which are prescribed by the very purposes for which it exists, the family has, at least, equal rights with the State in the choice and pursuit of those things which are needful to its preservation and its just liberty.

SOCIALISM REJECTED

The idea, then, that the civil government should, at its own discretion, penetrate and pervade the family and the household, is a great and pernicious mistake. . . .

Thus it is clear that the main tenet of Socialism, the community of goods, must be utterly rejected; for it would injure those whom it is intended to benefit, it would be contrary to the natural rights of mankind, and it would introduce confusion and disorder into the commonwealth. Our first and most fundamental principle, therefore, when we undertake to alleviate the condition of the masses, must be the inviolability of private property. . . .

THE CHURCH IS NECESSARY

Let it be laid down, in the first place, that humanity must remain as it is. It is impossible to reduce human society to a level. The Socialists may do their utmost, but all striving against nature is vain. There naturally exists among mankind innumerable differences of the most important kind; people differ in capability, in diligence, in health, and in strength; and unequal fortune is a necessary result of inequality of condition. Such inequality is far from being disadvantageous either to individuals or to the community; social and public life can only go on by the help of various kinds of capacity and the playing of many parts, and each man, as a rule, chooses the part which peculiarly suits his case. . . .

EMPLOYER AND EMPLOYEE

The great mistake that is made in the matter now under consideration, is to possess oneself of the idea that class is naturally hostile to class; that rich and poor are intended by nature to live at war with one another. So irrational and so false is this view, that the exact contrary is the truth. Just as the symmetry of the human body is the result of the disposition of the members of the body, so in a State it is ordained by nature that these two classes should exist in harmony and agreement, and should, as it were, fit into one another, so as to maintain the equilibrium of the body politic. Each requires the other; capital cannot do without labor, nor labor without capital. Mutual agreement results in pleasantness and good order; perpetual conflict necessarily produces confusion and outrage. Now, in preventing such strife as this, and in making it impossible, the efficacy of Christianity is marvelous and manifold.

First of all, there is nothing more powerful than Religion (of which the Church is the interpreter and guardian) in drawing rich and poor together, by reminding each class of its duties of justice. Thus Religion teaches the laboring man and the workman to carry out honestly and well all equitable agreements freely made, never to injure capital, nor to outrage the person of an employer; never to employ

violence in representing his own cause, nor to engage in riot and
disorder; and to have nothing to do with men of evil principles, who
work upon the people with artful promises, and raise foolish hopes
which usually end in disaster and in repentance when too late. Religion teaches the rich man and the employer that their work people
are not slaves; that they must respect in every man his dignity as a
man and as a Christian; that labor is nothing to be ashamed of, if we
listen to right reason and to Christian philosophy, but is an honorable employment, enabling a man to sustain his life in an upright
and creditable way; and that it is shameful and inhuman to treat
men like chattels to make money by, or to look upon them merely
as so much muscle or physical power. Thus again, Religion teaches
that, as among the workmen's concerns are Religion herself, and
things spiritual and mental, the employer is bound to see that he has
time for the duties of piety; that he be not exposed to corrupting influences and dangerous occasions; and that he be not led away to neglect his home and family or to squander his wages. Then, again the
employer must never tax his workpeople beyond their strength, nor
employ them in work unsuited to their sex or age.

His great and principal obligation is to give to every one that which
is just. Doubtless before we can decide whether wages are adequate
many things have to be considered; but rich men and masters should
remember this—that to exercise pressure for the sake of gain, upon
the indigent and destitute, and to make one's profit out of the need
of another, is condemned by all laws, human and divine. To defraud
any one of wages that are his due is a crime which cries to the avenging anger of Heaven. "Behold, the hire of the laborers . . . which by
fraud has been kept back by you, crieth; and the cry of them hath
entered the ears of the Lord of Sabaoth." Finally, the rich must religiously refrain from cutting down the workman's earnings, either by
force, fraud, or by usurious dealing; and with the more reason because
the poor man is weak and unprotected, and because his slender means
should be sacred in proportion to their scantiness.

Were these precepts carefully obeyed and followed would not strife
die out and cease?

THE GREAT TRUTH

But the Church, with Jesus Christ for its Master and Guide, aims
higher still. It lays down precepts yet more perfect, and tries to bind
the classes in friendliness and good understanding. The things of this
earth cannot be understood or valued rightly without taking into consideration the life to come, the life that will last forever. Exclude the
idea of futurity, and the very notion of what is good and right would

perish; nay, the whole system of the universe would become a dark and unfathomable mystery. The great truth which we learn from nature herself is also the grand Christian dogma on which Religion rests as on its base—that when we have done with this present life then we shall really begin to live. God has not created us for the perishable and transitory things of earth, but for things which men call good and desirable—we may have them in abundance or we may want them altogether; as far as eternal happiness is concerned, it is no matter; the only thing that is important is to use them aright. Jesus Christ, when He redeemed us with plentiful redemption, took not away the pains and sorrows which in such large proportion make up the texture of our mortal merit; and no man can hope for eternal reward unless he follows in the blood-stained footprints of his Savior. "If we suffer with Him, we shall also reign with Him." His labors and His suffering accepted by His own free will, have marvelously sweetened all suffering and all labor. And not only by His example, but by His grace and by the hope of everlasting recompense, He has made pain and grief more easy to endure; "for that which is at present momentary and light of our tribulation, worketh for us above measure exceedingly an eternal weight of glory."

THE WORKMAN'S RIGHTS

But if the owners of property must be made secure, the workman, too, has property and possessions in which he must be protected; and, first of all, there are his spiritual and mental interests. . . .

From this follows the obligation of the cessation of work and labor on Sundays and certain festivals. . . .

WORKMEN'S ASSOCIATIONS

The most important of all are Workmen's Associations; for these virtually include all the rest. History attests what excellent results were effected by the Artificer's Guilds of a former day. They were the means not only of many advantages to the workmen, but in no small degree of the advancement of art, as numerous monuments remain to prove. Such associations should be adapted to the requirements of the age in which we live—an age of greater instruction, of different customs, and of more numerous requirements in daily life. It is gratifying to know that there are actually in existence not a few societies of this nature, consisting either of workmen alone, or of workmen and employers together; but it were greatly to be desired that they should multiply and become more effective.

VIOLENT OPPRESSION

. . . Under these circumstances the Christian workmen must do one of two things: either join associations in which their religion will be exposed to peril or form associations themselves—unite their forces and courageously shake off the yoke of an unjust and intolerable oppression. No one who does not wish to expose man's chief good to extreme danger will hesitate to say that the second alternative must by all means be adopted.

WALTER RAUSCHENBUSCH

Walter Rauschenbusch (1861-1918) came into national prominence with the great popularity of *Christianity and the Social Crisis,* published in 1907. *Christianity and the Social Crisis* is a book "on social questions for the Lord Christ and the people." It was written for the working people of New York to whom Rauschenbusch had preached for 11 years.

Rauschenbusch here appeals to both religious and social sympathies. He provides a sweeping interpretation of history which some may find facile. Throughout Rauschenbusch offers his ideal of the kingdom of God as a new horizon for a generation troubled by industrial questions. Though mocked by some, *Christianity and the Social Crisis* has inspired American Christians for 75 years. Martin Luther King Jr. remembered the impact of the book: "[It] left an indelible imprint on my thinking. . . . in spite of [its] shortcomings Rauschenbusch gave to American Protestantism a sense of social responsibility that it should never lose."

From Walter Rauschenbusch, **Christianity and the Social Crisis**

To most thoughtful men today the social question is the absorbing intellectual problem of our time. To the working class it is more. Socialism is their class movement. The great forward movement inaugurated by the French Revolution was the movement of the business men who wrested political control from the feudal nobility and clergy. The wage-workers were then neither strong nor intelligent enough to force a readjustment of rights in their favor. That class is now in its birththroes. The rest of us may be sympathetic onlookers and helpers, but to them it is a question of life and death.

Every great movement which so profoundly stirs men, unlocks the depths of their religious nature, just as great experiences in our personal life make the individual susceptible to religious emotion. When the chaotic mass of humanity stirs to the throb of a new creative day, it always feels the spirit of God hovering over it. The large hope which then beckons men, the ideal of justice and humanity which inspires them, the devotion and self-sacrifice to the cause which they exhibit—these are in truth religious.

As long as the people are still patriotic and religious, their first impulse is to march under the banner of their inherited religion, sure that it must be on their side. When the German peasants in 1525 set forth their simple and just demands in the celebrated "Twelve Articles," they based them all on the Bible and offered to surrender any demand which should be proved out of harmony with God's word. Thus again the people of St. Petersburg on January 22, 1905, moved to the Winter Palace to present their petition to "the little Father," led by a priest in the vestments of religion, and bearing before them the portrait of the Czar and the cross of Christ. In both cases the response to their petition was a massacre.

It is humiliating to say that the confidence with which the people at the beginning of such risings have turned to their religion for moral backing has not been justified in the past. Luther had scant sympathy with the peasants at the outset, and as soon as they used force against the castles of the barons and the monasteries, he called for forcible repression in the most violent language. The pope, too, wrote a congratulatory letter to those who had been most active in repressing the movement. The state Church in Russia is certainly not on the side of the revolution, though many of her priests may be. The churches in Europe were almost universally hostile to the French Revolution. . . .

In *our own country we are still at the parting of the ways.* Our social movement is still in its earliest stages. The bitterness and anger of their fight has not eaten into the heart of the working classes as it has abroad. Many of them are still ready to make their fight in the name of God and Christ, though not of the Church. Populistic conventions used to recite the Lord's Prayer with deep feeling. The Single Tax movement utilized religious ideas freely. A Cooper Union meeting cheered Father McGlynn when he recited the words: "Thy kingdom come! Thy will be done on earth!" Some of the favorite speakers and organizers of the socialists in our country are former Christian ministers, who use their power of ethical and religious appeal. In Labor Lyceums and similar gatherings, ministers are often invited as speakers, though perhaps quite as much in the hope of converting them as with a desire to hear what they have to say. The divorce between the new class movement and the old religion can still be averted.

It is a hopeful fact that in our country the Church is so close to the common people. In many of the largest denominations the churches are organized as pure democracies, and the people own and run them.

Our ministry is not an hereditary pundit class, but most ministers have sprung from plain families and have worked for their living before they became ministers. The Church is not connected with the State and is not tainted, as in Europe, with the reputation of being a plainclothes policeman to club the people into spiritual submission to the ruling powers. The churches of monarchical countries have preached loyalty to the monarchy as an essential part of Christian character. The Church in America believes heartily in political democracy. But a Church which believes in political democracy can easily learn to believe in industrial democracy as soon as it comprehends the connection. It has one foot in the people's camp. The type of Christianity prevailing in America was developed in the Puritan Revolution and has retained the spirit of its origin. It is radical, evangelical, and has the strong bent towards politics which Calvinism has everywhere had. American ministers naturally take a keen interest in public life, and, as well as they know, have tried to bring the religious forces to bear at least on some aspects of public affairs.

As a result of these characteristics, the Christian Church in America is actually deeply affected by sympathy with the social movement. It stands now, at the very beginning of the social movement in America, where the repentant Church of Germany stands after a generation of punishment by atheistic socialism. No other learned profession seems to be so open to socialist ideals as the ministry. Several years ago the New York Evening Post began to lament that the Church had gone over to socialism.

Nevertheless the working class have not as yet gained the impression that the Church is a positive reinforcement to them in their struggle. The impression is rather the other way. The eminent ministers whose utterances are most widely disseminated are usually the pastors of wealthy churches, and it is natural that they should echo the views taken by the friends with whom they are in sympathetic intercourse. Even those ministers who are intellectually interested in social problems are not always in sympathy with the immediate conflicts of the working class. They may take a lively interest in municipal reform or public ownership, and yet view dubiously the efforts to create a fighting organization for labor or to end the wages system. We are of a different class and find it hard to sympathize with the class struggle of the wage-workers. . . .

In its struggle the working class becomes keenly conscious of the obstacles put in its way by the great institutions of society, the courts, the press, or the Church. It demands not only impartiality, but the kind of sympathy which will condone its mistakes and discern the justice of its cause in spite of the excesses of its followers. When our sympathies are enlisted, we develop a vast faculty for making excuses. If two dogs fight, our own dog is rarely the aggressor. Stealing peaches is a boyish prank when our boy does it, but petty larceny when that dratted boy of our neighbor does it. If the other political party grafts, it is a flagrant shame; if our own party does it, we regret it politely or deny the fact. If Germany annexes a part of Africa, it is brutal aggression, if England does it, she "fulfills her mission of civilization." If the business interests exclude the competition of foreign merchants by a protective tariff, it is a grand national policy; if the trade-unions try to exclude the competition of non-union labor, it is a denial of the right to work and an outrage.

The working class likes to get that kind of sympathy which will take a favorable view of its efforts and its mistakes, and a comprehension of the wrongs under which it suffers. Instead of that the pulpit of late has given its most vigorous interest to the wrongs of those whom militant labor regards as traitors to its cause. It has been more concerned with the fact that some individuals were barred from a job by the unions, than with the fact that the entire wage-working class is debarred from the land, from the tools of production, and from their fair share in the proceeds of production.

It cannot well be denied that there is an increasing alienation between the working class and the churches. That alienation is most complete wherever our industrial development has advanced farthest and has created a distinct class of wage-workers. Several causes have contributed. Many have dropped away because they cannot afford to take their share in the expensive maintenance of a church in a large city. Others because the tone, the spirit, the point of view in the churches, is that of another social class. The commercial and professional classes dominate the spiritual atmosphere in the large city churches. As workingmen grow more class-conscious, they come to regard the business men as their antagonists and the possessing classes as exploiters who live on their labor, and they resent it when persons belonging to these classes address them with the tone of moral superiority. When ministers handle the labor question, they often seem to the working class partial against them even when the ministers think they are most impartial. Foreign workingmen bring with them the long-standing distrust for the clergy and the Church as tools of oppression which they have learned abroad, and they perpetuate that attitude here. The churches of America suffer for the sins of the churches abroad. The "scientific socialism" imported from older countries through its literature and its advocates is saturated with materialistic philosophy and is apt to create dislike and antagonism for the ideas and institutions of religion.

Thus in spite of the favorable equipment of the Church in America there is imminent danger that the working people will pass from indifference to hostility, from religious enthusiasm to anti-religious bitterness. That would be one of the most unspeakable calamities that could come upon the Church. If we would only take warning by the fate of the churches in Europe, we might avert the desolation that threatens us. We may well be glad that in nearly every city there are a few ministers who are known as the outspoken friends of labor. Their fellow-ministers may regard them as radicals, lacking in balance, and very likely they are; but in the present situation they are among the most valuable servants of the Church. The workingmen see that there is at least a minority in the Church that champions their cause, and that fact helps to keep their judgment in hopeful suspense about the Church at large. Men who are just as one-sided in favor of capitalism pass as sane and conservative men. If the capitalist class have their court-chaplains, it is only fair that the army of labor should have its army-chaplains who administer the consolations of religion to militant labor.

Thus the Church has a tremendous stake in the social crisis. It may try to maintain an attitude of neutrality, but neither side will permit it. If it is quiescent, it thereby throws its influence on the side of things as they are, and the class which aspires to a fitter place in the organization of society will feel the great spiritual force of the Church as a dead weight against it. If it loses the loyalty and trust of the working class, it loses the very class in which it originated, to which its founders belonged, and which has lifted it to power. If it becomes a religion of the upper classes, it condemns itself to a slow and comfortable death. Protestantism from the outset entered into an intimate alliance with the intelligence and wealth of the city population. As the cities grew in importance since the Reformation, as commerce overshadowed agriculture, and as the business class crowded the feudal aristocracy out of its leading positions since the French Revolution, Protestantism throve with the class which had espoused it. It lifted its class, and its class lifted it. On the other hand, the Anabaptist movement in Germany, which propagated within the lower classes, was crushed with the class that bore its banner. If the present class struggle of the wage-worker is successful, and they become the dominant class of the future, any religious ideas and institutions which they now embrace in the heat of their struggle will rise to power with them, and any institution on which they turn their back is likely to find itself in the cold. The parable of the Wise and Foolish Virgins holds of entire nations and institutions as well as of individuals.

We have seen that the crisis of society is also the crisis of the

Church. The Church, too, feels the incipient paralysis that is creeping upon our splendid Christian civilization through the unjust absorption of wealth on one side and the poverty of the people on the other. It cannot thrive when society decays. Its wealth, its independence, its ministry, its social hold, its spiritual authority, are threatened in a hundred ways.

But on the other hand, the present crisis presents one of the greatest opportunities for its own growth and development that have ever been offered to Christianity. The present historical situation is a high summons of the Eternal to enter on a larger duty, and thereby to inherit a larger life.

In all the greatest forward movements of humanity, religion has been one of the driving forces. The dead weight of hoary institutions and the resistance of the caked and incrusted customs and ideas of the past are so great that unless the dormant energies of the people are awakened by moral enthusiasm and religious faith, the old triumphs over the new. "Mighty Truth's yet mightier man-child" comes to the hour of birth, but there is no strength to bring forth.

But in turn the greatest forward movements in religion have always taken place under the call of a great historical situation. Religious movements of the first magnitude are seldom purely religious in their origin and character. It is when nations throb with patriotic fervor, with social indignation, with the keen joy of new intellectual light, with the vastness and fear of untried conditions, when "the energy sublime of a century bursts full-blossomed on the thorny stem of Time," that religion, too, will rise to a new epoch in its existence. . . .

Thus in past history religion has demonstrated its capacity to evoke the latent powers of humanity, and has in turn gained a fresh hold on men and rejuvenated its own life by supporting the high patriotic and social ambitions of an age. We, too, are in the midst of a vast historical movement. The historians of the future will rank it second to none. It is one of the tides in the affairs of men. If rightly directed, a little effort in this time of malleable heat will shape humanity for good more than a huge labor when the iron is cold. If Christianity would now add its moral force to the social and economic forces making for a nobler organization of society, it could render such help to the cause of justice and the people as would make this a proud page in the history of the Church for our sons to read. And in turn the sweep and thrill of such a great cause would lift the Church beyond its own narrowness. If it would stake its life in this cause of God, it would gain its life. If it follows the ways of profit and prudence, it will find its wisdom foolishness. At the beginning of the modern foreign missionary movement the Church was full of timid scruples about its call and

its ability for such a work. Today there are few things in the life of
the Church which so inspire its finest sons and daughters and so in-
tensify the Christ-spirit in its whole body as this movement in which
it seems to scatter its strength abroad. If the social movement were
undertaken in a similar spirit of religious faith and daring, it would
have a similar power to re-christianize the Church. . . .

"No religion gains by the lapse of time; it only loses. Unless new
storms pass over it and cleanse it, it will be stifled in its own dry
foliage." *Men are so afraid of religious vagaries, and so little afraid of
religious stagnation.* Yet the religion of Jesus has less to fear from
sitting down to meet with publicans and sinners than from the immac-
ulate isolation of the Pharisees. It will take care of itself if mixed into
the three measures of meal; but if the leaven is kept standing by itself, it will sour hopelessly. If the Church tries to confine itself to
theology and the Bible, and refuses its larger mission to humanity, its
theology will gradually become mythology and its Bible a closed
book. . . .

The gospel, to have full power over an age, must be the highest expressions of the moral and religious truths held by that age. If it lags
behind and deals in outgrown conceptions of life and duty, it will lose
power over the ablest minds and the young men first, and gradually
over all. In our thought to-day the social problems irresistibly take the
lead. If the Church has no live and bold thought on this dominant
question of modern life, its teaching authority on all other questions
will dwindle and be despised. It cannot afford to have young men
sniff the air as in a stuffy room when they enter the sphere of religious
thought. When the world is in travail with a higher idea of justice,
the Church dare not ignore it if it would retain its moral leadership.
On the other hand, if the Church does incorporate the new social terms
in its synthesis of truth, they are certain to throw new light on all the
older elements of its teaching. The conception of race sin and race
salvation become comprehensible once more to those who have made
the idea of social solidarity in good and evil a part of their thought.
The law of sacrifice loses its arbitrary and mechanical aspect when
we understand the vital union of all humanity. Individualistic Christianity has almost lost sight of the great idea of the kingdom of God,
which was the inspiration and centre of the thought of Jesus. Social
Christianity would once more enable us to understand the purpose
and thought of Jesus and take the veil from our eyes when we read
the synoptic gospels.

The social crisis offers a great opportunity for the infusion of new
life and power into the religious thought of the Church. It also offers
the chance for progress in its life. When the broader social outlook

widens the purpose of a Christian man beyond the increase of his church, he lifts up his eyes and sees that there are others who are at work for humanity besides his denomination. Common work for social welfare is the best common ground for the various religious bodies and the best training school for practical Christian unity. The strong movement for Christian union in our country has been largely prompted by the realization of social needs, and is led by men who have felt the attraction of the kingdom of God as something greater than any denomination and as the common object of all. Thus the divisions which were caused in the past by differences in dogma and church polity may perhaps be healed by unity of interest in social salvation.

As we have seen, the industrial and commercial life to-day is dominated by principles antagonistic to the fundamental principles of Christianity, and it is so difficult to live a Christian life in the midst of it that few men ever try. If production could be organized on a basis of cooperative fraternity; if distribution could at least approximately be determined by justice; if all men could be conscious that their labor contributed to the welfare of all and that their personal well-being was dependent on the prosperity of the Commonwealth; if predatory business and parasitic wealth no longer made us all feverish with covetousness and a simpler life became the fashion; if our time and strength were not used up either in getting a bare living or in amassing unusable wealth and we had more leisure for the higher pursuits of the mind and the soul—then there might be a chance to live such a life of gentleness and brotherly kindness and tranquility of heart as Jesus desired for men. It may be that the cooperative Commonwealth would give us the first chance in history to live a really Christian life without retiring from the world, and would make the Sermon on the Mount a philosophy of life feasible for all who care to try.

This is the stake of the Church in the social crisis. If society continues to disintegrate and decay, the Church will be carried down with it. If the Church can rally such moral forces that injustice will be overcome and fresh red blood will course in a sounder social organism, it will itself rise to higher liberty and life. Doing the will of God it will have new visions of God. With a new message will come a new authority. If the salt loses its saltness, it will be trodden under foot. If the Church fulfills its prophetic functions, it may bear the prophet's reproach for a time, but it will have the prophet's vindication thereafter.

The conviction has always been embedded in the heart of the Church that "the world"—society as it is—is evil and some time is to make way for a true human society in which the spirit of Jesus Christ shall rule. For fifteen hundred years those who desired to live a truly

Christian life withdrew from the evil world to live a life apart. But the principle of such an ascetic departure from the world is dead in modern life. There are only two other possibilities. The Church must either condemn the world and seek to change it, or tolerate the world and conform to it. In the latter case it surrenders its holiness and its mission. The other possibility has never yet been tried with full faith on a large scale. All the leadings of God in contemporary history and all the promptings of Christ's spirit in our hearts urge us to make the trial. On this choice is staked the future of the Church. . . .

The ideal of a fraternal organization of society is so splendid that it is today enlisting the choicest young minds of the intellectual classes under its banner. Idealists everywhere are surrendering to it, especially those who are under the power of the ethical spirit of Christianity. The influence which these idealists exert in reinforcing the movement toward solidarity is beyond computation. They impregnate the popular mind with faith and enthusiasm. They furnish the watchwords and the intellectual backing of historical and scientific information. They supply devoted leaders and give a lofty sanction to the movement by their presence in it. They diminish the resistance of the upper classes among whom they spread their ideas. . . .

The question is whether the ideal of cooperation and economic fraternity can to-day depend on any great and conquering class whose self-interest is bound up with the victory of that principle. It is hopeless to expect the business class to espouse that principle as a class. Individuals in the business class will do so, but the class will not. There is no historical precedent for an altruistic self-effacement of a whole class. Of the professional class it is safe to expect that an important minority—perhaps a larger minority in our country than in any country heretofore—will range themselves under the new social ideal. With them especially the factor of religion will prove of immense power. But their motives will in the main be idealistic, and at the present stage of man's moral development the unselfish emotions are fragile and easily chafe through, unless the coarse fibre of self-interest is woven into them. But there is another class to which that conception of organized fraternity is not only a moral ideal, but the hope for bread and butter; with which it enlists not only religious devotion and self-sacrifice, but involves salvation from poverty and insecurity and participation in the wealth and culture of modern life for themselves and their children. . . .

As long as the working class simply attempts to better its condition somewhat and to secure a recognized standing for its class organization it stands on the basis of the present capitalistic organization of industry. Capitalism necessarily divides industrial society into two classes,—those who own the instruments and materials of production, and those who furnish the labor for it. This sharp division is the peculiar characteristic of modern capitalism which distinguishes it from other forms of social organization in the past. These two classes have to cooperate in modern production. The labor movement seeks to win better terms for the working class in striking its bargains. Yet whatever terms organized labor succeeds in winning are always temporary and insecure, like the hold which a wrestler gets on the body of his antagonist. The persistent tendency with capital necessarily is to get labor as cheaply as possible and to force as much work from it as possible. Moreover, labor is always in an inferior position in the struggle. It is handicapped by its own hunger and lack of resources. It has to wrestle on its knees with a foeman who is on his feet. Is this unequal struggle between two conflicting interests to go on forever? Is this insecurity the best that the working class can ever hope to attain?

Here enters socialism. It proposes to abolish the division of industrial society into two classes and to close the fatal chasm which has separated the employing class from the working class since the introduction of power machinery. It proposes to restore the independence of the workingman by making him once more the owner of his tools and to give him the full proceeds of his production instead of a wage determined by his poverty. It has no idea of reverting to the simple methods of the old handicrafts, but heartily accepts the power machinery, the great factory, the division of labor, the organization of men in great regiments of workers, as established facts in modern life, and as the most efficient method of producing wealth. But it proposes to give to the whole body of workers the ownership of these vast instruments of production and to distribute among them all the entire proceeds of their common labor. There would then be no capitalistic class opposed to the working class; there would be a single class which would unite the qualities of both. Every workman would be both owner and worker, just as a farmer is who tills his own farm, or a housewife who works in her own kitchen. This would be a permanent solution to the labor question. It would end the present insecurity, the physical exploitation, the intellectual poverty to which the working class is now exposed even when its condition is most favorable.

If such a solution is even approximately feasible, it should be hailed with joy by every patriot and Christian, for it would put a stop to our industrial war, drain off the miasmatic swamp of undeserved poverty, save our political democracy, and lift the great working class to an altogether different footing of comfort, intelligence, security and moral strength. And it would embody the principle of solidarity and fraternity in the fundamental institutions of our industrial life. All the elements of cooperation and interaction which are now at work in our great establishments would be conserved, and in addition the hearty interest of all workers in their common factory or store would be immensely intensified by the diffused sense of ownership. Such a social order would develop the altruistic and social instincts just as the competitive order brings out the selfish instincts.

Socialism is the ultimate and logical outcome of the labor movement. When the entire working class throughout the industrial nations is viewed in a large way, the progress of socialism gives an impression of resistless and elemental power. It is inconceivable from the point of view of that class that it should stop short of complete independence and equality as long as it has the power to move on, and independence and equality for the working class must mean the collective ownership of the means of production and the abolition of the present two-class arrangement of industrial society. If the labor movement in our country is only slightly tinged with socialism as yet, it is merely because it is still in its embryonic stages. Nothing will bring the working class to a thorough comprehension of the actual status of their class and its ultimate aim more quickly than continual failure to secure their smaller demands and reactionary efforts to suppress their unions.

We started out with the proposition that the ideal of a fraternal organization of society will remain powerless if it is supported by idealists only; that it needs the firm support of a solid class whose economic future is staked on the success of that idea; and that the industrial working class is consciously or unconsciously committed to the struggle for the realization of that principle. It follows that those who desire the victory of that ideal from a religious point of view will have to enter into a working alliance with this class. Just as the Protestant principle of religious liberty and the democratic principle of political liberty rose to victory by an alliance with the middle class which was then rising to power, so the new Christian principle of brotherly association must ally itself with the working class if both are to conquer. Each depends on the other. The idealistic movement alone would be a soul without a body; the economic class movement alone would be a body without a soul. It needs the high elation and faith that come through religion. Nothing else will call forth that self-sacrificing devotion and lifelong fidelity which will be needed in so gigantic a struggle as lies before the working class.

The cooperation of professional men outside the working class would contribute scientific information and trained intelligence. They would mediate between the two classes, interpreting each to the other, and thereby lessening the strain of hostility. Their presence and sympathy would cheer the working people and diminish the sense of class isolation. By their contact with the possessing classes they could help to persuade them of the inherent justice of the labor movement and so create a leaning toward concessions. No other influence could do so much to prevent a revolutionary explosion of pent-up forces. It is to the interest of all sides that the readjustment of the social classes should come as a steady evolutionary process rather than as a social catastrophe. If the laboring class should attempt to seize political power suddenly, the attempt might be beaten back with terrible loss in efficiency to the movement. If the attempt should be successful, a raw governing class would be compelled to handle a situation so vast and complicated that no past revolution presents a parallel. There would be widespread disorder and acute distress, and a reactionary relapse to old conditions would, by all historical precedents, be almost certain to occur. It is devoutly to be desired that the shifting of power should come through a continuous series of practicable demands on one side and concessions on the other. Such an historical process will be immensely facilitated if there are a large number of men in the professional and business class with whom religious and ethical motives overcome their selfish interests so that they will throw their influence on the side of the class which is now claiming its full rights in the family circle of humanity.

On the other hand the Christian idealists must not make the mistake of trying to hold the working class down to the use of moral suasion only, or be repelled when they hear the brute note of selfishness and anger. The class struggle is bound to be transferred to the field of politics in our country in some form. It would be folly if the working class failed to use the leverage which their political power gives them. The business class has certainly never failed to use political means to further its interests. This is a war of conflicting interests which is not likely to be fought out in love and tenderness. The possessing class will make concessions not in brotherly love but in fear, because it has to. The working class will force its demands, not merely because they are just, but because it feels it cannot do without them, and because it is strong enough to coerce. Even Bismarck acknowledged that the former indifference of the business class in Germany to the sufferings of the lower class had not been overcome by philanthropy, but by fear of the growing discontent of the people and the spread of social democracy. Max Nordau meant the same when he said, "In spite of its theoretical absurdity, socialism has already in thirty years wrought greater amelioration than all the wisdom of statesmen and philosophers of thousands of years." All that we as Christian men can do is to ease the struggle and hasten the victory of the right by giving faith and hope to those who are down, and quickening the sense of justice with those who are in power, so that they will not harden their hearts and hold Israel in bondage, but will "let the people go." But that spiritual contribution, intangible and imponderable though it be, has a chemical power of immeasurable efficiency. . . .

The force of the religious spirit should be bent toward asserting the supremacy of life over property. Property exists to maintain and develop life. It is unchristian to regard human life as a mere instrument for the production of wealth. . . .

In asking for faith in the possibility of a new social order, we ask for no Utopian delusion. We know well that there is no perfection. In personal religion we all look with seasoned suspicion at any one who claims to be holy and perfect, yet we always tell men to become holy and to seek perfection. We make it a duty to seek what is unattainable. We have the same paradox in the perfectibility of society. We shall never have a perfect social life, yet we must seek it with faith. We shall never abolish suffering. There will always be death and the empty chair and heart. There will always be the agony of love unreturned. Women will long for children and never press baby lips to their breasts. Men will long for fame and miss it. Imperfect moral insight will work hurt in the best conceivable social order. The strong will always have the impulse to exert their strength, and no system can be devised which can keep them from crowding and jostling the weaker. Increased social refinement will bring increased sensitiveness to pain. An American may suffer as much distress through a social slight as a Russian peasant under the knout. At best there is always but an approximation to a perfect social order. The kingdom of God is always but coming.

But every approximation to it is worth while. Every step toward personal purity and peace, though it only makes the consciousness of imperfection more poignant, carries its own exceeding great reward, and everlasting pilgrimage toward the kingdom of God is better than contented stability in the tents of wickedness.

And sometimes the hot hope surges up that perhaps the long and slow climb may be ending. In the past the steps of our race toward progress have been short and feeble, and succeeded by long intervals of sloth and apathy. But is that necessarily to remain the rate of advance? In the intellectual life there has been an unprecedented leap forward during the last hundred years. Individually we are not more gifted than our grandfathers, but collectively we have wrought out more epoch-making discoveries and inventions in one century than the whole race in the untold centuries that have gone before. If the twentieth century could do for us in the control of social forces what the nineteenth did for us in the control of natural forces, our grandchildren would live in a society that would be justified in regarding our present social life as semi-barbarous. Since the Reformation began to free the mind and to direct the force of religion toward morality, there has been a perceptible increase of speed. Humanity is gaining in elasticity and capacity for change, and every gain in general intelligence, in organizing capacity, in physical and moral soundness, and especially in responsiveness to ideal motives, again increases the ability to advance without disastrous reactions. The swiftness of evolution in our own country proves the immense latent perfectibility in human nature.

Last May a miracle happened. At the beginning of the week the fruit trees bore brown and greenish buds. At the end of the week they were robed in bridal garments of blossom. But for weeks and months the sap had been rising and distending the cells and maturing the tissues which were half ready in the fall before. The swift unfolding was the culmination of a long process. Perhaps these nineteen centuries of Christian influence have been a long preliminary stage of growth, and now the flower and fruit are almost here. If at this juncture we can rally sufficient religious faith and moral strength to snap the bonds of evil and turn the present unparalleled economic and intellectual resources of humanity to the harmonious development of a true social life, the generations yet unborn will mark this as that great day of the Lord for which the ages waited, and count us blessed for sharing in the apostolate that proclaimed it.

ROMANO GUARDINI

The Awakening of the Church in the Soul (1922) is the influential manifesto of Romano Guardini (1885-1968). It is a call for the emancipation of European culture from machines, dictators, and atheists. Here there is a basic assumption that the West is in a state of deep anarchy. Guardini diagnoses the crisis of the 1920s to be the death-rattle of individualism, the heritage of the Enlightenment. The church is depicted as the institution which will erect a new objective order upon the graves of Kantians and Idealists, as well as the captains of industry whose factories have destroyed the old organic forms of life and separated human from human. Guardini points to a growing awareness among Germans that "religious life comes no more from the I, but grows out of the objective form of the community." The liturgy insures the communal character of the Catholic Church. Guardini said this in his greatest and shortest work, *The Spirit of the Liturgy*, which came out in the Benedictine *Ecclesia Orans* series in 1918. The collectivity which is wanting in society can be achieved in communally celebrated worship. The individual yields place to the universal. Liturgical acts are a "manifestation of restrained and elevated social solidarity."

How different is the mood of *The End of the Modern World* (1956), called "the most somber book to come out of Germany since the Third Reich died." Guardini's reflections on the post-war world were composed as a set of lectures on the meaning of Pascal's vision of man and the world and were delivered in 1947-1948 at the University of Tübingen.

From Romano Guardini, **The Awakening of the Church in the Soul**

A religious process of incalculable importance has begun—the Church is coming to life in the souls of men. . . . With the development of individualism since the end of the Middle Ages, the Church has been thought of as a means to true religious life—as it were a God-designed framework or vessel in which that life is contained—a viaduct of life but not as life itself. It has, in other words, been thought of as a thing into which men must be incorporated that they may live with its life. Religious life tended increasingly away from the community and towards the individual sphere.

What was the basis of this attitude? The answer has already been indicated—the subjectivism and individualism of the modern age.

Religion was considered as something which belonged to the subjective sphere—it was simply something within a man, a condition of his soul. We are not speaking of conscious scientific theories, but of the spiritual tendency of the age. Objective religion represented by the Church was for the individual primarily the regulation of this individual and subjective religion; a protection against its inadequacies. That which remained over and above—the objective religion in its disinterested sublimity, and the community as a value in itself often left the individual cold and aroused no response in his heart. Even the acceptance and the enthusiasm which the Church evoked were largely external and individualistic, and psychologically had a strong affinity with an earlier 'patriotism.' When we look more closely we see that often there was no genuine belief in the existence of objective religious realities. This subjectivism dominated religious life all through the second half of the nineteenth century and during the beginning of the twentieth. Man felt imprisoned within himself.

Religious life was thus individualistic, disintegrated, and unsocial. The individual lived for himself. 'Myself and my Creator' was for many the exclusive formula. The community was not primary; it took the second place. It no longer was a natural reality which existed from the first by its own right. It had to be thought out, willed, and deliberately set up. One individual, it was believed, approached another, and went into partnership with him. But he was not from the outset bound up with a group of his fellows, the member of an organic community, sharing its common life. There was indeed no community, merely a mechanical organization, and this in the religious sphere as in every other. How little in Divine worship were the faithful aware of themselves as a community! How inwardly disintegrated the community was! How little was the individual parishioner conscious of the parish, and in how individualistic a spirit was the very Sacrament of community—Communion—conceived! . . . And the supra-personal unity of the community was not seen at all. The community was not seen at all. The community was regarded as a mere aggregate of individuals, as an organization of ends and means. Its mysterious substance, its creative power, and the organic laws governing communal growth and development, remained inaccessible.

All this naturally exerted its influence upon men's conception of the Church. She appeared above all as a legal institution for religious purposes. There was no limited perception of the mystical element in her; everything in fact which lies behind her palpable aims and visible institutions, and is expressed by the concept of the kingdom of God, the mystical Body of Christ.

This entire attitude, however, is now undergoing a profound change. New forces are at work busy in those mysterious depths of human nature where the intellectual and spiritual movements which now shape the life of a human culture receive their origin and direction. We are conscious of reality as a primary fact. It is no longer something dubious from which it is advisable to retreat upon the logical validity which seems more solid and more secure. Reality is as solid, indeed more solid, because prior, richer and more comprehensive.

Community is admitted just as directly. The attitude of withdrawal into the barred fortress of self no longer passes, as it did twenty years ago, for the only noble attitude. On the contrary, it is regarded as unjustifiable, barren and impotent. Just as powerful as the experience that things exist and the world exists, is the experience that human beings exist. Indeed, the latter is by far more powerful, because it affects us more closely. There are human beings like myself. Each one is akin to me, but each one is also a separate world of his own, of unique value. And from this realisation springs the passionate conviction that we all belong one to another; are all brothers. It is now taken as self-evident that the individual is a member of the community. The latter does not originate through one man attaching himself to another, or renouncing part of his independence. The community is just as primary a fact as individual existence. And the task of building up the community is just as primary and fundamental as that of perfecting personality.

And this consciousness of interdependence assumes a most significant expression; it develops into the consciousness of nationality. 'The people' does not mean the masses, or the uncultured, or the 'primitives,' whose mental and spiritual life, and whose system of facts and values are as yet undeveloped. All these uses of the term derive from the ideas of liberalism, the *Aufklärung* and individualism. An entirely new note is now being sounded; something essential is being born. 'The people' is the primary association of those human beings, who by race, country, and historical antecedents share the same life and destiny. The people is a human society which maintains an unbroken continuity with the roots of nature and life, and obeys their intrinsic laws. The people contains—not numerically or quantitatively, but in essential quality—the whole of mankind, in all its human variety of ages, sexes, temperament, mental and physical condition; to which we must add the sum total of its work and spheres of production as determined by class and vocation. The people is mankind in its radical comprehensiveness. And a man is of 'the people' if he embraces, so to speak, this whole within himself. His opposite number is the 'cultured' man. He is not the people, developed and intellectualized, but a malformation, a one-sided, debased and uprooted being. He is a product of humanism, and above all of the *Aufklärung*. He is a human type which has cut itself adrift from the ties which make man's physical and mental life organic. He has fallen away on the one hand into a world of abstraction, on the other into the purely physical sphere; from union with nature into the purely scholastic and artificial; from the community into isolation. His deepest longing should be to become once more one of the people; not indeed by romantic attempts to conform with popular ideas and customs, but by a renewal of his inmost spirit by a progressive return to a simple and complete life. The Youth Movement is an attempt in this direction.

And already a new reality is beginning to appear above the horizon. Here also the use of the word needs to be purified. It need not denote the rationalist conception of 'humanity,' but the living unity of the human race, of blood, destiny, responsibility, and labour; that solidarity which is postulated by the dogma of original sin and vicarious redemption, mysteries which no rationalist can understand.

The individual self is conscious of enrichment not only by the experience of real things, but also by the community, which expands its self-consciousness into a consciousness of a communal self. By direct sympathy, what belongs to another becomes mine own, and what belongs to me becomes his.

This life is also stirring in our consciousness of the community. We
are as immediately and acutely conscious of the communal life bearing us on its current, of those creative depths from which the being
and work of the community arise, as we are of the form it assumes and
the logic that form expresses.

Those revolutionary changes must necessarily have their repercussions in the religious community. . . . In this religious relation our
fellow men have a vital part. The religious community exists. Nor is it
a collection of self-contained individuals, but the reality which comprehends individuals—the Church. She embraces the people; she embraces mankind. She draws even things, indeed the whole world, into
herself. Thus the Church is regaining that cosmic spaciousness which
was hers during the early centuries and the Middle Ages. The conception of the Church as the *Corpus Christi mysticum* which is developed
in the Epistles of St. Paul to the Ephesians and Colossians, is acquiring
a wholly new power. Under Christ the Head the Church gathers together 'all which is in Heaven, on earth, and under the earth.' In the
Church everything—angels, men and things—are linked with God. In
her the great regeneration is already beginning for which the entire
creation 'groaneth and is in travail.' . . .

An event of tremendous importance has happened. The religious
life no longer rises solely in the self, but at the same time at the opposite pole, in the objective and already formed community. . . .

The religious life is being released from its fatal confinement within
the subject, and draws into itself the entire fulness of objective reality.
As once in the Middle Ages, all things are re-entering the religious
sphere, and moreover with a religious coloring and as religious values.
The rest of mankind and the things of this world once more are invested with a religious atmosphere and a profound religious significance. As a result the feeling for symbolism is coming back; concrete
objects once more become the vehicles and expressions of spiritual
reality. We understand how every department of the real world could
find a place in the cathedrals of the Middle Ages, in its *Summas,* universal histories, encyclopedias and cycles of legend, and moreover not
as an incongruous accessory, not as an allegory stuck on from without,
but filled with religious content and itself invested with a spiritual
character. Many signs point towards the re-emergence of a religious
world. This, however, is the Church, which gathers together under
one head 'what is in heaven, on the earth, and under the earth.' The
moment seems near for a genuine religious art, which will not be content to depict religious subjects with an unconsecrated brush, but will
see the whole world spiritually as a vast kingdom of realities, com-

prising good and evil powers, and in which the Kingdom of God is taken by storm.

All this, however, can be summed up in one word—'the Church.' That stupendous Fact that is the Church is once more becoming a living reality, and we understand that she truly is the One and the All. We dimly guess something of the passion with which great saints clung to her and fought for her. In the past their words may sometimes have sounded empty phrases. But now a light is breaking. The thinker, with rapture of spirit, will perceive in the Church the ultimate and vast synthesis of all realities. The artist with a force that moves his heart to the depths, will experience in the Church the overwhelming transformation, the exquisite refinement, and the sublime transfiguration of all reality by a sovereign radiance and beauty. . . .

All this, however, must not be confined to books and speech, but must be put with effect where the Church touches the individual most closely—in the parish. If the process known as the 'Church Movement' makes progress, it is bound to lead to a renewal of parochial consciousness. This is the appointed way in which the Church must become an object of personal experience. The measure of the individual's true—not merely verbal—loyalty to the Church lies in the extent to which he lives with her, knows that he is jointly responsible for her, and works for her. And conversely the various manifestations of parish life must in turn be such that the individual is able to behave in this way. Hitherto parish life itself has been deeply tainted by that individualistic spirit of which we have spoken above. How, indeed, could it have been otherwise?

It is in the light of what has already been said that we can understand the Liturgical Movement. This is a particular powerful current and one more exceptionally visible from outside than within the 'Church Movement'; indeed, it is the latter in its contemplative aspect. Through it the Church enters the life of prayer as a religious reality, and the life of the individual becomes an integral part of the life of the Church. . . .

The liturgy is essentially not the religion of the cultured, but the religion of the people. If the people are rightly instructed, and the liturgy is properly carried out, they display a simple and profound understanding of it. For the people do not analyze concepts, but contemplate. The people possess that inner integrity of being which corresponds perfectly with the symbolism of the liturgical language, imagery, action and ornaments. The cultured man has first of all to accustom himself to this attitude; but to the people it has always been inconceivable that religion should express itself by abstract ideas and logical developments, and not by being and action, by imagery and ritual.

From Romano Guardini, **The Spirit of the Liturgy**

The Catholic liturgy is the supreme example of an objectively established rule of spiritual life. It has been able to develop *kata ton holon*, that is to say, in every direction, and in accordance with all places, times, and types of human culture. Therefore, it will be the best teacher of the *via ordinaria*—the regulation of religious life in common, with, at the same time, a view to actual needs and requirements. . . .

The liturgy does not say 'I,' but 'We.' . . . The liturgy is not celebrated by the individual, but by the body of the faithful.

It is on the plane of liturgical relations that the individual experiences the meaning of religious fellowship. The individual—provided that he actually desires to take part in the celebration of the liturgy—must realise that it is as a member of the Church that he, and the Church within him, acts and prays; he must know that in this higher unity he is at one with the rest of the faithful, and he must desire to be so.

All this is particularly difficult for modern people, who find it so hard to renounce their independence. And yet people who are perfectly ready to play a subordinate part in state and commercial affairs are all the more susceptible and the more passionately reluctant to regulate their spiritual life by dictates other than those of their private and personal requirements. . . .

From the man of individualistic disposition, then, a sacrifice for the good of the community is required; from the man of social disposition, submission to the austere restraint which characterises liturgical fellowship. While the former must accustom himself to frequenting the company of his fellows, and must acknowledge that he is only a man among men, the latter must learn to subscribe to the noble, restrained forms which etiquette requires in the House and at the Court of the Divine Majesty.

From Romano Guardini, **The End of the Modern World**

Modern man's dishonesty was rooted in his refusal to recognize Christianity's affirmation of the God-man relationship. Even as the modern world acclaimed the worth of personality and of an order of personal values, it did away with their guarantor, Christian Revelation. This parallel affirmation and negation can be illustrated in modern history in the case of German classicism. Carried forward by truncated attitudes and values, German classicism was noble, humane and beautiful, but it lacked the final depth of truth. It had denied Revelation although it drew everywhere upon its effects. By the next generation the classical attitude toward man had also begun to fade, not because that generation did not occupy an equally high plane, but because an uprooted personal culture is powerless against the breakthrough of positivism. Thus the process of dissolution gained momentum. Suddenly the "value system" of the last two decades broke into history. In its sweeping contradiction of the whole modern tradition it proved that culture to have been only an apparent culture. That vacuum, however, had been created long before; now it was made evident to all men. With the denial of Christian Revelation genuine personality had disappeared from the human consciousness. With it had gone that realm of attitudes and values which only it can subsume.

The coming era will bring a frightful yet salutary preciseness to these conditions. No Christian can welcome the advent of a radical un-Christianity. Since Revelation is not a subjective experience but simple Truth promulgated by Him Who also made the world, every moment of history which excludes that Revelation is threatened in its most hidden recesses. Yet it is good that modern dishonesty was unmasked. As the benefits of Revelation disappear even more from the coming world, man will truly learn what it means to be cut off from Revelation.

The question of the temper of the religious sensibility of the new age remains before us. Although the content of Revelation is eternal, its historical realization, its incarnation in man, varies with the passage of time. We could offer many implications about the religious temper of the new man, but it is necessary to restrict our meditations.

The rapid advance of a non-Christian ethos, however, will be crucial for the Christian sensibility. As unbelievers deny Revelation more decisively, as they put their denial into more consistent practice, it will become the more evident what it really means to be a Christian. At the same time, the unbeliever will emerge from the fogs of secularism. He will cease to reap benefit from the values and forces developed by the very Revelation he denies. He must learn to exist honestly without Christ and without the God revealed through Him; he will have to learn to experience what this honesty means. Nietzsche has already warned us that the non-Christian of the modern world had no realization of what it truly meant to be without Christ. The last decades have suggested what life without Christ really is. The last decades were only the beginning.

A new paganism differing from that of earlier ages will appear in the new world. Again contemporary man labors under illusory attitudes. In many cases, the non-Christian today cherishes the opinion that he can erase Christianity by seeking a new religious path, by returning to classical antiquity from which he can make a new departure. He is mistaken. No man can retrace history. As a form of historic existence classical antiquity is forever gone. When contemporary man becomes a pagan he does so in a way completely other than that of the pre-Christian. Even at the height of their cultural achievement the religious attitudes of the ancients were youthful and naive. Classical man only lived before that crisis which was the coming of Christ. With the advent of Christ man confronted a decision which placed him on a new level of existence. Søren Kierkegaard made this fact clear, once and for all. With the coming of Christ man's existence took on an earnestness which classical antiquity never knew simply because it had no way of knowing it. This earnestness did not spring from a human maturity; it sprang from the call which each person received from God through Christ. With this call the person opened his eyes, he was awakened for the first time in his life. This the Christian is whether he wills it or not. This earnestness prevailed, springing from the historic realization of the centuries that Christ is Being. It springs from man's common experience, frightful in its clarity, that He "knew what is in man," from the awareness in men of all the ages of that super-human courage with which He mastered existence. When men deny this awareness we gain an impression that they suffer an immaturity, one common to the anti-Christian faiths of the ancient world.

Just as the renewal of the ancient classic myths against early Christianity was lifeless, so was the attempted rejuvenation of the Nordic myths. Seldom was either of those renewals the camouflage for a drive for power as it was with National Socialism. Nordic paganism had existed prior to the decision man had to make before God's call through Christ, as had classical paganism. On the other hand, which ever way contemporary man decides, he must enter the depths of the person as revealed in Christ, leaving behind the secure but static life of immediate existence with its false rhythms and images.

This exact judgment must be made against all those attempts which would create a new myth through secular affirmation of the true Christian vision. Consider what happened in the later poetry of Rilke for instance. Basic to Rilke's poetry is the will to shed the transcendence of Revelation and to ground existence absolutely on earth. Rilke's desire reveals its utter powerlessness when we note its total lack of harmony with the world now dawning. His attempts to adjust himself to the new world have a moving helplessness in a poem like the "Sonnette an Orpheus," an alienating helplessness in the "Elegien." In respect to French existentialism, too, its negation of an intelligible existence is so violent that it seems to be an especially despairing kind of Romanticism made possible by the convulsions of the last decades.

A totally different realism would be needed to maneuver human attitudes before they could contradict Christian Revelation or build a fortress out of the world fully independent of Revelation. It remains to be seen to what extent the East can develop this other realism and to what exigencies man will be subjected as a consequence.

The Faith of Christian men will need to take on a new decisiveness. It must strip itself of all secularism, all analogies with the secular world, all flabbiness and eclectic mixtures. Here, it seems to me, we have solid reasons for confidence. The Christian has always found it difficult to come to an understanding of modern attitudes, but we touch an issue here which needs more exact consideration. We do not mean that the Middle Ages was an historic epoch fully Christian in nature, nor do we mean that the modern world was an age fully un-Christian. Such assertions would resemble those of Romanticism, which have caused enough confusion. The Middle Ages were carried forward by forms of sensibility, thought and action which were basically neutral to the question of Faith, insofar as one can say such a thing at all. Similarly the modern world was carried by neutral forms. Within the modern era Western man created as his own an attitude of individual independence, yet that attitude said nothing about either the moral or the religious use which he made of his independence.

To be a Christian, however, demands an attitude toward Revelation; this demand can be found in every era of Western history. As far as this Christian attitude was concerned, Revelation remained equally near and equally distant for each epoch. Thus the Middle Ages contained its share of unbelief at every stage of decision, similarly the modern world demonstrated its share of full Christian affirmation. The modern Christian differed in character from his medieval ancestor, since he was forced to incarnate his faith within an historic situation which espoused individual independence, but he often succeeded as well as did the man of the Middle Ages. Indeed, the modern Christian faced obstacles which made it difficult for him to accept his age in the simple way that the medieval Christian could accept his. The memory of the revolt made against God by the modern world was too vividly impressed on the modern Christian. He was too aware of the manner in which his age had forced all cultural values to contradict his Faith. He knew too well the dubious and inferior position into which the world had forced that Faith. Besides these indignities there remained that modern dishonesty of which we have spoken, that hypocrisy which denied Christian doctrine and a Christian order of life even as it usurped its human and cultural effects. This dishonesty made the Christian feel insecure in his relation to the modern age. Everywhere within the modern world he found ideas and values whose Christian origin was clear, but which were declared the common property of all. How could he trust a situation like that? But the new age will do away with these ambivalences; the new age will declare that the secularized facets of Christianity are sentimentalities. This declaration will clear the air. The world to come will be filled with animosity and danger, but it will be a world open and clean. This danger within the new world will also have its cleansing effect upon the new Christian attitude, which in a special way must possess both trust and courage.

Men have often said that Christianity is a refuge from the realities of the modern world, and this charge contains a good measure of truth, not only because dogma fixes the thought of a Christian on an objective, timeless order and creates a life which survives the passing of the ages but also because the Church has preserved a full cultural tradition which would otherwise have died. The world to come will present less basis for objecting to Christianity as a refuge.

The cultural deposit preserved by the Church thus far will not be able to endure against the general decay of tradition. Even when it does endure it will be shaken and threatened on all sides. Dogma in its very nature, however, surmounts the march of time because it is rooted in eternity, and we can surmise that the character and conduct of coming Christian life will reveal itself especially through its old dogmatic roots. Christianity will once again need to prove itself deliberately as a faith which is not self-evident; it will be forced to distinguish itself more sharply from a dominantly non-Christian ethos. At that juncture the theological significance of dogma will begin a fresh advance; similarly will its practical and existential significance increase. I need not say that I imply no "modernization" here, no weakening of the content or of the effectiveness of Christian dogma; rather I emphasize its absoluteness, its unconditional demands and affirmations. These will be accentuated. The absolute experiencing of dogma will, I believe, make men feel more sharply the direction of life and the meaning of existence itself.

In this manner, the Faith will maintain itself against animosity and danger. At the forefront of Christian life, man's obedience to God will assert itself with a new power. Knowing that the very last thing is at stake, that he has reached that extremity which only obedience could meet—not because man might become *heteronom* but because God is Holy and Absolute—man will practice a pure obedience. Christianity will arm itself for an illiberal stand directed unconditionally toward Him Who is Unconditioned. Its illiberalism will differ from every form of violence, however, because it will be an act of freedom, an unconditional obedience to God; nor will it resemble an act of surrender to physical or psychic powers which might command one. No, man's unconditional answer to the call of God assumes within that very act the unconditional quality of the demand which God makes of him and which necessitates maturity of judgment, freedom and choice.

Here too we dare to hope. This trust is not based at all upon an optimism or confidence either in a universal order of reason or in a benevolent principle inherent to nature. It is based on God Who really is, Who alone is efficacious in His Action. It is based in this simple trust: that God is a God Who acts and Who everywhere prevails.

If I am right in my conclusions about the coming world, the Old Testament will take on a new significance. The Old Testament reveals the Living God Who smashes the mythical bonds of the earth, Who casts down the powers and the pagan rulers of life; it shows us the man of faith who is obedient to the acts of God according to the terms of the Covenant. These Old Testament truths will grow in meaning and import. The stronger the demonic powers, the more crucial will be that "victory over the world" realized in freedom and through Faith. It will be realized in the harmony between man's freedom freely returned to God from Whose own Creative Freedom it was gained. This will make possible not only effective action but even action itself. It is a strange thing that we should glimpse this holy way, this divine possibility, rising out of the very midst of universal power as it increases day by day.

This free union of the human person with the Absolute through unconditional freedom will enable the faithful to stand firm—God-centered—even though placeless and unprotected. It will enable man to enter into an immediate relationship with God which will cut through all force and danger. It will permit him to remain a vital person within the mounting loneliness of the future, a loneliness experienced in the very midst of the masses and all their organizations.

If we understand the eschatological text of Holy Writ correctly, trust and courage will totally form the character of the last age. The surrounding "Christian" culture and the traditions supported by it will lose their effectiveness. That loss will belong to the danger given by scandal, that danger of which it is said: "It will, if possible, deceive even the elect" (Matthew xxiv, 24).

Loneliness in faith will be terrible. Love will disappear from the face of the public world (Matthew xxiii, 12), but the more precious will that love be which flows from one lonely person to another, involving a courage of the heart born from the immediacy of the love of God as it was made known in Christ. Perhaps man will come to experience this love anew, to taste the sovereignty of its origin, to know its independence of the world, to sense the mystery of its final *why?* Perhaps love will achieve an intimacy and harmony never known to this day. Perhaps it will gain what lies hidden in the key words of the providential message of Jesus: "that things are transformed for the man who makes God's Will for His Kingdom his first concern" (Matthew vi, 33).

These eschatological conditions will show themselves, it seems to me, in the religious temper of the future. With these words I proclaim no facile apocalyptic. No man has the right to say that the End is here, for Christ Himself has declared that only the Father knows the day and the hour (Matthew xxiv, 36). If we speak here of the nearness of the End, we do not mean nearness in the sense of time, but nearness as it pertains to the essence of the End, for in essence man's existence is now nearing an absolute decision. Each and every consequence of that decision bears within it the greatest potentiality and the most extreme danger.

EMIL BRUNNER

"Man in the Universe" and "Personality and Humanity" contain the summation of the theme of modern Christian humanism: the balance of matter and spirit, individual and community, and freedom and limits wrought on earth in the incarnation of Jesus Christ. The essays are taken from *Christianity and Civilization* delivered by Emil Brunner (1889-1966) as the Gifford Lectures in the University of St. Andrews, Scotland, in 1947 and 1948.

The lectures are an attempt at a Christian doctrine of the foundations of civilization. Brunner justifies his conviction that only Christianity is capable of furnishing the basis of a civilization which can rightly be described as human upon an incarnational theology of culture. He presents a synoptic view of the whole relationship of the incarnation to "some of the problems of civilization, . . . of which the urgency is felt by every live Christian."

From Emil Brunner, **Christianity and Civilization**
MAN IN THE UNIVERSE

With this lecture we enter the field of those questions which may be called problems of humanism or the humane. The first of these problems comes from without; it is raised for us by the universe in which we find ourselves. All humanism, whether of a Christian or idealistic type, draws its life from the conviction that man's position within this Cosmos is a distinctive and, indeed, a unique one, and that man has to vindicate against nature something which belongs to himself alone. . . . Therefore there is an inescapable either/or between this opposition of man and nature on the one hand, and on the other a conception of continuity which ranges man entirely with nature, and thus destroys the foundations of humanism. . . .

Now it is curious that this nature-continuum, which denies the uniqueness of man and thereby sinks the human element in nature, stands at the beginning as well as at the end of the human history which we can survey. For the primitive mind there is no demarcation between man and surrounding nature. On the contrary, man and nature form one unbroken continuum. . . . Primitive man is, so to speak, a pre-scientific Darwinian, and the Darwinian of our time, by the same token, is a scientific primitive, if by Darwinism we understand a popular evolutionary philosophy rather than a strictly scientific hypothesis. There is, however, this considerable difference between the primitive and the modern nature-continuum, that in the world of primitive man the continuity is not established entirely at the cost of man. In the same measure that man is akin to the animal, the animal in its turn is akin to man. For the primitive mind, nature as a whole is somehow human. In this primitive world there are no "natural forces" in the present meaning of the word, but only forces which are at once of a personal and in some measure of a spiritual nature. Nature behaves in a way similar to man. You can talk with it, and it talks to you. All this is foreign to the conception of the modern Darwinist. Nature for him is conceived of as an object, i.e., it is radically non-personal. Nature is primarily a mechanism, and this is an idea entirely foreign to the primitive mind. The nature-continuum of modern times is established exclusively at the cost of man. Man has ceased to be something particular within a world which is conceived of in terms of mechanism. Therefore he is himself something like a highly-complicated mechanism. Whilst the primitive mind arrives at its scheme of continuity by the personification of nature, the modern mind arrives at it by a depersonification of man. It must now be our task to discover the background of this change in trying to summarise the history of man's thought about his place in the universe.

It is by a slow process that man has overcome the primitive nature-continuum. I would suggest that the best guide for the discovery of the history of human emancipation from nature is plastic art. The continuum is still living in all that mythological art which represents natural forces, understood as deities, in human shape as well as in animal— such art as we find in India as well as in old Egypt and Babylon. The decisive breach within this continuum happened in two distinct places: in Israel and in Greece. Leaving apart for the moment the Biblical concept of man, we may say that it is the unique contribution of the Greek mind to have abolished the animal shape of deity. In the mythological struggle of the Olympic gods against the semi- and totally bestial monsters, against the figures of the dark regions, there comes to the fore something of this unique inner liberation which takes place within the Greek conception of man. Man rises above the animal world; man becomes conscious of his uniqueness as a spiritual being distinct from a natural world.

But now, alongside this emancipation from and destruction of the nature-continuum, another process takes place, expressing itself again in plastic art, namely the rapproachement between deity and humanity which appears in an anthropomorphic deity and in the apotheosis of the human hero. This double process, first taking place in the subconscious forms of mythology, enters the full light of consciousness in philosophical reflection. Man discovers in himself that which distinguishes him from the animal and nature as a whole and elevates him above it, the Nous or the Logos, that spiritual principle which underlies all specifically human activity and gives man's work the character and content of human dignity. Now, this Nous or Logos is, at the same time, the principle which links mankind with the divine; the Logos is not merely the principle of human thought and meaningful action, but also that divine force which orders the world and makes it a Cosmos. It is the divine spark in human reason by which alone man emancipates himself from nature and places himself above it. It is that same divine spark in his reason in which he experiences the divinity of his innermost being. The continuum, then, is not broken, but shifted. Just as the divine Logos permeates nature and orders it, so it also permeates and orders man. But in man this divine principle becomes conscious knowledge. It is in the recognition of himself as partaker in the divine Logos that man becomes conscious of his specific essence and value; his humanity is, at the same time, divinity. This is the fundamental conception of Greek humanism in its conscious reflected form, freed from mythology.

In Biblical revelation the continuum of primitive mind is disrupted in an entirely different manner. A three-fold barrier is erected here: the barrier between God and the world, between God and man, and between man and nature. God is no more the immanent principle of the world, but is Lord and Creator. He, the Lord-creator, alone is divine. Everything which is not Himself is creature, product of His will. Therefor He is opposite the world. His essence, His divine Being, is other-than-world, He is the Holy One. That is why He does not allow Himself to be depicted in any form: "Thou shalt not make unto thee any graven image nor any likeness of any thing that is in heaven above or that is in the earth beneath, or that is in the water under the earth." But now—and this is the second barrier—it is not merely the nature-image of godhead which is forbidden to man, but equally the man-image. By that same character of holiness by which God is distinguished from nature, He is also distinguished from and placed opposite to man. Man, in spite of everything he has and is, with all his spiritual as well as natural powers, is not divine. He is a creature. The barrier which separates God and the world also separates God and man.

All the same, in spite of this sharp separation from God, man is not placed on the same level as the rest of the world and not seen in continuity with nature. Although man is not at all God, and God is not at all man, man is distinguished from all other creatures and elevated above them by a criterion of a specific kind. Man alone is created in the image of God. This likeness of man to God is the third barrier which is erected here. For man alone is created *in* the image and *to* the image of God. And this *imago dei* is the principle of Christian humanism as distinguished from Greek. At first sight it might appear as if this concept of *imago dei* meant something similar to the Greek idea that man is raised above the level of nature by his participation in the divine Nous or Logos dwelling in his reason. But the similarity between the two principles of humanism is merely apparent, for man's being created in the image of God does not imply any kind of divine spiritual substance in man, but only the relation to God. That which gives man his specific place in the Universe and specific dignity is not something which he has in his rational nature but his *relation* to the Creator. This relation is established by God's calling man to Himself and is realised by man's hearing this call and answering it by his own decision. That is to say, between God and man there exists the relation of calling, and responsibility founded in the divine Word and man's faith, a faith which works through love.

Christian humanism therefore, as distinguished from the Greek, is of such a kind that the humane character of existence is not automatically a possession of man, but is dependent on his relation to God, and remains a matter of decision. The humane character of man is not guaranteed in advance like a natural disposition. It realises itself only in that answer of man which corresponds to the divine call. There is a possibility of its not realising itself but of being perverted through a false decision into an untrue inhumane humanity. Even more: not only can this happen, but it has actually happened. It is the case that man has made the wrong decision and has thereby lost his true humanity, and can regain it only by a new act of creation of God, by redeeming grace. However, even the man who has lost his true humanity has not altogether lost his distinctive human character. In spite of his wrong decision, he still is and remains within that primary relation of responsibility and therefore retains—if not the truly humane content—at least the structure of human being. He is still distinguished from the rest of creation by the fact that he, and he alone, is a responsible person. Furthermore, to this man who has lost his true humane character, God, by His revelation of divine redeeming love in the God-man, Jesus Christ, has offered the possibility of reacquiring the true image of God; and, lastly, to those who accept this offer in obedient faith, the perfection and realisation of their eternal divine destiny is promised as the final goal of all history. That, in a few words, is the basis and content of Christian humanism.

Although the great difference between Christian and idealistic Greek humanism is quite obvious, they have at least this in common, that in both man is given a pre-eminent position in the Universe and is set over against and above nature on the sub-human level. In both man has a higher destiny, lifting him above the natural sphere and functions, and making him a partaker of a divine eternal meaning. In both the *humanum* has a rich content and is distinctly separated from the animal world. Therefore it is not surprising that where these two great streams of humanism met each other in history they did not merely flow alongside one another, but merged into one. Thus there was formed in the first centuries of our era something like a Christian-Greek or a Christian-idealistic humanism, a synthesis in which sometimes the classical, sometimes the Biblical element was predominant. But these two kinds of humanism were never clearly seen in their specific nature and so distinguished or separated from each other. It was only in the middle of the second millenium that a double-sided process of disentanglement or dissociation took place, on the one side from a genuinely Christian or Biblical conception of man, on the other side from a renewed classical idealistic humanism. The one we call Reformation, the other Renaissance. In previous lectures we mentioned the fact that the spiritual history of recent centuries is on the whole characterised by a progressive emancipation from Biblical revelation, and, hence, by a progressive domination of the rational element. The question which we have to answer is why this process led to a complete dissolution of humanism in the naturalist nihilism of our own day.

It is customary to answer this question by pointing to two epoch-making scientific discoveries, namely the revolutionary change within the conception of the spatial universe connected with the name Copernicus, and that other no less revolutionary re-establishment of the nature continuum connected with the name of Darwin. There is no doubt that both the destruction of the geo-centric world picture and the expansion of the spatial world into the infinite, as well as the doctrine of the descent of man from animal forms of life, came as a tremendous shock to the generations which these discoveries took by surprise. But in both cases it has become clear that this shock was of a

psychological rather than of a spiritual nature. For, if we contemplate
these discoveries dispassionately, it becomes clear that, whilst they
were bound to shake the frame of the traditional world-picture, they
could not by their own truth destroy or even endanger the substance
of humanism, whether Christian or idealistic.

In defending themselves against unconsidered consequences drawn
from these discoveries, idealistic and Christian humanism have a common interest. They have to make clear the difference between the
results of scientific research and the false interpretation of these results
by a naturalist philosophy. The Copernican destruction of geo-centrism
could, if I may use the phrase, be easily digested both by Christian
and idealistic humanism. For, after all, what has the assertion of the
independence and superiority of man over nature to do with the quantitative extension of the spatial world or with the destruction of an astronomical geo-centrism? That man, quantitatively considered, is a mere
nothing in the Universe was known before Copernicus and often found
expressed in the language of Homer as well as in that of the Old Testament. To anyone who understands that the human character of existence is no matter of quantities, but of quality, the multiplication of
man's quantitative disproportion with the Universe, involved in the
new cosmology, cannot make any difference. . . .

The case of Darwinism seems more dangerous. Granted that the
hypothesis of the descent of man from animal forms of life has become
a scientifically established fact—whether this is the case or not, science
alone can decide and seems as yet not to have decided definitely—does
this not mean that the continuity between man and animal is established and therefore that man has lost any claim to an exceptional
position? If this were so, this would no doubt mean that humanism has
lost its basis. . . . But once again dispassionate contemplation of the
facts and their implications shows that to draw such a consequence
from the zoological data is entirely illegitimate. The specifically human
can never be derived from the animal, even if it is true that the specifically human element begins to appear in such a minimal form that
its distinction from the animal is difficult. After Darwin, just as before
him, there is between man and animal the same unbridgeable gulf,
included in the concepts of spirit, culture, responsible personality. . . .
Man alone produces cultural life: this is the argument of idealistic
humanism. Man alone can hear the word of God: this is the argument
of Christian humanism. It is not science, but an unconsidered and
scientifically unsound philosophical speculation, which claims to have
shattered the pre-eminent position of man within nature by discovering man's animal past. The true scientist experiences his exceptional
position as *humanus* in his own field. It is the privilege of man alone

to produce science, to investigate truth for the sake of truth, regardless
of animal appetites and necessities.

If this is true . . . it is all the more surprising that Copernicanism
. . . in the largest sense of the word, as well as Darwinism, *has* contributed to the dissolution of humanism and to the rise of present-day
nihilism. Again, it is our task to try to understand this process and its
causes in order to come to a true understanding of our present spiritual situation. . . . Copernicanism had this effect because the Church
did and had done for centuries what it should not have done. The
Church had mixed up truth-of-God with world-truth. It had established
and dogmatically canonised the Biblical world-picture of antiquity,
which because of its origin we call the Babylonian world-picture, with
its three stories: the flat plate of the earth; above it and on the same
axis, so to speak, the sky or heaven; below it the underworld. This
ancient world-picture is merely the vessel in which the divine revelation is given to man, but has itself nothing to do with that revelation.
The Church and its theology therefore were forced by science to withdraw from a realm which was not theirs. Natural science has helped
the Church to understand its own truth and essence better than it had
understood them in the course of preceding centuries.

Nevertheless, Christian theology was not altogether wrong in its
apprehension with regard to Copernicanism. Theology should not have
opposed science, but it was right in opposing a certain philosophical
consequence drawn from the Copernican discovery within the rational-
istic humanism of the time. This Renaissance humanism in its turn
used the new world-picture as a weapon against the Christian doctrine
of revelation as such. It used the Copernican theory, as we see it, for
instance, in the example of Giordano Bruno, as a foundation of Pantheistic philosophy and mysticism. . . . However, whilst the Church
recognized her error in course of time, the philosophy of Enlightenment, the heir and successor of Renaissance humanism, continued the
fight on the same level, and does so to this day. . . .

The case of Darwinism is analogous. Once again Christian theology
confused God-knowledge and world-knowledge, and fought fiercely
against a strictly scientific hypothesis, i.e., the theory of evolution. In
particular, it was Darwin's idea of man's animal origin which the
Christian Church at first misconceived as a death-blow against a central Christian doctrine, namely man's being created in the image of
God. . . . This mistaken opposition to Darwinism on the part of Christian theology has, however, a positive side. It was not without reason
that the Church was afraid of the false and most dangerous philosophical use that would be made of this scientific discovery—a use which,
if it became victorious, would mean no less than the end of any kind

of humanism. This erroneous and, in its consequences, totally dangerous exploitation of Darwin's theory took place indeed in the development of an evolutionist system of philosophy in the latter part of the
19th century. The quintessence of this was the thesis that man is
nothing but a highly differentiated animal. This "nothing but" theory
was indeed the end of any kind of humanism and the beginning of the
naturalistic nihilism of our day.

How was this evolutionist pseudo-scientific philosophy possible? It
is necessary here to return to something which we have noted in a
previous connection, namely to that transition from a truly idealist
humanism grounded in an idealistic metaphysics to a positivistic anti-
metaphysical philosophy. It is best understood if we take Kant as our
starting point. From Kant's critical idealism, which gave rise to such
genuine forms of humanism as that of Humboldt and Schiller, two
very different philosophical schools developed: the absolute or speculative idealism of Fichte and Hegel on the one side, and an anti-meta-
physical critical philosophy on the other, which led on to positivism. In
Auguste Comte's *Religion de l'humanité* a remainder of ethical idealism survives, a reflection, so to speak, or idealistic light without a
source of its own. The same is true in thinkers like John Stuart Mill
and Herbert Spencer. They all hold a kind of ethical idealism cut off
from its roots. All these philosophers eagerly and sincerely intend to
salvage some kind of humanism, but cannot give it any satisfactory
theoretical foundation. It was into this philosophical context that the
Darwinist theory was launched, and by it developed into a system of
evolutionism with the essential doctrine that man is *nothing but* a
highly differentiated animal. It is obvious—although there are still
many who do not know it—that on such a basis humanism of any kind
is impossible. Humanism degenerates, if I may use the word, into a
mere hominism. The human becomes a mere natural datum. On such
a naturalistic basis it is impossible to distinguish the human from the
animal and to vindicate for man any kind of independence against
nature. If the nature-continuum is the only reality, there can be no
spiritual norms, no conscience, no higher destiny. The talk of "higher"
and "lower" is then a mere *façon de parler;* it simply means biological
differentiation which, as such, has nothing to do with value or norm.
It is, then, easy to understand why, in the generation following Comte,
Mill and Spencer, further development of the evolutionary system
caused the last remainders of the idealistic humanism of earlier times
to disappear. If man is nothing but the highly developed brain-species
of the mammal-family, ideas such as man's dignity, personality, the
rights of man, human destiny lose their meaning. The bankruptcy
which, theoretically, already existed in the generation of Spencer was

declared in the following decades; it only remained for the last generation to put it into execution. . . .

But why did it come about that idealistic humanism degenerated
more and more into positivist naturalistic "hominism"? I think the
answer must be that the germ of degeneration lies in the very foundation of idealistic humanism itself, firstly, in its anthropology; secondly,
in its metaphysics.

Idealism, in order to keep its conception of man, inevitably splits
human personality into two parts: into an animal or sensual, and a
spiritual or divine part. But what am I, this concrete individual man?
If, according to the principle, *principium individuationis est materia,*
my individual personality belongs to the lower parts, then it has no
spiritual foundation and dignity. If, however, personality belongs to
the divine part, how then could it be individual and plural? Idealism
separates spirit and nature. But am I the spirit, or is the spirit my spirit?
Since the days of the Stoics the attempt has been made to solve this
problem by the idea of a divine spark. Man's mind is a spark of the
divine spiritual fire. If that is so, its combination with an individual
must be a kind of banishment, a state of imprisonment, according to
the old Pythagorean phrase: *sōma, sēma* (the body is a tomb). This
individual spirit, and individual personality is merely a provisional,
not an essential and definitive, state of being. Then I, this individual
personality, am destined to perish, my higher part being consumed
within the divine spirit, my lower part going back to nature. Therefore,
it is not I, this individual person, who stands over against the natural
world; but there are two general, impersonal entities opposite one
another, the universal divine mind or reason and material nature. But
I, this individual Ego, am destined to vanish into these two universal
impersonal entities. I, as personal individuality, am not superior to
nature; my individual self is lost either way. What does it matter
whether it is lost in the divine mind or in material nature? It is this
doubt of the value of individual personality which is inherent in all
idealism, and this is one of the sources of the further degeneration.
What interest can individual man have in a kind of humanism which
is so disinterested in the metaphysical value of individual personality?

The second point is closely related to the first. Ancient humanism
grew out of ancient religion; its metaphysics was a rational transformation of pre-Christian religion and mythology. Now this religion was
destroyed by Christianity and no enthusiasm for classical Greece could
revive it. Modern idealistic humanism grew out of the Christian tradition. It was, so to speak, a rational by-product of Christian theology.
In so far as this humanism, following its tendency to rationality, detached itself from its Christian foundation, its metaphysical content

became thin and uncertain. True, there were some powerful thinkers who were able to develop an idealistic metaphysic as the foundation of this humanism. But these systems were, first, altogether comprehensible only to a small elite of qualified thinkers and could not affect the large majority. Apart from this, such a theoretical idealism was too abstract, not to say abstruse, to be a plausible solution of the problem of reality. Already in the first half of the 19th century this idealism had played out its role. It was, as we have already seen, only the non-metaphysical idealism which remained, and which formed also the transition to that positivist philosophy which was the grave of all true humanism. An idealism which was only capable of holding fast ideal values and postulates, without any foundation in being, had no power of resistance against the wave of naturalist realism with its causal explanation of everything, including man. Thus the emancipation from Christianity, which in the time of the Renaissance was begun with so much enthusiasm, ended in a stark, crude naturalism within which there was no room for genuine human values.

True *Christian* humanism is, however, still an unfinished project in a world hitherto called Christian. . . . Its basis can be found only in Biblical revelation. . . .

The Christian doctrine of man's being created in the image of God does two things: it places man within nature and at the same time elevates him above it. Like all nature, man in his totality is a creature. . . . The truly Christian conception of man does not reject the idea that the human race has its origins in a pre-human realm. . . . A truly Christian conception of man does not exclude the idea that in the spatial Universe there is no above and no below and no middle. At the same time, the Christian knows that God has called him to the dominion over all the earth, because he has created man, and man alone, in such a way that he has to execute God's will, not in blind, dumb and ignorant necessity, but in hearing God's word and answering Him by his own decision. In this call he recognises the deepest foundation of his personal being and his elevation over all the rest of creation. It is through this God-given dominion over nature that he is given the power and the right not merely to use natural forces, but also to investigate nature by his own God-given reason. But the man who knows himself as bound by the word of the Creator and responsible to Him, will not misuse his scientific knowledge of the world by using his reason to raise himself up against the Creator and to emancipate himself from Him by a false pretence of autonomy. He will not become one who, detached from God, is the prisoner of his own technical achievements. . . .

This doctrine of the *imago dei* does not, however, stand on its own right, but is comprehensible in its deepest meaning only from the centre of divine self-revelation. Behind Christian humanism stands, as its basic foundation, the faith in that Man in whom both the mystery of God and the secret of man have been revealed in one; the belief that the Creator of the Universe attaches Himself to man; that He, in whose creative word the whole structure of the Universe has its foundation, has made known as His world purpose the restoration and perfection of His image in man; that therefore not only the history of humanity, but the history of the whole Cosmos shall be consummated in God-humanity. It is this aspect of the Christian conception of man that gives him his incomparable and unique place in the Universe. . . .

If it is true that God created man in His image, and that this image is realised in Christ's God-manhood—and faith knows this to be true— then nothing, either in the sphere of nature or in that of history, can uproot this humanism, unless it be the loss of this faith. But where this faith is kept, where it is alive in the power and purity of its origin in the revelation of the New Testament, there Christian humanism does not merely consist of a humanistic conception of man and his place in the Universe, but is at the same time a power which must stamp all aspects of daily life as well as cultural life at large with the mark of true humanity.

PERSONALITY AND HUMANITY

The history of mankind begins with collectivism. Primitive man and primitive society do not know individual personality. . . . The oldest civilisations which we know, those of Egypt and Babylon, are thoroughly collectivist. . . .

In the discovery of individual personality Greece is the pioneer nation. . . . This is the significance of philosophical reflection as it originated on the shores of Asia Minor and in Sicily and which significantly developed from the start as a rival to myth. Now, for the first time, there are some bold individuals who dare to think independently, to criticise mythology and to emancipate themselves from tradition. . . . Single creative individualities come to the fore; works of culture are called after their creators; individual fame is no longer limited to military bravery, that is, to action in favour of collective security, but passes over to thinkers, poets, artists. . . . It is by this process that classical antiquity becomes a model which has never been surpassed for individualised cultural activity and individualised humanity. The human face presents itself in an innumerable plurality of markedly individual faces.

. . . The emancipation of the individual seems to end in a complete, sceptical dissolution of all objective norms. But, thanks to unspent moral and religious reserves, to a prevailing sense of social necessity, and last—but not least—thanks to the great achievement of Platonic and Aristotelian philosophy, this subjectivist sophism remained an episode or a crisis which was overcome. It is only after this that Greek humanism reasserts itself, and the concept of humanity and the human is formed.

In the full sense this is not yet true of Plato and Aristotle, because for them the humane is identical with the Hellenic. Beyond the realm of the Greek language begins that of the barbarians, which cannot be considered as truly human. And for those great thinkers the existence of the slave—that is, the man without dignity or rights—is taken for granted. But this limitation of classical philosophy is soon overcome in Hellenistic, particularly Stoic, philosophy. The vision extends itself beyond the Greek into the human as such; the sense of humanity as a whole is formed for the first time; . . .

All the same, it was not this Greek humanism which became the main foundation of Western humanism. That was kept in store for another power of a totally different character—for Christianity. . . .

I should like to formulate this fundamental difference between the Christian and the Greek conception of humanity in three points: in the idea of personality, in that of community, and in the relation between body and spirit. It will appear that those three points are in close necessary relation, so that we might call them rather three aspects of one and the same thing.

1. We have been trying to show how much the Greek mind has done for the discovery and appreciation of individual personality. But the Greek idea of man is threatened by a fatal either/or, which can be seen by a comparative study of the older Platonic-Aristotelian and the later Stoic concepts of the human. In Plato and Aristotle a certain appreciation of individual personality becomes possible by envisaging the articulation of reason, proportional to its different functions. The consequence of this individualising view is a scale or hierarchy of different groups like the Greeks and the barbarians, the men and the women, the free and the slaves. In Plato's state we are faced with a real caste-system based on this idea. Now the Stoics dropped this hierarchical conception, and by that gave the principle of humanity its full universality. Every man is essentially equal to every other man, because the same divine reason is indwelling in every one. But whilst this idea is the cause of the universality of humanity, it also produces the impersonal, abstract concept of man which strikes us in Stoic writings. . . .

The Christian concept of personality is entirely different. Here it is the call of God, summoning me, this individual man, to communion with Him, which makes me a person, a responsible being. "I have called Thee by Thy name, Thou art mine." A divine *I* calls me *Thou* and attests to me that I, this individual man, being here and being so, am seen and called by God from eternity. This dignity of human personality is not grounded in an abstract, general element in all men, namely reason, but individual personality as such is the object of this appreciation because it is deemed worthy of being called by God. Only the personal God can fundamentally establish truly personal existence and responsibility, responsibility being the inescapable necessity to answer God's creative call, and to answer it so that this answer is also a decision. God's call in love shall be answered by man's response in love. By doing this—by loving God as he is loved by God—man is similar to God. The loving man, having received God's love, is God's image. The love of the personal God does not create an abstract, impersonal humanity; it calls the individual to the most personal responsibility.

2. With this first element, the second is in the closest connection, namely the relation to community. As in Greek philosophy reason is the *principium humanitatis,* no relation to communion is based on it. Abstract reason does not tend to communion, but to unity. In thinking I am related to general truth, to ideas, not to the Thou of my neighbor. Activity of reason has its meaning in itself, the wise man is self-sufficient, he has no desire to go out from himself to another. In Christian faith, however, it is the same thing that makes me an individual person, which also leads me necessarily to my fellow-man: the love of God. God in His free grace gives man His love and calls him to receive it in order to give it back.

Not reason, but love is the *principium humanitatis.* In such a way, this love, given on the part of God, determines both the relation to God and the relation to the fellow-man. "Thou shalt love the Lord thy God," and the command that follows is equal with it: "Thou shalt love thy neighbor as thyself." More than that, it is not the divine commandment but the divine gift of love which is the basis of true personality. God gives man His own love, but He gives it in such a way that it cannot be received save in a free act of reception, in responsive love, which is faith. Greek idealism is a system of *unity;* Christianity, however, is revealed communion.

This means the creation of a humanism of a very different character from that of Greek idealism. Not reason, but love is the truly human. Reason, spiritual activity, is subordinate to love. It is an instrument of love. This is to say, also, that civilisation is not in itself the essentially human, but is, in its turn, an instrument, an expression, not in itself a purpose. In the same way the rational principle of *autarkia,* self-sufficiency, characteristic of the wise philosopher, is here impossible. Man cannot become truly human except by entering into community. He is called by the loving God into a loving relation to his fellow-man.

3. This opposition in the basis of the idea of humanity—immanent divine reason on the one hand, the transcendent divine call of love on the other—expresses itself in a third sense in a most characteristic and momentous manner. The Greek principle of reason brings with it a dualistic conception of man. Man is composed of two parts. By his reason, that is his higher element, he shares in the divine being; by his body, that is his lower element, man partakes of animal nature, out of which comes evil. The one is the basis of his dignity; the other is the cause of his ignominy which can be mitigated only by the fact that this lower part may be called unessential or accidental. The Christian faith, answering the call of love of the Creator, produces quite a different view of man's structure. The whole man, body and mind, is God's creation. There is no more reason to despise the body than there is to consider human rationality as divine. The whole man, body and mind, is called into communion with God and into the service of God. Therefore there is no question here of the ascetic ideal, inherent in idealism since Plato's *Phaedo,* that the spiritual is to be delivered out of its entanglement with the body, or that this spiritual freedom is to be maintained over against the world outside. Here the task is to cooperate in the totality of this corporal-spiritual personality with the work of God in the world, to give oneself in love into this service, which is at the same time a service for God and for man, and which is the expression of the freedom and nobility of the children of God. We can guess even now what a different conception of manual work must result from these two different anthropologies. The ascetic spiritualism, however, as we find it in the medieval Church, is not of Christian but of Hellenistic origin, and is an exact parallel to the Neoplatonic element in medieval philosophy.

Now taking these elements in their unity—the principle of immanence on the one hand, the divine relation of love and reciprocal service on the other—a further essential difference is revealed. In one of the most beautiful passages of Aristotle's Nicomachaean ethics, the chapter on friendship, the great thinker pronounces as a matter of course that one can love only those who are worthy of being loved. To love someone unworthy would be a sign of an ignoble mind, a sign of a lack of the sense of value. Now, Christian love is founded in God's love for sinful and unworthy man. This love, then, is received in the consciousness of being unworthy of it; that means that underlying the Christian *humanitas* we find *humilitas.* Humility is the most unambigu-

ous sign of true love, just as love for the unworthy is its most genuine
expression. This is the trait which distinguishes Christian humanity
most markedly from the idealistic Greek, and which is also the great
scandal for many humanists. It is, at bottom, the scandal and foolishness of the Cross which become apparent here.

During the first fifteen centuries of the Christian era these two forms
of humanism—the Christian and the idealistic Greek—lived together in
a kind of association or amalgam without any awareness of the specific
character of either of them. Then, in the middle of the second millenium, that double-sided process of disassociation took place, of which
we were speaking in the last lecture, and which is the essence of the
two principal movements, the Renaissance and the Reformation. In the
course of the following centuries it became apparent that the temper
of the modern age favoured the first of these two movements. Mankind
was out to find an immanent and rational basis of civilisation, and
therefore gave preference to the Renaissance conception of humanism.
This, however, meant a progressive detachment of European civilisation from its previously Christian basis. The phases of this movement
have already been sketched. The starting point is a theism still closely
connected with the Christian; it is therefore a humanism based on a
religious-metaphysical foundation, whilst the terminus of this movement is a naturalist positivism, which is not capable of giving a basis
to any kind of humanism, whether Christian or Greek. The question
consequently arises as to why the original programme of Renaissance
humanism, i.e., the restoration of the Greek idea of humanity, was
not carried out; or to put it better, why the process of emancipation
from Christianity was not successfully arrested in a revived classical
humanism.

The answer to this question comes from what was said in the last
lecture. Greek humanism had not been a *creatio ex nihilo*. It had been
the rational transformation of ancient pagan religion and drew much
of its power of conviction from this religious-metaphysical presupposition. Now this presupposition could not be reproduced, pre-Christian
religion having been completely destroyed by Christianity. The humanism of the Renaissance and even of the beginning of the Enlightenment
could remain unconscious of this fact as long as it still drew its life
from the metaphysical substance of the Christian tradition. But in so far
as this connection was lost, or consciously cut, the idealistic humanism
was hanging in the air. The systems of philosophical metaphysics could
not be an equivalent substitute for the lost religious basis, if only for
the reason that they were accessible only to a small elite of philosophical thinkers. This metaphysical background was definitely and purposely pushed aside by the positivist movement and from that moment

humanism had lost its basis. More and more it was replaced by a naturalistic inhumanism, by a materialist collectivism, by a pseudo-Dar-
winian principle of ruthless extinction of the weaker by the stronger, or
by a pseudo-romantic principle of the powerful individual dominating
the mass of the herd-people.

I should like to illustrate this general movement more concretely by
showing the effect of this process within those same three spheres in
which we have just been defining the difference between Greek and
Christian humanism. The first of these points was the Christian foundation of personality in divine election, in the personal call of God. Now,
for this transcendent basis of personality was first substituted the immanent principle of divine reason. . . . The principle of reason was more
and more divested of its transcendent content. . . .

We can observe this change from a half-transcendental to a flatly
secularist interpretation of human nature in the development of the
three most important pupils of Hegel, namely Feuerbach, Strauss, and
Marx. Whilst they all started as followers of Hegel's absolute idealism,
they all ended in a flat naturalism of a more or less materialistic character. But all of them tried to retain some humanistic elements, although without any theoretical justification. . . . [Friedrich Nietzsche's]
programme is the total "transvaluation of values," by declaring war on
all "backworlders," as he calls the adherents of any kind of religion or
metaphysics, and the proclamation of the powerful individual rising
above the average mass and using it as the material of his will to power.
Behind these conceptions of Marx and Nietzsche we see already dawning upon mankind the monstrous figure of the totalitarian state, either
in its post-Marxian Communist or in its post-Nietzschean Fascist form—
that totalitarian state in which human personality is practically denied
and abolished. . . .

Contemporaneously with that materialistic development of Hegelian-
ism, there arises in France Auguste Comte's "philosophie positive,"
with its negation of all metaphysics and its proclamation of a *Religion
de l'humanité.* In England there was a similar school of thought, led
by men like Stuart Mill and Herbert Spencer, with a similar tendency
to interpret man from merely immanent presuppositions, and still to
try to keep some humanistic elements within a naturalistic context
which was incapable of affording a basis for them. The idea of evolution, forming the backbone in the French as well as in the English
system of positivist philosophy, was incapable of safeguarding anything
like an idea of personality, either in the Greek or in the Christian
meaning of the word. A highly differentiated animal is no personality,
personality being—in distinction from a differentiated brain-animal—a
certain relation to transcendent truth, be it (as in the Greek concep-

tion) the relation to the divine Logos, or (as in the Christian conception) the relation to the person of the Creator. All the readiness of individual positivists to retain the moral values of the Greek-Christian tradition was in vain. . . .

The change from idealism to naturalistic positivism becomes particularly intelligible if we view it from the second stand-point, the problem of community. Those early humanists of the Renaissance and Enlightenment, who consciously or unconsciously tried to emancipate humanism from its Christian basis, were certainly not conscious of the fact that they thereby created a sociological alternative of the gravest consequences. In the Christian faith these two things are simultaneously and equally granted: the independent standing of personality and the necessity of community. It is the same call of God which summons the individual to his freedom and independent dignity and which summons him into communion and mutual responsibility. The unity of personality and community is rooted in the Christian God-idea alone. Apart from this basis the two cannot co-exist. Apart from the Christian foundation this unity breaks up into an either/or of individualist liberalism and collectivist authoritarianism.

Idealistic humanism in itself has always been an aristocratic doctrine. . . .

With the middle of the 19th century there begins a fierce reaction against this individualism, and this collectivist reaction in its turn is worked out logically from a naturalist philosophy. The alternative to idealistic individualism is not free communion, but primitive tribal, not to say animal, collectivism. It is the depersonalised mass-man, the man forming a mere particle of a social structure and the centralised, automatic, mechanical totalitarian state, which inherits the decaying liberal democracy. . . .

The third point—namely the relation between spirit and nature—remains to be taken into consideration in order to see these things clearly. In Christian faith man is seen as a spiritual-corporeal unity; God is the creator not only of man's spirit, but also of his body. Therefore the bodily life has its own dignity in the sight of God, and man is called into the service of bodily needs as into a sacred service. The body is "the temple of the Holy Spirit." In the Christian Sacrament an indissoluble connection of material bread and spiritual eating is expressed. In the middle of the Lord's Prayer stands the petition for daily bread. All this works together to make impossible a one-sided spirituality. Man need not be ashamed of his body and his bodily needs.

For idealist humanism, on the other hand, this bodily constitution of man—this animal part, as he calls it—is the *partie honteuse* of his existence, his dignity resting entirely on his spirit, which is his divine part. . . . The whole humanistic system of values is based upon this contrast or opposition of animal nature and divine spirit. It is therefore the liberation of the spirit from the body which is the guiding idea of humanistic culture. It is obvious that such a humanism cannot have much interest in the economic conditions of man's life. . . .

So exalted a spirituality could never be the spiritual home of the average man. Much less could it be so, when—through the Industrial Revolution—the economic element became the dominating feature of his life. In the middle of the 19th century this aristocratic spirituality had become impossible. The reaction against this spirituality was inevitable. And come it did, primarily in the form of a doctrine which placed the economic element in the very centre of the whole of human life, making it the very essence of human history, as did the historical materialism of Karl Marx. The change could not be more dramatic. Marx, the pupil of the philosopher who had proclaimed the spirit as the only reality, became the creator of a theory in which ideas and spiritual values were but an *Überbau*, a superstructure, an appendix or reflex of economic processes. But Marx is not the only one to make such a sudden volte-face. There was also Friedrich Nietzsche, a solitary thinker and poet, who came from a most dignified tradition of humanism and scholarship, and yet proclaimed with prophetic vehemence that doctrine of the transvaluation of all values, which means the primacy of instinct above the spirit and the will to power as the new principle of ethics. Aristocrat and individualist through and through, he could not prevent his teaching from becoming the programme of a mass movement, comparable in size and vehemence only to the one which Karl Marx had produced. Was it to be wondered at that the masses getting hold of this programme took literally Nietzsche's prophecy of the emancipation of instinct from the fetters of metaphysics and religion, and understood his doctrine of the will to power to mean what it said, namely that it was a practical application of the Darwinian principle of the struggle for life in which the strong survive at the cost of the weak?

Marx and Nietzsche are the fathers of the totalitarian revolutions and totalitarian states. It seems paradoxical that the extremest collectivism and the extremest individualism should flow together in one stream. But upon closer inspection this fact is not at all paradoxical. The common denominator of both systems is the complete depersonalisation of man. Whether you understand man primarily as the animal, that has hunger, or by the two categories of the herd-animals and the solitary beasts of prey terrorising the herds, you come to the same result, namely the elimination of man's personality, human dignity, and the rights of man, placing them all on the level of nature-phenomena.

Naturalistic philosophy, whether of the Marxist rationalist or of the Nietzschean romantic type, necessarily means depersonalisation. In Communist totalitarianism, on the one hand, and in National-Socialist totalitarianism on the other, the seed of Karl Marx and Friedrich Nietzsche has germinated, and in these two monstrosities, which are one in essence, the movement of emancipation from Christianity has reached its goal. This goal is, in both cases, the annihilation of the truly human, the end of humanism.

Christian faith itself, understood in its purity, is the only sure basis for, and an inexhaustible fountain of, a true humanism. But it is no exception to that rule: *corruptio optimi pessima*. The history of empirical Christianity is unhappily not only a testimony of truest, and purest, and sublimest humanity, but also in many cases it affords the sad spectacle of incredible inhumanity. Therefore the Gospel of Jesus Christ is not only a judgment upon the secularised godless, but also upon the godlessness of the Church, and of the pious, who so often forgot that faith in the Crucified implies the willingness to sacrifice, and that the ultimate criterion of faith is faithfulness in the service of the fellow-man.

But, whilst all this is true with regard to empirical Christendom taken as a whole, it does not touch the Christian Gospel as such. All these short-comings are due to a misunderstanding of God's revelation in Christ and to the failure of the Christian Church to be truly Christian. It does not disprove in the least that the Gospel of God's love is the only solid basis of a true humanism which safeguards the dignity of individual personality, essential, non-accidental community, and the unity of mankind. . . .

We should not close this survey without one further observation. Why did that whole movement of emancipation arise? Is it *entirely* due to man's unwillingness to bow his head before the divine revelation, because he wants to hold his head high as his own lord? Is the modern movement away from Christianity exclusively caused by the desire for an autonomous reason? Is not a cause also to be found within the presentation of this Christian revelation by empirical Christianity? In other words, should not the Christian Church take on its own shoulders a part of the burden of responsibility for this tragic history? If we think of that third point about which we have just been speaking—the false separation of body and spirit, of bread and divine will—we cannot ignore the fact that empirical Christianity has been untrue to its own truth. The Christians of almost all centuries have been guilty of a one-sided, false spiritualism which neglected the daily bread for the spiritual bread and by a false monastic or puritan disparagement of the body and its impulses brought about the revolt of an ill-treated human nature. The same could be said with regard to the other two points. If the modern age is characterized by a false secularism or this-worldliness, traditional Christianity certainly has to accept the verdict of a false other-worldliness which, in its interest in the eternal life, forgot the task of this earthly life. And finally, whilst it is true that the unity of the truly personal and the truly communal is grounded in the Christian revelation taken in its original truth, empirical Christianity has failed to a large extent to prove this unity practically. On the one hand, it has produced an authoritarian, pseudo-sacred collectivism, a Church of power and spiritual slavery; on the other hand, it has produced an orthodox misunderstanding of faith, i.e., a kind of faith which was not united with love but was morally sterile, and which therefore could not but repel those who had grasped something of the gospel of love. It is a provable fact that the shortcomings of Christianity were among the main impulses of the humanistic emancipation-movement. Thus, the de-Christianisation characteristic of the modern age is, to a large extent, the product of the infidelity of the Christians to their own faith.

REINHOLD NIEBUHR

"Ten Years That Shook My World" appeared in the *Christian Century* April 26, 1939. Since 1925 the name of Reinhold Niebuhr (1892-1971) had been appearing as a regular contributing editor to this Chicago-based Protestant weekly. The editor had proposed a series of articles to survey the currents of theological thought and life during the previous decade in autobiographical terms. Niebuhr was to express his own reactions to theological winds of doctrine and give some account of how he had arrived at his convictions.

Niebuhr reveals that the "simple little moral homilies" that he had preached in Detroit in accordance with the social gospel had become irrelevant in the face of the brutal facts of life in industrial America. Such sermons did not change human conditions or actions or attitudes in any problem of collective behavior "by a hair's breadth." Niebuhr criticizes "modern religious liberalism" for its "sentimental optimism" which still spoke of "the essential goodness of men without realizing how evil good men can be." Niebuhr seeks to re-establish a transcendent religious perspective because "reality slowly approaches the ideals which are implicit in it."

From Reinhold Niebuhr, "Ten Years That Shook My World"

The editor has suggested that this series of articles shall survey the currents of theological thought and life during the past decade in autobiographical terms, in the sense that they shall express the author's own reactions to theological winds of doctrine and give some account of how he arrived at his own convictions.

I

I can do this most simply by confessing that about midway in my ministry, which extends roughly from the peace of Versailles to the peace of Munich, measured in terms of Western history, I underwent a fairly complete conversion of thought which involved rejection of almost all the liberal theological ideals and ideas with which I ventured forth in 1915. I wrote a book, my first, in 1927 which when now consulted is proved to contain almost all the theological windmills against which today I tilt my sword. These windmills must have tumbled shortly thereafter for every succeeding volume expresses a more and more explicit revolt against what is usually known as liberal culture.

While my critics accuse me of inconsistency my own biased judgment is that there is no inconsistency in the development of my thought since that day, though there is a gradual theological elaboration of what was at first merely socio-ethical criticism. Since the war was the revelation of the internal anarchy of Western civilization, the existence of which bourgeois culture was inclined to deny, and since the peace of Versailles was the revelation of vindictive passions which liberalism imagined were banished from the world, and since the peace of Munich proves that one cannot simply correct the injustices of conquest by the injustice which results from capitulation to tyranny, I conclude that the whole of contemporary history proves that liberal culture has not seen the problem of mankind in sufficient depth to understand its own history. Its too simple moralism has confused issues at almost every turn.

The contemporary problem is brought into theological focus if it is recognized that liberal Christianity is essentially an appropriation of the genuine achievements, and an accommodation to the characteristic prejudices, of this bourgeois culture which first came to flower in the Renaissance, which gained some triumphs and suffered some checks in the Reformation, which reached its zenith in the early part of this century, which revealed its internal anarchy in the World War and its inability to defend itself against lower forms of civilization in the present hour. In terms of politics and economics the bourgeois world is the world of the businessman, of expanding commerce and industry, of economic imperialism, transmuted in a period of decay into economic nationalism.

II

In terms of culture, the bourgeois civilization produced what is generally known as liberalism. This liberalism, I must hasten to add, is something more than either the spirit of tolerance on the one hand, or liberal economic theory on the other hand. The liberalism of classical economics, upon which capitalism is built (though it must disavow its own presuppositions in its period of decay) is only one characteristic fruit of the liberal culture. The faith of classical economic theory, that economic activity left to itself, without political interference, would gradually achieve a perfect harmony and justice, was merely one, though a very fateful, error derived from the general liberal assumption that man is essentially a very harmless animal, if only he can be held within the harmonies of nature and of reason from which the fanaticism of religion had beguiled him.

The spirit of tolerance in the liberal culture is of course a real gain. It belongs by right to any profound Christianity which understands the ambiguity of all human actions, the imperfection of all human ideals and the peril of self-righteous fanaticism in all human conflict. It must be admitted, however, that traditional Christianity, both Catholic and Protestant, had so frequently allowed the loyalty and worship, which belongs to God alone, to be appropriated for relative, social, political, economic and theological positions, that it had given rationalists good reason to believe that fanatic cruelty was the chief by-product, or possibly even the chief product, of religion.

It may be observed, however, that those who move away from a liberal culture have both the obligation and the possibility of proving that they have a securer foundation for the spirit of tolerance than traditional liberalism afforded. In secular liberalism the spirit of tolerance is either rooted in a deep skepticism and pessimism which must finally culminate in the intolerable sneer of Pilate, "What is truth?" or it is based on an untenable optimism which believes, with Professor Dewey, that men of good will must, if they meditate upon the issues of life long and profoundly enough, arrive at a "common faith." Professor Dewey's notion that divisions in the human family are chiefly derived from anachronistic religious dogmas ought, incidentally, to be fairly well refuted now by the force of the tragic events of contemporary history.

In any profound Christianity the spirit of tolerance must be derived from the knowledge that, however necessary it may be to judge one another and even to fight one another on the moral and political level, we are all sinners who stand under God's ultimate judgment. It is this consciousness of a divine judgment which must persuade us to recognize the validity of Christ's admonition, "Judge not that ye be not judged," or of St. Paul's exhortation: "Therefore thou art inexcusable, O man, whosoever thou art that judgest; for wherein thou judgest another, thou condemnest thyself; for thou that judgest doest the same thing."

III

If liberalism as a creed is more than the liberal spirit of toleration on the one hand and more than laissez faire economics on the other, what is it? I should say primarily faith in man; faith in his capacity to subdue nature, and faith that the subjection of nature achieves life's final good; faith in man's essential goodness, to be realized either when man ceases to be spiritual and returns to nature (romanticism), or when he ceases to be natural and becomes rational; and finally, faith in human history which is conceived as a movement upward by a force immanent within it. Whether this faith rests upon Darwin or upon Hegel, that is, whether nature is believed to guarantee progress or whether progress is conceived of as man's "gradual spiritualization" and his emancipation from natural impulses, prejudices and parochial attachments, the optimistic conclusion is the same.

It is instructive to note that liberal culture was always divided against itself on the question whether it should regard human nature and human history primarily from the standpoint of man's relation to nature or from the standpoint of his rational transcendence over nature. In this conflict between the naturalists and idealists, the idealists had something of the Christian doctrine of the dignity of man as made in the image of God, and the naturalists had something of the Christian doctrine of man as a creature who must not pretend to be more than he is. But between them they lost the uneasy conscience of the Christian and expressed themselves in terms of an easy conscience. Whatever was wrong with man, the cause was some defect in his social organization or some imperfection in his education which further social history and cultural development would correct.

I may say that though I express my opposition to liberal civilization politically in terms of Marxian politics, I regard Marxian culture as participating essentially in all the liberal illusions. It also believes in the goodness of man, once capitalism has been destroyed. It also believes in an inevitable progress on the other side of the revolution. It has a catastrophic view of history, but only provisionally so. The destruction of capitalism is, for it, the final destruction of evil. This error must not be taken lightly, even by those of us who believe that the Marxian analysis of the relation of economics to politics is essentially correct.

The Marxian misunderstanding of man has contributed to the development of a tyranny in Russia which almost, though not quite, rivals fascist tyranny. Objectively it cannot be as bad, because it is impossible to destroy all the universal hopes in communism, which distinguish it from the franker tribal mania of fascism. Subjectively, this decay in Russia may be worse, because it extinguishes a new hope in which all the old lights are going out. I feel genuinely sorry for my friends who seem to be under a spiritual necessity to deny obvious facts about Russian tyranny.

IV

In a sense, the really tragic end of a liberal culture is to be found in the peace of Munich. What was best in that culture was outraged by the peace of Versailles and what was shallowest in it came to the conclusion that the horrors of a peace of conquest could be expiated by a peace of capitulation. Thus it lost its last chance to save what is genuine and universal in its life against the threat of a new barbarism. It fondly imagines that the decay of the modern world may still be healed by belatedly yielding "justice" to Germany, when it is obvious that Germany, and the fascist world in general, is no longer interested in justice, but bent upon the display of its power and the exercise of a dominion which asks no questions about justice in either the Christian or the liberal sense.

Liberal moralism is, in short, unable to cope either with man's immediate political or with his ultimate religious problems. It does not know how to check evil and historical injustice in politics, because it would like to operate against injustice in terms of perfect moral purity. The ultimate religious problem of evil in man does not arise for it, because it is always waiting for the perfect education or perfect social order which will make man moral. It does not understand man in the full dimension of his spirit, and does not see that precisely because he is a child of God and made in God's image, he cannot be contained in, or easily checked by, either the harmony of nature or the prudence of reason.

It would, of course, be grossly unfair not to recognize that liberal Christianity made a genuine contribution to true Christianity by appropriating some of the achievements of this culture. Through some of these appropriations liberal Christianity purified Christian theology of some of its grievous historical errors. One of these was the insistence of Christian orthodoxy that a religious explanation of natural events was also a scientific explanation and obviated the necessity of tracing the natural sequence of events and their secondary causation.

But religion is constitutionally indifferent to the problem of secondary causation. This indifference becomes a sin when theology is made into a bad science and the sense of ultimate meaning and creation is allowed to obscure the problem of natural causation. In accommodating itself to the "scientific spirit," liberal Christianity therefore rightly clarified an ancient confusion, though it must be admitted that it was frequently betrayed thereby into a world view in which its essential theism was transmuted into a vague pantheism.

A second great gain of liberal Christianity, derived from the achievements of modern culture, was the application of the scientific historical method to its own records. Ethically, this emancipated Christianity from the necessity of regarding any moral attitude, fortuitously enshrined in its own canon, as final and authoritative. It permitted the Christian law of love to stand out in Christian ethics as the only final norm. Theologically, this scientific spirit saved Christianity from the corruption of the profound principle, *credo ut intelligam*, into a tyranny of theological authority over human reason. These gains of liberal Christianity must not be imperiled. It would be truer to say that they must not be sacrificed, though they will be imperiled. Frantic and hysterical retreats to orthodoxy are bound to imperil them. This advance must be protected against those who think it a gain to return to theological obscurantism from the shallows of a too simple rationalism.

But liberal Christianity quite obviously accepted the prejudices as well as the achievements of modern culture. It was pathetically eager to justify itself before the "modern mind" and failed to realize that this modern mind was involved in a very ancient human sin. It imagined itself the final mind. It thought of itself as God, the final arbiter of truth and destiny.

V

In seeking to persuade the modern mind that Christianity is respectable and intelligent, the liberals sacrificed most of the essential Christian positions. Christ was transmuted into the good man Jesus, who could charm all men to become as good as he was. The classic Christology of the God-man was repudiated, though innumerable reservations sought to hide the repudiation. It was not recognized that this absurd doctrine of the God-man Christ contains the whole essence of the Christian faith—its belief that God transcends history and yet makes himself known in history; that history measured by Christ is tragic and ends tragically for it crucifies Christ; that only God is able to resolve the conflict between what man is and what he ought to be, a conflict in which all men stand; that God cannot do this by

simply wiping out history and transmuting it into eternity, but by redeeming history, but that the redemption of history involved more
than persuading man to follow the law of God. It involved God's taking upon himself the inevitable violation of that law.

Liberal Christianity, in short, tended to follow modern culture in
estimating both the stature and the virtue of man. It did not recognize that man is a spirit who can find a home neither in nature nor in
reason, but only in God. The power of human self-transcendence
(the true image of God) is such that man can and does break every
restraint set by nature or reason. His very capacities are occasions
for sin in him. It is because he is made in the image of God that man
can be tempted to make himself God, to seek to overcome his natural
insecurity by pretensions of power which involve him in more insecurity; to seek to hide the finiteness of his intelligence by pretensions
of absolute truth, which involve him in cruel fanaticisms; to seek to
transcend his insignificance by claims of importance which are both
ridiculous and dangerous.

All these things man does, not because his pure mind is impeded
by the inertia of his animal nature, but because he is the only animal
who is involved in history and yet stands outside of it, the only creature who has a glimpse of the eternal beyond the finite and is incited
to pretend an eternal significance for all his finite interests, values
and ideals.

For this reason, the simple reinterpretation of the Kingdom of God
into the law of progress, in the thought of liberal Christianity, is an
equally serious betrayal of essential insights of the Christian faith to
the prejudices of modern culture. Obviously there is progress of all
kinds in human history, including progress in aerial bombing and the
effective use of the radio for the dissemination of political lies.
There is progress from immaturity to maturity in every field of endeavor. But there is not a single bit of evidence to prove that good
triumphs over evil in this constant development of history. History
points to a goal beyond itself, and not merely to an eternity which
negates history.

This is what all biblical religion tries to say in words and symbols
which outrage reason, as they must. For reason cannot contain this
idea, though, if it is astute enough, it can uncover the absurdity of
alternative propositions. Liberal Christianity sought to efface these
irrationalities of biblical apocalypticism by discovering that Jesus
had, indeed, some difficulty in freeing his thought about the Kingdom
of God from outworn forms of Jewish thought, but that he is to be
commended for almost achieving this desirable emancipation in the

end and thus approximating what an enlightened modern man believes about history.

Yet from the standpoint of mere history the final story about this Jesus is that he was crucified. That he was raised from the dead and will come again in glory—that faith belongs to another dimension which is beyond history, and yet without which history would be either meaningless or filled with tragic meaning only.

VI

Christianity, in short, faces the tremendous task of extricating itself from the prejudices and illusions of a culture which is rapidly sinking with the disruption of the civilization which gave it birth. This is not yet fully realized in America, because the prospects and hopes of our civilization are sufficiently brighter than in Europe to give liberal illusions a tougher vitality and slower death here. This task of emancipation is a tremendous one, partly because liberalism as a culture is still superior to many of the cultures which threaten to displace it politically. It is certainly superior to the primitive and Nietzschean romanticism which expresses itself in fascist politics. It may even prove superior to socialism, if socialism sacrifices the achievements of democracy as it has done in Russia.

One of the real tragedies of our era is that the very democracy which is the great achievement of liberalism cannot be maintained if liberalism is not transcended as a culture. The problem of achieving economic justice is obviously more difficult than liberalism had imagined. The prerequisite of economic justice is a tolerable equilibrium of economic power, which in a technical age means the socialization of property. The excessive moralism of liberalism makes it impossible to see either the necessity of this end or the rigorous means which will be required to achieve it. Liberalism seems unable to move toward the economic democracy which is required to maintain its political democracy. Nor does it seem able to protect what is still left of its political democracy against the threat of a new barbarism; which is what makes the peace of Munich so significant.

If I believe that the Christian understanding of man could help solve some of these crucial issues and could conserve the best achievements of liberalism better than traditional liberalism can conserve them, I do not for that reason wish merely to hitch Christian faith to this or to that political task. Christianity faces ultimate issues of life which transcend all political vicissitudes and achievements. But the answer which Christian faith gives to man's ultimate perplexities and the hope which it makes possible in the very abyss of his despair, also throw light upon the immediate historical issues which he faces. Christianity is not a flight into eternity from the tasks and decisions of history. It is rather the power and the wisdom of God which makes decisions in history possible and which points to proximate goals in history which are usually obscured either by optimistic illusions or by the despair which followed upon the dissipation of these illusions. Christianity must therefore wage constant war, on the one hand against political religions which imagine some proximate goal and some conditioned good as man's final good, and on the other hand against an otherworldliness which by contrast gives these political religions a seeming validity.

VII

For this reason, any new orthodoxy which seeks to persuade men that because all men must finally be made manifest before the judgment seat of Christ, they are not to regard the momentary judgments, the proximate goals and the relative values of history seriously, must be regarded as a heresy as dangerous as any simple optimism. In every experience of life, Christ appears in many guises to the believer. He is the judge in comparison with whom I am found to fall short and to be an unprofitable servant. He is the redeemer who gives my life a new center of loyalty and a new source of power. He is, however, also the law, the logos, the essential structure of life, which I must seek to obey, even though I fall short in my obedience. He is what I am essentially, and therefore what I ought to be.

Liberal Christianity emphasized that fact rather too simply. The new orthodoxy rightly insists that he is also what I can never be. He is therefore the source of my despair. Only in that despair and in repentance can he become the source of a new hope. This second emphasis is true enough. Only it will tempt us "to continue to sin that grace may abound" if we do not preserve what is genuinely Christian in liberal Christian moralism: the insistence that Christ is our law, our ideal, our norm, and the revelation of our essential being.

All this is not very autobiographical, after all. The only autobiographical note which I can add, in conclusion, is that such theological convictions which I hold today began to dawn upon me during the end of a pastorate in a great industrial city. They dawned upon me because the simple little moral homilies which were preached in that as in other cities, by myself and others, seemed completely irrelevant to the brutal facts of life in a great industrial center. Whether irrelevant or not, they were certainly futile. They did not change human actions or attitudes in any problem of collective behavior by a hair's breadth, though they may well have helped to preserve private amenities and to assuage individual frustrations.

These convictions which dawned in my pastorate have been further elaborated in a teaching position in a theological seminary. Greater leisure has given me opportunity to discover the main currents and emphases of the classical ages of Christian thought, and to find insights there which have been long neglected and which are yet absolutely essential to modern man, or indeed to man of any age.

However, since I am not so much scholar as preacher, I must confess that the gradual unfolding of my theological ideas has come not so much through study as through the pressure of world events. Whatever measure of Christian faith I hold today is due to the gradual exclusion of alternative beliefs through world history. As did Peter, I would preface my confession, "Thou hast words of eternal life," with the question, "Lord, to whom shall we go?" Even while imagining myself to be preaching the gospel, I had really experimented with many modern alternatives to Christian faith, until one by one they proved unavailing.

DOROTHY SAYERS

In 1940 Dorothy Sayers (1893-1957) was establishing herself in the public eye as an authority not only on crime but also on Christianity. She described herself in early 1940 as "trying to do a little mild propaganda in the way of articles and lectures": a review in *Spectator,* an article on "The Contempt of Learning in Twentieth-Century England," an address to the Festival of Church Tutorial Classes, three more articles in *Time and Tide* and *Spectator.*

Amidst all this activity "Creed or Chaos?" was broadcast as two talks on the BBC. The theme of the radio talks is the necessity for an intelligent and informed faith amid the conditions of wartime. Sayers argues against the notion that the churches are empty because the clergy insist too much upon doctrine. The fact is the exact opposite. The Christian faith is the most exciting drama that ever staggered the human imagination—"and the dogma is the drama." Beyond this Sayers maintains that theology is an exact science with a specific vocabulary of its own which must be clearly defined for any discussion to be worthwhile.

The essay centers on the incarnation. From the incarnation springs the whole doctrine of sacraments—the indwelling of the mortal by the immortal, of the material by the spiritual, the phenomenal by the real. Sayers discusses the creative, the sacramental, the incarnational nature of work. Man, made in the image of God the creator, should take seriously his call as man the maker, *homo faber*.

If Sayer's language is hard, uncompromising, and elitist, we must remember that these words were broadcast to an island that stood alone before Hitler's might.

From Dorothy L. Sayers, "**Creed or Chaos?**"

It is worse than useless for Christians to talk about the importance of Christian morality, unless they are prepared to take their stand upon the fundamentals of Christian theology. It is a lie to say that dogma does not matter; it matters enormously. It is fatal to let people suppose that Christianity is only a mode of feeling; it is vitally necessary to insist that it is first and foremost a rational explanation of the universe. It is hopeless to offer Christianity as a vaguely idealistic aspiration of a simple and consoling kind; it is, on the contrary, a hard, tough, exacting, and complex doctrine, steeped in a drastic and uncompromising realism. And it is fatal to imagine that everybody knows quite well what Christianity is and needs only a little encouragement to practise it. The brutal fact is that in this Christian country not one person in a hundred has the faintest notion what the Church teaches about God or man or society or the person of Jesus Christ. If you think I am exaggerating, ask the Army chaplains. Apart from a possible one per cent of intelligent and instructed Christians, there are three kinds of people we have to deal with. There are the frank and open heathen, whose notions of Christianity are a dreadful jumble of rags and tags of Bible anecdote and clotted mythological nonsense. There are the ignorant Christians, who combine a mild gentle-Jesus sentimentality with vaguely humanistic ethics—most of these are Arian heretics. Finally there are the more or less instructed church-goers, who know all the arguments about divorce and auricular confession and communion in two kinds, but are about as well equipped to do battle on fundamentals against a Marxian atheist or a Wellsian agnostic as a boy with a pea-shooter facing a fan-fire of machine-guns. Theologically, this country is at present in a state of utter chaos, established in the name of religious toleration, and rapidly degenerating into the flight from reason and the death of hope. We are not happy in this condition and there are signs of a very great eagerness, especially among the younger people, to find a creed to which they can give wholehearted adherence.

This is the Church's opportunity, if she chooses to take it. So far as the people's readiness to listen goes, she has not been in so strong a position for at least two centuries. The rival philosophies of humanism, enlightened self-interest, and mechanical progress have broken down badly; the antagonism of science has proved to be far more apparent than real, and the happy-go-lucky doctrine of laissez-faire is completely discredited. But no good whatever will be done by a retreat into personal piety or by mere exhortation to a "recall to prayer." The thing that is in danger is the whole structure of society, and it is necessary to persuade thinking men and women of the vital and intimate connection between the structure of society and the theological doctrines of Christianity.

The task is not made easier by the obstinate refusal of a great body of nominal Christians, both lay and clerical, to face the theological question. "Take away theology and give us some nice religion" has been a popular slogan for so long that we are apt to accept it, without inquiring whether religion without theology has any meaning. And however unpopular I may make myself I shall and will affirm that the reason why the Churches are discredited today is not that they are too bigoted about theology, but that they have run away from theology. The Church of Rome alone has retained her prestige because she puts theology in the foreground of her teaching. Some of us may perhaps think it a rather unimaginative and confined theology; but that is not the point. The point is that the Church of Rome is a theological society, in a sense in which the Church of England, taken as a whole, is not, and that because of this insistence on theology, she is a body disciplined, honoured, and sociologically important.

I should like to do two things. First, to point out that if we really want a Christian society we must teach Christianity, and that it is absolutely impossible to teach Christianity without teaching Christian dogma. Secondly, to put before you a list of half a dozen or so main doctrinal points which the world most especially needs to have drummed into its ears at this moment—doctrines forgotten or misinterpreted, but which (if they are true as the Church maintains them to be) are cornerstones in that rational structure of human society which is the alternative to world chaos.

I will begin with this matter of the inevitability of dogma, if Christianity is to be anything more than a little mild wishful-thinking about ethical behaviour. . . .

If Christian dogma is irrelevant to life, to what, in Heaven's name is it relevant?—since religious dogma is in fact nothing but a statement of doctrines concerning the nature of life and the universe. If Christian ministers really believe it is only an intellectual game for theologians and has no bearing upon human life, it is no wonder that their congregations are ignorant, bored, and bewildered. . . .

Between Humanism and Christianity and between Paganism and Theism there is no distinction whatever except a distinction of dogma.

That you cannot have Christian principles without Christ is becoming increasingly clear, because their validity as principles depends on Christ's authority; and as we have seen, the Totalitarian States, having ceased to believe in Christ's authority, are logically quite justified in repudiating Christian principles. If "the average man" is required to "believe in Christ" and accept His authority for "Christian princilpes," it is surely relevant to inquire who or what Christ is, and why His authority should be accepted. But the question, "What think ye of Christ?" lands the average man at once in the very knottiest kind of dogmatic riddle. It is quite useless to say that it doesn't matter particularly who or what Christ was or by what authority He did those things, and that even if He was only a man, He was a very nice man and we ought to live by His principles: for that is merely Humanism; and if the "average man" in Germany chooses to think that Hitler is a nicer sort of man with still more attractive principles, the Christian humanist has no answer to make.

It is not true at all that dogma is "hopelessly irrelevant" to the life and thought of the average man. What is true is that ministers of the Christian religion often assert that it is, present it for consideration as though it were, and, in fact, by their faulty exposition of it make it so. The central dogma of the Incarnation is that by which relevance stands or falls. If Christ was only a man, then He is entirely irrelevant to any experience of human life. It is, in the strictest sense, necessary to the salvation of relevance that a man should believe rightly the Incarnation of Our Lord Jesus Christ. Unless he believes rightly, there is not the faintest reason why he should believe at all. And in that case, it is wholly irrelevant to chatter about "Christian principles."

If the "average man" is going to be interested in Christ at all, it is the dogma that will provide the interest. The trouble is that, in nine cases out of ten, he has never been offered the dogma. What he has been offered is a set of technical theological terms which nobody has taken the trouble to translate into language relevant to ordinary life. . . .

Teachers and preachers never, I think, make it sufficiently clear that dogmas are not a set of arbitrary regulations invented *a priori* by a committee of theologians enjoying a bout of all-in dialectical wrestling. Most of them were hammered out under pressure of urgent practical necessity to provide an answer to heresy. And heresy is, as I have tried to show, largely the expression of opinion of the untutored average man, trying to grapple with the problems of the universe at the point where they begin to interfere with his daily life and thought. To me, engaged in my diabolical occupation of going to and fro in the world and walking up and down in it, conversations and correspondence bring daily a magnificent crop of all the standard heresies. As practical examples of the "life and thought of the average man" I am extremely well familiar with them, though I had to hunt through the Encyclopedia to fit them with their proper theological titles for the purposes of this address. For the answers I need not go so far: they are compendiously set forth in the Creeds. But an interesting fact is this: that nine out of ten of my heretics are exceedingly surprised to discover that Creeds contain any statements that bear a practical and comprehensible meaning. If I tell them it is an article of faith that the same God who made the world endured the suffering of the world, they ask in perfect good faith what connection there is between that statement and the story of Jesus. If I draw their attention to the dogma that the same Jesus who was the Divine Love was also Light of Light, the Divine Wisdom, they are surprised. Some of them thank me very heartily for this entirely novel and original interpretation of Scripture, which they never heard of before and suppose me to have invented. Others say irritably that they don't like to think that wisdom and religion have anything to do with one another, and that I should do much better to cut out the wisdom and reason and intelligence and stick to a simple gospel of love. But whether they are pleased or annoyed, they are interested; and the thing that interests them, whether or not they suppose it to be my invention, is the resolute assertion of the dogma. . . .

I believe it to be a grave mistake to present Christianity as something charming and popular with no offence in it. Seeing that Christ went about the world giving the most violent offence to all kinds of people it would seem absurd to expect that the doctrine of His Person can be so presented as to offend nobody. We cannot blink at the fact that gentle Jesus meek and mild was so stiff in His opinions and so inflammatory in His language that He was thrown out of church, stoned, hunted from place to place, and finally gibbeted as a firebrand and a public danger. Whatever His peace was, it was not the peace of an amiable indifference; and He said in so many words that what He brought with Him was fire and sword. That being so, nobody need be too much surprised or disconcerted at finding that a determined preaching of Christian dogma may sometimes result in a few angry letters of protest or a difference of opinion on the parish council. . . .

I find by experience there is a very large measure of agreement among Christian denominations on all doctrine that is really ecumenical. . . . But what is urgently necessary is that certain fundamentals should be restated in terms that make their meaning—and indeed, the mere fact that they *have* a meaning—clear to the ordinary uninstructed heathen to whom technical language has become a dead letter.

May I now mention some of the dogmas concerning which I find there is most ignorance and misunderstanding and about which I believe the modern world most urgently needs to be told? Out of a very considerable number I have selected seven as being what I may call "key-positions," namely, God, man, sin, judgment, matter, work, and society. They are, of course, all closely bound together—Christian doctrine is not a set of rules, but one vast interlocking rational structure—but there are particular aspects of these seven subjects which seem to me to need special emphasis at the moment.

1. GOD.—At the risk of appearing quite insolently obvious, I shall say that if the Church is to make any impression on the modern mind she will have to preach Christ and the cross.

Of late years, the Church has not succeeded very well in preaching Christ: she has preached Jesus, which is not quite the same thing. I find that the ordinary man simply does not grasp at all the idea that Jesus Christ and God the Creator are held to be literally the same person. They believe Catholic doctrine to be that God the Father made the world and that Jesus Christ redeemed mankind and that these two characters are quite separate personalities. The phrasing of the Nicene Creed is here a little unfortunate—it is easy to read it as: "being of one substance with the-Father-by-whom-all-things-were-made." The Church Catechism—again rather unfortunately—emphasizes the distinction: "God the Father who hath made me and all the world, God the Son who hath redeemed me and all mankind." The distinction of the Persons within unity of the Substance is philosophically quite proper, and familiar enough to any creative artist: but the majority of people are not creative artists, and they have it very firmly fixed in their heads that the Person who bore the sins of the world was not the eternal creative life of the world, but an entirely different person, who was in fact the victim of God the Creator. It is dangerous to emphasize one aspect of a doctrine at the expense of the other, but at this present moment the danger that anybody will confound the Persons is so remote as to be negligible. What everybody does is to divide the substance—with the result that the whole Jesus-history becomes an unmeaning anecdote of the brutality of God to man.

It is only with the confident assertion of the creative divinity of the Son that the doctrine of the Incarnation becomes a real revelation of the structure of the world. And here Christianity has its enormous advantage over every other religion in the world. It is the *only* religion which gives value to evil and suffering. It affirms—not, like Christian Science, that evil has no real existence, nor yet, like Buddhism, that good consists in a refusal to experience evil—but that perfection is attained through the active and positive effort to wrench a real good out of a real evil.

I will not now go into the very difficult question of the nature of evil and the reality of not-being, though the modern physicists seem to be giving us a very valuable lead about that particular philosophic dilemma. But it seems to me most important that, in face of present world conditions, the doctrines of the reality of evil and the value of suffering should be kept in the very front line of Christian affirmation. I mean, it is not enough to say that religion produces virtues and personal consolations side by side with the very obvious evils and pains that afflict mankind, but that God is alive and at work within the evil and suffering, perpetually transforming them by the positive energy which He had with the Father before the world was made.

2. MAN.—A young and intelligent priest remarked to me the other day that he thought one of the greatest sources of strength in Christianity today lay in the profoundly pessimistic view it took of human nature. There is a great deal in what he says. The people who are most discouraged and made despondent by the barbarity and stupidity of human behavior at this time are those who think highly of *homo sapiens* as a product of evolution, and who still cling to an optimistic belief in the civilizing influence of progress and enlightenment. To them, the appalling outbursts of bestial ferocity in the Totalitarian States, and the obstinate selfishness and stupid greed of Capitalist Society, are not merely shocking and alarming. For them, these things are the utter negation of everything in which they have believed. It is as though the bottom had dropped out of their universe. The whole thing looks like a denial of all reason, and they feel as if they and the world had gone mad together. Now for the Christian, this is not so. He is as deeply shocked and grieved as anybody else, but he is not astonished. He has never thought very highly of human nature left to itself. He has been accustomed to the idea that there is a deep interior dislocation in the very centre of human personality, and that you can never, as they say, "make people good by Act of Parliament," just because laws are man-made and therefore partake of the imperfect and self-contradictory nature of man. Humanly speaking, it is not true at all that "truly to know the good is to do the good"; it is far truer to say with St. Paul that "the evil I would not, that I do"; so that the mere increase of knowledge is of very little help in the struggle to outlaw evil. The delusion of the mechanical perfectibility of mankind through a combined process of scientific knowledge and unconscious evolution

has been responsible for a great deal of heartbreak. It is, at bottom, far more pessimistic than Christian pessimism, because, if science and progress break down there is nothing to fall back upon. Humanism is self-contained—it provides for man no resources outside himself. The Christian dogma of the double nature in man—which asserts that man is disintegrated and necessarily imperfect in himself and all his works, yet closely related to a real unity of substance with an eternal perfection within and beyond him—makes the present parlous state of human society seem both less hopeless and less irrational. I say "the present parlous state"—but that is to limit it too much. A man told me the other day: "I have a little boy of a year old. When the war broke out, I was very much distressed about him, because I found I was taking it for granted that life *ought* to be better and easier for him than it had been for my generation. Then I realized that I had no right to take this for granted at all—that the fight between good and evil must be the same for him as it had always been, and then I ceased to feel so much distressed." As Lord David Cecil has said: "The jargon of the philosophy of progress taught us to think that the savage and primitive state of man is behind us; we still talk of the present 'return to barbarism.' But barbarism is not behind us, it is beneath us." And in the same article he observes: "Christianity has compelled the mind of man, not because it is the most cheering view of human existence, but because it is truest to the facts". I think this is true; and it seems to me quite disastrous that the idea should have got about that Christianity is an other-worldly, unreal, idealistic kind of religion which suggests that if we are good we shall be happy—or if not, it will all be made up to us in the next existence. On the contrary, it is fiercely and even harshly realistic, insisting that the Kingdom of Heaven can never be attained in this world except by unceasing toil and struggle and vigilance: that, in fact, we cannot be good and cannot be happy, but that there are certain eternal achievements that make even happiness look like trash. It has been said, I think by Berdyaev, that nothing can prevent the human soul from preferring creativeness to happiness. In this lies man's substantial likeness to the Divine Christ who in this world suffers and creates continually, being incarnate in the bonds of matter.

3. SIN.—This doctrine of man leads naturally to the doctrine of sin. One of the really surprising things about the present bewilderment of humanity is that the Christian Church now finds herself called upon to proclaim the old and hated doctrine of sin as a gospel of cheer and encouragement. The final tendency of the modern philosophies—hailed in their day as a release from the burden of sinfulness—has been to bind

man hard and fast in the chains of an iron determinism. The influences of heredity and environment, of glandular make-up and the control exercised by the unconscious, of economic necessity and the mechanics of biological development, have all been invoked to assure man that he is not responsible for his misfortunes and therefore not to be held guilty. Evil has been represented as something imposed upon him from without, not made by him from within. The dreadful conclusion follows inevitably, that as he is not responsible for evil, he cannot alter it; even though evolution and progress may offer some alleviation in the future, there is no hope for you and me, here and now. I well remember how an aunt of mine, brought up in an old-fashioned liberalism, protested angrily against having continually to call herself a "miserable sinner" when reciting the Litany. Today, if we could really be persuaded that we *are* miserable sinners—that the trouble is not outside us but inside us, and that therefore, by the grace of God, we can do something to put it right, we should receive that message as the most hopeful and heartening thing that can be imagined.

Needless to say, the whole doctrine of "original sin" will have to be restated, in terms which the ordinary man, brought up on biology and Freudian psychology, can understand. These sciences have done an enormous amount to expose the *nature* and *mechanism* of man's inner dislocation and ought to be powerful weapons in the hand of the Church. It is a thousand pities that the Church should ever have allowed these weapons to be turned against her. . . .

5. MATTER.—At this point we shall find ourselves compelled to lay down the Christian doctrine concerning the material universe; and it is here, I think, that we shall have our best opportunity to explain the meaning of sacramentalism. The common man labours under a delusion that for the Christian, matter is evil and the body is evil. . . . But so long as the Church continues to teach the manhood of God and to celebrate the sacraments of the Eucharist and of marriage, no living man should dare to say that matter and body are not sacred to her. She must insist strongly that the whole material universe is an expression and incarnation of the creative energy of God, as a book or a picture is the material expression of the creative soul of the artist. For that reason, all good and creative handling of the material universe is holy and beautiful, and all abuse of the material universe is a crucifixion of the body of Christ. The whole question of the right use to be made of art, of the intellect, and of the material resources of the world is bound up in this.

6. WORK.—The unsacramental attitude of modern society to man

and matter is probably closely connected with its unsacramental attitude to work. The Church is a good deal to blame for having connived at this. From the eighteenth century onwards, she has tended to acquiesce in what I may call the industrious apprentice view of the matter: "Work hard and be thrifty, and God will bless you with a contented mind and a competence." This is nothing but enlightened self-interest in its vulgarest form and plays directly into the hands of the monopolist and the financier. Nothing has so deeply discredited the Christian Church as her squalid submission to the economic theory of society. The burning question of the Christian attitude to money is being so eagerly debated nowadays that it is scarcely necessary to do more than remind ourselves that the present unrest, both in Russia and in Central Europe, is an immediate judgment upon a financial system that has subordinated man to economics, and that no mere readjustment of economic machinery will have any lasting effect if it keeps man a prisoner inside the machine.

This is the burning question; but I believe there is a still more important and fundamental question waiting to be dealt with, and that is, what men in a Christian society ought to think and feel about work. Curiously enough, apart from the passage in Genesis that suggests that work is a hardship and a judgment on sin, Christian doctrine is not very explicit about work. I believe, however, that there is a Christian doctrine of work, very closely related to the doctrines of the creative energy of God and the divine image in man. The modern tendency seems to be to identify work with gainful employment; and this is, I maintain, the essential heresy at the back of the great economic fallacy that allows wheat and coffee to be burned and fish to be used for manure while whole populations stand in need of food. The fallacy is that work is not the expression of man's creative energy in the service of society, but only something he does in order to obtain money and leisure. . . .

I will only add to this one thing that seems to me very symptomatic. I was shown a "scheme for a Christian society" drawn up by a number of young and earnest Roman Catholics. It contained a number of clauses dealing with work and employment—minimum wages, hours of labor, treatment of employees, housing, and so on—all very proper and Christian. But it offered no machinery whatever for ensuring that the work itself should be properly done. In its lack of a sacramental attitude to work, that is, it was as empty as a set of trade-union regulations. We may remember that a medieval guild did insist, not only on the employer's duty to his workmen, but also on the laborer's duty to his work.

If man's fulfillment of his nature is to be found in the full expression of his divine creativeness, then we urgently need a Christian doctrine of work, which shall provide, not only for proper conditions of employment, but also that the work shall be such as a man may do with his whole heart, and that he shall do it for the very work's sake. But we cannot expect a sacramental attitude to work, while many people are forced, by our evil standard of values, to do work that is a spiritual degradation—a long series of financial trickeries, for example, or the manufacture of vulgar and useless trivialities.

7. SOCIETY.—Lastly, a word or two about the Christian doctrine of society—not about its translation into political terms, but about its dogmatic basis. It rests on the doctrine of what God is and what man is, and it is impossible to have a Christian doctrine of society *except* as a corollary to Christian dogma about the place of man in the universe. This is, or should be, obvious. The one point to which I should like to draw attention is the Christian doctrine of the moral law. The attempt to abolish wars and wickedness by the moral law is doomed to failure, because of the fact of sinfulness. Law, like every other product of human activity, shares the integral human imperfection: it is, in the old Calvinist phrase: "of the nature of sin." That is to say: all legality, if erected into an absolute value, contains within itself the seeds of judgment and catastrophe. The law is necessary, but only, as it were, as a protective fence against the forces of evil, behind which the divine activity of grace may do its redeeming work. We can, for example, never make a positive peace or a positive righteousness by enactments against offenders; law is always prohibitive, negative, and corrupted by the interior contradictions of man's divided nature; it belongs to the category of judgment. That is why an intelligent understanding about sin is necessary to preserve the world from putting an unjustified confidence in the efficacy of the moral law taken by itself. It will never drive out Beelzebub; it cannot, because it is only human and not divine.

Nevertheless, the law must be rightly understood or it is not possible to make the world understand the meaning of grace. There is only one real law—the law of the universe; it may be fulfilled either by way of judgment or by the way of grace, but it must be fulfilled one way or the other. If men will not understand the meaning of judgment, they will never come to understand the meaning of grace. If they hear not Moses or the Prophets, neither will they be persuaded, though one rose from the dead.

DIETRICH BONHOEFFER

Dietrich Bonhoeffer (1906-1945) was a German Lutheran pastor imprisoned by the Nazis. His correspondence from prison reveals some provocative conjectures about the place of theology, church, and the Christian in a world "come of age." More than most theologians, he was sensitive to the growing secularity of the times and the necessity of new theological interpretation and direction.

Bonhoeffer here discusses a "religionless Christianity," a striking phrase that must be understood in terms of the problem of being an authentic Christian in Germany during the holocaust years of 1933-1945, and by which Bonhoeffer emphasizes being a Christian disciple in a world that no longer depends on "religious" support and interpretation. Unfortunately, he did not have time to work out the implications of these controversial proposals which have caught the attention of the modern world since his death.

From Dietrich Bonhoeffer, Letters and Papers from Prison

April 30, 1944

The thing that keeps coming back to me is, what *is* Christianity, and indeed what *is* Christ, for us today? The time when men could be told everything by means of words, whether theological or simply pious, is over, and so is the time of inwardness and conscience, which is to say the time of religion as such. We are proceeding towards a time of no religion at all: men as they are now simply cannot be religious any more. Even those who honestly describe themselves as "religious" mean something quite different. Our whole nineteen-hundred-year-old Christian preaching and theology rests upon the "religious premise" of man. What we call Christianity has always been a pattern—perhaps a true pattern—of religion. But if one day it becomes apparent that this *a priori* "premise" simply does not exist, but was an historical and temporary form of human self-expression, i.e., if we reach the stage of being radically without religion—and I think this is more or less the case already, else how is it, for instance, that this war, unlike any of those before it, is not calling forth any "religious" reaction?—what does that mean for "Christianity"?

It means that the linchpin is removed from the whole structure of our Christianity to date, and the only people left for us to light on in the way of "religion" are a few "last survivals of the age of chivalry," or else one or two who are intellectually dishonest. Would they be the chosen few? Is it on this dubious group and none other that we are to pounce, in fervour, pique, or indignation, in order to sell them the goods we have to offer? Are we to fall upon one or two unhappy people in their weakest moment and force upon them a sort of religious coercion?

If we do not want to do this, if we had finally to put down the western pattern of Christianity as a mere preliminary stage to doing without religion altogether, what situation would result for us, for the Church? How can Christ become the Lord even of those with no religion? If religion is no more than the garment of Christianity—and even that garment has had very different aspects at different periods—then what is a religionless Christianity? Barth, who is the only one to have started on this line of thought, has still not proceeded to its logical conclusion, but has arrived at a positivism of revelation which has nevertheless remained essentially a restoration. For the religionless working man, or indeed, man generally, nothing that makes any real difference is gained by that. The questions needing answers would surely be: What is the significance of a Church (church, parish, preaching, Christian life) in a religionless world? How do we speak of God without religion, i.e., without the temporally-influenced presuppositions of metaphysics, inwardness, and so on? How do we speak (but perhaps we are no longer capable of speaking of such things as we used to) in secular fashion of God? In what way are we in a religionless and secular sense Christians, in what way are we the *Ekklesia*, "those who are called forth," not conceiving of ourselves religiously as specially favoured, but as wholly belonging to the world? Then Christ is no longer an object of religion, but something quite different, indeed and in truth the Lord of the world. Yet what does that signify? What is the place of worship and prayer in an entire absence of religion? Does the secret discipline, or, as the case may be, the distinction (which you have met with me before) between penultimate and ultimate, at this point acquire fresh importance? I must break off for today, so that the letter can be posted straight away. In two days I will write to you further on the subject. I hope you have a rough idea of what I'm getting at, and that it does not bore you. Goodbye for the present. It isn't easy to keep writing without any echo from you. You must excuse me if that makes it rather a monologue!

I find after all I can carry on writing.—The Pauline question whether circumcision is a condition of justification is today, I consider, the question whether religion is a condition of salvation. Freedom from circumcision is at the same time freedom from religion. I often ask myself why a Christian instinct frequently draws me more to the religionless than to the religious, by which I mean not with any intent of evangelizing them, but rather, I might almost say, in "brotherhood". While I often shrink with religious people from speaking of God by name—because that Name somehow seems to me here not to ring true, and I strike myself as rather dishonest (it is especially bad when others start talking in religious jargon; then I dry up completely and feel somehow oppressed and ill at ease)—with people who have no religion I am able on occasion to speak of God quite openly and as it were naturally. Religious people speak of God when human perception is (often just from laziness) at an end, or human resources fail; it is really always the *Deus ex machina* they call to their aid, either for the so-called solving of insoluble problems or as support in human failure—always, that is to say, helping out human weakness or on the borders of human existence. Of necessity, that can only go until men can, by their own strength, push those borders a little further, so that God becomes superfluous as a *Deus ex machina*. I have come to be doubtful even about talking of "borders of human existence." Is even death today, since men are scarcely afraid of it any more, and sin, which they scarcely understand any more, still a genuine borderline? It always seems to me that in talking thus we are only seeking frantically to make room for God. I should like to speak of God not on the borders of life but at its centre, not in weakness but in strength, not, therefore, in man's suffering and death but in his life and prosperity. On the borders it seems to me better to hold our peace and leave the problem unsolved. Belief in the Resurrection is not the solution of the problem of death. The "beyond" in the midst of our life. The Church stands not where human powers give out, on the borders, but in the centre of the village. That is the way it is in the Old Testament, and in this sense we still read the New Testament far too little on the basis of the Old. The outward aspect of this religionless Christianity, the form it takes, is something to which I am giving much thought, and I shall be writing to you about it again soon.

May 5, 1944

A few more words about 'religionlessness.' I expect you remember Bultmann's essay on the 'demythologizing' of the New Testament? My view of it today would be, not that he went 'too far,' as most people thought, but that he didn't go far enough. It's not only the 'mythological' concepts, such as miracle, ascension, and so on (which are not in principle separable from the concepts of God, faith, etc.), but 'religious' concepts generally, which are problematic. You can't, as Bultmann supposes, separate God and miracle, but you must be able to interpret and proclaim *both* in a 'non-religious' sense. Bultmann's approach is fundamentally still a liberal one (i.e., abridging the gospel), whereas I'm trying to think theologically.

What does it mean to 'interpret in a religious sense'? I think it means to speak on the one hand metaphysically, and on the other hand individualistically. Neither of these is relevant to the biblical message or to the man of today. Hasn't the individualistic question about personal salvation almost completely left us all? Aren't we really under the impression that there are more important things than that question (perhaps not more important than the *matter* itself, but more important than the *question!*)? I know it sounds pretty monstrous to say that. But, fundamentally, isn't this in fact biblical? Does the question about saving one's soul appear in the Old Testament at all? Aren't righteousness and the Kingdom of God on earth the focus of everything, and isn't it true that Romans 3.24ff. is not an individualistic doctrine of salvation, but the culmination of the view that God alone is righteous? It is not with the beyond that we are concerned, but with this world as created and preserved, subjected to laws, reconciled, and restored. What is above this world is, in the gospel, intended to exist *for* this world; I mean that, not in the anthropocentric sense of liberal, mystic, pietistic, ethical theology, but in the biblical sense of the creation and of the incarnation, crucifixion, and resurrection of Jesus Christ.

May 29, 1944

Weizsacker's book on the world view of physics is still keeping me busy. It has brought home to me how wrong it is to use God as a stop-gap for the incompleteness of our knowledge. For the frontiers of knowledge are inevitably being pushed back further and further, which means that you only think of God as a stop-gap. He also is being pushed back further and further, and is in more or less continuous retreat. We should find God in what we do know, not in what we don't; not in outstanding problems, but in those we have already solved. This is true not only for the relation between Christianity and science, but also for wider human problems such as guilt, suffering and death. It is possible nowadays to find answers to these problems which leave God right out of the picture. It just isn't true to say that Christianity alone has the answers. In fact the Christian answers are no more conclusive or compelling than any of the others. Once more, God cannot be used as a stop-gap. We must not wait until we are at the end of our tether: he must be found at the centre of life: in life, and not only in death; in health and vigour, and not only in suffering; in activity, and not only in sin. The ground for this lies in the revelation of God in Christ. Christ is the centre of life, and in no sense did he come to answer our unsolved problems. From the centre of life certain questions are seen to be wholly irrelevant, and so are the answers commonly given to them—I am thinking for example of the judgment pronounced on the friends of Job. In Christ there are no Christian problems. Enough of this; I have just been disturbed again.

June 8, 1944

You have asked so many important questions on the subjects that have been occupying me lately, that I should be happy if I could answer them all myself. But I'm afraid the whole thing is very much in the initial stages. As usual, I am led on more by an instinctive feeling for the questions which are bound to crop up rather than by any conclusions I have reached already. I will try to define my position from the historical angle.

The movement beginning about the thirteenth century (I am not going to get involved in any arguments about the exact date) towards the autonomy of man (under which head I place the discovery of the laws by which the world lives and manages in science, social and political affairs, art, ethics and religion) has in our time reached a certain completion. Man has learned to cope with all questions of importance without recourse to God as a working hypothesis. In questions concerning science, art, and even ethics, this has become an understood thing which one scarcely dares to tilt at any more. But for the last hundred years or so, it has been increasingly true of religious questions also: it is becoming evident that everything gets along without "God," and just as well as before. As in the scientific field, so in human affairs generally, what we call "God" is being more and more edged out of life, losing more and more ground.

Catholic and Protestant historians are agreed that it is in this development that the great defection from God, from Christ, is to be discerned, and the more they bring in and make use of God and Christ in opposition to this trend, the more the trend itself considers itself to be anti-Christian. The world which has attained to a realization of itself and of the laws which govern its existence is so sure of itself in what seems to be an uncanny way. False starts and failures do not make the world deviate from the path and development it is following; they are accepted with fortitude and detachment as part of the bargain, and even an event like the present war is no exception. Christian apologetic has taken the most varying forms of opposition to this self-assurance. Efforts are made to prove to a world thus come of age that it cannot live without the tutelage of "God." Even though there has been surrender on all secular problems, there still remain the so-called ultimate questions—death, guilt,—on which only "God" can furnish an answer, and which are the reason why God and the Church and the pastor are needed. Thus we live, to some extent, by these ultimate questions of humanity. But what if one day they no longer exist as such, if they too can be answered without "God"? We have of course the secularized off-shoots of Christian theology, the existentialist philosophers and the psychotherapists, who demonstrate to secure, contented, happy mankind that it is really unhappy and desperate, and merely unwilling to realize that it is in severe straits it knows nothing at all about, from which only they can rescue it. Wherever there is health, strength, and security, simplicity, they spy luscious fruit to gnaw at or to lay their pernicious eggs in. They make it their object first of all to drive men to inward despair, and then it is all theirs. That is secularized methodism. And whom does it touch? A small number of intellectuals, of degenerates, of people who regard themselves as the most important thing in the world and hence like looking after themselves. The ordinary man who spends his everyday life at work, and with his family, and of course with all kinds of hobbies and other interests too, is not affected. He has neither time nor inclination for thinking about his intellectual despair and regarding his modest share of happiness as a trial, a trouble or a disaster.

The attack by Christian apologetic upon the adulthood of the world I consider to be in the first place pointless, in the second ignoble, and in the third un-Christian. Pointless, because it looks to me like an attempt to put a grown-up man back into adolescence, i.e., to make him dependent on things on which he is not in fact dependent any more, thrusting him back into the midst of problems which are in fact not problems for him anymore. Ignoble, because this amounts to an effort to exploit the weakness of man for purposes alien to him and not freely subscribed to by him. Un-Christian, because for Christ himself is being substituted one particular stage in the religiousness of man, i.e., a human law. Of this more later.

June 30, 1944

You see, that is the attitude that I am contending against. When Jesus blessed sinners, they were real sinners, but Jesus did not make everyone a sinner first. He called them away from their sin, not into their sin. It is true that encounter with Jesus meant the reversal of all human values. So it was in the conversion of Paul, though in his case the encounter with Jesus preceded the realization of sin. It is true that Jesus cared about people on the fringe of human society, such as harlots and tax-collectors, but never about them alone, for he sought to care about man as such. Never did he question a man's health, vigour, or happiness, regarded in themselves, or regard them as evil fruits; else why would he heal the sick and restore the weak? Jesus claims for himself and the Kingdom of God the whole of human life in all its manifestations.

July 18, 1944

Man is challenged to participate in the sufferings of God at the hands of a Godless world.

He must therefore plunge himself into the life of a godless world, without attempting to gloss over its ungodliness with a veneer of religion or trying to transfigure it. He must live a "worldly" life and so participate in the suffering of God. He *may* live a worldly life as one emancipated from all false religions and obligations. To be a Christian does not mean to be religious in a particular way, to cultivate some particular form of asceticism (as a sinner, a penitent or a saint), but to be a man. It is not some religious act which makes a Christian what he is, but participation in the suffering of God in the life of the world.

This is *metanoia*. It is not in the first instance bothering about one's own needs, problems, sins, and fears, but allowing oneself to be caught up in the way of Christ, into the Messianic event, and thus fulfilling Isaiah 53. Therefore, "believe in the Gospel," or in the words of St. John the Baptist, "Behold the Lamb of God that taketh away the sin of the world." (By the way, Jeremias has recently suggested that in Aramaic the word for "lamb" could also mean "servant"—very appropriate, in view of Isaiah 53). This being caught up into the Messianic suffering of God in Jesus Christ takes a variety of forms in the New Testament. It appears in the call to discipleship, in Jesus' table fellowship with sinners, in conversions in the narrower sense of the word (e.g., Zacchaeus), in the act of the woman who was a sinner (Luke 7), an act which she performed without any specific confession of sin, in the healing of the sick (Matthew 8.17, see above), in Jesus' acceptance of the children. The shepherds, like the wise men from the east, stand at the crib, not as converted sinners, but because they were drawn to the crib by the star just as they were. The centurion of Capernaum (who does not make any confession of sin) is held up by Jesus as a model of faith (cf. Jairus). Jesus loves the rich young man. The eunuch (Acts 8), Cornelius (Acts 10), are anything but "existences over the abyss." Nathanael is an Israelite without guile (John 1.47). Finally, Joseph of Arimathaea and the women at the tomb. All that is common between them is their participation in the suffering of God in Christ. That is their faith. There is nothing of religious asceticism here. The religious act is always something partial, faith is always something whole, an act involving the whole life. Jesus does not call men to a new religion, but to life. What is the nature of that life, that participation in the powerlessness of God in the world? More about that next time, I hope.

Just one more point for today. When we speak of God in a non-religious way, we must not gloss over the ungodliness of the world, but expose it in a new light. Now that it has come of age, the world is more godless, and perhaps it is for that very reason nearer to God than ever before.

July 21, 1944

During the last year or so I have come to appreciate the "worldli-ness" of Christianity as never before. The Christian is not simply a *homo religiosus,* but a man, pure and simple, just as Jesus was a man, compared with John the Baptist anyhow. I don't mean the shallow this-worldliness of the enlightened, of the busy, the comfortable or the lascivious. It's something much more profound than that, something in which the knowledge of death and resurrection is ever present. I be-lieve Luther lived a this-worldly life in this sense. I remember talking to a young French pastor at A. thirteen years ago. We were discussing what our real purpose was in life. He said he would like to become a saint. I think it is quite likely he did become one. At the time I was very much impressed, though I disagreed with him, and said I should prefer to have faith, or words to that effect. For a long time I did not realize how far we were apart. I thought I could acquire faith by trying to live a holy life, or something like it. It was in this phase that I wrote *The Cost of Discipleship.* Today I can see the dangers of this book, though I am prepared to stand by what I wrote.

Later I discovered and am still discovering up to this very moment that it is only by living completely in this world that one learns to believe. One must abandon every attempt to make something of one-self, whether it be a saint, a converted sinner, a churchman (the priestly-type, so-called!), a righteous man or an unrighteous one, a sick man or a healthy one. This is what I mean by worldliness—taking life in one's stride, with all its duties and problems, its successes and failures, its experiences and helplessness. It is in such a life that we throw ourselves utterly in the arms of God and participate in his suf-ferings in the world and watch with Christ in Gethsemane. That is faith, that is *metanoia,* and that is what makes a man and a Christian.

WALKER PERCY

"The Message in the Bottle" appeared in 1959 in *Thought.* The article is a parable of a man without memory who finds himself a castaway on an island of some culture. The parable illustrates three topics: "the nature of science," "the nature of religious faith," and "the use of language to convey knowledge." Percy analyzes the uselessness of arguments between scientists and Christians. He demonstrates that some situations call for scientific knowledge. Other situations call for "news." Men and women are hungry for "news" and confuse "news" with science. "News" deals with the concrete human predicament. It cannot be evaluated by the criteria of science. It is information about man's existential condition.

For Percy, Christian faith is the news from across the sea that a castaway craves. Christ's "good news," propagated by "newsbearers" of sober mien, is the "message in the bottle" which Percy finds responsive to the castaway's own situation.

Walker Percy, "The Message in the Bottle"

The act of faith consists essentially in knowledge and there we find its formal or specific perfection.

—Thomas Aquinas, *De Veritate*

Faith is not a form of knowledge; for all knowledge is either knowledge of the eternal, excluding the temporal and the historical as indifferent, or it is pure historical knowledge. No knowledge can have for its object the absurdity that the eternal is the historical.

—Søren Kierkegaard, *Philosophical Fragments*

Suppose a man is a castaway on an island. He is, moreover, a special sort of castaway. He has lost his memory in the shipwreck and has no recollection of where he came from or who he is. All he knows is that one day he finds himself cast up on the beach. But it is a pleasant place and he soon discovers that the island is inhabited. Indeed it turns out that the islanders have a remarkable culture with highly developed social institutions, a good university, first-class science, a flourishing industry and art. The castaway is warmly received. Being a resourceful fellow, he makes the best of the situation, gets a job, builds a house, takes a wife, raises a family, goes to night school, and enjoys the local arts of cinema, music, and literature. He becomes, as the phrase goes, a useful member of the community.

The castaway, who by now is quite well educated and curious about the world, forms the habit of taking a walk on the beach early in the morning. Here he regularly comes upon bottles which have been washed up by the waves. The bottles are tightly corked and each one contains a single piece of paper with a single sentence written on it.

The messages are very diverse in form and subject matter. Naturally he is interested, at first idly, then acutely—when it turns out that some of the messages convey important information. Being an alert, conscientious, and well-informed man who is interested in the advance of science and the arts, and a responsible citizen who has a stake in the welfare of his island society, he is anxious to evaluate the messages properly and so take advantage of the information they convey. The bottles arrive by the thousands and he and his fellow islanders—by now he has told them of the messages and they share his interest—are faced with two questions. One is, Where are the bottles coming from?—a question which does not here concern us; the other is, How shall we go about sorting out the messages? which are important and which are not? which are more important and which less? Some of the messages are obviously trivial or nonsensical. Others are false. Still others state facts and draw conclusions which appear to be significant.

Here are some of the messages, chosen at random:

Lead melts at 330 degrees.
$2 + 2 = 4.$
Chicago, a city, is on Lake Michigan.
Chicago is on the Hudson River or Chicago is not on the Hudson River.°
At 2 p.m., January 4, 1902, at the residence of Manuel Gomez in Matanzas, Cuba, a leaf fell from the banyan tree.
The British are coming.
The market for eggs in Bora Bora [a neighboring island] is very good.
If water John brick is.
Jane will arrive tomorrow.
The pressure of a gas is a function of heat and volume.
Acute myelogenous leukemia may be cured by parenteral administration of metallic beryllium.
In 1943 the Russians murdered 10,000 Polish officers in the Katyn forest.
A war party is approaching from Bora Bora.
It is possible to predict a supernova in the constellation Ophiuchus next month by using the following technique—
The Atman (Self) is the Brahman.
The dream symbol, house with a balcony, usually stands for a woman.
Tears, idle tears, I know not what they mean.
Truth is beauty.
Being comprises essence and existence.

As the castaway sets about sorting out these messages, he would, if he followed conventional logical practice, separate them into two large groups. There are those sentences which appear to state empirical facts which can only be arrived at by observation. Such are the sentences

---

° Some of the bottles must have been launched by Rudolf Carnap, since the sentences are identical with those he uses in the article "Formal and Factual Science."

Chicago is on Lake Michigan.
Lead melts at 330 degrees.

Then there are those sentences which seem to refer to a state of affairs implicit in the very nature of reality (or some would say in the very structure of consciousness). Certainly they do not seem to depend on a particular observation. Such are the sentences

Chicago is on the Hudson River or Chicago is not on the Hudson River.
$2 + 2 = 4.$

These two types of sentences are usually called synthetic and analytic.

For the time being I will pass over the positivist division between sense and nonsense, a criterion which would accept the sentence about the melting point of lead because it can be tested experimentally but would reject the sentences about the dream symbol and the metaphysical and poetic sentences because they cannot be tested. I will also say nothing for the moment about another possible division, that between those synthetic sentences which state repeatable events, like the melting of lead, and those which state nonrepeatable historical events, like the murder of the Polish officers.

It is possible, however, to sort out the messages in an entirely different way. To the islander indeed it must seem that this second way is far more sensible—and far more radical—than the former. The sentences appear to him to fall naturally into two quite different groups.

There are those sentences which are the result of a very special kind of human activity, an activity which the castaway, an ordinary fellow, attributes alike to scientists, scholars, poets, and philosophers. Different as these men are, they are alike in their withdrawal from the ordinary affairs of the island, the trading, farming, manufacturing, playing, gossiping, loving—in order to discover underlying constancies amid the flux of phenomena, in order to take exact measurements, in order to make precise inductions and deductions, in order to arrange words or sounds or colors to express universal human experience. (This extraordinary activity is first known to have appeared in the world more or less simultaneously in Greece, India, and China around 600 B.C., a time which Jaspers calls the axial period in world history.)

In this very large group, which the islander might well call "science" in the broadest sense of knowing, the sense of the German word *Wissenschaft*, the islander would put both synthetic and analytic sentences, not only those accepted by positive scientists, but the psychoanalytic sentence, the metaphysical sentence, and the lines of poetry. (He might even include paintings as being, in a sense, sentences.) If the physicist protests at finding himself in the company of psychoanalysts, poets, Vedantists, and Scholastics, the islander will reply that he is not saying that all the sentences are true but that their writers appear to him to be engaged in the same sort of activity as the physicist, namely, withdrawal from the ordinary affairs of life to university, laboratory, studio, mountain eyrie, where they write sentences to which other men assent (or refuse assent), saying, Yes, this is indeed how things are. In some sense or other, the sentences can be verified by the readers even if not testable experimentally—as when the psychiatric patient hears his analyst explain a dream symbol and suddenly realizes that this is indeed what his own dream symbol meant.

In the second group the islander would place those sentences which are significant precisely in so far as the reader is caught up in the affairs and in the life of the island and in so far as he has *not* withdrawn into laboratory or seminar room. Such are the sentences

> *There is fresh water in the next cove.*
> *A hostile war party is approaching.*
> *The market for eggs in Bora Bora is very good.*

These sentences are highly significant to the islander, because he is thirsty, because his island society is threatened, or because he is in the egg business. Such messages he might well call "news."

It will be seen that the criteria of the logician and the positive scientist are of no use to the islander. They do not distinguish between those messages which are of consequence for life on the island and those messages which are not. The logician would place these two sentences

> *A hostile war party is approaching.*
> *The British are coming [to Concord].*

in the same pigeonhole. But to the islander they are very different. The islander lumps together synthetic and analytic, sense and nonsense (to the positivist) sentences under the group "science." Nor is the division tidy. Some sentences do not seem to be provided for at all. The islander is fully aware of the importance of the sentence about the melting point of lead and he puts it under "science." He is fully aware of the importance of the sentence about the hostile war party and he puts it under "news." But where does he put the sentence about the approach of the British to Concord? He does not really care; he would be happy to put it in the "science" pigeonhole if the scientists want it. All he knows is that it is not news to him or the island.

If the islander was asked to say what was wrong with the first division of the logician and scientist, he might reply that it unconsciously assumes that this very special posture of "science" (including poetry, psychoanalysis, philosophy, etc.) is the only attitude that yields significant sentences. People who discover how to strike this attitude of "science" seem also to decide at the same time that they will only admit as significant those sentences which have been written by others who have struck the same attitude. Yet there are times when they act as if this were not the case. If a group of island logicians are busy in a seminar room sifting through the messages from the bottles and someone ran in crying, "The place is on fire!" the logicians would not be content to classify the message as a protocol sentence. They would also leave the building. The castaway will observe only that their classification does take account of the extraordinary significance which they as men have attributed to the message.

To the castaway it seems obvious that a radical classification of the sentences cannot abstract from the concrete situation in which one finds oneself. He is as interested as the scientist in arriving at a rigorous and valid classification. If the scientist should protest that one can hardly make such a classification when each sentence may have a different significance for every man who hears it, the castaway must agree with him. He must agree, that is, that you cannot classify without abstracting. But he insists that the classification be radical enough to take account of the hearer of the news, of the difference between a true piece of news which is not important and a true piece of news which is important. In order to do this, we do not have to throw away the hard-won objectivity of the scientist. We have only to take a step further back so that we may see objectively not only the sentences but the positive scientist who is examining them. After all, the objective posture of the scientist is in the world and can be studied like anything else in the world.

If the scientist protests that in taking one step back to see the scientist at work, the castaway is starting a game of upstaging which has no end—for why not take still another step back and watch the castaway watching the scientist—the castaway replies simply that this is not so. For if you take a step back to see the castaway classifying the messages, you will only see the same thing he sees as he watches the scientist, a man working objectively.

Then, if the castaway is a serious fellow who wants to do justice both to the scientists and to the news in the bottle, he is obliged to become not less but more objective and to take one step back of the scientist, so that he can see him at work in the laboratory and seminar room—and see the news in the bottle too.

What he will see then is not only that there are two kinds of sentences in the bottles but that there are two kinds of postures from which one reads the sentences, two kinds of verifying procedures by which one acts upon them, and two kinds of responses to the sentences.

The classification of the castaway would be something like this:

THE DIFFERENCE BETWEEN A PIECE OF KNOWLEDGE AND A PIECE OF NEWS

(1) *The Character of the Sentence*

By "piece of knowledge" the castaway means knowledge *sub specie aeternitatis*. By *sub specie aeternitatis* he means not what the philosopher usually means but rather knowledge which can be arrived at anywhere by anyone and at any time. The islanders may receive such knowledge in the bottle and be glad to get it—if they have not already gotten it. But getting this knowledge from across the seas is not indispensable. By its very nature the knowledge can also be reached, in principle, by the islander on his island, using his own raw materials, his own scientific, philosophical, and artistic efforts.

Such knowledge would include not only the synthetic and analytic propositions of science and logic but also the philosophical and poetic sentences in the bottle. To the logician the sentence "Lead melts at 330 degrees" seems to be empirical and synthetic. It cannot be deduced from self-evident principles like the analytic sentence "2 + 2 = 4." It cannot be arrived at by reflection, however strenuous. Yet to the castaway this sentence is knowledge *sub specie aeternitatis*. It is a property of lead on any island at any time and for anyone.

The following sentences the castaway would consider knowledge *sub specie aeternitatis* even though they might not have been so considered in the past. Notice that the list includes a mixture of synthetic, analytic, normative, poetic, and metaphysical sentences.

Lead melts at 330 degrees.
Chicago is on the Hudson River or Chicago is not on the Hudson River.
2 + 2 = 4.
The pressure of a gas is a function of temperature and volume.
Acute myelogenous leukemia may be cured by parenteral administration of metallic beryllium.
The dream symbol, house and balcony, usually represents a woman.
Men should not kill each other.
Being comprises essence and existence.

He is not saying that all the sentences are true—at least one (the one about leukemia) is probably not. But they are all pieces of knowledge

which can be arrived at (or rejected) by anyone on any island at any
time. If true they will hold true for anyone on any island at any time.
He has no quarrel with the positivist over the admissibility of poetic
and metaphysical statements. Admissible or not, it is all the same to
him. All he is saying is that this kind of sentence may be arrived at (has
in fact been arrived at) independently by people in different places and
can be confirmed (or rejected) by people in still other places.

By a "piece of news" the castaway generally means a synthetic sentence expressing a contingent and nonrecurring event or state of affairs
which event or state of affairs is peculiarly relevant to the concrete
predicament of the hearer of the news.

It is a knowledge which cannot possibly be arrived at by any effort
of experimentation or reflection or artistic insight. It may not be arrived
at by observation on any island at any time. It may not even be arrived
at on this island at any time (since it is a single, nonrecurring event or
state of affairs).

Both these sentences are synthetic empirical sentences open to verification by the positive method of the sciences. Yet one is, to the castaway, knowledge *sub specie aeternitatis* and the other is a piece of
news.

> *Water boils at 100 degrees at sea level.*
> *There is fresh water in the next cove.*

The following sentences would qualify as possible news to the castaway.

> *At 2 p.m., January 4, 1902, at the residence of Manuel Gomez in Ma-
>   tanzas, Cuba, a leaf fell from the banyan tree.*
> *The British are coming.*
> *The market for eggs in Bora Bora [a neighboring island] is very good.*
> *Jane will arrive tomorrow.*
> *In 1943 the Russians murdered 10,000 Polish officers in the Katyn forest.*
> *A war party is approaching from Bora Bora.*
> *There is fresh water in the next cove.*

What does the positive scientist think of the sentences which the
castaway calls news? Does he reject them as being false or absurd? No,
he is perfectly willing to accept them as long as they meet his standard
of verification. By the use of the critical historical method he attaches
a high degree of probability to the report that the British were approaching Concord. As for the water in the next cove, he goes to see
for himself and so confirms the news or rejects it. But what sort of

significance does he assign these sentences as he sorts them out in the seminar room? To him they express a few of the almost infinite number of true but random observations which might be made about the world. The murder of the Polish officers may have been a great tragedy, yet in all honesty he cannot assign to it a significance qualitatively different from the sentence about the leaf falling from the banyan tree (nor may the castaway necessarily). This is not to say that these sentences are worthless as scientific data. For example, the presence of water in the next cove might serve as a significant datum for the descriptive science of geography, or as an important clue in geology. This single observation could conceivably be the means of verifying a revolutionary scientific theory—just as the sight of a star on a particular night in a particular place provided dramatic confirmation of Einstein's general theory of relativity.

The sentences about the coming of the British and the murder of the Polish officers might serve as significant data from which, along with other such data, general historical principles might be drawn—just as Toynbee speaks of such and such an event as being a good example of such and such a historical process.

In summary, the castaway will make a distinction between the sentences which assert a piece of knowledge *sub specie aeternitatis* and the sentences announcing a piece of news which bears directly on his life. The scientist and logician, however, cannot in so far as they are scientists and logicians, take account of the special character of these news sentences. To them they are empirical observations of a random order and, if significant, they occupy at best the very lowest rung of scientific significance: they are the particular instances from which hypotheses and theories are drawn.

(2) *The Posture of the Reader of the Sentence*

The significance of the sentences for the reader will depend on the reader's own mode of existence in the world. To say this is to say nothing about the truth of the sentences. Assuming that they are all true, they will have a qualitatively different significance for the reader according to his own placement in the world.

(a) The posture of objectivity. If the reader has discovered the secret of science, art, and philosophizing, and so has entered the great company of Thales, Lao-tse, Aquinas, Newton, Keats, Whitehead, he will know what it is to stand outside and over against the world as one who sees and thinks and knows and tells. He tells and hears others tell how it is there in the world and what it is to live in the world. In so far as he himself is a scientist, artist, or philosopher, he reads the sentences in the bottles as stating (or coming short of stating) knowledge *sub*

specie aeternitatis. It may be trivial knowledge; it may be knowledge
he has already arrived at; it may be knowledge he has not yet arrived
at but could arrive at in time; it may be false knowledge which fails
to be verified and so is rejected. It cannot be any other kind of
knowledge.

(b) The posture of the castaway. The reader of the sentences may
or may not be an objective-minded man. But at the moment of finding
the bottle on the beach he is, we will say, very far from being objective-
minded. He is a man who finds himself in a certain situation. To say
this is practically equivalent, life being what it is, to saying that he finds
himself in a certain predicament. Let us say his predicament is a simple
organic need. He is thirsty. In his predicament the sentence about the
water is received not as a datum from which, along with similar data,
more general scientific conclusions might be drawn. Nor is it received
as stating a universal human experience, even though the announcement were composed by Shakespeare at the height of his powers. The
sentence is received as news, news strictly relevant to the predicament
in which the hearer of the news finds himself.

So with other kinds of news, ranging from news relevant to the most
elementary organic predicament to news of complex cultural significance.

Here are some other examples of news and their attending contexts.

Mackerel here!	(*Malinowski's Trobriand Island fisherman announcing a strike to his fellows*)
Jane is home!	(*I love Jane and she has been away*)
The market is up $2.00.	(*I am in the market*)
The British are coming!	(*I am a Minute Man. The context here is not organic but cultural. I thrive under British rule but I throw in my lot with the Revolution for patriotic reasons*)
The light has turned green!	(*I have stopped at a red light*)
Eisenhower is elected!	(*I voted for Stevenson*)

News sentences, in short, are drawn from the context of everyday
life and indeed to a large extent comprise this context.

Insofar as a man is objective-minded, no sentence is significant as a
piece of news. For in order to be objective-minded one must stand outside and over against the world as its knower in one mode or another.
As empirical scientists themselves have noticed, one condition of the
practice of the objective method of the sciences is the exclusion of
oneself from the world of objects one studies.° The absent-minded pro-

---

° See, for example, the physicist Erwin Schrödinger in *What Is Life?* and
the psychiatrist C. G. Jung in *Der Geist der Psychologie*.

fessor, the inspired poet, the Vedic mystic, is indifferent to news, some-times even news of high relevance for him, because he is in a very real sense "out of this world." †

In summary, the hearer of news is a man who finds himself in a pre-dicament. News is precisely that communication which has bearing on his predicament and is therefore good or bad news.

The question arises as to whether news is not the same thing as a sign for an organism, a sign directing him to appropriate need-satisfac-tions, like the buzzer to Pavlov's dog, or warning him of a threat, like the lion's scent to a deer. The organism experiences needs and drives and learns to respond to those signs in its environment which indicate the presence of food, opposite sex, danger, and so on.

This may very well be a fair appraisal of the status of the news we are talking about here—providing the notions of "organism" and "sign" be allowed sufficiently broad interpretation. For the organism we speak of here is not only the physiological mechanism of the body but the encultured creature, the economic creature, and so on. The sign we speak of here is not merely the environmental element; it is the sen-tence, the symbolic assertion made by one man and understood by another.

The scientist—I use the word in the broadest possible sense to include philosophers and artists as well as positive scientists—has abstracted from his own predicament in order to achieve objectivity.° His objec-tivity is indeed nothing else than his removal from his own concrete situation. No sentence can be received by him as a piece of news, there-fore, because he does not stand in the way of hearing news.

(3) *The Scale of Significance*

The scale of significance by which the scientist evaluates the sen-tences in the bottles may be said to range from the particular to the general. The movement of science is toward unity through abstraction,

---

† I wish to make an objective distinction here without pejoration to cast-aways on the one hand or scientists, scholars, mystics, and poets, on the other —while at the same time readily admitting we could use a few more of the absent-minded variety at this time.

° If the depth psychologist objects that the scientist and artist is no differ-ent from anyone else: he undertakes his science and his art so that he may satisfy the deepest unconscious needs of his personality by "sublimating" and so on—the castaway will not quarrel with him. He will observe only that whatever his psychological motivation may be, the scientist and artist—and depth analyst—undertake a very extraordinary activity in virtue of which they stand over against the world as its knowers.

toward formulae and principles which embrace an ever greater number of particular instances. Thus the sentence "Hydrogen and oxygen combine in the ratio of two to one to form water" is a general statement covering a large number of particular cases. But Mendeleev's law of periodicity covers not merely water but all other cases of chemical combination. A theory of gravitation and a theory of radiation are conceived at very high levels of abstraction. But a unified field theory which unites the two occurs at an even higher level.

The scale of significance by which the castaway evaluates news is its relevance for his own predicament. The significance of a piece of knowledge is abstracted altogether from the concrete circumstances which attended the discovery of the knowledge, its verification, its hearing by others. The relationship of Mendeleev's law of periodicity to Lavoisier's discovery of the composition of water is a relation *sub specie aeternitatis*. Its significance in no way depends upon Lavoisier's or Mendeleev's circumstance in life or on the circumstance of him who hears it.

But in judging the significance of a piece of news, everything depends on the situation of the hearer. The question is not merely, What is the nature of the news? but, Who is the hearer? If a man has lost his way in a cave and hears the cry "Come! This way out!" the communication qualifies as news of high significance. But if another man has for reasons of his own come to the cave to spend the rest of his life, the announcement will be of no significance. To a man dying of thirst the news of diamonds over the next dune is of no significance. But the news of water is.

The abstraction of the scientist from the affairs of life may be so great that he even ignores news of the highest relevance for his own predicament. When a friend approached Archimedes and announced, "Archimedes, the soldiers of Marcellus are coming to kill you," Archimedes remained indifferent. He attributed no significance to a contingent piece of news in comparison with the significance of his geometrical deductions. In so doing it may be that he acted as an admirable martyr for science or it may be that he acted foolishly. All that we are concerned here to notice are the traits of objectivity.

The castaway, on the other hand, can only take account of knowledge *sub specie aeternitatis* if it is significant also as news. If his island stands to win international honor providing one of its scientists discovers the secret of atomic energy, or if indeed such a discovery means survival, then the announcement of his scientist friend

$$E = MC^2!$$

is news of the highest significance.

In summary, the scale of significance by which one judges sentences expressing knowledge *sub specie aeternitatis* is the scientific scale of particular-general. The scale of significance by which a castaway evaluates the news in the bottle is the degree of relevance for his own predicament.

(4) *Canons of Acceptance*

The operation of acceptance of a piece of knowledge *sub specie aeternitatis* is synonymous with the procedure of verification.

We need not review the verification procedures of formal logic or positive science. The truth of analytic sentences is demonstrated by a disclosure of the deductive process by which they are inferred. The truth or probability of synthetic sentences is demonstrated by a physical operation repeatable by others.

What about the verification procedures of our other "scientific" sentences, those of psychoanalysts, artists, philosophers, *et al.*? For example, a neurotic physicist is able to verify the suggestion of his analyst that his dream symbol means such and such, and to do so without resorting to a physical operation. These and other such sentences, I suggest, are verifiable not experimentally but experientially by the hearer on the basis of his own experience or reflection. These sentences

> *Your dream symbol, house and balcony, represents a woman.*
> *The whole is greater than the part.*
> *We are such stuff as dreams are made on, and our little life is rounded with a sleep.*

can only be verified (or rejected) by the immediate assent or assent after reflection of him who hears, on the basis of his own experience.

The criteria of acceptance of a news sentence are not the same as those of a knowledge sentence. This is not a pejorative judgment. To say this is not to say that news is of a lower cognitive order than knowledge—such a judgment presupposes the superiority of the scientific posture. It is only to say that once a piece of news is subject to the verification procedures of a piece of knowledge, it simply ceases to be news.

If I am thirsty and you appear on the next sand dune and shout, "Come with me! I know where water is!" it is not open to me to apply any of the verification procedures mentioned above, experimental operations, deduction, or interior recognition and assent to the truth of your statement. A piece of news is neither deducible, repeatable, or otherwise confirmable *at the point of hearing*.

You may deny this, saying that the thirsty man is not really different from the scientist: The only way to verify a report in either case is to go and see for yourself. Very true! But what we are concerned with is not the act, going and seeing for yourself, as a verification procedure, but how one decides to heed the initial "Come!" The scientist does not need to heed the "Come!" For he does not have to come. He is in no predicament whatever and any knowledge that he might wish to arrive at can be arrived at anywhere and at any time and by anyone. Whatever he wants to find out can be found out in his laboratory, on his field trip, in his studio, on his grass mat.

But the castaway must act by a canon of acceptance which is usable *prior* to the procedure of verification. He is obliged to contrive some standard. Otherwise he is easy prey for any clever scoundrel who knows how to take advantage of his predicament to lead him into a den of thieves. What is this standard? What elements does it comprise?

Clearly there are at least two elements. One is the relevance of the news to my predicament. If the stranger in the desert approaches me and announces, "I know what your need is. It is diamonds. Come with me. I know where they are"—I reject him on two counts. One, because it is not diamonds I need; two, because, if he is such a fool or knave as to believe it is diamonds I want, he is probably lying anyway. But if he announces instead, "Come! I know your need. I will take you to water" —then this very announcement is an earnest of his reliability. Yet he might still be a knave or a fool.

Two men are riding a commuter train. One is, as the expression goes, fat, dumb, and happy. Though he lives the most meaningless sort of life, a trivial routine of meals, work, gossip, television, and sleep, he nevertheless feels quite content with himself and is at home in the world. The other commuter, who lives the same kind of life, feels quite lost to himself. He knows that something is dreadfully wrong. More than that, he is in anxiety; he suffers acutely, yet he does not know why. What is wrong? Does he not have all the goods of life?

If now a stranger approaches the first commuter, takes him aside, and says to him earnestly, "My friend, I know your predicament; come with me; I have news of the utmost importance for you"—then the commuter will reject the communication out of hand. For he is in no predicament, or if he is, he does not know it, and so the communication strikes him as nonsense.

The second commuter might very well heed the stranger's "Come!" At least he will take it seriously. Indeed it may well be that he has been waiting all his life to hear this "Come!"

The canon of acceptance by which one rejects and the other heeds the "Come!" is its relevance to his predicament. The man who is dying of thirst will not heed news of diamonds. The man at home, the satisfied man, he who does not feel himself to be in a predicament, will not

heed good news. The objective-minded man, he who stands outside
and over against the world as its knower, will not heed news of any
kind, good or bad—in so far as he remains objective-minded. The castaway will heed news relevant to his predicament. Yet the relevance of
the news is not in itself sufficient warrant.

A second canon of acceptance of news is the credentials of the newsbearer. Such credentials make themselves known through the reputation or through the mien of the newsbearer. The credentials of the
bearer of knowledge *sub specie aeternitatis* are of no matter to the
scientist. It doesn't matter whether Wagner, in writing his music, is a
rascal or whether Lavoisier, in speaking of oxygen, is a thief. The
knowledge sentence carries or fails to carry its own credentials in so far
as it is in some fashion affirmable. If the newsbearer is my brother or
friend and if I know that he knows my predicament and if he approaches me with every outward sign of sobriety and good faith, and
if the news is of a momentous nature, then I have reason to heed the
news. If the newsbearer is known to me as a knave or a fool, I have
reason to ignore the news.

If the newsbearer is a stranger to me, he is not necessarily disquali-
fied as a newsbearer. In some cases indeed his disinterest may itself be
a warrant, since he does not stand to profit from the usual considerations of friendship, family feelings, and so on. His sobriety or foolishness, good faith or knavery may be known through his mien. Even
though he may bring news of high relevance to my predicament, yet a
certain drunkenness of spirit—enthusiasm in the old sense of the word—
is enough to disqualify him and lead me to suspect that he is concerned
not with my predicament but only with his own drunkenness. If a
Jehovah's Witness should ring my doorbell and announce the advent
of God's kingdom, I recognize the possibly momentous character of his
news but must withhold acceptance because of a certain lack of
sobriety in the newsbearer.[*]

If the newsbearer is a stranger and if he meets the requirements of
good faith and sobriety and, extraordinarily enough, knows my predicament, then the very fact of his being a stranger is reason enough
to heed the news. For if a perfect stranger puts himself to some trouble

---

[*] If one thinks of the Christian gospel primarily as a communication between a newsbearer and a hearer of news, one realizes that the news is
often not heeded because it is not delivered soberly. Instead of being delivered with the sobriety with which other important news would be delivered
—even by a preacher—it is spoken either in a sonorous pulpit voice or at a
pitch calculated to stimulate the emotions. But emotional stimuli are not
news. The emotions can be stimulated on any island and at any time.

to come to me and announces a piece of news relevant to my predicament and announce it with perfect sobriety and with every outward
sign of good faith, then I must say to myself, What manner of man is
this that he should put himself out of his way for a perfect stranger—
and I should heed him. It was enough for Jesus to utter the one word
Come! to a stranger—yet when he uttered the same word in Nazareth,
no one came.

The message in the bottle, then, is not sufficient credential in itself
as a piece of news. It is sufficient credential in itself as a piece of knowledge, for the scientist has only to test it and does not care who wrote
it or whether the writer was sober or in good faith. *But a piece of news
requires that there be a newsbearer.* The sentence written on a piece
of paper in the bottle is sufficient if it is a piece of knowledge but it is
hardly sufficient if it is a piece of news.

A third canon of acceptance is the possibility of the news. If the
news is strictly relevant to my predicament and if the bearer of the
news is a person of the best character, I still cannot heed the news
if (1) I know for a fact that it cannot possibly be true or (2) the report
refers to an event of an unheralded, absurd, or otherwise inappropriate
character. If I am dying of thirst and the newsbearer announces to me
that over the next dune I will discover molten sulfur and that it will
quench my thirst, I must despair of his news. If the castaway arrived
at his South Sea island in 1862 and found his adoptive land in bondage
to a tyrant and if a newsbearer arrived and announced that Robert E.
Lee and the Army of Northern Virginia were on their way to deliver
the island—such a piece of news would lie within the realm of possibility yet be so intrinsically inappropriate that the most patriotic of
islanders could hardly take it seriously. If, however, there had been
promises of deliverance for a hundred years from a neighboring island
and if, further, signs had been agreed upon by which one could recognize the deliverer, and if, finally, a newsbearer from this very island
arrived and announced a piece of news of supreme relevance to the
predicament of the islanders and announced it in perfect sobriety and
with every outward sign of good faith, then the islander must himself
be a fool or a knave if he did not heed the news.

(5) Response of the Reader of the Sentence

The response of a reader of a sentence expressing a piece of knowledge is to confirm it (or reject it). The response of a hearer of a piece
of news is to heed it (or ignore it) by taking action appropriate to
one's predicament. In the sphere of pure knowledge, knowledge in
science, philosophy, or art, the act of knowing is complete when the
sentence (or formula or insight or poem or painting) is received, un-

derstood, and confirmed as being true. Other consequences may follow. Physics may lead to useful inventions; a great philosopher may invigorate his civilization and prolong its life for hundreds of years; a great artist may lower the incidence of neurosis. But science is not necessarily committed to technics; philosophers do not necessarily philosophize in order to preserve the state; art is not a form of mental hygiene. There is a goodness and a joy in science and art apart from the effects of science and art on ordinary life. These effects may follow and may be good, but if the effect is made the end, if science is enslaved to technics, philosopy to the state, art to psychiatry—one wonders how long we would have a science, philosophy, or art worthy of the name.

The appropriate response of the reader of a sentence conveying a piece of knowledge—a piece of knowledge which, let us say, falls in the vanguard of the islander's own knowledge—is to know this and more. The movement of science is toward an ever-more-encompassing unity and depth of vision. The movement of the islander who has caught the excitement of science, art, or philosophy is toward the attainment of an ever-more encompassing unity and depth of vision. The man who finds the bottle on the beach and who reads its message conveying a piece of knowledge undertakes his quest, verification and extension of the knowledge, on his own island or on any island at any time. His quest takes place *sub specie aeternitatis* and, in so far as he is a scientist, he does not care who he is, where he is, or what his predicament may be.

The response of a hearer of a piece of news is to take action appropriate to his predicament. The news is not delivered to be confirmed— for then it would not be a piece of news but a piece of knowledge. There would be no pressing need to deliver it for it is not relevant to the predicament of the islander and it can, theoretically, be arrived at by the islander himself on his own island. The piece of news is delivered to be heeded and acted upon. There is a criterion of acceptance of a piece of news but this acceptance procedure is strictly ancillary to the action to be taken. In science, however, the technical invention which may follow the discovery is optional.°

If a congress of scientists, philosophers, and artists is convening in

---

° Einstein's discovery of the equivalence of matter and energy and of the ratio of the equivalence was a momentous advance of science. As it happened, it was also a piece of good news for the Allies in World War II. Indeed, pure science, research *sub specie aeternitatis,* may be undertaken under the pressure of a historical predicament. But the point is that it may also be undertaken—and Einstein's research was undertaken—with no thought of its possible bearing on politics.

an Aspen auditorium in order to take account of the recent "sentences" of their colleagues (hypotheses, theories, formulae, logics, geometries, poems, symphonies, etc.), and if during the meeting a fire should break out, and if then a man should mount the podium and utter the sentence "Come! I know the way out!"—the conferees will be able to distinguish at once the difference between this sentence and all the other sentences which have been uttered from the podium. Different as a bar of music is from a differential equation, it will be seen at once that the two share a generic likeness when compared with a piece of news. A radical shift of posture by both teller and hearer has taken place. The conferees will attach a high importance to the sentence even though it conveys no universal truth and *even though it may not be verified on hearing.* A different criterion of acceptance becomes appropriate. It is not an inferior or makeshift criterion—as when a castaway makes do with a raft but would rather have a steamship. It is the criterion appropriate to news as a category of communication. If a criterion of verification could be used, then the communication would cease to be news relevant to my predicament; it would become instead a piece of knowledge *sub specie aeternitatis.*†

The conferees at Aspen apply an appropriate criterion. They are not gullible—for bad advice at this juncture could get them killed. If the newsbearer had announced, not that he knew the way out, but that world peace had been achieved, they would hardly heed him. If he commanded them to flap their arms and fly out through the skylight, they would hardly heed him. If he spoke like a fool with all manner of ranting and raving, they would hardly heed him. If they knew him to be a liar, they would hardly heed him. But if he spoke with authority, in perfect sobriety, and with every outward sign of good faith and regard for them, saying that he knew the way out and they had only to follow him, they would heed him. They would heed him with all dispatch. They would, unless there were an Archimedes present, give his news priority over the most momentous and exciting advance in science. They would heed him at any cost, even though as scientists they must preserve a low regard for sentences bearing news of a contingent event.

---

† True, after the announcement, the way out could then be seen by the conferee from where he sits, and so the news verified before it is heeded and acted upon. The event takes place at an organic level of animal response. But the difference still holds: the prime importance which the hearer attaches to the announcement, even though it is of no greater scientific significance than the sentence, "There is a fly on your nose"; the response of the hearer of the sentence, the getting out rather than the verification in situ.

THE MISTAKING OF A PIECE OF KNOWLEDGE FOR A PIECE OF NEWS FROM ACROSS THE SEAS

What if it should happen that a scientist should assign a high order of significance to a piece of knowledge and a low order of significance to a piece of news? He could make a serious mistake. Having assigned all news sentences to a low order of significance, he could make the mistake of attending only to scientific sentences in the belief that since they are so important in the sphere of knowledge, they might also do duty as pieces of news. Thus, if it should happen that he experiences a predicament of homelessness or of anxiety without cause, he may seek for its cause and cure within the sphere of scientific and artistic knowledge or from the satisfaction of his island needs. He may resort to analysis or drugs or group therapy or creative writing or reading creative writing, all of which may assuage this or that symptom of his loneliness or anxiety. Or he may seek a wife or new friends or more meaningful relationships. But what if it should be the case that his symptoms of homelessness or anxiety do not have their roots in this or that lack of knowledge or this or that malfunction which he may suffer as an islander but rather in the very fact that he is a castaway and that as such he stands not in the way of one who requires a piece of island knowledge or a technique of island treatment or this or that island need satisfaction but stands rather in the way of one who is waiting for a piece of news from across the seas? Then he has deceived himself and, even if his symptoms are better, is worse off than he was.

THE DIFFERENCE BETWEEN ISLAND NEWS AND NEWS FROM ACROSS THE SEAS

My purpose here is not apologetic. We are not here concerned with the truth of the Christian gospel or with the career in time of that unique Thing, the Jewish-People-Jesus-Christ-Catholic-Church. An apologetic would deal with the evidences of God's entry into history through His covenant with the Jews, through His own incarnation, and through His institution of the Catholic Church as the means of man's salvation. It would also deal with philosophical approaches to God's existence and nature. My purpose is rather the investigation of news as a category of communication.

In the light of the distinction we have made, however, it is possible to shed light on some perennial confusions which arise whenever Christianity is misunderstood as a teaching *sub specie aeternitatis*. As Kierkegaard put it, the object of the student is not the teacher but the teaching, while the object of the Christian is not the teaching but the

teacher.° I say perennial because the misunderstanding by the Athenians of Saint Paul and the offense they took is not essentially different
from the misunderstanding of modern eclectics like Whitehead, Huxley,
and Toynbee, and the offense they take. Not being an apostle and, as
Kierkegaard again would say, having no authority to preach, I should
hope not to give further offense and to propose only a small clarifying
distinction—not a piece of news in the bottle but only a minor "scientific" sentence—which should offend neither believer nor unbeliever.
Whitehead, for one, should not take offense. He pronounced that gen-
erality is the salt of religion just as it is the salt of science. And if one
should propose therefore that Christianity is not a teaching but a
teacher, not a piece of knowledge *sub specie aeternitatis* but a piece
of news, not a member in good standing of the World's Great Religions
but a unique Person-Event-Thing in time—then the eclectic should not
mind, because to say this is hardly to advance the case of Christianity
in his eyes; it is rather to admit the worst that he has suspected all
along. I do not mean that a mistaking of the Judeo-Christian Thing for
a piece of knowledge *sub specie aeternitatis* leads always to hostility
and rejection. Indeed it is more common nowadays to accept Christianity on such grounds—as being confirmed by Buddhism in this
respect or by psychiatry in some other respect—or as in the case of the
Look magazine article which announced that one might now believe in
miracles because the Law of Probability allowed that once in a great
while a body might fly straight up instead of falling down.

We might then be content here to agree to disagree about what salt
is and whether or not in becoming general it loses its savor. Nevertheless the peculiar character of the Christian claim, its staking everything
on a people, a person, an event, a thing existing here and now in time—
and on the news of this Thing—and its relative indifference to esoteric
philosophical truths such as might be arrived at by Vedantists, Bud-
dhists, idealists, existentialists, or by any islanders anywhere or at any
time—might serve here to quicken our interest in news as a category
of communication.

But to return to the castaway and the message in the bottle. The
castaway has, we have seen, classified the messages differently from
the scientist and logician. Their classifications would divide the sentences accordingly as they were analytic or synthetic, necessary or contingent, repeatable or historic, etc. But the castaway's classification
divides them accordingly as some express a knowledge which can be
arrived at anywhere and at any time, given the talent, time, and incli-

---

° Although primarily a teacher, a Person, Christianity, of course, involves
a teaching too.

nation of the student—and as others tell pieces of news which cannot be so arrived at by any effort of observation or reflection however strenuous and yet which are of immense importance to the hearer. Has the castaway's classification exhausted the significant communications which the bottles contain? If this is the case, then we seem to be saying that the news which the islander finds significant is nothing more than signs of various need-satisfactions which the organism must take account of to flourish. These needs and their satisfactions are readily acknowledged by the objective-minded man. Indeed, the main concern of the biological, medical, and psychological sciences is the discovery of these various needs and the satisfying of them. If a man is thirsty, then he had better pay attention to news of water. If a culture is to survive, it had better heed the news of the approach of the British or a war party from a neighboring island. Also, if a man is to live a rich, full, "rewarding" life, he should have his quota of myths and archetypes.

Are we saying in short that the predicament which the islander finds himself in and the means he takes to get out of it are those very needs and drives and those very satisfactions and goals which the objective-minded man recognizes and seeks to provide for every island everywhere? It is not quite so simple. For we have forgotten who it is we are talking about. As we noted earlier, the significance of news depends not only on the news but on the hearer, who he is and what his predicament is.

Our subject is not only an organism and a culture member; he is also a castaway. That is to say, he is not in the world as a swallow is in the world, as an organism which is what it is, never more or less. Our islander may choose his mode of being. Thus, he may choose to exist as a scientist, outside and over against the world as its knower, or he may choose to exist as a culture member, that is, an organism whose biological and psychological needs are more or less satisfied by his culture. But however he chooses to exist, he is in the last analysis a castaway, a stranger who is in the world but who is not at home in the world.

A castaway, everyone would agree, would do well to pay attention to knowledge and news, knowledge of the nature of the world and news of events that are relevant to his life on the island. Such news, the news relevant to his survival as an organism, his life as a father and husband, as a member of a culture, as an economic man, and so on—we can well call *island news*. Such news is relevant to the everyday life of any islander on any island at any time.

Yet even so all is not well with him. Something is wrong. For with all the knowledge he achieves, all his art and philosophy, all the island news he pays attention to, something is missing. What is it? He does not know. He might say that he was homesick except that the island is his home and he has spent his life making himself at home there. He knows only that his sickness cannot be cured by island knowledge or by island news.

But how does he know he is sick, let alone homesick? He may not know. He may live and die as an islander at home on his island. But if he does know, he knows for the simple reason that in his heart of hearts he can never forget who he is: that he is a stranger, a castaway, who despite a lifetime of striving to be at home on the island is as homeless now as he was the first day he found himself cast up on the beach.

But then do you mean that his homesickness is one final need to be satisfied, that the island news has taken care of 95 percent of his needs and that there remains one last little need to be taken care of—these occasional twinges of nostalgia? Or, as the church advertisements would say, one must have a "church home" besides one's regular home? No, it is much worse than that. I mean that in his heart of hearts there is not a moment of his life when the castaway does not know that life on the island, being "at home" on the island, is something of a charade. At that very moment when he should feel most at home on the island, when needs are satisfied, knowledge arrived at, family raised, business attended to, at that very moment when by every criterion of island at-homeness he should feel most at home, he feels most homeless. Not one moment of his life passes but that he is aware, however faintly, of his own predicament: that he is a castaway.

Nor would it avail to say to him simply that he is homesick and that all he needs is to know who he is and where he came from. He would only shake his head and turn away. For he knows nothing of any native land except the island and such talk anyhow reminds him of Sunday school. But if we say to him only that something is very wrong and that after fifty years on the island he is still a stranger and a castaway, he must listen, for he knows this better than anyone else.

Then what should he do? It is not for me to say here that he do this or that or should believe such and such. But one thing is certain. He should be what he is and not pretend to be somebody else. He should be a castaway and not pretend to be at home on the island. To be a castaway is to be in a grave predicament and this is not a happy state of affairs. But it is very much happier than being a castaway and pretending one is not. This is despair. The worst of all despairs is to imagine one is at home when one is really homeless.

But what is it to be a castaway? To be a castaway is to search for news from across the seas. Does this mean that one throws over science, throws over art, pays no attention to island news, forgets to eat and sleep and love—does nothing in fact but comb the beach in search of the bottle with the news from across the seas? No, but it means that one searches nevertheless and that one lives in hope that such a message will come, and that one knows that the message will not be a piece of knowledge or a piece of island news but news from across the seas.

It is news, however, this news from across the seas, and it is as a piece of news that it must be evaluated. Faith is the organ of the historical, said Kierkegaard. Faith of a sort is the organ for dealing with island news, and faith of a sort is the organ for dealing with news from across the seas.

But what does it mean to say that faith is the organ of the historical? For Kierkegaard it means two things. For an ordinary historical truth —what we here call "island news"—faith is the organ of the historical because the organ of the historical must have a structure analogous to the historical. The nature of the historical is becoming. The nature of belief is a "negated uncertainty which corresponds to the uncertainty of becoming." By historical Kierkegaard means the existing thing or event, not only that which existed in the past, but that which exists here and now before our very eyes. One sees that star rightly enough, but one must also confirm by another act that the star has come into existence. Faith is the organ which confirms that an existing thing has come into existence.° The Christian faith, however—the news from across the seas—is an embrace of the Absolute Paradox as such, a setting aside of reason, a *credo quia absurdum est.* It is well known that Kierkegaard, unlike Saint Thomas, denies a cognitive content to faith— faith is not a form of knowledge. His extreme position is at least in part attributable to his anxiety to rescue Christianity from the embrace of the Hegelians.

Yet we must ask whether Kierkegaard's antinomy of faith versus reason is any more appropriate to the situation of the castaway than the logician's classification of synthetic and analytic. For the castaway, or anyone who finds himself in a predicament in the world, there are two kinds of knowledge, knowledge *sub specie aeternitatis* and news bearing on his own predicament. The classification of the castaway would correspond roughly to the two knowledges of Saint Thomas: (1) scientific knowledge, in which assent is achieved by reason, (2) knowledge of faith, in which scientific knowledge and assent are undertaken simultaneously. The fact is that Kierkegaard, despite his passionate dialectic, laid himself open to his enemies. For his categories

---

° A similar distinction is made by Newman between real assent and notional assent.

of faith, inwardness, subjectivity, and Absolute Paradox seem to the objective-minded man to confirm the worst of what he had thought all along of the Christian news.

To Kierkegaard the Absolute Paradox was that one's eternal happiness should depend on a piece of news from across the seas. He still remained Hegelian enough ("scientist" enough in our terminology) to accept the scientific scale of significance which ranks general knowledge *sub specie aeternitatis* very high and contingent historical knowledge very low. Yet the curious fact is that the philosophical movement of which he has been called the founder has developed an anthropology, a view of man, which is very much more receptive to such news than Kierkegaard ever allowed one could be—*even though this movement has in most cases disavowed the Christian setting Kierkegaard gave it.* The Jasperian notion of shipwrecked man, Heidegger's notion of man's existence as a *Geworfenheit,* the state of being a castaway, allows the possibility of such news as a significant category of communication, as indeed the most significant.

To put it briefly: When Kierkegaard declares that the deliverance of the castaway by a piece of news from across the seas rather than by philosophical knowledge is the Absolute Paradox, one wonders simply how the castaway could be delivered any other way. *It is this news and this news alone that he has been waiting for.* Christianity cannot appear otherwise than as the Absolute Paradox once one has awarded total competence to knowledge *sub specie aeternitatis,* once one has disallowed the cognitive content of news as a category of communication.

The stumbling block to the scientist-philosopher-artist on the island is that salvation comes by hearing, by a piece of news, and not through knowledge *sub specie aeternitatis.* But scandalized or not, he might at least realize that it could not be otherwise. For no knowledge which can be gained on the island, on any island anywhere at any time, can be relevant to his predicament as a castaway. The castaway is he who waits for news from across the seas.

It is interesting to see what criteria of acceptance Kierkegaard does allow to faith. Clearly he removes faith from the sphere of knowledge and science in any sense of these words. Is it not then simply a matter of God's gift, a miraculous favor which allows one to embrace the Absolute Paradox and believe the impossible? No, there is more to be said. Kierkegaard recognizes that a category of communication is involved. Faith comes from God, but it also comes by hearing. It is a piece of news and there is a newsbearer. But why should we believe the newsbearer, the apostle? Must the apostle first prove his case to the scientist in the seminar room? No, because this would mean that God and the apostle must wait in the porter's lodge while the learned upstairs settle the matter.

Why then do we believe the apostle? We believe him because he has the authority to deliver the message. The communication of the genius (the scientific message in the bottle) is in the sphere of immanence. "A genius may be a century ahead of his time and therefore appear to be a paradox but ultimately the race will assimilate what was once a paradox in such a way that it is no longer a paradox." Given time, knowledge may be arrived at independently on any island. It is otherwise with the apostle. His message is in the sphere of transcendence and is therefore paradoxical. It cannot be arrived at by any effort and not even eternity can mediate it.

How then may we recognize the divine authority of the apostle? What, in other words, are the credentials of the newsbearer? The credential of the apostle is simply the gravity of his message: "I am called by God; do with me what you will, scourge me, persecute me, but my last words are my first; I am called by God and I make you eternally responsible for what you do against me."

Kierkegaard recognized the unique character of the Christian gospel but, rather than see it as a piece of bona fide news delivered by a newsbearer, albeit news of divine origin delivered by one with credentials of divine origin, he felt obliged to set it over against knowledge as paradox. Yet to the castaway who becomes a Christian, it is not paradox but news from across the seas, the very news he has been waiting for.

Kierkegaard, of all people, overlooked a major canon of significance of the news from across the seas—the most "Kierkegaardian" canon. One canon has to do with the news and the newsbearer, the nature of the news, and the credentials of the newsbearer. But the other canon has to do with the hearer of the news. Who is the hearer when all is said and done? Kierkegaard may have turned his dialectic against the Hegelian system, but he continued to appraise the gospel from the posture of the Hegelian scientist—and pronounced it absurd that a man's eternal happiness should depend not on knowledge *sub specie aeternitatis* but on a piece of news from across the seas. But neither the Hegelian nor any other objective-minded man is a hearer of news. For he has struck a posture and removed himself from all predicaments for which news might be relevant. Who is the hearer? The hearer is the castaway, not the man in the seminar, but the man who finds himself cast into the world. For whom is the news not news? It is not news to a swallow, for a swallow is what it is, no more and no less; it is at home in the world and no castaway. It is not news to unfallen man because he too is at home in the world and no castaway. It is not news to a fallen man who is a castaway but believes himself to be at home in the world, for he does not recognize his own predicament. It is only news to a castaway who knows himself to be a castaway.

Once it is granted that Christianity is the Absolute Paradox, then, according to Kierkegaard, the message in the bottle is all that is needed. It is enough to read "this little advertisement, this *nota bene* on a page of universal history—'We have believed that in such and such a year God appeared among us in the humble figure of a servant, that he lived and taught in our community, and finally died.' "

But the message in the bottle is not enough—if the message conveys news and not knowledge *sub specie aeternitatis*. There must be, as Kierkegaard himself saw later, someone who delivers the news and who speaks with authority.

Is this someone then anyone who rings the doorbell and says "Come!" No indeed, for in these times everyone is an apostle of sorts, ringing doorbells and bidding his neighbor to believe this and do that. In such times, when everyone is saying "Come!" when radio and television say nothing else but "Come!" it may be that the best way to say "Come!" is to remain silent. Sometimes silence itself is a "Come!"

Since everyone is saying "Come!" now in the fashion of apostles— Communists and Jehovah's Witnesses as well as advertisers – the uniqueness of the original "Come!" from across the seas is apt to be overlooked. The apostolic character of Christianity is unique among religions. No one else has ever left or will ever leave his island to say "Come!" to other islanders for reasons which have nothing to do with the dissemination of knowledge *sub specie aeternitatis* and nothing to do with his own needs. The Communist is disseminating what he believes to be knowledge *sub specie aeternitatis*—and so is the Rockefeller scientist. The Jehovah's Witness and the Holy Roller are bearing island news to make themselves and other islanders happy. But what if a man receives the commission to bring news across the seas to the castaway and does so in perfect sobriety and with good faith and perseverance to the point of martyrdom? And what if the news the newsbearer bears is the very news the castaway had been waiting for, news of where he came from and who he is and what he must do, and what if the newsbearer brought with him the means by which the castaway may do what he must do? Well then, the castaway will, by the grace of God, believe him.

THE DOCUMENTS OF VATICAN II

When the Second Vatican Council opened in 1962 many wondered how long it would take the Council Fathers to begin publishing documents that had been planned after years of labor by preparatory commissions of theologians, historians, and liturgists. The first collection of Vatican II documents was not promulgated until 1963, and further "constitutions," or major statements, continued to pour out of the Vatican until the last, *Gaudium et Spes,* the *Constitution on the Church in the Modern World* of December 7, 1965.

The paragraphs of *Gaudium et Spes* reproduced here are some of the most pastoral products of the Vatican Council. They present the kernel of modern Christian humanism. Key themes are Christ, the Light of the World, and Church, Servant of the People. The words *Gaudium et Spes* look to compassionate dialogue with modern men and women, to peace, to social justice, to whatever concerns the dignity and unity of humankind. The message is one of awareness of the world's problems and a strong desire to help. The constitution emphasizes the Christian quest for a community of peoples, the motivation that comes from Christ's love, and the need for cooperation, among all men of good will.

Gaudium et Spes was literally released to all of humanity. That very fact made it a remarkable first among Vatican documents and a landmark of Christian humanism.

From Vatican II, **The Church in the Modern World**
THE SITUATION OF MAN IN THE WORLD TODAY
Man's Deeper Questionings

The dichotomy affecting the modern world is, in fact, a symptom of the deeper dichotomy that is in man himself. He is the meeting point of many conflicting forces. In his condition as a created being he is subject to a thousand shortcomings, but feels untrammeled in his inclinations and destined for a higher form of life. Torn by a welter of anxieties he is compelled to choose between them and repudiate some among them. Worse still, feeble and sinful as he is, he often does the very thing he hates and does not do what he wants. And so he feels himself divided, and the result is a host of discords in social life. Many, it is true, fail to see the dramatic nature of this state of affairs in all its clarity for their vision is in fact blurred by materialism, or they are prevented from even thinking about it by the wretchedness of their plight. Others delude themselves that they have found peace in a world-view now fashionable. There are still others whose hopes are set on a genuine and total emancipation of mankind through human effort alone and look forward to some future earthly paradise where all the desires of their hearts will be fulfilled. Nor is it unusual to find people who having lost faith in life extol the kind of foolhardiness which would empty life of all significance in itself and invest it with a meaning of their own devising. Nonetheless, in the face of modern developments there is a growing body of men who are asking the most fundamental of all questions or are glimpsing them with a keener insight: What is man? What is the meaning of suffering, evil, death, which have not been eliminated by all this progress? What is the purpose of these achievements, purchased at so high a price? What can man contribute to society? What can he expect from it? What happens after this earthly life is ended?

The Church believes that Christ, who died and was raised for the sake of all, can show man the way and strengthen him through the Spirit in order to be worthy of his destiny: nor is there any other name under heaven given among men by which they can be saved. The Church likewise believes that the key, the center and the purpose of the whole of man's history is to be found in its Lord and Master. She also maintains that beneath all that changes there is much that is unchanging, much that has its ultimate foundation in Christ, who is the same yesterday, and today, and forever. And that is why the Council, relying on the inspiration of Christ, the image of the invisible God, the firstborn of all creation, proposes to speak to all men in order to unfold the mystery that is man and cooperate in tackling the main problems facing the world today.

THE DIGNITY OF THE HUMAN PERSON

Man as the Image of God

Believers and unbelievers agree almost unanimously that all things on earth should be ordained to man as to their center and summit.

But what is man? He has put forward, and continues to put forward, many views about himself, views that are divergent and even contradictory. Often he either sets himself up as the absolute measure of all things, or debases himself to the point of despair. Hence his doubt and his anguish. The Church is keenly sensitive to these difficulties. Enlightened by divine revelation she can offer a solution to them by which the true state of man may be outlined, his weakness explained, in such a way that at the same time his dignity and his vocation may be perceived in their true light. . . .

The Essential Nature of Man

Man, though made of body and soul, is a unity. Through his very bodily condition he sums up in himself the elements of the material world. Through him they are thus brought to their highest perfection and can raise their voice in praise freely given to the creator. For this reason man may not despise his bodily life. Rather he is obliged to regard his body as good and hold it in honor since God has created it and will raise it up on the last day. Nevertheless man has been wounded by sin. He finds by experience that his body is in revolt. His very dignity therefore requires that he should glorify God in his body, and not allow it to serve the evil inclinations of his heart.

Man is not deceived when he regards himself as superior to bodily things and as more than just a speck of nature or a nameless unit in the city of man. For by his power to know himself in the depths of his being he rises above the whole universe of mere objects. When he is drawn to think about his real self he turns to those deep recesses of his being where God who probes the heart awaits him, and where he himself decides his own destiny in the sight of God. So when he recognizes in himself a spiritual and immortal soul, he is not being led astray by false imaginings that are due to merely physical or social causes. On the contrary, he grasps what is profoundly true in this matter.

The Excellence of Freedom

It is, however, only in freedom that man can turn himself towards what is good. The people of our time prize freedom very highly and strive eagerly for it. In this they are right. Yet they often cherish it improperly, as if it gave them leave to do anything they like, even when it is evil. But that which is truly freedom is an exceptional sign of the image of God in man. For God willed that man should "be left in the hand of his own counsel" so that he might of his own accord seek his creator and freely attain his full and blessed perfection by cleaving to him. Man's dignity therefore requires him to act out of conscious and free choice, as moved and drawn in a personal way from within, and not by blind impulses in himself or by mere external constraint. Man gains such dignity when, ridding himself of all slavery to the passions, he presses forward towards his goal by freely choosing what is good, and, by his diligence and skill, effectively secures for himself the means suited to this end. Since human freedom has been weakened by sin it is only by the help of God's grace that man can give his actions their full and proper relationship to God. Before the judgment seat of God an account of his own life will be rendered to each one according as he has done either good or evil.

Christ the New Man

In reality it is only in the mystery of the Word made flesh that the mystery of man truly becomes clear. For Adam, the first man, was a type of him who was to come, Christ the Lord, Christ the new Adam, in the very revelation of the mystery of the Father and of his love, fully reveals man to himself and brings to light his most high calling. It is no wonder, then, that all the truths mentioned so far should find in him their source and their most perfect embodiment.

He who is the "image of the invisible God" (Col. 1:15), is himself the perfect man who has restored in the children of Adam that likeness to God which had been disfigured ever since the first sin. Human nature, by the very fact that it was assumed, not absorbed, in him, has been raised in us also to a dignity beyond compare. For, by his incarnation, he, the son of God, has in a certain way united himself with each man. He worked with human hands, he thought with a human mind. He acted with a human will, and with a human heart he loved. Born of the Virgin Mary, he has truly been made one of us, like to us in all things except sin. . . .

THE COMMUNITY OF MANKIND

Need to Transcend an Individualistic Morality

The pace of change is so far-reaching and rapid nowadays that no one can allow himself to close his eyes to the course of events or indifferently ignore them and wallow in the luxury of a merely individualistic morality. The best way to fulfil one's obligations of justice and love is to contribute to the common good according to one's means and the needs of others, even to the point of fostering and helping public and private organizations devoted to bettering the conditions of life. There is a kind of person who boasts of grand and noble sentiments and lives in practice as if he could not care less about the needs of society. There are many in various countries who make light of social laws and directives and are not ashamed to resort to fraud and cheating to avoid paying just taxes and fulfilling other social obligations. There are others who neglect the norms of social conduct, such as those regulating public hygiene and speed limits, forgetting that they are endangering their own lives and the lives of others by their carelessness.

Let everyone consider it his sacred duty to count social obligations among man's chief duties today and observe them as such. For the more closely the world comes together, the most widely do men's obligations transcend particular groups and gradually extend to the whole world. This will be realized only if individuals and groups practice moral and social values and foster them in social living. Then, under the necessary help of divine grace, there will arise a generation of new men, the molders of a new humanity.

The Word Made Flesh and Human Solidarity

Just as God did not create men to live as individuals but to come together in the formation of social unity, so he "willed to make men holy and save them, not as individuals without any bond or link between them, but rather to make them into a people who might acknowledge him and serve him in holiness." At the outset of salvation history he chose certain men as members of a given community, not as individuals, and revealed his plan to them, calling them "his people" (Ex. 3:7-12) and making a covenant on Mount Sinai with them.

This communitarian character is perfected and fulfilled in the work of Jesus Christ, for the Word made flesh willed to share in human fellowship. He was present at the wedding feast at Cana, he visited the house of Zacchaeus, he sat down with publicans and sinners. In revealing the Father's love and man's sublime calling he made use of the most ordinary things of social life and illustrated his words with expression and imagery from everyday life. He sanctified those human ties, above all family ties, which are the basis of social structures. He willingly observed the laws of his country and chose to lead the life of an ordinary craftsman of his time and place. . . .

MAN'S ACTIVITY IN THE UNIVERSE
What the Church Offers to Individuals

Modern Man is in a process of fuller personality development and of a growing discovery and affirmation of his own rights. But the Church is entrusted with the task of opening up to man the mystery of God, who is the last end of man; in doing so it opens up to him the meaning of his own existence, the innermost truth about himself. The Church knows well that God alone, whom it serves, can satisfy the deepest cravings of the human heart, for the world and what it has to offer can never fully content it. It also realizes that man is continually being aroused by the Spirit of God and that he will never be utterly indifferent to religion—a fact confirmed by the experience of ages past and plentiful evidence at the present day. For man will ever be anxious to know, if only in a vague way, what is the meaning of his life, his activity, and his death. The very presence of the

Church recalls these problems to his mind. The most perfect answer to these questionings is to be found in God alone, who created man in his own image and redeemed him from sin; and this answer is given in the revelation in Christ his Son who became man. Whoever follows Christ the perfect man becomes himself more a man.

Relying on this faith the Church can raise the dignity of human nature above all fluctuating opinions which, for example, would unduly despise or idolize the human body. There is no human law so powerful to safeguard the personal dignity and freedom of man as the Gospel which Christ entrusted to the Church; for the Gospel announces and proclaims the freedom of the sons of God, it rejects all bondage resulting from sin, it scrupulously respects the dignity of conscience and its freedom of choice, it never ceases to encourage the employment of human talents in the service of God and man, and, finally, it commends everyone to the charity of all. This is nothing other than the basic law of the Christian scheme of things. The fact that it is the same God who is at once saviour and creator, Lord of human history and of the history of salvation, does not mean that the autonomy of the creature, of man in particular, is suppressed; on the contrary, in the divine order of things all this redounds to the restoration and consolidation of this autonomy.

In virtue of the Gospel entrusted to it the Church proclaims the rights of man: she acknowledges and holds in high esteem the dynamic approach of today which is fostering these rights all over the world. But this approach needs to be animated by the spirit of the Gospel and preserved from all traces of false autonomy. For there is a temptation to feel that our personal rights are fully maintained only when we are exempt from every restriction of divine law. But this is the way leading to the extinction of human dignity, not its preservation.

What the Church Offers to Society

The union of the family of man is greatly consolidated and perfected by the unity which Christ established among the sons of God.

Christ did not bequeath to the Church a mission in the political, economic, or social order: the purpose he assigned to it was a religious one. But this religious mission can be the source of commitment, direction, and vigor to establish and consolidate the community of men according to the law of God. In fact, the Church is able, indeed it is obliged, if times and circumstances require it, to initiate action for the benefit of all men, especially of those in need, like works of mercy and similar undertakings.

The Church, moreover, acknowledges the good to be found in the social dynamism of today, particularly progress towards unity, healthy socialization, and civil and economic cooperation. The encouragement of unity is in harmony with the deepest nature of the Church's mission, for it "is in the nature of a sacrament—a sign and instrument —that is of communion with God and of unity among all men." It shows to the world that social and exterior union comes from a union of hearts and minds, from the faith and love by which its own indissoluble unity has been founded in the Holy Spirit. The impact which the Church can have on modern society amounts to an effective living of faith and love, not to any external power exercised by purely human means.

By its nature and mission the Church is universal in that it is not committed to any one culture or to any political, economic or social system. Hence it can form a very close unifying effort on the various communities of men and nations, provided they have trust in the Church and guarantee it true freedom to carry out its mission. With this in view the Church calls upon its members and upon all men to put aside, in the family spirit of the children of God, all conflict between nations and races and to consolidate legitimate human organizations in themselves.

PROPER DEVELOPMENT OF CULTURE

Faith and Culture

In their pilgrimage to the heavenly city Christians are to seek and relish the things that are above: this involves not a lesser, but rather a greater commitment to working with all men towards the establishment of a world that is more human. Indeed, the mystery of the Christian faith provides them with an outstanding incentive and encouragement to fulfil their role even more eagerly and to discover the full sense of the commitment by which human culture becomes important in man's total vocation.

By the work of his hands and with the aid of technical means man tills the earth to bring forth fruit and to make it a dwelling place fit for all mankind; he also consciously plays his part in the life of social groups; in so doing he is realizing the design, which God revealed at the beginning of time, to subdue the earth and perfect the work of creation, and at the same time he is improving his own person: he is also observing the command of Christ to devote himself to the service of his fellow men.

Furthermore, when man works in the fields of philosophy, history, mathematics and science and cultivates the arts, he can greatly contribute towards bringing the human race to a higher understanding of truth, goodness, and beauty, to points of view having universal value; thus man will be more clearly enlightened by the wondrous Wisdom, which was with God from eternity, working beside him like a mastercraftsman, rejoicing in his inhabited world, and delighting in the sons of men. As a consequence the human spirit, freed from the bondage of material things, can be more easily drawn to the worship and contemplation of the creator. Moreover, man is disposed to acknowledge, under the impulse of grace, the Word of God, who was in the world as "the true light that enlightens every man" (Jn. 1:9), before becoming flesh to save and gather up all things in himself.

There is no doubt that modern scientific and technical progress can lead to a certain phenomenism or agnosticism; this happens when scientific methods of investigation which of themselves are incapable of penetrating to the deepest nature of things, are unjustifiably taken as the supreme norm for arriving at truth. There is a further danger that in his excessive confidence in modern inventions man may think he is sufficient unto himself and give up the search for higher values.

But these drawbacks are not necessarily due to modern culture and they should not tempt us to overlook its positive values. Among these values we would like to draw attention to the following: study of the sciences and exact fidelity to truth in scientific investigation, the necessity of teamwork in technology, the sense of international solidarity, a growing awareness of the expert's responsibility to help and defend his fellow men, and an eagerness to improve the standard of living for all men, especially of those who are deprived of responsibility or suffer from cultural destitution. All these can afford a certain kind of preparation for the acceptance of the message of the Gospel and can be infused with divine charity by him who came to save the world.

ECONOMIC AND SOCIAL LIFE

An End to Excessive Economic and Social Differences

To fulfil the requirements of justice and equity, every effort must be made to put an end as soon as possible to the immense economic inequalities which exist in the world and increase from day to day, linked with individual and social discrimination, provided, of course, that the rights of individuals and the character of each people are not disturbed. Likewise in many areas, in view of the special difficulties of production and marketing in agriculture, country people must be helped to improve methods of production and marketing, to introduce necessary developments and renewal, and to achieve a fair return for their products, lest they continue, as often happens, in the state of inferior citizens. Farmers themselves, especially young farmers, ought to apply themselves eagerly to bettering their professional skill, without which the advancement of farming is impossible.

Justice and equity also demand that the livelihood of individuals and their families should not become insecure and precarious through a kind of mobility which is a necessary feature of developing economies. All kinds of discrimination in wages and working conditions should be avoided in regard to workers who come from other countries or areas and contribute their work to the economic development of a people or a region. Furthermore, no one, especially public authorities, should treat them simply as mere tools of production, but as persons; they should facilitate them in having their families with them and in obtaining decent housing conditions, and they should endeavor to integrate them into the social life of the country or area to which they have come. However, employment should be found for them so far as possible in their own countries.

Nowadays when the economy is undergoing transition, as in new forms of industrialization, where, for example, automation is being introduced, care must be taken to ensure that there is sufficient and suitable employment available; opportunities of appropriate technical and professional training should be provided, and safeguards should be placed so that the livelihood and human dignity should be protected of those who through age or ill health labor under serious disadvantages.

Work, Working Conditions, Leisure

Human work which is exercised in the production and exchange of goods or in the provision of economic services, surpasses all other elements of economic life, for the latter are only means to an end.

Human work, whether exercised independently or in subordination to another, proceeds from the human person, who as it were impresses his seal on the things of nature and reduces them to his will. By his work a man ordinarily provides for himself and his family, associates with others as his brothers, and renders them service; he can exercise genuine charity and be a partner in the work of bringing divine creation to perfection. Moreover, we believe by faith that through the homage of work offered to God man is associated with the redemptive work of Jesus Christ, whose labor with his hands at

Nazareth greatly ennobled the dignity of work. This is the source of every man's duty to work loyally as well as his right to work; moreover, it is the duty of society to see to it that, according to the prevailing circumstances, all citizens have the opportunity of finding employment. Finally, remuneration for work should guarantee man the opportunity to provide a dignified livelihood for himself and his family on the material, social, cultural and spiritual level to correspond to the role and the productivity of each, the relevant economic factors in his employment, and the common good.

Since economic activity is, for the most part, the fruit of the collaboration of many men, it is unjust and inhuman to organize and direct it in such a way that some of the workers are exploited. But it frequently happens, even today, that workers are almost enslaved by the work they do. So-called laws of economics are no excuse for this kind of thing. The entire process of productive work, then, must be accommodated to the needs of the human person and the right of his life, with special attention to domestic life and of mothers of families in particular, taking sex and age always into account. Workers should have the opportunity to develop their talents and their personalities in the very exercise of their work. While devoting their time and energy to the performance of their work with a due sense of responsibility, they should nevertheless be allowed sufficient rest and leisure to cultivate their family, cultural, social and religious life. And they should be given the opportunity to develop those energies and talents, which perhaps are not catered for in their professional work.

CONCLUSION

A World to Be Built Up and Brought to Fulfillment

Mindful of the words of the Lord: "By this all men will know that you are my disciples, if you have love for one another" (Jn. 13:35), Christians can yearn for nothing more ardently than to serve the men of this age with ever growing generosity and success. Holding loyally to the Gospel, enriched by its resources, and joining forces with all who love and practice justice, they have shouldered a weighty task here on earth and they must render an account of it to him who will judge all men on the last day. Not everyone who says "Lord, Lord," will enter the kingdom of heaven, but those who do the will of the Father, and who manfully put their hands to the work. It is the Father's will that we should recognize Christ our brother in the persons of all men and love them with an effective love, in word and deed, thus bearing witness to the truth; and it is his will that we should share with others the mystery of his heavenly love. In this way men all over the world will awaken to a lively hope (the gift of the Holy Spirit) that they will one day be admitted to the haven of surpassing peace and happiness in their homeland radiant with the glory of the Lord. . . .

Epilogue

Human Liberation and Limits

In the 1970s and 1980s, when limitations of many kinds drew attention to the international and national economy, it was easy to overlook the human revolutions of the recent past. Human liberation and limits are properly seen as interconnected, but from the standpoint of Christian humanism the struggle for humanity is primary and of more lasting significance. Limits are not a new fact in human experience; they have been the norm for most people through most of human history. To the affluent, accustomed to plenty as the norm, limits may seem to pose a new problem. Perhaps the revolution yet to come, already experienced by some, will be the discovery by the comfortable and well-fed of the world that quality of life can be deepened in the midst of restraints and limits.

The latter part of the twentieth century has been characterized by significant movements of human liberation. The readings that follow reflect the nature of several of these. In 1962 Barbara Ward (Lady Jackson), an early leader in the analysis of world poverty and economics, wrote about the rich nations and the poor nations. In a chapter entitled "Not by Bread Alone" she hails the revolutions going on in the world but notes with regret that the Western world has buried, instead of used, the greatest revolution of all, that of freedom.

In his famous letter from the Birmingham city jail in 1963, Martin Luther King Jr., explains why direct, nonviolent action against segregation was necessary, how he understands the citizen's responsibility toward the laws, and why he was disappointed by the responses of the white moderates and the white church. The letter movingly portrays the struggle for liberation from racial prejudice.

Women's liberation is the concern of Monika Hellwig in "Hope and Liberation." Unlike some feminists who regard the Christian tradition as fundamentally sexist and beyond reform, Ms. Hellwig argues for a change of consciousness, a new humanization, within Christian theology and ethics.

Liberation in concrete terms of political and economic change, undergirded by a fresh perception of Christ as the liberator from hunger and

627

oppression, is the message of Latin American liberation theology, represented by selections from an important book by Gustavo Gutiérrez, *A Theology of Liberation*. Like King and Hellwig, Gutiérrez is keenly aware that the needed changes in the social order are not merely external adjustments but transformations of the human participants themselves. The Christian life, he writes, is a passover, "a transition from sin to grace, . . . from the subhuman to the human."

E. F. Schumacher, British economist, coined a valuable, if not entirely original humanistic phrase in the title of his book, *Small Is Beautiful*. The excerpts from this 1973 publication question the profit orientation of modern economic theory and apply the four cardinal virtues to a world faced with limitations of resources. An organization called "Bread for the World" has issued a policy statement, "The Right to Food," in which it outlines specific steps which the United States government ought to take to alleviate world hunger. The language and motivation of the statement are explicitly Christian: "By creating us and redeeming us through Jesus Christ, he [God] has given us a love that will not turn aside from those who lack daily bread. The human wholeness of all of us . . . is at stake."

In the final selection, theologian Langdon Gilkey comments on the religious dilemmas of a scientific culture. In freeing persons from natural fates, technology seems to have subjected them to "a new kind of social and historical fate." Technology must be complemented by the religious dimension of human beings. "From religion alone has traditionally come the concern with the human that can prevent the manipulation of men and the dehumanization of society." Such a religion, which is inclusive of the transcendent and also of nature and the human, must be related to history and to social existence.

This final set of readings, it will be seen, gives clear indication of the vitality of Christian humanistic thought in an era characterized by pressing human problems of enormous dimensions. Christian humanism is not a triumphalistic doctrine, but it is a significant witness to the truth in any period of human history. In the latter part of the twentieth century it presents itself as a living, compassionate perspective on humanity and the world with resources of faith and reason to be applied to the quest for human fulfilment.

BARBARA WARD

When Barbara Ward (1914-1981) died, National Public Radio honored her memory by broadcasting the address she gave at the United Nations Conference on the Human Environment held in Stockholm in June, 1972. In that speech she discussed three new ways in which people had begun to think about their planetary existence: by recognizing the risk of irreversible planetary damage to airs and oceans; by beginning to doubt the economics of growth and the "trickle-down" effects of capitalism when that economic system rewards the already affluent; by suspecting that the nationalistic approach to making the planet work is not adequate.

Barbara Ward (Lady Jackson), British economist, was Albert Schweitzer Professor of International Economic Development at Columbia University. She collaborated with René Dubos in writing *Only One Earth: The Care and Maintenance of a Small Planet* as a background document for the Stockholm Conference. Among her other writings are *Faith and Freedom, Five Ideas That Change the World, India and the West,* and *The Lopsided World.* Concerning *The Rich Nations and the Poor Nations* (1962), the book from which the following reading is taken, the late President Lyndon Johnson reportedly said, "I read it like I do the Bible" (*Newsweek,* June 15, 1981, p. 107).

The humanism of Barbara Ward was both practical and visionary. She looked squarely at the facts of revolution, poverty, hunger, modern science, global communication, and the threat of atomic devastation. But she did not lose her hope for "a community of moral purpose." Language and insight drawn from the New Testament inform her comments on using material things to serve the needs of humankind. She sees science as a means of liberty, but for liberty to be realized requires economic changes and these, in turn, require that nations become aware of the moral dimensions of freedom. "Am I free if my brother is bound by hopeless poverty and ignorance?"

From Barbara Ward, **The Rich Nations and the Poor Nations**
NOT BY BREAD ALONE

We recognize the principles more or less inside our own domestic community. We do not have private wars. The rich do indeed contribute to the advancement of the poor. And while I am not concerned here with the whole great issue of world law and of disarmament, I am deeply concerned with the second aspect of good order: the ability of the rich to recognize their obligations and to see that in an interdependent world—and Heaven knows our interdependence cannot be denied when we all stand under the shadow of atomic destruction—the principles of the general welfare cannot stop at the limits of our frontiers. It has to go forward; it has to include the whole family of man.

And having said so much, I begin to wonder whether there are any forces inside our comfortable, cosy, complacent Western world that will make us accept this challenge and see that we now face thirty to forty years of world-building on a scale never known in human history, since all our forefathers lived without the community of science, the speed of transport, the whole interconnectedness of the modern globe. What will spur us to face this kind of decision? Facts? The facts are there. We cannot wish away the great revolution of modernization that is sweeping round the world; we cannot say it would be easier or more pleasant if it had not happened. Perhaps so; but we started the revolution and we can hardly ignore the forces that we unleashed upon the world.

Should we be guided by fear? Fear can indeed be the beginning of wisdom. Those who can live comfortably and without perturbation under the hideous threat of atomic destruction do not seem to me to be very wise. But blind fear is not a constructive force. Fear will serve us only if it drives us on to find a way out of our fears. And there is only one: to leave behind our present community of potential annihilation and build a community of moral purpose in its place. In such a world public law would take the place of private violence and the general welfare would be accepted over and above the particular interests of particular communities; above all, mankind would discover, beneath the clash of ideology, some minimum standards of trust rooted in the fact that we are all men, that we all stand under the judgment of history, and that we all love and seek to live and know that we must die.

It is just because the task before us is the positive task of building a peaceful home for the human family that I doubt whether realism or fear is enough to set us to work. We need resources of faith and vision as well. Do we have them? Or have the revolutions of our day, while increasing our physical powers, damped down the ardours of our spirit?

I do not believe it. Every one of the revolutions we have discussed goes beyond our material concerns and offers a challenge to the quality of our mind and spirit. The equality of men which is such a driving force all round the world sprang originally from the Western sense that men, as souls of infinite metaphysical value, stand equal before the throne of God. And if we feel this equality of man as a profound, moral fact, can we really be content to see men hungry, to see men die, to see men continue in starvation and ill-health when we have the means to help them? Is this our concept of equality? If it is, do we not betray our faith?

Then, again, our concern with worldly things is not mere materialism. It has in it an essential element of religious insight. God looked on his universe and found it good. The materials offered us in farm and factory can be set to work to create a community in which no one need starve or go naked and unhoused. We can 'redeem the time' by setting matter to work for the greater good of all our brothers, who are all mankind. The Christian God who bade His followers feed the hungry and heal the sick and took His parables from the homely round of daily work gave material things His benediction. It has not faded because material things are more abundant now.

Science itself—this vision of an orderly world in which matter does not respond to chaotic promptings but to some vast harmony of universal law—is in no way incompatible with a vision of moral order in which it can be the tool of a better life for all mankind. Science has removed us from the heaviest bondage of the past: the fact that material resources were always too scarce to match even the greatest goodwill. Only a hundred years ago, if we had wished to give covering, food, shelter, and a simple education to the mass of mankind, we could not have done so because our material means were not equal to the task. What science has done has been to set us free. It has delivered us from the bondage of our material poverty and opened a great area of choice where vision and will can operate because they have the physical means at hand.

Science understood in this sense, is indeed a means of liberty. Perhaps you have wondered why I have not mentioned freedom as the greatest revolution of our time. Quite frankly, the reason is that I am not sure whether it *is* one of the spreading revolutions of this century. There are times when I feel that, in our Western world, freedom rather resembles the Biblical talent that was put in a napkin and buried in the ground. We have it—but do we use it? On the issue of freedom, the revolution of equality does not necessarily imply freedom. All prisoners in a jail are equal. But they are not free. The revolution of science offers the means of freedom. But it can be used as well for making dictatorship more efficient and war more dire. And materialism, misunderstood as a false overconcern with the things of this world, a false worship of 'the idols of the market place and the idols of the tribe,' can create the reverse of true freedom if men and women become more and more entangled in their own clamant and unassuageable wants. Our revolutions will not do our work for us. They can yield us freedom or its opposite. The outcome depends on us, and I sometimes wonder whether we have made any very fundamental attempt to interpret the revolutions of our time in the light of freedom. Have we measured the margin of choice given us by our new capital resources, our new technology, our new ability to create the means of wealth? Have we understood that this liberty of action must be used? It cannot, it must not be left to rust with us. And given our ability to assist in the process of modernization, have we really grasped its relevance to the grand question of our time: whether the developing world society will be closed or open, slave or free?

After all, constitutional liberty is a sophisticated concept. Between Magna Charta and our present-day democracy there lie eight hundred years of experience and feeling our way. I am not a determinist. I do not believe that economic forces necessarily create political forms. On the contrary, I believe freedom to have been one of the innate formative ideas of our Western way of life. But equally I observe that its incorporation in concrete institutions did presuppose some economic and social changes. The emergence of a strong middle class after the Middle Ages helped to secure rights and liberties to a larger and larger group of articulate and responsible citizens. In the nineteenth century, the growth of wealth and the spread of literacy encouraged the extension of democratic privileges even further, and complete adult suffrage and complete adult literacy arrived at about the same time.

I think it is probably a safe assumption that something of the same pattern must be expected in emergent societies; though they need not wait so long since models of change already exist. A strong expanding professional and managerial class, a strong thrust of literacy, and the expanding resources both presuppose are almost certainly pre-conditions of political development in freedom. We are, I think, irrational when we suddenly expect those who emerge from primitive societies to seize our concepts of liberty intact, forgetting the long intervening history of our own experiments. If we are not to be disappointed, I think we must seek with new energy and commitment to fill in the historical gap. We need to be far more active in the way of economic aid, capital investment, and educational assistance. We need to work with far more purpose to create the framework of general literacy and personal responsibility. We need to be far more imaginative in showing that we regard the right of nations to govern themselves as only the first, essential, but preliminary, step in creating the conditions in which nations can be truly free. But the next step is equally vital: to give concrete substance to the experience of national liberty and not permit it to become a time of lessening opportunity and hope.

But I have the impression that when we talk so confidently of liberty, we are unaware of the awful servitudes that are created by the ancient enemies of mankind: the servitude of poverty when means are so small that there is literally no choice at all; the servitude of ignorance when there are no perspectives to which the mind can begin to work; the servitude of ill-health which means that the expectation of life is almost too short to allow for any experience of freedom, and the years that *are* lived are dragged out without the health and strength which are themselves a liberation.

Because we have interpreted freedom in too narrow a sense and assumed that people will find the outer form of freedom natural when none of its actual substantial content has been realized, there has been something empty about our advocacy of the free way of life. What is the free way of life to a tribal society which does not know whether it can eat next week? What is the free way of life to an ancient society where illiteracy bars most people from any of the benefits of freedom? What, above all, can freedom be said to mean when the nations who talk of it most incessantly seem to have so little awareness of its wider moral dimensions? Am I free if my brother is bound by hopeless poverty and ignorance? Am I a prophet of the free way of life if I reveal perfect indifference to the plight of the man who has 'fallen among thieves,' the man whom the good Samaritan helped while the others passed him by?

If we want to spread the revolution of liberty round the world to complete and reconcile the other great revolutions of our day, we have to re-examine its moral content and ask ourselves whether we are not leaving liberty as a wasted talent and allowing other forces, not friendly to liberty, to monopolize the great vision of men working in brotherhood to create a world in which all can live. But God is not mocked. We reap what we sow and if freedom for us is no more than the right to pursue our own self-interest—personal or national—then we can make no claim to the greatest vision of our society: 'the glorious liberty of the sons of God.' Without vision we, like other peoples, will perish. But if it is restored, it can be as it always has been the profoundest inspiration of our society, and can give our way of life its continuing strength.

MARTIN LUTHER KING JR.

Martin Luther King Jr. (1929-1968) has an honored place in America as one of its outstanding religious and social thinkers and activists. He can fairly be said to be responsible, more than any other single American, for at least the partial ending of racial segregation and for the passage of the Civil Rights Act of 1964. Born in Atlanta in 1929 in a minister's family, he grew up during a period when the black protest movement was reaching maturity and power but was divided. The militants advocated protest. The accommodators counseled resignation, hard work, service and sacrifice; the separatists urged creation of a black state; and the moderates sought a path between protest and accommodation in litigation and lobbying. King was instrumental in uniting most of these diverse wings of the movement into an effective force which awakened the American conscience to the vestiges of black enslavement remaining in America. He led the Montgomery bus boycott and the March on Washington and inspired "sit-ins" and "freedom rides." The federal government was galvanized into action in several ways.

King entered Morehouse College in Atlanta at the unprecedented age of 15 years. He decided on the ministry at 18 and in 1947 was ordained and made assistant pastor of his father's church. He took his theological education at Crozer Seminary in Philadelphia, and earned his doctorate at Boston University. He excelled as a scholar. During these years, he was inspired by the method of civil disobedience employed by Asa Philip Randolph in protest against the segregated U.S. Army. Of the two basic approaches to power, resistance or submission, King's concern for the masses led him to reject the submissiveness of the black middle class in which he was raised and to search for another method to eliminate the social evil of racism. He turned from the legal approach of the NAACP to the "third way" of reconciliation through nonviolent and civil disobedience, inspired by the teaching of Jesus and the example of Mahatma Gandhi, whose nonviolent movement had led to the liberation of India.

Intellectually and ethically, he was influenced strongly by the writings of Reinhold Niebuhr, Marx, the Existentialists (Sartre, Jaspers, and Heidegger), by the philosopher Hegel (from whose writings on the dialectical process of history he learned that progress comes only through conflict and suffering), and by Walter Rauschenbusch, from whom King took the idea that the church should take a direct, active part in the struggle for social justice. From Gandhi (who was inspired by Jesus and by Henry David Thoreau), he learned the tactic of nonviolent resistance and his philosophy of "war without violence" with the aim of reconciliation of the races. From Gandhi he also gained his key concept of "soul force"—the vindication of truth not by inflicting suffering on others but on one's self. He often quoted Gandhi's famous saying: "Rivers of blood may have to flow before we gain our freedom, but it must be our blood." This clearly reflects Jesus' way of redemptive suffering. In this way, and by his own oratorical gifts, King rallied his people and harnessed the deep and powerful reservoirs of spiritual energy in black people for the bitter struggle.

The opportunity came following King's completion of his doctoral study in Boston and during his first pastorate at the Dexter Avenue Baptist Church in Montgomery, Alabama. It was in Montgomery, the heart of the old Confederacy and of segregationism, that King was catapulted into national prominence and to the forefront of the black struggle for equal rights. He emerged as the leader of the 382-day Montgomery Bus Boycott, which was the first break in the stranglehold of "Jim Crow" laws that had kept blacks in an inferior status in the South for nearly 100 years after the Civil War. The story of the Montgomery struggle is told in his autobiographical *Stride Toward Freedom*. Here he evolved the unique spirit and tactics of nonviolent resistance to unjust laws, which evoked the hatred and violence of the whites who were entrenched in power. After the boycott broke the grip of segregation on city buses, and the city laws enforcing that practice were declared unconstitutional by the U.S. Supreme Court, King formed the Southern Christian Leadership Conference and went on to attack other segregationist laws and practices in the South, and *de facto* segregation in the North.

King was arrested several times, and it was during one such period of incarceration that he composed his eloquent *Letter from Birmingham City Jail*. It was a response to the urgings of white church leaders in Birmingham that blacks should negotiate and be patient and not protest or resist. King expanded these ideas at greater length in his book *Why We Can't Wait*. President Kennedy was compelled to act to protect nonviolent protesters from the organized violence of local and state governments.

King was honored by universities, communities, and foreign governments for his contributions to human rights and was awarded the Nobel Peace Prize in 1965. He reached the highest pinnacle of prophetic witness in the March on Washington in 1963 to pressure Congress to pass a strong Civil Rights Act, where he delivered his inspired "I Have a Dream" speech before hundreds of thousands at the Lincoln Memorial. He was assassinated in Memphis, Tennessee, in 1968 and died a martyr to the struggle for human rights, inspired in his case by Christian faith.

From Martin Luther King Jr.
Letter from Birmingham City Jail

Martin Luther King Jr.
Birmingham City Jail
April 16, 1963

Bishop C. C. J. Carpenter
Bishop Joseph A. Curick
Rabbi Milton L. Grafman
Bishop Paul Hardin
Bishop Nolan B. Harmon
The Rev. George M. Murray
The Rev. Edward V. Ramage
The Rev. Earl Stallings

My dear Fellow Clergymen,

While confined here in the Birmingham City Jail, I came across your recent statement calling our present activities "unwise and untimely." . . . Since I feel that you are men of genuine goodwill and your criticisms are sincerely set forth, I would like to answer your statement in what I hope will be patient and reasonable terms.

I think I should give the reason for my being in Birmingham, since you have been influenced by the argument of "outsiders coming in." I have the honor of serving as president of the Southern Christian Leadership Conference, an organization operating in every Southern state with headquarters in Atlanta, Georgia. We have some eighty-five affiliate organizations all across the South—one being the Alabama Christian Movement for Human Rights. Whenever necessary and possible we share staff, educational and financial resources with our affiliates. Several months ago our local affiliate here in Birmingham invited us to be on call to engage in a nonviolent direct action program. We readily consented. . . . Beyond this, I am in Birmingham because injustice is here. Just as the eighth century prophets left their little villages and carried their "thus saith the Lord" far beyond the boundaries of their home town, and just as the Apostle Paul left his little village of Tarsus and carried the gospel of Jesus Christ to practically every hamlet and city of the Graeco-Roman world, I too am compelled to carry the gospel of freedom beyond my particular home town. . . .

Moreover, I am cognizant of the interrelatedness of all communities and states. I cannot sit idly by in Atlanta and not be concerned about what happens in Birmingham. Injustice anywhere is a threat to justice everywhere. . . . Never again can we afford to live with the narrow, provincial "outside agitator" idea. . . .

You deplore the demonstrations that are presently taking place in Birmingham. But I am sorry that your statement did not express a similar concern for the conditions that brought the demonstrations into being. . . . It is unfortunate that so-called demonstrations are taking place in Birmingham at this time, but I would say in more emphatic terms that it is even more unfortunate that the white power structure of this city left the Negro community with no other alternative.

In any nonviolent campaign there are four basic steps: (1) collection of the facts to determine whether injustices are alive; (2) negotiations; (3) self-purification; and (4) direct action. We have gone through all of these steps in Birmingham. There can be no gainsaying of the fact that racial injustices engulf this community. Birmingham is probably the most thoroughly segregated city in the United States. Its ugly record of police brutality is known in every section of this country. Its unjust treatment of Negroes in the courts is a notorious reality. There have been more unsolved bombings of Negro homes and churches in Birmingham than any city in this nation. These are the hard, brutal, and unbelievable facts. On the basis of these conditions Negro leaders sought to negotiate with the city fathers. But the political leaders consistently refused to engage in good faith negotiation.

Then came the opportunity last September to talk with some of the leaders of the economic community. In these negotiating sessions certain promises were made by the merchants—such as the promise to remove the humiliating racial signs from the stores. On the basis of these promises Rev. Shuttlesworth and the leaders of the Alabama Christian Movement for Human Rights agreed to call a moratorium on any type of demonstrations. As the weeks and months unfolded we realized that we were the victims of a broken promise. . . . So we had no alternative except that of preparing for direct action, whereby we would present our very bodies as a means of laying our case before the conscience of the local and national community. We were not unmindful of the difficulties involved. So we decided to go through a process of self-purification. We started having workshops on nonviolence and repeatedly asked ourselves the questions, "Are you able to accept blows without retaliation?" "Are you able to endure the ordeals of jail?"

We decided to set our direct action program around the Easter season, realizing that with the exception of Christmas, this was the largest shopping period of the year. Knowing that a strong economic withdrawal program would be the byproduct of direct action, we felt that this was the best time to bring pressure on the merchants for the needed changes. . . .

This reveals that we did not move irresponsibly into direct action. . . .

You may well ask, "Why direct action? Why sit-ins, marches, etc.? Isn't negotiation a better path?" You are exactly right in your call for negotiation. Indeed, this is the purpose of direct action. Nonviolent direct action seeks to create such a crisis and establish such creative tension that a community that has constantly refused to negotiate is forced to confront the issue. . . . This may sound rather shocking. But I must confess that I am not afraid of the word tension. I have earnestly worked and preached against violent tension, and there is a type of constructive nonviolent tension that is necessary for growth. Just as Socrates felt that it was necessary to create a tension in the mind . . . we must see the need of having nonviolent gadflies to create the kind of tension in society that will help men rise from the dark depths of prejudice and racism to the majestic heights of understanding and brotherhood. . . . We, therefore, concur with you in your call for negotiation. . . .

One of the basic points in your statement is that our acts are untimely. Some have asked, "Why didn't you give the new administration time to act?" The only answer that I can give to this inquiry is that the new administration must be prodded about as much as the outgoing one before it acts. . . . My friends, I must say to you that we have not made a single gain in civil rights without determined legal and nonviolent pressure. History is the long and tragic story of the fact that privileged groups seldom give up their privileges voluntarily. Individuals may see the moral light and voluntarily give up their unjust posture; but as Reinhold Niebuhr has reminded us, groups are more immoral than individuals.

We know through painful experience that freedom is never voluntarily given by the oppressor; it must be demanded by the oppressed. Frankly I have never yet engaged in a direct action movement that was "well-timed," according to the timetable of those who have not suffered unduly from the disease of segregation. For years now I have heard the word "Wait!" It rings in the ear of every Negro with a piercing familiarity. This "wait" has almost always meant "never." . . . We must come to see with the distinguished jurist of yesterday that "justice too long delayed is justice denied." We have waited for more than three hundred and forty years for our constitutional and God-given rights. . . .

I guess it is easy for those who have never felt the stinging darts of segregation to say wait. But when you have seen vicious mobs lynch your mothers and fathers at will and drown your sisters and brothers at whim; when you have seen hate-filled policemen curse, kick, brutalize, and even kill your black brothers and sisters with impunity; when you see the vast majority of your twenty million Negro brothers smothering in an air-tight cage of poverty in the midst of an affluent society; when you suddenly find your tongue twisted and your speech stammering as you seek to explain to your six-year-old daughter why she can't go to the public amusement park that has just been advertised on television, and see tears welling up in her little eyes when she is told that Funtown is closed to colored children, and see the depressing clouds of inferiority begin to form in her little mental sky, and see her begin to distort her little personality by unconsciously developing a bitterness toward white people; when you have to concoct an answer for a five-year-old son asking in agonizing pathos: "Daddy, why do white people treat colored people so mean?"; when you take a cross country drive and find it necessary to sleep night after night in the uncomfortable corners of your automobile because no motel will accept you; when you are humiliated day in and day out by nagging signs reading "white" men and "colored"; when your first name becomes "nigger" and your middle name becomes "boy" (however old you are) and your last name becomes "John," and when your wife and mother are never given the respected title "Mrs."; when you are harried by day and haunted by night by the fact that you are a Negro, living constantly at tip-toe stance never quite knowing what to expect next, and plagued with inner fears and outer resentments; when you are forever fighting a degenerating sense of "nobodiness";—then you will understand why we find it difficult to wait. There comes a time when the cup of endurance runs over, and men are no longer willing to be plunged into an abyss of injustice where they experience the bleakness of corroding despair. I hope, sirs, you can understand our legitimate and unavoidable impatience.

You express a great deal of anxiety over our willingness to break laws. This is certainly a legitimate concern. Since we so diligently urge people to obey the Supreme Court's decision of 1954 outlawing segregation in the public schools, it is rather strange and paradoxical to find us consciously breaking laws. One may well ask, "How can you advocate breaking some laws and obeying others?" The answer is found in the fact that there are two types of laws; there are *just* laws and there are *unjust* laws. I would be the first to advocate obeying just laws. One has not only a legal but moral responsibility to obey just laws. Conversely, one has a moral responsibility to disobey unjust laws. I would agree with Saint Augustine that "An unjust law is no law at all."

Now what is the difference between the two? How does one determine when a law is just or unjust? A just law is a man-made code that squares with the moral law or the law of God. An unjust law is a code that is out of harmony with the moral law. To put it in the terms of Saint Thomas Aquinas, an unjust law is a human law that is not rooted in eternal and natural law. Any law that uplifts human personality is just. Any law that degrades human personality is unjust. All segregation statutes are unjust because segregation distorts the soul and damages the personality. It gives the segregator a false sense of superiority and the segregated a false sense of inferiority. To use the words of Martin Buber, the great Jewish philosopher, segregation substitutes an "I-it" relationship for the "I-thou" relationship, and ends up relegating persons to the status of things. So segregation is not only politically, economically, and sociologically unsound, but it is morally wrong and sinful. Paul Tillich has said that sin is separation. Isn't segregation an existential expression of man's tragic separation, an expression of his awful estrangement, his terrible sinfulness? So I can urge men to obey the 1954 decision of the Supreme Court because it is morally right, and I can urge them to disobey segregation ordinances because they are morally wrong.

Let us turn to a more concrete example of just and unjust laws. An unjust law is a code that a majority inflicts on a minority that is not binding on itself. This is *difference* made legal. On the other hand a just law is a code that a majority compels a minority to follow that it is willing to follow itself. This is *sameness* made legal.

Let me give you another explanation. An unjust law is a code inflicted upon a minority which that minority had no part in enacting or creating because they did not have the unhampered right to vote. Who can say the legislature of Alabama which set up the segregation laws was democratically elected? Throughout the state of Alabama all types of conniving methods are used to prevent Negroes from becoming registered voters and there are some counties without a single Negro registered to vote despite the fact that the Negro constitutes a majority of the population. Can any law set up in such a state be considered democratically structured?

These are just a few examples of unjust and just laws. There are some instances when a law is just on its face but unjust in its application. For instance, I was arrested Friday on a charge of parading without a permit. Now there is nothing wrong with an ordinance which requires a permit for a parade, but when the ordinance is used to preserve segregation and to deny citizens the First Amendment privilege of peaceful assembly and peaceful protest, then it becomes unjust.

I hope you can see the distinction I am trying to point out. In no sense do I advocate evading or defying the law as the rabid segregationist would do. This would lead to anarchy. One who breaks an unjust law must do it *openly, lovingly* (not hatefully as the white mothers did in New Orleans when they were seen on television screaming "nigger, nigger, nigger") and with a willingness to accept the penalty. I submit that an individual who breaks a law that conscience tells him is unjust, and willingly accepts the penalty by staying in jail to arouse the conscience of the community over its injustice, is in reality expressing the very highest respect for law.

Of course there is nothing new about this kind of civil disobedience. . . . It was practiced superbly by the early Christians who were willing to face hungry lions and the excruciating pain of chopping blocks, before submitting to certain unjust laws of the Roman Empire. . . .

We can never forget that everything Hitler did in Germany was "legal" and everything the Hungarian freedom fighters did in Hungary was "illegal." . . .

I must make two honest confessions to you, my Christian and Jewish brothers. First I must confess that over the last few years I have been gravely disappointed with the white moderate. I have almost reached the regrettable conclusion that the Negroes' greatest stum-

bling block in the stride toward freedom is not the White Citizens'
"Counciler" or the Ku Klux Klanner, but the white moderate who is
more devoted to "order" than to justice; who prefers a negative peace
which is the absence of tension to a positive peace which is the presence of justice; who constantly says 'I agree with you in the goal you
seek, but I can't agree with your methods of direct action"; who
paternalistically feels that he can set the time-table for another man's
freedom; who lives by the myth of time. . . .

I had hoped that the white moderate would understand that law
and order exist for the purpose of establishing justice, and that when
they fail to do this they become dangerously structured dams that
block the flow of social progress. I had hoped that the white moderate
would understand that the present tension in the South is merely a
necessary phase of the transition from an obnoxious negative peace,
where the Negro passively accepted his unjust plight, to a substance-
filled positive peace, where all men will respect the dignity and worth
of human personality. Actually, we who engage in nonviolent direct
action are not the creators of tension. We merely bring to the surface
the hidden tension that is already alive. . . .

In your statement you asserted that our actions, even though peaceful, must be condemned because they precipitate violence. But can
this assertion be logically made? Isn't this like condemning the robbed
man because his possession of money precipitated the evil act of rob-
bery? . . . Isn't this like condemning Jesus because His unique God
consciousness and never-ceasing devotion to His will precipitated
the evil act of crucifixion? . . .

I had also hoped that the white moderate would reject the myth
of time. . . . Actually time is neutral. It can be used either destructively
or constructively. I am coming to feel that the people of ill will have
used time much more effectively than the people of good will. We will
have to repent in this generation not merely for the vitriolic words and
actions of the bad people, but for the appalling silence of the good
people. We must come to see that human progress never rolls in on
wheels of inevitability. It comes through the tireless efforts and persistent work of men willing to be co-workers with God, and without this
hard work time itself becomes an ally of the forces of social stagnation.

We must use time creatively, and forever realize that the time is always ripe to do right. Now is the time to make real the promise of
democracy, and transform our pending national elegy into a creative
psalm of brotherhood. Now is the time to lift our national policy from
the quicksand of racial injustice to the solid rock of human dignity.

You spoke of our activity in Birmingham as extreme. At first I was
rather disappointed that fellow clergymen would see my nonviolent

efforts as those of the extremist. I started thinking about the fact that I stand in the middle of two opposing forces in the Negro community. One is a force of complacency made up of Negroes who, as a result of long years of oppression, have been so completely drained of self-respect and a sense of "somebodiness" that they have adjusted to segregation, and of a few Negroes in the middle class who, because of a degree of academic and economic security, and because at points they profit by segregation, have unconsciously become insensitive to the problems of the masses. The other force is one of bitterness and hatred and comes perilously close to advocating violence. It is expressed in the various black nationalist groups that are springing up over the nation, the largest and best known being Elijah Muhammad's Muslim movement. This movement is nourished by the contemporary frustration over the continued existence of racial discrimination. It is made up of people who have lost faith in America, who have absolutely repudiated Christianity, and who have concluded that the white man is an incurable "devil." I have tried to stand between these two forces saying that we need not follow the "do-nothingism" of the complacent or the hatred and despair of the black nationalist. There is the more excellent way of love and nonviolent protest. I'm grateful to God that, through the Negro church, the dimension of nonviolence entered our struggle. If this philosophy had not emerged I am convinced that by now many streets of the South would be flowing with floods of blood.

Oppressed people cannot remain oppressed forever. The urge for freedom will eventually come. This is what has happened to the American Negro. Something within has reminded him of his birthright of freedom; something without has reminded him that he can gain it. Consciously and unconsciously, he has been swept in by what the Germans call the Zeitgeist, and with his black brothers of Africa, and his brown and yellow brothers of Asia, South America, and the Caribbean, he is moving with a sense of cosmic urgency toward the promised land of racial justice. Recognizing this vital urge that has engulfed the Negro community, one should readily understand public demonstrations. The Negro has many pentup resentments and latent frustrations. He has to get them out. So let him march sometime; let him have his prayer pilgrimages to the city hall, understand why he must have sit-ins and freedom-rides. If his repressed emotions do not come out in these nonviolent ways, they will come out in ominous expressions of violence. This is not a threat; it is a fact of history. . . .

But as I continued to think about the matter I gradually gained a bit of satisfaction from being considered an extremist. Was not Jesus an extremist in love? . . . Was not Amos an extremist for justice? . . . Was not Paul an extremist for the gospel of Jesus Christ? . . . Was not Martin

Luther an extremist? . . . Was not John Bunyan an extremist? . . . Was not Abraham Lincoln an extremist? . . . Was not Thomas Jefferson an extremist? . . . So the question is not whether we will be extremist but what kind of extremist we will be. Will we be extremists for the preservation of injustice—or will we be extremists for the cause of justice? . . .

I had hoped that the white moderate would see this. Maybe I was too optimistic. Maybe I expected too much. I guess I should have realized that few members of a race that has oppressed another race can understand or appreciate the deep groans and passionate yearnings of those that have been oppressed, and still fewer have the vision to see that injustice must be rooted out by strong, persistent, and determined action. I am thankful, however, that some of our white brothers have grasped the meaning of this social revolution, and committed themselves to it. . . .

Let me rush on to mention my other disappointment. I have been so greatly disappointed with the white Church and its leadership. Of course there are some notable exceptions. . . .

But despite these notable exceptions I must honestly reiterate that I have been disappointed with the Church. I do not say that as one of those negative critics who can always find something wrong with the Church. I say it as a minister of the gospel, who loves the Church, who was nurtured in its bosom; who has been sustained by its spiritual blessings and who will remain true to it as long as the cord of life shall lengthen.

I had the strange feeling when I was suddenly catapulted into the leadership of the bus protest in Montgomery several years ago that we would have the support of the white Church. I felt that the white ministers, priests, and rabbis of the South would be some of our strongest allies, instead, some have been outright opponents. . . .

I came to Birmingham with the hope that the white religious leadership of this community would see the justice of our cause. . . . But again I have been disappointed.

I have heard numerous religious leaders of the South call upon their worshippers to comply with a desegregation decision because it is the law, but I have longed to hear white ministers say follow this decree because integration is morally right and the Negro is your brother. In the midst of blatant injustices inflicted upon the Negro, I have watched white churches stand on the sideline and merely mouth pious irrelevancies and sanctimonious trivialities. In the midst of a mighty struggle to rid our nation of racial and economic injustice, I have heard so many ministers say, "Those are social issues with which the Gospel has no real concern," and I have watched so many churches commit them-

selves to a completely other-worldly religion which made a strange
distinction between body and soul, the sacred and the secular.

So here we are moving toward the exit of the twentieth century with
a religious community largely adjusted to the status quo, standing as a
taillight behind other community agencies rather than a headlight leading men to higher levels of justice. . . .

In deep disappointment, I have wept over the laxity of the Church.
But, be assured that my tears have been tears of love. There can be no
deep disappointment where there is not deep love. Yes, I love the
Church. . . . Yes, I see the Church as the body of Christ. But oh! How
we have blemished and scarred that body through social neglect and
fear of being nonconformist.

There was a time when the Church was very powerful. It was during
that period when the early Christians rejoiced when they were deemed
worthy to suffer for what they believed. In those days the Church was
not merely a thermometer that recorded the ideas and principles of
popular opinion; it was a thermostat that transformed the mores of
society. Wherever the early Christians entered a town the power structure got disturbed and immediately sought to convict them for being
"disturbers of the peace" and "outside agitators." But they went on with
the conviction that they were a "colony of heaven" and had to obey
God rather than man. They were small in number but big in commitment. They were too God-intoxicated to be "astronomically intimi-
dated." They brought an end to such ancient evils as infanticide and
gladiatorial contest.

Things are different now. The contemporary Church is so often a
weak, ineffectual voice with an uncertain sound. It is so often the arch-
supporter of the status quo. . . .

But the judgment of God is upon the Church as never before. If the
Church of today does not recapture the sacrificial spirit of the early
Church, it will lose its authentic ring, forfeit the loyalty of millions,
and be dismissed as an irrelevant social club with no meaning for the
twentieth century. I am meeting young people every day whose disappointment with the Church has risen to outright disgust.

Maybe again I have been too optimistic. Is organized religion too
inextricably bound to the status quo to save our nation and the world?
Maybe I must turn my faith to the inner spiritual Church, the church
within the Church, as the true *ecclesia* and the hope of the world. But
again I am thankful to God that some noble souls from the ranks of
organized religion have broken loose from the paralyzing chains of
conformity and joined us as active partners in the struggle for freedom. . . .

I hope the Church as a whole will meet the challenge of this decisive hour. But even if the Church does not come to the aid of justice, I have no despair about the future. I have no fear about the outcome of our struggle in Birmingham, even if our motives are presently misunderstood. We will reach the goal of freedom in Birmingham and all over the nation, because the goal of America is freedom. Abused and scorned though we may be, our destiny is tied up with the destiny of America. . . . If the inexpressible cruelties of slavery could not stop us, the opposition we now face will surely fail. We will win our freedom because the sacred heritage of our nation and the eternal will of God are embodied in our echoing demands. . . .

One other point . . . You warmly commended the Birmingham police force for keeping "order" and "preventing violence." I don't believe you would have so warmly commended the police force if you had seen its angry dogs literally biting six unarmed nonviolent Negroes. I don't believe you would so quickly commend the policemen if you would observe their ugly and inhuman treatment of Negroes here in the city jail, if you would watch them push and curse old Negro women and young Negro girls; if you would see them slap and kick old Negro men and young Negro boys; if you will observe them, as they did on two occasions, refuse to give us food because we wanted to sing our grace together. I'm sorry that I can't join you in your praise for the police department.

It is true that they have been rather disciplined in their public handling of the demonstrators. In this sense they have been rather publicly "nonviolent." But for what purpose? To preserve the evil system of segregation. Over the last few years I have consistently preached that nonviolence demands that the means we use must be as pure as the ends we seek. So I have tried to make it clear that it is wrong to use immoral means to attain moral ends. But now I must affirm that it is just as wrong, or even more so, to use moral means to preserve immoral ends. . . . T. S. Eliot has said that there is no greater treason than to do the right deed for the wrong reason.

I wish you had commended the Negro sit-inners and demonstrators of Birmingham for their sublime courage, their willingness to suffer, and their amazing discipline in the midst of the most inhuman provocation. One day the South will recognize its real heroes. They will be the James Merediths, courageously and with a majestic sense of purpose, facing jeering and hostile mobs and the agonizing loneliness that characterizes the life of the pioneer. They will be old, oppressed, battered Negro women, symbolized in a seventy-two year old woman of Montgomery, Alabama, who rose up with a sense of dignity and with her people decided not to ride the segregated buses, and responded to one who inquired about her tiredness with ungrammatical profundity:

"My feets is tired, but my soul is rested." They will be young high school and college students, young ministers of the gospel and a host of the elders, courageously and nonviolently sitting in at lunch counters and willingly going to jail for conscience sake. One day the South will know that when these disinherited children of God sat down at lunch counters they were in reality standing up for the best in the American dream and the most sacred values in our Judeo-Christian heritage, and thus carrying our whole nation back to great wells of democracy which were dug deep by the founding fathers in the formulation of the Constitution and the Declaration of Independence. . . .

If I have said anything in this letter that is an overstatement of the truth and is indicative of an unreasonable impatience, I beg you to forgive me. If I have said anything in this letter that is an understatement of the truth and is indicative of my having a patience that makes me patient with anything less than brotherhood, I beg God to forgive me.

I hope this letter finds you strong in the faith. I also hope that circumstances will soon make it possible for me to meet each of you, not as an integrationist or a civil rights leader, but as a fellow clergyman and as a Christian brother. Let us all hope that the dark clouds of racial prejudice will soon pass away . . . the radiant stars of love and brotherhood will shine over our great nation with all of their scintillating beauty.

Yours for the cause of Peace and Brotherhood,
MARTIN LUTHER KING JR.

MONIKA HELLWIG

Monika H. K. Hellwig is a professor of theology at Georgetown University, Washington, D.C. She received the Ph.D. degree from the Catholic University of America. Among her published works is a book, *What Are the Theologians Saying?* (1970), in which she introduces Roman Catholic lay readers to basic theological issues as treated by such progressive Roman Catholic theolgians as Karl Rahner, Hans Küng, and Edward Schillebeeckx.

The women's movement of the past few decades constitutes a highly important part of the worldwide quest for human liberation. Monika Hellwig joins other feminist theologians, such as Rosemary Ruether, in relating the liberation of women to the parallel concerns of Latin American liberation theology. In both cases, the problems to be faced are those of oppression, alienation, and dehumanization.

In the following article, which appeared in the journal *Liturgy* in October 1970, Hellwig expresses the hope that women will band together in a common effort to identify and destroy the stereotypes which alienate and oppress women to the end that persons, men as well as women, may be liberated. She takes up the theological issues related to human liberation. What is truly human must be found in the freedom of the creative process. "Humanization" as taught by Third World experience means being the subject of one's own history. Redemption from the forces of evil calls, not for projecting problems onto others, but for a change of consciousness, a conversion to God and to the welfare of others. Liberation from unjust powers and structures is fired by the hope of a common destiny for all humankind in Christ.

From Monika Hellwig, "Hope and Liberation"

Women's liberation is truly a movement rather than an organization. Hard to define and almost impossible to understand, it has as many streams as an eddying fast-flowing river. Many superficial manifestations are so whimsical and extravagant that they are easily discounted. Underneath these there is a powerful current flowing rather steadily and gathering colossal force.

It may be worthwhile to attempt a description of the alienation experience on which women's liberation is based, and then to ask whether there are theological issues involved.

In our own society at least, there are two levels of experience for a person, namely an intimate and immediate level and a public one, which tend to structure themselves by different criteria. In the intimate and immediate level, as a woman I experience myself as central, stable, important and normal. While I may be clearly aware that the world does not revolve around me, that there are many other centers, I feel quite comfortably "in place" as the center of my particular world, my life, my family. As a woman, I experience myself very much as a living body constantly becoming more alive, bursting all kinds of barriers into greater reflexive self-awareness, deeper mutual awareness with others and more far-reaching freedom and creativity. As a woman, I have been looked at with interest and approval a great deal in my life, far more than most men. As a woman, I am kissed and embraced more often and by more people than most men. As a woman, I am at ease with a wide show of emotions; I even have "social permission" to show fear and to weep, though if I am angry instead it will not be held against me, and if I am fearless it will be admired. At this intimate level, I am superbly free, or ought to be, because I have almost limitless possibilities of becoming and relating, with almost minimal risk of rejection, frustration, failure.

WOMAN AS ACCESSORY: THE PUBLIC EXPERIENCE

At the public level of experience, a person is answerable to society at large, not in terms of one-to-one personal relationships, but in terms of economic, social and political function in relation to the whole society. As our society functions today, a woman may find the intimate level of experience invaded and disrupted by the public level, and this may give rise to a fearful experience of alienation and oppression. That is because at the public level she is frequently not seen as person, but as attachment to another person. As consumer, tax-payer, traveller, home-owner, and in public ceremonial functions, she has a self-image imposed on her which does not correspond to her experience of herself as person, but mirrors her back to herself as an accessory to another person or if she is single, as an unclaimed, unattached accessory. Because as person she experiences herself as reflexive self-awareness and creative freedom, she feels threatened when society tells her she is something less than person. Similarly, as worker, active contributor and wage or salary earner in the society, she often finds that the patterns of interaction in the larger society have been set up so as to preclude her from contributing at her full capacity in terms of aptitude or training, and that she is not paid in direct proportion to her contribution. Again, if she is aware of her abilities and the true worth of her services, she is threatened because society systematically undervalues her in the public arena.

A woman can react to this threat in several ways. One is to withdraw into the intimate level of experience where she can live authentically. This becomes less possible today, because our technology draws us all inexorably into the public arena of the larger society all the time. Moreover, both our formal school education and our informal diffuse education for life orient all of us, men and women, to seek our identity in terms of our functional relation to the society at large. Under these circumstances, retreat may be cut off, because a woman's intimate world may be effectively destroyed if she cannot combat the dehumanizing image projected onto her by the society at large.

A second response is open to very few. Some women are basically secure enough as persons that they can live authentically and creatively, sure of their self-image and accepting their full potential. They are able to recognize derogatory, institutionalized stereotypes as artificial and mistaken, no matter how often and how convincingly they are repeated. Some women are secure and adaptable and fortunate enough to be able to move into areas of employment where there is relatively little discrimination and to settle in circles where the stereotypes are not hurled at them as crudely or damagingly as elsewhere.

A third reaction is apparently more frequent. Many women seem to collapse psychically under the sheer weight of the stereotypes dumped upon them. They lose their nerve and cannot believe in the truth of their own experience as persons. They settle for a prefabricated destiny and proceed to try to fulfill the stereotype, in the vain hope of gaining acceptance and approval. So they set out to be manageable accessories —shapeless, brainless, helpless, but efficient instruments for someone else's purpose. Anyone who resorts to this type of role-playing has to suppress frightening amounts of conflict and hostility, because she is utterly alienated from her true self and cannot afford to admit it. She may find free women a direct and intolerable threat to herself. She may need to be catty and underhanded to try to pull them down and destroy them.

A fourth possibility is of course a banding together of women in a common endeavor to destroy the stereotypes and liberate the persons. This is the deep current of the women's liberation movement—to identify the alienation and oppression correctly, to bring many women to a conscious awareness of the alienation, to grow together toward a consciousness of freedom and a will to rebel against the stereotypes, and to collaborate in strategies to overthrow those stereotypes.

THEOLOGY: BEYOND STEREOTYPES

In this deep current of the movement, there are several theological issues. First among them is the question of what is truly human. There has been much theologizing in the past about the "nature of woman" which has missed the mark in several ways. Often it has defined woman as function of society rather than as person and therefore end in herself. More significantly, such theologizing has often attempted to lock women into existing stereotypes drawn from the experiences of a particular culture at a particular stage of its development. As long as we look for what is truly human in terms of discovering a blueprint written by the creator within his creation, we are unlikely to escape the stereotypes. Only if we accept a definition of the truly human in terms of freedom, in terms of collaborating with God in creation by the imaginative projection of what is not yet, can we escape the stereotypes. In these terms we do not yet know what it is to be woman or to be man, because we are still being created. This process of creation is not passive; rather it is one in which we are self-creating in response to the liberating call of God and in interaction with the world and with one another. We may not blame God for the limitations of what we are, much less invoke the name of God as the guarantee of the status quo, because God is not the watchmaker of the beginning but the infinite and exigent freedom of the future.

In this context, when we try to determine the true nature of woman, we are asking what women can become, and we are asking it in the context of redemption, in the context of biblical faith, in the context of the category of the *novum* or radically new, in the context of the theology of hope as presented, for instance, by Jurgen Moltmann. (See his *Religion, Revolution and the Future.*) This means that we are not making an estimate on empirical grounds of the possibilities implicit in the existing situation. We are asking what promises, contained in our revelatory experiences of Christ Jesus, offer quantum leaps of personal freedom toward the creation of a radically new world of human relationships.

TOWARD CONFRONTATION

If we define the future in terms of freedom to project and become what is not yet and therefore cannot be spelled out beforehand, a further theological issue arises of criteria for what is desirable. The revolutions of the third world have given us the concept of "humanization," that is, becoming the subject of one's own history, rather than the object of someone else's history, assuming full personal participation in the shaping of one's own destiny, living one's own life creatively and purposefully rather than experiencing oneself as a machine that is being run by another.

This raises the question of the individual's freedom in society where other individuals are also looking for their freedom to choose and shape their own destiny. Albert Camus, in his book, *The Rebel,* writing from an atheist humanist position, has pointed out by painful and laborious logic that such humanization, such liberation can only be authentic if it is desired and is possible for all men. The alienation and oppression can only be overcome by a very arduous, radical and total rebellion against what is not human in the name of all that is human and all who are human.

This precludes the identification of any group of persons as the enemy. We are thrown back to the Pauline principle that the battle is not against flesh and blood but against principalities and powers. Men are not the enemy of the liberation of women. It is the organization of this world in terms of power struggle, competition, coercive relationships, and untruths, the organization of this world that resists the kingdom of God that is to come, that is the enemy of freedom both for men and for women. However, it is a time-honored principle of Christian spirituality that in order to identify correctly the principalities and powers—the forces that resist the kingdom—one should place oneself at the bottom of any given hierarchy in the power struggle; one should be on that side of the discrimination where it hurts. In this case, what is wrong with our society's attitude to persons is much more clearly apparent from the women's vantage point.

CREATING FREEDOM AND EQUALITY

A third theological issue concerns what may be the hope for redemption from the forces of evil; in concrete terms, what we must do to be saved. Clearly, the basic task is not one of external force or persuasion but one of conversion in the root sense of *metanoia,* a change of consciousness, a process of "conscientiation" as the Medillin conference called it, a move from lassitude to commitment to change, a move from the first three attitudes listed above to the fourth. The most important move, pointed out by Rubem Alves in *A Theology of Human Hope* and by other Latin American authors, is the conversion of the oppressed and alienated away from a neat projection of the problem onto persons outside of themselves who become the enemy. It is the painful conversion toward recognizing the problem within one's own attitudes and expectations. It means the realization that it has become more comfortable to accommodate to the stereotypes than to challenge them, because accommodation requires less effort and no risk. To challenge them requires constant effort and attention and involves considerable risk in personal relationships and personal peace of mind.

Such risk, however, is not only worthwhile but of the very substance of the redemptive process in the world. Wolfhart Pannenberg has pointed out that the Christian conversion to God is the conversion to the world, commitment to the improvement of human life and the quality of structures and relations of human society. This is implemented in Pannenberg's view through a dynamic of love that fearlessly summons the self-determining freedom and independence of the other, supports the weakest, and searches for peace in the full confidence that the welfare of others is in the last resort one's own welfare because we have a common destiny. This view, as Pannenberg himself points out, has nothing to do with evolutionary optimism. Equality and freedom are in our destiny, yet to be created; they are not a starting point or a natural outcome.

One might also add that the very strategy of women's liberation is a theological and ethical issue. Clearly, whatever polarizes, whatever divides the world into camps is ruled out, because this is the very condition that must be overcome. In terms of the gospel promise, it would seem that this is precisely a moment that offers the possibility of the quantum leap of freedom through a movement of non-violent resistance in the tradition of Gandhi, in the footsteps of Martin Luther King, but in a unique mode suitable precisely to the problem at hand. The fact that many men are also cruelly stereotyped and alienated by society at large by lack of education, lack of connections, ethnic identity and other factors—must be clearly taken into account. Such men may see the stereotyping of women as necessary self-defense. To make them more insecure will not transform human relations into more positive channels. Moreover, for some time our society has been making it very difficult for men to be comfortably and fully at ease with themselves in the intimate immediate level of experience, and it has been necessary for them to search for a basic personal identity at the public level. It is at least worth some reflection that the most productive efforts in women's liberation may be those directed to sympathetic reconstruction of a satisfying personal identity for men at the intimate level.

Be this as it may, seen in Christian theological perspective, all human liberation is an arduous, long term task involving *metanoia* or radical change of consciousness. It focuses its hostility not on other persons but on structures, relationships and attitudes that are unjust, because it looks in hope to a common destiny for all mankind in Christ.

GUSTAVO GUTIERREZ

Gustavo Gutiérrez is a leading Latin American theologian who is credited with coining the term, "liberation theology," of which Avery Dulles has written that it "arises out of deep compassion and critical reflection on the situation of the poor and oppressed."

Born in Lima, Peru, in 1928, Gutiérrez studied medicine in his home country, then turned to philosophical and theological studies in preparation for the priesthood, traveling first to Chile, then to Belgium, where he spent four years at the University of Louvain, and to France, where he studied theology for four years at Lyon. He was ordained to the priesthood in Lima in 1959. He is professor of theology in the Catholic University of Peru, chaplain to the National Union of Catholic University Students, and advisor to the Latin American Bishops Conference.

His book, *A Theology of Liberation* (English translation, 1973), is regarded as the classic presentation of liberation theology, described by Gutiérrez as "critical reflection on historical praxis" which he distinguishes from theology as "wisdom" or as "rational knowledge." "Historical praxis" refers to the actual conditions of oppression, poverty, and alienation found in Latin America and the activity of the church and others in the struggle for freedom and human dignity.

The Latin titles in the first paragraph of the selection refer to an encyclical by Pope Paul VI, *Populorum progressio* (1967), which Gutiérrez regards as an advance toward the idea of liberation, going further than the Vatican II document, *Gaudium et spes* (*Pastoral Constitution on the Church in the Modern World*, 1965), but still not direct and decisive enough "in favor of the oppressed, encouraging them to break with their present situation and take control of their own destiny" (*A Theology of Liberation,* p. 35). Liberation, as Gutiérrez sees it, means freeing the oppressed, forming a new man and a new society, and being delivered from sin by Christ.

From Gustavo Gutiérrez, **A Theology of Liberation**
THE HORIZON OF POLITICAL LIBERATION

The texts of the magisterium of the Church to which we have referred (with the exception of some points in *Populorum progressio*) are typical of the way contemporary theology treats this question. The approach seems to preclude the question regarding the ultimate meanings of man's action in history or, to express it in the terms of *Gaudium et spes,* of the relationship between temporal progress and the growth of the Kingdom. Temporal progress is seen preferably in the dominion of nature by science and technology and in some of the repercussions on the development of human society; there is no radical challenge to the unjust system on which it is based. The conflictual aspects of the political sphere are absent; or rather they have been avoided.

Theologically, therefore, we will consider temporal progress as a continuation of the work of creation and explore its connection with redemptive action. Redemption implies a direct relation to sin, and sin—the breach of friendship with God and others—is a human, social, and historical reality which originates in a socially and historically situated freedom.

"Creation," the cosmos, suffers from the consequence of sin. To cite Rom. 8 in this regard is interesting and does broaden our perspective, but this passage is not directly related to the question at hand. The immediate relationship between creation and redemption easily leads to a juxtaposition or to an artificial inclusion of the former into the latter, in which creation is granted autonomy and yet struggles to escape from the strait-jacket it is thus put into. It will be necessary to look at the question from a greater distance, or in other terms, to penetrate it more deeply, in order to capture in a single view or to establish on a single principle the creation-redemption relationship. In the way the problem has previously been stated, there is a curious omission of the liberating and protagonistic role of man, the lord of creation and coparticipant in his own salvation.[89] As we have already pointed out in this chapter, only the concept of the mediation of man's self-creation in history can lead us to an accurate and fruitful understanding of the relationship between creation and redemption. This line of interpretation is suggested by the outstanding fact of the Exodus; because of it, creation is regarded as the first salvific act and salvation as a new creation. Without the perspective of political liberation we cannot go beyond a relationship between two separate "orders," that of creation and that of redemption.[90] The liberation approach subverts also the very "order" involved in the posing of the question.

The work of man, the transformation of nature, continues creation only if it is a human act, that is to say, if it is not alienated by unjust socio-economic structures. A whole theology of work, despite its evident insights, appears naive from a political point of view. Teilhard de Chardin is among those who contributed most to a search for a unity between faith and the "religion of the world," but he does so from a scientific point of view. He values the dominion over nature man has achieved and speaks of it as the penetration point of evolution, enabling man to control it. Politically his vision is, on the whole, neutral.[91] This focus had a definite impact, as could be expected, on the views of theologians of the developed world. The faith-science conflict and the application of science to the transformation of the world have sapped most of their energy. This is why concern for human society is translated into terms of development and progress.[92] In other areas the problems are different. The concerns of the so-called Third World countries revolve around the social injustice-justice axis.[93] Thus there is a great challenge to the faith of Christians in these countries. In contradistinction to a pessimistic approach to this world which is so frequent in traditional Christian groups and which encourages escapism, there is proposed in these other countries an optimistic vision which seeks to reconcile faith and the world and to facilitate commitment. But this optimism must be based on facts. Otherwise, this posture can be deceitful and treacherous and can even lead to a justification of the present order of things. In the underdeveloped countries one starts with a rejection of the existing situation, considered as fundamentally unjust and dehumanizing. Although this is a negative vision, it is nevertheless the only one which allows us to go to the root of the problems and to create without compromises a new social order, based on justice and brotherhood. This rejection does not produce an escapist attitude, but rather a will to revolution.

The concept of political liberation—with economic roots—recalls the conflictual aspects of the historical current of humanity. In this current there is not only an effort to know and dominate nature. There is also a situation—which both affects and is affected by this current—of misery and despoliation of the fruit of man's work, the result of the exploitation of man by man; there is a confrontation between social classes and, therefore, a struggle for liberation from oppressive structures which hinder man from living with dignity and assuming his own destiny. This struggle is the human activity whose ultimate goal must in the first place be enlightened by faith. Once this has been achieved, other

facets will likewise be illuminated. The horizon of political liberation
allows for a new approach to the problem, it throws new light on it,
and it enables us to see aspects which had been but dimly perceived;
it permits us also to get away from an alleged apolitical science and
provides a different context for the crucial role of scientific knowledge
in the historical praxis of man. Other religions think in terms of cosmos
and nature; Christianity, rooted in Biblical sources, thinks in terms of
history. And in this history, injustice and oppression, divisions and con-
frontations exist. But the hope of liberation is also present.

CHRIST THE LIBERATOR

The approach we have been considering opens up for us—and this is
of utmost importance—unforeseen vistas on the problem of sin. An
unjust situation does not happen by chance; it is not something branded
by a fatal destiny: there is human responsibility behind it. The prophets
said it clearly and energetically and we are rediscovering their words
now. This is the reason why the Medellin Conference refers to the state
of things in Latin America as a "sinful situation," as a "rejection of the
Lord." [94] This characterization, in all its breadth and depth, not only
criticizes the individual abuses on the part of those who enjoy great
power in this social order; it challenges all their practices, that is to
say, it is a repudiation of the whole existing system—to which the
Church itself belongs.

In this approach we are far, therefore, from that naive optimism
which denies the role of sin in the historical development of humanity.
This was the criticism, one will remember, of the Schema of Ariccia
and it is frequently made in connection with Teilhard de Chardin and
all those theologies enthusiastic about human progress. But in the
liberation approach sin is not considered as an individual, private, or
merely interior reality—asserted just enough to necessitate a "spiritual"
redemption which does not challenge the order in which we live. Sin
is regarded as a social, historical fact, the absence of brotherhood and
love in relationships among men, the breach of friendship with God
and with other men, and, therefore, an interior, personal fracture. When
it is considered in this way, the collective dimensions of sin are rediscovered. This is the Biblical notion that Jose Maria Gonzalez Ruiz calls
the "hamartiosphere," the sphere of sin: "a kind of parameter or structure which objectively conditions the progress of human history itself." [95] Moreover, sin does not appear as an afterthought, something
which one has to mention so as not to stray from tradition or leave oneself open to attack. Nor is this a matter of escape into a fleshless spiritualism. Sin is evident in oppressive structures, in the exploitation of

man by man, in the domination and slavery of peoples, races, and social classes. Sin appears, therefore, as the fundamental alienation, the root of a situation of injustice and exploitation.[96] It cannot be encountered in itself, but only in concrete instances, in particular alienations.[97] It is impossible to understand the concrete manifestations without understanding the underlying basis and vice versa. Sin demands a radical liberation.[98] Only by participating in the historical process of liberation will it be possible to show the fundamental alienation present in every partial alienation.

This radical liberation is the gift which Christ offers us. By his death and resurrection he redeems man from sin and all its consequences, as has been well said in a text we quote again: "It is the same God who, in the fullness of time, sends his Son in the flesh, so that He might come to liberate all men from *all* slavery to which sin has subjected them: hunger, misery, oppression, and ignorance, in a word, that injustice and hatred which have their origin in human selfishness." [99] This is why the Christian life is a passover, a transition from sin to grace, from death to life, from injustice to justice, from the subhuman to the human. Christ introduces us by the gift of his Spirit into communion with God and with all men. More precisely, it is *because* he introduces us into this communion, into a continuous search for its fullness, that he conquers sin—which is the negation of love—and all its consequences.

In dealing with the notion of liberation in Chapter 2, we distinguished three levels of meaning: political liberation, the liberation of man throughout history, liberation from sin and admission to communion with God. In the light of the present chapter, we can now study this question again. These three levels mutually affect each other, but they are not the same. One is not present without the others, but they are distinct: they are all part of a single, all-encompassing salvific process, but they are to be found at different levels.[100] Not only is the growth of the Kingdom not reduced to temporal progress; because of the Word accepted in faith, we see that the fundamental obstacle to the Kingdom, which is sin, is also the root of all misery and injustice; we see that the very meaning of the growth of the Kingdom is also the ultimate precondition for a just society and a new man. One reaches this root and this ultimate precondition only through the acceptance of the liberating gift of Christ, which surpasses all expectations. But, inversely, all struggle against exploitation and alienation, in a history which is fundamentally one, is an attempt to vanquish selfishness, the negation of love. This is the reason why any effort to build a just society is liberating. And it has an indirect but effective impact on the fundamental alienation. It is a salvific work, although it is not all of salvation. As a human work it is not exempt from ambiguities, any more than what is considered to be strictly "religious" work. But this does not weaken its basic orientation nor its objective results.

Temporal progress—or to avoid this aseptic term, the liberation of man—and the growth of the Kingdom both are directed toward complete communion of men with God and of men among themselves. They have the same goal, but they do not follow parallel roads, not even convergent ones. The growth of the Kingdom is a process which occurs historically *in* liberation, insofar as liberation means a greater fulfillment of man. Liberation is a precondition for the new society, but this is not all it is. While liberation is implemented in liberating historical events, it also denounces their limitations and ambiguities, proclaims their fulfillment, and impels them effectively towards total communion. This is not an identification. Without liberating historical events, there would be no growth of the Kingdom. But the process of liberation will not have conquered the very roots of oppression and the exploitation of man by man without the coming of the Kingdom, which is above all a gift. Moreover, we can say that the historical, political liberating event *is* the growth of the Kingdom and *is* a salvific event; but it is not *the* coming of the Kingdom, not *all* of salvation. It is the historical realization of the Kingdom and, therefore, it also proclaims its fullness. This is where the difference lies. It is a distinction made from a dynamic viewpoint, which has nothing to do with the one which holds for the existence of two juxtaposed "orders," closely connected or convergent, but deep down different from each other.

The very radicalness and totality of the salvific process require this relationship. Nothing escapes this process, nothing is outside the pale of the action of Christ and the gift of the Spirit. This gives human history its profound unity. Those who reduce the work of salvation are indeed those who limit it to the strictly "religious" sphere and are not aware of the universality of the process. It is those who think that the work of Christ touches the social order in which we live only indirectly or tangentially, and not in its roots and basic structure. It is those who in order to protect salvation (or to protect their interests) lift salvation from the midst of history, where men and social classes struggle to liberate themselves from the slavery and oppression to which other men and social classes have subjected them. It is those who refuse to see that the salvation of Christ is a radical liberation from all misery, all despoliation, all alienation. It is those who by trying to "save" the work of Christ will "lose" it.

In Christ the all-comprehensiveness of the liberating process reaches its fullest sense. His work encompasses the three levels of meaning which we mentioned above. A Latin American text on the mission seems to us to summarize this assertion accurately: "All the dynamism of the cosmos and of human history, the movement towards the creation of a more just and fraternal world, the overcoming of social inequalities among men, the efforts, so urgently needed on our continent, to liberate man from all that depersonalizes him—physical and moral misery, ignorance, and hunger—as well as the awareness of human dignity (*Gaudium et spes*, no. 22), all these originate, are transformed, and reach their perfection in the saving work of Christ. In him and through him salvation is present at the heart of man's history, and there is no human act which, in the last instance, is not defined in terms of it." [101]

NOTES

89. According to the famous text of St. Augustine of Hippo, quoted in the Schema of Ariccia but not found in the final version, "He who made you without you does not justify you without you. He created you without your knowing it: he will justify you if you will it."

90. The text of Ariccia does not escape these reproaches. In it there is a tendency to oversimplify by identifying the "order" of creation with the natural order and redemption with the supernatural order.

91. The well-documented work of P. L. Mathieu, *La pensée politique et économique de Teilhard de Chardin* (Paris: Éditions du Seuil, 1969), gathers and synthesizes the thinking of Teilhard in this regard. In spite of the effort of the author, the impression that one gets from this work is clear: the questions of social justice, or the exploitation of man by man, do not occupy an important place in the concerns of the illustrious Jesuit.

92. This is the basis for certain works like the theologies of development, progress, etc. It is not a matter merely of the title, but also, especially, of the fashion of posing and resolving the question. The greater part of these authors recognize the influence of Teilhard in the posing of the problem.

93. As André Gunder Frank correctly points out, the term *dependence* is definitely nothing more than a euphemism for oppression, injustice, and alienation (*Lumpenburgesia*, p. 18).

94. See "Peace," nos. 1 and 14, in *Medellin*.

95. *Pobreza evangélica y promocion humana*, p. 29.

96. The religious resonances of Hegel's use of the term *alienation* (*Entäusserung und Entfremdung*) are well known. See George Cottier, *L'athéisme du jeune Marx* (Paris: Librairie Philosophique J. Vrin, 1959), pp. 34-43; and Albert Chapelle, *Hegel et la religion, Annexes, Les textes théologiques de Hegel* (Paris: Éditions Universitaires, 1967), pp. 99-125.

97. See Christian Duquoc, "Qu'est-ce que le salut?," pp. 101-2.

98. Without overestimating its importance, it is interesting to recall here the comparison that Marx establishes between sin and private ownership of

the means of production. Because of this private ownership the worker is separated, alienated, from the fruit of his work: "This primitive accumulation plays in political economy about the same part as original sin in theology. Adam bit the apple, and thereupon sin fell on the human race" ("Capital," Part 8, Chapter 26, in *Marx*, Great Books of the Western World, 50:354).

99. "Justice," no. 3, in *Medellin*. The italics are ours. See also the interesting reflections of Eduardo Pironio, *La Iglesia que nace entre nosotros* (Bogota: Indo-American Press Service, 1970).

100. This is what was implied, partially and in other terms, in the text of *Populorum progressio* which we have already quoted.

101. *La pastoral en las misiones de América Latina*, p. 16.

E. F. SCHUMACHER

Ernest Friedrich Schumacher (1911-1977), born in Germany, pursued his interests as an economist on British soil for much of his career, and received international attention, especially when his book, *Small Is Beautiful: Economics as If People Mattered* (Harper & Row, 1973), became well known. For 20 years Schumacher was chief advisor to Britain's National Coal Board. He established the Intermediate Technology Development Group to put into practice his theory that what Third World economies need is not the heavy, power-consuming equipment used in rich countries, but a lighter, cheaper, human-scaled technology designed for local villages where labor is abundant and certain resources limited or unavailable.

Schumacher's main contention in *Small Is Beautiful* is that economic systems should bring benefit to qualitative human life, not simply profit. He challenges the "religion of economics" and its commandment that a good bargain must be sought even if it is the result of exploitation. But he does not simply preach the importance of nonmaterial values. He says that world events are now demonstrating that unless one discards the metaphysic of materialism, the material things which humans need will become unavailable.

In the epilogue to the book, Schumacher introduces for discussion the Four Cardinal Virtues as "relevant and appropriate to the modern predicament." They are prudence, justice, fortitude, and temperance. This traditional wisdom of the human race can be a guide in making economics serve as the means for the betterment of human existence instead of as the end.

From E. F. Schumacher, **Small Is Beautiful**
THE ROLE OF ECONOMICS

To say that our economic future is being determined by the economists would be an exaggeration; but that their influence, or in any case the influence of economics, is far-reaching can hardly be doubted. Economics plays a central role in shaping the activities of the modern world inasmuch as it supplies the criteria of what is "economic" and what is "uneconomic," and there is no other set of criteria that exercises a greater influence over the actions of individuals and groups as well as over those of governments. It may be thought, therefore, that we should look to the economists for advice on how to overcome the dangers and difficulties in which the modern world finds itself, and how to achieve economic arrangements that vouchsafe peace and permanence.

How *does* economics relate to the problems discussed in the previous chapters? When the economist delivers a verdict that this or that activity is "economically sound" or "uneconomic," two important and closely related questions arise: First, what does the verdict mean? And second, is the verdict conclusive in the sense that practical action can reasonably be based on it?

Going back into history we may recall that when there was talk about founding a professorship for political economy at Oxford 150 years ago, many people were by no means happy about the prospect. Edward Copleston, the great Provost of Oriel College, did not want to admit into the University's curriculum a science "so prone to usurp the rest"; even Henry Drummond of Albury Park, who endowed the professorship in 1825, felt it necessary to make it clear that he expected the University to keep the new study "in its proper place." The first professor, Nassau Senior, was certainly not to be kept in an *inferior* place. Immediately, in his inaugural lecture, he predicted that the new science "will rank in public estimation among the first of moral sciences in interest and in utility" and claimed that "the pursuit of wealth . . . is, to the mass of mankind, the great source of moral improvement." Not all economists, to be sure, have staked their claims quite so high. John Stuart Mill (1806-73) looked upon political economy "not as a thing by itself, but as a fragment of a greater whole; a branch of social philosophy, so interlinked with all the other branches that its conclusions, even in its own peculiar province, are only true conditionally, subject to interference and counteraction from causes not directly within its scope." And even Keynes, in contradiction to his own advice (already quoted) that "avarice and usury and precaution must be our gods for a little longer still," admonished us not to "overestimate the importance of the economic problem, or sacrifice to its supposed necessities other matters of greater and more permanent significance."

Such voices, however, are but seldom heard today. It is hardly an exaggeration to say that, with increasing affluence, economics has moved into the very centre of public concern, and economic performance, economic growth, economic expansion, and so forth have become the abiding interest, if not the obsession, of all modern societies. In the current vocabulary of condemnation there are few words as final and conclusive as the word "uneconomic." If an activity has been branded as uneconomic, its right to existence is not merely questioned but energetically denied. Anything that is found to be an impediment to economic growth is a shameful thing, and if people cling to it, they are thought of as either saboteurs or fools. Call a thing immoral or ugly, soul-destroying or a degradation of man, a peril to the peace of the world or to the well-being of future generations; as long as you have not shown it to be "uneconomic" you have not really questioned its right to exist, grow, and prosper.

But what does it *mean* when we say something is uneconomic? I am not asking what most people mean when they say this; because that is clear enough. They simply mean that it is like an illness: you are better off without it. The economist is supposed to be able to diagnose the illness and then, with luck and skill, remove it. Admittedly, economists often disagree among each other about the diagnosis and, even more frequently, about the cure; but that merely proves that the subject matter is uncommonly difficult and economists like other humans, are fallible.

No, I am asking what *it* means, *what sort of meaning the method of economics actually produces*. And the answer to this question cannot be in doubt: something is uneconomic when it fails to earn an adequate profit in terms of money. The method of economics does not, and cannot, produce any other meaning. Numerous attempts have been made to obscure this fact, and they have caused a very great deal of confusion; but the fact remains. Society, or a group or an individual within society, may decide to hang on to an activity or asset *for noneconomic reasons*—social, aesthetic, moral, or political—but this does in no way alter its uneconomic character. The judgement of economics, in other words, is an extremely *fragmentary* judgement; out of the large number of aspects which in real life have to be seen and judged together before a decision can be taken, economics supplies only one— whether a thing yields a money profit *to those who undertake it* or not.

Do not overlook the words "to those who undertake it." It is a great error to assume, for instance, that the methodology of economics is normally applied to determine whether an activity carried on by a group within society yields a profit to society as a whole. Even nationalised industries are not considered from this more comprehensive point of view. Every one of them is given a financial target—which is, in fact, an obligation—and is expected to pursue this target without regard to any damage it might be inflicting on other parts of the economy. In fact, the prevailing creed, held with equal fervour by all political parties, is that the common good will necessarily be maximised if everybody, every industry and trade, whether nationalised or not, strives to earn an acceptable "return" on the capital employed. Not even Adam Smith had a more implicit faith in the "hidden hand" to ensure that "what is good for General Motors is good for the United States."

However that may be, about the *fragmentary* nature of the judgements of economics there can be no doubt whatever. Even within the narrow compass of the economic calculus, these judgements are necessarily and *methodically* narrow. For one thing, they give vastly more weight to the short than to the long term, because in the long term, as Keynes put it with cheerful brutality, we are all dead. And then, second, they are based on a definition of cost which excludes all "free goods," that is to say, the entire God-given environment, except for those parts of it that have been privately appropriated. This means that an activity can be economic although it plays hell with the environment, and that a competing activity, if at some cost it protects and conserves the environment, will be uneconomic.

Economics, moreover, deals with goods in accordance with their market value and not in accordance with what they really are. The same rules and criteria are applied to primary goods, which man has to win from nature, and secondary goods, which presuppose the existence of primary goods and are manufactured from them. All goods are treated the same, because the point of view is fundamentally that of private profit-making, and this means that it is inherent in the methodology of economics *to ignore man's dependence on the natural world.*

Another way of stating this is to say that economics deals with goods and services from the point of view of the market, where willing buyer meets willing seller. The buyer is essentially a bargain hunter; he is not concerned with the origin of the goods or the conditions under which they have been produced. His sole concern is to obtain the best value for his money.

The market therefore represents only the surface of society and its significance relates to the momentary situation as it exists there and then. There is no probing into the depths of things, into the natural or social facts that lie behind them. In a sense, the market is the institutionalisation of individualism and non-responsibility. . . .

To be relieved of all responsibility except to oneself, means of course an enormous simplification of business. We can recognise that it is practical and need not be surprised that it is highly popular among businessmen. What may cause surprise is that it is also considered virtuous to make the maximum use of this freedom from responsibility.

If a buyer refused a good bargain because he suspected that the cheapness of the goods in question stemmed from exploitation or other despicable practices (except theft), he would be open to the criticism of behaving "uneconomically," which is viewed as nothing less than a fall from grace. Economists and others are wont to treat such eccentric behaviour with derision if not indignation. The religion of economics has its own code of ethics, and the First Commandment is to behave "economically"—in any case when you are producing, selling, or buying. It is only when the bargain hunter has gone home and becomes a consumer that the First Commandment no longer applies: he is then encouraged to "enjoy himself" in any way he pleases. As far as the religion of economics is concerned, the consumer is extra-territorial. This strange and significant feature of the modern world warrants more discussion than it has yet received.

In the market place, for practical reasons, innumerable qualitative distinctions which are of vital importance for man and society are suppressed; they are not allowed to surface. Thus the reign of quantity celebrates its greatest triumphs in "The Market." Everything is equated with everything else. To equate things means to give them a price and thus to make them exchangeable. To the extent that economic thinking is based on the market, it takes the sacredness out of life, because there can be nothing sacred in something that has a price. Not surprisingly, therefore, if economic thinking pervades the whole of society, even simple non-economic values like beauty, health, or cleanliness can survive only if they prove to be "economic."

To press non-economic values into the framework of the economic calculus, economists use the method of cost/benefit analysis. This is generally thought to be an enlightened and progressive development, as it is at least an attempt to take account of costs and benefits which might otherwise be disregarded altogether. In fact, however, it is a procedure by which the higher is reduced to the level of the lower and the priceless is given a price. It can therefore never serve to clarify the situation and lead to an enlightened decision. . . . The logical absurdity, however, is not the greatest fault of the undertaking: what is worse, and destructive of civilisation, is the pretence that everything has a price or, in other words, that money is the highest of all values.

Economics operates legitimately and usefully within a "given" framework which lies altogether outside the economic calculus. We might say that economics does not stand on its own feet, or that it is a "derived" body of thought—derived from meta-economics. If the economist fails to study meta-economics, or, even worse, if he remains unaware of the fact that there are boundaries to the applicability of the economic calculus, he is likely to fall into a similar kind of error as that of certain medieval theologians who tried to settle questions of physics by means of biblical quotations. Every science is beneficial within its proper limits, but becomes evil and destructive as soon as it transgresses them.

The science of economics is "so prone to usurp the rest"—even more so today than it was 150 years ago, when Edward Copleston pointed to this danger—because it relates to certain very strong drives of human nature, such as envy and greed. All the greater is the duty of its experts, the economists, to understand and clarify its limitations, that is to say, to understand meta-economics.

What, then, is meta-economics? As economics deals with man in his environment, we may expect that meta-economics consists of two arts —one dealing with man and the other dealing with the environment. In other words, we may expect that economics must derive its aims and objectives from a study of man, and that it must derive at least a large part of its methodology from a study of nature. . . .

In this chapter, I confine myself to a discussion of the second part of meta-economics, i.e., the way in which a vital part of the methodology of economics has to be derived from a study of nature. As I have emphasised already, on the market all goods are treated the same, because the market is essentially an institution for unlimited bargain hunting, and this means that it is inherent in the methodology of modern economics, which is so largely market-oriented, to ignore man's dependence on the natural world. Professor E. H. Phelps Brown, in his Presidential Address to the Royal Economic Society on "The Underdevelopment of Economics," talked about "the smallness of the contribution that the most conspicuous developments of economics in the last quarter of a century have made to the solution of the most pressing problems of the times," and among these problems he lists "checking the adverse effects on the environment and the quality of life of industrialism, population growth and urbanism."

As a matter of fact, to talk of "the smallness of the contribution" is to employ an euphemism, as there is no contribution at all. . . .

Economics deals with a virtually limitless variety of goods and services, produced and consumed by an equally limitless variety of people. It would obviously be impossible to develop any economic theory at all, unless one were prepared to disregard a vast array of qualitative distinctions. But it should be just as obvious that the total suppression of qualitative distinctions, while it makes theorising easy, at the same time makes it totally sterile. Most of the "conspicuous developments of economics in the last quarter of a century" (referred to by Professor Phelps Brown) are in the direction of quantification at the expense of the understanding of qualitative differences. . . . For example, having established by his purely quantitative methods that the Gross National Product of a country has risen by, say, five per cent, the economist-turned-econometrician is unwilling, and generally unable, to face the question of whether this is to be taken as a good thing or a bad thing. He would lose all his certainties if he even entertained such a question: growth of GNP must be a good thing, irrespective of what has grown and who, if anyone, has benefited. The idea that there could be pathological growth, unhealthy growth, disruptive or destructive growth, is to him a perverse idea which must not be allowed to surface. A small minority of economists is at present beginning to question how much further "growth" will be possible since infinite growth in a finite environment is an obvious impossibility; but even they cannot get away from the purely quantitative growth concept. Instead of insisting on *the primacy of qualitative distinctions*, they simply substitute non-growth for growth, that is to say, one emptiness for another.

It is of course true that quality is much more difficult to "handle" than quantity, just as the exercise of judgement is a higher function than the ability to count and calculate. Quantitative differences can be more easily grasped and certainly more easily defined than qualitative differences; their concreteness is beguiling and gives them the appearance of scientific precision, even when this precision has been purchased by the suppression of vital differences of quality. The great majority of economists is still pursuing the absurd ideal of making their "science" as scientific and precise as physics, as if there were no qualitative difference between mindless atoms and men made in the image of God.

The main subject matter of economics is "goods." Economists make some rudimentary distinctions between categories of goods from the point of view of the *purchaser,* such as the distinction between consumers' goods and producers' goods; but there is virtually no attempt to take cognisance of what such goods actually are; for instance, whether they are man-made or God-given, whether they are freely reproducible or not. . . .

It is a fact, however, that there are fundamental and vital differences between various categories of "goods" which cannot be disregarded without losing touch with reality. The following might be called a minimum scheme of categorisation: (See diagram, next page)

There could hardly be a more important distinction, to start with, than that between primary and secondary goods, because the latter presuppose the availability of the former. An expansion of man's ability to bring forth secondary products is useless unless preceded by an expansion of his ability to win primary products from the earth; for man is not a producer but only a converter, and for every job of con-

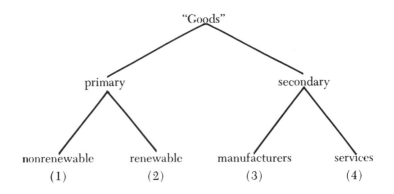

version he needs primary products. In particular, his power to convert depends on primary energy, which immediately points to the need for a vital distinction within the field of primary goods, that between non-renewable and renewable. As far as secondary goods are concerned, there is an obvious and basic distinction between manufactures and services. We thus arrive at a minimum of four categories, each of which is *essentially* different from each of the three others.

The market knows nothing of these distinctions. It provides a price tag for all goods and thereby enables us to pretend that they are all of equal significance. Five pounds' worth of oil (category 1) equals five pounds' worth of wheat (category 2), which equals five pounds' worth of shoes (category 3) or five pounds' worth of hotel accommodation (category 4). The sole criterion to determine the relative importance of these different goods is the rate of profit that can be obtained by providing them. If categories 3 and 4 yield higher profits than categories 1 and 2, this is taken as a "signal" that it is "rational" to put additional resources into the former and withdraw resources from the latter. . . .

In fact, without going into any further details, it can be said that economics, as currently constituted, fully applies only to manufactures (category 3), but it is being applied without discrimination to all goods and services, because an appreciation of the essential, qualitative differences between the four categories is entirely lacking.

These differences may be called meta-economic, inasmuch as they have to be recognised before economic analysis begins. Even more important is the recognition of the existence of "goods" which never appear on the market, because they cannot be, or have not been, privately appropriated, but are nonetheless an essential precondition of all human activity, such as air, water, the soil, and in fact the whole framework of living nature.

Until fairly recently the economists have felt entitled, with tolerably good reason, to treat the entire framework within which economic activity takes place as *given*, that is to say, as permanent and inde-structible. It was no part of their job and, indeed, of their professional competence, to study the effects of economic activity upon the frame-work. Since there is now increasing evidence of environmental deterio-ration, particularly in living nature, the entire outlook and methodology of economics is being called into question. The study of economics is too narrow and too fragmentary to lead to valid insights, unless com-plemented and completed by a study of meta-economics.

The trouble about valuing means above ends—which, as confirmed by Keynes, is the attitude of modern economics—is that it destroys man's freedom and power to choose the ends he really favours; the development of means, as it were, dictates the choice of ends. Obvious examples are the pursuit of supersonic transport speeds and the im-mense efforts made to land men on the moon. The conception of these aims was not the result of any insight into real human needs and aspira-tions, which technology is meant to serve, but solely of the fact that the necessary technical means appeared to be available. . . .

EPILOGUE

In the excitement over the unfolding of his scientific and technical powers, modern man has built a system of production that ravishes nature and a type of society that mutilates man. If only there were more and more wealth, everything else, it is thought, would fall into place. Money is considered to be all-powerful; if it could not actually buy non-material values, such as justice, harmony, beauty or even health, it could circumvent the need for them or compensate for their loss. The development of production and the acquisition of wealth have thus become the highest goals of the modern world in relation to which all other goals, no matter how much lip-service may still be paid to them, have come to take second place. The highest goals require no justification; all secondary goals have finally to justify themselves in terms of the service their attainment renders to the attainment of the highest.

This is the philosophy of materialism, and it is this philosophy—or metaphysic—which is now being challenged by events. There has never been a time, in any society in any part of the world, without its sages and teachers to challenge materialism and plead for a different order of priorities. The languages have differed, the symbols have varied, yet the message has always been the same: "Seek ye *first* the kingdom of God and all these things [the material things which you also need] shall be *added* unto you." They shall be added, we are told, here on earth where we need them, not simply in an after-life beyond our imagination. Today, however, this message reaches us not solely from the sages and saints but from the actual course of physical events. It speaks to us in the language of terrorism, genocide, breakdown, pollution, exhaustion. We live, it seems, in a unique period of convergence. It is becoming apparent that there is not only a promise but also a threat in those astonishing words about the kingdom of God—the threat that "unless you seek first the kingdom, these other things, which you also need, will cease to be available to you." As a recent writer put it, without reference to economics and politics but nonetheless with direct reference to the condition of the modern world:

> If it can be said that man collectively shrinks back more and more from the Truth, it can also be said that on all sides the Truth is closing in more and more upon man. It might almost be said that, in order to receive a touch of It, which in the past required a lifetime of effort, all that is asked of him now is not to shrink back. And yet how difficult that is! [1]

We shrink back from the truth if we believe that the destructive forces of the modern world can be "brought under control" simply by mobilising more resources—of wealth, education, and research—to fight pollution, to preserve wildlife, to discover new sources of energy, and to arrive at more effective agreements on peaceful coexistence. Needless to say, wealth, education, research, and many other things are needed for any civilisation, but what is most needed today is a revision of the ends which these means are meant to serve. And this implies, above all else, the development of a life-style which accords to material things their proper, legitimate place, which is secondary and not primary.

The "logic of production" is neither the logic of life nor that of society. It is a small and subservient part of both. The destructive forces unleashed by it cannot be brought under control, unless the "logic of production" itself is brought under control—so that destructive forces cease to be unleashed. It is of little use trying to suppress terrorism if the production of deadly devices continues to be deemed a legitimate employment of man's creative powers. Nor can the fight against pollution be successful if the patterns of production and consumption continue to be of a scale, a complexity, and a degree of violence which, as is becoming more and more apparent, do not fit into the laws of the universe, to which man is just as much subject as the rest of creation. Equally, the chance of mitigating the rate of resource depletion or of bringing harmony into the relationships between those in possession of wealth and power and those without is non-existent as long as there is no idea anywhere of enough being good and more-than-enough being evil.

It is a hopeful sign that some awareness of these deeper issues is gradually—if exceedingly cautiously—finding expression even in some official and semi-official utterances. A report, written by a committee at the request of the Secretary of State for the Environment, talks about buying time during which technologically developed societies have an opportunity "to revise their values and to change their political objectives." [2] It is a matter of "moral choices," says the report; "no amount of calculation can alone provide the answers. . . . The fundamental questioning of conventional values by young people all over the world is a symptom of the widespread unease with which our industrial civilisation is increasingly regarded." [3] Pollution must be brought under control and mankind's population and consumption of resources must be steered towards a permanent and sustainable equilibrium. "Unless this is done, sooner or later—and some believe that there is little time left—the downfall of civilisation will not be a matter of science fiction. It will be the experience of our children and grandchildren." [4]

But how is it to be done? What are the "moral choices"? Is it just a matter, as the report also suggests, of deciding "how much we are willing to pay for clean surroundings"? Mankind has indeed a certain freedom of choice: it is not bound by trends, by the "logic of production," or by any other fragmentary logic. But it is bound by truth. Only in the service of truth is perfect freedom, and even those who today ask us "to free our imagination from bondage to the existing system" [5] fail to point the way to the recognition of truth.

It is hardly likely that twentieth-century man is called upon to discover truth that has never been discovered before. In the Christian tradition, as in all genuine traditions of mankind, the truth has been stated in religious terms, a language which has become well-nigh incomprehensible to the majority of modern men. The language can be revised, and there are contemporary writers who have done so, while leaving the truth inviolate. Out of the whole Christian tradition, there is perhaps no body of teaching which is more relevant and appropriate to the modern predicament than the marvellously subtle and realistic doctrines of the Four Cardinal Virtues—*prudentia, justitia, fortitudo,* and *temperantia.*

The meaning of *prudentia,* significantly called the "mother of all other virtues—*prudentia dicitur genitrix virtutum*—is not conveyed by the word "prudence," as currently used. It signifies the opposite of a small, mean, calculating attitude to life, which refuses to see and value anything that fails to promise an immediate utilitarian advantage.

The pre-eminence of prudence means that realisation of the good presupposes knowledge of reality. He alone can do good who knows what
things are like and what their situation is. The pre-eminence of prudence means that so-called "good intentions" and so-called "meaning
well" by no means suffice. Realisation of the good presupposes that
our actions are appropriate to the real situation, that is to the concrete
realities which form the "environment" of a concrete human action;
and that we therefore take this concrete reality seriously, with clear-
eyed objectivity.[6]

This clear-eyed objectivity, however, cannot be achieved and prudence
cannot be perfected except by an attitude of "silent contemplation" of
reality, during which the egocentric interests of man are at least temporarily silenced.

Only on the basis of this magnanimous kind of prudence can we
achieve justice, fortitude, and *temperantia,* which means knowing when
enough is enough. "Prudence implies a transformation of the knowledge
of truth into decisions corresponding to reality." [7] What, therefore,
could be of greater importance today than the study and cultivation
of prudence, which would almost inevitably lead to a real understanding of the three other cardinal virtues, all of which are indispensable
for the survival of civilisation? [8]

Justice relates to truth, fortitude to goodness, and *temperantia* to
beauty; while prudence, in a sense, comprises all three. The type of
realism which behaves as if the good, the true, and the beautiful were
too vague and subjective to be adopted as the highest aims of social or
individual life, or were the automatic spin-off of the successful pursuit
of wealth and power, has been aptly called "crackpot-realism." Everywhere people ask: "What can I actually *do?*" The answer is as simple
as it is disconcerting: we can, each of us, work to put our own inner
house in order. The guidance we need for this work cannot be found
in science or technology, the value of which utterly depends on the
ends they serve; but it can still be found in the traditional wisdom
of mankind.

NOTES

1. *Ancient Beliefs and Modern Superstitions* by Martin Lings (Perennial
Books, London, 1964).

2. *Pollution: Nuisance or Nemesis?* (HMSO, London, 1972).

3. *Ibid.*

4. *Ibid.*

5. *Ibid.*

6. *Prudence* by Joseph Pieper, translated by Richard and Clara Winston (Faber & Faber Ltd., London, 1960).

7. *Fortitude and Temperance* by Joseph Pieper, translated by Daniel F. Coogan (Faber & Faber Ltd., London, 1955).

8. *Justice* by Joseph Pieper, translated by Lawrence E. Lynch (Faber & Faber Ltd., London, 1957). No better guide to the matchless Christian teaching of the Four Cardinal Virtues could be found than Joseph Pieper of whom it has been rightly said that he knows how to make what he has to say not only intelligible to the general reader but urgently relevant to the reader's problems and needs.

BREAD FOR THE WORLD

The reading entitled "The Right to Food" is a policy statement published by a Christian citizens' movement called Bread for the World. The organization concentrates on securing U.S. government policies that will deal with the basic causes of hunger. It has gathered public support for congressional Right-to-Food resolutions; it has urged legislation for a United States grain reserve program; and it has sought revisions in foreign aid legislation aimed at enabling the poor to become more self-reliant.

The executive director of Bread for the World is Arthur Simon, author of the award-winning book *Bread for the World* (1975) and coauthor with his brother, Congressman Paul Simon of Illinois, of *The Politics of World Hunger* (1973). Bread for the World approaches the problem of hunger with carefully assembled facts, the unsentimental conviction that Christians have an obligation toward their starving brothers and sisters throughout the world, a pronounced commitment to the effort to influence public policy, and a program of action in which ordinary citizens may participate.

The World Food Conference, held in 1974, implicitly replied to those who ask, "What can I do besides give?" that private giving is still needed but more important is to "influence government policy." In "The Right to Food" the same position is taken: "the extent of hunger makes large-scale government assistance essential." A United Nations report in 1974 indicated that 460 million people were permanently hungry. Yet, during the 1970s, when world hunger was commanding greater attention, the United States increased its earnings from farm exports by billions of dollars while it decreased the amount of food assistance to poor countries.

The principles set forth in "The Right to Food," though written in 1975, are not outmoded. Rather, the scale of tragic hunger in the world and the disposition of political leaders to spend more on military weapons and less on food for the poor make even more urgent a republication of "The Right to Food."

From Bread for the World, **The Right to Food**

Our response to the hunger crisis springs from God's love for all people. By creating us and redeeming us through Jesus Christ, he has given us a love that will not turn aside from those who lack daily bread. The human wholeness of all of us—the well-fed as well as the starving—is at stake.

As Christians we affirm the right to food: the right of every man, woman, and child on earth to a nutritionally adequate diet. This right is grounded in the value God places on human life and in the belief that "the earth is the Lord's and the fulness thereof." Because other considerations, including the importance of work, flow from these, we cannot rest until the fruit of God's earth is shared in a way that befits his human family.

Today hundreds of millions suffer from acute hunger. Emergency food aid is imperative . . . But emergency aid is not enough. We need to think in terms of *long-range strategies* that deal with the causes of hunger. These causes include poverty, illiteracy, lack of health services, technical inadequacy, rapid growth of population, and unemployment, to name some of the more serious. Church relief agencies have increasingly sponsored development projects that address these problems. But again, although there are small models of excellence on the part of those agencies, the extent of hunger makes large-scale government assistance essential.

Hunger is also rooted in privileges that may, in securing wealth for some, perpetuate the poverty of others. Because they reflect sinful human nature and are usually sanctioned by custom and law, these privileges are often the most obstinate causes of hunger. The rich can resist taxes that could generate jobs for the poor. Landless peasants may be forced to work for a few pennies an hour. Tenant farmers are often kept in perpetual debt. The powerful, with privileges to protect, can use repression to prevent change.

The problem of privileges for some at the cost of hunger for others applies not only to persons and groups within a country, but also to nations. Because the United States earns more than twice the income of the entire poor world, U.S. Christians need to be especially alert to the possibility that our privileges may come at high cost to others.

The policies of the U.S. government are especially crucial regarding world hunger. Our nation can lead countless persons out of hunger or lock them into despair and death. Citizen impact on U.S. policies is, therefore, our most important tool in the struggle against hunger.

In affirming the right to food, Bread for the World seeks:

1. *An end to hunger in the United States.* It supports:

A. a floor of economic decency under every U.S. citizen through measures such as minimum income and guaranteed employment;

B. steps to improve existing programs, such as (1) food stamps; (2) school lunches; and (3) nutritional assistance for especially vulnerable persons, along with steps to enroll in these programs all who qualify; and

C. a national nutrition policy that enables every citizen to get an acceptably nutritious diet.

2. *A U.S. food policy committed to world food security and rural development, as proposed by the World Food Conference.*

The United States clearly shoulders a special responsibility regarding global food needs. Our country controls most of the world's grain exports. U.S. commercial farm export earnings from poor countries alone jumped from 1.6 billion in 1972 to 6.6 billion in 1974—an increase double the amount of our entire development assistance to those countries. While this happened, U.S. food assistance declined sharply. We now need to respond in a way that reflects the more generous U.S. tradition of two decades following World War II. . . .

3. *The reform and expansion of U.S. development assistance.*

The United States currently ranks near the bottom of Development Assistance Committee nations, when assistance is measured as a percentage of GNP. By official (and somewhat exaggerated) figures, U.S. developmental assistance to poor countries amounts to one-fifth of 1 percent of our GNP. We can do better than that. What is true for the United States is true for all countries: "To whom much has been given, much will be required." Further, the *quality* of assistance is crucial. Assistance should deliver self-help opportunities primarily to those living in hunger and poverty, especially the rural poor. It should be aimed at developing self-reliance, not dependency on the part of the recipient nations and people. And rather than imposing capital-intensive western technologies on those countries, assistance should make possible the development of locally appropriate technologies, usually geared to small-scale, labor-intensive methods. Bread for the World therefore supports:

A. a U.S. contribution, in proportion to our share of the world's income, to the International Fund for Agricultural Development as a major attempt to increase the food production capacity and living standards of impoverished rural families;

B. rapid movement toward the 1-percent-of-GNP assistance goal;

C. the "untying" of assistance. Economic strings that put burdens on recipient nations should be cut;

D. honest accounting of U.S. assistance. Loans are counted as grants in aid figures. Either repayments from previous loans should be subtracted, or only a percentage of loans counted, because they are made on below-market terms; . . .

4. *The separation of development assistance from all forms of military assistance.*

Most U.S. aid is either military assistance or assistance in which political and military considerations are uppermost. This mixing of humanitarian assistance with military and political aid gives the public an exaggerated impression of real U.S. aid to hungry and poverty-ridden countries. Bread for the World therefore proposes legislation to sever completely the connection between humanitarian development assistance and military and political assistance.

5. *Trade preferences for the poorest countries.*

Trade is not perceived by the public as a "hunger" issue, but trade, even more than aid, vitally affects hungry people. In the past poor countries have been compelled to export their raw materials at bargain prices, and import high-priced manufactured products. The terms of such trade have progressively deteriorated over the past two decades. Recent food, fertilizer, and oil price hikes have left the 40 poorest countries, representing a billion people, in a desperate position. For them in particular trade opportunities are more important than ever. Bread for the World therefore supports the following positions, which are partly embodied in the Trade Act of 1974:

A. the lowering of trade barriers such as tariffs and quotas, especcially on semi-processed and finished products. It has been estimated that these barriers cost U.S. consumers 10 to 15 billion a year;

B. special trade preferences for the poorest countries. These countries need markets for their products, if they are to work their way out of hunger; and

C. greatly increased planning for economic adjustment, including assistance for adversely affected U.S. workers and industries. Without this, U.S. laborers are made to bear an unfair burden and are increasingly pitted against hungry people.

6. *Reduced military spending.*

U.S. defense spending alone exceeds the total annual income of the poorest billion people on earth, the truly hungry children of God. Our thinking begins with them. During his presidential years, Dwight D.

Eisenhower said, "Every gun that is made, every warship launched, every rocket fired signifies, in the final sense, a theft from those who hunger and are not fed, those who are cold and are not clothed." Bread for the World supports:

A. greater U.S. initiative in pressing for arms limitation agreements and mutual cutbacks in existing arms as well as greater public access to information surrounding negotiations;

B. curtailment of the sale of arms, if possible by international agreement, and

C. adoption of a U.S. defense budget that would reduce military spending. For example, a 10 percent reduction could provide $9 billion for financing long-range measures against hunger.

7. *Study and appropriate control of multinational corporations, with particular attention to agribusiness.*

Multinationals are playing an increasingly influential global role. They transcend national boundaries and often bring jobs and needed development opportunities to poor countries. But they create empires that are not accountable to host countries and often impose a type of development that reinforces inequalities and, consequently, the problem of hunger, as well. Bread for the World therefore supports:

A. the principle that each country has the right to determine its own path to human and social development, including legitimate control over outside investments;

B. efforts to study and analyze the role of multinational corporations, especially as they relate positively or negatively to the problem of hunger;

C. national and international measures that seek fair means of accountability on the part of such companies; and

D. special examination of the role of corporate farming, with a view toward adequate safeguards for low-income consumers and small family farm holders.

8. *Efforts to deal with the population growth rate.*

Rapid population growth is putting great pressure on the world's food supply and on the capacity of countries to absorb the increase into their economies. Population growth will not be effectively curbed if it is dealt with in isolation, but only if placed in the context of total development needs. For example, hungry people usually have large families, in part because surviving sons provide security in old age. Only where social and economic gains include the poor, and where the rate of infant mortality begins to approximate that of the affluent nations, do people feel secure enough to limit family size. Bread for the World therefore supports:

A. greatly expanded U.S. efforts to enable the poor of the world to work their way out of hunger and poverty;

B. additional U.S. assistance for health programs abroad aimed at reducing infant mortality and increasing health security;

C. additional support for research to develop family planning methods that are dependable, inexpensive, simple, safe, and morally acceptable to all; and

D. efforts to modify our own consumption, which strains the carrying capacity of the earth no less than population increases.

9. Christian patterns of living.

The growing scarcity of several key resources—grain, fuel, and fertilizer in particular—that directly affect the food supply has prompted many to reassess their habits of consumption. This country, with 6 percent of the world's population, consumes one-third or more of the world's marketed resources. On the average each person in the United States buys about 4.5 times more grain—most of it indirectly as meat and dairy products—along with alcohol and pet food—than persons in poor countries do. There is often no direct connection between our using less and others having more. Nevertheless there are important psychological, symbolic and spiritual values in reexamining our patterns of consumption. Bread for the World invites Christians to:

A. remember that along with changes in habits of consumption we have to change government policies, without which life-style modifications do little more than give us a misleading sense of accomplishment;

B. reconsider our personal spending and consuming, with a view toward living more simply and less materialistically;

C. reconsider a way of life in which billions of dollars are spent annually to make us crave, and in turn spend countless additional billions on products we do not need, and which in fact often harm us—all this while sisters and brothers perish for lack of bread.

These things we seek because we affirm for others a right that we enjoy: the right to food. We seek to extend to all this God-given right in obedience to Christ who has called us to follow him in loving our neighbor as ourselves.

LANGDON GILKEY

Langdon Gilkey is professor of theology at the Divinity School of the University of Chicago. He received the A.B. degree from Harvard College and the Ph.D. from Columbia University. He has taught at Union Theological Seminary in New York, Vassar College, Vanderbilt University, and, early in his career, at Yenching University in China. During World War II, Gilkey was one of several hundred Westerners confined by the Japanese in a civilian internment camp in Shantung Province in North China. On the basis of that experience, Gilkey wrote *Shantung Compound* (1966).

Other books by Langdon Gilkey include *Maker of Heaven and Earth, Naming the Whirlwind, Religion and the Scientific Future, Catholicism Confronts Modernity, Reaping the Whirlwind,* and *Message and Existence.*

In a passage in *Shantung Compond,* Gilkey reflected on what the internment in China had revealed about human nature. "First, it seemed certain enough that man is immensely creative, ingenious, and courageous in the face of new problems. But it was also equally apparent that under pressure he loves himself and his own more than he will ever admit."

In the selection following, from Gilkey's chapter in *Being Human in a Technological Age,* the question explored is how religious categories are to be applied to a culture which has long since become characterized by its confidence in science and technology. The new factors causing uneasiness about technological culture are its dehumanizing effects and its ecological implications. Writes Gilkey, "Modern culture in the development of its science and technology has not made religion irrelevant. It has made religious understanding and the religious spirit more necessary than ever if we are to be human and even if we are to survive." Religion offers "a new understanding of the unity of nature, history and mankind." Without the category of the ultimate, humans are either subordinated to nature or tempted to exploit it.

THE RELIGIOUS DILEMMAS OF A SCIENTIFIC CULTURE: THE INTERFACE OF TECHNOLOGY, HISTORY AND RELIGION by Langdon Gilkey

From **Being Human in a Technological Age**

Our title may well seem puzzling. We can certainly understand that a scientific culture poses dilemmas for traditional religion of any sort. This has been assumed ever since our culture became scientific in the sixteenth and seventeenth centuries, and it became a virtual certainty in the nineteenth. But can a scientific culture as it develops raise its own religious dilemmas and show itself to be in need of religion in the way agricultural and nomadic societies were? This is the question I would like to investigate. We shall begin by exploring a middle term, history, and our understanding of history. For science has greatly influenced our sense of history, of where we are all going—and wishes to do so. And with the question of the meaning of history, religion inevitably enters the scene. . . .

The Anxiety and Ambiguity Attending
Science/Technology

A change both in mood and in reflection, in feelings and in explicit thought, has occurred in the last decades with regard to this fundamental confidence in science and technology, and all that they imply about freedom, history and the future—like a sudden cover of storm clouds shutting out the bright sun. A chill, thematized in art, drama, novels and films and felt, if not thematized by most people, has settled over much of the West. The scientific community in particular is uncertain in an unprecedented way about its role and worried about its future and the future of the society it helped to create. Such anxiety appears whenever a "religious" confidence becomes shaky. The center of this new *Angst* is, I believe, a new intuition of the *ambiguity* of science and technology as forces in history. This is not primarily an uncertainty about the validity of scientific knowledge or about the reliability of technological skills. About these there are few new doubts—except among small (but growing) mystical and religious communities in the counterculture. It is rather a radical doubt about their "saving" character and an anxious feeling that they create as many new problems and dilemmas for human life as they resolve and even that they compound our ills rather than dissolve them.

Beneath this anxiety, but rarely explicitly expressed, lie deeper and more devastating questions. If a valid science and a reliable technology can really compound our problems rather than dissolve them, what does *that* mean about man and about the history he helps to create? Do we really increase our dilemma by using our intelligence, our inquiry, our techniques? What does *that* mean about us? When these questions are asked, it becomes evident that the *user* of knowledge and technology, and so man himself, is the cause of this ambiguity. Possibly knowledge, informed intelligence and the freedom to enact human purposes that they give are not enough. Something seems to be radically wrong with the ways we use our intelligence, our knowledge, and with the ways we enact our control. Can it be true that human creativity in which we have so deeply believed, is in some strange way self-destructive, that there is in human freedom an element of the "demonic," and that intelligence and informed freedom, far from exorcising the fates of history, can create their own forms of fate over which they also have no control? As is evident, all the great philosophical and especially religious problems about human life are implicitly raised here, problems unanswerable by science and unresolvable by technology, and yet raised by both of them the moment the future they seem to create becomes apparently oppressive and menacing rather than bright and promising.

As we all know, these deeper questions about scientific knowledge and control have been brewing for some time. They began with the development and use of the terrible new weapons and the threat to human life itself which the technological power evidenced in those weapons represented. These questions continued with the realization that technology provides the political authorities and a potential scientific elite with new and dangerous powers over ordinary people: political powers based not only on weapons and communications systems unavailable to the people, but also on the possibility of psychological and even genetic control of entire populations. Technology seemed now not so much to guarantee freedom and self-determination, individuality of life-style and privacy of personal existence, freedom from *natural* fates and freedom for becoming human, but rather it seemed to open up the possibility of an all-encompassing totalitarianism that could crush individuality and humanity, a possibility in which the human would be subordinated to a new kind of *social* and *historical* fate. These fears have been expressed for some decades in the Western consciousness—for example by Huxley and Orwell. However, two new factors have recently become visible that have widely increased this uneasiness about a technological culture: one of them since World War II and the other in the last decade.

The Dehumanization Attending a Technological Culture

The first can be referred to as the dehumanizing effects of a technological culture. As Jacques Ellul has pointed out, technology is not only a matter of tools, instruments, machines and computers. It also characterizes a society in so far as it is organized, systematized or rationalized into an efficient organization: as in an army, an efficient business or a bureaucracy. Here all the human parts are integrated with each other into a practical, efficient smooth-running organization where no time, effort or materials are wasted, where the product or the service is quickly, correctly and inexpensively created, and where a minimum of loss, error and cross-purpose is achieved. Thus are homes put up all alike by a single company and according to a single plan—for efficiency's sake. Thus is local government submerged in national bureaucracy. Thus do individual farms give way to farming combines. Thus is every small industry swallowed up by large, unified business or state concerns. The beneficial results of this technologizing or rationalizing of society are obvious: the rising standards of living of America, Europe and Japan have directly depended on the development of this sort of efficient, centralized administration of industry, distribution, services and government. And every developing country seeks to increase as rapidly as possible its rationalization of production and organization in order to feed, clothe, house and defend its people.

In the midst of these benefits, however, there have appeared other, negative consequences. As every advanced technological society has discovered, human beings are now not so much masters as the servants of the organizations they have created, servants in the sense that they find themselves "caught" and rendered inwardly helpless within the system in so far as they participate in it at all. By this I mean that they experience their personness, their individuality, their unique gifts, creativity and joy, their sense of their being and worth sacrificed to the common systematic effort—an effort in which all that their own thought and ingenuity can contribute is to devise more practical means to an uncriticized end. Any considerations they might raise concerning creativity, aesthetics or the moral meaning of what is being done, any suggestions that might compromise the efficiency, the smooth-running of the whole team, are ipso facto "impracticable" and so by these standards irrational. Thus does the individuality of each lose its transcendence over the system; individual minds and consciences cease to be masters and become servants, devoted only to the harmony and success of the system. Human beings are present and are creative, but only as parts of a system, their worth is judged only with regard to their contribution as an efficient part; they are lured into being merely *parts* of a machine.

Society as a unified system has, moreover, proved ruthlessly destructive of many of the other less public grounds of our identity as persons. It uproots us from that in which much of our identity, or sense of it, is founded, namely, our identification with a particular place and with a particular community. For it gathers us into ever larger groups of people similarly organized, and then it moves us about from here to there, from these people to those, within the larger society. It rewards and satisfies us only externally by giving us things to consume or to watch. After all, such things are all that efficient organization can produce. Having dampened our creative activity in the world into the rote work expected of a mere part of a system, it now smothers the intensity of our private enjoyments by offering us the passive pleasures of mere consumption. Thus does it stifle our inwardness.

Ironically the West had in its spiritual career discovered and emphasized, as had no other culture, the reality, uniqueness and value of the inwardness of each human being, or what was once called the "soul."

But a concurrent theme, its affirmation of the goodness of life, the intelligibility of the world and the possibility through knowledge of the latter's manipulation and control, has gradually achieved an almost exclusive dominance. The combination of these two themes had promised to reshape human existence in relation both to nature and to the forms of social life, culminating in technology, democracy and socialism. Thus in comparison with the Eastern world, the West had creatively learned to manipulate the external, objective world and done much to humanize and rationalize the objective social order. But it has in the process endangered its own inward soul, the reality and creativity of the spirit. Thus having through science, technology, democracy and socialism helped to rescue the Orient's social orders, it now must turn back to the Orient in order to rediscover its own inwardness. And it is doing so in great numbers—ironically just when the Orient is itself grasping after the lures of Western technology and external progress!

Technological society promised to free the individual from crushing work, from scarcity, disease and want, to free him to become himself by dispensing with these external fates. In many ways, on the contrary, it has emptied (or threatens to do so) rather than freed the self by placing each person in a homogeneous environment, setting him as a replaceable part within an organized system, and satisfying his external wants rather than energizing his creative powers. Thus appears the first paradox: the organization of modern society necessary to the survival and well-being of the race seems now to menace the humanity, the inwardness and the creativity, of the race. In seeking to live by means of a surplus of goods unknown before and for the sake of such goods, we have found that men and women are in danger of losing themselves inwardly and so of dying in the process. What had been seen clearly with regard to individual life by the wisdom of almost every religious tradition, has been proved objectively on a vast scale by modern consumer culture: men and women cannot live by bread alone.

The Ecological Crisis Attending Advanced Technology

Consciousness of the second menacing face of technology is astoundingly recent, within the last half-decade. This may be termed the "ecology" crisis in its widest connotations. It refers not only to the problems of technological and industrial pollution of the water, air and earth and the despoilation of whatever natural beauties are left— though these are serious enough problems, and with energy and resources short will only get worse! It refers centrally to the exhaustion

through expanded industrial production of the earth's available resources, in the end a far more serious problem. Medicine and greater
production of food have increased the population; technology in both
agriculture and industry has at an accelerating pace increased our use
of nature's resources of fuels, metals and chemicals. In order to feed
and care for that mounting population, such agricultural and industrial
growth must itself expand almost exponentially. And yet if it does, an
absolute limit or term will soon be reached; these resources will come
to an end, if not in two or three generations, then surely in four or five.
The seemingly infinite expansion of civilization and its needs is in collision course with the obstinate finitude of available nature and threatens to engulf both civilization and nature. For the first time man's
freedom in history menaces not only his fellow humans but nature as
well. In the past, with the development of the techniques of civilization, history was freed from the overwhelming power of nature and
its cycles and submitted nature to her own control. Now civilization
and history have become so dominant in their power that they threaten
to engulf nature in their own ambiguity.

In this case that ambiguity is very great. A world economy, whether
its domestic forms be socialist or capitalist, facing the combination of
expanded populations and both depleted and diminishing resources,
is a world facing even more bitter rivalries and conflicts than the past
has known. It is also, ironically, a world facing in new forms precisely
those "fates" from which technology had promised to save us: scarcity,
crowding, want and undue authority. . . . Freedom of experiment,
freedom for new and radical thoughts and techniques, freedom for
individual life-styles, may well be unaffordable luxuries in that age.
Perhaps most important, such rational and peaceful solutions will require from the nations with power an extraordinary self-restraint in
the use of their power, a willingness to sacrifice their affluence lest
they be tempted to use their power to grab all that is left for the sake
of that affluence. All of this bespeaks an increase of authority in our
future undreamed of in the technological utopias of the recent past.
Whether we desire it or not we seem headed for a less free, less affluent, less individualistic, less dynamic and less innovative world. The
long-term results of science and technology seem ironically to be
bringing about anything but the individualistic, creative, secure world
they originally promised. In fact this progressive, dynamic, innovative civilization seems to be in the process of generating its own anti-
thesis: a stable, even stagnant society with an iron structure of rationality and authority, with a minimum of goods, of self-determination,
of intellectual and personal freedom. Such a new and grim world is by
no means a certainty, for nothing in history is fated. But unless our

public life—technological, political, and economic—is directed by more reason and more self-sacrifice than in the past, such a future has a disturbingly high probability. . . .

The Ambiguities of Technology and Religious Response

I need not in conclusion underline that these paradoxes arising out of the role of science and technology in modern life raise religious issues. It is obvious that all these questions make direct contact with the themes, meanings, questions and answers of speculative philosophy and high religion. If it is the way we use our creativity, our intelligence and freedom—not our lack of them—that is at fault, then is there any recourse for us from this estrangement of our own most treasured and precious powers, from this bondage of our wills to self-destruction? We seem to need rescue not so much from our ignorance and our weakness as from our own creative strength—not so that either our creativity or intelligence is lost, but so that their self-destructive power is gone. Thus the religious question of a transcendent *ground* of renewal, not from ourselves but from beyond ourselves, is raised by the most impressive of modernity's achievements—its scientific intelligence and its technological capacities. The creative role of religion is not to replace intelligence and technology with something else, but to enable us to be more intelligent, more rational, more self-controlled, and more just in our use of them. Further, if it is our use of creativity which threatens the meaning of our history—because it renders ambiguous our common future—then again the question of a meaning in *history* which is more than meaning which we can create or give to history appears. In the face of the fate with which our own creativity seems able to dominate us, the religious question arises whether there is any other providence that can rule the fates that seem to rule over us. Our history and our future are not threatened by the stars of the blind gods—by forces beyond us. Ironically they are threatened by a fate which our own freedom and ingenuity have themselves created. Here too, therefore, for us to be able to face our future with confidence —for we can no more live without technology than we can apparently live humanely with it—we must trust in a power that tempers and transmutes the evil that is in our every good and the unreason that is in our highest intelligence.

Such issues as these, raised not against science and technology but precisely by them, cannot be understood or even discussed without religious categories. Moreover, on the existential as well as the reflective level, they cannot be handled without a confidence and a trust born of religion. The anxieties involved in facing such a potentially

menacing future require the serenity, the courage and the willingness
to sacrifice which only touch with the transcendent can bring. Modern culture in the development of its science and technology has not
made religion irrelevant. It has made religious understanding and
the religious spirit more necessary than ever if we are to be human
and even if we are to survive. Technology by itself, technical-manipu-
lative reason, if made the exclusive form of reason and of creativity,
has been clearly shown to possess a built-in element that leads to its
own destruction and the destruction of all it manipulates. It must be
complemented by the religious dimension of man and by the participating, uniting function of reason if it, and we, are to survive at all.

Specifically, science, technology and the society they constitute
must be tempered and shaped by the religious dimension of man, not
with regard to their own modes of inquiry, their conclusions or even
their specific programs—though the latter do need ethical as well as
"practical" assessment; rather this tempering and shaping has to do
with the humans who use them and on whom they are used. From
religion alone has traditionally come the concern with the human
that can prevent the manipulation of men and the dehumanization
of society; and from religion alone can come the vision or conception
of the human that can creatively guide social policy. From religious
confidence alone has come the courage in the face of fate and despair—especially when these two arise from the distortion of *our own*
creativity—concerning a future that will by no means be easier than
the past. For humanism can count on only our own deepest creativity; when that too reveals itself as ambiguous, then despair and
cynicism rather than humanistic confidence appear. From religion
alone can come the healing of desire and concupiscence, that demonic
driving force behind our use of technology that ravishes the world.
And from religion alone can come a new understanding of the unity
of nature, history and mankind—not in human subservience to nature
and her cycles, but in an attitude which, recognizing the unique
spiritual creativity of mankind, can still find human life a dependent
part of a larger spiritual whole that includes the natural world on
which we depend. Such a unity with nature has been expressed in
much traditional religion, especially in the Orient. It must be re-
expressed and reintegrated in the light of the modern consciousness
of human freedom, technology and of history. Naturalistic humanism
cannot achieve such a unity with nature through spirit. Without the
category of the ultimate, the transcendent, or the divine beyond and
yet inclusive of both nature and human being, man is either subordinated to nature or, recognizing his transcendence uses her for his own

"superior" ends. Thus religion is necessary in a technological society if such a society and the nature on which it depends are to survive.

But—and religion both East and West should take note—it is only a religion related to history, to social existence and to the human in its social and historical context that can complement, shape and temper technology. A religion that lifts us out of time or gives us only individual peace, that vacates society and history in favor of transcendence alone, will only encourage an irresponsible and so a demonic technology and will foster and not conquer a sense of fate within history. We are, whether we will or not, *in* history, immersed in historical and social process; and here our lives for good or ill are led. On our response to the social and historical destiny of our time—in this case a technological destiny of vast ambiguity—rests the validity and meaning of our inward spiritual life, of our religion. Only a religion that responds to a transcendence beyond our own self-destructive powers and yet that finds its task centered in our common historical and social future can become a genuine means of grace to us.